MW01107150

WORK HORSE OF THE WESTERN FRONT

The Story of The 30th Infantry Division

By ROBERT L HEWITT

WASHINGTON
INFANTRY JOURNAL PRESS

Copyright, 1946, by

INFANTRY JOURNAL, INC

First edition

AUGUST 1946

WORK HORSE OF THE

WESTERN FRONT

On the Rhine with the 30th Infantry Division, March 24—(AP)—
The American Army's work horse division, which the Germans nick-
named "Roosevelt's SS," more than made up for missing the Normandy
landing by spearheading the Ninth Army's drive across the Rhine One
of the finest divisions in the American Army, the 30th has taken more
than its share of tough fighting on the Western Front

—Wes Gallagher, in an Associated Press dispatch

CONTENTS

APPENDICES

All photographs in this section, unless specifically credited to other
organizations, were taken by official Signal Corps photographers

MAPS

DIAGRAMS

INTRODUCTION

To the Veterans of the 30th·

In this history of your fight on the Western Front I take my final opportunity to tell you once more the pride with which I commanded the Old Hickory Division in battle.

It is not necessary for me to remind you of the trials and triumphs we shared through France, Belgium, Holland and Germany, for they are covered in the body of this work

But I do feel it necessary to convey once more the appreciation my superiors and I felt for the tremendously difficult tasks you completed so successfully during the course of our campaigns Time and again, corps and army commanders commended your work in official correspondence

Our Division was awarded a Fourragére by the Belgian Government for its contribution to the early work of liberation in Belgium and for the fighting in the Ardennes In addition, at least twelve separate units within the Division received the Distinguished Unit Citation The pride I feel in these citations turns first to you, the men of the 30th whose strength and courage and tenacity carried you through to one victory after another.

I sincerely trust you will have as much success in your future activities as you have had in your past campaigning By your actions in war, you have earned happiness in peace. May you enjoy it.

Leland S Hobbs

LELAND S HOBBS
Major General, U S Army

PREFACE

More than 60 American divisions participated in the defeat of Germany in 1944-45. This is the story of one of the best of them, a division which fought continually from the Normandy beachhead to the banks of the Elbe River in the heart of Germany.

In a narrow sense this is a single unit's story. If it conveys to the men who fought Old Hickory's battles a better understanding of how they worked together and gained skill in what was, for most, an alien profession, it will have succeeded in its primary purpose.

In another sense, however, the 30th's history illustrates what happened to a million other men in Europe. They fought with and were loyal to other divisions. But they struggled against approximately the same obstacles of terrain, enemy and the sheer complexity of their jobs. They too, were mainly civilian soldiers.

"Work Horse of the Western Front" is as accurate and honest an account as the writer could make it under the circumstances. Waging war is an exacting business undertaken under conditions which make for confusion and "snafu." The writer has taken the facts as he saw them, the bad as well as the good, with the conviction that he would slight the very real achievements of the Division if he attempted to present a saccharine picture of inevitable triumphs. The measure of a great fighting unit is not that it never runs into difficulties but that it minimizes its errors and gains by experience. By these standards, Old Hickory was a great division—as is evidenced by the caliber of the tasks it was called upon to perform.

Much of the book is based on the official after-action reports of the units concerned and of the Division staff sections. These reports, prepared monthly in the rush of battle conditions, are necessarily condensed and occasionally in error. They have been supplemented as much as possible by personal interviews, by the recollections of the writer, who was Assistant Intelligence Officer of the Division during the entire fighting period, and by all additional data he could obtain in Europe In this connection, the information obtained by the Theater Historical Section, through interviews with all ranks from buck privates on up, has been extremely valuable. The excellent stenographic record of the Commanding General's telephone conversations provided vital data on the exercise of command. Much of the manuscript was reviewed by the commanders of the principal units of the Division and by the chiefs of Division staff sections. The wide scattering of personnel of the Division even before its deactivation in November 1945, however, made complete review of this type impractical

As a history issued under Division auspices, the entire manuscript was reviewed and approved by Major General Leland S Hobbs, the 30th's commander in combat However, the writer was given virtually *carte blanche* in preparation of the manuscript and must consider any errors of fact or emphasis his own. Undoubtedly the descriptions here of some engagements will vary from the recollections of some readers who participated in the actions involved It is hoped that these discrepancies will be confined to minor details.

So many members of the Division assisted in the preparation of the book by supplying information and advice that it is impossible to name them all However, the author wishes in particular to acknowledge the work of First Lieutenant William E. McKenzie, who planned and edited the photograph section, and Sergeant Charles L Cassar, who prepared the imaginative route diagrams which appear on the inside covers Majors Frank Ferris and Kenneth W. Hechler, Captain John Henderson, and First Lieutenants George Tuttle and Robert Merriam, all of the Theater Historical Section, were most helpful in supplying material, much of which they had obtained themselves in the field First Lieutenant Haley F. Thomas has handled sales and distribution of the book to members and ex-members of the Division.

R L H

Part One

THE BEGINNINGS

Chapter I

THE OLD 30TH

This book is the story of a division in battle and is almost entirely concerned with the eleven months between June 1944, when the 30th Infantry Division landed on Omaha Beach in Normandy, and May 1945, when—sitting in place on the Elbe River at Magdeburg—it learned that the war in Europe was over So, in a sense, the previous phases of Old Hickory's story—its record in World War I, and its history as a National Guard organization during the two decades that intervened between the two wars, and even the long months of training in the United States and England—are somewhat foreign to the purpose of this narrative. Nevertheless, they deserve some mention. Only a handful of the men who fought with the Division in 1918 were on hand to fight again with it in 1944-45. Most of the National Guardsmen who formed the bulk of the Division when it was mustered into Federal service in 1940 had departed elsewhere by the time the 30th landed in France. Many of the men who fought with the 30th in Europe joined it in the heat of battle. Yet knowledge of the past history of the organization, stretching back even before World War I, had its influence on the 30th's conduct in battle. And the training period at least set up most of the key figures of the Division team and moulded the way that Old Hickory would go about its business.

The 30th Infantry Division was created on July 18, 1917, three months after the United States entered World War I. However, many of its components, State Militia and National Guard units of Tennessee and the Carolinas, even then had long and colorful records of participation in every American war, from the Battle of King's Mountain in the Revolutionary War to the Battles of San Juan Hill and Santiago in the Spanish-American War.

Most of them fresh from active duty on the Mexican border, the units making up the 30th assembled for the first time on August 3, 1917, when they went into training at Camp Sevier, near Greenville, South Carolina From the beginning the new division was known as the "Old Hickory" Division, in honor of Andrew Jackson, who was born near the North Carolina-South Carolina boundary and rose to military and political fame in Tennessee The Division shoulder patch, a blue H within a blue O, against a red background, with a Roman "thirty" across the cross-bar of the H, was inadvertently worn at first on its side and this practice persisted through World War I.

The 30th remained in training at Camp Sevier until May 1, 1918, sailing for Europe from New York After passing through rest camps in England, the Division shipped to Le Havre, France, and, after training with the British in Picardy and Flanders, went into battle The Division made an outstanding record, its most notable achievement being the cracking of the Hindenburg Line During its four months of fighting, Old Hickory earned more than half of the decorations awarded American troops by the British and 12 of the 78 Medals of Honor awarded for World War I service

The Division entered battle on July 9 when, with the 27th (New York) Division, it was assigned to the defense of the East Poperinghe Line and defensive positions in the Dickebusch Lake and Scherpenberg sectors

It then moved into offensive front line positions in Flanders and remained there until August 9, when it was called back for specialized training Shortly afterwards the Division returned to the Flanders front and played a major role in the Ypres-Lys action from August 19 to September 4. On the night of August 31 patrols from the Division investigated a rumor that the Germans were withdrawing troops from the area As a result on the next day the Division attacked and captured Moated Grange, Voormezeele, Lock No 8, and Lankhof Farm A line was occupied connecting these localities with the original front at Gunner's Lodge, with the American 27th Division on the right, and the British 14th on the left

During this time the Division's 55th Field Artillery Brigade, which had departed under separate orders before the Division was committed, had participated in the occupation of the Lucy sector in support of the American 89th Division and fought in the St Mihiel operation On September 15, the artillery was detached from the 89th and sent to the V Corps to support the 37th Division in the Avocourt sector It fought there until September 25

On September 21 the 30th joined the Somme offensive, occupying the Lincourt–Bouchy sector with the British Fourth Army On September 26 it attacked from a line of departure about 400 meters east of La Haute Bruyére, with its old friend, the 27th, on its left This attack was to end in the breaking of the Hindenburg Line on September 29, 1918.

In organizing the Hindenburg Line on that portion of the front opposite the 30th Division, the Germans had taken advantage of the St Quentin Canal, which entered a tunnel about $4\frac{1}{2}$ kilometers north of Bellicourt, passed under the town and emerged at a point about 1 kilometer south of the town. This tunnel contained many underground connections with various trenches of the Hindenburg Line The canal south of the tunnel had high banks and was well suited for defensive purposes.

The 119th and 120th Infantry Regiments of the 60th Infantry Brigade, were designated as the assault units. The 117th Infantry Regiment of the 59th Infantry Brigade was assigned to follow up the 120th and protect the Division's right flank The 118th Infantry Regiment was held in divisional reserve

Following a rolling artillery barrage, the Division attacked and, after overcoming stubborn resistance, penetrated the concrete Hindenburg defenses Immediately after the penetration, the Division crossed the canal and captured Bellicourt, then entered Nauroy. The Australian 5th Division moved up with the 30th to relieve it, but the 30th tenaciously kept on fighting Together the two divisions advanced, and, although the command passed to the Australians on the following morning, the 30th continued to fight until noon

During this advance of 20 miles, the Division captured 98 officers, 3,750 men, 72 artillery pieces, 26 trench mortars, and 426 machine guns. It suffered 8,415 casualties

On October 1, the 30th moved to the Serbecourt and Mesnil-Bruntel areas and went back into the lines on the 5th Again it attacked, capturing Brancourt-le-Grand and Prémont, and, on October 9, it captured Busigny and Recquigny

While the Division was participating in this heavy fighting, the 55th Field Artillery Brigade was engaged in the Meuse–Argonne sector, where the German Army was making one of its most powerful defensive stands of the war Between October 11 and November 11, the brigade supported the 33d and 79th Divisions in the Troyon sector

On October 11 the Division took Vaux-Andigny, La-Haie-Mennercasse, and reached the outskirts of St Martin Rivière. Here it was given a short rest but returned to the fight on the night of October 15, when it relieved the 27th Division and crossed the La Selle River, capturing Molain and Ribeauville

On the night of the 19th, it was relieved and sent to the rear for a well earned rest, and for rehabilitation and training. The Division had suffered heavy casualties On October 23, the 30th moved to the Querrieu area near Amiens, where it was undergoing rehabilitation at the time of the Armistice On November 19 the Division, less the artillery brigade, moved to the American Embarkation Center at Le Mans The artillery brigade rejoined the Division on January 20, 1919 and on February 18 the first unit of Old Hickory sailed from Brest for the United States The last elements of the Division arrived at Charleston, S C, on April 18

The 30th was disbanded after the war, but was reactivated by the War

Department in 1925 as a National Guard Division, with troops from Georgia added to the original components. Thereafter, until 1941, its story was the usual one of annual summer encampments and peacetime maneuvers. It participated in the first post-war mobilization at Camp Jackson, South Carolina, in 1928, and participated in the DeSoto National Forest maneuvers in Mississippi in 1938 and in the Third Army maneuvers in Louisiana in 1940. Within a month after its return from the Louisiana maneuvers it was recalled to full-time duty in September 1940, its ranks filled to wartime strength by volunteers. Conscription had not yet been established.

Chapter II

THE NEW 30TH

One of the first four National Guard Divisions to be called into Federal service when the Army of the United States began expanding in 1940, the 30th Infantry Division trained for almost four years before it was committed to battle. During that period it underwent innumerable transformations and emerged, like most of the other National Guard divisions, with its pristine sectional and National Guard character all but buried under the influx of selectees, Reserve officers, Regular Army men and Officer Candidate School graduates from all sections of the country.

For two years the Division trained at Fort Jackson, near Columbia, South Carolina. In June 1941 the Division participated in Second Army maneuvers in Tennessee and in the fall of 1941 it took part in the First Army maneuvers in the Carolinas before returning to Fort Jackson. The first big exodus from the Division occurred then, when approximately 6,000 men left at the end of one-year enlistments or because of hardship cases. At this time the 121st Infantry Regiment was transferred to the 8th Infantry Division.

During the spring of 1942 the changes in the Division's personnel continued to be drastic. The Division was reorganized from an old-style square division, with two brigades and a total of four infantry regiments, into a triangular division, of three infantry regiments, its present form. Newly activated divisions, officer candidate schools, and Air Forces training continued to draw many men away from the Division. Major General Henry D Russell, the National Guard division commander, was replaced by Major General William H. Simpson, a Regular Army officer, on May 1, 1942, and he in turn was succeeded on September 12, 1942, by another Regular, Major General Leland S. Hobbs, Old Hickory's commander in battle. By that time the Division had been cut down to a strength of approximately 6,000 men—about forty per cent of its normal strength—having lost within a year the equivalent of a full division in both officers and men.

During the fall of 1942 the Division was filled up to full strength again, with the 119th Infantry Regiment and the 197th Field Artillery Battalion constituted to replace the 118th Infantry Regiment and the 115th Field Artillery Battalion, which had been sent overseas during the summer as a combat team. The 117th Infantry Regiment went to Fort Benning, Georgia, September 13 and remained there on instructional and demonstration duty for The Infantry School until February 28, 1943. The Division, which had been transferred to Camp Blanding, Florida, at the beginning of October, began training anew in December, with two-thirds of its enlisted personnel fresh from the reception center

Training at Camp Blanding followed the usual pattern of training camps throughout the country—thirteen weeks emphasizing individual training, followed by a like period of small-unit training As far as tests could determine, the Division was progressing well In May, just before the Division was ready for its first real field work, the Division Artillery, under Brigadier General Arthur McK Harper, set a new Army Ground Forces record in field firing tests at Camp Gordon, Georgia Meanwhile the rest of the Division was proceeding by train and motors to Camp Forrest, Tennessee, where it set up a tent encampment on the edge of the post and went to work on intradivisional field maneuvers near Lynchburg, Tennessee By the end of September it was ready for large-scale maneuvers, and joined the 94th and 98th Infantry Divisions, the 12th Armored Division, IV Armored Corps, and a host of corps and army troops in a two-month maneuver period This period was particularly valuable in training commanders and staffs, and although the problems, which usually lasted for about a week at a time, were not officially won or lost, the Division showed considerable alertness and skill, and was credited with knocking out several "enemy" battalions in succession by double envelopments Aside from the training afforded staffs in how to function, this success provided the chief value of the maneuver period The Division entered the maneuvers with good morale, it left them with the conviction that it had "won" and was now ready to do some real fighting.

From the maneuver area the 30th, in November, moved north by truck to Camp Atterbury, Indiana, where it concentrated on preparation for movement overseas At Atterbury, Division Artillery again set a new Army Ground Forces record for battalion firing tests

In February 1944, the Division started its trip by train for Camp Myles Standish, Massachusetts, one of the staging camps serving the Boston Port of Embarkation On February 12, loaded on three transports, the *John Ericsson,* the *Brazil* and the *Argentina,* it left Boston Harbor in a blinding snowstorm to join its convoy for Europe An advance party led by Brigadier General William K. Harrison, the assistant division commander, had previously sailed on the *Queen Mary.*

The repeated inspections and pressure of the period, just before sailing, left most of the men with a feeling of finality, almost as though they would come off the ships fighting and would leave civilian pleasures behind until the war was over Crowded as they were on the boats, they had little room for training, although troop commanders went through the motions of trying to set up instruction.

The convoy was an impressive sight, with ships spread out over the ocean as far as the eye could see, shepherded by a battleship and by destroyers frisking around the edges of the great pattern of ships Periodically naval gun crews on the transports held gunnery practice, and blackout instructions were strict Rumors of submarines went the rounds

Nevertheless, the passage had been unusually uneventful as the convoy headed into the Irish Sea and split up The 120th Infantry landed on the Clyde in Scotland, the 117th at Liverpool and the 119th at Bristol. February 22, Washington's birthday, the Division was in port Some of the troops were given a brief introduction to the air war on their first night ashore, as their blacked-out trains were sidetracked and re-routed through marshalling yards of London because of a German air raid. In their new area the men of the Division were to find air raids almost a nightly affair, with the enemy raiders flying over their heads from the English Channel toward London.

The 30th's first training area in England was on the south coast, with the division headquarters at the ancient town of Chichester, two of the regiments, the 119th and 120th, billetted on Channel coast towns to the south; while the 117th, Division Artillery and other troops spread northward toward London In April the Division moved north to the London suburbs, with headquarters at Chesham

All of the billets had previously been used by British troops Most of them were private houses, although some units lived in Nissen huts

England, somewhat begrimed and shabby after four years of war, was no foxhole Men adjusted themselves to the wartime weakness of British beer, made friends with the British and attempted to cope with the perils of British pronunciation and idiom and with the endless pit-falls of trying to keep warm in wintertime without central heating Gradually, even before they were initiated into the plans for invasion then being made, the troops began to sense the urgency in what was going on in England that spring Closer to the war already, if only because they were in a land being bombed, the men of the 30th began to see more and more military equipment around the countryside Some main roads were so monopolized by trucks and tanks that a stray civilian vehicle seemed almost to have arrived there by mistake

There was work to be done First was the fundamental task of restoring the fine edge of technique and endurance dulled by days in transit. The infantry marched and marched and marched The artillery fired problem after problem on tiny ranges as full of local ground rules as a tricky golf course One shell broke a civilian's wooden leg, the civilian himself was unhurt Another shell hit a bull that had strayed onto the range These were the exceptions

Small-unit techniques were practiced. Weapons were fired. For the first time the 30th's infantrymen practiced in earnest working with tanks. Special teams visited the troops to demonstrate German uniforms and methods The. military police platoon, practicing the handling of prisoners, tried out close-order drill in German. The higher-ups came around on visits of inspection, trying to be cordial and friendly, but looking the men over appraisingly—General Eisenhower, General Montgomery, General Bradley, the Secretary of War, General Corlett of XIX Corps. And so the spring wore on. Soon there were other jobs to be done—waterproofing of vehicles so that they could wade across the sandy beaches of Normandy without stalling. Invasion rumors were everywhere, one penny if one wanted to read them in the newspapers, otherwise free

Sometime in March 1944, when the Division was still in the vicinity of Chichester, and more than two months before the actual invasion, an armed officer-courier delivered a bundle of documents containing a plan known as "Neptune," published by U.S. First Army. It was perhaps the most breathtaking document ever received at the 30th Division: "The object of NEPTUNE is to secure a lodgement area on the continent from which further offensive operations can be developed It is part of a large strategic plan designed to bring about the total defeat of Germany" From there it went on—the places, the troops, the method. Everything but the time. D-day was to be announced. Y-day, the target day, was May 30.

The First Army was to land on D-day, H-hour, at Utah Beach, on the east side of the Cherbourg Peninsula north of Carentan and at Omaha Beach facing north into the English Channel just east of Isigny. The VII Corps would assault Utah Beach, the V Corps, led by the 1st and 29th Infantry Divisions, Omaha Beach. Two airborne American divisions would make a vertical envelopment behind the western assault areas The British would attack with three divisions initially, their first objectives Caen and Bayeux Overwhelming air and naval power would support the assault. The 30th would land on Omaha Beach as a part of XIX Corps, after the initial beachhead had been established. XIX Corps on landing would consist principally of the 30th, 2d and 3d Armored Divisions. After it was all ashore it was contemplated that the XIX Corps would pick up the 29th Division and lose the 2d Armored Division.

This was the secret the 30th Division guarded zealously and effectively, as did many other units, during that restless spring. A planning room was set up under armed guard. Special lists were made of those who could enter the room and consult the documents there. Countless details had to be worked out at division level—particularly the problems

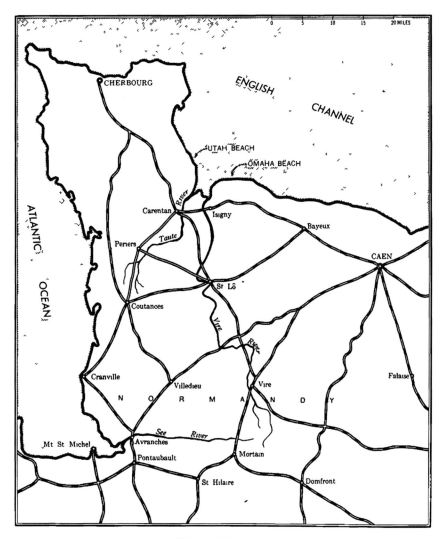

Map 1—Normandy

of supply, administration, and equipment. Study by the commanding general and his operational staff officers at first was generalized, then became more specific In mid-May XIX Corps issued a tentative field order—the 30th must be prepared for one of three jobs (1) to assist VII Corps (101st Airborne Division) in capturing Carentan, (2) to pass through elements of the 29th Division, advancing on the west to seize Marigny and the high ground near Montpichon or to help the 29th take St. Lô, (3) to pass through the 29th to take St Lô, frontally

The area along the Vire-et-Taute Canal just south of the beach area had been deliberately flooded by the Germans Air photographs of the area showed the fields neatly ticked off by hedgerows, many of the ancient roads worn down into ruts yards below the general ground level In the entire area of the American assault were four German divisions, three of them so-called static divisions, weak in transportation and numerical strength and heavily padded with Russian and Polish troops This was the set-up before the invasion It would be hard to predict what the situation would be by the time the 30th landed.

The days passed slowly or quickly, depending on one's mood Gradually more and more of the Division's commanders were brought into the planning room and introduced to the plan and the terrain, outlined on huge curtained maps in a special wing of the headquarters building in Chesham Bets were made; wry jokes about a Second Front were repeated in the pubs Nobody except perhaps General Hobbs knew when the invasion was supposed to take place

May gave way to June The weather was unsettled June 5 looked as though it might be the day General Hobbs scheduled talks to the troops, reminding them with especial seriousness of the simple basic things they must keep in mind in battle But the 5th passed quietly, under cloudy skies

There were two things particularly noticeable about Tuesday, June 6, as the troops woke up and looked outside. The first important thing was that the sun was shining, the skies were clear The second thing was that those skies were filled with more planes than anyone had ever seen before, not the heavy four-motor bombers of normal times, but light twin-engine attack bombers Almost all of them were flying purposefully south All of them carried black stripes on the undersides of their wings The invasion was on

For the next few days, the men of the 30th felt curiously out of touch with things Packed and ready to go, they remained in place, listening to the radio and reading the newspapers Corps was swallowed up in the elaborate staging area system and ceased to be a source of information. Then the Division itself was alerted, and, unit by unit, moved down into the sprawling tent cities of the staging areas in southern England Here their sense of isolation increased. They were briefed, but with information days old They waited, were alerted, were told to forget about the alert order The Division was split up into separate groups, with communication between them all but impossible. Finally, they moved down to the Southampton docks and were loaded into their transports Then they waited more, with the unhurried personnel of the dock area seemingly unaware of the fact that a war was being fought on the other side of the Channel Thus it is always with impatient men At last the convoys gathered themselves together and started across the channel, protected by E-boats and with a grotesque little barrage balloon floating above each ship

Part Two

THE BATTLE OF FRANCE

Chapter III

FIRST ACTION

The beach at last! The strange and battered cliffs of France brought some misgivings, true In the crowded anchorage offshore churning with the activity of landing boats, many of the ships of the vast armada would sail no more The beach itself was littered with the hulks of abandoned landing craft, their wounds gaping, and beneath the shadow of the shell-torn heights more than one American tank hulk rusted motionless on the sands, the escape ports of its turret flung open toward the sky as if in supplication Over on the cliff, near where the C-47s were already shuttling wounded back to England from an improvised landing strip, puffs of smoke and heavy explosions alternated interminably, signalling either the explorations of a German long-range gun or the clearing of mines, and many of the soldiers—still spectators—were inclined to accept the first explanation At night, as the German raiders flew over the beach, the curving lines of tracer bullets crackling into the sky from every direction were ominous as well as beautiful, while that useful tool of night raiders, the parachute flare, seemed the essence of evil as it drifted down, grinning yellowly, trailing gray smoke The bomb-shattered towns of the landing area were a mixture of death and dust and nothing else

But, the suspense was over Here was the actuality of specific Germans to fight and specific places to fight for, in place of the multicolored promises of the planning maps and the somber apparitions of the G-2's possibility chart. Here was an end to the uneasiness of vomit bags and speculation, to the isolation of the transit camps and the transports, to the incomprehensible mysteries of the Transportation Corps and the Navy Here at last was a job to be done

The 230th Field Artillery Battalion was the first unit of the Division to land, coming ashore on the afternoon of June 10—D Plus 4 It had been specially alerted late in the afternoon of June 8 to replace a battalion of the 29th Division which had lost most of its pieces in the swirling waters off Grandcamps-les-Bains, and by virtue of the special urgency for its arrival missed most of the tedious delays of crossing. Forty-five minutes after it had been alerted it was rolling through a cold drizzly rain direct to the docks, bypassing the transit areas, and by morning of the 9th had been loaded in two Landing Ships, Tank That night it waved a solemn goodbye to General McLain and sailed with the convoy

Reconnaissance for positions took place toward nightfall on the 10th and 5 00 o'clock the next morning found the cannoneers digging-in their 105mm howitzers. By noon the battalion had fired a registration to determine firing corrections, using its Cub airplane observer, and had captured its first prisoner, a sniper.

On the 12th the battalion fired a dawn preparation for 29th Division troops and remained attached to that division until the morning of the 14th.

The main body of the Division, led by the 120th Infantry, began to come ashore the night of the 13th-14th, much to the relief of General Hobbs, who had been using up cigars somewhat faster than rationing would permit since his arrival via destroyer at Vierville-sur-Mer on the 10th. Arrival of 30th troops by bits and pieces was virtually completed on the 17th, although the Quartermaster Company had to wait until the 27th before writing "Somewhere in France" at the top of its letters home.

Except for damage in handling to a few pieces of matériel, the crossing had been without mishap for almost everyone The 113th Field Artillery Battalion, however lost 30 men to the Nazis' offshore defenses when the LST carrying three of its batteries struck a mine, which had probably been planted by E-boats the previous night. Two men were known dead at the time, eight more were wounded and 20 additional were missing

* * *

While the troops of the 30th were fighting the administrative struggles of getting to the battlefield, the beautifully printed phase lines, boundaries between units and goose eggs of the invasion plan were being erased and redrawn on the ground On the west, the VII Corps landing at Utah Beach, along the east coast of the Cotentin Peninsula just north of Carentan and the mouth of the Taute River, had achieved good initial success. The 101st Airborne Division's fight for Carentan appeared won, although one of the strong reserves pulled up from Brittany, the 17th SS Panzer Grenadier Division *Goetz von Berlichingen,* had already counterattacked the town unsuccessfully on the 13th. But the British, who had seemed on the verge of gaining their D-day objective, Caen, on schedule, were already feeling the presence of the 21st Panzer Division, which like a defensive fullback had inched up close to the first line of defenders along the coast. The protracted armored battles in the narrow strip of open country around that historic town were already joined.

Farthest behind schedule was the V Corps' assault at Omaha Beach, where the 30th was landing Those treacherous shoals, the Rochers d'Isigny, had taken an even greater toll of men and matériel than had been previously expected The originally weak coastal garrison there had

THE STORY OF THE 30th INFANTRY DIVISION   17

been unexpectedly (and, it turned out, quite accidentally) reinforced by the D-day presence of the entire German 352nd Infantry Division, up from its reserve assembly area west of St. Lô for an anti-invasion drill. By the time the dour and sceptical Norman peasantry was getting its first real glimpses of the Old Hickory shoulder patch, fairly good progress had been made on the east, where the 1st and 2d Divisions were fighting toward the St Lô–Bayeux highway, the remains of the key town of Isigny had been cleared and a tenuous link-up effected between the 29th Division and the 101st Airborne Division, with elements of the 501st Parachute Infantry spread along the Carentan–Isigny road

The first goal was attained—a lodgement had been won on the shores of *Festung Europa* and the first line of defenders had been shattered. But the beachhead was shallow, the assault units weary and reduced in size, the line thin. Phase II—the inevitable battle with Von Rundstedt's powerful mobile reserves—was beginning.

Thus the Division's first action was not a full-dress attack to St. Lô or Marigny, as discussed so often in the planning room at Chesham. Rather it was a one-combat-team assault to the line of the Vire-et-Taute Canal, some 10 miles north of those two cities. Such an operation was vitally necessary to give depth and strength, against possible German countermeasures, to the most vulnerable stretch of the American front, the single road between Isigny and Carentan linking the two United States beachheads A German drive to the coast in the Isigny-Carentan area, splitting these forces, would prevent the movement of troops and ammunition from one area to a critical point in the other. It would throw additional responsibilities on the already heavily taxed beach facilities If through bad weather or other mishap, the buildup lagged at any one beach, there would be no assistance from the other Such an attack would be the almost necessary opening blow in any drive to defeat the Allies in detail Finally, Allied failure to hold the hinge north of the Vire-et-Taute Canal, so close to the vital supply areas of the beach itself, would be a strong deterrent to the projected American drive southwest toward Avranches Without such a drive the Cotentin Peninsula might be sealed off and neutralized by the Germans and the later capture of Cherbourg a thoroughly empty triumph

*   *   *

The 30th's attack was made the morning of June 15, while over half the Division was still afloat or moving through assembly areas on the beach and thus out of touch with the skeleton Division headquarters set up in a field a half mile south of Isigny It was made by an improvised combat team assembled around the 120th Infantry, the only

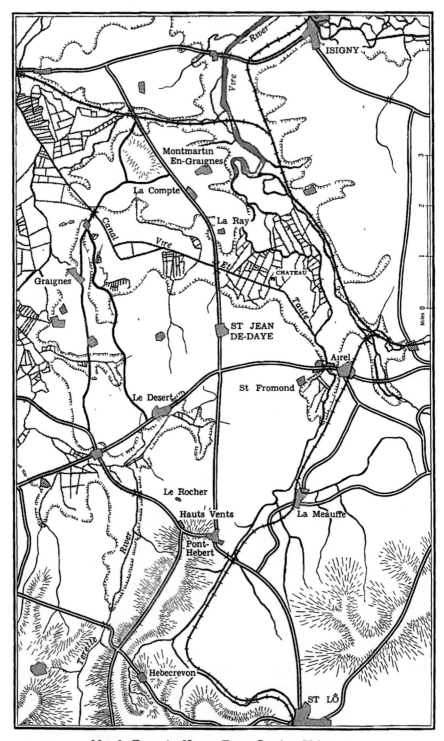

Map 2—From the Vire-et-Taute Canal to Hebecrevon

complete regiment available, which had taken over the sprawling 7500-yard sector of the 501st at 1.00 A M on the 15th [1] Twice previously the area had been the scene of sharp fighting. The presence of enemy troops in the regimental zone of action was well established, their strength and unit allegiances were matters for investigation

The "investigation" started at 6 30 A M with an artillery preparation by the 230th and four other field artillery battalions supported by the battleships of the Western Naval Task Force, which had naval forward-observer shore parties on hand. Previously the regimental and battalion commanders and their staffs had made their reconnaissance and plans An hour later fighter-bombers struck at probable enemy positions in the path of advance and at 8:00 o'clock the infantry and tanks jumped off

(The truck convoy of the Division command post, stumbling in the gathering dawn down a strange road to where General Hobbs and his key staff officers were supposed to be located, all but furnished a spearhead for the assault, reaching the forward assembly area of the tanks before deciding that it was on the wrong road)

Difficult opposition was encountered as soon as the leading squads had crept past the line of the railroad leading east from Carentan Lenauderie, a tiny settlement about a thousand yards south of the tracks, proved to be a center from which the whirring of German machine guns and the monotonous and maddeningly accurate plopping of mortar shells was coming, but was cleared by 2d Battalion after a forty-minute battle. By the end of the morning the battalion had inched up another quarter-mile to the outskirts of Montmartin-en-Graignes, a larger hamlet which boasted a church steeple projecting above the mud-colored old farm buildings In another hour of hard fighting American infantrymen were in possession That was the end of the day's progress for the 2d Battalion, which set about consolidating for the night In midafternoon the fresh 1st Battalion worked its way down through the intermittent artillery fire and passed through the 2d's positions, swinging to the southeast to threaten the group of houses on the Vire River known as La Ray. Meantime the 3rd Battalion of the 120th Infantry was making equally painstaking progress on the west side of the main southward road Resistance continued stiff from hedge-row to hedgerow, reaching its peak at the village of La Compte, astride the highway a half mile south of Montmartin A wide sweep to the west by a platoon of tanks and a reinforced platoon of infantry brought pressure on the town from the flank, however, and by the end of the

---

[1]Company D was attached to the 3d Battalion because neither the latter's heavy weapons company nor the 1st Battalion's rifle company had arrived Later both the 1st Battalion and Company M arrived in time to join the attack The 743rd Tank Battalion furnished tank support

afternoon it had been mopped up. A small party continued south to the main highway bridge over the Vire-et-Taute Canal but discovered that it had been blown.

The next day the 120th finished the job of clearing the canal. The 1st Battalion pushed cautiously through the hedgerows downhill toward the exposed swamplands of the Canal–Vire River junction, while F Company extracted the last enemy resistance from the barnyards and ditches around La Ray. The 3d Battalion turned its attention to the western stretches of the sector, moving over by motor to clear out the Deville area and sending a patrol to the bridge at Graignes, which also proved to have been blown. That night the regiment was digging in along the gentle slope leading down to the naked and watery no man's land along the canal.

The Germans had a last spasm of aggressiveness at 10:30 that night, when a company of the 38th SS Panzer Grenadier Regiment (from the *Goetz von Berlichingen* Division) made a raid across the canal. It was driven back by massed infantry and artillery fire

Interrogation of the 50-odd prisoners taken during the two-day action revealed that they included troops of the 984th Grenadier Regiment, last heard of as part of the 275th Division in Brittany, as well as some battered specimens from the already dying 352d Division. Blown bridges on the canal indicated that the German plans were, at least for the moment, defensive. But the 88mm. shells that raced north along the main highway at any signs of movement, the artillery that crashed intermittently, and the presence of snipers seemingly everywhere indicated that the canal was no boundary of safety.

While the 120th was getting a rude introduction to the intricacies of hedgerow fighting, the other regiments of the Division were moving into line along the east bank of the Vire. The 117th, which began arriving June 15, was assigned a position along the railroad tracks just east of the river and north of Airel, encountering slight opposition taking over, except at the short concrete bridge over the Vire opposite Airel. This was intact but convincingly covered by machine-gun fire from the far side. Only one battalion was in line; the others, which were placed in XIX Corps reserve on the 17th, were bivouacked about a mile to the rear. The 119th set up shop equally quietly until it sent a platoon into La Mèauffe on the 18th, to take over guard duties from friendly troops supposedly in the town. La Meauffe, however, proved to be occupied by Germans who showed no desire to change billets, and a strange disjointed battle continued through the darkness. Company B came down the next morning to tidy up and occupied the northeast half of the town, and finally all of the 1st Battalion took up positions in the area Protected by dug-in positions along the wooded knoll to the south of the village, the enemy however reaffirmed with fire his interest in the place, and finally on the 19th the battalion was pulled back to less exposed ground outside the village Perhaps later La Meauffe would be worth a fight although the opposition might then be stronger Neither regiment nor Division, however, was convinced that immediate possession of the town was worth the cost in men

As June 16 wore on and the 120th's leading troops were working their way down to within sight of the canal, the feeling at Division headquarters was that the attack would continue to the south, with an initial crossing, however, not across the soggy and naked approaches to the canal but westward across the Vire River south of Airel There the artificial flooding effected by the Germans prior to invasion had been less drastic and there the approach of troops to the water would be less exposed to the interested eyes of German machine gunners and artillery observers A warning order to that effect had already been issued and a rapid engineer reconnaissance of the proposed site completed before word came through from XIX Corps that signals were off, that further advances were postponed indefinitely pending arrival of more men and equipment Thus began a three-week interlude while the Transportation Corps and engineer troops on the beach wrestled with the problems of supply for a steadily increasing number of human mouths and for howitzers and guns whose appetites at times seemed monstrous

* * *

The Division's first action had been good without being brilliant The tight little squares of field surrounded by earthen walls topped by scraggly hedges—the *bocage* which was to stretch ahead constrictingly until the glorious days of late August—required a new technique of fighting which the training the men had had with the ground-level British hedges had not warned of When men were halted by the inevitable burp of a machine pistol or chatter of a machine gun from the next hedgerow, German mortar shells arrived with deadly promptness and seeming comprehension of where they were The best assurance of safety was continued advance—a point which Colonel Birks and his battalion commanders spent two sweaty days all along the front lines selling to the dusty doughboys on whom success depended Infantry-tank teamwork was perhaps as good as might be expected between newly acquired teammates but was far from perfect in numerous instances

By far the most important thing about the action, however, was the fact that it had been successful For in the plowed-up fields near Montmartin hundreds of Americans learned, as did many times that number elsewhere during that fateful month of June, that they could win battles, that they were equal to their task

To some, such feelings may now seem trite, to others, strange and overdrawn. They were very real indeed in the days of the beachhead, when St Lô seemed months away and Germany itself almost unattainable.

The Division's activities for the next three weeks were faithfully summarized in the standardized language of the G-3 (Operations Officer) periodic reports as "vigorous patrolling and active defense " But while the infantrymen were taking their turns in the first line of foxholes facing the river and canal or venturing forth in the late twilight toward the enemy positions, other doughboys were practicing, platoon by platoon, new hedgerow techniques for working with tanks, or undertaking meticulous rehearsals of the coming river crossing The 30th Signal Company aided the creation of the tank-infantry team by developing a way to mount telephones on the outside of tanks so that accompanying infantry could talk to the tank commander, and also installed 'infantry type radios in the tanks which tied in with infantry radio nets Engineers not engaged in river reconnaissance were busy minesweeping, or making up explosive charges for blasting tank-sized openings in the hedgerows, or building sections of foot bridge for the coming crossing. The 743d Tank Battalion, which had preceded the infantry to the beach by 10 hours on D-day and which later was to receive the Distinguished Unit Citation for its gallantry during the terrible fighting of those first days, was preoccupied with long-overdue maintenance It had come to the 30th for June 15's attack after supporting the 1st Division at Caumont and remained a part of the Old Hickory team through the entire campaign on the Continent. The 823d Tank Destroyer Battalion arrived with the Division June 24, but spent a week fighting with the 29th Division before returning to the 30th on July 3. About every man in the Division practiced the manual of the shovel and was glad to have a foxhole when the enemy planes came over at night. Sniper fire was still prevalent throughout the area, though some liaison officers and messengers alleged that they were more afraid of nervous sentries in the rear areas than of Germans. On June 17 the first mail on the Continent was distributed. The British Broadcasting Corporation, blaring forth from Special Service radios in trucks, jeeps and a thousand other incongruous places, featured a song called "Holiday for Strings" and a place called Caen.

The 197th Field Artillery Battalion's surgeon, an obstetrician in civilian life, delivered a peasant woman's baby And on June 27 the harried S-4 of the 117th Infantry finally rescued his Service Company from the clutches of the cross-Channel ferry service

Meanwhile the picture of the enemy peering so watchfully from the hills enclosed by the canal and river was being slowly and painfully sketched—a necessary prelude to a successful assault crossing That the enemy was there was certain, for he sniped with 88s and crashed in other artillery. At night his machine gunners moved up into the swamplands and German patrols roamed in the mucky darkness just north of the canal Islanded by the artificial floods, on the American side of the canal, was a time-worn chateau of sorts still occupied by Germans, its ancient masonry all but impervious to artillery and proof against everything but a full-scale infantry assault.

Some information came free Two young University of Paris students, who had pounded the highways all the way from the Sorbonne, somehow found their way through the lines and across the shattered highway bridge to talk volubly if inexpertly of what they had seen A courageous Frenchman from Graignes came circuitously by boat to report that there were SS men in his town and went back to get more specific locations His reward ? He asked for (and received) a certificate stating that he had helped in the task of liberation A number of deserters, most of them Russians and Poles impressed into the *Wehrmacht,* crossed the river and provided new locations for the enemy situation map They were so insistent on the eagerness of Germany's sorry foreign legions to desert, that propaganda shells and a public-address system were employed to cause further desertions, but with little success Control by the German officers and non-commissioned officers was still too effective

Our artillery provided more information, particularly the fragile observation planes which hovered above the battlefield So gleefully did the artillery respond to signs of enemy activity, however, the enemy redoubled his efforts to stay out of sight. Daylight motion diminished sharply Prisoners later were to speak with horror of the losses that the early days of shelling had inflicted, of whole companies afraid to leave their foxholes by daylight, of shell-wrecked kitchen wagons and days of hunger.

Aerial photographs provided more data. But the total would not have been enough without patrols which went out night after night And bit by bit the information came in.

Patrolling proved difficult because of several things. Daylight reconnaissance was impossible because of the vast open spaces to be negotiated The nights were at their shortest, and in some cases three to four hours had to be spent crossing the watery front lines, leaving only an hour for investigation of enemy positions Inexperience played a part at first.

Many of the first patrols were unsuccessful All three regiments lost some of their most resourceful men Staff Sergeant John J Gilson, intelligence noncommissioned officer of the 120th, was killed Lieutenants Martin F. Missimer, Robert J Kane and Robert J. Hawling of the 119th, were captured (and long afterward returned) First Lieutenant Henry C Payne, I&R platoon leader of the 117th, was wounded Twice, however, 36-hour patrols led by Lieutenant Carl C Harnden, of the 120th, penetrated to within a few hundred yards of St Jean-de-Daye, and other groups developed the perimeter defenses being built up by the Germans Several raids were made during the waiting period Three were made by the 2d Battalion of the 120th near Graignes Two knocked out several enemy machine guns at a cost of few American casualties A third lost ten out of 15 men but inflicted heavier losses on the enemy Another raid, by a platoon of the 117th, worked into the little town of Pont-du-St Fromond opposite Airel but was deterred by darkness and short rounds of friendly artillery fire A raid by the 1st Battalion, 120th Infantry, to the chateau was driven off by heavy fire

The remoter echelons of Corps and Army saw the enemy picture develop in Old Hickory's sector with only slightly less interest than did the Division itself The Cotentin Peninsula had been cut on June 18, and by the 26th the commander of the great port of Cherbourg had surrendered A deep-water harbor was now in American hands The beaches were steadily disgorging vast quantities of supplies despite a three-day storm beginning June 18 which had all but wrecked them The entire American force in France could now face south and drive down out of the flooded lowlands to the good roadnet of the St Lô–Coutances line

The picture that did emerge in front of the 30th—a well knit enemy line low along the forward slopes of the hills, but without depth, with the garrison heavily sprinkled on the east with Polish and Russian levies—was encouraging, for the crossing of the Vire and the Canal was to be the opening blow in the drive for St Lô Terrain would make the crossing difficult, the Germans had relied heavily on that Once the first line had been breached, a bridge installed and secured from artillery fire, however, part of the 3d Armored Division could be moved across And perhaps the armor could streak down to cut the St Lô–Coutances highway before the counterblow fell

Chapter IV

VIRE CROSSING

Three weeks after it had driven the enemy back behind the protection of the Vire-et-Taute Canal and the Vire River, Old Hickory launched its first full-scale divisional offensive, an assault crossing of a defended river line in which it drove seven bitterly contested, costly miles through the hedgerows during the next fortnight

Riverlines are obstacles, not insurmountable barriers The reason why they are difficult to assault is because in addition to the main problem of fighting and defeating the enemy there is another problem, that of physically making a way across the stream, and the two problems affect each other The combat men must seek out and destroy the enemy while trying to cross the water or while their supporting weapons or supplies are immobilized on the other side The engineers, military police, and signalmen making and maintaining a route for men, supplies, and communications across the stream must do so while they themselves are among the most important targets for the enemy to shoot at

The problems of the river and of the enemy soldiers already in place to defend it can be minimized, though not eliminated, by careful planning, fire power, and skill But afterward come the counterattacks The important thing is to get past the fixed defenses, have bridges operating and reinforcements and supplies flowing, all with a minimum of losses For the counterattacks, coming when men are tired and their ranks depleted, are often more dangerous than the assault itself

Thus it was with the Vire crossing The days preceding the assault had been well spent in reconnaissance and planning, in construction of improvised footbridges and ladders to scale the steep banks on the far shore, in thorough and repeated rehearsals of what men were to do under fire Division Artillery, reinforced by the 203d Field Artillery Battalion, the 92d Chemical Battalion's mortars and the 3-inch guns of the 823d Tank Destroyer Battalion, delivered a thunderous barrage which left many of the enemy still cowering in their foxholes when our infantrymen charged with bayonets gleaming at the end of their rifles The crossing was made, the enemy's fixed defenses were shattered as cheaply in American lives as possible Then, as the Division struggled south, the enemy brought up successively the bulk of two crack panzer divisions and then part of a cocky parachute division to try to plug, with counterattacks, the gap Old Hickory's thrust had achieved

Division planned a converging attack The 117th Infantry, which had demonstrated river crossings in the old days for Infantry School

25

students at Fort Benning, was to lead off, slashing to the southwest across the Vire just north of the little town at the St Fromond bridge. This attack was to begin before dawn Then, early in the afternoon, the 120th Infantry was to attack due south with two battalions, along the axis of the main highway leading south to Pont Hebert and St. Lô. The attached 113th Cavalry Group was to cross as soon as possible after the 120th to protect the Division's right flank. The 119th Infantry, along the Vire south of Airel, and the 2d Battalion of the 120th Infantry, far to the west opposite Graignes, would have to remain in place until the enemy facing them across the water was driven back. They would support the attack with fire. Corps had the 3d Armored Division ready to cross as soon as it could be used. The 247th Engineer Combat Battalion and the 503d Light Ponton Company would support the Division's own 105th in bridging the river and canal. The 743d Tank Battalion was divided between the two assault regiments.

At 3:30 A M on July 7, Division Artillery, backed up by four corps artillery battalions sited to support the widely separated crossing forces, began its preparatory concentrations. Low-hanging clouds, from which a drizzle had been seeping, eclipsed the full moon Hedges were dripping wet The clay banks of the river were slick and slippery Half an hour previously the infantry of the 2d Battalion, 117th Infantry, had started moving from its assembly area Engineer guides met the assault companies at the last hedgerow on the near side of the river, 400 yards from the bank, and the engineers and infantry carried their rubber assault boats and scaling ladders down to the water's edge The banks were steep and the boats shipped water as they were lowered At 4·20 the first wave of 32 boats was on its way across the 70-foot stream The mortar squad of F Company dumped its weapons in the boat and then paddled alongside so as to avoid swamping the boat. On the far shore the men scrambled up the six-foot bank on the scaling ladders the engineers had built for them and followed their instructions to move fast to the first hedgerow 400 yards away. As the engineer boats returned for their second load enemy 88mm. guns opened up By the time the second wave started out thirty minutes later artillery and mortar fire was crashing into the stream

The 3d Platoon of Company B, 105th Engineer Battalion, started carrying the heavy preassembled footbridge it had constructed down to the water's edge as the first wave moved out Six bays were in the water when direct artillery hits on the bridge destroyed it Another concentration, almost simultaneously, killed four men and wounded four more of a section carrying parts of the bridge down to the river The remaining members of the platoon grimly started construction again, still under fire The last bay of the bridge had just been put in place on the second try when artillery found its target again, tearing the bridge loose from its moorings and wounding several more men. Forty per cent of the platoon were casualties by now, but there was still a bridge to be installed. Some of the men swam into the stream, which was 9 to 14 feet deep, and secured the bridge. By 5:30 repairs had-been completed and the bridge was ready for use. The first three waves of infantry used assault boats Thereafter they moved swiftly over the bridge. The engineer platoon, which lost 17 men, was later awarded the Distinguished Unit Citation for this action

On the far shore the 2d Battalion of the 117th was struggling to keep up with its artillery barrage, rolling ahead 100 yards every five minutes. E and F Companies headed straight up the hill. G Company, following, executed a difficult maneuver in the gathering dawn, cutting sharply to the left to fight with rifle grenades and bazookas through St. Fromond, then pivoting to the right to protect the battalion's left flank E Company reached its first phase line by 8:00 A.M. F had more trouble. Its command group of 14 men ran into some 25 to 30 men and were in a hot fire fight when the support platoon arrived and mopped up the enemy. A machine-gun nest opened up; four volunteers called for by the battalion commander cleaned it out and the company moved on. A Company followed the 2d Battalion to swing into St. Fromond. Then the 3d Battalion started crossing

The engineers were still busy at the river. At 7:30 an infantry support bridge was ordered An hour later it was complete—at a cost of 15 casualties. The heavier bridges were also going in The damaged stone bridge at Airel had to be cleared of a wrecked truck before its ruined sections could be bridged. At 8:30 the work began Four hours later the bridge was open for business The leading company of tanks supporting the attack, A of the 743d, cleared the bridge at 2 05 P M Meanwhile another treadway bridge had been installed near the stone bridge at Airel.

The enemy opposition became stronger as the morning wore on, particularly artillery and mortar fire, as the 117th drove eastward along the axis of the highway By 2:30 the battalion was 400 yards from the crossing of the main north-south road and the westward road it was skirting, and, as the battalion executive put it, "sticking out like a sore thumb " G Company swung too far to the left and had to fight its way back to tie in with the rest of the battalion. Communications from battalion to the rear were tenuous. But, by midnight the battalion had secured the crossroads

At 1·45 P M the 120th jumped off on its assault to the south, first objective St Jean-de-Daye, a mile north of the crossroads toward which the 117th was heading The canal was not as deep as the river and could be forded in places In addition, footbridges built by Company C, 105th Engineer Battalion, were used. These preconstructed bridges proved too short and had to be doubled up. The artillery fired on schedule despite this delay and the enemy was back in position to fire heavy final protective line fires when the infantry assaulted When the bridgehead was only 600 yards deep Company C's engineers began installing a treadway bridge, with the fire on the canal still intense. Enemy opposition slackened noticeably after the first line of defense was breached The regiment first bypassed St Jean-de-Daye, then swung back to take it By 10 00 P M the town was liberated and the 113th Cavalry was crossing the 120th's bridge to swing to the west to protect the flank

Meanwhile the command post of the 2d Battalion, 117th Infantry, was driving off its first counterattack of tanks and infantry Enemy artillery fire was still causing casualties at the bridge sites.

The next day complications set in Corps committed Combat Command B of the 3d Armored Division, and its long, heavy columns crowded across the Airel bridge to operate on the 30th's left, jamming the 30th's roadnet and cutting its telephone wires Also, the enemy brought up the 2d SS Panzer Division *Das Reich* to counterattack Identifications of the 2d SS were made on the 8th in minor counterattacks but its presence was principally manifested in strong resistance to the 120th's advance to the high ground north of Le Desert, southwest of St Jean-de-Daye. The 117th made little progress on that day as its 3d Battalion pinched out the 2d Battalion, but the 119th Infantry, attacking in midafternoon, made substantial advances on the left to the neighborhood of Bordigny New arrangements for use of the 3d Armored Division were made Combat Command B, which was to attack the next day, was attached to the 30th, although General Hobbs asked to be allowed to continue without the armor Combat Command A, meanwhile, was to strike to the southwest for Le Desert, under 3d Armored Division control

The complications hinted at the previous day became very real indeed on July 9 On the left the 119th's projected attack in conjunction with the armor was stalled by tanks sitting on roads and fields everywhere. Combat Command B's spearheads didn't get going and the rest of the armored columns stayed in place Late in the morning reports of enemy armor moving up from the St Lô area arrived from reconnaissance aviation In midafternoon the 2d SS, its artillery now in place, struck hard at the leading elements of the 117th and 120th Infantry Regiments, with an estimated 15 tanks and infantry

What happened after the attack began is not entirely clear Two battalions were definitely hit, the 2d Battalion of the 120th Infantry, which lost its commander and executive as casualties, and the 2d Battalion of the 117th. Three tanks of the 743d Tank Battalion supporting the 120th were knocked out almost immediately At approximately the same time a column of Combat Command A's tanks made a wrong turn which led them north instead of south, running into a twenty-minute fire fight with emplaced friendly antiaircraft guns Leading elements of both battalions engaged began to fall back, and this combination of circumstances apparently was responsible for conditions bordering on panic which affected the 3d Battalion, 117th Infantry, command post, then under the direction of its executive, and other troops as far back as St Jean-de-Daye The Division Artillery fire direction center was on the road to a new command post near St Fromond, along with Division headquarters when the attack struck, but on call from the direct support battalions, the 118th and 230th, it quickly set up and soon was blanketing enemy approaches with up to 18 battalions of artillery firing maximum rate This volume of fire was chiefly responsible for halting the enemy, who apparently had had more tanks waiting to be used Energetic leadership, particularly by Lieutenant Colonel Hugh I Mainord of the 3d Battalion, 120th Infantry, and Lieutenant Colonel Mac Dowell of the 3d Battalion, 117th Infantry, dispelled the impending panic The 823d Tank Destroyer Battalion firmly instructed its three-inch gun crews to stay in place despite their pleas that the infantry was pulling out, and the 743d's tanks with the 3d Battalion, 120th Infantry, on being instructed to stay in place, remained to assist considerably After the excitement had died down and troops reorganized, the ground was regained the same evening The right flank of the Division, where 9th Infantry Division units were moving in, was still exposed, however, for two miles

The fury of the 30th's response, particularly the artillery fire poured into the enemy positions, apparently hurt and discouraged the enemy badly, for the next day the Division made relatively rapid progress to the long ridge which ran along the western side of the Vire River from Pont Hébert to the south Sluggishness of Combat Command B the previous day had culminated in the relief of its commander, and now the tankers set the pace, driving down to the hill crossroads at Hauts-Vents The 119th Infantry, though harassed by enemy fire from the east side of the Vire River, in front of the 35th Division, which relieved the 29th Division there the same day, pressed on through the hedgerows to the outskirts of Pont Hebert The 117th was by now pinched out, the 120th plowed on through the hedgerows

But the enemy was far from through. *Das Reich's* panzers had evidently withdrawn, their whereabouts to be an enigma for days to come. But Panzer Lehr Division, which had demonstrated the approved solution in armored warfare tactics to countless budding *panzertruppen* before the invasion diverted it to less academic duties, was on hand. July 8 it was reported in the St. Lô area. On the night of July 10-11 it attempted to infiltrate into the 120th Infantry's positions. And on the next day it mounted a bold two-pronged attack which left the rear areas of the 30th and 9th Divisions littered with burned-out German tanks The 902d Panzer Grenadier Regiment and a battalion of tanks struck the 30th, the other armored infantry regiment and the other battalion of Lehr's tank regiment operated against the 9th Division. Lehr's ambitious mission, according to captured documents: the recapture of Isigny, on the Norman coast

During the evening of July 10 the 3d Battalion, 120th Infantry, was ordered to advance to Le Rocher, a little town on the northwest edge of the long ridge stretching south, parallel to the Vire River. The foot columns, leading the advance met stiff resistance in some places en route, and were digging in when the vehicular column arrived. Both flanks were exposed. Road blocks were sent out, with the information that the friendly armor of Combat Command B was working in the vicinity of Hauts-Vents, to the south At 1:30 in the morning, as the Cannon Company and Antitank Company officers working with the battalion were conferring with Lieutenant Colonel Paul W. McCollum, the battalion commander, two reports came in K Company phoned that a flame-throwing tank was in action against it and a nearby 3d Armored Division tank At the same time a runner arrived from one of the road-blocks to the east tanks and armored vehicles followed by at least 20 infantrymen were moving along the road toward the command post Two enemy tanks actually moved past the command post just after messages alerting the companies had been sent out. Then a third German tank approached in cautious bounds, followed at an interval by another, and then another, and finally by an armored car. A German was standing in the open turret of the lead tank trying to send a message

Then things began to happen One American lieutenant ran to a jeep-mounted machine gun and started to fire Someone fired a bazooka and then worked around for another shot. Two officers started lobbing hand grenades into the turret and at the accompanying German infantry on the road The first tank exploded into flames, the enemy screaming for mercy. A German tried to warn the second tank but was cut down by a hail of fire. An American officer picked up a light machine gun, throwing the ammunition belt over his shoulder, and went after the third tank and the armored car. The tank escaped, with some of its metalwork knocked off. The armored car burned.

The two visiting officers started for their guns but were both wounded and captured, as the action swirled around at close quarters in the dark. Another officer leading a small ammunition party approached an armored car down the road, thinking it was American, and drew deadly fire The prisoners were lined up behind the armored car with the accompanying German infantry, and the vehicle moved toward the command post. It never got there At a crossroads just short of the command post caliber .50 slugs and rockets from two bazookas set it on fire. By morning the battalion had 60 prisoners, the toll paid by the enemy in dead and wounded was never calculated accurately Outposts reported the rumbling of armor dying off in the distance—evidently this had been the spearhead of a larger force A total of five enemy tanks and four armored cars were knocked out in the fight.

The attack on the 119th Infantry was first noticed at 6.00 A M , as the German tanks and infantry infiltrated into the American lines The attack was broken up during the morning with the aid of a task force from Combat Command B. Four enemy tanks were knocked out in the 119th sector. One engineer lieutenant working on road clearance far to the rear near Bahais recruited a tank and infantrymen to knock out one tank and then drive 20 enemy out of a house near the river, which they had occupied. Not all of the enemy armor reached our lines During the morning one group of 13 tanks was reported burning as the result of an air strike by P-47's Meanwhile the 1st Battalion of the 119th moved up and during the afternoon passed through the 2d Battalion to take the Pont Hebert bridge The 120th, still extended along the Division's exposed right flank, made local gains The 9th Division on the right had lost about 800 yards before the counterattack against it was halted

July 12 the 117th Infantry moved out of its assembly area down to the 120th Infantry zone to continue the movement south, with the 120th still spread out in roadblocks along the Division's right flank The 119th made local gains. The Division was still stuck out, with its flanks curving back on both right and left Fire from the left, across the Vire River into the 119th, was particularly heavy. The Division was almost entirely committed and would be vulnerable to counterattacks

*   *   *

The Division started south again on July 13, as the 35th Division on its left started its own attack. Panzer Lehr counterattacked again early in the morning, smacking the 117th Infantry with infantry and tanks.

The 117th organized defenses in depth and held Harassed by heavy artillery fire observed from the enemy-held heights on the east side of the Vire, the 119th made only slight gains

Thus began a week of slow intermittent progress which brought the Division down to a streamline two and a half miles away from St Gilles, the objective for the armored thrust projected so optimistically before the Vire assault started The pattern of the hedgerow war was firmly established dug in enemy tanks, well sited enemy machine guns and anti-tank guns, local counterattacks When the enemy came out of his dugouts to counterattack by daylight we scored heavily When the Americans attacked, they did so with full knowledge that their own casualties would be serious In the first seven days of the Vire attack, from July 7 to July 13, the Division lost 3,200 officers and men in dead, wounded and missing The left flank battalion of the 119th sustained 50 per cent casualties

The trouble with the hedgerows was not so much the hedges themselves as the fact that they were planted on high earthen walls which surrounded every field Men had to advance single file To get past the hedgerows the infantryman would eventually have to scale one of the earthen walls, exposed to the possible fire of a machine gun or a tank, which may or may not have been knocked out by the time he got there Tanks were easy victims on the roads, which were well covered by anti-tank guns During July, the 743d Tank Battalion had 38 tanks out of the running, one time or another, as the result of enemy action To go across country, tanks had to move slowly preceded by tankdozers to knock a passage through the earthen walls or by infantrymen with blasting charges to detonate a passageway This procedure was safer than going down the roads, but it was, like the necessary form of infantry advance, slow The opposing lines were frequently so close that we could not use artillery, with safety—too many shells would burst among friendly troops Artillery forward observers and liaison officers had to remain with the leading infantry units to obtain any terrestrial observation and there would have been no effective fire on deep targets if it had not been for the artillery spotting planes Forward observers and liaison officers were about as expendable as company and platoon leaders, who had to expose themselves to keep in contact with their men The 197th Field Artillery Battalion lost most heavily—15 killed and 23 wounded during July, including three liaison officers These casualties were negligible when compared to infantry losses, but these represented the most highly skilled men in the artillery—its eyes

On July 14 a prisoner brought rumors that the half of Panzer Lehr Division on the 30th Division front would be replaced by the cocky 14th

Parachute Regiment of the 5th Parachute Division On the 16th the strapping German paratroopers appeared in savage counterattacks, with about a battalion of them supported by tanks and backed up by exceptionally heavy artillery fire The 120th Infantry massacred about a company of them in the open as they crossed a field Sixteen enemy tanks were knocked out on the 16th, eight by observed artillery fire Panzer Lehr's armored infantrymen remained around as did remnants of the Battle Group Heintz which had opposed the Division back along the line of the Vire-et-Taute Canal Already the enemy was manifesting what was one of his greatest achievements during the entire campaign —mastery of the art of piecing together a coherent fighting team from a heterogeneous mass of troops

In preparation for the next operation, Old Hickory at midnight of July 15 was placed under control of VII Corps, which controlled the 9th Division on the right of the 30th Two days later, as the Division continued its way slowly south, a task force from the 29th Division captured St Lô, which was by then being threatened from three sides The 30th pushed down to the Terette River on the west to help pull the 9th Division along By July 20 Old Hickory's forward motion had ceased and it began reorganizing for its next major effort The Division had led the way as the Allied line swung south out of the swamplands onto solid ground. It was an exhausting effort It was costly in men and tanks, and would have been even more expensive save for expenditure of artillery ammunition undreamed of during the planning stages of the invasion

But, perhaps the expenditure was worth it First Army had a plan "for piercing the enemy line with great power on a narrow front," which was based on preliminary seizure of the ground the 30th now held The code name of the plan was "Cobra"

Chapter V

MAKING THE ST. LÔ BREAKTHROUGH

Costly, in men and matériel, as hedgerow fighting was for the Allies, it was equally expensive for the Germans in Normandy United States First Army later estimated that the enemy had lost, by the latter part of July 1944, 160,000 men, close to 400 tanks and approximately 2,500 vehicles to the invasion forces and French resistance groups The *Wehrmacht's* personnel replacement system was strained, more and more the enemy went into battle with makeshift *Kampfgruppen*. Enemy tank replacements trickled in, unequal to the losses. His gasoline and ammunition stocks in the battle area were low. The enemy defended with great tenacity and skill, constantly pruning and regrouping to maintain an unbroken front. His defense was linear, not disposed in depth. Only one division, 2d SS Panzer Division *Das Reich,* was uncommitted on First Army's front and thus available for immediate counterattack. *Oberbefehlshaber West* still had substantial reserves east of the Seine, where the German Fifteenth Army waited for a new invasion across the Dunkerque beaches There were also a number of divisions scattered through southern France Even if such troops were ordered to the battlefield, however, they would be slow to arrive, because of already shattered road and rail lines and because of direct air attack on moving columns Troops coming from the south would probably have to fight the Maquis on the way.

Operation Cobra was tailored to meet these conditions. VII Corps was to make the main effort along the St Lô–Periers highway just west of St Lô. The primary job was to drive clear through the enemy's crustlike defensive position before he could reform. For this purpose, Army planned a saturation bombing by fighter-bombers, mediums, and heavies over an area from the front lines back through the enemy's artillery positions Following this bombing, three battle-tried divisions, the 30th, 4th and 9th, were to attack southward on a narrow front, clearing the way for the three divisions which would then pour through the opening— the 2d and 3d Armored Divisions and the 1st Infantry Division, entirely motorized This last trio, the exploitation group of VII Corps, was to advance rapidly south and then turn to the southwest into the rear of the forces opposing VIII Corps along the western portion of the Cotentin Peninsula. VIII Corps on the right and XIX and V Corps on the left were ordered to maintain pressure during the VII Corps attack, first containing the enemy opposing them, later driving forward to exploit along the flanks of the breakthrough

The 30th was the easternmost of the three divisions assigned to make the breakthrough and therefore was given a second mission, that of fanning out to the southeast along the west bank of the Vire River as far south as Tessy-sur-Vire, 12 miles from the line of departure. The 30th was thus charged with protecting the entire left flank of the breakthrough, a task of particular importance because the strongest enemy counterattacks would probably be made from the east by troops from the British front or from the German Fifteenth Army.

The Division plan called for an assault by two regiments abreast, the 120th on the right, along the axis of the main highway to St. Gilles, along which the 2d Armored Division would travel; the 119th on the left, with Hebecrevon the first objective. Two battalions of the 117th were loaned to the attacking regiments. The 117th itself was to be in reserve, initially, prepared to pass through on the left to clean out the curve of the Vire River opposite St Lô

The air preparation was a key feature of the assault plan. For a month and a half progress through Normandy had been measured almost yard by yard. Air enthusiasts in particular felt that a massive carpetlike air attack before the ground troops jumped off would virtually annihilate the main enemy position by reason of concussion or sheer destruction, so that the attacking infantry could swiftly secure the breach and hold it for the following armor and motorized infantry. The air plan—the heaviest ever used in direct support of ground troops in France—called for two and a half solid hours of bombing, first by 350 fighter-bombers hitting the enemy front lines, then by 1,500 heavy bombers assigned a target area 2,500 yards deep and 6,000 yards wide, this followed by another 350-plane dive-bombing raid on the enemy front lines, and finally, as the assault troops moved forward, by forty-five minutes of bombing by 396 medium bombers hitting the rear portion of the target area assigned the heavies. The Division was particularly anxious that this rear area be well hit because it appeared to be full of emplacements—probably artillery positions but possibly the real main line of resistance.

The assault troops were to withdraw 1,200 yards behind their lines of departure before the heavy bombers attacked, for their own protection. Front lines would be marked with panels and smoke. The bombers were to come in from east to west and guide on the St Lô–Periers road.

The attack was first scheduled for July 18, but was postponed because of rains which left the roads and fields doubly treacherous for tanks and trucks and which prevented the air attack which bulked so large in the assault plan. The attack of the 18th was cancelled before the 30th ever heard of it, but the Division was set to go on the 21st, when bad weather forced another postponement.

July 24, the first of the two terrible days which opened the St Lô breakthrough, dawned clear, with a slight haze over the ground At 11 30 A M , on schedule, the 350 P-47's arrived for their preliminary dive-bombing, followed by the heavy steady drone signalling the approach of the 1,500 heavy bombers Scarcely had the men in the rear echelons caught sight of the seemingly endless tight patterns of heavy bombers glistening in the sun when the first alarming reports began to arrive, some of the dive bombers were hitting friendly troops Within twenty minutes the entire show had been called off The visibility apparently was not good enough for accurate bombing But in that period the damage was done—the one heavy squadron to dump its bombs splashed them squarely on friendly troops Dead and wounded were reported throughout the area, but most of the bombs fell where the 2d Battalion, 120th Infantry, was waiting above ground for the word to lead the regiment's attack Men already in foxholes were not hurt except for close hits which either buried them or so scattered them as to render burial impossible The toll was 24 men killed, 128 wounded

New instructions were given for the 25th The infantry attack would start at 11 00 o'clock Artillery would cover the no man's land from which the troops were to withdraw prior to the bombing, in the 9th Division zone, the previous day, the enemy had advanced as the Americans pulled back temporarily There were assurances from Corps that this time the bombers would fly from east to west rather than from north to south over the troops Airmen were to be instructed to bomb south of the St Lô–Periers road only, and if they couldn't see the road not to bomb at all

But the 25th proved to be even more of a slaughter than the previous day Both of the assault groups were hit badly The 92d Chemical Battalion was knocked out of action The 2d Battalion of the 120th was not only badly hurt in personnel but had all of its battalion radios and some of its company radios knocked out The regimental commander considered substituting another battalion in the assault but decided against it because he didn't want to risk the attendant confusion Forty of the 119th's 133 casualties were sustained near the regimental command group, on the road near Le-Mesnil-Durand Hurriedly the 1st Battalion of the 117th was substituted for the bomb-disorganized 3d Battalion, in support of the 120th's attack

Miraculously, despite the morale effect and physical disorganization of two successive bombings, the attack of the infantry proceeded almost on schedule, and continued despite further bombings by mediums, which were supposed to be instead striking at the enemy's artillery and reserve area two and a half miles farther south The 119th Infantry passed its line of departure at 11:14, only fourteen minutes later than the scheduled H-hour. The 120th jumped off at 11:30.

The bombing of the 25th caused the Division as many casualties as the most severe day of combat. The 30th suffered, in that brief bombing, 662 casualties—64 killed, 374 wounded, 60 missing and 164 cases of combat fatigue, thus raising the two-day total to 814. Not included in the totals and not then known to be a casualty by most of the 30th's troops was Lieutenant General Lesley J. McNair, who had come to Europe from his post of Commanding General, Army Ground Forces, to take a new assignment in Europe. Like Brigadier General Harrison, the assistant division commander, who had deliberately returned to the forward area on July 25, lest those who had seen him there on the 24th lose heart, General McNair had been with the assault troops on both days General McNair was killed instantly, while with the 2d Battalion of the 120th Infantry.

That portion of the bombardment that fell on the Germans shook some of them up and caused some damage. But, unlike the hapless Americans, they had had the advantage of shelters deep enough to withstand the uniformly heavy concentrations which seemed to characterize American artillery tactics When the assault troops approached they found the enemy doing business at the same old stand with the same old merchandise—dug-in tanks and infantry Enemy artillery was splattering on the main routes of approach

*   *   *

The 120th Infantry, hurriedly restoring some order out of the chaos and destruction left by the bombing, ran into tanks right off the bat. The regiment advanced in column of battalions down a long ridge toward its first objective, the junction of the north-south secondary road and the St. Lô–Periers highway, led by Company F of the hard-hit 2d Battalion Three Mark Vs and a liberal assortment of German infantrymen were in the way. Company E and then G deployed around the left flank, but were unable to get past. A platoon of light tanks from Company D of the 743d was in direct support. One of the lights had been set ablaze during the friendly bombing, but although it was restored to action, the 37 mm guns in Company D's tanks were not good enough to handle the ponderous German Panthers One American tank fired two quick shots at one of the Mark Vs The German slowly began to wheel the 88mm gun in its turret around toward the source of annoyance The American gunner fired once more and his despairing voice was heard over the radio: "Good God, I fired three rounds and they all bounced off."

The regimental plan called for deployment of the support battalions, in turn, on the left if there was a holdup. By this time, therefore, the 1st Battalion with another platoon of light tanks was starting to come around the flank, with the mission of taking a road junction a little south of the one the 2d Battalion was after. There wasn't much room between the 119th Infantry and the spread-out elements of the 2d Battalion, the 119th was already using the line of departure that the 1st Battalion commander had hoped to employ. Most of the battalion squeezed through Company E's positions on the regimental left flank, a platoon at a time, though along the regimental boundary military police methods were necessary to separate the 119th and 120th soldiers. Getting through was a slow process—besides the congestion there was enemy fire to contend with, particularly from machine guns along a sunken road at the battalion objective. But Company B and most of Company C managed to keep moving and worked on down to the battalion objective.

The 3d Battalion went into action last, advancing in column of companies on the right. Opposition was stiff at first but lessened as the battalion plowed on through. Three enemy tanks held up the advance for a while but the remaining two withdrew after artillery fire knocked out one of the trio. By nightfall the 3d Battalion was as far south as La Roque. The regimental right flank, which had been guarded by the Intelligence and Reconnaissance Platoon, extended to the Terette River.

The 2d Battalion was still held up late in the day. The medium tanks of Company A of the 743d had followed Company D's lights. Already one of the Shermans had been knocked out and one of the platoon leaders killed by a hit through the turret of his tank. Lieutenant Ernest Aas, the Company A tank commander, went on a foot reconnaissance. He located one Mark V on the left of the road and this was knocked out. Another one of the original three enemy tanks fell back to the south. Aas couldn't locate the third, but he came back with a plan for breaking through which might mean the loss of three of his five tanks to antitank fire, but was worth trying. The plan was to attack boldly across country to the left of the road, thus avoiding the mines and covering enemy fire. This plan was approved by both the regimental commander and Lieutenant Colonel Duncan, commander of the 743d, who was on hand. Lieutenant Aas' tanks attacked as planned, one at a time, and soon were engaged with no less than five Mark Vs, on both sides of the road. Company A's tank guns knocked out one enemy Panther, and the others were chased into the woods. The 2d Battalion could now advance with confidence. The American tanks swung around to work with the 1st Battalion, knocking out two more tanks before the day was over. Infantry-tank co-operation was excellent.

The 119th, also attacking in column of battalions, had a terrain problem from the start, for the front lines were along the steep-banked gully of the little stream flowing eastward into the Vire north of the road center of Hebecrevon, the initial objective for the regiment and the key feature of the high ground along which the enemy main line of resistance was located.

Thus, the 3d Battalion, leading the attack with two companies abreast, soon found itself in a slow, bitter fight Two companies of Battle Group Kentner, which had withdrawn to the west side of the Vire River as the 35th Division forced a passage southward toward St. Lô, were dug-in in the path of the battalion. The two enemy companies were supported by artillery fire and by dug-in tanks. Finally, a sizable force scrambled across the stream, but even the commitment of Company L around the right flank failed to shake the attack loose.

The 2d Battalion was sent far around the right flank, but it was the 1st Battalion which played the main role in the 119th's breakthrough. The 1st Battalion attacked in column of companies around the left flank of the 3d Battalion at 1.13 P.M , its progress notably assisted by a rolling barrage by the 197th Field Artillery Battalion and by counter-battery fire. Two or three fields south of the stream, the battalion encountered the enemy main line of resistance, which was centered on a cluster of buildings named La Huberderie Enemy mortar fire, in particular, fell heavily on the attackers. The battalion deployed, closed up to within hand-grenade range and began hand-to-hand fighting. The battalion commander ordered Company B to sideslip to the left On doing so it found a soft spot and began to threaten the enemy flank. Company C was still embroiled, however, and it therefore swung right and advanced up a gully so steep that only one man could get into it at a time.

This maneuver, although slow, succeeded in flushing the enemy out of his main line positions, now threatened from both flanks The trailing platoon of Company C drove through the group of buildings which had furnished the core of the enemy positions. The two companies captured about 50 prisoners in the action, and re-established contact with each other as they reached the top of the hill. Enemy resistance slackened as the battalion came over the brow of the hill and dug in facing the south and southwest, but German artillery and mortar fire increased proportionately In addition to the riflemen of the battalion, the mortars and the following troops of the 117th Infantry were hit hard by enemy fire

Artillery remained the most reliable of the supporting arms In some instances the bombardment had shaken up the enemy, but its favorable effects were noticeable more on the rest of VII Corps front than in front of the 30th Some of the medium bombers struck again at the assault troops after the attack began, instead of bombing the artillery positions area near St. Gilles, and it became increasingly evident that these enemy guns had not been neutralized by the air attack. Unfortunately, even with both VII and XIX Corps artillery batteries active, there was not enough ammunition available for a really heavy counterbattery program. The VII Corps commander, anxious that Hebecrevon be secured that day so that the armor could roll on the 26th, suggested at 3:50 P.M. an air attack on the town, but General Hobbs didn't dare use the planes for close support: "If we should have any more of the same [bombing of friendly troops], then our troops are finished."

Attempts by the 119th to get friendly tanks into the action were initially unsuccessful, because of terrain and the extremely heavy volume of fire put out by German tanks and antitank guns [1]

A task force consisting of a platoon of light tanks and a platoon of mediums from Company C of the 743d attacked at 1:00 P M., but it was halted both by mines and by heavy fire from three dug-in enemy tanks. Engineers attempted to remove the mines, but they were chased away by intense fire. At 4:00 P.M. the two tank platoons withdrew

The regiment at first tried to get tanks around to flank Hebecrevon from the right. The Shermans of Company C were able to get across the stream but couldn't negotiate the sharp right turn required up an old thickly overgrown road In midafternoon the tank liaison officer at regimental headquarters was ordered out on foot to reconnoiter a route that the tanks could use to support the 1st Battalion's attack on the left. He found the roads impassable, but finally figured out a path involving a left turn at the stream, movement up a steep slope and then cross-country travel to the south. When he led the tanks back to the stream, however, the first tank turned the wrong way, and within a few minutes two tanks were out of action—one knocked out by 88mm. gun fire, the other sprawled in the ditch on the north side of the stream where it had slipped off the road. The liaison officer, still on foot, cajoled the remainder through that unpleasant spot and finally at sunset got them into an assembly area in an orchard near the 1st Battalion They had come too late to be used in the attack, but their presence heartened the infantry and perhaps had helped persuade the enemy to fall back.

Hebecrevon was vital to the Corps plan of passing the armor through on the next day, as General Hobbs had been reminded at the end of the afternoon. Colonel Sutherland of the 119th gave the assignment of taking the town "at once and at all costs" to the 1st Battalion. Company A had not fought with the rest of the battalion but had advanced from the

---

[1] Later the 743d executive stated that the enemy fire received on July 25 was even heavier in volume than that received at Mortain, where the enemy had a much higher fire power potential present

northwest along with tanks from Company C of the 743d. The battalion commander ordered this group—Task Force A—to make the attack from its positions still northwest of the town. He held the rest of the battalion in position, fearing to make a converging attack in the dark. Dusk was giving way to night when the task force received the orders. It moved out led by a platoon of tanks and a platoon of infantry, with infantry scouts in front and a skirmish line of doughboys on both sides of the road. It was a nerve-wracking advance. The tanks on the road traveled with 20-yard distance between vehicles, passing down by word of mouth warning of the deep craters left by the air bombardment. The doughboys were particularly helpful in guiding the leading tanks

About a mile out of Hebecrevon an enemy roadblock came to life with 88 mm guns and machine guns blazing. One of the Shermans silenced an 88, aided by a German flare which inadvertently illuminated the enemy position. Infantrymen went forward in the dark to remove the mines in the road. Luckily they were not booby-trapped. By 1:00 A.M. the infantry-tank team had passed entirely through Hebecrevon as far as a roadblock on the other side of town. Both the rest of the 1st Battalion and the 2d Battalion moved up to the town before the 3d Battalion, which had been heavily engaged since the attack began, entered Hebecrevon at dawn on July 26.

By the morning of July 26 the howitzer had replaced the machine gun and the 88mm. gun as the most important German weapon in action against the 30th. Hebecrevon, in particular, was steadily pounded by enemy artillery, and proved a remunerative target because of the concentration of 119th Infantry troops which had to pass that way.

At 9:00 A M the tanks of the 2d Armored Division started passing through the 120th on their long dash southward. The 117th, with all of its elements back under regimental control, except for the 3d Battalion, took up positions on the left of the 119th Infantry and joined with that regiment in attacking southward alongside the armor. For perhaps a mile the enemy held with some firmness. During the latter part of the day the action resembled pursuit more than attack.

The 117th Infantry swung far to the east to the knob in the bend of the Vire River opposite St. Lô, continuing the attack far into the night. The 119th swept generally southeast, took its objective and continued south to the rail line running west from St Lô. Its, then record, bag of 236 prisoners included Colonel Kentner, who had commanded a battle group of the German 275th Infantry Division. Fleeing westward with his adjutant in a staff car after dark, he was captured, fatally wounded, by a soldier from Company I.

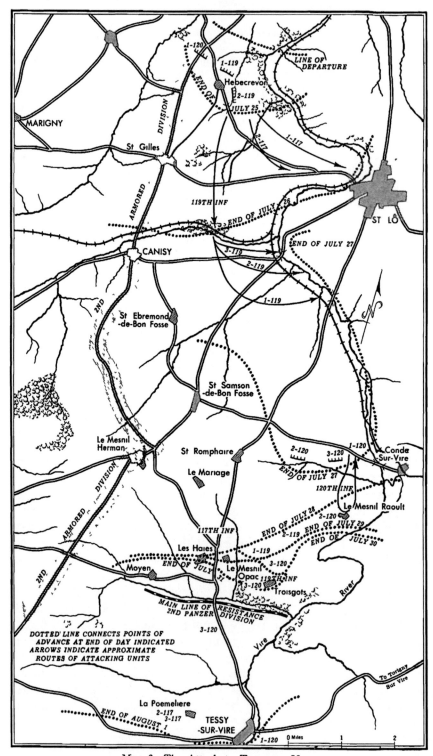

Map 3—The Attack to Tessy-sur-Vire

The fastest progress of the entire operation took place on July 27. What had borne the semblance of a fairly well organized enemy withdrawal on the previous day had degenerated into a rout. Most of the prisoners were from overrun artillery batteries and other strays The 120th Infantry came back into the battle with a long slash southward to the crossing of the Vire at Condé-sur-Vire, while the 119th turned east to hold the crossings farther north until the 35th Infantry Division covered them. The 117th remained in place cleaning out the river bend until that night, when it moved down to a new assembly area under heavy attack from the Luftwaffe.[2]

The most significant event of the day for Old Hickory did not, however, take place within its boundaries, but miles farther east This was a daylight move westward by the 2d Panzer Division, which had been pulled out of line on the British front for a well deserved rest but now found itself en route to the area of the breakthrough, with orders to cross the Vire River and attack to the north and northwest The 2d Panzer, an old and well-trained regular army division, crossed the Vire at 4:00 A.M., July 28. It was advancing northward, still in approach formation, when it ran headlong into the leading elements of the Division near St. Romphaire.

First contact with the 2d Panzer Division was made by the 2d Battalion, 120th Infantry, which attacked south at 7:00 A M on July 28, from its positions about a half-mile southeast of St Romphaire, about three and a half miles distant from the rest of the regiment covering the Condé crossing The battalion advanced about 900 yards without difficulty, then halted in the face of strong fire from the 2d Panzer Grenadier Regiment of 2d Panzer By afternoon the battalion was engaged in repelling counterattacks The 1st Battalion, which contacted 35th Infantry Division elements across the river in midafternoon sent a column southwest to aid the 2d Battalion and another column into Le-Mesnil-Raoult, across a small east-west tributary of the Vire. Company A of the latter column entered the town in the evening but withdraw under orders so that friendly artillery could hammer the town and vicinity. Identification on the regimental front, by now, included elements of the 304th Panzer Grenadier Regiment of 2d Panzer as well as the 2d Panzer Grenadier Regiment

By early afternoon the 117th Infantry, off on the left, where it had taken over from troops of the 2d Armored Division and 4th Armored Division north of Le-Mesnil-Opac, had also encountered the 2d Panzer The regiment had at first started to dig in after its overnight move for-

---

[2] Enemy planes were active over the Division area 16 out of 31 days in July, and some 10 20 planes bombed the Division several times during each of the last four nights of the month

ward but was ordered to attack at 11:30. The attack began at 1:00 P M,
and soon the leading 3d Battalion was engaged in a bitter fire fight with
the enemy's tanks, 88s, and armored infantry at a road junction just
north of Le-Mesnil-Opac, about 1,000 yards from its line of departure

By early morning the 1st Battalion of the 120th had re-entered Le-
Mesnil-Raoult, this time to stay, but that was the last major gain for the
Division for some time to come The Germans, according to prisoner
testimony, entered the battle with only the vaguest of ideas as to the
strength and location of the forces opposing them, whereas the 30th had
been warned at 10:00 P.M the night before of the probable approach
of the 2d Panzer. But after the surprise of the initial contacts, the German units settled down to skillful defense and succeeded in holding the
streamline south of Moyen–Le-Mesnil-Opac–Troisgots for three days
before they were forced to fall back and yield the important Vire crossing at Tessy-sur-Vire The enemy position was generally along the ridge
just south of the stream, with additional positions in the towns and along
the reverse slopes north of the stream Liberally equipped with machine guns, tanks, and artillery, the veteran 2d Panzer troops created
more respect for their fighting ability than had even the SS and parachute
men who had opposed the 30th north of St. Lô.

The 119th Infantry rejoined the battle on July 29, passing through
the 120th. It managed to fight its way to within a mile of Troisgots, in
the center of the still extended division battle line. But this was the only
success of the day: the 117th Infantry was being fought almost to a
standstill. The assault troops gained the top of the hill near Le-Mesnil-
Opac but got no farther Company C was committed around the left
flank to stop persistent German infiltration.

July 30 brought some of the bitterest fighting the 30th ever engaged
in. Twice, at 7·00 A M. and at 3:15 P M, Old Hickory attempted a
co-ordinated attack employing all three regiments. The artillery fired
three times as much ammunition as it normally expended, but failed to
halt the heavy fire poured out by enemy howitzers and guns The German panzer grenadiers seemed to be attacking as much as the American
infantry, taking full advantage of the strong fire power of the panzer
division The 30th Division's losses were heavy—a couple of hundred in
one battalion alone Six of the 16 tanks supporting the 119th Infantry
were knocked out. Both American attacks were stopped in their tracks.

The tide began to turn on the 31st The 117th, on the right, made a
scant 300 yards in the face of heavy fire and the 120th also was held to
painfully short gains But the 119th, in the center, finally cracked the
crust protecting Troisgots, and the 2d Battalion and supporting tanks

triumphantly entered the town. The 743d Tank Battalion knocked out five strategically located Panther tanks and its Lieutenant Harry F. Hansen guided infantry bazooka teams to two others that his 75mm. tank guns could not reach.

Time as well as strength was running short for the 2d Panzer Division. The 35th Infantry Division was slowly advancing south along the east bank of the Vire River, menacing its supply route. The main body of the American exploitation force was still running wild south and west of the 2d Panzer's island of resistance, threatening to veer into its left flank and rear. During the night of the July 31-August 1, its battered troops withdrew to the south and east. It was not yet willing, however, to give up Tessy-sur-Vire without a fight.

*   *   *

The XIX Corps moved west of the Vire River, taking the 29th Division with it, and at noon on July 28 reassumed control of the 30th. By August 1, therefore, both the 29th Division and the 2d Armored Division were operating on the 30th's right. Old Hickory jumped off as usual at 6:00 A. M. that day in its old zone, but five hours later the Division zone was narrowed to facilitate a concentration of power against Tessy-sur-Vire, outside which 2d Armored Division elements approaching from the west were reported heavily engaged.

Tessy was originally the 117th Infantry's objective, but on the morning of August 1 it was transferred to the 120th's zone and promptly assigned to the 1st Battalion and then to Company B, at the time about three miles from the town. "We were suddenly ordered early in the morning to take off for Tessy, so we took off," the company commander explained. Without even an artillery observer to furnish supporting fire, the company moved across country along a sunken road to within a mile of the town, where its appearances on the ridge leading down into Tessy prompted enemy artillery and mortar fire. There was also a machine-gun nest, but this was soon knocked out by Private Carlos J. Ruiz, the lead scout, who killed two German machine gunners in position and then leaped over the hedge to kill the third man of the enemy group as he attempted to escape. With this key machine gun out of action, the enemy fell back, firing green flares as they withdrew to mark Company B's current positions for the German artillery. The company advanced another 400 yards, firing at the flare points, before an antitank gun opened up—and then was knocked out with a rifle grenade at close range by Private First Class Lonnie M. Groves.

At 7:30 the company entered Tessy, only to come under fire from all directions. Two platoons fought house by house down the main street while the weapons platoon paralleled them on the flank. A Browning automatic-rifle man knocked out a half-track towing an 88mm. gun. Someone else used a rifle grenade to wreck an armored car with an anti-aircraft gun. The company commander had thought at first that his job was primarily to set up roadblocks and that the 2d Armored Division had already done the rough work of taking the town. Already he had his doubts about the accuracy of those ideas and soon it was a lot more than a doubt. A counterattack supported by 88s and mortars from across the Vire shoved the company back to the edge of town, where it dug in under heavy artillery fire. A wire patrol was attempting to work its way forward to Company B, but there was still no contact with the rest of the battalion, which was fighting its way forward to help the company. But somehow, artillery fire was brought to bear on the enemy mortar positions and they shut up.

Combat Command A of the 2d Armored Division was not in Tessy but some of its troops were nearby. About this time an officer from the tankers showed up He thought the artillery fire in Tessy was too heavy for tank fighting, but was persuaded to provide four Shermans.

The arrival of the tanks made the second attack on Tessy successful—as much for their psychological effect on friend and foe as for their considerable fire power. "The tanks could have been wooden guns," the Company B commander commented Friendly morale soared and enemy morale declined sharply. B Company charged back into town and set up to stay

Enemy artillery continued to thunder profusely into the buildings of Tessy, directed from the high ground flanking the town. One 150mm. shell, fortunately a dud, landed in the company command post Some of the fire was eliminated by the 117th Infantry's drive to the high ground west of Tessy, cutting the roads to the west and south The town remained unhealthy, however, until the 35th Division seized the town and high ground east of the Vire which overlooked Tessy.

*   *   *

Thus ended the costliest month of fighting the 30th experienced in Europe. Some later battles were as bitter as those fought in July and some were perhaps even more savage. But, the three weeks of fighting between the assault of the Vire and the capture of Tessy provided a sustained nightmare of losses Platoon leaders, forward observers, riflemen —they are always expendable in war, it seems, but never did they pass in and out of the battle area with such speed and regularity as in July's fighting. There were many instances where, three days after a replacement had jumped off a truck to report at the division rear echelon, he would be stricken off the division's rosters—evacuated by the clearing station or dead.

On August 2, Old Hickory passed out of direct contact with the enemy for the first time in 49 days. Enemy artillery fire and air raids continued, but the Division's troops concentrated on snatching a well deserved rest. A quartermaster bath unit set up shop on the banks of the Vire near Condé. Movies, USO shows, Red Cross doughnut wagons came into the area. Many doughboys just wandered about aimlessly in the sunlight. General Hobbs toured the unit bivouacs with praise for success and a grim reminder: "If there is any running to be done in this Division we run forward. And if we should ever have to temporarily move back, we move step by step, with our faces to the front and our guns blazing, every inch of the way."

Whether or not speeches influence fighting men is an open question. This speech may well have done some good. For, six days after the 30th passed to XIX Corps reserve, it was engaged in nothing less than a struggle for survival.

Chapter VI

THE BATTLE OF MORTAIN

Operation Cobra was, of course, the weapon which broke the back of the German position in Normandy. Indeed, one might conclude from a casual examination of the record that the St. Lô breakthrough signalled the end of serious enemy resistance until the heavy fighting of the fall

If, however, we accept the textbook dictum that warfare is directed at the enemy will to resist, and if we take at face value the testimony of the German High Command, the decisive battle of the entire hedge-row campaign took place a full two weeks after the St. Lô breakthrough occurred. Not the operation beginning July 25, but the Battle of Mortain a fortnight later, convinced the enemy that he had lost the Battle of France and that there was no alternative to precipitate flight all the way back to the Westwall. One trio of German generals went so far as to declare that the Battle of Mortain was one of the two critical operations leading to the defeat of Germany in the West.[1]

The battle itself, as we hope to show, was as dramatic and hazardous a struggle as one might wish to read about but not engage in. Even aside from its general importance, Mortain was Old Hickory's epic battle. Almost as interesting as the action itself, however, was the pattern of its staging, in which the 30th, unwarned and without time to prepare for a major battle, was drawn to the Mortain area, as if by a puppeteer's strings, just in time to be struck by four panzer divisions

* * *

The story of the Mortain operation properly begins on the last day of July. The St. Lô breakthrough was then a week old. German casualties in prisoners alone were mounting by leaps and bounds, and would eventually be calculated as approximately 20,000 men for Operation Cobra alone. Losses in matériel—tanks, guns, trucks—were even more serious. Worst of all for the Germans, the Americans now had an open corridor through which fresh troops could pass to circle westward into Brittany and eastward, in rear of the entire German position, toward Paris The next day, August 1, General Patton's Third Army swung into action for the first time, for that very purpose

---

[1]"Failure of the German attempt to cut off the Americans at Avranches and the loss of the Remagen Bridge were two of the biggest reasons for Nazi defeat, according to a high ranking SHAEF [Supreme Headquarters, Allied Expeditionary Forces] officer, who interviewed Colonel General Gustav Jodl, supreme planner for the Germans and a close associate of Hitler, Field Marshal Wilhelm Keitel, and General Albert von Kesselring The German High Command, the Nazis said, was astonished that the attack of their four divisions   failed to reach Avranches to cut off the American Third Army " *Stars and Stripes,* June 24, 1945 This statement is typical of many others obtained in interviews with captured high ranking German officers

By July 31, the German commanders in Normandy were badly handicapped by disrupted communications and the relative immobility, under constant air attack, of the few reserves available to them The telephone journals of German Commander in Chief West's headquarters indicate that Field Marshal von Kluge, in supreme command of the Germans in France and the Low Countries, did not learn of the fall of Avranches and Villedieu until 9:20 A.M. on the 31st, although these two road centers had passed into American hands the previous day, and the report announcing this bad news characterized the situation in the Avranches–Villedieu area as "completely unclear." A few minutes later the Field Marshal and the Chief of Staff of the German Seventh Army were agreeing that "obviously the enemy is still very weak in Avranches We are dealing with an advanced enemy spearhead there."

An hour later, however, as von Kluge reported to General Warlimonts, Hitler's personal representative, he demonstrated full realization of the plight of his armies:

> The enemy is in Avranches and may be [!] also in Villedieu These key positions for future operations must be held at all costs .   Commander in Chief West describes the seriousness of the situation with impressive eloquence Whether the enemy can be stopped at this point is still questionable The enemy air activity is terrific, and smothers almost every one of our movements Every movement of the enemy, however, is prepared and protected by its air force. Losses in men and equipment are extraordinary. The morale of the troops has suffered very heavily under constant murderous enemy fire, especially, since all infantry units consist of only haphazard groups which do not form a coordinated force any longer In the rear areas of the front, terrorists, feeling the end approaching, grow steadily bolder This fact and the loss of numerous signal installations makes an orderly command extremely difficult LXXXIV Corps has reached a certain degree of disintegration   Fresh troops must be brought up from the Fifteenth Army or from somewhere else. Commander in Chief West recalls herewith World War I for example, in which Parisian buses were used to bring up troops to the Allied front Now, as then, all available means must be exhausted It is, however, still impossible to determine whether it would be possible to stop the enemy

The situation obviously called for immediate action to close the Avranches Gap, but so great was the disorganization of enemy front-line troops and reserves alike, in the face of incessant ground and air attack, that an entire week passed before sufficient German forces could be gathered for that purpose. Meanwhile the exploitation was proceeding at full gallop Most of the United States Third Army raced through the corridor, now widened to approximately 20 miles, during the first week of August, and part of First Army also charged into the clear Pontorson, controlling the northern highway to Brest, fell August 1, and during the week General Patton's tanks and motorized infantry captured Rennes, the ancient provincial capital, and fanned out across the peninsula. From Caen to Vire the German line still manifested some cohesiveness, but unless something were done to choke off the flood of men and equipment moving south past Avranches, not only would Brittany fall but the Germans still fighting in place in Normandy would be enveloped from the south. Also, the road to Paris was undefended

Hitherto the German High Command had employed its armor stingily, a division or even a battle group of a division at a time. Now, with survival itself at stake, it decided to employ no less than four panzer divisions, plus attachments, for the counterattack. These were the 1st SS Panzer Division *Leibstandarte Adolf Hitler,* the remnants of 2d SS Panzer Division *Das Reich,* filled up with what was left of the 17th SS Panzer Grenadier Division *Goetz von Berlichingen,* the 2d Panzer Division and the 116th Panzer Division All were under XLVII Panzer Corps

Flowing almost due west into the Baie-du-Mont-St-Michel at Avranches is the Sée River. Just south of the river is a sharply rising ridge which follows the stream through the entire 20 miles of the Allied corridor. Just north of the river is a good secondary road running westward to Avranches, roughly paralleled by another one a few miles farther south just behind the ridge. The counterattack plan, which bore the code name Luttich,[2] contemplated an attack along the axis of these roads, evidently with the thought of reestablishing a defensive line facing northward along this excellent terrain. A secondary objective was the tactically important Hill 314, rising sharply from the eastern edge of Mortain, a few miles south of the intended breakthrough corridor. In German hands, Hill 314 would not only provide excellent observation of American dispositions south of the Sée River, but would serve to deny the Americans almost equally good observation eastward.

Except for the towering hills, which contrasted notably with the rolling, half-flooded lowlands northeast of St Lô, the Mortain battlefield was typical hedgerow country The Germans would rely on surprise and mass to keep their attack rolling in such constricting terrain.

*   *   *

While Operation Luttich was being projected onto the map boards of the German planning sections, the 30th Infantry Division was finishing up its brief rest period. The 2d Battalion of the 119th Infantry pro-

---

[2]Luttich is the German name for the Belgian city of Liège Thus, curiously, the first of the two major German counterblows in the west was named after the main object of the second—the great winter counteroffensive through the Ardennes

ceeded south by motors on the night of August 3-4 to join Combat Command A of the 2d Armored Division near Vire. The 3d Battalion, 119th
Infantry, planned to join its sister unit the next morning, but the orders
were cancelled when it was learned that the 30th would pass to V
Corps, for operations east of the Vire River, on the evening of the 4th
Routes and assembly areas were reconnoitered, but, approximately half
an hour before the scheduled 11:00 A M., August 5, commencement of
the move, the orders were changed. The Division was placed under
VII Corps effective at 9:30 P M. that night. At 8:30 P M. First Army
phoned down new orders a combat team should move as soon as possible
through Percy to Villedieu, where VII Corps guides would pick it up
and lead it to its destination. General Harrison, who had gone to VII
Corps to receive instructions, reported shortly after midnight that the
mission was to take over from the 1st Division near Mortain as soon as
possible VII Corps, intent on exploitation, was stretching southward
as fast as it could. Arrival of the 30th would permit the 1st Division
to continue to extend the American line, now curling into the German
rear.

As soon as the trucks promised by Army arrived the 120th Infantry
climbed aboard and at 1:30 in the morning began its 40-mile road march
By morning of August 6, the entire Division was on the road Most of
the trip was more like a celebration than a move into battle August 6
was a warm bright Sunday, and the local citizenry thronged the roads
to wave, throw flowers and offer drinks to the passing soldiers. At
Mortain itself hotels and cafés were open and crowded with customers
The only signs of trouble came late in the afternoon, as the later convoys
pulling into their respective areas were strafed by several flights of
German fighter-bombers.

Relief of the 1st Division, begun during the morning as the 120th
Infantry Regimental Combat Team arrived, continued through the
afternoon and evening The 120th took over the positions held by the
18th Infantry in and near Mortain and on Hill 314. The 117th occupied
the 26th Infantry's positions in St. Barthelmy, a couple of miles north
of Mortain and on the ridge back of the former town The artillery
moved into the positions of the 1st Division Artillery. The 119th Infantry, in Division reserve, moved into an assembly area just north of
the ridge road to Avranches, about three miles west of Juvigny.

The local situation when the 30th arrived might almost have been
described in the words the German generals had used a week previously
"completely unclear," although at the time it seemed perhaps no more
obscure than was natural in an exploitation period. The 30th itself
physically occupied an arc beginning at Mortain on the south, swinging

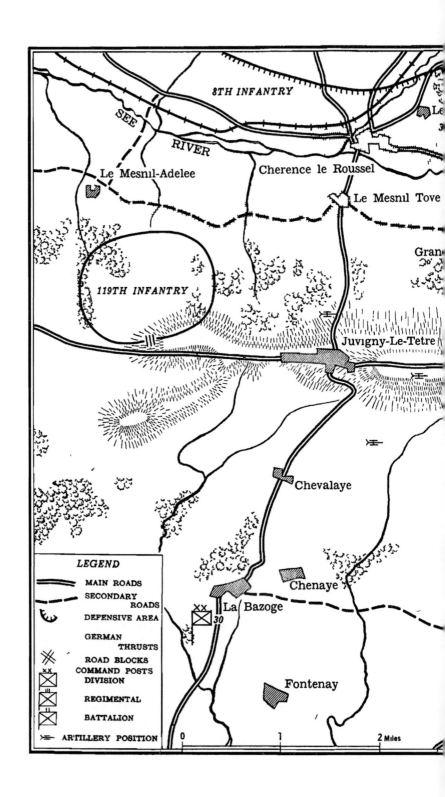

8TH INFANTRY

SEE RIVER

Le Mesnil-Adelee

Cherence le Roussel

Le Mesnil Tove

Gran

119TH INFANTRY

Juvigny-Le-Tetre

Chevalaye

Chenaye

La Bazoge

Fontenay

LEGEND

——— MAIN ROADS

– – – SECONDARY ROADS

DEFENSIVE AREA

GERMAN THRUSTS

ROAD BLOCKS

COMMAND POSTS
DIVISION

REGIMENTAL

BATTALION

ARTILLERY POSITION

0   1   2 Miles

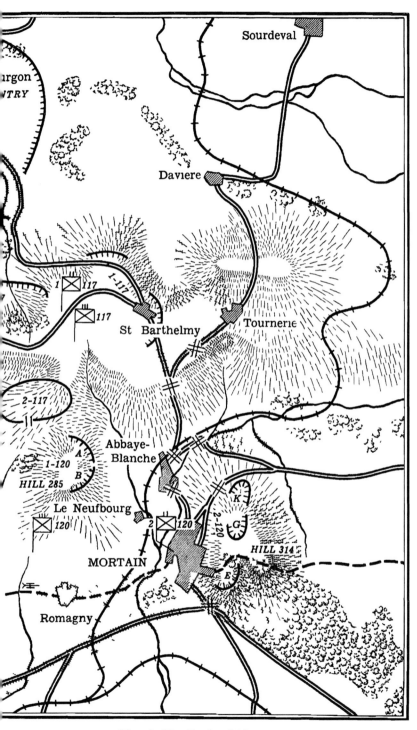

Map 4—The Battle of Mortain

north through St. Barthelmy and then curving westward along the high
ground south of the Sée River. VII Corps cavalry was reported present
on the Division's right flank as far south as Le Teileul, a town about
eight miles south of Mortain. A task force of the 2d Armored Division
was reported in Barenton, about six miles southeast of Mortain on the
road to Domfront. The 39th Infantry of the 9th Infantry Division was
somewhere north of the 117th Infantry in the Grand-Dove–Le-Mont-
Turgon area, facing north toward the enemy pocket west of Vire.[3] Just
north of Cherence-le-Roussel, and west of the 39th Infantry, was the 8th
Infantry Regiment of the 4th Division.

If the Division's knowledge of friendly dispositions and responsibilities
was vague, its knowledge of the enemy situation near Mortain and of
the probable course of events was very close to being guesswork, neither
VII Corps nor the departing 1st Division could furnish any information
as to actual enemy dispositions in the sector. Elements of three enemy
divisions, including the 2d Panzer, were known to be pocketed north
of Cherence-le-Roussel, and the Division's G-2 periodic report for the
period ending at midnight on August 6 noted that the enemy was "highly
capable" of counterattacking southwest out of the pocket However, it
seemed probable that the 9th and 4th Division north of the Sée River,
not the 30th, would bear the brunt of such an attack if it did take place.
Corps' plans for the 30th tied in more closely with the theory that the
enemy was intent on withdrawal eastward, for a reinforced battalion of
the 120th was ordered to relieve the 2d Armored Division elements in
Barenton, and the 119th Infantry had been alerted to make a long
sweep eastward to seize Domfront. The situation map showed almost
nothing directly in front of the 30th area save elements of two enemy
divisional reconnaissance battalions According to one report, a warning of an imminent attack reached the 30th Division command post
from VII Corps approximately twenty minutes before the first definite
signs of trouble appeared, but even this warning—which never
reached the regiments—was couched in the vaguest of terms—"Enemy
counterattack expected vicinity Mortain from east or north within
twelve hours."

As we have seen above, the Germans achieved some surprise in a
purely psychological sense, when they attacked at Mortain. But the
important factors that handicapped the defenders there were not psychological but physical Most of them stemmed from lack of time in
which to get set Some are attributable to sheer lack of troops

The plan for the relief of the 1st Infantry Division was based on the

---

[3]The 117th sent patrols to contact the 39th Infantry but they did not succeed in getting through
before the enemy attack began

theory that regiments, battalions, companies, platoons and even squads would take over positions occupied by 1st Division troops Even the telephone wire nets laid by 1st Division wiremen were left in place. The trouble with this plan was that the 1st Division had never planned to fight a major battle when it paused near Mortain Its field works, adequate for their original purpose, were utterly inadequate for defense against a major attack. The field artillery positions were uniformly far forward, so that later 30th Division Artillery was unable to mass its fire power on both the northern and southern portions of the front Most infantry units of the 30th arrived too late for their commanders to make thorough reconnaissance, and almost no one had time to dig in completely. Large-scale maps did not arrive at the Division until about 11:00 P M on August 6, although the Division Engineer had been attempting ever since the alert order had been received to obtain them As a result the Division went into battle with a few small-scale maps given it for the motor movement and with the crumpled large-scale maps the 1st Division's men pulled out of their pockets and off of their mapboards, and turned over to the Old Hickory soldiers before departing By the time the artillery arrived there was no opportunity to redispose the Division's howitzers in depth even if the idea had been presented, and by the time the need for realignment of the artillery became apparent, some of the batteries were already engaged at close quarters with enemy tanks and infantry. Many of the wire circuits left by the 1st Division soon developed trouble and had to be duplicated In accordance with the 1st Division's mission, no direct telephone lines had been laid from Division Artillery to the artillery battalions, although such lines, paralleling the connection through Division headquarters and the infantry regiment, were normal and urgently needed portions of the communications scheme in all but light actions

Fatigue was also a by-product of the shortage of time: most of the men had been up all day and some the night before when they began digging in their new positions.

The strength situation may be quickly summarized. At the end of July the Division plus normal attachments was approximately 1,900 men under strength. Between August 3 and 5, it received 780 replacements; even counting these new men, unassimilated into the organization, the 30th still lacked approximately 1,000 men, or almost a battalion and a half in fighting strength In addition, two of the nine infantry battalions of the Division were absent when the fight started With its seven remaining battalions spread over a 7-mile front, the Division was soon perilously low in reserve strength. Except for cavalry, its right flank was open. Soon the left flank materialized into another weak point.

By 10:00 P.M. of August 6, the preliminaries were over. Digging in, improving communications—all the little local acts of taking over a position continued until more pressing matters happened along, but the bigger units were all in place. The 3d Battalion, 120th Infantry, accompanied by a company of 743d tanks and a platoon each from the Reconnaissance Troop and the 823d Tank Destroyer Battalion, was just leaving on its detached mission in Barenton. The 119th Infantry, studying plans to seize far-off Domfront, was still without the services of its 2d Battalion All the other units of the Division were now where they were supposed to be, as the G-3 officer informed VII Corps. Everyone was ready, that is to say, except the Germans, who alone had seen the program beforehand.

While VII Corps was being informed that the 30th Infantry Division had "closed into present area at 062000B Aug '44," a somewhat more interesting message was being transmitted over a German field telephone system. The speaker was the commanding General of XLVII Panzer Corps, his audience the commander of the German Seventh Army. General Funk, it seemed, had some troubles: the 1st SS Panzer Division's leading elements had gotten no farther than Tinchebray, a dozen miles away from the front, as of only forty minutes previously. The 2d Panzer Division still hadn't received the assault guns, Panther tanks and artillery it was supposed to get from II Parachute Corps Least tolerable of all was the failure of 116th Panzer Division to show up with the units promised to work with the 2d Panzer Division Evidently this was an old source of complaint, for the corps commander requested that Count von Schwerin be relieved as commander of the 116th, adding that his division "practically always mucks up the situation."

All this the army commander listened to without comment. When General Funk went on to suggest that the attack on the right wing would probably be delayed for hours, however, he received a curt reply: "This does not alter the fact that Lüttich will be executed as ordered "

The 3d Battalion of the 120th Infantry advancing to Domfront, was bombed and strafed by nine German Focke-Wulf 190s almost as soon as it got on to the road, losing 25 men and four trucks and a precious half hour's time. As the battalion was departing, about 10 enemy tanks were observed moving eastward ahead of the American column, just west of Barenton. At 10:17 P.M. the 120th received a report that enemy tanks were in position northwest of Barenton, and a little later learned that the friendly armor in the town had been ejected.

Advance elements of the 3d Battalion task force contacted Task Force X of the 2d Armored Division—80 men and 10 tanks—at 11:10 P.M. just outside of Barenton, learning that the enemy then holding the town had arrived during the last half hour—that it would have been able to enter the town unopposed had it not been for the air attack enroute The battalion took up positions for the night and prepared to retake Barenton the next day. It did not rejoin the rest of the Division until six days later

*   *   *

H-hour for the German general attack must have been midnight or soon afterward About 1:00 A M a forward observer of the 26th Field Artillery Battalion (supporting the 30th Infantry Regiment) heard tanks moving along the northern road paralleling the Sée River where it bends south toward St Barthelmy and Mortain At first the battalion was told it was friendly armor, but soon began to shoot, starting at ranges of about 4,000-5,000 yards from its positions near Juvigny, then cutting down the range until it was shooting its lowest powder charge at sound-located targets only 1,000 yards away The Cannon Company of the 39th Infantry, in Le-Mesnil-Tove, was forced to abandon its trucks and weapons. Soon a column of about 20 tanks, accompanied by dismounted elements of the 1st SS Panzer Reconnaissance Battalion, was driving down the secondary road just south of the Sée toward Le-Mesnil-Adelée, more than three miles west of where the front lines were supposed to be

Within an hour the enemy attack had begun along the entire length of the Division front. At 1:25 A.M. the 2d Battalion of the 120th Infantry, its line elements up on Hill 314, reported small-arms fire to the east. Five minutes later German tanks and infantry advanced along a good dirt road through the Forêt de Mortain, swept around and engulfed the road-blocks guarding Mortain from the south, and penetrated the town itself At 2:00 A M. a new enemy threat from the east was reported by the roadblocks around Abbaye Blanche which guarded the northern entrance to Mortain; some of the enemy were succeeding in by-passing the blocks and were entering the town. Other Germans were painstakingly insinuating themselves among our positions up on Hill 314.

*   *   *

During the night the first attempts to eliminate the enemy penetrations took place. The commander of the 120th Infantry at 2:50 sent Company C, which had moved into positions on the regimental right flank when the 3d Battalion departed, to re-establish contact with the 2d Battalion command post, located in a Mortain hotel. The company reached Lieutenant Colonel Hardaway, commander of the 2d Battalion, but was unable to perform its second mission of re-establishing a road-block in the south end of Mortain This was the last real reserve open to the regiment; when Colonel Hardaway reported at 3:45 that part of

Hill 314 was now German-held, he was ordered to use his own Company G to retake the ground. Later the 2d Battalion, 117th Infantry, was made available to Colonel Birks of the 120th, but it was several miles away and could not be put into action until later in the day.

The northern threat, knifing past the 117th Infantry toward Le-Mesnil-Adelée, was a divisional problem. The two-thirds strength 119th Infantry was ordered into action at 3:00 A M with instructions to set up a company-strength roadblock at Le-Mesnil-Adelée, to drive west into the rear of the armored spearhead with another company, from La Preventerie, and to send the 3d Battalion north from Juvigny to retake Le-Mesnil-Tove and contact the 8th Infantry.

Company B of the 119th, reinforced by two 57mm antitank guns from 1st Battalion Headquarters Company, set out on the Le-Mesnil-Adelée mission, arriving between 5.30 and 6:30 in the morning The German spearhead had stopped; enemy tanks could be discerned off the road under camouflage nets. One of the 57s, commanded by Sergeant Richard Waller, was manhandled into position while the other covered it, and with three rounds set a Panther tank afire After this the AT guns, unequal in fire power or numbers to the enemy, pulled back.

*   *   *

At 3:15 A M a combat observer from VII Corps, reporting the counterattack, noted that "Division G-3 states [30th] Division not yet greatly concerned," and an hour or so later indicated that 30th Division headquarters was still optimistic; another example of the fact that rapidly assessing the strength of an enemy attack is one of the most difficult feats in the business of warfare [4] Actually the full force of the enemy attack did not appear until just before dawn; the deep penetration along the north flank and the steady pressure around Mortain were essentially preliminary operations As darkness gave way to fog-laden daylight the deep penetration at the north had stopped and was tenuously blocked, but it had not been expelled. The situation around Mortain was unsatisfactory indeed And, in the center, approximately 50 tanks of the 1st SS and their supporting infantry from the 2d SS Panzer Grenadier Regiment were moving in on the positions of the 1st Battalion, 117th Infantry, in St. Barthelmy.

*   *   *

"With a heavy onion breath that day the Germans would have achieved their objective," General Hobbs later said of the fighting on the 7th. Excited civilians reported German tanks and infantry within a

---

[4] *Infantry in Battle,* a series of accounts of World War I actions edited by General (then Colonel) George C Marshall, contains a classic case the leader of a platoon hit by one of the major German thrusts at the American sector thought he was facing a combat patrol

mile of the Division command post, and the 1st Battalion of the 119th and Company D of the 743d were pulled south to help protect it, only to be sent away a little later on another mission. The Reconnaissance Troop, ordered to set up roadblocks on the highway leading southwest from Mortain encountered six Mark IV tanks and infantry four miles farther west, lost an armored car but succeeded in halting the enemy force. Near Romagny, C Battery of the 197th Field Artillery found itself embroiled in a short range fight with tanks and infantry. A telephone switchboard operator at the 120th Infantry command post, Private First Class Joseph O. Shipley, slipped away from his post in midafternoon long enough to knock out, with a bazooka, one of two enemy tanks which had penetrated to within 250 yards of the regimental headquarters.

These were the spearheads. Farther forward the battle raged even more heavily, while P-47s and RAF rocket-firing Typhoons slugged at the enemy tank waves, often inadvertently hitting friendly positions. The 120th was hit by aircraft ten times during the day. With enemy tanks and infantry all through the American positions, some troops were hit by friendly artillery and small-arms fire. Smoke from the bombs obscured the battlefield As one tank destroyer man put it, "We didn't have a friend in the world that day."

At St. Barthelmy the enemy tank-infantry teams followed a heavy barrage and soon overran Companies A and C of the 117th, which fought doggedly in place. The 1st Battalion command group was surrounded and had to fight its way out; Colonel Frankland killed a tank commander with his pistol. Company B was flung into line along with clerks, messengers and drivers of headquarters company. Regimental headquarters of the 117th was about 400 yards south of the 1st Battalion command post and approximately as close to the front lines. Lieutenant Colonel Walter M. Johnson, who had jumped from regimental executive to regimental commander when Colonel Kelly left just before the move from Tessy, called his farmhouse command post "Château Nebelwerfer." Artillery fire knocked out the regimental switchboard, and all of the larger vehicles at the command post were evacuated under small-arms and artillery fire Enemy tanks reached a point about a quarter of a mile from the building A four-man volunteer detail took care of one of them, two men exposing themselves to draw its fire, the other two then lobbing two bazooka rounds through its turret. About a company of enemy infantry maneuvered to the rear of the headquarters, was discovered by the Intelligence and Reconnaissance Platoon, and finally driven away by the platoon—after one man had held them back with hand grenades to gain time in which his comrades could maneuver. Both enemy and friendly planes struck the area In effect, the command post was isolated for the next six days, although liaison officers managed occasionally to slip through the German infiltrations along the road to the rear.

Towed tank-destroyer guns of Company B of the 823d played an important part in halting the Germans, although particularly vulnerable to the well co-ordinated panzergrenadier-tank attack and handicapped by the fog. At the start the gunners were firing at nothing more tangible than the flashes of the enemy tank guns. Tank destroyers knocked out two Panthers early in the fight, but three of the four guns in the 3d Platoon were soon casualties: the heavy towed guns were sitting ducks when they revealed their locations by firing. Lieutenant Neel brought forward a replacement gun from the 1st Platoon under heavy fire. This gun, from its position just west of St. Barthelmy, knocked out a Mark V, killed a tank commander and mowed down supporting enemy infantry with small-arms fire before an enemy 88 found the range, knocked out the gun and wounded most of the crew. Another Company B gun was brought forward—and had an equally short but useful career. One enemy tank approached and was promptly knocked out. Two more German tanks appeared and halted out of gun range Then one of them advanced while the other covered it. The Company B crew destroyed the first tank. But, just as anticipated, the second tank opened fire, knocking out the 823d's gun. Company B lost seven of its 12 guns and their half-track prime movers during the day, though one intrepid crew ventured out past the friendly front lines and extricated one of the abandoned guns Other members of Company B fought alongside the infantrymen with their carbines or joined bazooka teams stalking tanks. Company B accounted for at least eight Mark V tanks during the day and probably knocked out an additional two.

The infantry casualties at St Barthelmy were heavy The 1st Battalion, 117th Infantry, lost 350 men during the day, but was crippled even more than this high figure indicates by disorganization and isolation of its small units. Some men of the battalion fought and hid in isolated bands for two days before they succeeded in rejoining their companies. The battalion, its fighting capacity something like 50 per cent of normal, fell back about a thousand yards during the morning and grouped itself on the hill overlooking St. Barthelmy, now strewn with dead German tanks and soldiers. By noon, however, the battalion appeared to have won the battle of survival. Harried by air and ground resistance, the enemy push came to a halt.

While the 117th was absorbing the main enemy drive in the St Barthelmy area, the nocturnal thrust to Le-Mesnil-Adelée which preceded it was hammered back from three sides during daylight fighting of August 7. Combat Command B of the 3d Armored Division, which was attached to Old Hickory at 7:30 A.M., passed through the Company B, 119th Infantry, roadblock at Adelée and struck due east along the road during the day, aided by the ubiquitous Typhoons overhead Company I of the 119th, it may be recalled, had been given the ambitious mission of hitting westward into the rear of the German column. With two of its accompanying tanks knocked out by Allied dive bombing, Company I was too frail a plug for the German escape route and had to get off the road as the German spearhead fell back to its own lines. The rest of the 3d Battalion, attacking northward from Juvigny toward Le-Mesnil-Tove, was no match for the German force either, especially since it was being harassed on its right (east) flank. However, it massed fires on the German withdrawal with sufficient effect to drive it north of Le-Mesnil-Tove, and to permit a junction with the 3d Armored tankers near Tove. The 30th Division forces were not yet in contact with the 8th Infantry, which had withdrawn north toward Cherence-le-Roussel, but the most threatening of the German thrusts was now reduced to a tough cleanup problem The 3d Battalion, 119th Infantry, sent out a small task force of doughboys and engineers, plus a pair of 57mm anti-tank guns, to guard its right rear as it faced north, and the sector settled down to a temporary stability.

The first blows against the 120th Infantry, as we have seen, principally threatened the 2d Battalion, stuck out in the Mortain–Hill 314 area As the day wore on, not only Mortain but the integrity of the entire regimental position, as well, was seriously challenged. North of Mortain, a task force of doughboys and tank destroyers held a long, critically important road block near Abbaye Blanche The 1st Battalion was in a full-scale fight on Hill 285, about a half-mile west of Abbaye Blanche. The south flank, originally defended by the 3d Battalion before its dispatch to Barenton, and then by C Company, was now almost denuded of troops. The regimental Intelligence and Reconnaissance Platoon ventured into the little town of Romagny on the south flank just before dawn—and was ambushed. The platoon fought for two hours, taking some prisoners, interrogating them, and radioing valuable information back to regiment until the very last minute But, finally, the Germans swallowed up all but two vehicles and a few men. In full possession of Romagny, they could now attack directly into the command post and artillery position area of the American rear. Luckily, their spearheads were discouraged by the vigorous reactions to their presence by the 120th Infantry command post and Battery C of the 197th Field Artillery Battalion.

Action on the barren forward slope of Hill 285 began in the mist at about 5:00 A.M. A bazooka team led by a 1st Battalion lieutenant went forward about 500 yards after a Mark IV tank moving out from behind a house. The tank was finally stalked down and knocked out by Sergeant Ames Broussard of the 823d Tank Destroyer Battalion. Broussard wasn't able to get back to his own lines for 14 hours. At 9:00 A.M two other German tanks approached, and were knocked out at 150 yards by one of the tank destroyer guns of the 2d Platoon of the 823d's Company A. Another tank moved up, firing at the American position, but was set afire by a shot at only 50 yards from a well concealed tank destroyer gun. It was later found abandoned Two self-propelled German guns and an armored car also fell victim to the Hill 285 position.

Meanwhile the Abbaye Blanche roadblock, under constant tank, artillery and small-arms fire, was destroying nine vehicles, six of them armored and all of them carrying German infantrymen.

By late afternoon the problem of communication between elements of the regiment was acute—shell fire had knocked out many of the wire lines and physical infiltration of German infantrymen and tanks made messenger service precarious

The fighting elements of the 2d Battalion were isolated, not only from the rest of the regiment but from their own battalion headquarters. At dawn Colonel Hardaway had radioed back that the Germans occupied Mortain in strength with tanks and infantrymen. About 9:00 A M., with enemy troops approaching the building he was using as a command post, he attempted to move his party by infiltration through the German positions to his men on Hill 314 He was forced into hiding after proceeding only 400 yards, under heavy fire. The vital Abbaye Blanche position was threatened with isolation by the enemy troops engaging the 1st Battalion on Hill 285.

At about the same time, however, reinforcements finally reached the 120th commander, who had exhausted his own reserves soon after the start of the operation The reinforcements had been physically en route since early morning.

The 2d Battalion of the 117th Infantry was split when it arrived near the 120th Infantry command post. Most of it, together with four tanks from the 743d's Company A, was sent to contact the 2d Battalion in Mortain. Company F, together with four more tanks, attacked south to retake Romagny. The attempt to relieve the besieged Mortain–Hill 314 garrison was unsuccessful, but by fighting its way to the outskirts of the town, the 117th Infantry group secured the supply route to the Abbaye Blanche block, and picked up remnants of the Company C platoon still in town The attack to the south bogged down against strong opposition Evidently a lot more than a reinforced company would be needed to retake Romagny.

Another reinforcement arrived late in the afternoon. This was the 1st Battalion of the 119th Infantry, which had been shifted from its temporary defense of the Division command post to the pressing problem in the south. It attacked eastward on the secondary road toward Romagny, with instructions to first clean out that town and vicinity and then drive on toward contact with the 2d Battalion of the 120th Infantry. Two platoons of light tanks, two medium tanks and a tankdozer, all from the 743d, were attached.

This task force penetrated to within 500 yards of Romagny before encountering serious opposition. Four rounds of armor-piercing shell then swished in from the north among the 743d's tanks, signalling the end of the approach march. Lieutenant Heglein then led an infantry patrol out, discovered two enemy tanks, and disabled one of them, a Mark VI, with two bazooka rounds By this time night was falling Romagny itself was a little too hot for comfort and both sides backed off for the night.

The Division was assigned assistance during August 7, although none of it was in action before the next day. At noon Corps had told the 30th that its sector extended all the way down to the line Le Teilleul–Domfront. Three hours later the Corps commander cut down its size He reported that the 35th Infantry Division, previously earmarked for Third Army, was to attack toward Mortain on the right of the 30th, with the main road leading southwest from that town as the division boundary The 12th Infantry Regiment of the 4th Infantry Division and the 629th Tank Destroyer Battalion, a self-propelled gun unit, were attached to Old Hickory in midafternoon and started toward the 30th's zone.

* * *

The events of August 7 brought the 30th Infantry Division to the brink of disintegration. But it had not been a happy day for the Germans, either. The attack had inflicted severe damage on the defenders, but it won no decisive advantage. German losses, particularly in panzers, were heavy Ground force soldiers—infantrymen, tank destroyer crews, artillerymen, engineers—accounted for 52 German tanks, in addition to many other vehicles How great was the toll exacted by Allied dive bombers is not known, but it must have been severe.

Part of the story appears in German Seventh Army's telephone journals. At 11:45, Seventh Army passed on an urgent request from XLVII Panzer Corps for air support And when, at 3:00 P.M, the Army chief of staff attempted to reassure Colonel Reinhard of Corps with word that German planes should then be arriving over the battlefield, he was told acidly that the colonel hadn't seen a German plane all day

The Colonel went on:

> The activities of the [Allied] fighter-bombers are said to be almost unbearable The *Leibstandarte* [1st SS Panzer Division] also reports that fighter-bomber attacks, of such caliber, have never been experienced
> The attack of the *Leibstandarte* has been stopped

Later, the Army chief of staff explained to Corps that the German planes had been in dogfights from the moment they left their airdromes. He expressed the hope that thus they at least diverted some of the Allied planes from the battlefield proper. "There was no noticeable relief," was the curt reply.

The 116th Panzer Division finally began its long-overdue attack on the south flank at 4:30 P.M., but without success. According to an 8:35 P.M report by the XLVII Panzer Corps commander: "There is bitter fighting in the Mortain area The situation of our tanks is becoming very alarming. Schwerin [116th Panzer] has not advanced one step today, neither have the other units."

By about 10.00 P M. the postmortem report for the supreme commander of the German forces in the west had been composed, although the battle on the ground continued Field Marshal von Kluge learned that "We were unsuccessful mainly because of the sizable fighter-bomber activity and also because the 116th Panzer muffed their job. Resistance was stronger than expected but probably not more than one or two divisions, which by the way were being constantly reinforced." (At this time the only reinforcement in action was Combat Command B of the 3d Armored Division.) Another report spoke of "terrific fighter-bomber attacks and considerable tank losses" Von Schwerin, who, rightfully or not, had seemed destined from the start to be the scapegoat, now stood stripped of his command of the 116th Panzer Division Colonel Reinhard had been sent from Corps to take charge of the Division.

Commander in Chief West directed that the attack continue, although both Von Kluge and the Army commander, significantly, now referred to the "remnants of the *Leibstandarte*." At the beginning of the day 1st SS was the strongest division in the attack "Each man must give his best," said the supreme commander. "If we have not advanced considerably by this evening or tomorrow morning, the operation will have been a failure."

Both sides attacked on August 8. The result was another day of heavy fighting at close quarters in which the positions of the opposing lines remained almost unchanged. The 1st Battalion of the 120th Infantry was attacked by infantry and at least eight tanks beginning about 1:30 A.M. Some time after 4 30 Company A was forced to fall back across the road traversing the hill, under pressure from about a reinforced company of infantry. Two flamethrowers prevented the tank destroyer crews from manning their guns, and tank destroyer men fought as infantry. Heavy American artillery fire brought this attack to a standstill, but at 8:15 Company B, just to the south, in turn came under attack by tanks and flame throwers.

By that time the German attack had become general, with the main thrust centering on St. Barthelmy and extending from Abbaye Blanche northwest to Cherence-le-Roussel. This assault was handicapped by the tank losses sustained the previous day, but this disadvantage was matched by an increase in supporting fires. Evidently more artillery and Nebelwerfer batteries were in action for the Germans. There were still plenty of tanks in the enemy push. Fighter-bombers struck at two 100-tank concentrations, one near St. Barthelmy and one a few miles to the rear.

Meanwhile the 12th Infantry Regiment was moving forward between the 117th Infantry, back of St. Barthelmy, and the 120th road block at Abbaye Blanche. The 117th, with the 12th Infantry's 3d Battalion and Company A of the 629th Tank Destroyer Battalion attached, attempted to advance back toward St. Barthelmy at 8:00 A.M., but was soon locked in a static battle with enemy tanks and infantry, under heavy artillery and mortar fire. The 12th Infantry, less its 3d Battalion, attacked early in the afternoon, with a plan of taking Road Junction 278, just south of St Barthelmy, and then turning south toward Abbaye Blanche Its approach met no opposition, but, as soon as it had advanced into line with the American troops on its flanks, the 12th's attack bogged down under blistering enemy fire. The regiment ended operations for the day still a third of a mile away from the road junction.

On the south, the 1st Battalion of the 119th Infantry spent most of the day extending to its left to strengthen the link with the 117th Infantry's Company F, having established patrol contact at 1:25 A.M. At 3:00 P.M. it attacked eastward and picked up 400 yards before being forced to halt to reorganize its infantry elements, scattered out among the high-walled hedgerows. The tanks with the battalion were sent back to remain under cover while the reorganization went on, but one medium tank was hit by enemy shellfire. The attack was resumed at 7:30 but again was stopped by dark.

In the meantime the joint attack by the 3d Battalion of the 119th Infantry and two task forces of Combat Command B, 3d Armored Division, was meeting determined opposition, although some of the tankers now held Le-Mesnil-Tove, and a link-up was being effected nearby with some troops of the 8th Infantry who had crossed the Sée River west of Cherence-le-Roussel. The high ground of Le-Mesnil-Tove remained in enemy hands.

By noon, while the battle on the ground raged unabated, the German commanders were beginning to concede that their great offensive had failed. Colonel Kleinschmidt of XLVII Panzer Corps, reporting to the Seventh Army chief of staff at 12:30, was asked: "Do you believe it is possible to continue operations?" "Not at all," he answered, "not with the forces on hand   . Under protection of his air superiority, the enemy has been able to reinforce himself considerably yesterday   Our combat strengths have been greatly reduced."[5]

Despite the pessimism at German Corps headquarters, and despite the heavy unremunerative losses which that night prompted the 30th Division G-2 to list withdrawal as the foremost enemy capability, the German higher commanders decided not to abandon the attack   The Seventh Army commander at 6.45 P.M. reported American reinforcements, as well as American counterattacks west of Mortain and near Juvigny and breakthrough all along the LXXXIV Corps front further north   Field Marshal von Kluge nevertheless replied: "We have to risk everything. Besides a breakthrough has occurred near Caen the like of which we have never seen   .." The two officers then discussed preparations to be made the next day for resumption of the attack on the 10th

*   *   *

The waning of German chances for decisive success focussed the attention of the 30th on what was now its No   1 problem—relieving the 2d Battalion of the 120th Infantry on Hill 314, and also keeping the lost battalion alive until the relief columns could make physical contact with it   Colonel Hardaway's command post group was by this time correctly presumed to be captured; his last radio transmission, fixing a schedule on which he would listen for messages, had taken place at 9.15 A M   At 11:00 A.M. the men on the hill radioed an urgent request for radio batteries, food, medical supplies, ammunition. Until these supplies could be furnished, or until the battalion could be rescued, there was nothing to do save continue to place a ring of artillery fire around the position and hope for the best.

---

[5] In the same telephonic report, Colonel Kleinschmidt estimated that "about three infantry divisions (30, 9, and one presently not identified) and one armored division" were facing XLVII Panzer Corps   This estimate is approximately one and a half times too large—an unconscious tribute to the American ground troops in the battle   The Army chief of staff himself was quick to note that "the main body of the 9th [Infantry Division] is opposing [German] 84th Infantry Division", that is, that the 9th Division was north of the See River, which constituted XLVII Panzer Corps' right boundary   Opposing the Panzer Corps in actuality were the 30th Division, swelled by one attached infantry regiment and a combat command of armor, a combat command of the 2d Armored Division, far off on the flank at Barenton, a regimental combat team of the 35th Infantry Division, driving northeast toward Mortain but still miles away, and elements of the 9th Division just over the Corps boundary at Cherence le Roussel   Thus, the total American troops in action was an equivalent two infantry divisions at most and two thirds of an armored division   More than sixty per cent of this force was under 30th Division control

The first plan for getting supplies to the lost battalion contemplated dropping them by parachute from Division Artillery's light liaison planes Two such planes, piloted by Lieutenants Trigg and Johnson, attempted to fly over Hill 314 on August 9, but both were hit by flak. Evidently slow, low-flying aircraft could not penetrate the umbrella of antiaircraft fires set up over the German panzer divisions

Air drop of supplies by C-47 cargo airplanes was attempted next, with incomplete success. Slow-working channels for scheduling such flights and time needed by the Air Corps for reconnaissance flights delayed the first drop until 4·30 P M. on August 10, after the Division G-4 section had placed the request for air supply by dual channels of communication no less than four times The 4:30 payload consisted of two days' supply, but it was only about fifty per cent effective· many of the bundles parachuted into enemy-held territory. After much phoning another day's supply was dropped between 7:30 and 8:00 P M. on August 11; most of this, according to radio reports from the isolated battalion, fell into enemy hands. Plans to try again as soon as possible on August 12 were cancelled when they proved no longer necessary.

Meanwhile local ingenuity was providing a more successful if less comprehensive solution Lieutenant Colonel Lewis D Vieman, commander of the 230th Field Artillery Battalion, decided to try smoke shell cases, of the sort used to fire propaganda leaflets, to fire medical supplies to the cut-off men. The 105mm howitzers fired the first of these shells at 10:40 P.M on the 10th and later similar rounds were fired by the 105 mm assault guns of the 743d Tank Battalion None of the first six shells fired could be recovered Five of the next six reached their destination On the third salvo the score was three for three. None of the blood plasma so delivered reached it destination intact, although additional plasma was fired by the 155 mm howitzers of the 113th Field Artillery Battalion Bandages, adhesive tape, some morphine and other medical items, however, were successfully salvaged by the besieged men

*   *   *

The progress of the rescue expeditions was slow and discouraging. Two units were involved—the 1st Battalion of the 119th Infantry, advancing almost due east through Romagny, and the 320th Regimental Combat Team of the 35th Infantry Division, driving northeast toward Mortain. Both units used tanks and hoped, in the final stages, to make contact with the 120th Infantry's 2d Battalion with the armor alone, even if the unprotected doughboys couldn't keep pace Two factors limited the maneuverability of the tanks, however. One was the hedgerow terrain, which tended to confine the tanks to the heavily mined roads. The other was the abundance of German antitank guns In addition, the approach of the 35th Division task force from so far south of the division boundary meant that both units had to be especially wary about infiltration around their flanks. The 320th Infantry was forced to expend valuable time fighting its way out of such a trap.

At the end of August 8, after repeated attacks, the 1st Battalion of the 119th Infantry still was held up in the outskirts of Romagny A knocked-out German tank, mined and well covered with enemy antitank fire, blocked the road. During the next two days the battalion fought its way past this stumbling block but found the enemy still strong before it. Romagny, by this time, was almost levelled by American gunfire; the church steeple had been deliberately knocked down because of its use by the enemy as an observation post and snipers' nest The Germans had at first raised a white flag on the steeple but then resumed their fire as the Americans approached. Heavy and accurate enemy artillery fire was not stopped until the American tanks began delivering regular fire every fifteen minutes at a tall building to the southwest which served as a German artillery observation post.

Eight medium tanks of Company B of the 743d were assigned to the 1st Battalion on August 9, and a pair of them were placed on the road, to pace the attack A rifle company was in the walled fields on either side and the third rifle company of the battalion was behind them It was the old story of hedgerow fighting all over again: channelized on the road by inability to move across country through the fields, the tanks were smothered in well placed German antitank-gun fire. The principal satisfaction of these two days came from seeing a German counter-attack with light armored cars and infantry thoroughly chewed up on the 10th The German panzer grenadiers advanced erect and were mowed down by the American guns.

On August 11, Lieutenant Colonel Robert A. Herlong, commanding the 1st Battalion, found a solution. At 8·00 A M, with Companies B and C in position flanking the road east to Mortain, the battalion made what appeared to be a repetition of the previously unsuccessful attack, preceded by a ten-minute artillery and heavy weapon preparation Meanwhile Company A and six medium tanks were unobtrusively going into a jump-off position about 800 yards south of the road

The ruse was successful. Company A's thrust forced the enemy opposing the battalion along the road to withdraw; by 9:30 A M the Germans had fallen back to a road junction east of Romagny Here the advance came to a temporary halt on orders from Division the battalion was getting too far ahead of friendly units on the flanks for safety

Forward motion was resumed, however, at 3:30 P.M., with the infantry-men taking the lead and the tanks and tank destroyers furnishing fire support.

Progress was slower now because of enemy pressure on the flanks as well as on the face of the attack. German fire seemed to come from every direction but the rear. The battalion came to a point where the road led through a draw. Concentrated enemy artillery fire, here, could have inflicted heavy losses as the men came together to get through. But the troops moved through without unusual trouble. As darkness fell the leading doughboys were in the edge of Mortain. About 500 yards back, on their right, were the leading elements of the 320th Infantry.

At this point a difficult decision had to be made: whether to push on in the darkness with men who had been on the offensive for almost five full days, or whether to dig in for the night. The plight of the men on the hill was clear; at 10:34 that night they stated their case bluntly: "We can hold out until tomorrow."

General Hobbs himself suggested digging in, but left the final decision to the man on the ground, Colonel Herlong. The latter dared not remain where he was, for his positions in the hollow invited both ground attack and concentrated artillery fire. He ordered the battalion to pull back to higher ground, voluntarily abandoning some of the territory won that day.

His judgement proved correct. That night the enemy abandoned his positions in Mortain, his truck columns hammered by artillery fire directed by the lost battalion. The Germans covered their retreat with heavy artillery fire and night bombing of the position which Herlong's battalion had first occupied. By noon of August 12, first the 320th Infantry and then the 1st Battalion of the 119th Infantry made contact with the hollow-eyed Americans on Hill 314. The lost battalion's struggle for existence was at an end.

* * *

The story of the lost battalion begins as not one story but many. Three rifle companies of the 120th Infantry were in place on Hill 314 when the German drive began. Company K, on loan from the 3d Battalion, and Company G occupied a knob on the northern part of the hill, with K on the left as the men faced eastward into enemy territory. Company E's foxholes were a couple of hundred yards away on the southern knob of the hill, across the main east-west road. H, the heavy-weapons company, was split between the two defensive areas Company F, down in the valley, was split three ways. One platoon formed the infantry core of the Abbaye Blanche roadblock. The company had another roadblock about 500 yards east of Abbaye Blanche, where two roads intersected Another Company F block was in place south of Mortain. On the northwest slope of the hill was a block set up by the 1st Platoon of the Antitank Company. South of Mortain, near the Company F men, the 3d Platoon of Company A, 823d Tank Destroyer Battalion, was in position. 2d Battalion headquarters, it may be recalled, was in a hotel in Mortain itself.

These scattered units under the 2d Battalion's control were hit almost simultaneously at about midnight of August 6-7. One of the very first problems to face them was how to link themselves together in a common defense against the heavy pressure of German guns, tanks, and infantrymen. The bulk of them succeeded in maintaining contact with each other. Others did not and ended in German prisoner-of-war cages

The tank destroyer platoon south of Mortain is a good example It fended off the first German attack with the caliber .50 machine guns in its half-tracks but was then split asunder in the dark when the Germans swept around its positions, making the platoon's 3-inch guns untenable with close-in small-arms fire Sixteen men reached the 1st Platoon's positions north of Mortain after five days fighting. Nine others joined nearby infantry and fought their way into friendly lines on Hill 314 One man, off by himself, remained hidden in a ditch for five days Thirteen men were still missing when the battle ended.

Nothing much seems to have happened before midnight of August 6 Second Lieutenant Robert L. Weiss, one of the two forward observers of the 230th Field Artillery Battalion on the hill, shot at a few enemy infantrymen during the afternoon of the 6th from his observation post in the Company E area, but reported everything quiet when he bedded down for the night in the draw just west of the hill, using old 1st Division foxholes. Company K, up at the other end of the hill, noted nothing unusual as August 6 ended.

After midnight, however, things were anything but quiet. German planes were overhead, enemy tanks were moving around east of Hill 314 and German infantrymen were infiltrating in among the hill positions. One group of Germans swept around Company E's right flank, seized 19 out of 21 quarter-ton trucks there and overran the lone 57mm antitank gun which guarded the road

Two squads of the 1st Platoon of Company K were captured as enemy patrols armed with machine guns and flamethrowers moved up Lieutenant Ronald Woody, commanding Company G, lost contact with his company at first When he rejoined it, after scaling a cliff to get up to the front positions, he found that its strength had dwindled to 100 men, although his company (including rear elements) had gone into battle with 212 men. High-velocity fire, probably from German tanks, was causing heavy casualties, mainly from tree bursts. Lieutenant Woody led his men back about 150 yards across open ground to get away from the trees, cleverly using covering fire by the first men to withdraw, so that even the wounded could be taken back.

Captain Erichson of Company F lost telephone communications with his scattered company at 3:00 A.M. Reporting to his battalion commander, he was given a platoon of Company C and told to move up on the hill to furnish contact between Company E and the larger group farther north. Up on the heights it was dark and misty. As the platoon moved along a trail leading north, "we walked right up on 30 Germans before we could see them. My scouts were so near to the enemy that we could have shaken hands with them. The Germans cut loose with their machine pistols, and I jumped over a hedgerow and managed to set the platoon up in a hasty defense."

But that was not all. When Captain Erichson reached Company G and reported by phone to his battalion commander, he received new orders. Germans were breaking into the northern part of Mortain; Captain Erichson was to come back to town to combat them. And when the detachment finally got back into town, under heavy enemy machine-gun fire, it received still another set of orders; to attempt to rejoin the rest of Company C in the southern part of Mortain.

By this time, however, disintegration of the American position in the town had proceeded far. En route south, the platoon ran into opposition from three sides. Only on the east was its way relatively clear. It climbed the hill again to the Company G area, moving again when direct fire from enemy guns made the position untenable. It was by then late in the afternoon. The whole group—Company G, elements of C, F, and the Antitank Company—moved northward and tied in with Company K.

Lieutenant Weiss and First Lieutenant Charles A. Barts, the other forward observer from the 230th on the hill, had started firing prepared defensive concentrations early in the attack, supplementing them with sound-located targets sent in by the infantry scouts and outposts. Foggy weather obscured the field of observation until 9:30 or 10:00 A.M. "When the mist did clear," related Lieutenant Weiss, "it left us facing a German attack." Part of the hill behind Company E was in enemy hands. Enemy machine-gun fire at the observation post rendered it useless; Weiss crawled back to the draw, where a runner sent by Lieutenant Kerley directed him to the south end of the hill. This was the highest point on the hill and probably furnished the best all-around observation." By 2:00 P.M. air bursts from time and ricochet fire discouraged the infantrymen furnishing the bulk of the enemy attack, and the artillerymen settled down to keeping out of the way of an 88mm. gun sniping at the rock outcropping where they were dug in.

Nightfall found the situation discouraging. Sniper fire from the rear prevented use of the draw; the observation post party crawled behind the rock on the hill. Company H's detachment had one 81mm. mortar left; it could fire at only one elevation. One of the two 60mm mortars couldn't be traversed. The defenders possessed one bazooka and nine rounds of ammunition but no antitank guns. Most of the machine-gun ammunition was in the valley, covered by enemy guns The infantrymen had had no food or water since the previous day.

One enemy tank moved into the Company E area on the night of August 7, but luckily there was no follow-up: "We could have been driven off the hill with ease." Artillery fire and good work by the Cannon Company kept the enemy away.

2d Battalion headquarters, the reader will recall, sent its last message to Regiment on the morning of August 8, more than twenty-four hours after its communications with the line companies up on the hill had been broken. Its original command post threatened, the entire group of 29 men had moved toward the hill positions, being forced into a house about 400 yards away from its starting point. Colonel Hardaway's last message emanated from this point.

For two days and three nights the battalion staff remained there in hiding. One the morning of August 9 the Germans discovered them One man was captured as the enemy battered down the front door, the remainder of them escaped out the back way. For most, however, the escape was only temporary. The group was surrounded; all but Lieutenants Irby and Hagen, who tell the story, and four enlisted men were captured. Slipping down an embankment, these six hid in a wheatfield for a day and then infiltrated to a loft near the Mortain hospital The Germans almost immediately searched the hospital and the stable beneath their hideout, but without success. The men lived on carrots and radishes from a nearby garden and water brought by a Frenchman who worked in the stable On August 12, desperately hungry and deprived of their hideout by an incendiary shell, they raided the hospital larder twice, obtaining jam, bread, candy, and a raw ham. At 11:00 A.M they saw Americans advancing nearby. When they emerged they ran into Colonel Birks of the 120th Infantry.

Capture of the 2d Battalion staff formed the background for one of the most dramatic incidents of the lost battalion's stand During the 8th and most of the 9th the enemy had hammered away with every weapon in his armory Weiss, finding that observation was becoming "spotty" in view of the heavy enemy fire, moved twice, the 88s still on his trail. Three night attacks on August 8 had been driven back by American artillery fire; on the 9th the enemy took the roadblock on Company E's left but was expelled.

Then, at about 6:30 P.M., a German officer, accompanied by a soldier bearing a white flag, entered our lines in the edge of the Company E area. With great formality he told Lieutenant Rohmiller of Company E and Sergeant Wingate of Company G that he was an officer of the SS and prepared to give 'the Americans honorable conditions of surrender. The Germans knew they had the 2d Battalion of the 120th Infantry, 30th Infantry Division, surrounded, he said. They had captured a Lieutenant Pike (the battalion S-2) and a "one-star" officer (evidently Colonel Hardaway, whose silver leaves may have been confused with stars) among many other prisoners. The American position was hopeless If they did not surrender by 8 00 P. M. they would be "blown to bits"

The lieutenant and the sergeant refused the offer out of hand, but sent the message back to Lieutenant Kerley, the E Company commander According to one colorful story which later reached the newspapers, Lieutenant Kerley's reply, duly reported back to the surrender party, was that his men would not surrender as long as they had ammunition to kill Germans with or bayonets to stick in their bellies More reliable sources indicate his reply was shorter and less printable, but equally to the point Wounded Americans, lying near Lieutenant Kerley, cried "No, no, don't surrender," when they heard of the offer. The German officer returned to his lines That night German tanks attacked, accompanied by infantrymen who shouted "Surrender!" as they charged.

By then the pattern of the fighting was well fixed. The enemy pounded the American positions incessantly. When an organized attack was not being made, the enemy filled in with combat patrols, so that the depleted American units had to constantly rotate in position to get any rest at all. Operating without adequate supplies and without a medical officer, the aid men nevertheless did a noteworthy job. As many of the wounded as possible were bedded down in deep slit trenches in the center of the position, there to undergo the long wait for real medical care.

Food was an acute problem, as was water, until Company E men began dashing over to a nearby farmhouse on the second day. Most of the men lived off the land as best they could, scrounging potatoes, cabbages, and even a few chickens. Each man received two K-ration meals after the first air drop, on August 10. During the entire action, Lieutenant Weiss's party averaged close to two meals a day except on the 9th, when each man had four squares of D-ration chocolate and one-fifth of a K-ration meal. However he notes that "the field artillery observer without a doubt ate more and better than anyone else on the hill, because of the rations he carried with him and because of the solicitude of the infantry for the artillery."

The solicitude was deserved. Artillery fire, directed by the 230th observers, by the Cannon Company representative, and by company commanders through the Regimental Intelligence Officer, was probably the main factor in saving the situation. Every night the position was ringed around with American defensive fires· The excellent observation from the hill enabled the Americans to shoot at enemy columns forming up, with deadly effectiveness, and with deep satisfaction. "As sleepy, tired, and hungry as I am," one of the 230th men radioed back, after shooting up a German column on August 10, "I never felt so good as I feel right now."

The most remunerative target of all was satisfying in another way, for it was furnished by the Germans retreating, at last, from Mortain. Even before dawn on August 12 American guns were busy shooting at sounds of movement east of Hill 314. Visibility came early that morning, and the firing continued. The enemy columns contained all types of vehicles—horsedrawn wagons, trucks, about 30 to 50 tanks. Well more than 50 enemy vehicles were destroyed. For hours afterward, while they waited for the relief columns, the besieged men could see smoke from burning vehicles The road leading east before them was strewn with wreckage.

The Abbaye Blanche roadblock also aided greatly in defense of Hill 314, for it controlled the main road which curled around the north edge of the hill, as well as three other roads Lieutenant Andrew of Company F, 120th Infantry, the commander, estimated, when he moved in, that he needed a company and a half of infantry to hold the position properly Instead he had about 70 men, aided by the 1st Platoon of Company A, 823d Tank Destroyer Battalion, and a platoon of his regiment's Antitank Company. By the end of the battle incoming stragglers had raised his strength to 150 men, but many of the newcomers were battle fatigue cases and thus non-effective.

One of the most noteworthy things about the Abbaye Blanche block was its low casualties—23 in six days—although the only positions which could be used to do the job had been prepared by the 1st Division, were presumably known to the Germans, and were heavily and accurately shelled. Despite this, however, the enemy brought tanks, trucks and half-tracks up to the position day after day. By the end of the week 24 German vehicles were piled up on one road alone. The total for the entire Abbaye Blanche position was in the neighborhood of 40 German vehicles and tanks knocked out.

Three hundred and seventy men came down off Hill 314 when the 119th relieved it August 12. Another 300 men had become casualties—dead, wounded, missing.

*   *   *

The Battle of Hill 314 was not the only one in which Old Hickory was engaged during the latter part of the week. The renewed offensive, which Field Marshal von Kluge and the German Seventh Army commander were so busily arranging on the evening of August 8, never really materialized. On the other hand, neither did the American prediction of enemy withdrawal, at least not until very late in the battle. Day after day the 30th attempted to restore its original positions, in response to insistent orders from Corps Its path remained blocked by an abundance of German men and guns, powerless to reassume the initiative generally, but thoroughly capable of thwarting the increasingly weary American attacks.

On Tuesday, August 9, enemy artillery fire attained an intensity unprecedented in the 30th's experience. Shells from approximately 200 German heavy guns thickened the mass of fire poured out over American positions by machine guns, mortars, and tank guns. Nebelwerfers were in action. An artillery air observer, flying over the battlefield at about 6:00 P.M. saw gun flashes from 42 different enemy batteries in the course of a few minutes. In an hour's time that evening, firing as fast as it could, Division Artillery responded with concentrations against 30 different gun positions its observers could see. On the next day, its observers located and directed fire against 20 active batteries during the course of an hour and a half.

All up and down the front the nasty in-fighting of the hedgerows continued Near Hill 285 what later appeared to have been about 300 Germans, some of them wearing parts of American uniforms, had moved into an orchard early in the battle. This group proved troublesome, until the end, in support of repeated local German attacks On August 9 the hill appeared to be safe in American hands; the next morning the struggle to hold it was being waged all over again.

Little by little the enemy was pushed out of the remains of his northern salient—the one that had briefly stretched to Le-Mesnil-Adelée. On August 9 the 119th's 3d Battalion and two task forces of Combat Command B were to have tried a new plan to eject the Germans. An enemy shell landing in a field where Task Force 2 was having a pre-attack conference eliminated most of its officers; Lieutenant Colonel Cornog, the task force commander was killed. The tanks could not function effectively with their command system wrecked The 3d Battalion and the 1st Battalion, 33d Armored Regiment, jumped off without accompanying tanks at 8:00 P.M. By dark they were embroiled in German machine-gun fires. For another two days they made their way forward with difficulty, from one limited objective to another. On August 11 the armored doughboys contacted the 39th Infantry for the first time. A solid line now existed as far as the Division north boundary.

In the center the tired 117th attempted to slug its way back down the hill to recapture St. Barthelmy, with negligible success. The 12th Infantry, on its right, was equally frustrated by the tight-knit German defenses and heavy defensive fires. It, too, was tired, for it had been scheduled for a much needed rest when it was called upon to help the 30th. Far to the east, the 120th's 3d Battalion, having taken Barenton on August 8, was fighting to get through the passes north of that town, along with tanks of the 2d Armored Division, to break into the enemy's rear.[6]

On Friday, August 11, the picture began to change. The main body of the German forces began its retreat back toward the Falaise Gap, leaving strong rearguards behind from the 1st and 2d SS Panzer Divisions to cover the withdrawal. August 12, all along the line, as at Mortain, the 30th's attack proved successful. While Colonel Birks was up on Hill 314 greeting his men, Colonel Johnson of the 117th was leading the advance into the tank scrap heap that was St. Barthelmy.

*   *   *

Thus ended the battle of Mortain. The Division lost approximately 1,800 men during the six-day engagement, most of them fairly equally divided among the three infantry regiments. However, it had been a hard battle for almost everyone Engineer troops fought side by side with their infantry combat-team partners. The antiaircraft artillery with the Division spent the first part of the battle engaging tanks and infantry on the ground The constant shelling by enemy artillery kept Signal Company wire teams out all the time repairing wire lines, and the company had to furnish one regiment switchboard operators and linemen to replace battle casualties. After the capture of Colonel Hardaway's headquarters the Division Signal Office turned out a complete new set of codes in four hours' time Two vehicles of B Company, 105th Medical Battalion were captured on August 7 en route to the 117th Infantry area. On the same day Germans halted two ambulances from

[6]One of the most interesting members of the Barenton task force was a Frenchman named Barthoneuf, an ex Foreign Legion man and a member of the local police Barthoneuf was an avid hunter of Nazis, reporting many enemy locations, including one of 180 men He also operated, with his friends, a runner service at the incredible speed of six miles per hour

Company C en route from Barenton back to the rear, removing lightly wounded passengers before allowing them to proceed.

For the Germans, too, it was a costly battle. Ground troops with the Division knocked out 69 German tanks, aside from those shelled east of Mortain. Thirty more enemy tanks, blasted from the air, lay abandoned around St. Barthelmy alone. German infantry losses are unknown, but they must have kept pace with the destruction of enemy matériel.

As important to the Germans as their immediate losses was the precious time lost. In taking the desperate gamble of an attack toward Avranches, they sent some of their best units even deeper into the Normandy trap. The enemy men and machines which escaped intact from the Mortain battlefield still had to run the gauntlet of artillery fire and bombs near Falaise. As a result of the battle, they reached the escape gap days later than they would have done otherwise. By then the fires had thickened and the German route of withdrawal had become a narrow one indeed.

Six units of the 30th received the Distinguished Unit Citation for their actions at Mortain. They were the 1st Battalion, 117th Infantry, for its work near St. Barthelmy; the 2d Battalion, Company K, and the 1st and 2d Platoons of the Antitank Company, 120th Infantry, for the Hill 314–Abbaye Blanche action; and Companies A and B, 823d Tank Destroyer Battalion, in action near Mortain and St. Barthelmy, respectively. To the Division as a whole came a letter of commendation from Major General (later Lieutenant General) J. Lawton Collins, commander of VII Corps.

Chapter VII

THE RACE TO BELGIUM

The ending of the Mortain battle marked the end of the slow hedge-row battles for Old Hickory. In the next month the Division ranged more than 520 road miles, driving across France, Belgium and the southern tip of Holland, and finally thrusting across the German border. Here and there hard fighting took place, but casualties were generally light. These were the days of the great liberation, when the dusty convoys passed through village after village gaily hung with home-made French, Belgian, Dutch, and American flags, to be presented with flowers, fruit, liquor, and kisses from a grateful populace.

The Division took up the pursuit on August 14, having passed to the control of XIX Corps the previous morning. Its first move brought it more than 10 miles by motors eastward past the stern heights of Mortain to detrucking areas on the road to Domfront. The 113th Cavalry Group, against negligible opposition, had already cleared the way that far the previous day.

The enemy offered no serious resistance to the Division's advance Only rear guards were left to delay, and the principal difficulties were provided by mines, strewn in great profusion, and by demolitions at the small bridge sites in the area. By the end of the 14th the infantry had moved more than four miles from its detrucking points and was up to the sharply rising ground on the far side of the Varenne River, at the outskirts of the major road center of Domfront.

The next day Domfront itself fell. Situated behind the protection of the Varenne River and extending up the abrupt nose of an imposing razorback hill, it might have been tenaciously held. Instead it was garrisoned by the odds and ends of the retreat—depot companies, labor troops, a flak battalion. Many of the defenders were drunk when they were captured.

Local resistance cropped up at various critical points along the hills leading eastward, but it was ineffectual. The regiments averaged a three-mile gain on the 15th. On August 16 the Division easily reached a "no advance" line set up to prevent entry into the zone of a British division sweeping south across the face of the American advance. Before the day was over the infantry regiments and the Reconnaissance Troop had established contact with the British along the entire front. At the little town of Ferrières-aux-Étampes, where the Reconnaisance Troop halted, a wild celebration took place. Every villager, it appeared, had a gardenful of buried treasure in bottled form, and Frenchmen, Americans and Britishers toasted each other with vintage wine or the fiery native drink of Calvados.

Replacements for the men lost at Mortain and for about a third of the men lost during the grinding St. Lô breakthrough operation arrived at the Division just before the departure from the Mortain area, and they badly needed refresher work on weapons and small-unit instruction with the squads and platoons to which they had been assigned. A little of this training had been squeezed in during the advance past Domfront, but most of it was accomplished on the 17th and 18th, while the Division—pinched out by the British—awaited new orders.

Meanwhile the fate of the German Seventh Army was being sealed farther west at the Falaise gap, where a desperate enemy tried to hold an escape route open with local counterattacks while other German troops hazarded the storm of artillery fire and bombs which saturated the few escape routes. The western end of the pocket, already sliced down by attacks from almost every direction, was an empty bag, and the closely packed Allied troops there unneeded.

On August 19, led by the 113th Cavalry Group and the 30th Reconnaissance Troop, Old Hickory, took to the road to catch up with the battle, its infantry motorized by the attachment of six quartermaster truck companies. The orders from XIX Corps had been terse and uninformative—to move approximately 115 miles to an assembly area near Dreux, 42 miles west of Paris, prepared to move either to the north or to the east. The 2d Armored Division and the 28th Infantry Division were to follow.

As the 30th's troops loaded up in their trucks, there was wild speculation about taking Paris, for American troops were reported past Chartres and almost to the outskirts of Versailles. As it turned out upon arrival in the new area that night, the pessimists were right. Paris was taken, not by the 30th but by the French. And Old Hickory, plumped down in territory where Allied troops had, at best, thrown away K ration boxes in passing through, was instructed to protect itself against enemy attack from any direction and assume the more prosaic duties of driving north toward the busy ferries of the lower Seine, where the remnants of a German army were elbowing each other trying to escape.

The Division launched its attack to the north at 8:00 A.M. on August 20, while the last of its infantry regiments, the 117th, was still en route. Little was known of enemy strength or disposition, although Corps had warned of an enemy main line of resistance being set up along the east-west line of the Avre River, about two miles north of the 30th's assembly area south of Nonancourt.

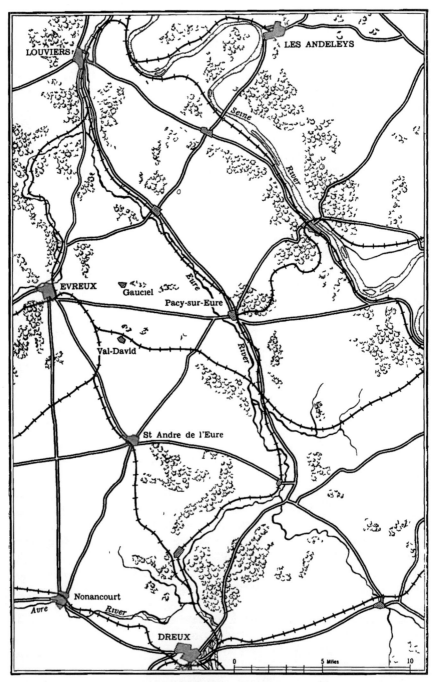

Map 5—Evreux and Vicinity

Enemy resistance was spotty from the start. The bridges across the Avre had been blown, but enemy defenses protecting the crossing sites were weak and ineffective. Both the 120th Infantry, on the right, and the 119th Infantry successfully crossed the Avre just west of Nonancourt. The highpoint of the action was a reported counterattack of tanks and infantry which did some damage to Company C of the 119th This turned out to be an *ad hoc* formation of infantry and three tanks trying to escape to the east.

During the six-day drive northward, the 30th moved forward 30 miles. The enemy had brought the 17th Luftwaffe Division from across the Seine to block in the 30th's area while other troops escaped eastward across the Seine near Elbeuf and Rouen, but the air force troops, most of them originally ground crews converted into infantry, were among the weakest ever encountered by the 30th. The desire to fight, of many, was dubious, to say the least, and they further were handicapped by a drastic lack of information about the strength and location of the American troops opposing them. Twice on the night of August 20-21 enemy groups blundered into the Division's roadblocks. Occasionally strongpoints, especially those supported by tanks or antitank guns, required hard work to clean out, but the actions were disconnected.

The speed of the advance made it impossible for the infantry to clean out all of the enemy troops on hand. Twice this situation led to unexpected battles for the artillery. On the afternoon of August 21, C Battery of the 197th Field Artillery Battalion, on the road in march column along with supporting weapons from C Battery of the 531st Antiaircraft Artillery Battalion, ran into a fire fight with a force of about 100 men armed with bazookas, rifles and machine guns and supported by two antitank guns The artillerymen, aided materially by the 40mm. antiaircraft guns, opened fire from the road while a 531st half-track advanced toward the strong point to draw fire away from the column. By the time the action was over approximately 40 of the enemy were prisoners and another 25 killed, with the remainder dispersed. There were three American casualties.

During the next night the 230th Field Artillery Battalion had a fight of its own. The battalion had been leapfrogging forward so that some of its guns were always in position to provide fire on call Late in the evening of August 22 the first echelon, consisting of A and B Batteries and part of the command post group, arrived at an abandoned airfield near Gauciel, about two miles to the east of the large town of Evreux C Battery, a battery of six 105mm assault guns from the 743d Tank Battalion and part of the battalion staff were about three miles to the rear at Val David.

About midnight the sounds of horse-drawn vehicles proceeding westward on the road just south of the Gauciel area were heard, and sentries were sent out to challenge them as they approached, to determine if they were French or German. The first challenge was answered with enemy fire. Some sounds of movement continued but it appeared that the enemy column had dispersed in the fields east and southwest of the battalion command post. At 3:00 A.M. a German approached with a cry of *"Kamerad!"* but turned on a flashlight on being challenged and ran to the rear. A little later the battalion commander and one of his noncommissioned officers attempted to obtain the surrender of the Germans by shouting from one of the outpost positions, having been instructed over the telephone in what to say by a German-speaking lieutenant at the rear echelon. This attempt failed, and orders were issued for A and B Batteries and a detachment from Battery D of the 531st to attack from their positions in the enemy's rear at dawn.

Meanwhile the Germans, too, were preparing, and at 5:40 A M they attacked the command post's outposts with mortar, small-arms and 20mm. fire. At this point the battalion commander called for fire from the two batteries at Val David, first warning the men who had already started to attack the enemy rear. This artillery fire proved persuasive The enemy raised a white flag and many were rounded up by A Battery's men, who had been advancing in the face of strong fire. Others surrendered to the battalion executive, who had commandeered a half-track from nearby tank destroyers. Ninety-six enemy were taken prisoner in the action and the bodies of five more were found dead. Nine loaded wagons, a truck, a 20mm antiaircraft gun, and considerable small arms were captured.

On the same day, August 23, the Division headquarters quartering party picked up 47 prisoners.

Progress was rapid on the 21st. Some elements of the Division advanced as much as 11 miles, with the crossroads town of St. André-de-l'Eure, captured by the 120th, the principal prize. The troops moved forward in an upside-down U formation, with the 120th on the right and the 119th on the left. The 117th protected the left flank of the formation and the 30th Reconnaissance Troop patrolled the right flank as far east as the northward-flowing Eure River, beyond which the 5th Armored Division was also advancing northward. During the day four intact planes were captured on an airport overrun by the Division.

The next day the doughboys toiled northward about nine miles more to positions on high ground overlooking the city of Evreux from the east. Corps passed on a tip that four panzer divisions—the 1st SS, 2nd

SS, 12th SS and 116th—could be expected to counterattack by evening on the 23d, but such fears were unfounded A French liaison officer infiltrated into Evreux with instructions for the resistance groups to eject the Germans in town, and on the morning of the 23d, before the 117th's troops headed for the town had reached its outskirts, both the Division Counterintelligence Corps detachment commander and Colonel Johnson of the 117th entered Evreux. Most of the Germans there had already fled; the remainder were being rounded up by the French resistance groups Meanwhile the 119th Infantry was moving over to positions on the ridge north of Evreux, with the 120th Infantry spreading westward to take over the 119th's old positions northeast of the town.

A day of rest for all units except the Reconnaissance Troop, cleaning out the woods along the Eure River on the Division right boundary, intervened before the final day of the drive, in which the 117th and 119th advanced about six miles against light resistance to cut the roads leading west from Louviers. The German pocket west of the Seine was almost extinct. The 2d Armored Division was moving forward to capture the Seine city of Elbeuf, where aerial reconnaissance had reported the streets jammed with abandoned German vehicles. The Canadians were advancing rapidly from the west toward the lower Seine. The same day, August 25, Paris was liberated.

*   *   *

The Seine, which had been such a strong barrier to the Germans in their movements both toward and away from the battlefield, was proving no real obstacle to the Allied advance. While French armored troops, Americans and resistance groups finished rounding up German snipers in a Paris delirious with joy, Third Army was crossing in strength upstream, heading toward the traditional battlefields of the Marne. And on the other side of the French capital, 25 miles or so to the west, XV Corps' 79th Infantry Division was fighting to hold its bridgehead at Mantes-Gassicourt, where the undulating Seine bends south.

During the early evening of August 24, the XIX Corps commander told the 30th to disregard rumors that Old Hickory would be placed under XV Corps control; XIX Corps had just been told to look toward Belgium, and it expected to have plenty of work for the 30th. But the next day, as the 30th was finishing its clean-up job near Louviers, the plans changed. The 30th was to be loaned to XV Corps long enough to extend the 79th's bridgehead.

The Seine near Mantes-Gassicourt is shaped something like the end of a dog biscuit, with the town of Mantes itself at the little indentation in the middle. This loop, facing southwest, was an advantage to the Americans attacking from that direction, for it enabled them to converge fire on the bridgehead area. Northeast of the river, however, were two ridges more or less paralleling the stream course. The one closest to the Seine towered 600 feet above its banks. The second ridge was slightly higher. These ridges were important, not only because they covered the Seine, giving the Germans superior observation and cutting off the Mantes bend in the river from the area above it, but because they dominated the rolling plains farther north.

Thus, the enemy had two good reasons for trying hard to contain the Mantes bridgehead at the double ridgeline. First, if successful, such an attempt would prevent Allied troops from breaking into the open and racing into the rear of the German forces retreating northeast along the Channel coast. Secondly, if the attempt failed, the attacking forces would have superior terrain and observation for many miles.

The Germans certainly did their best to hold the ridgelines, and the fact that their effort was no better than it was is indicative of their plight at the time. Most of two divisions had been rushed up to keep the 79th Infantry Division south of the ridgelines. One was the 18th Luftwaffe Division, the other the German 49th Infantry Division. A regiment of the German 353d Infantry Division had also been identified at the northwest corner of the bridgehead. The enemy counterattacked three times before the 30th came up on August 27th to take over the eastern part of the 79th Division's sector. One of these counterattacks had involved two battalions of enemy infantry as well as a few tanks. All of the counterattack forces lost heavily, principally to our artillery fire.

The 30th began moving south into position to perform its new mission on August 26, with the 120th Infantry left behind near Evreux because there just weren't enough trucks available to move all the infantry at once. During the morning of August 27 the 117th and 119th crossed the Seine and relieved elements of the 79th Division in line. By the end of the day the 117th Infantry, on the left, had driven up on the high ground of the first ridgeline. The 119th, driving northeast almost parallel to the Seine, ran into heavy mortar and heavy-weapons fires in the rising ground, and was forced to hold up short of its objective.

Two more days of fighting were required to make a clean breakthrough of the enemy position. The 117th drove through the valley between the two ridges and finally, late on the 29th, after waiting for the forces on its flanks to catch up, shoved a battalion over the second of the two ridge lines. The 119th Infantry worked itself forward on the 117th's right against strong mortar, small-arms, and high-velocity gun fire, repulsing two counterattacks, one from the north and one from the east, with artillery fire on the 29th In the battle that day about 200 enemy troops were killed, wounded or captured and five antitank guns were knocked out. Four tanks of the 743d's Company B were knocked out by enemy fire during the day.

This action brought the 197th Field Artillery Battalion close to exhausting its ammunition. Forward observers with the 119th Infantry reported two counterattacks forming up almost simultaneously on both flanks, and the Battalion pumped out about 1,200 rounds within an hour. The 197th's ammunition train was out getting ammunition, but meanwhile the ready reserve on hand was dropping to almost nothing and the observers kept calling for fire. The battalion operations officer sent out a hurry call for ammunition to the other artillery battalions of the Division. In a matter almost of minutes, the situation was reversed. Ammunition convoys from the 118th and 230th reported in. And then, what would have been just in the nick of time, the 197th's ammunition officer led his train into the battalion area.

The 120th Infantry joined the fight on August 28, taking up a place in line on the right flank, along the Seine. Here opposition was less formidable than along the high ridge positions, and progress was steady

Meanwhile changes were taking place in the enemy order of battle At first, the 30th had appeared to be opposed entirely by elements of the 18th Luftwaffe Division, but on the second day, August 28, two battalions of a Parachute Lehr (Demonstration) Regiment appeared. This turned out to be a part of the 6th Parachute Division, which had been lurking in the rear. After the stiff fighting of August 29, in which both regiments of the 18th Luftwaffe Division and the Parachute Lehr Regiment were in action, the enemy withdrew the 18th Luftwaffe Division toward Beauvais, leaving the 6th Parachute Division to hold the bag. Evidently the hammering given the two counterattacks against the 119th Infantry had been convincing.

As a result, the infantry advanced on the last two days of the month almost as fast as their legs would carry them. On the 30th the line swung forward 11 miles, well past the Oise River town of Pontoise, and on the 31st the Division picked up another 15 miles, with the Oise River on its right, past the Therain River. Three blown bridges and a little long-range artillery fire were encountered. There had been localized opposition, but at best by disorganized groups of Germans lost in the shuffle. The time for rapid motorized pursuit had arrived.

*   *   *

The operation which followed was pursuit with a capital "P"—one of the wildest and fastest advances ever made to catch up with a retreating enemy. For, as the XIX Corps order which arrived at the Division command post about midnight of August 31-September 1 made clear, this was to be no ordinary drive forward The objective was not the line of the Somme River, some 50 miles distant, which G-2s had been solemnly discussing as the Germans' next defensive position. It was nothing less than the Belgian border, more than 100 miles away.

What had happened on the 30th Division front—the crumbling of enemy opposition into nothingness—had been duplicated all along the battle line. The enemy was in headlong flight—divisions, regiments, battalions, companies, platoons bunched together as they found themselves The whole United States First Army, therefore, was going to advance northeast as far and as fast as its gasoline supply and the enemy opposition would allow.

The 30th Division was ordered to move up to an assembly area just north of the French-Belgian border, near Tournai, Belgium, as soon as possible. Corps artillery and antiaircraft artillery battalions were dumping their equipment on the ground and would be able to provide enough trucks to carry two of the Division's three infantry regiments. On the 30th's left would be the 2d Armored Division, under XIX Corps. On its right was the 28th Division of V Corps. The Division would use a single route through Roye, Péronne and Cambrai.

The headlong dash to Belgium began early on the afternoon of September 1, not quite as soon as had been planned, but soon enough to allow the 30th to become the first American infantry division to enter Belgium. The hours preceeding the start of the move had been hectic ones, for there was much to be done. gathering troops and commanders, issuing maps, obtaining gasoline. Where and in what strength the enemy's stragglers might be encountered was anyone's guess. It was important that the long column not be held up by minor opposition. Therefore a task force was set up under Brigadier General Harrison, consisting of the 125th Cavalry Squadron; the 30th Reconnaissance Troop; the 743d Tank Battalion; the 1st Battalion, 119th Infantry (entirely motorized); the 118th Field Artillery Battalion; Company A, 105th Engineer Battalion; and Company A, 823d Tank Destroyer Battalion. This force was powerful and highly mobile—just the thing to rapidly knock out anything but really strong opposition. Behind Task Force Harrison in the march order came the remainder of the 119th Infantry Regimental Combat Team, then the Division command post, the 120th Infantry Regimental Combat Team and then the rest of the division. Left behind, however, was the 117th Infantry: there just weren't enough trucks to go around.

The 125th Cavalry jumped off an hour before the rest of the task

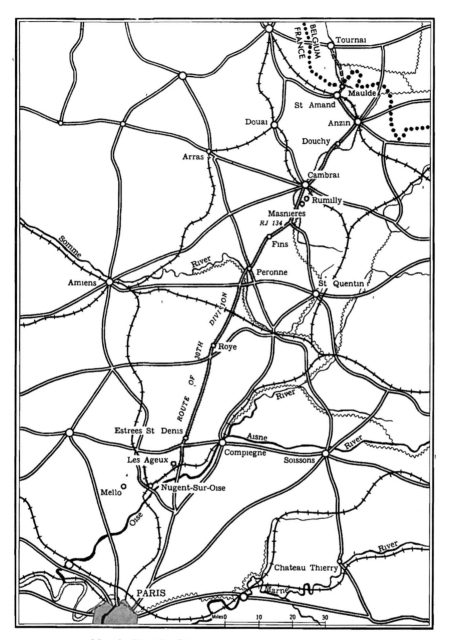

Map 6—The 30th Infantry Division's Route to Belgium

force. Enemy opposition during the day was almost negligible. Troop A, moving up the secondary roads on the left of the route the Division column was to use, easily knocked out the occasional blocks set up by machine gunners and riflemen, as did the platoon of Troop C on the right flank. There was no opposition at all on the main route for the first 35 miles At Roye, Troop C was met with a burst of small-arms fire as it passed through town and civilians reported large numbers of enemy equipped with tanks just northeast of the town. These reports proved exaggerated However, a column of German half-tracks were chased away and a Mark III tank and a German staff car were knocked out in three short actions by a few rounds from the assault-gun platoon attached to the troop, and a dozen Germans were captured and almost as many killed in a 45-minute action at Carrepuis, the next town past Roye Similar actions took place at almost every town along the way. The French Forces of the Interior took charge of the German weapons and the prisoners in most cases, and often assumed the task of mopping up the strays while the cavalrymen surged forward

By early evening Troop A had reached Péronne on the Somme River. Here the 82d Reconnaissance Battalion of the 2d Armored Division had been of great help. Having started before the 125th Cavalry, it had reached the Somme first, and after crossing in the 2d Armored zone had fanned out as far east as Péronne, where it knocked out a fairly strong enemy force stationed there and prepared to blow the bridge, before proceeding on its way. Thus, Troop A, now following the main road, crossed without difficulty, followed without an interval by the main body of the task force, which had been traveling rapidly Meanwhile, Troop C, which had had slower going over the secondary roads on the right, pulled into Péronne Gas was already getting to be a problem, but the troop managed to pick up some fuel and was prepared to continue at daybreak

Meanwhile Troop A was also worried about gas. About eight miles south of Cambrai, with the equivalent of 30 miles in its fuel tanks, the troop was ordered to stop to wait for the squadron fuel truck to catch up, but after a fruitless hour and a half wait the troop started up again at 11:00 P M —the squadron commander felt that the fuel truck would probably be able to catch up before the tanks ran dry

About three-quarters of a mile further on the point of the task force column caught up with a column of German horse-drawn carts and demolished it with machine-gun and 37mm. cannon fire from the five leading vehicles. Soon the column had advanced almost to the Escaut (Scheldt) River at Masnières, about four miles south of Cambrai Here began the only real holdup the task force encountered. By this time the entire Division column was on the road, stretched back almost to the initial point.

The lead cavalry platoon ran into 20mm gun fire at about 3:00 A.M. about 200 yards from the bridge over the stream As the cavalrymen reconnoitered for a bypass, four medium tanks from the 743d Tank Battalion came up past a burning German half-track spewing 20mm. shells and swiftly overran the antitank guns on the north side of the waterway. One tank hit a mine and had a track blown off. There were no other losses. Another cavalry platoon got a quarter-ton truck across the bridge without being fired on and then proceeded about a mile past Masnières to the outskirts of Rumillu Again the point was greeted with 20mm. gun fire, which knocked out the two leading armored cars. The drive was temporarily halted General Harrison, who had been at the front of the task force main body all the way, was wounded by a 20mm shell as he hit the ditch from his jeep, and Colonel Sutherland took over temporary command of the task force, until General Hobbs, on his way forward in his own jeep, arrived.

Medium tanks again came to the front to knock out the light anti-tank guns the enemy was using. It was decided to use them to capture Cambrai, where the enemy strength was unknown. Two companies of the 743d providing a base of fire on the hill south of Cambrai, another tank company swept in from the southeast and moved through the town. The cavalry was ordered to move up to the head of the column again as the advance was resumed.

Meanwhile, as the head of the task force column drove past Cambrai, a fire-fight developed in the town with an enemy column which had blundered into town from the east, evidently unaware of the presence of the Americans. The 3d Battalion of the 119th Infantry was called upon to clear the town, and as a precaution, Company A of the 823d Tank Destroyer Battalion was left in the town to secure the flank of the main route there. The head of the task force column resumed its march

Minor actions continued for the rest of the operation Near Iwuy, about five miles past Cambrai, the cavalry knocked out a column of six armored cars advancing along a sunken road from the southeast. Sniper fire was encountered at Denham, and some sniper and antitank fire was received at Valenciennes. By this time the fast moving point of the column had pulled away from the main body Many vehicles had been forced to drop out because of practically dry gasoline tanks Other detachments had been dropped off to clean out snipers.

At 6:30 P.M. Colonel Sutherland's party—a handful of jeeps and about a platoon of tanks—crossed the Belgian border at Maulde, with the rest of the column coming ahead as fast as it could—making the

30th the first American infantry division to enter Belgium. By 7:00 P.M. roadblocks had been established in the south part of Tournai and a rifle platoon of the 119th Infantry was in the center of the city. The 30th had còme 180 miles in 72 hours—118 of them in 30 hours. "This is believed to be one of the fastest opposed advances by an infantry division over a similar distance in the history of warfare," the XIX Corps commander noted September 6, in a letter of commendation to the Division.

Not all of the action took place at the head of the column. Part of the task force coming through Péronne ran into small-arms fire near the bridge there, and during the night of September 1-2 an enemy vehicle traveled with part of the 823d Tank Destroyer Battalion column for some distance before it was discovered and removed by the military police.

There was more excitement for many of the units as they closed into their assembly areas south of Tournai. The 30th Reconnaissance Troop, setting up road blocks southeast of the city, was attacked in the dark and sustained damage to two armored cars and lost a jeep, as well as three men killed and six wounded, including the troop commander. The 119th Infantry, closing into its assembly area at 10:00 P.M. on September 2, was forced to fight a half-hour long battle against anti-tank guns and infantry to clear out the assigned area. The 823d Tank Destroyer Battalion command post group found its wooded assembly area swarming with enemy, and, after pulling back temporarily to get assistance from infantry and artillery, returned to beat the bushes for a total of 91 prisoners and six enemy dead.

Only 236 prisoners were evacuated by the 30th Division's Military Police Platoon, most of the Germans instead being turned over to the French Forces of the Interior. Army finally credited the Division with 2,081 prisoners so evacuated, for a grand total of 2,317 for the operation.

Most of the Division was on hand in the new area on September 3, though vehicles which had dropped out en route with empty gas tanks and other detachments still trickled in. The 117th Infantry started moving up the next day on trucks sent back from the new assembly area in Belgium, arriving during the night of September 4-5.

The scattered and confused German columns were by this time far away on their blind retreat toward the German border. On September 3 a column of some 30,000 troops from a score of enemy divisions was trapped and virtually destroyed near Mons by the 1st Infantry Division and the 3d Armored Division, but this was the only large windfall in the fighting past the Seine. By now supply was the big problem, not the enemy. The usable ports were still back in Normandy, the nearest army depots back in the Paris area. Most of the 30th's trucks were deadlined, for there was scarcely enough gasoline for administrative duties alone. The pursuit was over for the time being, until gasoline and rations and ammunition could be moved up.

So the Division sat in place. Stray Germans continued to be flushed out of the woods and out-of-the-way villages. The city of Tournai, now in the British sector, was turned over on September 3 The infantry practiced the technique of assault on a fortified position, which might come in handy at the Meuse River or at the German border. Everyone waited for orders to move.

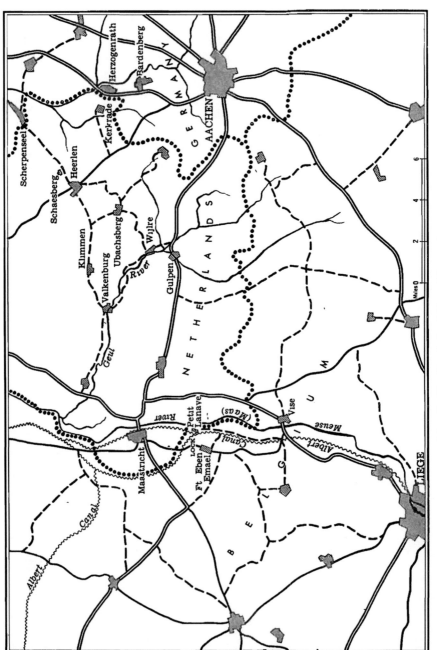

Map 7—The Borderland Near Maastricht

Chapter VIII

TO THE GERMAN BORDER

By September 7, two full days after the last combat elements of the 30th had reached Belgium and five days after its first vehicles had crossed the border, enough motor fuel had been accumulated for the pursuit to be resumed, with captured German stocks combined with American gasoline to provide a barely acceptable mixture. But those who had hoped for a repetition of the headlong dash from the Paris area were sadly disappointed. When the long motorized convoys set out eastward in the rain on the 7th their ambitiously selected march objectives were about 130 miles away—close to the Meuse River, where the Germans might be expected to stand temporarily, at last. The hoped-for fuel reserves, however, did not materialize, and early in the afternoon, after an advance of only 80 miles, the mud-spattered trucks pulled off the roads and halted near the Waterloo battlefield south of Brussels. And when Old Hickory moved out again next morning, its infantry was on foot, and the vehicles of the march columns moved in long bounds, so as to conserve gasoline. What should have been a one-day journey took three times as long. At that, the advance was made possible only by long, gruelling footslogging over the mucky country roads. On the 8th the doughboys plodded 27 miles to the vicinity of Jodoigne, on the 9th another 22 miles to their assembly area near Tongres. A 15-mile stint the next day brought the Division to the Meuse River

Enemy interference with the three-day approach march was entirely lacking, although Belgian Armée Blanche detachments reported occasional small bands in the woods and near isolated towns. Even the 113th Cavalry Squadron, sweeping ahead of the three regimental combat team columns, encountered almost no enemy. The first signs of German resistance appeared on September 10, as the Division secured the west bank of the Meuse River and Albert Canal. Even then these signs were pitifully weak.

The line of the Meuse River from Liège northward was the first line of defense for Belgium in both World Wars. At Liège, after flowing northeast from Namur for some 40 miles, the Meuse turns north into Holland, flowing past Maastricht, the chief city of southern Holland, 18 river miles from Liège On the outskirts of Liège the Meuse is joined by the Albert Canal, which parallels it in the river valley to a point four miles south of Maastricht, where it swings in an arc to the northeast through the Meuse bluffs to form, with other canals, a man-made island on which the western half of Maastricht is located Visé, about half way

to Liège, controls the first good crossing of the Meuse south of Maastricht
From here south the bluffs which flank the river become almost sheer,
especially on the east bank, and dominate the double waterway. The
Albert Canal, lying 160 feet below the surface of the hill it cuts through,
as it circles around Maastricht, is also characterized by very steep banks

This region was heavily fortified by Belgium, ironically enough
furnishing, in both World Wars, classical examples of the vulnerability
of fortresses. In 1914 unprecedentedly heavy German siege guns hammered the ring of forts around Liège into submission. In 1940 the successful German assault of the modern fortress Eben Emael, located on
the Albert Canal as it slants to circle around Maastricht, was a model
of combined operations. In both instances, however, reduction of the
forts required long planning and special equipment. Luckily for the
30th in 1944, the Germans were not prepared to use either the natural
barrier or the old Belgian emplacements as a defensive position.

For the approach to the Meuse on September 10, the 30th gathered
itself into two columns, with the 117th, which had originally provided
the center column, following the 119th Infantry on the south. The 113th
Cavalry Squadron still led An air strike had been scheduled to hit Fort
Eben Emael for the 120th but delay in completing arrangements developed, and the regimental commander decided not to wait for the planes
His judgment proved correct. The regiment advanced almost without
opposition, and Fort Eben Emael proved to have been abandoned. It
was later learned that about three hundred enemy troops had withdrawn
from the fort to Maastricht. The strongest enemy reaction to the seizure
of the fort was a 25-round light artillery concentration against the 3d
Battalion. Meanwhile the 119th moved up to the river line opposite
Visé entirely unopposed.

The Meuse itself never did become a defended obstacle to the 30th.
Early the next afternoon, after a night of engineer reconnaissance, the
119th boldly sent Company L across the two waterways just south of
the blown bridges at Visé, following it with the rest of the regiment by
nightfall. Some enemy artillery fire landed sporadically, but that was all.

While the 30th was getting its first elements across the river near
Visé, the major crossing at Liège was being forced by elements of the
VII Corps. This success enabled the dispatch of a company of tanks and
a company of tank destroyers via Liège, on the following day, to support
the 119th. The 113th Cavalry Squadron also crossed at Liège to maintain
contact with VII Corps.

Meanwhile the 120th Infantry was seizing the locks at the southern
tip of the Maastricht island which controlled the water level in the river
and canal. At 5:00 P.M. a platoon of Company E scrambled down the

steep banks of the canal just north of Fort Eben Emael and crossed in assault boats to take the Belgian town of Petit Lanaye against scattered small-arms fire, being joined in a couple of hours by another platoon.

This move was followed by an ingenious attack on the locks themselves from Fort Eben Emael. The big problem was that of getting down the steep bare banks of the canal. It was solved with the aid of a Belgian military engineer who pointed out two tunnels which could be used from within the fort. One large tunnel opened on the cliff beside the canal, but was about halfway up the bank. The other was a drainage pipe, barely large enough to crawl through, which opened on the canal one foot above water level. Both tunnels were used in the scheme En- gineers brought pneumatic boats through the upper tunnel and then lowered them to members of the Company K squad charged with seizing the locks, who had crawled 500 yards through the lower tunnel. They descended to the river and paddled across the canal.

The maneuver was a great success, completely surprising the small German party guarding the locks and neutralizing the German demoli- tion charges under the supervision of the engineer officer who came along for that purpose. The next morning, after the rest of the platoon which furnished the assault party had come down to the locks via Company E's positions at Lanaye, the Germans awoke to what had happened and sent an improvised company there to rectify the situation. Unfortunately for the Germans, their commander neglected to reconnoiter the route of approach, and the group was neatly ambushed by Company K's men All 96 were specifically accounted for: 76 prisoners, ten killed, six wounded and four more died of wounds

*   *   *

By September 12 the enemy authorities in Maastricht, who had been collecting the strays of the great retreat and sorting them into squad-, platoon- and company-sized bundles for defense of the sector, were aware of a far more potent threat than the 120th foray This was the bridge- head at Visé, now enlarged by the presence of the 117th Infantry, which had begun crossing at 3:30 A M. The enemy's efforts to set up a defensive line south of Maastricht, chiefly with makeshift infantry closely sup- ported by 20mm flak guns, was a notable failure, however Company A of the 117th crossed the Dutch-Belgian border at 10.00 A.M, Septem- ber 12, thus becoming the first Allied unit to enter Holland, and the eastern part of Maastricht fell on the 13th. Although handicapped at first by the absence of heavy supporting weapons (only one tank com- pany was in action on the 12th), the two regiments forged steadily forward, the 117th moving almost directly north and the 119th driving northeast on its right Where enemy resistance stiffened, it was broken down by artillery concentrations or by dispatch of a platoon of tanks. On the 12th, enemy reinforcements, including one group of 150 men, attempted to move south to the battle-line, but artillery observers in the 120th sector, west of the Meuse, scattered them with heavy concentrations. Advances of up to seven miles were registered on the 13th, as the 117th swept north to cut the roads out of Maastricht, as well as to enter the town, and the 119th Infantry made for the high ground overlooking the Geul River.

The Germans counterattacked in battalion strength during this operation to rescue a general's aide who was by that time a corpse in his command car, while the papers that had been in his dispatch case were being pored over at Division headquarters The dispatch case had been captured through the foresight of Lieutenant Elwood G Daddow of B Company, who dashed out under fire to get it. The papers proved to be an extremely valuable find, indicating missions and strengths of most of the units in the German Seventh Army. One map, for example, indicated not only the location of Army headquarters, but the command post locations of two corps and twelve divisions. These data were particularly important because of the far-reaching reorganization then going on in the *Wehrmacht* as it fell back to the German border.

During the night of September 13-14, virtually all the enemy troops in western Maastricht fled northward, although three of them were still busy burning papers in Gestapo headquarters when Captain Melvin Handville of the division Counterintelligence Corps detachment walked in the next morning. The enemy had blown the bridges over the Maas, and therefore Company F of the 117th Infantry had to use engineer boats to cross to the western part of the city. Otherwise, however, the occupation of the central portion of the Limbourg Province capital was easy. 120th Infantry troops and Company F men made contact on the Maastricht island.

While Maastricht was being cleared, thus furnishing a route for the 2d Armored Division to cross the Maas, other elements of the Division were closing down to the line of the Geul River, and the 120th Infantry's Intelligence and Reconnaissance Platoon was ranging out to the German border, which it crossed above five miles west of Aachen at 5:30 P M. before returning to its unit.

The toughest fighting was at Valkenberg, down in the valley of the Geul River. The 1st Battalion first sent a platoon into the town to seize it but before long the whole battalion had been gradually drawn into the fight there.

The line of the Geul River was evidently intended to be a major defensive position. At the time the enemy was opposing the Allied advance in two directions. The British, driving north, were halted generally along the line of the Albert Canal between Maastricht and Antwerp The American forces driving east were now slowing up as they hit the German border and the Siegfried Line. Between Aachen and Maastricht was the hinge linking the two positions, to be held until the Germans were' forced back to the Westwall north of Aachen. Air reconnaissance photos showed a few long trenches already dug in hills north and east of the Geul when the 30th arrived there, and the Division's combat troops were experiencing the first consistently heavy artillery fire in many weeks, particularly in Valkenberg. Nevertheless, the German defenses, though showing signs of cohesion for the first time since the gallop across France began, were still incomplete and undermanned. German LXXXI Corps' order to *Gruppe Jungklaus,* charged with building defensive positions between the Albert Canal and the Westwall, stated "The elimination of the still existing hole on the left [?] wing defense to the Westwall is of great importance." *Gruppe Jungklaus,* with a fighting strength, according to captured documents, of about 4,500 men, was supposed to control the front from the corps boundary at Valkenberg 'down to a wooded hill just west of Aachen until the staffs of the 275th and 49 Infantry Divisions could take over.

The switch position along the Geul River fell quickly and a three day advance left the 30th looking down, from the hills west of the Wurm River, at the Siegfried Line. The attack began September 16, with the 119th on the left, the 120th on the right The 117th, already earmarked for extending the Division zone northward once the Siegfried Line was reached, followed the 119th.

Valkenberg, favorite target of German artillery, provided the stiffest fight of the first day. Both small-arms fire and shelling were intense, as the 1st Battalion, 119th Infantry, cleaned out a pocket of enemy resistance in the town and splashed across the Geul headed for the railroad tracks paralleling the river. Here the enemy attempted to hold, but his infantry was forced back during the afternoon and the 1st Battalion reached Walem, just over the hill overlooking the river At Wiljre, further east, where the 3d Battalion was crossing, mortar and small-arms fire failed to stop the advance, and by nightfall the battalion had reached its objective, Ubachsberg. Meanwhile the 120th, making a steady five mile advance, was hard put to find an enemy to defeat. There was no contact on the southeast front at all until mid-morning, and the meager enemy positions encountered were easily overrun. So fast was the enemy withdrawing here that by nightfall the only contact with the Germans was through patrols.

Next day saw the job virtually completed. The 1st Battalion, 119th Infantry, ran into stubborn resistance around Klimmen, but the arrival of tanks, which had crossed the river at fords prepared by the 105th Engineer Combat Battalion, helped break up the opposition. By nightfall the 1st Battalion was entering Heerlen. The 3d Battalion, marching in column of companies, also faced delaying action, but its strongest opposition was broken up in twenty minutes after a double envelopment with the two follow-up companies took place The 120th, after advancing for an hour unopposed, became the first unit of the 30th to enter Germany in strength as elements of Company F crossed the border at 10:30 A.M. and headed for Horsbach.

Regrouping and mopping up occupied the Division on September 18 and 19. At noon on the 18th, the 117th began shifting north to positions facing the Siegfried Line near Scherpenseel Mortar, artillery, and antitank fire from a still uncleaned forest on the left, along the 30th Division–2d Armored Division boundary, forced a holdup short of the objective that night. By evening of the next day the regiment was in place. The 119th and 120th also sideslipped northward; Company G of the 119th Infantry flushed out some enemy near Schaesberg on the morning of the 18th, but, by noon, aided by a platoon of tanks, had restored order.

Thus, by the end of September 19 the Division was in contact with the Siegfried Line along its entire front except in the south, where the 120th Infantry was watching and probing, with patrols and fire, the close-in German positions in the Dutch borderline town of Kerkrade. Already the battle of the German border was in progress south of Aachen Both sides knew it would soon flare up along the Wurm River where the 30th was in place

*   *   *

Arrival at the German border marked the end of the honeymoon. It was an important change in the big terms of armies and campaigns, but it was also significant in countless little ways. Casualties were light in September; in the 120th Infantry the non-battle casualties were actually twice those sustained in combat, although some of the former were men who couldn't stand the long marches. Later, in the spring, the 30th took part in another "ratrace," but some of the carnival spirit was lacking the second time. Kisses were to be had later, but they were seldom public expressions of *joie de vivre* and enthusiasm. Liquor, thereafter, was confiscated, not received as a gift. So long as the Division remained on the border its men had friends in the rear areas, but ahead, until the end of February, Germany was a land of hostile, shell-torn, almost deserted towns, with few exceptions.

Hitherto information supplied by natives, either organized into resistance groups or individually, had played an important part in combat intelligence. Hereafter information from civilians was scanty, not so much because of hostility as because so many civilians had been evacuated from the forward areas.

The desire to prevent leakage of information probably prompted the forced evacuation of Kerkrade by the Germans on September 25—one of the last occasions, incidentally, on which resistance groups helped the Division. Soon after midnight of September 24-25 the Dutch *Ordre Dienst* reported to the 120th Infantry that the Germans planned to evacuate all of Kerkrade's population between 8:00 A.M. and noon that day, and estimated that 25,000 would be coming toward the Allied lines. At 7:20 the exodus began.

Kerkrade's evacuation was one of the most touching scenes of the war. Men, women and children, carrying their possessions on their backs or in baby carriages and carts, clogged the roads leading west, directed by military guides and by the Dutch OD, which kept a careful eye out for German sympathizers and agents. Blind men walked in the procession. Invalids were pushed along in their wheelchairs. On the way back the Germans shelled the helpless column, but blindly it circled around the dangerous points and kept going. That night an estimated 30,000-35,000 civilian refugees were being temporarily lodged in schools and offices and homes in the rear

Part Three

GERMANY: THE OPENING WEDGE

Chapter IX

SIEGFRIED BREAKTHROUGH

The hard-fought battle which the 30th Infantry Division waged al: most single-handed between October 2, 1944, when it assaulted the Siegfried Line east of Maastricht, and October 16, when it completed the encirclement of Aachen, occupies a special place in the annals of Allied victory in western Europe. It was a battle charged with political values second only to those of the Normandy invasion itself—a condition fully reflected in the bitterness of the fighting. The purely military stakes were similarly high. Technically it was a difficult and complicated operation undertaken on relatively short notice.

The time element is perhaps the most essential clue to the individuality of that action. It was fought in a period of major transition.

By the end of September 1944 the glorious days of the Battle of France were over almost everywhere. The German Seventh Army had been badly beaten. Most of its fighting men were either gathered together in Allied prisoner of war cages or scattered in lonely graves from the Normandy beaches to the German border The hulks of its tanks and trucks rested in the ditches where our bulldozers, clearing the roads, had shoved them. The German Fifteenth Army was in retreat to the watery fastnesses of northern Netherlands. In less than four months of fighting much of France and almost all of Belgium had been set free. Allied troops were in Holland. Others had reached the German border near Aachen. It had been a great victory

Already, however, there were signs that the pursuit was over. The American spearheads had halted for days at a time for ammunition, food and gasoline depots to be moved up toward the front, but supply lines were still dangerously long. Artillery and mortar ammunition was rationed. The line of forward troops was thin. Nor were the Germans content to "collapse or surrender," as one high-ranking intelligence officer had begun hinting broadly at the first of the month. A miracle of reorganization was taking place in the retreating *Wehrmacht* South of Aachen, where the American V Corps had probed tentatively through the concrete barriers of the Siegfried Line, the American troops were being pushed back over the border by counterattacks of increasing vehemence. VII Corps, which had moved through one of the two lines of Westwall fortifications enclosing Aachen, was now locked in a costly standstill battle. The daring airborne attempt to outflank the Siegfried Line and the Rhine simultaneously, at Arnhem, had been brought to a standstill under the blows of the German panzers. Never again would the German armies be as strong as they were on June 6 But every night as the 30th waited in the shadow of the Westwall new troops came up to occupy pillboxes, and the same process was taking place all along the far-flung battle line. From the ashes of defeat in France, from the bombed-out factories of the Reich, from the idle warships of the fleet, Germany was rallying a new army for defense of the Fatherland And every day, in its concrete and steel fortifications along the border, it was getting stronger

*   *   *

When Old Hickory's leading foot soldiers fought to within sight of the Siegfried Line in the middle third of September, it was just beginning to reassume a dual character, as a symbol as well as a series of specific places and structures on the ground. The Westwall, as the Germans called it, dated back to 1936, when Nazi Germany took a deep breath and moved its then inadequate army into the Rhineland in defiance of the Versailles Treaty. German leaders feared then that France's massive military strength would strike quickly against them But it did not, and acquiescence thus was the original line of defense for the re-arming Reich. In the years that followed, however, something more substantial was created—thousands of Organizasion Todt workers built the Westwall, emplacing pillboxes and dragon's teeth and antitank ditches along the natural barriers of the German border. It never was as elaborate a static defense as that of the Maginot Line, which faced it for many miles along the Franco-German border. It did not have to be. The Maginot Line was a defensive symbol of a defensive-minded nation The Westwall was the defensive symbol of an offensive-minded nation, a sign to Germans and non-Germans alike that it would brook no interference with the Third Reich's renascent *Wehrmacht* or with its expansionist schemes in eastern Europe.

The Westwall ceased abruptly to be a symbol in the spring of 1940, when the German legions poured westward to the speedy glory of *Sieg im Westen*. During the lush years of Nazi triumph which followed, the Siegfried Line was neglected. Then, after the abysmal defeat in France in 1944, it became again a magic name to be shouted over the German radio and printed in fiery exhortations to the men of the *Wehrmacht*. The battle of the Atlantic Wall had ended in disaster for Germany, but back at the borders of the Reich there could be no further retreat. Brave German soldiers inspired by Teutonic loyalty would fight to the last man to keep the invaders from the holy soil of the Fatherland. The Westwall would be their fortress.

Aachen also figured heavily in the propaganda war. A communications and industrial center of 160,000, it was the first large German city to be threatened with capture by the Allies Aachen was an ancient city with a long and colorful history during the incessant border wars of the middle ages. It had been glorious, too, in 1940, for it was there that staff officers had paced up and down the night of May 9, watches and march tables in their hands, as their convoys rolled west to the blitz victory over the Western Powers Aachen would be held, though it prove to be another Stalingrad. Like the Westwall, which enclosed it in two concrete arms, it would be a watchword of German resistance

Sound military considerations, of course, were also involved in the decision to defend at the Westwall The Siegfried Line was the strongest position west of the Rhine. In the mountains of Alsace-Lorraine to the south, the Germans possessed an additional covering position of great power The Siegfried Line could be easily extended to the north of the Aachen plain along the line of the Maas River. Holding the Westwall would require fewer troops than any other line short of the Rhine, allowing the bulk of the reforming German armies to devote themselves to the dual problems of reorganization and rearward displacement of their supply installations Holding the Siegfried Line, further, would keep the Allies away from the vital industrial establishments of the Rhine and Ruhr valleys. By the testimony of prisoners and the evidence of the fighting itself, it became clear during that fall of 1944 that the Westwall would be the German winter line, behind which the *Wehrmacht* hoped to nurse its wounds and gather strength for the inevitable Allied offensive of the spring.

During the battles which punctured it, the Siegfried Line assumed the popular character of a barrier beyond which there were no stopping points short of the Rhine itself, leading to the impression that once it was breached the Allied armies could stream through to the gates of Cologne and Dusseldorf without opposition. That was, of course, not true At the time of the Siegfried breakthrough frenzied community digging by villagers along the Roer River and the Erft River was taking place—and the Roer eventually was the scene of the longest stalemate of the Western campaign. These positions were not occupied before or during the breakthrough operation and showed signs of having been dug with more zeal than skill But if sufficient troops had been available to man them they could have been a considerable obstacle

Moreover the Siegfried Line was never intended for static linear defense In accordance with German aggressive tactical doctrine, its prime function was to soften up the attacker for a strong counterattack by mobile reserves waiting behind the line Even if an assaulting force were able to get through the pillboxes and barriers, it would be so weakened and channelized by the narrowness of its penetrations that it could be hit effectively.

As it existed in the Division zone, the Siegfried Line consisted of a heavy belt of pillboxes, entrenchments and obstacles. Because the Aachen plain was a logical avenue of armored attack into Germany, this portion of the line was highly developed. The fortifications were closely tied in with existing terrain obstacles. The first of these was the Wurm River, a 30-foot-wide stream some 3-6 feet deep with steep banks 4-6 feet high. In some cases the Germans had evidently cut the bank to make it more steep. Both the banks of the stream and the bottom were soft, making the approaches difficult for supporting tanks and tank destroyers. Behind the Wurm was a railroad line stretching north from Aachen. Because of the numerous cuts and fills along the line of track, it was also an obstacle and in addition it was covered with heavy small-arms defensive fires. Both river and railroad were under enemy observation from the high ground north of Palenberg, from the slag pile near Palenberg and from the Rimberg Castle.

Another terrain obstacle of importance in the southern part of the assault zone was the belt of woods which extended over the slope of the hill south of the Rimberg Castle. Generally, the terrain to the east was fairly flat, with rises in the ground offering limited observation. The prevalence of slag piles in that coal-mining section, however, considerably extended the range of observation.

Behind the river and the railroad was a belt of pillboxes facing generally west and sited up to three kilometers in depth, with the strongest grouping along the more difficult terrain to the west and other clusters of concrete emplacements farther east. The standard pillbox was about 20 to 30 feet by 40 to 50 feet in size and 20 to 25 feet high, with most of the box under ground level Each pillbox had several rooms and was designed to accommodate a squad with its one or two machine guns A few pillboxes were large enough to house the 37mm. antitank gun, which was standard when the Line was constructed, but provisions for larger weapons were made in open emplacements to the rear for artillery. Dug-in tanks later encountered may have taken advantage of these positions Many of the pillboxes were carefully disguised as houses, barns, haystacks, and so forth, and even those not so disguised but merely covered with earth proved very difficult to spot after four years of overgrowth. In this connection British and French aerial photographs made during the construction period were invaluable in the successful location of over ninety per cent of the pillboxes in the Division zone before the attack was made. Some idea of the size of the job of pillbox reduction may be derived from the fact that 191 boxes were destroyed or sealed by the 30th Division's engineers during the month of October

During the two weeks before the attack, frantic German efforts were made to improve the Westwall defenses Minefields were planted, particularly in the southern portion of the zone, additional barbed wire was strung, and the fixed concrete positions supplemented by firing trenches. The strongpoint system developed in the Russian campaign and reflected in the Atlantic Wall defenses had not been worked out when the Westwall was constructed, and although the pillboxes were grouped in mutually supporting clusters, they had limited fields of fire and were not suitable for all around defense.

Thus the German 1944 concept of defense of the Line was that the men should occupy their living quarters in the boxes and retire to them during artillery concentrations and bombings, but that at least part of the crew must return to the field fortifications outside when the infantry attack came, to prevent the boxes being assaulted from the rear by special assault detachments in the approved textbook fashion.

At that, the Palenberg–Rimberg section of the line was the most favorable area for an assault, for farther north near Geilenkirchen the pillbox clusters were even thicker and farther south toward Aachen the enemy had a strong covering position in the Dutch town of Kerkrade, with the additional obstacles of built-up areas and a line of dragon's teeth as well to slow up the attacker The place where the actual assault was made had been selected before our leading troops had reached the German border, the 117th swinging north to get into position.

Two missions were involved in the Division's prospective attack: first, to make a breakthrough in the Westwall defenses before they could be further strengthened; and second, to swing south toward the VII Corps troops south of Aachen, relieving the heavy pressure on them and enabling them to close in on that city. The American positions in the Aachen–Geilenkirchen sector were extended by great curving lines of front. Capture of Aachen would allow both VII Corps and XIX Corps to redistribute troops more economically and further would reduce the threat of a determined German drive to cut the vital supply link at Liège on the Meuse River The airborne attempt to flank the line had failed. Other troops that had pushed into the line were stalled A new effort was necessary to open up Germany's border defenses—a gap which the Ninth Army would later extend and use to pour through a great mass of troops and supplies for the drive to the Rhine.

*   *   *

If the overtaxed supply troops had been able to sustain an uninterrupted motorized advance across Belgium and the tip of southern Holland, the Allies might have pressed to the Rhine without decisive opposition. If the 30th had had supplies and fresh troops to back it up when it did reach the German border, there might never have been a battle of the pillboxes But the facts were otherwise The 30th reached the Siegfried Line on September 19. The Army plan, then, was for the 30th to push on through the Westwall the next day and turn south to relieve the pressure on the VII Corps around Aachen. On the 20th, however, air was not available for the assault and the Division was forbidden to attack without air support. The attack was discussed back and forth from Army to Division level until finally, on the 22d, it was decided to postpone the attack for several days.

Several specific reasons for the fortnight's postponement can be given but they can be summarized by the word "overextension." Even back of the Dutch border the line of troops was dangerously thin. The forested areas north of the 30th's zone had not been cleared and to the south a sleeve of enemy territory extended invitingly west from Aachen toward Liège, the vital supply bottleneck over the Meuse River which months later was the target of the Germans' Ardennes winter counteroffensive. Troops could not be made available to clean out this area before the fall of Aachen, and it remained a calculated risk—and a source of worry Even if these rearward problems could be solved, an attack through the Westwall would require troops and fire power to even hold the breakthrough against counterattack, let alone expand and exploit it The 29th Infantry Division was en route from Brittany but would not be available for several days. Artillery ammunition supply was critically short and it would be severely rationed even after a breathing spell to the end of the month, during which Army service troops and the Communications Zone could move their dumps forward. A rainy spell was forecast which would delay until the beginning of October effective air support to supplement the reduced artillery expenditure possible General Hobbs and the Corps and Army commanders could only surmise then how vigorous would be the opposition to a breakthrough operation. They found out later how correct their apprehensions had been

By the time the attack did jump off on October 2, the Germans had brought enough troops into the Siegfried Line to make the operation, not another normal attack but a full-scale "set piece," the reduction of a fortified position. Even the most impromptu attacks require some degree of planning and reconnaissance. This one required in addition specialized assault training

The major planning had been accomplished for the most part even before the waiting period began. The Division plan was for the 117th Infantry on the left and the 119th Infantry on the right to attack together

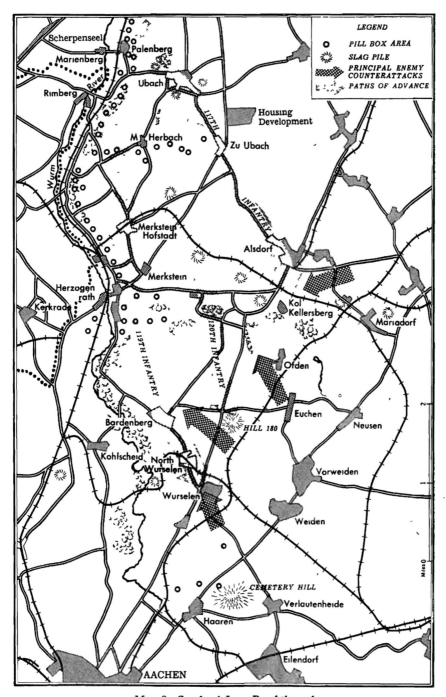

○ PILL BOX AREA
☼ SLAG PILE
▨ PRINCIPAL ENEMY
COUNTERATTACKS
∴ PATHS OF ADVANCE

Scherpenseel
Palenberg
Marienberg
Rimberg
Ubach
Mr Herbach
Zu Ubach
Housing
Development
117TH
INFANTRY
Merkstein
Hofstadt
Alsdorf
Merkstein
Herzogen
rath
Kerkrade
119TH INFANTRY
120TH INFANTRY
Kol
Kellersberg
Mariadorf
Ofden
Euchen
Neusen
Bardenberg
HILL 180
Kohlscheid
North
Wurselen
Vorweiden
Wurselen
Weiden
CEMETERY HILL
Verlautenheide
Haaren
Eilendorf
AACHEN

Map 8—Siegfried Line Breakthrough

on a narrow front at the northern edge of the Division zone, which had been extended for that purpose, and then swing south to take in flank the more difficult portions of the Siegfried Line down to the Division south boundary, where a linkup could be made with the 1st Division The 30th could then face east in preparation for further operations The 2d Armored Division would follow through the gap as soon as possible to take over the northern portion of the bridgehead through the line and extend it further north and east. Meanwhile the 120th Infantry would make a holding attack against the German defenses in Kerkrade and be prepared to either go on to attack eastward or come through the gap and join the attack to the south within the Westwall.

However, the detailed planning which would get individual platoons and squads to their objectives was still to be done This planning was performed mainly on the basis of terrain and fixed defenses rather than on detailed knowledge of enemy dispositions. The latter sort of information was hard to get because of the difficulty of working patrols into the German lines and it rapidly became outdated as new enemy units moved in piecemeal. Enough information had come in to indicate that, except for the German 183d Division, which moved into the northern part of the XIX Corps zone astride the breakthrough area, enemy reinforcements were arriving in very small packages, usually company strength. It was assumed that most, if not all, of the pillboxes would be occupied by the time the assault took place. The amount of enemy artillery which could oppose the attack was a disturbing unknown. Only four battalions were known to be on hand, but it was assumed in planning that enemy fire on the approaches to his position would be extremely heavy.

Thus, the Division intelligence officers concentrated on the problem of disseminating detailed information of terrain and defense locations. This was done through distribution of annotated vertical and oblique air photographs and preparation and distribution on a large scale of photomaps with defenses overprinted on them. Information coming in from civilians and prisoners on locations of minefields was almost too much to handle—the intelligence periodic report for September 27 stated: "So extensive have reports of minefields become that it is almost impossible to plot them all. Minefields appear in every conceivable position along the front and in some depth to the enemy's rear. Troops should be cautioned to expect both antitank and antipersonnel mines in profusion."

Patrols, as always, played a key role in getting information of how rough the terrain was, how steep the banks of the river were, how formidable an obstacle the barbed wire was. "I can still remember the first patrol conducted by Lieutenant Cushman, platoon leader of Company B," said Lieutenant Colonel Robert E. Frankland of the 117th's

1st Battalion. "He came back dripping wet from the shoulders down, having waded across the Wurm River. He found, by reconnoitering the river on both sides, the best places to cross—eventually used on October 2 by B Company."

First reports revealed an almost impassable hedge along the side of the railroad, but one of the patrols found a gap. Another patrol located a place at the end of the barbed wire where troops could advance.

Meanwhile the troops were studying their sectors. Lieutenant Colonel Frankland's intelligence officer, Lieutenant D. W. Morgan, made a sand-table by boarding up the sides of a table in the battalion command post, using inked wooden blocks for houses, cabbage leaves for vegetation and depicting the pillboxes, barbed wire, company and platoon zones, the river, the railroad, and other terrain features. Not only the riflemen but the tank destroyer and tank commanders, the heavy-weapons men and the engineers studied the table, so that by the time the operation started they were thoroughly familiar with where they were to go and what they were to do. Individual riflemen were able to refer to pillboxes by number. A Company, in battalion reserve, had to be prepared to operate anywhere in the battalion sector. "Night after night, Captain John Kent, A Company commander, would pull his support platoon out of the line and come back to the battalion CP to pore over the sandtable until close to midnight," Lieutenant Colonel Frankland noted.

Although all three regiments were still in line, they managed to provide all the assault troops with intensive training. All three battalions of the 117th and 119th went through a two-day training period in assault tactics, supervised by the 105th Engineer Battalion and the Division Chemical Officer. The 3d Battalion of the 120th, in Division reserve, spent most of its time in such practice. The line companies of the other two battalions of the 120th were also rotated so as to get assault training. The work covered use of flamethrowers, demolition charges, bazookas, and other weapons of the special assault detachments; review of the tactics of assault of pillboxes; and dry runs in pillbox reduction and in the equally important preliminary job of getting across the Wurm River rapidly. Engineers, tanks, and tank destroyers also practiced their part in the attack. All the men reviewed the use of all infantry weapons in the training areas.

This training proved invaluable. In one of the assault battalions only one man was left after four months' fighting who knew how to operate a flamethrower before the training period began. As the battalion commander put it, "All the training we had in the States and in England was now useless, because all of our assault detachments had been wiped out and there was a complete turnover in battalion personnel. This time instead of training only the assault detachments, we set out to familiarize all personnel with all tools That proved fortunate on the day of the assault, for whenever the leading elements were cut down, the nearest man could always pick up the weapon and do the job "

The initial plan was for the 117th's leading troops to cross the Wurm River using assault boats However, Lieutenant William J O'Neill, the Ammunition and Pioneer Platoon leader of the 1st Battalion, talked his battalion commander into using duckboard ladders some 4 feet wide and 15-20 feet long, which were constructed by the 105th Engineer Battalion. Meanwhile the engineers were developing expedient bridges by which tanks and tank destroyers could be swiftly moved across the stream to support the assault on the pillboxes

There was no let-up for other elements of the Division either The supply troops were busy building up ammunition and other stores for the operation. The Signal Company laid alternate wire lines to the regimental command posts and established a wirehead at an alternate Division CP, to be used in the event the operating command post in Heerlen was shelled out. Lateral lines were laid as well, so that wire communication was maintained throughout the initial phases of the assault

During the waiting period, artillery fires were kept up as much as possible, considering the ammunition shortage, with the 823d Tank Destroyer Battalion's guns also being used for indirect fires Light artillery and even high-velocity tank destroyer shells were not sufficient to reduce pillboxes, though they helped clear away pillbox camouflage. The best weapons for the purpose were the self-propelled 155mm. guns of the 258th Field Artillery Battalion, which fired on a total of 45 pillboxes from short ranges, often venturing into exposed positions to do so. This shelling, which hit all of the pillboxes which could be reached, did not necessarily knock out a pillbox but often succeeded in widening the firing aperture, making later destruction easier.

It was during this period that one of the regiments reported· "Fired at haystack with machine gun. Shots bounced off "

*   *   *

The opening blow in the assault, the air strike, was a disappointment. Saturation bombing by medium and fighter bombers had been counted on to shake up the opposition, to knock out pillboxes facing the assault troops, and to disorganize the enemy firing positions around the breakthrough area. It was to have compensated for the shortages in artillery ammunition available Even prior to D-day, October 2, the number of planes available had been cut to nine groups of mediums (324 planes) and only two groups (72 planes) of fighter-bombers The sky was intermittently overcast when the mediums came over from due west instead of from the southwest over enemy territory, and all but four groups dropped their bombs entirely outside the target area, to the east. At that, two of these groups bombed Palenberg, where red smoke shells were landing to mark pinpoint targets for the more accurate dive bombers. This bombing had little effect. The fighter bombers were well on target when they dropped their inflammable jelly bombs, but their effect was not up to expectations In the north some field fortifications were hit In the wooded region farther south the vegetation was too green for fire bombs to be of much use. Psychological effect on the defenders, which had been so noticeable after the huge air preparation for the St. Lô breakthrough, was non-existent. Some prisoners who had been in pillboxes at the time later asked, "What bombing?" when questioned as to the effect of the air preparation.

And that was that. Perhaps in the future the delicate technique of ground support by medium bombers could be made more foolproof—that was something for higher echelons to study. A few bombs had cascaded into friendly territory but few had been hurt. H-hour for the ground troops was approaching. They would go regardless.

Thus the artillery, which had plastered the German antiaircraft batteries into complete silence before the air strike, turned to its long list of prepared fires, lengthened it and went to work, with more than 400 tubes in the Division sector belching forth high explosive shells, and additional VII Corps artillery in support. Targets were enemy batteries, assembly areas, strongpoints The thirty-six 4.2-inch mortars of the attached 92d Chemical Battalion chewed up the barbed wire that protected the enemy positions and then shortened range to begin their rolling barrage for the infantry, while the 81mm. mortars of the regiments hammered at still other targets At 11:00 o'clock, H-hour, the doughboys moved out

In the 117th sector to the north, where the initial barrier of the Wurm River had to be approached over the top of an open hill in full view of the enemy, most of the men were thinking about the need to keep moving to avoid casualties—a point that Lieutenant Colonel Frankland, of the leading 1st Battalion, and others of his officers had stressed over and over again during the preparation period. "I told them we'd have to get down to the river between a fast walk and a dogtrot and that's just what they did in battle," Colonel Frankland said later

Enemy artillery and mortar fire was heavy and constant as soon as the brow of the hill was reached. B Company, which was on the left, suffered its first casualty on the edge of the hill when a shell crashed in "Its only result was more speed," said one of the officers present On the way down the hill the company faltered once but rushed ahead again when a lieutenant smashed a shovel down on a barbed-wire fence and yelled, "Jesus! Let's get out of here." Some of them jogging along carrying heavy wooden footbridges were so tired they wanted to stop and dig in—and were glad later they didn't The surge carried past the river. Big Lieutenant Don Borton, who reached the stream first, waded across, slapped a single footbridge length into place and shouted, "There's yer goddamned bridge "[1] B Company rushed across, with some impatient men splashing across the stream beside the bridge, and headed for the railroad tracks

C Company, following a still more exposed route, had heavy losses from artillery on the approach, just over the top of the hill "They were zeroed in and a dozen big babies spattered right in the middle of the 2d Platoon, practically wiping it out. There were only six boys left unwounded and alive," said one survivor. In the first hour C Company had 87 casualties, and although some of the company was across the river and moving forward, the battalion commander decided to use his reserve company, A, which had been held well back to avoid the artillery and mortar fire falling behind the assault companies. A Company moved rapidly forward along B Company's route and by 12:25 P.M. Regiment had been informed that it was on line, continuing the assault.

The next obstacle, the railroad track, was swiftly overrun, to the surprise and discomfiture of a 25- to 30-man German outpost dug in there. It was quickly mopped up, and the special assault detachments in each platoon gathered and advanced for the slow, meticulous work of knocking out pillboxes.

E Company advanced on the left of 1st Battalion at 11:00 A.M., took a bridge site over the river on the Marienberg–Palenberg road, using bazookas to overpower the two pillboxes blocking its way, and then moved through Marienberg in hand-to-hand fighting. At 1:00 P.M. the other two rifle companies of the 2d Battalion followed 1st Battalion across the river and pushed to the north, with F Company working its way up to the foot of a fiercely defended cliff north of Palenberg and G Company driving through the northeast part of the town. I Company of the 3d Battalion also crossed that day, to protect the south flank of the regimental front.

By nightfall the regiment's initial objectives had been taken, entirely without tank or tank destroyer support, at a cost to the enemy of 11 pillboxes and numerous strongly defended positions in the houses of Palenberg.

---

[1]In training three lengths had been used, the bottom two resting V like in the stream forming a foundation for the third

There weren't many of the old Tennessee National Guard gang left in the 117th by the time the Siegfried Line was reached—normal attrition of three and a half years in the States and the violent attrition of three and a half months of combat had cleaned out most of the old-timers. But the regiment certainly lived up to the straight-shooting mountaineer tradition. Aimed small-arms fire is scarcely mentioned in the Field Manual instructions on attack of a fortified position, but in this case gunfire at the apertures of the pillboxes played a large part in their reduction. A surprising number of enemy machine gunners in the pillboxes were later found shot between the eyes. One officer prisoner said that every time a pillbox embrasure was opened to fire the machine gun, the gunner got shot, so that they had to keep the ports closed. The heavy machine guns of 1st Battalion, up on the hill overlooking the Wurm, did a good job and a dangerous one. Five of the eight machine guns were knocked out by mortar fire, their positions given away by tracers they fired to zero in on the pillbox openings.

There were other factors. Speed meant surprise as well as fewer casualties, and speed in getting past the barrier of river and railroad paid off in the pillbox belt as well as on the shell-torn slope west of the river. Mortar and artillery shells had kept the defenders out of their trenches and penned up in the pillboxes, and some of them had been hurt even there. Like most good jobs it was a combined weapons job and one based on almost instinctively knowing what to do next. "Even when we got a new pillbox to take, we just pushed out our support and assault detachments mechanically," said Staff Sergeant Howard King of A Company. And so they went in with a variety of tools and played the situation for what it was worth. Sometimes rifle and hand grenades did a lot of good. In two cases portable flamethrowers turned the trick. Bazookas knocked out some pillboxes, as in the E Company sector.

A Company's first big job was to knock out a pillbox north of Rimberg. The assault detachment rushed in while Browning automatic rifles blazed from the road. "Put it in low, Gus," someone shouted to Private First Class Pantazapulos as he took aim with his bazooka "The shot sure caused a lot of commotion," Pantazapulos reflected later, "and tore a hole three feet wide in the firing slit I put in another one and the dust was still thick when Private Sirotkin ran right up to the pillbox and shoved a pole charge into the hole. That finished most of them."

"All except that one that right away tossed out a grenade and tore this piece out of my cheek," added Lieutenant Theodore Foote, the platoon leader "But we shot him pretty quick "

"What were you thinking about when you plugged that bazooka, Gus?"

"I wasn't thinking; I was praying."

*   *   *

To many of the men of the 119th Infantry, October 1944 provided the nastiest fighting they encountered on the Continent. The operation was sticky from the start. Advancing across exposed ground to the Wurm as did its neighbor to the north, the regiment's leading battalion, the 1st, moved down to the river rapidly before artillery fire on its approach route became really heavy, hurried across the river and had pushed A Company to the railroad track by noon, an hour after the jump-off. But there it was forced to hold up, with B and C Companies still west of the river, because of the strong fire from the woods to the front and the heavy flanking fire from the medieval masonry of Rimberg Castle to the northeast and from the village of Rimberg itself on the west side of the Wurm. A platoon of C Company sustained 15 casualties including the platoon leader and all NCOs, under cross fire from twin pillboxes. The 2d Battalion was soon committed to eliminate this threat. E Company, advancing under heavy German artillery concentrations, fought its way into Rimberg by 12 25, while F Company worked on until 10:45 that night before it could clean out the ten machine guns and the pillbox guarding the approach to the castle walls. Late in the afternoon L Company of the 3d Battalion crossed the river and went into position on 1st Battalion's south flank, but it too was all but immobilized in short order by the heavy fire coming from the woods.

These woods in front of the 119th possessed a number of defensive advantages, and the German fortress machine-gun battalion which occupied them displayed an unusual determination, even a few days later when its positions had been outflanked The pillboxes in the forest were so well covered that many of the positions were first disclosed by the fire coming from them The self-propelled 155mm guns had been unable to snipe at them during the preparation period Numerous trenches had been dug around the pillboxes, when American artillery shells crashed in the trees the defenders retired to their concrete shelters, but returned to the firing line when the infantry approached Later, when tanks were available to the attackers, the steep slopes in the forested area made use of direct tank fire difficult During most of the fighting in the woods, until they were cleared, the opposing forces were no more than 25 to 50 yards apart, so that the 119th could not get artillery or mortar support without pulling back Tree bursts caused many casualties

*   *   *

Both regiments had hoped to have tanks and self-propelled tank destroyers to help them in the difficult job of knocking out pillboxes and, equally important, to protect against the counterattacks that everyone knew were coming. To speed the crossing of friendly armor, the 105th Engineer Battalion had designed expedient bridges. These consisted of culverts lashed together and covered by a log roadbed, all mounted on a sledlike arrangement. The plan, which was successfully demonstrated in the practice runs, was to push them into the stream with bulldozers, which would then level the banks so as to provide a continuous roadway. But the wet weather preceding the attack proved too much. One bridge stuck in the mud; in the case of the other, the bulldozer itself became mired. Soggy ground continued to delay operations even after the engineers had speedily finished a treadway bridge in the 119th sector only slightly over four hours after the infantry had jumped off. Five of the ten tanks that used the bridge that first day promptly bogged down and both of the recovery vehicles that tried to pull them out got into trouble. One also became mired; the other broke a cable trying to pull a tank out. Meanwhile heavy enemy artillery fire was falling. Both platoons of tanks were ordered to remain on the west side of the river, and made hasty arrangements with the infantry for mutual protection during the night.

The company of 743d tanks with the 117th was ordered down to the river twenty minutes after H-hour and remained there under fire until the 117th's treadway bridge was completed at 6:30 that night— crossing too late to participate in the day's fighting Another platoon of tanks worked with G Company of the 119th protecting the engineers putting in the southern bridge.

Except for 2d Battalion, 119th Infantry, which worked late fighting its way up to the Rimberg Castle, the assault troops spent the night consolidating against counterattack, their penetration protected throughout the night by a continuous curtain of artillery and mortar fires. Only one counterthrust did come in during the hours of darkness, against the 1st Battalion, 117th Infantry. The battalion commander called it a "minor effort"—but, as the Army historian put it, "you can still see tank tracks that stopped exactly two feet from the leading A Company foxhole, where you find the helmet and effects of Private Marvin Sirotkin, who had put in the pole charge earlier in the day and then was killed in the first counterattack." Later interrogation of prisoners disclosed that a battalion-strength counterattack had been launched. The German battalion commander refused, however, to continue it through such heavy artillery fire.

On the north, where the enemy had observed the construction of the 117th's first bridge from the high ground past Palenberg, artillery, mortar, and Nebelwerfer shells rained in during the night in a vain attempt to knock out the bridge, while attached troops of the 247th

Engineer Combat Battalion were working in the dark to install a Bailey bridge near Marienberg and another treadway bridge farther downstream near Rimberg A lone German plane made a bombing run over the northern bridge without success

Enemy artillery fire had been bad enough the first day, it was ominously heavy on October 3. It whistled in throughout the assault area, but particularly in Ubach, which the 3d Battalion of the 117th ground through during the morning, after clearing the eastern outskirts of Palenberg. The Bailey bridge was in at 9.30 in the morning and at 1 30 Task Force Heintz of the 2d Armored Division started moving over the Wurm toward Ubach, where it was to fan out to the north and northeast, rolling up the flank of the pillbox belt Thus, congestion on the roads lent added importance to the shells crashing in in numbers unequalled since the days of the beachhead in Normandy

The only other substantial gain of the day was the capture of the Rimberg Castle, which fell to the 2d Battalion of the 119th after bitter room-to-room fighting. It was a valuable prize, for it had not only contributed to the deadlock in the regiment's sector but had delivered fire into the 117th Infantry's bridgehead area. The sharply rising high ground north of Palenberg which dominated the crossing sites was proof against the attack of the 117th's 2d Battalion, and during the morning about 50 Germans supported by strong artillery fire tried to force the battalion's leading troops back. A little progress was made in the woods in the south. The 1st Battalion of the 119th worked across the railroad tracks just south of the castle and pushed out to the south with its assault detachments. Three pillboxes were taken in this effort but the remaining defenders, well protected by trenches and firing positions which honeycombed the woods, held their ground against this flank attack and a frontal attack from the west, displaying strong resistance at the antitank ditch that crossed the railroad.

The regiment tried swinging a task force of two rifle companies and a company each of tanks and tank destroyers around through the 117th sector and south along the east side of the woods, but without too much success, though the task force knocked out two pillboxes, found two more unoccupied and took 100 prisoners Some of the tanks of the 743d pulled back west of the river for servicing after contact had been made with 2d Battalion, and though the task force circled around the woods defenses to make contact with 3d Battalion on the south, the Germans stayed put and kept on shooting. Meanwhile direct-fire weapons near Merkstein Hofstadt to the south were making it hot for any troops on the exposed slopes on the east of the woods

Slow as the progress was at many points on the ground the picture was beginning to look encouraging as the second day of the attack ended. A clear break had been made in the Palenberg–Ubach sector, and a captured enemy document indicated that 39 pillboxes had been knocked out The 2d Armored Division was in the fight and would help enlarge the gap to the north by rolling up the flank of the belt of pillboxes. 30th Division troops had pushed in deep enough to start turning south to clear out the line down to the Corps' south boundary.

Enemy artillery fire was again heavier on October 4, with the heaviest concentrations around Ubach, where the long columns of the 30th and the 2d Armored Division were trying to disentangle themselves and get about their business. But artillery wasn't all.

"All day on the 4th it was one counterattack after another. Tanks busted in and cut off a platoon, only two men came back. Then we counterattacked and recaptured seven of our guys," related Captain Wayne Culp of the 117th's K Company in Ubach.

That story was typical of the whole Division front I Company of the 119th, posted at the east edge of the woods on the regiment's right flank, was hit by a battalion of infantry supported by 4 tanks at 5 00 o'clock in the morning after a two-hour artillery preparation The tanks came down the road leading northwest into the woods spraying machine-gun fire into the American positions and I Company was forced back through the 1st Battalion positions. Two D Company heavy machine-gun crews remained in position when I Company withdrew at noon, though both guns had been hit and could be traversed only by dragging the tripod from side to side. Lieutenant Seymour Shefrin, a Cannon Company observer, was wounded before the counterattack began but insisted on staying in place. He was later listed as missing in action. Total casualties for I Company were 26 wounded, 6 killed and 46 missing. As the German infantrymen reached the edge of the woods, however, they were hurt badly by tree bursts from their own artillery and the 119th rallied to drive back to its old positions in bitter fighting. Farther north some positions were still holding out in the center of the woods B Company helped the 1st Battalion, 119th Infantry, advance by knocking out two mutually supporting pillboxes. After several men had been lost trying to close with the forts, Staff Sergeant Harley Carson twice dashed 85 yards across a fire lane covered by one of them to attack the other with a satchel charge and hand grenades.

Up under the cliff north of Palenberg, where two preliminary counter-attacks had struck during the night, the 117th's 2d Battalion had a difficult time with an enemy battalion which attacked accompanied by engineers with explosives to blow the bridges over the Wurm, again with a powerful artillery preparation. The first daylight attack struck at 7:00

A.M. and dragged out fiercely until 10 00, and another one was launched at 3:00 in the afternoon It was during this action that Technical Sergeant Fred Leno, who took over command of a platoon in E Company during the fight, saw the enemy attack drive so close that drastic action was necessary "Dig deep," he notified his men—and called for artillery fire on his own position. The fire poured in as directed, one shell landing in the yard of the house where Leno's observation post was located Twelve Germans were killed by the concentration, 32 more surrendered, and the counterattack receded

In the Ubach sector the enemy pressure started at 3 50 in the morning and continued through the forenoon, with two separate attacks discernible Two battalions of infantry plus tanks, and the inevitable artillery, were involved in this threat, which was broken up with the aid of heavy American artillery fire The light machine guns of L Company were cut off all day in a house on the eastern edge of Ubach "There was a Jerry tank with his aerial in our second story window and another who forced us to look down the barrel of his 88 on the other side of the house We had a field day sniping at Jerries but those tanks were no fun," testified Private Ira Reeder

The counterattacks of the 4th were noteworthy for more than their persistence and strength Identified during the day's fighting were two battalions from the German 246th Infantry Division, which had been fighting a bitter battle of attrition against VII Corps troops near Aachen. One of the purposes of the 30th's breakthrough attempt was to relieve pressure against the 1st and 9th Divisions around Aachen Here was tangible proof that that purpose was being accomplished. The previous afternoon General Hobbs had told General Corlett, "I do not think it is too early to advise our neighbors on the right it is about time they plan to start the thing tomorrow morning . . . If Army could get one more infantry division behind us we can go to hell and breakfast." But the friendly troops to the south were too thin for effective pushing And another division just wasn't available.

On October 5, with 2d Armored Division working to the north and Old Hickory definitely turned south to drive down toward the Corps' boundary and junction with the 1st Division, enemy artillery fire reached an even greater intensity that it had the previous day. Ninety-nine counterbattery missions were fired by the American artillery but still the enemy shells arrived in almost unparalleled numbers Perhaps the main reason why the fire against enemy artillery was not completely effective was the ammunition shortage which had plagued Division Artillery and Corps Artillery ever since they had reached Germany. Even in the big counterbattery program fired on October 2 just before the infantry attacked, the average dose administered to each enemy battery position had been 24 rounds—about a third of the normal prescription and far less than the unusually heavy fires needed in this situation Thus, enemy batteries were at best silenced for a minute or two without significant loss in cannoneers or guns, and after the American fire had lifted could go back to work. Even a direct support battalion like the 118th, backing up the 117th Infantry, began to feel the ammunition rationing on the afternoon of October 5, according to its commander

Best advances of the day were made by the 2d Battalion, 119th Infantry, which, spearheaded by Technical Sergeant Harold L. Holycross's E Company platoon, attacked south out of the shell-ravaged buildings of Ubach with the 3d Battalion of the 117th Infantry on its left. By the end of the day the 2d Battalion had advanced close to 2000 yards to the high ground east of Merkstein-Herbach and had captured 11 pillboxes, eight of them taken by Sergeant Holycross's platoon [2]

The operation was an excellent example of cooperation, with infantry, tanks and self-propelled tank destroyers working together to get the defenders into a vulnerable position and then smash at them. Four scouts of Sergeant Holycross's platoon, leading the rest of the battalion by 800 yards, found a pillbox, directed tank destroyer fire on it until they were 100 yards away and then continued the advance to 20 yards from the box, where one man threw grenades into the opening.

---

[2] American soldiers entering one captured pillbox on October 4 were surprised to hear the telephone ring and were able to hear a conversation over the party line between two then German held boxes, one of which was a company command post The line was monitored for the next twenty four hours, with interesting results

5 00 A M —October 5—*Unidentified bunker calls CP* Sir, out of four men counting myself, two have become casualties Furthermore a dead man has been brought to my bunker What can I do?— Evacuate them —The dead one too?—Yes, of course the dead one too

6 00 A M —Is that you Heinrich?—Yes, how is the general situation?—Don't worry! [lowers his voice to confidential tone], our stuff has been rolling since 0215 —Thank God, I hope they make it

10 30 A M —*Bunker* 240 *calls CP* Sir, I counted 80 tanks coming over the bridge and I have one casualty The Tommies are running back but the tanks keep on coming —Did you say eight tanks?— No, sir Eighty! They came over the bridge in close column —*Himmel, Donnerwetter!* I'll request artillery barrage immediately

12 00—Lt Hofner, sir, the Americans shoot smoke shells along the whole line I think they prepare to attack

12 40—*Bunker* 240 *to CP* We received enemy fire Three of my men are badly hurt   My strength is now two or three men The Americans apparently try to attack the coal mine under the cover of smoke We will hold the bunker as long as possible and then?

2 00 P M —What are we going to do now? American troops passed us and are already at the power station   3 30—Sir, the Americans are at the battalion CP and we are receiving fire —Hell, yes, so are we 3 40—Sir, we are receiving machine gun fire from the coal mine —Just get inside

4 00 P M —I can't get connection with the CP any more How about you?—Hell, we can't get in touch with them either That son of a · · · · · beat it, without notifying us Ten tanks approaching from the power station What the hell are we going to do?—Let's try to make it back to our lines after dark

The line went dead after 8 00 P M

Twenty-nine enemy surrendered, including four who were wounded.

On the east, however, the 117th had difficulty in getting out of Ubach because of strong fire from a German barracks 1,000 yards to the southeast. Five of our supporting tanks were hit by direct fire from the barracks in this operation, three of them burning. Over on the right the 1st Battalion of the 119th continued the slow work of mopping up in the woods, knocking out an additional three pillboxes, while the 3d Battalion pushed out to the east across the railroad tracks and into the open.

Meanwhile the 120th Infantry was moving into Kerkrade and up to the German border some 4,000 yards to the south of the leading elements of the other units, enabling artillery batteries and OPs to move forward to work on the flank of enemy troops facing the rest of the Division. The 120th had made a feint attack on October 2 to divert pressure from the main assault area, had patrolled in strength on the 3d and on the following day had nosed into the closely knit town defenses along the German-Dutch border, encountering many mines. The pressure was too much for the Germans, although they put up strong resistance that day, and during the night of October 4-5 most of the defenders had withdrawn, after a small counterattack of theirs in the late afternoon had been severely dealt with. The 3d Battalion of the 120th, which had been in Division reserve, did not participate in its regiment's action but moved up behind the 119th, and in the afternoon of October 5 took its place in line on the right of that regiment's 2d Battalion, reducing three pillboxes en route. Lieutenant Colonel Paul W. McCollum, the battalion commander, was killed that afternoon by artillery fire.

October 6, D plus 5 of the operation, provided the last serious German attempt to hold the Siegfried Line in the Division sector. Attacking at 7:10 in the morning, two battalions of the enemy's 148th Grenadier Regiment slashed northward at the newly won pillboxes of the 2d Battalion 119th Infantry, supported by eight tanks and assault guns and backed up by strong artillery and mortar fire. The German drive surged over 800 yards in the first 45 minutes, retaking six pillboxes, with some of the enemy troops piling into the pillboxes while others moved on forward. Many of the pillboxes were not occupied by American troops when the counterthrust came and they had been taken too recently to be destroyed. The leading platoon of E Company, which had taken eight pillboxes the previous day, occupied only three of them, and enemy riflemen moved into the other five as their tanks rolled past. Staff Sergeant Harry L. Robinson of that platoon, who personally used up 22 Browning automatic rifle clips in an hour, said that his squad fired its own rifles and Browning automatic rifles until they were too hot to handle and then kept on firing with German weapons left behind in the previous day's attack "We thought we were goners," he said "After we got out of that scrap alive we figured nothing could stop us," Private First Class Nicholas Caroccia, the platoon runner, added.

At one point a squad used a borrowed heavy mortar to knock out six enemy soldiers setting up a pair of machine guns on a recaptured pillbox Two shells were needed Lieutenant Walter D Macht of C Company, 743d Tank Battalion, helped stem the tide by knocking out three enemy tanks and mowing down the enemy infantry as it approached.

Capture seemed imminent to many of the men and they got rid of the German knives and pistols they had picked up. "But what hurt most," said Staff Sergeant Robert R. Allen, whose men later went on to recapture pillboxes for a second time, "was destroying a whole batch of letters—twenty-two of them—which I hadn't had time to read." He and all of the others destroyed all papers which might give away their unit designation.

F Company lost about 65 men and E about 35 as the enemy advanced during the morning; effective strengths of the two companies went down to 40 and 35 men respectively.

"Do you feel the situation is favorable?" General Hobbs asked Colonel Sutherland of the 119th late in the morning "I don't think it's alarming," the Colonel countered. All morning fighter-bombers, artillery and friendly tanks had hammered at the counterattack Two particular artillery concentrations were shot over and over again, and the air contributed a pair of "beautiful" air strikes. Meanwhile, the 1st Battalion of the 117th had swung to its right to help and by early afternoon 2d Battalion of the 119th, reinforced with two additional companies, started the drive south again Eight hours later the job was completed—all of the ground had been retaken, all of the pillboxes were once again in American hands. After their tanks and infantry, which had pushed deepest, were destroyed or turned back in open fighting, the Germans of this counterattacking force who had reoccupied the pillboxes were cut off and offered little further resistance.

Meanwhile the 117th had driven south to zu Ubach, past the barracks which had held it up the previous day, softening that obstacle with two air strikes and artillery concentrations before moving through. On the right of the counterattack the 3d Battalion of the 120th Infantry grabbed the high ground south of Merkstein-Herbach, the 1st Battalion of the 119th worked slowly through the town and the 3d Battalion of the 119th cleaned out the rest of the pillbox belt in the woods south of the Rimberg Castle.

Other and larger counterattacks were to arrive later, but they were tied in closely with the defense of Aachen. By the end of the 6th the local enemy reserves had been committed and beaten, and the German defenses seemed to disintegrate.

Thus, October 7 was a day of exploitation against a beaten and disorganized enemy. 843 prisoners passed through the Division cage that day and others arrived too late to be counted in the official tabulations. The 3d Battalion of the 120th Infantry alone took 406 prisoners, including a battalion commander and his staff. The 1st and 3d Battalions of the 117th charged 5,000 yards south, led by tanks of the 743d Tank Battalion, to capture Wilhelmschacht and Alsdorf on the main road between Aachen and Linnich on the Roer, while the 2d Battalion cleaned out snipers in the by-passed barracks area. Another battalion of the German 246th Division was identified on the dash, which yielded 471 prisoners, but it had come too late. The 119th, with the 3d Battalion of the 120th still under its control, also made rapid progress. Its only real stumbling block was at Merkstein-Hofstadt, where still another battalion of the 246th Division had arrived only that morning from the Aachen area and was hit before it ever had a chance to get set. Heavy small-arms and mortar fire came from the town at first, but after the town had been hit by dive bombers the attack moved forward. Eighty out of the 90 men in one defending company surrendered.

Another good reason for speedy success at Merkstein was Private Salvatore Pepe, a scout for the leading platoon of the battalion. After the platoon was pinned down by fire from a large building and surrounding barns, Pepe crawled ahead firing his rifle and then tossing grenades. He wounded four Germans and induced the surrender of 53 enemy. Captured in Pepe's exploit, which won him the Distinguished Service Cross, were two mortars, two machine guns and other weapons.

"We had real infantry-tank cooperation after we shook loose from that Ubach artillery and started rolling to Alsdorf," said Lieutenant Dewey Sandell, platoon leader in I Company, 117th Infantry. "The tanks just machine gunned the Jerries in their holes and when the doughs came up it was mass surrender." The 3d Battalion of the 120th Infantry, using similar methods, took 386 prisoners as it moved cross-country opposite the 117th. Friendly artillery time fire, bursting above the fieldworks around the pillboxes in the battalion's path, caused many casualties and forced the defenders into their pillboxes. The tanks machine gunned others as they tried to escape across the fields.

So ended the battle for the Siegfried Line. It was an end that no one fighting out there on the ground could recognize as such, for there was no break in the around-the-clock routine of moving, fighting, digging and moving again. Next morning the attack moved forward once more —but this time the stakes were different A clean break had been made in the Westwall defenses; as General Hobbs informed Corps, "We have a hole in this thing big enough to drive two divisions through. I entertain no doubts that this line is cracked wide open." What had started out as the battle of the Siegfried Line was now becoming part of the battle of Aachen. And that ancient city, that imperial city as the German radio called it, was approaching its most critical hour.

Chapter X

THE BATTLE OF THE AACHEN GAP

The 30th's rupture of the Siegfried Line focused the attention of both Allied and German headquarters on Aachen. If Old Hickory's breakthrough could be joined with VII Corps' penetration and the City of the Kaisers taken, the Allies would possess a large consolidated breakthrough of Germany's main line of defense and a road center capable of supporting a large-scale drive toward the Rhine. The screams of Nazi propagandists that Aachen would never fall committed both sides to extra effort.

North of Aachen the tired 30th Division appeared on the verge of breaking into the clear. The 1st Division, spread thin on the dual mission of seizing and holding the east-west ridges just east of the city and containing Aachen itself, was being held by repeated counterattacks. In place of the 246th Division, which had moved north to oppose the 30th, the Germans had brought up the 12th Division A major decision was in the making. Both high commands sought speedy victory, before the balance of power could swing the other way.

While Old Hickory was fighting its way through the pillboxes, the struggle along the rest of the Western Front was slowing almost to a standstill, as the Germans consolidated behind natural barriers Aachen was the only sensitive spot along the entire battle line; it had no rivals for the services of the German reserves

This was the background for the battle of the Aachen Gap, a battle which grew alarmingly in size and ferocity When it started, the 30th Division had all but completed its assigned mission and was looking forward to rest and reorganization. Before it was over, the Division had acquired new responsibilities and new, powerful opposition which came desperately close to denying it success.

On October 8 the Division continued its motion southward in what appeared to be the relatively easy task of closing down to the Division boundary, which ran east and west through Wurselen. No one had any illusions that there would be no fighting to be done, but the advances of the previous day had badly disorganized the enemy and exhausted his local reserves. To move the 4,000 yards to the Division boundary appeared at worst a two day job. The 1st Division then was simultaneously attacking north to take Crucifix Hill, just north of Aachen. After the two divisions had linked up along their mutual boundary the 30th could face east, then regroup and rest its battered line units prior to the next operation.

Over on the west that day, the 119th Infantry was feeling its way through Herzogenrath, which was heavily strewn with booby traps and mines, some under the cobblestones of its streets, others merely placed on the open pavement. Leading elements of the regiment were beginning to run into tank and pillbox fire in the rugged country just south of the town. The 120th Infantry, attacking across the Herzogenrath–Alsdorf road, was encountering strong fire from infantry and antitank guns dug in along the rising ground in its path but was making progress The 117th Infantry on the left, which at Alsdorf had cut one of the two main highways running northeast out of Aachen on the previous day, was moving ahead with two battalions to the southeast toward Maria- dorf and control of the enemy's other main supply route

It was no pushover. The forward elements of the 117th's 1st and 3d Battalions had moved through Kol Kellersberg and had worked some of their tanks and infantry past the German emplacements along the railroad line by midmorning, but the enemy fire was getting worse and worse. The tanks, which led by 100 to 150 yards, were experiencing trouble in getting at the Germans they uncovered in foxholes; one tank crew resorted to tossing hand grenades into the German field works when its machine guns could no longer be used The 117th's dough- boys had difficulty in keeping up across the open ground. Direct fire as well as intense small-arms fire was coming from the enemy positions —two tanks and an assault gun were knocked out, their crews contin- uing the fight as infantrymen. I Company, in the lead for 3d Battalion, lost the bulk of its rifle strength crossing the railroad tracks, returning with only 33 men in its three rifle platoons.[1]

Then, with the assault elements of the regiment extended and heavily engaged, came the opening blow in the crescendo of armored counter- attacks which the Germans mounted in their attempt to save Aachen. "While the 3d and 1st Battalions shoved off for Mariadorf, four tanks and a company of German doughs slipped in behind them and headed for our OP," said Lieutenant Colonel MacDowell of the 3d Battalion. "We manned every window and took pot shots, I got four sures and three probables. The tankers knocked out three of the tanks but the fourth and another from somewhere wandered up and down the streets of Alsdorf all day."

It was one of these last two tanks which was dubbed by regimental headquarters, then in Alsdorf, the "Reluctant Dragon." Lieutenant C. M Spilman, looking out of an upstairs window in Alsdorf, first saw

---

[1]The action produced one grim joke After Company I had been stopped, a German officer rose up to full height and waved his men into an open skirmish line Company I held its fire as the Germans approached, then mowed them down

the tank, with the heads of two Germans sticking out of the turret. He shot both, but the Dragon belched fire, turning its turret immediately on his position and knocking him down two flights of stairs with a single shot His ankle twisted, the lieutenant limped over to the coal bin serving as a command post and breathlessly reported to his regimental commander, "Sir, I wanted you to know about this before I go back to get those unprintables."

But the Dragon escaped For the rest of the day doughboys and tank destroyer crews shuffled around setting up traps for the loose tank at street corner after street corner. There weren't enough tank destroyer guns or bazooka teams available to handle every possibility, so that every time the Dragon put in a new appearance and then backtracked, the guns would be moved to a new and likely position to intercept it That night it was gone.

German infantrymen also penetrated into town, getting within 100 yards and a street away from the regimental command group, but the real battle was going on in the open ground east of Alsdorf and just north of Kol Kellersberg The German attack came from behind a huge slag pile beside a coal mine in the north outskirts of Mariadorf, with the enemy tanks and infantry circling up through the southern edge of Schauffenberg to strike across the open ground into the flank of the American advance Significantly, the 118th Field Artillery Battalion was able to impose heavy losses with time fire placed expertly behind our own assault troops, between them and the battalion OPs in the buildings to the rear.

The force of the first counterthrust was broken by 11:30 A.M., but hostile tanks and infantry continued to press in for the rest of the day. Meanwhile, the 117th's 2d Battalion was moving up from positions in the rear to expel the enemy from Alsdorf. Faced by strong fire from the front and counterattack on its exposed left flank, the 117th was given permission to pull back, with the 1st Battalion taking up defensive positions in Kol Kellersberg and the 3d Battalion digging in on a small open rise of ground to the northeast.

That night, when the prisoner-of-war stories began to come in, the story became clear The attack had been made by two of the three battalions of the Von Fritschen Mobile Regiment, with seven tanks and 20 assault guns at their disposal. This unit had arrived in Mariadorf the previous night. Even more interesting were the mission and the origin of *Kampfgruppe Von Fritschen*. Its job was to recapture Alsdorf at all costs, to reopen the road between Aachen and Linnich. And it had come 100 miles from Luxembourg to do it

The next day, the 9th, provided further proof that Aachen would not fall by default This time the center of gravity of the German counter-measures shifted to the south and west into the 120th Infantry's zone

The 117th improved its positions facing the enemy's emplacements along the railroad track in front of Mariadorf, finished clearing out Alsdorf and, with its 2d Battalion, G Company leading, secured Schauffenberg after moderate house-to-house fighting.

The 120th, attacking in the fog at 7:00 A M, attained considerable surprise at first, capturing a self-propelled 88mm. gun and seven *"pupchen"*—large, wheeled bazookas—belonging to the newly arrived German 7th Antitank Battalion. Then at 1.00 P.M, without artillery preparation to give warning, an enemy force of infantry and 10 tanks slashed up from Euchen toward the 2d Battalion, which was setting up on the newly acquired high ground to the northwest of the town But the 2d Battalion was even then too well organized to be overrun, and in the next two hours the weight of the attack shifted over to the west into the zone of the 1st Battalion, which was having difficulty in securing its objective on the high ground near Birk. Seven enemy tanks were knocked out during the afternoon and the counterattack had been definitely repulsed by 6:45 P M, but the end of the day found the 1st Battalion still short of its objective and starting to pull around to the west through the 119th area near Bardenberg for a thrust toward Birk from the flank.

The 119th meanwhile was moving rapidly south. I Company of the 3d Battalion struck early to the southwest to take the little town of Pley, thus setting up a converging attack through Bardenberg, with the 3rd Battalion and its supporting tanks coming in from the north-west and the 1st Battalion moving through the eastern portion of the town By the end of the day both battalions had passed through Barden-berg and were up on the high ground of their objectives on the out-skirts of North Wurselen. For all practical purposes the Division south boundary had been reached, and plans were being readied for 119th patrols to cross the boundary to contact the 1st Division. There was supposed to be a link-up between the 119th and 120th near Bardenberg, but actually there was a gap.

Then, just as twilight yielded to darkness, the Germans struck again. For two days they had been feeling along the front of the Division, moving steadily westward, looking for a weak spot. This time they found it, in Bardenberg. It was a discovery that cost the Division two days to cancel out.

First warning of the thrust, which was made without artillery preparation, came from A Company of the 120th, which was moving across the Bardenberg–Birk road just east of Bardenberg getting into position to envelop the high ground position which had held up the 1st Battalion during the day A Company's trailing platoon, strung out along the road, was suddenly struck by half-tracks spraying 20mm. shells in the dark.

Soon after the first fragmentary story came from the 120th, the 119th also reported trouble Its A Company, which had been dropped off on the way to North Wurselen to put up road blocks on the east edge of Bardenberg, was also encountering direct fire from 20mm guns mounted on half-tracks The first enemy effort was reported repulsed, but almost immediately another drive came in, this involving, according to a prisoner, 300 infantry and 5 tanks A Company, 119th Infantry, withdrew 300 yards by echelon. The situation remained obscure all night, but this much was evident: the enemy had retaken part of Bardenberg, and the supply route to the two battalions to the south had been severed.

The 119th's reserve battalion, the 2d, was a mile back at Herzogenrath when the Bardenberg counterattack struck, not to be committed without authority of Division. It started moving down that night, with regimental headquarters and service companies alerted for line duty if necessary.

The first report on the 10th relieved the tension somewhat The 120th's 1st Battalion, attacking at 5:30 A.M. without an artillery preparation so as to achieve surprise, had enjoyed complete and speedy success. The objective, Birk, fell with only one shot fired and that by accident; the defenders were caught literally asleep. As a result the enemy's penetration into Bardenberg was in turn deprived of its supply route; reinforcements and stores for the German spearhead there would have to move over the open lip of ground sloping up from Birk toward North Wurselen. Furthermore, the 120th now had good ground all along its front from which to defend against attack from the south and east.

In Bardenberg itself, the 119th's 2d Battalion was also in contact with the enemy. The menace was definitely in the south portion of the town and in the woods between Bardenberg and North Wurselen. K Company attempted to move back into Bardenberg supported by three tanks but the infantry was fairly soon pinned down by 20mm. and mortar fire. I Company, to the west near Pley, was under tank fire. Between 10 and 20 German half-tracks, which corresponded to the American multiple mount caliber .50 machine-gun half-track, were in the town, along with five tanks. During the course of the day the 2d Battalion succeeded in working its way back into part of Bardenberg, but the enemy in the south end of the town proved to be expertly organized among the houses for mutual support—a precursor of the close-knit infantry-tank defenses which later made the fight in Wurselen so difficult During the afternoon the 119th attempted without success to advance tanks and bazooka teams to knock out key German vehicles, which were covering the channelized approaches through the streets with effective fire. By nightfall the regiment had reluctantly decided to pull back to the north edge of the town so as to hammer the enemy with artillery during the night.

None of the enemy units previously opposing the 30th, within Germany, had possessed self-propelled 20mm. antiaircraft guns Prisoners taken in Bardenberg and Birk on the 10th dispelled the mystery of whose they were; the 108th Panzer Brigade had arrived in the Aachen gap area October 5 with a battalion of tanks and another battalion of armored infantry riding in half-tracks mounting 20mm cannons, and had moved up to Euchen to attack on the 9th. The brigade had last been committed at Nijmegen on the Neder Rhein, 80 miles away—further proof that the German Commander in Chief West was rifling his entire front to provide troops to save Aachen.

Later it was learned that both the Von Fritschen Regiment and the 108th Panzer Brigade operated directly under the German LXXXVIII Corps Apparently, there was no division then available to take the responsibility for the sector.

Pressure against the 120th's positions continued all day North of Birk a B Company tank of the 743d and nearby infantry held off an attack by several hundred infantry and nine tanks, setting one enemy tank ablaze In the 15 minutes before help could arrive, the Sherman, commanded by Sergeant Kirksey, fired more than 60 rounds of high explosive and armor-piercing shells. Smaller attempts to find a weak point in our lines were made during the afternoon. At it appeared later in the morning, the penetration at Bardenberg, made by a newly arrived unit without prior reconnaissance, had an element of luck in it The enemy's failure to adequately defend the gateway of his penetration at Birk furnished strong evidence that he did not at once recognize the importance of his penetration So he spent the rest of the day in tentative thrusts with tanks, with some infantry support. They were unsuccessful. The 120th had wasted no time in putting newly acquired German antitank weapons to use, in addition to the artillery fire furnished with alacrity by the 230th Field Artillery Battalion's observers Infantrymen, never trained as cannoneers, mastered and manned the antitank gun captured the previous day; one enemy tank moved to within 200 yards of the 120th's positions before being knocked out— by an infantry-served *pupchen*. The 230th claimed six tanks destroyed that day, and artillery fire, some directed by tankers of the 743d, pursued about 20 enemy tanks during the day.

At the same time the troops of the 119th Infantry in North Wurselen were under pressure Several enemy advances from the south were discouraged by artillery fire and late in the afternoon a thrust by a battalion of the German 246th Division supported by tanks and artillery fire was repulsed

Army, however, feeling that the time was ripe for the final assault on Aachen, was beginning to get impatient about making contact with the 1st Division and physically sealing off the city. That day, as the 1st pressed forward to take some of its objectives, a long-prepared ultimatum demanding the surrender of Aachen was taken from the files and presented to the city's military commander under a flag of truce, by an intelligence officer of the 1st Division American prestige, as well as tactical considerations, were involved in a speedy link-up.

During the morning, patrols to contact 1st Division patrols somewhere in the bullet-whipped 3,000 yards still separating the two divisions, were planned by the 119th. Wurselen's shell-torn streets, however, appeared too generously supplied with German soldiers for such a deep patrol to succeed. Early in the afternoon permission was obtained from XIX Corps to instead pummel the town with artillery, to pave the way for a more secure junction.

In spite of the early morning success of the 120th's 1st Battalion, October 10 was very close to being a day of marking time. With the attention of the higher commanders focused on Wurselen and the problem of contact with the 1st Division, it had been hoped by Division that the Bardenberg penetration could be wiped out by the last uncommitted infantry reserves of the Division—the 119th's 2d Battalion—without thinning the line anywhere else. But at the end of the day more than half of the 119th Infantry was still virtually cut off in North Wurselen, with the rest of the regiment's line troops, ranged around the perimeter of Bardenberg, and under fire, in almost equally tenuous contact with the rear. The Germans, probing ceaselessly all day, had evidently not sensed the value of their wedge into the American lines. Were they to do so, the cancer at Bardenberg could lead not only to the elimination of the 30th's so-important spearhead but to a drive into the rear areas.

Corps had no troops available, so there was no alternative to weakening the already thin line of defenses elsewhere to take care of the Bardenberg menace. Thus that night the 3d Battalion of the 120th moved out of its positions on the regiment's left flank, and was attached to the 119th for the job of cleaning out Bardenberg. F Company of the 120th

moved in to assume responsibility for the battalion's old sector As
General Hobbs told Colonel Sutherland of the 119th on the morning
of October 11, "This thing *has* to drive through "

It did, but the job took all day to accomplish Little opposition was
encountered until the southern part of Bardenberg was reached, but
there and in the woods just south of the town, resistance was stubborn,
with German infantrymen and tankers covering each other expertly
from well coordinated positions Major Greer, commander of the 120th's
3d Battalion, personally did much to get the attack rolling during the
afternoon. Grabbing a bazooka, he worked his way up to within range
of one tank and knocked it out with one shot Almost at once another
tank fired, hitting the building in which he was and knocking off his
helmet. But a few minutes later he had reloaded and had moved to a
point of vantage for a shot at the second tank It worked He won the
Distinguished Service Cross for these actions

Staff Sergeant Anthony A Tempesta, A Company, 743d Tank Battalion, was another key figure in the Bardenberg fight Seeing a German
assault gun covering an intersection as he led his platoon south along
the main street of the town, Tempesta boldly knocked it out with three
shots, first swinging his tank cannon around toward the assault gun,
then moving fast into an open firing position in the center of the intersection the assault gun was covering, while an infantry bazooka team
also fired Enemy snipers dropped grenades from upstairs windows
but the tank moved ahead, knocking out another assault gun as it had
the first, and disabling six half-tracks Tempesta assumed command of
his company at 2:00 P M when all of the officers had been wounded

Similar crowbar tactics, here against a half-track spouting 20mm
shells, there against a machine gun or a tank, finally disassembled the
matrix of German defenses A total of 6 tanks and 16 half-tracks had to
be knocked out before the Bardenberg operation succeeded

While the Bardenberg pocket was being eliminated, the other line
troops of the Division were not suffering from want of attention by the
Germans The two battalions in North Wurselen were hit by German
tanks and infantry twice, at about 10 00 A.M and at 3 30 P M , but
artillery fire promptly squelched these efforts The 120th's positions,
curving to the southwest from just south of Kol Kellersberg, sustained
thrusts from tanks and infantry all day, with the most important one
at 3.20 P M The 230th Field Artillery Battalion, firing steadily,
claimed 7 tanks knocked out Two small infantry attacks, made without
benefit of enemy armor, were repulsed as darkness closed in The final
attacks of the day were made after nightfall, at 8 15 P M , by infantry
alone. One, which hit to the north into the thinly held left flank of the

120th, made a slight penetration along the regimental boundary before it was halted. The other, which struck the 117th's positions east of Kol Kellersberg from the southeast, also was soon neutralized in the dark.

Fourteen German tanks were knocked out by ground weapons during October 11, with others falling victim to the four squadrons of American fighter-bombers which struck at Bardenberg, Euchen, and other targets. Some of the prisoners taken in the 120th area spoke of disorganization of German infantry-tank teams as they advanced under American artillery fire. But despite the losses the enemy took, his position appeared to be improving. Observation posts reported ominously heavy traffic moving southwest into the Aachen gap along the highway through Mariadorf and the secondary roads to the rear. Corps warned that the 116th Panzer Division was expected momentarily.

*   *   *

"We are being attacked all along our front—being pecked at in some places, strong in others, and building up in others," the 30th's Commanding General reported to Corps at noon on October 12. That day, in fact, proved to be the turning point in the battle of the Aachen gap. Thereafter the enemy continued to fight with skill and stubbornness and strength, counterattacking many times. But it was on the 12th that the Germans launched their all-out general counterattack against the 30th and failed.

Where the main effort of the German counterthrust was being made is still obscure, for massed, almost continuous American artillery fire and the efforts of 14 squadrons of fighter-bombers, which all day swooped down on enemy tank concentrations and then went back to their bases for more bombs, did wonders in chewing up the German attack formations before they closed with the American lines. Bardenberg was still the center of attraction, however, with drives coming in from the east, from the south frontally against the 119th vanguard in North Wurselen, and even from the west near Kohlscheid. Perhaps the greatest massing of German troops took place in the open country between Euchen and Wurselen, but every American soldier all along the Division's battle line had his hands full that day.

Pressure was first felt by the 120th's 2d Battalion, northeast of Birk. At 7:00 A.M., with its area churned by a heavy German artillery preparation, 2d Battalion received an attack by infantry and tanks, which in the next half-hour swung westward toward the 1st Battalion's positions. B Company's position was hard hit in a three-hour battle. A tank from the 743d's B Company, commanded by Staff Sergeant Melvin H. Bieber, battled a German Mark V and a Mark VI simultaneously, forcing the VI's crew to run after two hits and destroying the V with 12 hits At this time the 57mm. gun guarding the area had been knocked out and another United States tank had gone to the rear to repair its gun When the latter tank returned the fog was lifting and many more tanks could be seen near the railroad along with infantry Five more enemy tanks were knocked out there during the morning

A Company of the 120th 'sustained 48 casualties and lost the four antitank guns protecting it. Even more serious was the loss of the artillery observation post on the exposed slope in front of it After the forward observer had been wounded by persistent enemy shelling of the OP and another observer wounded trying to reach it, Captain Michael S Bouchlas, the 1st Battalion's liaison officer from the 230th, started up the hill alone A Company's anxious riflemen couldn't see all of his journey, but finally "We knew he had made it when our own artillery, which up to this point had been firing spasmodically and was even throwing stuff in on us, stopped and then began adjusting its fire. We all felt good about it " Soon massed artillery fire was pounding the attackers and within half an hour the threat was over Thus, by 10.30 Regiment was willing to report that the situation was under control, but tanks roamed around in front of its positions all day, harried by artillery fire and dive bombers, and the enemy artillery fire continued heavy.

Two more threats, however, showed up elsewhere at 10.30 A.M One, involving tanks and infantry assembling just north of Wurselen and starting to move against the flank of the 119th in North Wurselen, was squashed by artillery fire Simultaneously other 119th elements, moving through the woods along the Wurm River between Bardenberg and North Wurselen, ran into a battalion of the 116th Panzer Division's 60th Panzer Grenadier Regiment, which had arrived from Arnhem on the lower Rhine River the previous day Still another major drive started to roll from the south at 11 05 A M against the North Wurselen salient—involving 200 infantry supported by at least 8 tanks This force proved to be another newcomer—a Combat Team Ring from the vaunted 1st SS Panzer Division *Leibstandarte Adolf Hitler*. This unit had come 50 miles from Trier, near the German-Luxembourg boundary, on October 9

Still other distinguished company was revealed by midday The enemy infantry charging in at the 120th's foxholes proved to be local talent—a battalion of the 246th Division and another of panzer grenadiers from the 108th Panzer Brigade The tanks were something different, however, belonging to the 506th GHQ Heavy Tank Battalion

Like the 116th Panzer Division, this battalion had also come down from Arnhem, 100 miles away, arriving during the night of October 11-12 Meanwhile the 1st Division to the south was also receiving pressure from the funnel of German-held territory extending northeast from Aachen and was later to report the presence of a battle group from the 2d Panzer Division.

To many the battle looked like another Mortain—in fact, of the major German armored units present there only 2d SS Panzer Division *Das Reich* was absent this time General Hobbs mentioned the parallel as he figuratively held hands with General Corlett over the telephone at noon discussing the possibility of using Corps artillery and antiaircraft crews, if necessary, to back up the main defenses Both men were frankly worried, they had made their disposition of troops and could only hope for the best

Meanwhile the battle raged As at Mortain, clear weather was a godsend, permitting the fighter-bombers to come back again and again to strike German armor, and, after the fog had lifted in late morning, allowing the little observation planes of the artillery to direct deadly masses of fire into the enemy's assembly areas At noon the dive-bombers were swooping down on a 40-tank concentration; after one attack during the day 18 tanks were seen burning Without good weather the battle might have turned out less fortunately

But in the last analysis the battle was fought by men on the ground. A platoon of the 823d Tank Destroyer Battalion, for example, lost two of its four guns and their half-track prime movers, but still knocked out two Mark V tanks, a ponderous Mark VI and a German quarter-ton car The most eloquent tribute to the fighting men that day was paid by Colonel Branner P. Purdue, who had commanded the 120th for only a few days [2] He was talking primarily about infantrymen but he might have said the same thing about many others—artillery observers, signalmen, tank destroyers, tank crews What he had to say is worth quoting.

> *General Hobbs* How do you think things are?
> *Colonel Purdue* I have no complaints These are the bravest men you ever saw That 1st Battalion fought them off with the outposts   I never did see men going like these have been going We are as strong as strong can be

Men of the 30th Signal Company stationed in the rear made an unusual contribution Soon after the Siegfried Line–Aachen Gap operation began, the special batteries used in bazookas became unobtainable. The Signal Company worked out an ingenious way of mounting ordinary flashlight batteries, still plentiful, on the bazooka Almost all the rocket

---

[2] Colonel Hammond D Birks, later a brigadier general, left the regiment October 6 to become assistant division commander of the 9th Division

launchers in the division, 507 in all, were thus modified and kept in service.

By midafternoon of the 12th the enemy legions appeared to be falling back under the terrific pounding inflicted upon them, though enemy shells continued to pour heavily into the forward areas and into Bardenberg, Bottleneck No 1 on the route to the south As General Hobbs put it at 3 00 P.M , "They are nibbling and pushing but no general attack "

But though the defensive struggle seemed to be easing up, at least for the moment, the problem of Aachen's encirclement still hung swordlike over the Division's head Three hours after Generals Hobbs and Corlett had talked in terms of another Mortain, about the battle's being one of the decisive ones of the war, the Corps commander phoned again "General Hodges tells me we have got to close the gap some way."

A plan was worked out that afternoon, with the Division clearly warned for the first time that it was responsible for making contact with VII Corps—regardless of boundaries and regardless of whether or not the 1st Division also attacked to make the junction The pressing problem was new troops, not only to attack south but to fill in the expanding line of front along the east After some desultory talk about an armored task force, General Corlett obtained Army's permission to give the 30th the two available battalions of the 29th Division's 116th Infantry, which had been posting the northwest edge of the no man's land west of Aachen, plus a company of tanks

General Corlett had at first suggested a drive along the Wurm River through Pley, but this idea was dropped because of the uncertainty of whether or not the rest of the 116th Panzer Division was moving in there. He had also hinted that a general advance might be ordered for the Division by Army, but this, too, did not eventualize The attack would be continued from North Wurselen

*   *   *

The next three days were bitterly disappointing for Old Hickory. Most of the Division's front, the area northeast of Wurselen, was dormant On the 13th General Corlett suggested that a task force drive south from the Alsdorf area General Hobbs, however, seconding the opinions of his regimental commanders, demurred—there were not enough troops available for a practicable assault and with enemy forces still strong in front of the Division the eastward regiments should not abandon the good defensive positions built up over a period of days and be caught in the open by German counterattacks Expansion of the assault to the west would involve another river crossing and the reduction of the possibly strong garrison at Kohlscheid (To avoid a river crossing by attacking from the west of the Wurm River would mean hitting the Siegfried Line pillboxes frontally again)

Thus everything depended on success on a narrow front through a maze of defenses in the buildings and streets of Wurselen As Bardenberg's reduction the second time had proved in that very area, street fighting against a determined enemy is a slow and painstaking process The defenses must be pried apart one by one During the 13th, 14th, and part of the 15th, the Division hoped that pressure would bring results, that the operation would loosen up It did not Little ground was gained.

An attack on so narrow a front was an invitation to the German artillery massing east of Wurselen, and the invitation was accepted with alacrity. Artillery and mortar fire on the 116th Infantry's advances was bitterly heavy, succeeding in neutralizing many approaches to the network of enemy positions and thus cutting down maneuverability. Some dug-in tanks were encountered, as well as four or five others employed in a mobile defensive role, pulling back to new positions after being ejected from their first hideouts Another armored infantry battalion and the engineer battalion of the German 116th Panzer Division were identified

Other factors contributed to the slowness of the advance. One battalion commander and his operations officer became casualties, disorganizing the attack Wire lines were constantly being shelled out and communications were frequently poor Finally, the action called, in high degree, for willingness to take losses in gaining ground—one of the most difficult things to communicate along the chain of command

On the 14th, with the 116th Infantry's 2d Battalion, on the west, about 1,000 yards past its original line of departure and the 1st Battalion, on the left, about half that distance from its starting point, the attack was renewed at 5:00 A.M The early start, however, was unsuccessful in establishing an initial momentum, almost as soon as the attack started the old pattern of enemy fires was resumed across the brief spaces separating the two forces

All day long, the regiment struggled with the problem of shaking the opposition loose, but with only modest success One enemy tank was knocked out by combined infantry-tank action, and the line of advance troops moved forward up to 300 yards during the day But as nightfall approached there were no signs that the opposition was weakening Progress would continue to depend on trying one technique after another to knock out the key points in the defense—and many of these key points had held out against everything tried against them that day. Progress was being made, but it wasn't enough The Army commander personally phoned to tell General Hobbs so, expressing great dissatisfaction that contact with the 1st Infantry Division had not been made on that day

* * *

Thus, the plan which took final form on the Division G-3's workmap on the morning of the 15th was one born of desperation The 116th had attacked again early in the morning toward its original objectives, with three dive-bombing missions and an artillery TOT preceding the jump-off, but the thrust through Wurselen could no longer be depended on

The new plan was for the 119th to sweep south on October 16 on the right of the 116th Infantry, with two battalions striking across the Wurm River through Kohlscheid and the other battalion shoving down along the east bank of the stream past the deadlocked Wurselen battlefield to the main highway, taking in flank the pillboxes facing westward across the Wurm River Attached to the regiment were two companies of the 743d Tank Battalion and the 99th Infantry Battalion, a separate unit which would be used to help hold the ground

The plan had to work and without waste motion, that was clear, and it became apparent during the afternoon and evening of the 15th that Corps was as worried as Division about getting the job done At 7.20 P.M General Corlett phoned again from Corps "I'm going to give you an order to attack all along the line and close the gap " In the brief conversation which followed, the words "close the gap" were spoken four more times by the Corps commander

The 116th had gained about 1,000 yards at the most in three days of bitter fighting. If the plan was to succeed on the 16th, the 119th's 2d Battalion would have to gain 3,000 yards in one day

The attack began at 5.00 A M , as the 1st and 3d Battalions of the 119th attacked west across the Wurm River to secure the flank of the main effort by the 2d Battalion Within half an hour the 1st Battalion on the north had reached the east edge of Kohlscheid and had begun the work of clearing out the northern portion of the town By 8 A M the 3d Battalion had also gained the eastern edge of Kohlscheid, where it was joined by tanks which had moved over one of two treadway bridges built over the Wurm River by the 105th Engineer Battalion Working in the dark, the engineers had completed the first bridge by 5 30 A M , half an hour after the infantry assault commenced, although the bridge site was under strong and accurate mortar fire During the morning the infantry-tank teams of the two battalions west of the Wurm cleared out Kohlscheid and the 3d Battalion started south out of town

The 2d Battalion moved out at 6 00 A M. against heavy resistance but by 7 30 had advanced over 1,000 yards past the slag piles on the west side of Wurselen to its first objective, just south of Teuterhof But enemy artillery fire and tank fire had been increasing ominously and after this first objective had been attained, the main effort battalion appeared stalled.

At this time the first of the diversionary efforts on the eastern part of the Division front took place For half an hour a smoke screen was maintained in front of the 117th and 120th Infantry Regiments and heavy small-arms, mortar and artillery fires were placed on enemy positions to the front there to suggest a preparatory barrage As a result all of the enemy's heavy defensive fires opened up in reply, to break up the attack that appeared imminent. Veterans of the entire European campaign reported that this enemy response was the heaviest fire they had ever experienced, with every caliber up to the 210mm German gun represented

As a result, much of the artillery which had been firing in front of the 119th was diverted Thus, the 2d Battalion, 119th Infantry and its attached tanks, further aided by flanking fire by the 3d Battalion, which had moved down approximately opposite it, were able to shake themselves into motion again during the morning.

A further and costly diversion was made during the afternoon by the flank companies of the 117th and 120th, for the purpose of drawing enemy artillery fire from the main effort E Company of the 117th, attacking through 500 yards of woods closely held by the enemy to the line of the railroad along which the enemy's main position was located, doggedly attacked no less than five times in full realization of the fact that its job was to be shot at, to convince the enemy that it was engaged in a major attack There had been no time for adequate prior reconnaissance, and on the first attempt both assault platoons lost direction in the heavy fire and thick underbrush The 3d Platoon on the left drove to within 50 yards of its objective, a cut on the railroad, but was cut off, losing all but six of its men in the process. The 2d Platoon, on the right, was unable to maintain direction and withdrew, still under fire, to reorganize and try again, this time with the 1st Platoon, previously in reserve, on the left. Twice again this happened. After the third attempt, the remaining men of the company tried to advance by infiltration, the right platoon laboriously moving up 200 yards Then Regiment ordered withdrawal The E Company commander, Captain George H. Sibbald, got permission to send a 10-man patrol on the left to contact the 3d Platoon, still isolated, but after a single unsuccessful attempt with this patrol, a final and definite order to withdraw came from Regiment, the mission having been accomplished Colonel Johnson, the 117th Regimental commander, characterized the action as the finest example of leadership by a company commander in the regiment The company was later awarded the Distinguished Unit Citation for this day's fine work.

K Company of the 120th, which moved out on the right of E Company, had less rugged but equally exposed ground to traverse, and also operated under withering fire Two platoons moved out to the objective and remained there for almost two hours before fighting their way back to friendly lines with the help of well-planned covering fire.

Meanwhile the 119th was grinding its way south At 3 44 P.M the 1st Division's chief of staff phoned to say that his observers reported friendly troops in the southern outskirts of Wurselen and that a patrol was being sent out During the afternoon the 119th's 2d Battalion reached a hill just south of Wurselen and across the main highway from the outposts of the 18th Infantry on Cemetery Hill about 1,000 yards away. The commanding generals of both VII and XIX Corps agreed that the gap had been closed for all practical purposes, but decided to wait until actual physical contact had been made before notifying Army

The 119th actually made physical contact with the 1st Division's 18th Infantry at 6:15 P.M The patrol that did the job was at first led by Private Frank A Karwel, but he was wounded en route and his comrades, Privates Edward Krauss and Evan Whitis, went on alone They crossed the highway where the patrol meeting was supposed to take place and moved toward Cemetery Hill They saw figures in American uniforms atop the hill and soon were within shouting distance

"We're from K Company Come on up," called the men on the hill

"We're from F Company Come on down."

"They out-talked us and we pushed on up," related Whitis

Within half an hour the meeting had been reported to Army The Aachen Gap was officially closed

Later, after Aachen had fallen, VII Corps and the 1st Division formally thanked the 30th for its vital work in enabling the city to be taken, and the Division received credit in the newspapers for its part in the battle But the tribute Old Hickory men will remember most warmly was not issued through official channels One day in late October Major General Clarence R. Huebner of the 1st Division appeared at a 119th Infantry outpost and introduced himself to the surprised doughboys "I wish you'd get it around to your people," he said, "that we never could have taken Aachen without your help "

*   *   *

With the physical isolation of Aachen complete, the focus of public attention shifted to the center of the city, where troops of the 1st Division were driving forward block by block to annihilate the entrapped garrison of the town. But there was plenty of work still to be done outside that smoldering mass of ruined masonry The German's Aachen escape gap was impermanently plugged on the 16th, during the next two days the 119th Infantry drove still farther to thicken the plug, taking Richterich, Laurensberg and Sors, with some of its troops south of 1st Division positions One small road block of the attached 99th Infantry Battalion in the cordon around the Aachen defenders was broken through by two German tanks supported by about 40 infantry, attempting to escape from the trap The greater danger, however, was from attempts to re-open the gap from the outside, where the enemy's 3d Panzer Grenadier Division, which had made contact with the 1st Division's positions east of Aachen on the 15th and 16th, was now out of contact On the same day more than a company of enemy infantry, supported by tanks, attacked unsuccessfully from Wurselen toward the 2d Battalion, 119th Infantry, during the afternoon, and late in the evening another infantry-tank thrust about 1,000 yards farther south was also repelled.

On the 19th, while the 119th Infantry's 3d Battalion moved north along the Aachen–Wurselen road to occupy positions near the 18th Infantry's positions on Cemetery Hill, there was another flurry of enemy activity during the afternoon, when infantry and five tanks attempted to take over some pillboxes at the foot of Cemetery Hill and virtually in 2d Battalion, 119th Infantry's front yard [3] Artillery fire did most of the work of discouraging this effort, though one tank of the 743d Tank Battalion, firing at 1,400 yards' range, set ablaze a retreating Mark V German tank 30th Division Artillery also worked over a concentration of hostile troops in the woods just to the north.

The prospects of a large-scale counterattack died slowly as the area of German-held Aachen was shaved down, block by block. On October 20, as the friendly forces pried their way into the western part of the city, the 30th's front was almost inactive—except for heavy movement of armored vehicles and trucks to the northeast—away from the battle

Any hopes that Wurselen would be lightly held thereafter, however, were quickly dispelled the next day, October 21, while the commander of Aachen, Colonel Gerhard M Wilck, was surrendering the remnants of his doomed command The 116th Infantry, with the 3d Battalion, 120th Infantry attached on its north flank, tried once again to drive to the east through Wurselen, with the 1st Battalion of the 119th joining the attack on the south to reach the main highway at the southern tip of the town.

---

[3] This was, of course, also of great concern to the 1st Division Observed fire by 30th Division Artillery harried enemy counterattack formations against the 1st Division through the entire Aachen gap battle, frequently on targets the 1st Division could not see General Huebner of the 1st Division told General Hobbs, "Without the aid of the 30th Division Artillery, counterattacks would probably have cost us that important hill"

The attack was most successful on the flanks The 1st Battalion of the 119th was up to the road by 9:45 A M. and the 3d Battalion of the 120th had good initial success, capturing 40 prisoners from the 116th Panzer Division even before the attack started, as the result of artillery persuasion But the attack lagged in the center, and beginning at 2.15 P M the exposed 3d Battalion, 120th Infantry, began to receive counterattacks from the flanks by tanks and infantry I Company was hard hit in this first attack, the 1st Platoon being cut off and then returning under cover of friendly artillery fire with only 14 of its 34 men The Security Company of the 116th Panzer Division struck again aided by 4 tanks and a 200-round artillery barrage an hour and a half later, attacking twice before being halted with the aid of friendly artillery and an air strike Finally, the battalion was ordered back out of its exposed position to its original line.

One more counterattack was received on the 21st, this by the 1st Battalion 119th Infantry. Attacking under cover of darkness at 9:00 P M. with 100 infantrymen and 2 tanks, the enemy was stopped with the aid of artillery fire, although some infiltrating Germans were not ejected from the position until after daybreak

October 22 marked the end of that attempt to clean out Wurselen The attack was renewed at 7 30 A M , but little progress was made against the tenacious house-to-house defenses, except by C Company, 119th Infantry, which gained 200 yards before being counterattacked on both flanks in early afternoon The enemy's counterblow, in weak company strength assisted by 2 tanks and plentiful artillery fire, was halted, but C Company withdrew nevertheless to conform to the line held by its neighbors Three enemy tanks had been knocked out, but the line was solidly held by elements of the 3d Panzer Grenadier Division The 116th Infantry withdrew from line and returned to the 29th Infantry Division The troops of the 30th readjusted their positions and settled down for a much deserved breathing spell. Typical entry in small unit records for October 24: "The big event of the day was showers—*hot showers*—the first the men had been able to get under since September 25, 1944! This was also the first opportunity in more than six weeks for personnel to launder their clothes " Or more cryptically "B rations!"

Chapter XI

THE PERFECT INFANTRY ATTACK

Even before the fall of Aachen, the Allied High Command was planning the opening phases of a winter war to keep the tattered *Wehrmacht* needy and off balance On October 21, the day on which that unhappy city fell, 12th Army Group issued instructions for the next move The springboard around and north of Aachen, which the 30th Division had started erecting when it drove through the Siegfried Line, would be used by the First and Ninth Armies for an attack to the Rhine. First Army, making the main effort, was to cross that great water barrier if possible Ninth Army, protecting the north flank of the offensive, would sweep to the north and co-operate with the British 21st Army Group in clearing the west bank of the Rhine of German soldiers

The conflicting demands of speed and adequate supply were still paramount The great port of Antwerp was in Allied hands but enemy resistance on Walcheren Island, dominating the water approaches to the city, did not cease until November 11, a day after the tentative target date for the new offensive, with the Channel itself still to undergo the long process of mine removal Thus, supply lines were long—back to the beaches and ports of Normandy—and many items were critical Tanks, so vulnerable in pitched battles with the heavy German Mark Vs and VIs, were hard to replace Fighting men to replace the inevitable losses of battle were present in the reinforcement depots in only limited numbers The ammunition shortage was so serious that General Simpson himself took over the rationing of ammunition within his Ninth Army. But despite these handicaps, despite the abnormally heavy fall rains which sharply reduced cross country movement of tanks and made difficult the maintenance of roads, an early large-scale offensive was deemed necessary to maintain the margin of superiority which the Allies had gained in their summer victory. Continued pressure would at least deny the enemy a chance to fatten and regroup his armies, and high hopes were entertained that the enemy could be beaten decisively before the harsh winter of northwest Europe set in.

The job assigned to the 30th, still under XIX Corps, was to wheel to the southeast, pivoting on Wurselen, and thus eliminate the enemy salient pointing westward toward Aachen Flanking the 30th were two recent arrivals which were to strike eastward—the 29th Infantry Division on the north and the 104th Infantry Division, which had relieved the 1st Infantry Division, on the south Speedy success by the 30th, by protecting their flanks, would aid greatly in their forward movement to the east.

Thus, there was nothing spectacular in the Division's assigned task It was something that was becoming almost routine—an attack through an enemy defensive position neither surpassingly strong nor notably weak, another problem in getting to assigned objectives with a minimum expenditure of time and human life That the operation proved to be one of the prouder achievements of the Division resulted from the manner in which it was executed rather than the uniqueness of the assignment

The day tentatively set for the attack, November 10, came and went, under leaden skies Back of the front lines trucks crawled up and down in the creamy black mud of the roads Facing the 117th and 120th Infantry positions stretching from Alsdorf to Euchen, there was little to be noticed except for occasional harassing fire and one or two signs of rotation of troops in line Patrols had found out most of the things to be known—that the enemy line of resistance was stretched along the railroad embankment, with minefields in the woods and fields covering the position In Wurselen, where the opposing lines were across the street from one another, the tempo was faster At night single tanks would move up to fire into the buildings occupied by the 119th Infantry, machine guns would open up with little or no provocation and little battles flared up as the patrols went out Everyone knew that the pie-shaped block of buildings along the main highway in the southwest part of town was called the "Bloody Triangle" and felt it was well named. The regimental intelligence officer gave up trying to plot enemy locations on a standard scale (1 25,000) map and began noting positions on a 1:10,000 scale aerial photograph, it was soon covered with red ink markings of minefields and machine guns and company command posts This building occupied—that building empty—these houses boobytrapped—they serve chow here at 1300—a tank holes up behind this house almost every night

The 116th Panzer Division had gone, November 4 it was located at Schmidt, in the Hurtgen Forest, where First Army troops were pressing perilously ahead toward the headwaters of the Roer River Many of its companions in the battle for Aachen were also absent In Wurselen the 3d Panzer Grenadier Division was still around, with its battalion command posts and heavy infantry weapons along the main highway through Weiden and Linden What enemy unit held Euchen was not quite clear, the area in front of the 117th Infantry was the responsibility of a battalion from the Von Fritschen Regiment, retitled 1st Battalion, 404th Infantry Regiment, under the German 246th Infantry Division Along the high ground 4,000 yards to the rear running through Kinzweiler and Schleiden, old artillery positions and the results of long-past community digging seemed to be undergoing renovation. The forward line was thin—perhaps, reasoned the Division intelligence officer, the Germans would for once attempt a defense in depth

Not until early in the morning of November 16 did word come through from Corps that the weather forecasts for air support were favorable and that D-day for the attack had arrived H-hour was 12 45.

*   *   *

Speed in the initial attack and detailed study of objectives by the assault troops, using a sandtable and aerial photographs, had paid big dividends in breaking through the Siegfried Line The same techniques worked handsomely on the 16th, although developments on the ground forced subsequent variations from the set plan of attack

On the Division's left, with the greatest distance to go as the 30th's front swung forward, the 117th Infantry struck first for Mariadorf The 2d Battalion headed southeast from Schaufenberg past the north edge of the massive 150-foot-high slag pile which protected the enemy's main line of resistance along the railroad embankment in front of the town, and the 3d Battalion attacked generally east from Kol Kellersberg through the little settlement of Mariagrube along the railroad tracks Following the air preparation and an intense artillery barrage, and with tanks and tank destroyers covering the flanks with fire, the leading waves doubletimed across the open flats of no man's land The enemy's defensive artillery fires did not begin falling until fifteen minutes after the jump-off and even then they were directed not at the assault waves but at the recently vacated line of departure. F Company, leading the 2d Battalion's advance, reached the slag pile before a machine gun opened up from the railroad embankment to the front In attempting to maneuver around it, F stumbled into a minefield—one of many later cleared by engineers near Mariadorf—and was immobilized. As a result G Company was ordered to move around the south edge of the slag pile and E Company, the battalion reserve, started to move from Alsdorf through Kol Kellersberg in the wake of the 3d Battalion

The 3d Battalion also moved fast and well spread out, with the enemy artillery falling well to the rear. The deeply dug-in enemy machine-gun and rifle pits along the 20-foot-high railroad embankment soon opened up with a strong fire, but the two assault companies of the battalion were able to maneuver to the northeast near the slag pile and into Mariagrube Nowhere in the regimental zone was the full force of the enemy's final protective line fires felt, because of the speed of our initial infantry attack.

Company A of the 105th Engineer Battalion found itself unexpectedly in the fight. A three-man engineer patrol, investigating the Mariagrube bridge, known to be mined for demolition, got there before it could be blown but soon discovered itself abreast of the infantry and in a fire fight with the enemy. Soon, however, other engineers came up to reinforce the patrol Four hundred pounds of explosives were removed from the bridge Later engineers helped to rout an enemy group out of a coal mine shaft by detonating explosives in the entrance after a surrender offer had been refused by the Germans.

By nightfall four line companies were in place on the objective, given close support by Company A of the 743d, whose first tanks had raced at top speed from Schanzenberg to Mariadorf at 2.00 P M , covered by fire of the other tanks of the company The tank movement, executed platoon by platoon, was finished half an hour later The struggle to extricate F Company from the minefield continued through the night Seven men were rescued during two hours of daylight work but heavy enemy mortar and artillery fire forced delay of the rescue work until dark. The engineers first used a light bulldozer on the job, but it too was immobilized by mines. Then a heavier dozer was employed, with a boom extension that permitted rescue with the dozer within 10 yards of a soldier During the night 40 men from F Company, rescued from the minefield, moved up to take their place in the still thin line in Mariadorf, and the 1st Battalion moved up for its attack of the following day.

The 120th's 1st Battalion reported similarly gratifying results within an hour of its concurrent attack for Euchen Moving rapidly, close behind an artillery and heavy weapons barrage, the battalion's riflemen swept through the line of defenses along the railroad and swallowed up the town in a combination of fire and movement later described by one of the regiment's officers as a "Field Manual writer's dream " Most of the defending troops had thought the planes of the preliminary air strike on positions to their rear were headed for Cologne, rather than presaging a ground attack against them and then had dived into their holes when the artillery preparation descended Thus surprised, they never had a chance to use their weapons effectively, and the 1st Battalion spent the rest of the afternoon digging them out of their cellars Also captured were 50 men of a night-shift trench-digging detail culled from the rear echelons of the 29th Panzer Grenadier Regiment They were still in bed when the attackers rounded them up Enemy artillery and mortar fire fell harmlessly behind the assault waves

Company F, attacking through the more rugged partly wooded country in the northern part of the regimental zone at 1.00 P.M , soon ran into heavy automatic-weapons fire from the towering railroad embankment, and although part of the company got up the embankment, it was shoved back by a counterattack This effort had succeeded, however, in keeping flanking fire off Euchen, and that night plans were laid to forego a frontal assault in the 2d Battalion's sector and exploit the Euchen success

The 119th's target, Wurselen, proved to be as troublesome as ever on the first day of the attack Weeks of firing by artillery, tank destroyers and tanks had knocked down many of the buildings, but the rubble still swarmed with German machine gunners and mortarmen, their positions carefully protected to withstand a month's incessant hammering German-held Wurselen was a key point, pinning in place the bandage of new defenses which the Germans had pressed over the gaping wound in the Siegfried Line The enemy knew its importance and kept two battalions of the crack 3d Panzer Grenadier Division there to hold it. In Wurselen, where localized fighting had flared up almost daily between the tight-packed opposing troops, there could be no hope of surprise

The 119th had hoped to jar loose the Wurselen defenses with its 3d Battalion, which had a sector centered on the north edge of town which possessed some open spaces and the possibility of maneuver The 1st Battalion, on its right, with its front line clearly defined along the buildings of the main highway, would have obvious difficulties in making a frontal assault But no sooner had the 3d Battalion jumped off than murderous cross fires from well positioned machine guns opened up and soon mortar fire was plopping on the halted American riflemen The front lines were too close for artillery to be used effectively, and American mortar fire had little effect on the enemy positions American tanks and tank destroyers were restricted to static fire support because of the ubiquitous mine fields One tank was knocked out by mines, another by a German bazooka team The fight broke down into a series of probing missions by small teams seeking a route past the enemy machine guns On one such mission Private Alexander Mastrobattista of Company L had one leg blown off by a Schu mine Private First Class Herbert A McKitrick, the company aid man, wormed his way through the machine-gun fire and dragged Mastrobattista back to comparative safety, where he applied a tourniquet Even this position was so exposed that Mastrobattista was forced to lie there four hours, calmly smoking cigarettes, before a litter team could approach to evacuate him The gallant medical corpsman was killed next day by another mine

That night the line of departure for the 119th's attack became the main line of resistance, with outposts up through the scanty 150 yards of ground the attack had gained, and the 1st Battalion still in its original positions

Despite the understandable stickiness in Wurselen, the Division had struck an auspicious opening blow on the 16th, probably the most dramatic of any along the length of the great offensive that day. Neither of the Division's neighbors had been able to keep pace: the 29th Division's assault waves in particular were seriously chewed up in their initial attempts to seize the exposed high ground between the interlocking village defenses in their path. Within an hour after the jump-off, the enemy's main line of resistance had been cracked along two-thirds of the 30th's front, and the threat of encircling Wurselen and the sheer need for troops farther north to contain Old Hickory's surge forward gave promise that the situation in Wurselen, too, would open up soon. Despite repeated assurances down the enemy chain of command that they would stay put for the winter, the troops facing the Division had long expected attack, but when it did come they were genuinely surprised and too overwhelmed by the combination of speed and carefully timed supporting fire to resist strongly. The cost to the Division was low—137 casualties, 60 of them in the 117th's unlucky F Company.

It was this day's work, the long prepared first round, which a XIX Corps staff officer admiringly described as "the perfect example of an infantry division in the attack," and which was so reported in the nation's newspapers. Other blows to follow soon were to prove almost equally classic.

During the night of November 16, the Germans made what adjustments they could, with 1st and 3d Battalions of the 8th Panzer Grenadier Regiment pulling back from Wurselen into the Linden–Neusen area along the main highway Even after nightfall the enemy was badly confused as to what had happened, the troops in Wurselen, for example, knew that Euchen had fallen but did not know that Mariadorf had also been lost This confusion was exploited the next morning, when the 120th Infantry at 7 00 o'clock literally charged from Euchen into the center of the Linden–Neusen settlement Swiftly reorganizing, the regiment's 2d Battalion pushed north to clean out Neusen under enemy artillery fire, while the 3d Battalion, previously in reserve, rapidly swept through Linden The panzer grenadiers from Wurselen, who had finished their night march just before dawn, had not had time to set up their defenses when the 120th's doughboys charged in, and although some resisted with small-arms fire, they never had a chance A total of 326 prisoners, including 201 from 1st Battalion of the 8th Panzer Grenadier Regiment (almost the entire battalion strength), were taken during a day of mopping up in Linden At 11·15 A M , a counterattack by infantry buttressed by seven tanks struck belatedly from the south at Linden, but was broken up by 3.00 P M , mainly by artillery fire.

The effects of the night withdrawal were felt in Wurselen, too, on November 17, though a profusion of mines unprecedented in the Division's experience made the advance ticklish (Mine clearance, by the supporting troops of the 105th Engineer Battalion and by the battalion ammunition and pioneer platoons, was speeded by capture of a marked map used by German engineers) The 3d Battalion advanced against rear-guard action to the eastern edge of the town and by 11 00 o'clock had made contact with Company B By midafternoon the 1st Battalion had completed moving up through the town to secure the new position.

Meanwhile the 117th Infantry was engaged in securing the left flank of the division. While the 3d Battalion stayed in place in Mariadorf, the 1st Battalion maneuvered almost due east toward a housing development on the far side of the main highway through the town in conjunction with the 120th's attack, and the 2d Battalion moved northeast to take Hongen, almost on the Division boundary. G Company started the push for Hongen by driving east to the main highway during the morning, flushing out some snipers and capturing a large amount of German small-arms ammunition and other supplies, which it set ablaze There it waited until almost midafternoon pending movement of the 1st Battalion Then, followed by tanks firing their machine guns and 75mm cannons, the company jogged astride the main highway into Hongen and had occupied it and outposted it within 22 minutes. Company E, also striking for Hongen just east of the railroad tracks, was held up at first by bitter fire from German barracks and trenches just northeast of Mariadorf, but after a five minute artillery and mortar concentration on the barracks began pulling itself through the position, with two attached tanks firing into the leading houses before the infantry rushed them By 3·15 P M the position had been taken and enemy troops still positioned along the railroad to the left front driven to cover by artillery time fire E Company then swiftly advanced into Hongen, with F Company, still well below strength, following to complete the circle of all-around defense there

Going was considerably tougher on November 18, the third day of the attack The 117th Infantry, with its 2d and 3d Battalions strung out in protection of the Division left flank, attacked with the 1st Battalion for Warden at 7 30 A M but had to try three times before taking the town, which later proved to have been well fortified and amply provided with ammunition and other supplies

The original plan, worked out with the 743d Tank Battalion well in advance, had been for tanks of Company A to attack with the infantry, but when the time came the tank commander refused to move them into the open, because of enemy AT guns he wanted first destroyed by artillery or dive bombers Thus the first attempt, made by B Company of the 117th without mobile tank support, soon bogged down under the heavy machine-gun fire that swept the flat approaches to Warden One of the assault platoons managed to crawl back to the housing project which had been the line of departure, but the other was marooned until the final attack, when the enemy fires lifted enough for it to join the charge into Warden A second attempt, again with the tanks firing from position only, jumped off in late morning, with the 3d Platoon of B Company reaching the edge of town before machine-gun and assault-gun fire drove it back with heavy casualties, including 15 men lost as prisoners. Only six men from the platoon got back

Finally Lieutenant Colonel Duncan, commanding the 743d Tank Battalion, and Colonel Johnson of the 117th acted to replace the tank company commander New plans were worked out, including screening smoke and artillery fires against the German AT guns Then, at 3.15 P M, with daylight already waning, tanks of A Company, each carrying four infantrymen, roared into Warden from the south, west and north with their machine guns blazing, while infantrymen of Companies A, C and F, brought up to replace B, also converged on the town from three directions An intense artillery and mortar concentration lifted just as the tanks neared the town Three enemy assault guns were knocked out, two by the tankers, and the town also yielded two anti-tank guns and 209 prisoners A few more Germans scuttled out of town crowded on four armored vehicles

Farther south, the enemy fought hard to retain control of Vorweiden, apparently to permit more orderly withdrawal that night The 120th's 3d Battalion, attempting to drive south along the line of houses flanking the highway, found the Germans well prepared with automatic weapons and maneuver difficult because of the openness of the surrounding country Progress was limited to 500 yards, but observer reports of enemy withdrawal to the east as darkness began to close in gave promise of better results the next day

Resistance stiffened, too, for the 119th in its assault on Weiden C Company attacked up the road from Wurselen and circled around to take the southeast portion of the town without much trouble, but A Company, following most of the way, was stopped at noon by fire from two pillboxes as it swung up to take the northwest part of the village. The attached tankers, who had already lost one, tank in a minefield and had bad memories of Wurselen's explosive-lined pavements, were hesitant about moving, but Technical Sergeant Francis M Cordle mounted the leading tank and directed it to a firing position A few

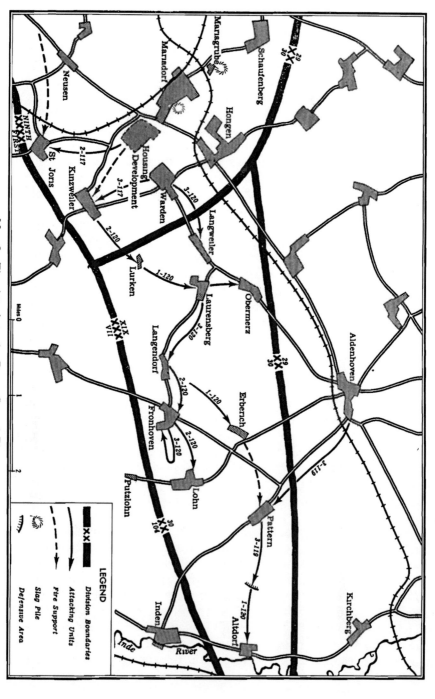

Map 9—The Attack to the Roer Second Phase

rounds from the tank's cannon brought surrender of each of the boxes in turn, and the doughboys moved on

During the evening Corps intercepted an enemy message designating the ridge running north from St Joris and Kinzweiler to Schleiden as the new main line of resistance This position, which was in the zone of the 117th Infantry, was gobbled up, however, in a matter of minutes on the next morning, by a carefully planned and coordinated combination of fire and movement The key points on the ridge were St Joris and Kinzweiler, within 1,000 yards of each other and thus capable of delivering deadly supporting fire Two battalions of the 117th had not been actively engaged the previous day, and Colonel Johnson decided to use both of them in a simultaneous attack, with the 3d Battalion moving south toward St Joris from the housing development that the 1st Battalion held and the 2d Battalion striking southeast toward Kinzweiler from Warden. With the regiment's attack the only major entry on the Division's schedule, ample artillery support and two of the 743d's tank companies were available for the attack In addition it was planned to plaster Kinzweiler with fire from the tank destroyers, tanks, and heavy weapons of both 1st and 2d Battalions, while all available weapons working with the 120th Infantry concentrated fires on St Joris. The plan was worked out well in advance, permitting detailed reconnaissance by the assault battalions and by the commanders of the support-fire weapons and meticulous mapping and timing of supporting fires The 120th Infantry gave enthusiastic assistance to the plan, its commander personally reconnoitering new weapon positions for support of the attack, and moving a task force up the slope just east of Neusen to provide gun locations

Thus, beginning at 8:00 A M, the two objectives were drenched in the fire of an overwhelming number of weapons of all types Artillery and mortar shells arched into the targets and the high-velocity projectiles of the tanks, tank destroyers, and machine guns, their flat trajectories marked by tracers, raced across the slightly rising ground The direct support 118th Field Artillery Battalion was dropped out of the program to permit execution of close support missions on call if needed

Simultaneously with the opening of the preparation, the infantry moved out for the 1,200-yard dash to the objectives The 3d Battalion streaked so fast that its supporting artillery preparation on St Joris, planned for 15 minutes, had to be lifted in 11 minutes, and at 8 12 A M the leading elements of Company G reached the outskirts of Kinzweiler. The nine attached tanks, each with four infantrymen aboard, continued to fire from the line of departure until the foot soldiers neared the towns, then raced ahead so as to arrive on the objective simultane-

ously with the infantrymen Four of the eight tanks working with the
2d Battalion were disabled by mines en route to Kinzweiler, but tankers
piled out and continued on foot to fight with the infantry

By 8:45 A M both objectives were consolidated The yield was
pleasing 223 prisoners (including two battalion commanders), an unknown number of enemy dead, three self-propelled guns, four 75mm
antitank guns, four half tracks, and large stores of ammunition The
enemy had been too dazed by the heavy preparation, and by the appearance of tanks and infantry from an unexpected direction as soon
as the supporting fires lifted, to resist One of the antitank guns was
found concealed in a haystack with 105 rounds of ammunition Not a
shot had been fired, the crew was found still hiding in its personnel
shelters The 3d Battalion suffered only eight casualties; a sniper
wounded three 2d Battalion men in Kinzweiler but there were no other
casualties until later in the day when harassing artillery fire came in

The remaining jobs for the Division were minor The 120th Infantry
rapidly finished cleaning out Vorweiden, now outflanked, white flags
were noted. The 119th Infantry used its 3d Battalion to finish mopping
up Weiden and to establish firm contact with the 104th Division on the
right The 30th was still poked out a little further than its neighbors,
but was well established on its objectives The opposition had disintegrated badly, aggressive enemy activity to the Division's front consisted
of light harassing artillery fire In four days, at a cost of 60 killed and
474 wounded, the Division had wrecked the 3d Panzer Grenadier Division and the 404th Infantry Regiment, German 246th Division, taking
1,595 prisoners and considerable matériel

On November 20th the 30th sat in place, on the 21st, pursuant to
orders from XIX Corps to seize a 2,000-yard-wide strip of territory east
to the Roer River along the Corps south boundary, it attacked again
On its flanks the attacks of the 104th and 29th Infantry Divisions were
beginning to get rolling against bitter opposition and constricting weather conditions, and north of the 29th Division, the 2d Armored Division,
with the 2d Battalion of the 119th Infantry attached, was pressing
ahead against almost crippling counterattacks by a crack panzer division.
- This time it was the 120th's show, with the entire 743d Tank Battalion attached to provide speedy mobile fire power. The first objectives
were Lurken, Laurensberg and Obermerz, along the line of field fortifications on the high ground running north from Kinzweiler, and Langweiler, just to the west The field fortifications faced generally northwest and were flanked by American-held Kinzweiler. Thus, the attack
was launched from the latter town, with lavish supporting fires by the

117th Infantry from there and from Warden covering the advance Enemy minefields forced both F Company, which attacked for Lurken and E Company, designated to take the high ground to the east, to swing to the right, but they closed in on their objective rapidly Heavy rains had left the fields treacherous for vehicle movement, and two of the eight light tanks moving cross-country bogged down The attached platoon of medium tanks moved along the secondary road to Lurken but were delayed by mines When they did move they were harassed from the east flank by tank fire, but moved ahead out of danger rapidly to enter Lurken 50 yards ahead of the infantry. Sixty prisoners were taken

At 9 30 A M. B Company, which had moved up to Warden, started the second phase of the attack, assaulting swiftly into Langweiler with a platoon of medium tanks Fifteen minutes later, with the enemy newly ejected from Langweiler streaming into Laurensberg, the remainder of the 1st Battalion struck at that town from Lurken with tanks and infantry By 11.00 A.M both Laurensberg and the little settlement of Obermerz to the north had been taken The whole operation, involving four towns, yielded about 200 prisoners and a probable 50 more enemy casualties, at a cost of 56 casualties, most of them resulting when B Company followed its own artillery barrage too closely

It was only noon, and the regiment had further objectives to the east. The 3d Battalion, which had been previously briefed about its role in the operation, was moving up through Warden to Langweiler, where it was to attack southeast toward Langendorf, about 1,500 yards away The 2d Battalion was alerted to support this thrust with an attack from Lurken, but it was not needed.

Flanking fire could not be used on this attack, but a 20-minute artillery preparation was fired as the troops moved out at 1 00 P M. along the axis of the road, with L Company on the right and K Company on the left Hostile small arms and automatic weapons opened up on the advancing troops from the edge of town, but within 40 minutes these companies were the victors Some enemy fire came from a little clump of farm buildings and orchards known as Hausen, just north of Langendorf, and a platoon of Company K was peeled off en route to Langendorf to capture it Enemy firing from there and from positions between there and Langendorf prevented capture of the place until later in the afternoon, when most of K Company was used to eject the enemy at close quarters with bayonets and grenades.

The 2d Battalion's turn was coming up again, and at 2 00 P M. the long battalion column advanced in the cold drizzle that had been falling all day to Langendorf almost on the heels of the 3d Battalion, to prepare for the short jump east to Fronhoven. Fronhoven was the largest of the seven places the regiment had to capture that day Enemy artillery and mortar fire on newly won Langendorf drove both battalions in the town to cover, delaying reorganization, and the intensity of the shelling along the line of departure at the eastern end of town held up the attack for an hour. Darkness was falling.

Ten minutes before 5.00 the 2d Battalion, weary after a full day of muddy combat and marching, began its attack, with the attached tanks advancing promptly at the same time They immediately met a storm of small-arms fire from positions at the edge of their objective which had missed the brunt of the artillery preparations on the center of the town With their regimental commander directing the right company and the battalion commander the left company, the infantrymen and tankers moved out together, however, forced their way into town, and by midnight had done enough night fighting to report it clear of enemy and prepared for defense The unearthing of isolated groups of enemy soldiers continued through the night

The Division had lashed out over three miles, halfway to the Roer, in its first day of its new attack, but there was still no rest in store for the 120th's doughboys Following the technique of leapfrogging battalions, which allowed the least tired troops to continue the assault and gave their commanders time for planning and reconnaissance, it was planned to use the 1st Battalion, still back in Laurensberg, to punch northeast to Erberich and the 3d Battalion to hit due east to the larger village of Lohn, while the 2d Battalion caught what rest it could in Fronhoven, the defended base The attack on Lohn was to be made in conjunction with an attack by the 104th Division on Putzlohn, which lay less than 1,000 yards to the south just over the Division boundary, and which was ideally located to churn up an attack on Lohn with enfilading fire

During the night of November 21-22, the enemy reinforced his disorganized troops still in the Division's path—mainly stragglers and rear-echelon groups from the 3d Panzer Grenadier Division—with a fresh replacement battalion, 300 men strong, and a battalion of assault guns The assault-gun battalion introduced Old Hickory to the newest weapon in the German armory, an 88mm. gun mounted on a Mark V tank chassis, known as the *Jagdpanther* (pursuit Panther). The replacement battalion moved into Lohn. The assault guns operated mainly on the flanks and caused considerable trouble

The 1st Battalion moved up to Hausen around daybreak and jumped off from there toward Erberich at 8 00 o'clock on the 22d, again with tanks Despite small-arms, mortar, and artillery fire which harried its advance, A Company, on the right, was soon in the southern part of the town. C Company, however, was slowed by some assault guns which were finally ejected from the northern part of the village, fleeing toward Pattern. By noon the battalion was well in possession of the town Three light tanks of the 743d were knocked out by enemy fire in the battle

The 3d Battalion, though it had a shorter distance to go, was soon in difficulty. Company L, assaulting on the right, was almost immediately brought under direct fire from Putzlohn, and observed artillery and mortar fire followed as soon as it was pinned down Company I advanced a short distance and also was halted Then the reserve company, K, moved forward around the left flank well spaced to avoid casualties from the brisk enemy artillery fire falling there This gave I Company a chance to move and both units drove into the edge of town

Meanwhile, L Company lay in the open waiting for the expected 104th Division attack on Putzlohn, which would eliminate the fire pinning it down. During this painful wait American tanks and tank destroyers battled three Mark VI Royal Tiger tanks which had shown up on the ridge between Lohn and Putzlohn, with the shells screaming over the heads of the prone men Two Shermans were knocked out at approximately 1,000 yards by one of the Germans' 88s, after running into friendly minefields which the tankers understood to have been removed, while direct hits by American 3-inch tank destroyers seemed to have no effect on the enemy armor After 10 minutes the enemy tanks pulled away to the east By 9 30 the Company L commander gave up on the Putzlohn attack, which later proved to have been halted almost in its tracks, and ordered his men to infiltrate back, crawling the painful 500 yards back to Fronhoven Not until 1 00 P M was the withdrawal complete

American troops were in the edge of Lohn, but the town was far from being taken. The close support of direct-fire weapons—tanks and tank destroyers—and supplies as well were urgently needed to convert the Lohn toehold into an asset Mud and mines ruled out cross country movement of vehicles High-velocity fire from the south and in addition from Pattern knocked out two tanks and a tank destroyer attempting to move up the road to reinforce the men in Lohn. Reluctantly, at 4.00 P M , the order was given for Companies I and K to withdraw by infiltration They were all back in Fronhoven four hours later

During the action six enemy tanks were knocked out, four by the 823d Tank Destroyer Battalion and two by infantry action. The tank destroyers also blew up two small radio controlled tanks loaded down with explosives, commonly called "doodlebugs"

November 23 was Thanksgiving Day, but it was also a fighting day, and dank and cold as well The 120th was to try again for Lohn, with the 104th Division attacking again for Putzlohn The 119th Infantry would circle up into the 29th Division's zone to attack from Aldenhoven to Pattern

The 2d Battalion of the 120th took over the task of taking Lohn It was a bitter struggle Before the troops jumped off from Fronhoven, enemy artillery crashed in on the line of departure there in unusually heavy volume, inflicting 35 casualties on E Company alone and a total of 70 in the battalion E Company's commander was killed by machine gun fire a few minutes later Lieutenant William P. Barenkamp, the battalion intelligence officer but an old E Company man, was on hand and without prompting took command Delayed half an hour by this artillery fire, F Company and the 20 men remaining in E Company attacked at 7·30 through heavy shelling, while the 1st Battalion delivered supporting fires from Erberich By 9 15 they held a precarious hold in Lohn, G Company and L, borrowed from the 3d Battalion, coming up to reinforce the weakly held position

Heavy fire was supposed to be delivered from Lohn on Pattern, to keep the Germans there faced away from the attack preparing at Aldenhoven Hardly had L Company closed into Lohn, closing a dangerous gap in the lines, however, than Lohn itself was the target for German counterattack The first thrust, apparently from Putzlohn, was broken up within an hour by artillery, which knocked out two of the enemy tanks and splashed the infantry with shell fragments At noon a company of the 3d Panzer Grenadier Division's reconnaissance battalion attacked L Company's position in the southeast part of Lohn Tank destroyers of the 823d knocked out two of the accompanying enemy tanks and their fire and heavy artillery concentrations pumped out by Division Artillery dispersed most of the attack while it was forming about 1,000 yards out of town The remaining armored vehicles of the counterblow fled into Pattern, arriving just in time to get in on the receiving end of an 11-battalion artillery TOT placed there to precede the 119th's attack

About 40 Germans worked into Lohn during the attack and about two hours elapsed before they could be cleaned out A regimental 57mm antitank gun accounted for seven of them as they moved around a corner High-velocity tank or assault-gun fire from the area to the south, continued to harass the supply route into Lohn during the afternoon. The eastern part of Putzlohn was still enemy-held

The 119th Infantry's 3d Battalion was back at the Division rest center having its Thanksgiving turkey for breakfast before dawn on the morning of the 23d Then it moved up to Aldenhoven, at the time under brisk artillery fire, and at 12.45 jumped off on schedule for Pattern The attack was a spectacular success Diverted and pinned down by a crushing twenty minutes of artillery fire and by the blazing infantry, tank destroyer, and tank fires that poured in upon them from the 1st Battalion, 120th Infantry, positions in Erberich, the defenders of Pattern were utterly unprepared for the attack from Aldenhoven Forty minutes later the town was completely in our hands Not a single American casualty was sustained in this assault At 1 05 A Company of the 743d Tank Battalion attacked from Pattern at 25 miles per hour so as to reach the edge of town alongside the infantry. About 500 yards away from the objective the company commander spotted a minefield across the road With the fields as muddy as they were there was nothing to do but wait under the threat of tank-destroying fire from the left, ahead of the 29th Division's forces, until a pioneer platoon sweeping the road could catch up When they resumed their dash 15 minutes later, they suddenly came upon prize game Captain David W Korrison in the first tank knocked out two new *Jagdpanthers* in rapid succession, at a range of about 50 yards, while the Germans were engaging B Company tanks firing from Erberich Another Panther was eliminated at close range after preliminary shots had created openings in the building behind which it was hiding Sixty-two prisoners were taken

During the next four days the front-line troops remained in place, while the 29th Division grappled with heavy resistance in Bourheim and Koslar on the left flank and the 104th Division advanced along the Inde River toward Inden on the right The only town remaining to be taken in the Division zone was Altdorf, a thin town stretched along the river controlling a second-rate crossing, and hidden from our troops by a steep slope down to the river which began 800 yards to the west Patrols located eight machine guns on the reverse slope spaced at fifty-yard intervals in front of the town so as to deliver interlocking bands of grazing fire over the crest The area facing Old Hickory forward elements in Pattern and Lohn was bald Two other towns along the river—Kirchberg, 2,000 yards to the north, and Inden, even closer on the south—were capable of being moulded into a three-position co-ordinated defense with Altdorf.

The question of joint pressure by the three American divisions was a delicate one. The 104th Division wanted the 30th to attack on the 25th In view of the probability that the 104th would not be able to take Inden at the same time the 30th attacked Altdorf, the XIX Corps commander permitted the 30th to support its neighbor's attack with fire alone On that day the 3d Battalion, 119th Infantry, outposted the woods just east of Pattern

General Hobbs and Colonel Purdue both felt that Altdorf was a difficult objective, because of the exposed approach over the hill, vulnerable to fire both from the town and from the far side of the river, and because of the poor roadnet and steep ground, which would not permit tracked vehicles to work with the infantry and which would make supply difficult They believed that the town should be ignored or neutralized until the more important towns of Kirchberg and Inden were taken If the town had to be assaulted, they favored a night attack to reduce the advantage which the exposed approach gave the enemy, and on November 24 Colonel Purdue started Lieutenant Colonel Williamson of his 1st Battalion working on plans for such an attack

By the 26th the 29th Division was ready to jump off for Kirchberg at 10·00 A M. the following day, and the 30th was ordered to attack with it The 104th Division, driving for Inden through Lamersdorf to the south, had not taken the latter town, but would continue the attack on the morning of the 27th

A reinforced company of the 3d Battalion, 120th Infantry, moved out before dawn on the 27th to seize an objective in the open, for a line of departure At 11 40 the 3d Battalion, 119th Infantry, attacked through this position for Altdorf, but as expected was soon pinned down by machine-gun fire from the positions outside the town and by direct tank fire from the edge of the town Artillery pummelled the enemy positions while the infantrymen dug in. Kirchberg fell to the 29th by 2 00 P M but the 30th's attack remained stalled. At 5·52 P M Colonel Purdue, who had the battalion of the 119th under his command, reported that he would try a new plan and would have Altdorf by morning The 1st Battalion, 120th Infantry, would make the long-planned night attack at 4 30 in the morning The 104th Division, which had driven from the south of Lamersdorf during the morning of the 27th, reverted to its original scheme and planned to assault Inden before dawn from the west, alongside the 120th

Careful planning and orientation preceded the attack Individual aerial photographs marked with zones of responsibility were distributed to each squad, so that every man could study in detail exactly where he was to go and what he was to do This also permitted the squads to move to their assigned objectives within the town knowing where adjacent units would be

B and C, the two assault companies, were formed into eight platoon files after the battalion moved on a compass course to the line of departure, and jumped off on time, preceded by four squads spread out in a skirmish line, with a grenade launcher on every man's rifle. To

achieve surprise, only the normal artillery harassing fires on enemy
rear areas were fired. The "natural" route of advance was avoided on
the correct assumption that it would be well covered with defensive
fires at the slightest hint of an attack, this route was constantly under
fire as the attack developed

Air bursts of artillery supporting the attack on Inden to the south
illuminated the area enough to give the enemy warning, after the
men had moved forward 100 yards from the line of departure, and the
machine guns outside Altdorf opened up They were quickly disposed
of by rifle grenades fired at the flashes by the entire line of skirmishers,
after the latter advanced under fire to within effective range During
the delay A Company, in reserve, moved up beside the assault units and
they all advanced swiftly into the town. For two hours an animated
battle raged in the darkness of the town In addition to the Germans
firing small-arms weapons at the men moving in the dark to the
buildings they were to seize, seven enemy tanks roamed the main street
of the town trying to escape A platoon of the reserve company had
moved into Altdorf laden with as many mines as it could hand-carry,
with the mission of placing hasty minefields at both ends of the settlement to keep tanks out These minefields trapped the tanks and the
bridge leading over the river to the east was also taken before the tanks
could escape Their consequent attempts to get out and those of the
infantrymen stalking them made a strange battle. Two enemy tank
commanders exposed themselves trying to peer through the darkness
and were picked off by riflemen One tank blundered into a building
and was trapped, after its lights had been shot out It was set ablaze
by a white phosphorus grenade. The attackers hit every tank at least
three times and some as often as 15 times with bazookas, rifle grenades,
and every other weapon at hand, but the heavy armor repelled even
bazooka rounds in all except one case Technical Sergeant Vincent
Bernier knocked out a half-track personnel carrier with a rifle grenade
and then accounted for a Mark V with a bazooka round at close range
Six of the tanks, however, were able to escape over the bridge which
was later destroyed by an enemy artillery round Seventy-four prisoners
were taken

During the morning of the 28th supporting tanks, tank destroyers
and other supporting vehicles moved up The small tracked M29,
cargo carriers were, however, the only vehicles which could be used
cross country

Meanwhile, elements of the 119th's 3d Battalion closed up to the
river north of Altdorf, capturing 20 men of a column attempting to
escape, and making contact with the 29th Division.

On November 30, the 17th Cavalry Squadron took over the Division's narrow stretch of front December 13, L Company of the 120th attacked north from a bridgehead which the 104th Division had established over the Inde River and cleaned out the desolate V-shaped flats between the Inde and the Roer River in the Division sector Most of the Division was far behind the front—the Division command post still at Herzogenrath, the 119th Infantry at Kohlscheid and the 117th near Warden.

*   *   *

Old Hickory had accomplished its part in the drive to the Roer with distinction, and, more important, at a total cost (including attached units) of only 160 killed and 1,058 wounded. Two engagements were such classic examples of technique in village fighting that they were re-enacted as demonstrations, at the express desire of General Simpson of Ninth Army, for the benefit of newly arrived commanders of divisional units ·These were the joint attack on Kinzweiler and St Joris and the assault that gobbled up Lurken, Langweiler, Laurensberg and Langendorf in the same day

But the offensive as a whole was a grave disappointment Nowhere had the advancing Americans been able to break into the open and exploit. The First Army's drive toward the great dams controlling the headwaters of the Roer River had bogged down in slow and costly fighting in the bitterly held Hurtgen Forest, so that the Ninth Army, in dragging itself to the Roer, had only attained a new and serious water barrier.

Advances had been expensive, in both men and equipment. The 29th Division, for example, had the line elements of two battalions at less than rifle-company strength when it finally cleared out the last stubborn opposition west of the Roer In fighting the 9th Panzer Division, the 2d Armored Division's lighter-armored and outgunned Sherman tanks sustained a high rate of loss, particularly serious in view of the continued shortage of tank and tank-crew replacements,· and the division's infantry had also suffered Nor could casualty figures express adequately the weariness of those who had fought and worked through rain and cold for the bleak waterlogged beetfields and shattered town of the Aachen plain.

The supply and reinforcement situation was even more·serious than before the operation began, with armor, bridging equipment, and ammunition particularly short, and skilled riflemen and tank crews almost unobtainable as replacements Heavy rains had flooded the Maas River, over which all supplies had to come The two British Second

Army bridges were rendered unusable and the main two-way Ninth Army bridge at Maastricht over which the British traffic was rerouted had to be restricted to one-way traffic and finally closed on November 22 Thus, the Ninth Army was left with only two one-way bridges over the Maas.

Especially galling was the realization that, despite the Allied offensive, which drew three panzer divisions into the fight in the northern part of the front, the Germans were amassing a potent mobile reserve Reports of an elite panzer array forming east of the Rhine in Westphalia began to drift in at the beginning of November On the eve of the November 16 assault it was identified as the Sixth SS Panzer Army under *Generaloberst* (Lieutenant-General) *der Waffen-SS* Sepp Dietrich, an old Hitler favorite On November 18 the 30th's G-2 periodic report announced that "much if not all of Sixth Panzer Army is now west of the Rhine " For the next four weeks Allied intelligence sections worried and sifted conflicting reports as to the whereabouts of the four tank divisions in that army—the 1st SS *Leibstandarte Ado'f Hitler,* the 2nd SS *Das Reich,* the 9th *Hohenstaufen* and the 12th SS *Hitler-Jugend.* On December 17 they knew

Early in December the Division began working on plans for a new operation The mission was still offensive XIX Corps' plan called for the 29th Infantry Division to establish a bridgehead at Julich opposite its current positions, with the 30th crossing the 29th's bridges and clearing out the heavy forested area southeast of that town and the 2d Armored Division crossing as soon as room could be made The 30th was also asked to work up plans for assaulting in the 29th's zone The sector facing Old Hickory, which had no first-class road, was considered unsuitable for an assault crossing in view of the water-soaked condition of the approaches to the river and the flooding of the Roer which heavy rains had already brought on

The German-held Roer dams upstream constituted a serious and unusual menace to any Allied operations across that stream and across the Maas below Roermond A captured map indicated that the Germans were fully aware of their capability of blowing the major dams after an assault crossing had been started, washing away the American bridges with a wall of water and isolating the troops on the far side for savage counterattack by the Sixth SS Panzer Army Controlled flooding of the Roer, alternatively, could be maintained for a considerable period by manipulation of the sluice gates.

Between December 4 and December 11 three RAF attempts to blow the two principal dams by air bombardment, involving some 2,000 tons of bombs, were made, so as to get the flooding of the Roer over with and out of the way Despite a number of hits the dams remained intact. When the German counteroffensive in the Ardennes was launched December 16, plans for an American attack across the Roer were still unsettled

Chapter XII

SITZKRIEG

For three of its eleven fighting months in Europe during World War II, Old Hickory remained in the Aachen area, with its center of gravity within a dozen miles of the Dutch-German border. Rear installations moved seldom or not at all during this period, between September 19, when the Division first entered German territory, and December 16, when it was drawn south into the battle of the Ardennes The Division command post spent approximately a month in a school building in Heerlen, Holland, and then moved to a glider factory in Herzogenrath, just over the boundary in Germany, for another two months. Though the combat troops participated in some of their bitterest fighting during the fall of 1944, two three-week-long periods—between the last spasms of the Aachen Gap battle and the drive to the Roer and from the time that drive slowed to a stop and the exodus for the Ardennes—gave them an opportunity to enjoy the comparative advantages of static warfare and their first real chance to relax from the strain of battle For the infantrymen, taking their turns in the front line foxholes and fortified buildings and then going to the rear, it was the closest sustained approach they ever made to the muddy cycle of trench warfare which figures so much in World War I reminiscences

The area that 30th men will remember, as particularly theirs, stretched from Maastricht east into Germany as far as Alsdorf Most of the towns in that area are mining towns, with the slag piles and gaunt mine buildings towering over the rolling fields There were a great many housing developments and the little villages often ran into each other as the lines of houses stretched out along the roads Later, with the attack to the Roer, began the pattern which would repeat itself across the central German plain—distinct little agricultural villages about half a mile to a mile apart which dotted the fields. Up to the border, destruction of buildings through battle was moderate and the troops which remained there were assured of watertight billets. The villages of the Siegfried Line zone were, of course, well battered, and most of them required patchwork.

The presence of the coal mines was a particular boon because of the shower facilities there available Washing in France and Belgium had depended on the quartermaster bath units and on local streams—both of limited capacity. The mines, however, were able to accommodate large numbers of men

On October 27 a Division recreation center was set up on twenty-four hours' notice in the outskirts of Kerkrade, Holland, in the buildings of the Rolduc College, which was founded in 1106 A D. and thus ranks as the oldest educational institution in the Netherlands. Most of the buildings were of eighteenth and nineteenth century construction Designed to accommodate a combat infantry battalion at a time, the rest center was an outstanding success in restoring a sense of well-being to weary, cold, muddy men Beds in the dormitories, showers, captured chinaware and silverware to do away with the need for messkits, tailor and barber service, writing facilities, legal aid, and Special Service entertainment were provided Those who wanted to go to Kerkrade for the evening obtained passes without difficulty The Division band, which had been mounting guard over the CP for many months, discovered some German Army instruments and went back to music-making

The outstanding feature of the rest center's program was the determination of Major George E Motz, the director of the center, that freedom from regimentation was as important as all the services and comforts that could be devised How right he was, was disclosed in a base censorship spot check of mail made in February when the rest center was still being operated "This is a soldier's dream," wrote one infantry sergeant "No regimentation, sleep as long as you want, do as you please, no orders, no schedule The food is good and three meals a day " "Boy! It sure is the next thing to paradise," wrote another infantryman "We sleep in beds in our own cubicles and the best part, you can sleep as long as you like No details, no training, no nothing " Another man pointed out "But there to [sic] much to do to sleep Breakfast from 0700-0800 with music and they have plates and cups and no KP. We have music at all meals Now comes the best part After the show I went to a tea-dance." "We're in the best damn rest camp in the ETO," another doughboy stated "Three different movies a day and good chow. I could stay here for the duration " "Like a dream or a fairy tale," another man wrote

The men very definitely wanted to forget the danger and the misery of front-line life in the rainy season, but they were decidedly interested in the progress of the war The walls of one large room were covered with maps and the front lines replotted daily One map was set up so that the men could follow their journey from the Normandy beach. Air photos of battlefields over which the Division had fought were also posted Daily talks were given by Sergeant Abram Gennett, who had fought in a line platoon of the 120th Infantry during the Siegfried Line battle and by Captain Robert J Kline, who had also been writing a daily newsletter, *Notes to Company Commanders,* ever since the days of the St Lô breakthrough. Like other facilities, the orientation program at the center was entirely voluntary. But a high proportion of the men attended the briefing sessions, to listen, ask questions, and express their own ideas

The no-rules policy created some difficulty at first. Some of the first units to arrive broke equipment and left the center littered with cast-off dirty clothing and pieces of personal equipment. The rest center staff held its peace and waited "Some of the men, when they arrived the first time, figured that they would never come back and didn't care how they left the place," Major Motz stated. "Then when they came back for a second or third time they decided that the place was theirs to come back to and worth keeping in good shape. We never had any trouble after that "

A smaller rest camp was maintained by XIX Corps at Valkenberg on the road back toward Maastricht, and small regular quotas were allocated to the 30th for its use The Division center was retained under Division control until early March, just before the Rhine crossing operation During the battle of the Ardennes the center serviced XIII Corps troops

Training, of course, was also a prominent feature of this period In the fourteen days between the launching of the attack on the Siegfried Line and the closing of the Aachen Gap on October 16, each of the infantry regiments had lost approximately a battalion, mainly from the line companies. The total Division casualties for this period were 2,030 In addition, although the drive to the Roer was made at a minimum cost in wounded, dead and missing, the 119th Infantry participated in heavy fighting with the 2d Armored Division Many of the replacements were "retreads," former Communications Zone personnel or antiaircraft troops given only a short course in infantry tactics before being shipped to the front These men required intensive training In addition, all small units needed practice and instruction in teamwork as they absorbed new men The 823d Tank Destroyer Battalion had the special problem of reconverting from towed guns to self-propelled mounts. By December 16 half of the battalion's weapons were self-propelled.

The 30th also assisted in "breaking in" troops of two divisions newly arrived in the combat zone. From October 25 to November 6 the 406th Infantry Regiment of the 102d Division was attached to the 30th and from November 10 to November 21 the 335th Infantry Regiment of the 84th Division was put under 30th Division control. Both regiments were split up and their battalions assigned defensive sectors in line, so as to gain experience in combat before going on to offensive missions with their own divisions.

The Division's entry into Germany permitted acquisition of extra needed equipment Noteworthy was the machinery for making dentures found by the Division Dental Surgeon in Aachen For combat men particularly, the mortality among dental plates and false teeth was high—men lost them or sat on them or otherwise managed to need replacement. During the remainder of the Division's stay on the Continent, a dental section of the 105th Medical Battalion kept busy replacing dentures far faster than they could have been supplied by rear installations

The engineers were kept busy maintaining the roads in the division area, most of which were unequal to the task of carrying heavy equipment in a rainy season In the morning one might find a dozen signal vehicles from as many units repairing the ravages of the previous night's German interdiction artillery fire. The service echelons of all units were busy with maintenance

Along the front itself, the action soon developed a regular pattern As the patrols gingerly worked in Wurselen, fights would spring up at night° Machine-gun duels took place sporadically along the entire Division front in late October and early December It was normal for a German tank or two to put in an appearance to shell our positions The cycle of patrolling began anew; a couple of 117th patrols demonstrated great dexterity in shepherding in prisoners with the aid of artillery fire directed by a forward observer with the patrol The artillery looked for targets and shot what it saw Outposts of the 120th Infantry discovered a German soldier who was wont to sit in the open combing his long hair. Inevitably named "Herman the German," he remained an amiable and unhittable target despite a long series of schemes to eliminate him Some of the 117th's front line men, becoming bored with the situation, rigged up a combination of bells and old pieces of metal, which they would clank for the benefit of the Germans across the way. The enemy's fire thus aroused was jubilantly greeted by waving a dirty red cloth mounted on a stick—the traditional "Maggie's Drawers" of the rifle range The night before Election Day, the German night raiders dropped anti-Roosevelt propaganda leaflets on the front-line troops Soon after Aachen had fallen the German radio reported that Bardenberg was being defended by the Germans against three divisions—which was taken as a belated tribute to the 119th "Axis Sal," the Division's favorite German broadcaster, announced that the 30th had been wiped out in the Siegfried Line and Aachen Gap fighting The announcement was received with some scepticism.

Part Four

THE BATTLE OF THE ARDENNES

Chapter XIII

DEFEAT OF THE 1st SS

In mid-December 1944, the quietest sector of the Western Front was the rugged 60 miles along the German border between the tip of Luxembourg on the south and the headwaters of the Roer River on the north. There, where the Belgian Ardennes merge with the German Eifel, the Americans had driven during the fall into contact with the log bunkers of the Siegfried Line and had stopped, setting up defensive positions on the hills and along the mountain roads With difficult territory to the front, the Allied Expeditionary Forces high command deemed this area unworthy of serious offensive effort, and was diverting its troops to the Aachen area in the north and to the Alsace-Lorraine battle in the south. The principal American units on line were the 99th and 106th Infantry Divisions, under V Corps, in front of Malmédy, and the 4th and 28th Infantry Divisions, under VIII Corps, to the south. They were connected by a cavalry group Both the 99th and 106th were getting their introduction to combat in this quiet sector. The 4th and 28th were resting after heavy duty in the Hurtgen Forest. Behind the latter two divisions was the 9th Armored Division, newly arrived in the battle area.

At 5:30 on the morning of December 16, these divisions had new troubles on their hands. For several days their widely scattered outposts had been plagued by persistent German infiltration behind their positions Now, in addition, the front-line troops were reporting heavy incoming artillery fire from the east and what appeared to be reconnaissance in force at several places.

Both the infantry and artillery action continued unabated all day. By nightfall communications to many forward positions had been cut, strongpoints had been isolated, withdrawals of up to three kilometers made on a 10-kilometer front. Six-new enemy divisions including the 2d and 116th Panzer Divisions, were identified in the action The battle of the Ardennes—the most massive German effort of the Western campaign and one which would eventually involve 29 enemy divisions —was under way.

During the night of December 16-17, the Germans dropped large numbers of paratroopers with sabotage missions in the Eupen–Malmédy area and next day began introducing more of their armor into the struggle Months later, Lieutenant General Kurt Dittmar, the German General Staff official commentator, described the Ardennes operation as a "poor man's choice " But, under the capable direction of Field Marshal Von Rundstedt, it was a bold and powerful measure With Sepp Dietrich's Sixth SS Panzer Army on the north making the main effort, and Manteuffel's Fifth Panzer Army supporting on the south, Von Rundstedt planned to drive to the great communications center of Liège —also a vital target in World War I—there overrunning huge Allied dumps of gasoline and ammunition and splitting the Allied forces New Volksgrenadier divisions had been earmarked for the offensive The élite panzers of the SS Army had been overhauled, filled up again with young fanatical troops A special sabotage unit under Skorzeny, Mussolini's kidnaper, was equipped with American uniforms and equipment Gasoline and equipment had been hoarded all fall for the operation and would be sufficient for the first surge Thereafter, using captured stores as Rommel had on occasion done in Africa, the *Wehrmacht* might be able to strike again, this time for Antwerp German ability to flood the Roer was counted on to prevent an American counterattack across the Roer into the right flank of the German drive

Poor weather which grounded reconnaissance planes, strict secrecy in the preparations, the choice of difficult terrain, and moderation in the first day's attack gave the Germans a "considerable degree of surprise" A similarly unexpected German thrust through the "impenetrable" Ardennes in 1940, also directed by Von Rundstedt, had shattered the French Ninth Army near Sedan, led to the breakthrough to the English Channel and proved the most important blow of that campaign This time, however, the Germans failed to anticipate the speed and determination of the Allied reaction.

*   *   *

To the 30th Infantry Division, sitting quietly behind the Roer River slightly north of Aachen, the events of December 16—two and more corps away—were remote The G-2 periodic report for the day, received by the units the next morning, did devote a laconic paragraph to the action, even noting that "it is considered to be a large-scale attack with an armored spearhead," but most divisional units receiving the report had to get out newspaper maps to find the scene of the action Colonel Johnson of the 117th started out on a seven-day leave in London on the afternoon of the 16th During the morning of the 17th the 30th mopped up stray parachutists who had descended into its zone during the night, then settled down to enjoy a quiet Sunday. At 10:00 General Hobbs was wondering about the plane that was supposed to take him to London for a short leave

At 11:15 A.M the XIX Corps chief of staff phoned General Hobbs: "Just got a call from General Simpson and he is taking you away from us . . . I guess you better pack up and get ready as soon as you can I don't know any details but you are going south. I think it is only temporary." By 4:25 that afternoon the 119th Regimental Combat Team was on the road to the V Corps sector leading the way for the rest of the Division. Colonel Johnson returned to his unit in time to lead the 117th out next. The 120th Infantry, the only unit in line, turned its sector over to the 29th Infantry Division and at 11:00 P.M. started out with the last of the Division's fighting elements The rear echelons remained behind. Billets and CP locations were left plastered with signs, "Reserved for ——————" Corps thought it would be a ten-day affair, though no one was sure of anything.

The trip south was a nightmare in both planning and execution The Commanding General and the operations officer left to report to V Corps and then continued south Orders arrived from both V Corps and First Army. Roads were clogged, particularly from Eupen to the south, where civilians and military refugees streamed back. In Eupen parked cars held up the convoys. During the night the Luftwaffe was active over the column, but fortunately dropped more flares than bombs and failed to hurt the column. Army needed a regimental combat team right away and tried to get the lead column. The 119th had detrucked for the night, however, and the second column, that of the 117th, was instead routed through, with instructions to seize and defend Stavelot and Malmédy. The 119th paused in Hauset, Belgium, just south of Aachen, the first night and then proceeded south on the afternoon of the 18th.

Most of the troops had little idea of what they were going to do. Some heard for the first time when the voice of Axis Sal, the German radio commentator, coming through jeep-mounted radios, told them that the "fanatical 30th Division, Roosevelt's SS troops," was going to the rescue of First Army.

The triangle Spa–Malmédy–Stavelot contained two installations of vital importance. One was the First Army headquarters in Spa. The other was a pair of Quartermaster Class III dumps containing one of the greatest concentrations of gasoline and allied products on the Continent—"sufficient to send his [the enemy's] motorized columns sweeping on to Antwerp with full tanks."[1] Depot No 3, about one-third of the way to Stavelot along the road leading south from Francorchamps, contained 997,730 gallons of motor fuel Depot No 2, about a mile or two south of Spa along the ridge roads, had no less than 2,110,920 gallons of gasoline alone, for a combined total of 3,108,250 gallons of motor fuel, as well as motor oils and greases

As a stopgap while the 30th was on the road, First Army ordered

1FUSA G 3 Journal V Corps 191508 December 44

the 99th Infantry Battalion to the Malmédy sector from Tilff late on the afternoon of December 17, with the 526th Armored Infantry Battalion and Company B of the 825th Tank Destroyer Battalion attached. The commander of the 99th arrived in Malmédy about 9 30 P.M on the 17th, ahead of the main body of his troops There he found about 60 men of the 291st Engineer Battalion, posted in hasty roadblocks and with some demolitions prepared. The rest of the task force arrived during the small hours of the morning. By the time the 30th Division's leading elements arrived the next morning, the task force under the 99th Infantry Battalion had performed valuable work. Already, however, it was running into more trouble than it could handle.

The 526th Armored Infantry Battalion arrived in Malmédy about 2:00 A M. on December 18, and immediately dispatched Company A to Stavelot. Company A arrived there about two hours later, found a few engineers, and within an hour was plunged into a stiff fight with enemy armor

The engineers had placed minefields on the south side of the river at Stavelot Company A sent out two platoons of doughboys and a pair of tank destroyer guns to cover these barriers. They never had a chance to get set. German infantry engaged them as they were moving into position. The enemy foot soldiers were turned back, but at dawn German tanks started rumbling toward the bridge across the Amblève River. Tank destroyer guns knocked out a pair of the enemy tanks at 800 yards. A 57mm antitank gun halted the new lead tank, but 88mm gun fire thereupon silenced one of the three 57s in action and forced a second to withdraw. The third kept firing until the enemy was only 40 yards away and the gun itself out of ammunition. After that the enemy began crossing in strength, and the armored infantrymen were forced back across the river.

*   *   *

Meanwhile the 30th's leading regimental combat team, the 117th, was butting its way south through the streams of withdrawing vehicles, through Eupen, through Spa, where First Army headquarters was in process of moving its unwieldy installations onto the road and out of immediate danger. Blazing headlights of some of the withdrawing vehicles helped mark the roads for the Luftwaffe Wrecked trucks were strewn alongside the road

By dawn of December 18 the regiment had reached an assembly area near Malmédy and, preceded by the Intelligence and Reconnaissance Platoon and by part of the 30th Reconnaissance Troop, was heading for its objective—Malmédy The 118th Field Artillery Battalion pulled away from infantry protection and went into positions on high ground ahead of the doughboys, about a kilometer north of Malmédy, fighting off snipers and two hostile tanks to get its howitzers into position.

Malmédy, nestled at the foot of towering snow-covered hills protecting Spa, had been reported in the hands of enemy paratroopers It was in friendly hands when the 117th arrived but the confusion left by units now absent was more noticeable than the small garrison grouped around the 99th Infantry Hospitals, supply installations, reinforcement depots—their signs were still there but the troops had fled, leaving behind food,[2] liquor, documents, footlockers, dress clothing, miscellaneous equipment.

The 3d Battalion set up roadblocks and prepared for business, gratefully picking up the troops that were on hand and ready to fight

The 1st Battalion moved down through Francorchamps, detrucked two miles north of Stavelot and set off for that town through knee-deep snow at 8:30 in the morning, without waiting for the artillery to finish setting up.

At 10:30 an officer from A Company, 526th Armored Infantry Battalion reported that his company had been ejected from Stavelot by a large number of enemy tanks, after knocking out three of the German monsters.

Before pulling out, the armored infantry ordered the guards at the gasoline dump to set it on fire. This act of destruction, later stopped, succeeded in halting 15 enemy tanks which sallied northward from Stavelot. Civilians later reported they returned to Stavelot and then headed west toward La Gleize.

The 2d Battalion, reinforced by the 291st Engineer Combat Battalion, which was on the scene in Malmédy, took up positions along the road and railroad which ran along the edge of the hills from Malmédy to Stavelot, setting up roadblocks and patrolling to the Amblève River, which ran generally westward past Stavelot. Footbridges over the Amblève River were already blown Two underpasses, where the railroad crossed, were prepared for demolition and minefields were laid.

At 11 00 A M. friendly troops were reported in the edge of Stavelot, but fighting there raged during the afternoon. The square in Stavelot was a no man's land At 2.55 P.M 10 enemy tanks and infantry surged forward to attack the 1st Battalion, and fighting was still bitter when American fighter-bombers appeared on the scene an hour later to strafe and bomb an estimated 40 enemy tanks south of the river The battalion drove on to take most of Stavelot northwest of the Amblève River.

---

[2] Some of the 117th's opportunistic mess sergeants served steak for days afterwards

The 2d Battalion knocked out three enemy tanks in counterattacks against its position on the flank

At 6:00 P.M , soon after dark, the Division command post was being set up in a small hotel in Francorchamps. This town, blocking the enemy approach to Spa and Verviers, was at the northwest corner of a triangle of main roads, with Stavelot and Malmédy at the other corners Thanks to wire left in place by First Army troops and the assistance of V Corps wire teams, 30th Signal Company had swiftly put in telephone communications to the regiments which had arrived in the battle area. Most of the Division's troops were still on the move, but with the re-establishment of a Division command post, unity of control was established

The 119th Combat Team had resumed its march south during the afternoon, circling around through Verviers and Remouchamps, on the north bank of the Amblève River southwest of Spa. There, under instructions delivered by General Hobbs en route, the 2d Battalion circled even farther west to Aywaille before continuing south to Werbomont and then to the east The rest of the regiment, led by the 3d Battalion, moved east toward Trois Ponts along the road skirting the north side of the river Time-space factors indicated that the enemy columns could thus be intercepted at Stoumont and Habiemont, respectively Identifications made during the day to the east indicated that the I SS Panzer Corps, controlling the 1st and 12th SS Panzer Divisions, was operating in the Malmédy–St. Vith sector

The 120th Infantry's reconnaissance elements reached Malmédy during the 18th, the main body arriving that night, prepared to take over defense of the Malmédy sector from the 3d Battalion, 117th Infantry, which was needed farther west The 823d Tank Destroyer Battalion, the 743d Tank Battalion, and the light field artillery battalions of the Division traveled in combat team attachments.

The 119th made contact with the enemy during the night At 9 45 P M. the 3d Battalion organized positions in the dark at Stoumont A patrol sent east to locate the enemy reported about 30 enemy tanks parked nearby The Germans were singing, talking loudly, and smoking, as though unaware of the presence of Americans to their front Later in the night an enemy half-track blew up in a hasty minefield laid by the 119th This, and possibly patrol reports, alerted the Germans to the presence of the 3d Battalion in Stoumont.

The 1st Battalion dug in about a mile to the rear of the Stoumont position, where a road from the south crossed the Amblève River to join the Remouchamps–Stoumont–Stavelot highway.

Another enemy spearhead, which had crossed to the south side of the

Amblève River just east of Stoumont, stumbled into the positions of the 119th's 2d Battalion near Habiemont just as Company F was setting up a roadblock in the dark at Chevron Enemy half-tracks carrying troops of the 2d SS Panzer Grenadier Regiment got past the first friendly position, after firing two rounds into the house occupied by most of the men of the detachment Then, forty yards from the nearest tank destroyer gun, the leading enemy half-track made the mistake of flashing on its running lights, evidently to illuminate a bend in the road Three rounds from the tank destroyer eliminated the lights and the half-track in a hurry Private First Class Mason H Armstrong of Company F reconnoitered, returned with a bazooka and a machine gunner to knock out two more half-tracks from a position in a vacant building Three others were abandoned as the enemy withdrew back toward the main body near Stoumont

Fighting still raged at Stavelot. At 9 15 P M fresh enemy infantry in American trucks and half-tracks approached and, although three loaded enemy personnel carriers were knocked out, the fighting continued bitter. The bridge at Stavelot, over which the enemy could approach from the east, was still intact, though it had been reported blown by army troops There were disquieting reports of tank concentrations at La Gleize and south of Stavelot

Two other events of the 18th are worth mentioning The first was the destruction by the 111th Engineer Group of the Trois Ponts bridge The second was the delaying action fought about noon by a 12-man detachment of Company B, 526th Armored Infantry Battalion This detachment set up a "daisy chain" of antitank mines and a 57mm gun on the highway just north of Trois Ponts The 57mm gun knocked out at least one and perhaps two of the enemy tanks which stopped when the "daisy chain" was pulled across the road in front of them After that they knocked out the 57 and proceeded on their way toward Stoumont This was evidently part of the spearhead which appeared opposite the 2d Battalion, 119th Infantry, that night. If so, the 119th and perhaps higher echelons than regiment should feel grateful for the delay thus afforded.

*   *   *

Daybreak of December 19 found Old Hickory stretched over 17 troubled miles of battle line, its little nodes of fighting men linked mainly by forested hillsides and the hope that they were impassable. There were no boundaries, only a handful of rudimentary blocking missions The fog of battle obscured much of what was going on, and blotted out almost completely the events in more distant parts of the

Ardennes battlefield Many supply installations had moved or were moving back miles over narrow, crowded mountain roads Paratroopers and sabotage agents were reported everywhere. Already the troops in Stavelot had uncovered the grisly evidence of some of the atrocities committed by SS troops against civilians and captured American soldiers [3] The atmosphere was charged with uncertainty and fear, which might in time infect even the spirited Old Hickory men coming in

The reaction of the Division was almost pure reflex There was little time to speculate on the successes of the German spearheads to the south, and, besides, no one knew much about what was happening, anyway Locally, there was a lot to be done before the area in which the 30th found itself could be considered up to even minimum standards of organization for defense Defiantly, almost cockily, the Division went to work.

Ammunition and troops were needed badly The 117th's Service Company had already sent a convoy by back roads to a supply point believed in enemy hands—and it had returned triumphantly laden with 81mm mortar ammunition, unobtainable at the assigned ammunition depots. Artillery ammunition train commanders foraged around and found huge stores of the shell which had been so drastically rationed in the north The 823d Tank Destroyer Battalion recruited four tanks and four wreckers from the rear echelon of the 7th Armored Division General Hobbs called for and received supporting artillery from Army The 740th Tank Battalion, fresh from the States and without equipment, raided an ordnance depot and returned in 16 hours with a crazy collection of tanks, tank destroyers, self-propelled guns, and half-tracks to fight gallantly with the 30th In its first action near Stoumont on the afternoon of December 19 one tank was to knock out

---

[3] Almost all of the atrocities against defenseless prisoners and civilians committed by the Nazis in their Ardennes counteroffensive took place in the 30th Division zone and were discovered by or reported to the Old Hickory troops in the midst of the fight against the SS men who had committed them They all appear to be the work of the *Leibstandarte Adolf Hitler's* 1st SS Panzer Reconnaissance Battalion

Here are typical examples Battery B, 285th Field Artillery Observation Battalion was intercepted and captured on the road leading south from Malmedy, on December 17 After the men had been disarmed and stripped of valuables, they were shot at by a German, possibly an officer When an American officer told his men, "Stand fast," the Germans opened up with automatic weapons and pistols As a parting gesture the Germans walked among the bodies, kicking them and shooting those that appeared still alive A few men feigned death and then escaped This testimony is by a survivor Civilian testimony, later corroborated by signed confessions obtained at the 117th Infantry prisoner of war cage, indicated that the engineer platoon of the 1st SS Panzer Reconnaissance Battalion, on instructions from the platoon leader, rounded up 20 civilians in Parfondruy en route to Stavelot on December 18, and shot them all in a barn Later the charred remains of a small shed there revealed about 10 or 12 completely burned corpses In the adjacent house the body of a middle aged woman had been stabbed and shot Two boys, aged 6 to 10 had bullet holes in their foreheads One old woman had been killed by a smash over the head Other bodies were in the vicinity, including those of a 13 year old boy and a 15-year-old girl A total of 117 bodies was found at Ster and Parfondruy

three Panther tanks with four shots and kill 70 enemy in ten blazing minutes, while another 740th tank was smashing up two more Panthers 150 yards away and a Tiger at 1,200 yards The 105th Engineer Battalion drew 15,400 mines, distributed two-thirds of them to the regiments and started laying the rest.

Contact evidently had been made with the German spearheads on the 18th Tactically, the next job would be to drive them back so that a coherent defense could be organized 30th Reconnaissance Troop patrols linked the Division's left flank with the 1st Infantry Division, which held an east-west line to the east of Malmédy. The obvious line to defend was from Malmédy to Stavelot, thence west along the north bank of the Amblève River to Stoumont, until the 82d Airborne Division, taking positions immediately south of the river, could tie in with the 30th and advance to the north-south line of the Salm River up to Trois Ponts, where it joined the Amblève Thus, the first efforts of the Division would be bent on cleaning out down the steep slopes to the river line.

The German target was clearly Liège, center of the vast supply area serving First and Ninth Armies The shortest route there was from the Malmédy–Stavelot sector, where good roads arched over the ridgeline of Hohe Venne toward Spa and then Liège This fact obsessed Division, Corps, Army. How much of the German armor had been committed, how much was still in reserve, was unknown. But the threat of a new enemy attack to the northwest was frightening in its implications. The Division, in cleaning out to the line of Amblève River to the south, had to keep an anxious eye on Malmédy.

At Stoumont on December 18, the paybook of a dead German revealed the presence of elements of the 1st SS Panzer Division *Leibstandarte Adolf Hitler*. Actually the whole of that division was stretched out in column across the Old Hickory front.

When the first elements of the Division made contact with the enemy at Stavelot on the 18th, the 1st SS Panzer Division was rolling westward in two columns, with the main force on the north. The stronger column was using the route Bullingen–Ligneuville–Stavelot–La Gleize–Stoumont–Aywaille. The southern column was traveling abreast via Pont–Trois-Ponts–Werbomont It was operating as part of the I SS Panzer Corps, spearheading the main effort Sixth SS Panzer Army. Its companion in I SS Panzer Corps, the 12th SS Panzer Division *Hitler-Jugend*, attacking on the right, was supposed to come through Malmédy, but had been stopped on the Butgenbach–Bullingen corner of the breakthrough area.

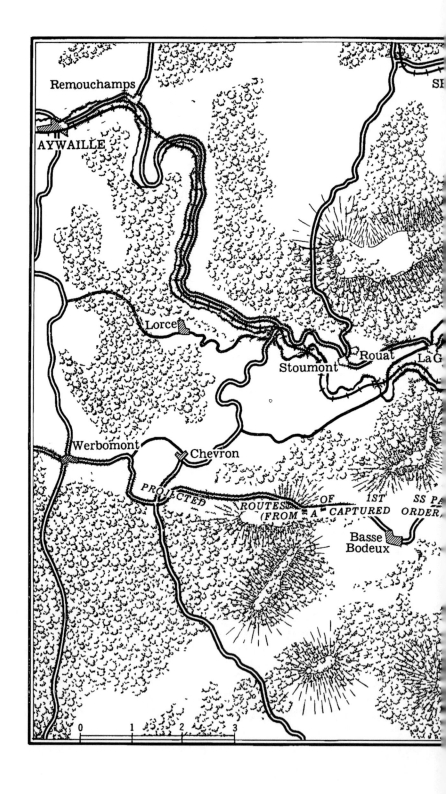

Remouchamps

SI

AYWAILLE

Lorce

Stoumont

Rouat

La G

Werbomont

Chevron

PROJECTED

ROUTES OF

(FROM A CAPTURED ORDER

1ST

SS P

Basse
Bodeux

SS P

La

0   1   2   3

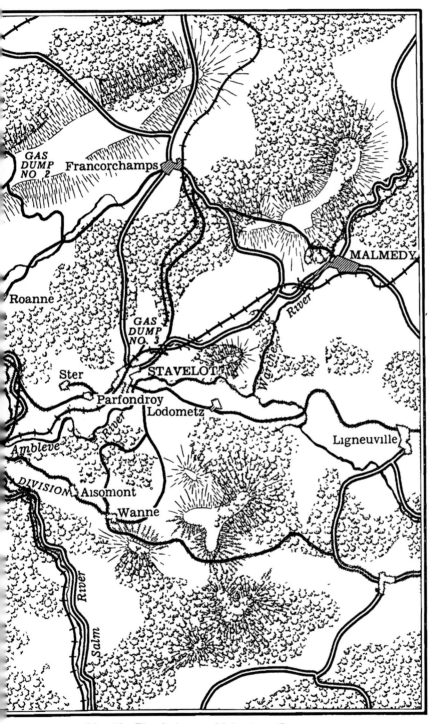

Map 10—The Ardennes   Malmedy to Stoumont

The spearhead of the northern column had already passed through Stavelot when the doughboys of the 117th Infantry put in an appearance there This advance guard, under command of Lieutenant Colonel Joachim Peiper, commander of the Nazi division's tank regiment, consisted of the 1st Battalion of the 1st SS Panzer Regiment plus a company of Royal Tiger tanks from the 501st GHQ Tank Battalion, the 3d Battalion of the 2d SS Panzer Grenadier Regiment, the 1st SS Panzer Reconnaissance Battalion, a company of engineers, a six-gun battery of self-propelled 105mm. howitzers, and two companies of a special parachute regiment, English-speaking and wearing American uniforms It was this formidable task force which had stopped for the night just east of Stoumont At Stavelot the fight had been waged by the main body of the column, which stretched back through Ligneuville.

Thus, while the American commanders were primarily concerned with a drive to the north and northwest in the Malmédy area, Hitler's own panzer division, in its turn, was worried about continued progress to the east and the threat to its flank at Stavelot.

Before dawn on the 19th Colonel Peiper's panzers were stirring in front of Stoumont. Fog and darkness limited visibility to 25-50 yards. Enemy tanks worked their way into the outskirts of town, and German armored infantry infiltrated under cover of darkness to positions on the high ground overlooking the town.

At 7 00 A M , just as two platoons from Company C of the 743d Tank Battalion were taking position with the infantry, the SS troops struck An estimated battalion of infantry, supported by 88 and machine-gun fire from at least 15 observed tanks, attacked Company I's roadblock on the east side of Stoumont.

The 3d Battalion held against two infantry attacks. Then five tanks each assaulted both I and L Companies, accompanied by infantry The situation went badly for the defenders Many of the positions, reconnoitered by night, proved to have poor fields of fire and were unable to hold out against the skillful infantry-tank assault. Company I withdrew to the center of the town and held for two hours At 10.00 A M battalion ordered Company L to withdraw under cover of smoke grenades More than 100 men were captured by the Germans as the battalion fell back, and as the doughboys withdrew, the immobile towed tank destroyers were one by one uncovered and surrounded The 743d's tanks put up a good fight but they soon were running short on ammunition, by the time they were relieved by the 740th Tank Battalion in the early afternoon, their supply of shells and bullets was almost exhausted.

The 3d Battalion and its attached troops accounted for a dozen German tanks and three half-tracks during the morning's action—the 823d knocked out a Royal Tiger, the 743d destroyed six Mark IVs and the half-tracks, 90mm antiaircraft guns disabled three Mark Vs, and bazookamen disabled two tanks The trouble was that the price was too high American losses in Stoumont included eight 3-inch tank destroyer guns, two 90mm antiaircraft guns, three 57mm antitank guns, 10 vehicles, and most of the machine guns of the battalion—in short almost all of its heavy armament. Personnel losses were also serious entering the battle with a total rifle company strength of 447—more than 100 men understrength—the 3d Battalion lost 241 men during the action, including 203 missing Ten men returned the next day.

Enemy control of Stoumont created a new menace, for a secondary road led over the ridge from Stoumont to connect up with the Spa–Verviers road—in rear of all Division installations This threat was blocked by the 80 men immediately available from the 3d Battalion, being reorganized by Captain Carleton E. Stewart, the assistant executive and soon to be battalion commander, supported by two 90mm. antiaircraft guns and a self-propelled tank destroyer Meanwhile, the 1st Battalion, which had furnished a company-strength infantry-tank task force to cover the withdrawal from Stoumont, prepared to counterattack, while the 2d Battalion, relieved by the 82d Airborne Division, rejoined the regiment. Early in the afternoon the 1st Battalion was counterattacked unsuccessfully. When the battalion in turn attacked at 3.00 P.M. it knocked out another three enemy tanks but made little headway The attack would have to be resumed the next morning [4]

In Stavelot, still one-third in enemy hands, the enemy attacked from the south at 8:30 with 10 tanks and two companies of infantry. This attack was beaten off by 9.40 and the 1st Battalion began moving slowly through the town. By noon it controlled all of the town but the last houses north of the river in the direction of La Gleize to the west. Early in the afternoon 10 tanks attempted to cross the river on the bridge but were driven back, though they were supported by heavy fire from the far shore. Later the enemy already across the river attacked from the southwest—back along their route of advance—and a similar attack took place at 10:55 P M. But the position held, supported by the 118th Field Artillery, which poured 3,000 shells into a 1,000-yard square area during the day, continuously dousing its guns with water to cool them off.

‡To facilitate control, the 119th Infantry was placed under XVIII Airborne Corps control from 3 30 P M December 19 to 3 00 P M December 20 Two hours before it returned to Division control, the Division itself was transferred from V Corps to XVIII Airborne Corps This headquarters had just been dramatically flown over from England to take charge of part of V Corps' expanding sector

All afternoon assault detachments from Company A of the 105th Engineer Battalion had been trying to get down to the Stavelot bridge to blow it, but had been driven back by intense small-arms and tank fire from the far shore After dark, however, a demolitions team finally succeeded, covered by smoke shells fired on the enemy bank of the river Close reconnaissance had been impossible in the heavy fire around the bridge site and the amount of explosives needed was a matter of conjecture The engineers took no chances and loaded 1,000 pounds of TNT in their truck for the dash to the river bank They proved quite sufficient the tank-heavy striking echelon of the 1st SS now was cut off from its supplies and reserves

On December 18 the Germans almost captured gasoline Depot No. 3, but were forced back when the first stacks of cans were set ablaze The next day they were bluffed out of an even greater prize—Depot No 2.

The 3d Battalion of the 117th partially blocked the enemy armor in the La Gleize–Stoumont area; the 119th was fighting desperately on the 19th to block at Stoumont. There was a gap of sorts in between. The only troops in this area were from Headquarters Company of the 9th Armored Group, which had been given the task of setting up close defense of Depot No 2 on the morning of December 18 At first it had only five half-tracks and three assault guns, plus some troops drafted from the personnel servicing the dump During the night it picked up two 90mm antiaircraft guns and four multiple-mount caliber .50 machine guns On the morning of December 19 a patrol from the company saw an enemy tank outside of Bourgamont About noon the attack came, from the west—two armored cars, two tanks and two self-propelled 88mm guns The enemy column halted 500 yards from the vast fuel dump, in front of a minefield, a caliber .50 machine gun opened up and in a moment or so everyone, on both sides, was blazing away After ten minutes of firing the enemy column withdrew "Jerry must have thought he hit a regiment "

This was his last chance for free gas, at least in the Stavelot–Spa sector Dump No. 3 was completely evacuated by 11 00 A M. on the 19th, and Dump No 2 was cleared out by 11 00 A M of the 22d

Bit by bit, in the next six days, the trapped column was chopped down, while Division Artillery hammered at efforts to relieve it from the outside During the 19th, the 117th's 3d Battalion had moved over to seize the tiny settlements controlling the roads north of La Gleize On the 20th, accompanied by Combat Command B of the 3d Armored Division, it struck to the south. La Gleize resisted strongly with tanks and infantry, but the American armor drove down the road to the river bend opposite Trois Ponts, setting up roadblocks, thus further splitting the enemy column: A tank column attacking Stoumont from the north was stopped on a road bend, its two leading tanks, unable to deploy, destroyed. Now there were two pockets—one from Stoumont to La Gleize, the other on the north side of the river between Trois Ponts and Stavelot

While the armored task force was driving down past La Gleize to the river bend opposite Trois Ponts, the Division had two other major battles on its hands, at Stavelot and Stoumont, and was preparing for a third on the line of road and railroad between the latter town and Malmédy The *status quo* was satisfactory to neither side, and attacks and counterattacks alternated incessantly.

American-held Stavelot, cutting the 1st SS column in two, was the key to the situation. The enemy conceded its loss reluctantly For two more days, on the 20th and 21st, he made desperate attempts, from both within and without the trap, to reestablish control of the town At 4 00 A M. on the 20th the enemy began wading the icy river opposite Company A of the 117th Infantry, in the southwest part of Stavelot The Americans responded with flares and gun fire Sergeant William Pierce swam the river, doused a house with gasoline and set it ablaze Bridge construction material was brought down to the far shore of the stream American riflemen, machine gunners, artillery and mortars slaughtered this attempt, although a small bridgehead was established for about an hour in the first row of houses, under cover of direct tank fire from across the river Almost simultaneously an all-out attack was launched from the southwest, north of the river, by three to five tanks and about a company of German infantry, advancing up the road laying down saturating fire One platoon leader of A Company was chased out of his command post three times by Tiger tanks that waddled up to the doorway, and the Americans were driven back about 100 yards along the axis of the highway Then they rallied and held No sooner had the enemy tanks been stopped than the enemy infantry drove forward again Fighting continued bitter among the buildings strung out along the road until darkness forced a let-up

Both attacks were resumed with the coming of daylight on the 21st, but without success. Well positioned to deal with the river crossing, the 2d Battalion wiped out about 80 of the first 100 men trying to cross the river opposite it on the second day and gleefully referred to the operation as "duck shooting" The fire in the southwest part of Stavelot continued fierce, but the enemy was never able to get into motion Meanwhile artillery smashed enemy tank concentrations southwest of the town

Generally, the Ardennes campaign provided the classic example in the West of Nazi violence and determination in battle. Confident of victory and imbued with doctrinaire fervor, the young fanatics of the SS drove themselves almost as ruthlessly as they had treated the civilians and prisoners whose mutilated bodies lay stiff in the snow near Malmédy.

Nowhere had they displayed more brute courage than at Stavelot. But even such costly measures were not enough. By December 22 the enemy had given up on Stavelot.

On the 20th the 1st Battalion of the 119th attacked again from the west against the tip of the enemy spearhead, coiled in Stoumont. Slowed by hasty antipersonnel and antitank minefields covered by intense tank and 20mm cannon fire from the SS formation in town, the battalion inched forward all day After nightfall it attained a sanitarium on commanding ground west of the town The enemy counterattacked through the night, screaming "Heil Hitler!" and recaptured part of the sanitarium in bitter room-to-room fighting After the third counterattack, at 4 00 A.M., many of our men were without ammunition During the action the battalion lost four tanks, five platoon leaders and about half the men in two companies, B and C, which had on the morning of December 21 only about 60 effectives each.

At noon the battalion attempted to resume the offensive, with an initial mission of cleaning out the enemy-held portion of the sanitarium. But it was no go General Harrison, who had been given command of the 119th Combat Team, Combat Command B and the 740th Tank Battalion in order to clean out the Stoumont pocket, ordered the infantry to hold up At 4 00 P M he reported, "The real picture is that two of these battalions [the 1st and 3d] are in pretty bad shape . . . We can stop them, all right, [but] . . . I don't think the troops we have now, without some improvement, can take the thing [Stoumont]." The American tanks attempting the drive down from the north, lighter armored and gunned than their German adversaries, could not function without exposing themselves to deadly fire

The '740th Tank Battalion put in a corduroy road to enable its tanks to get up the hill as far as the sanitarium. It knocked out a particularly troublesome Mark V in consequence, but the enemy clung to the high ground back of the sanitarium, thus denying us effective tank support.

There was further bad news The commander of the 2d Battalion, which was attempting to flank the Stoumont position to hit from the east, Major Hal D McCown, was captured on reconnaissance, and the battalion withdrew whence it had come He later was to escape with an amazing account of the action.

Discouraging as was the American picture at Stoumont, the enemy there was even more dismayed While the Americans regrouped and a self-propelled 155mm gun took up direct-fire positions to hurl its 95-pound shells into Stoumont, the German commander there was preparing to withdraw the bulk of his troops to La Gleize, according to Major McCown because of the appearance of the 2d Battalion in the German rear.

Thus, when Task Force Harrison's infantry, tank destroyers, and tanks resumed the attack the next afternoon, December 22, with converging blows from west and north, the sanitarium and then Stoumont itself fell. A hospital in town held wounded from all three battalions of the 2d SS Panzer Grenadier Regiment and from two battalions of the 1st SS Panzer Grenadier Regiment. Evidently the enemy had been reinforcing with infantry across the western portions of the Amblève River.

*   *   *

For two days after taking over on December 19, the 120th Infantry, swollen to include the 99th Infantry Battalion, most of the 526th Armored Infantry Battalion, and part of the 291st Engineer Battalion, prepared its positions for the attack northwest through Francorchamps and Spa, which everyone expected Behind its thin-stretched strongpoints and roadblocks, the 110th and 143d Antiaircraft Gun Battalions moved their heavy 90mm cannon into place along the roads and hooked up telephone communications

On the 19th deep patrols to Bellevaux and Geremont penetrated to within sight of the German route across the front of the Division and returned with the encouraging news that the enemy had only scattered roadblocks facing Malmédy The next day, however, the picture was disquieting. A prisoner reported that an attack to the northwest would be made that night by the 1st SS.

The attack was actually made on the morning of December 21. It was preceded by a diversion to the southeast of Malmédy, where a sabotage party more than 120 men strong attempted to break through the 1st Battalion's roadblocks and were driven back in confusion with a loss of 11 vehicles Prisoners wore American uniforms and had American vehicles They said their mission was to get at the American artillery positions which were hammering the stalled German columns. Then the real attack came, headed straight at the focal point of the entire Malmédy defense sector—the point where the road from Spa and Francorchamps winds down the hill to join the Malmédy–Stavelot highway.

At 4.30 two companies of infantry and 10 tanks, led by a captured American Sherman with United States markings, moved up in the misty darkness without being seen, and at 7:00 A M the attack was launched with infantry supported by three tanks. Two 3-inch towed tank destroyer guns and a pair of 57mm antitank guns were overrun, while supporting German machine guns which had attained a nearby height rained fire down upon the defenders A platoon of K Company, which was holding the bridge where the highway crosses the Warche River, finally fell back across the road into a paper factory after about six hours of fighting Some enemy infantry infiltrated through the thin defensive position and one armored vehicle also got through But the battered position finally held through hours of fighting and the enemy was repulsed

Private First Class Francis S. Currey earned the Medal of Honor in this action. Fighting constantly for twelve hours, he dashed in and out of cover, using almost every weapon in the infantryman's armory—the bazooka, the Browning automatic rifle, the heavy machine gun, the caliber .50 machine gun, and antitank grenades, knocking out a tank, forcing the abandonment of three others, killing 15 Germans and, scattering many more Five enemy tanks were knocked out during the action

This effort was the only one the enemy made in great strength to take the Malmédy–Spa road The next day a new attempt was made to drive in on the road to Malmédy from the east, but it was repelled by heavy fire. Thereafter the chief damage in the Malmédy sector was caused by American medium bombers, which burned out the middle of the town on the 23d, 24th, 25th and 27th—despite the frantic efforts of Division to convince headquarters to the rear that friendly forces occupied Malmédy The sense of uneasiness arising from these bombings and strafings were increased by stories in *Stars and Stripes,* the Army newpaper, stating Malmédy was held by the enemy

*   *   *

Enemy resistance in the pockets remained stubborn. The infantry-tank team which had driven south to the outskirts of La Gleize on the 20th was vigorously opposed the next day and finally forced to fall back Meanwhile other 117th troops sliced southeast through the woods from the La Gleize area to take three little towns just west of Stavelot On the 22d, as Stoumont was being taken, the 117th's La Gleize forces sideslipped to the east to outflank the town from the east and southeast This maneuver was answered with an enemy foray to the north of the town, which was broken up by artillery fire The same day Germans working through the woods in the deep salient stretching down toward Trois Ponts overran a roadblock near the river bend opposite that town, capturing an aid station. The next day, however, a platoon of the 105th Engineer Battalion and some Combat Command B tanks reopened the road. Another attack on newly won Ster during the 22d was driven back

By afternoon of the 23d the position of the 1st SS was critical indeed Between Stavelot and Trois Ponts two battalions of the 1st SS Panzer Grenadier Regiment had moved west over forest trails and then crossed the Amblève River from the south, over a reinforced footbridge a kilometer east of Trois Ponts, in an attempt to regain contact with Colonel Peiper's force in La Gleize Their best efforts, however, were being slowly beaten back by the 117th American artillery thundered into La Gleize incessantly The SS tanks were out of gas and running out of ammunition The besieged garrison held off the encircling attacks on the 23d and even mounted a defiant but short-lived counterattack to the north. But the end was approaching. Late in the afternoon, Major McCown—then still a prisoner—testified, Colonel Peiper stated he had been ordered by his commanding general to withdraw [5] At 3·00 in the morning preparations were complete and the enemy foot column, 800 men strong, moved silently south, crossed the river on a small highway bridge immediately under the railroad bridge. "At 0500 we heard the first tank blow up and inside of thirty minutes the entire area formerly occupied by Colonel's Peiper's command was a sea of fiercely burning vehicles, the work of the small detachment he had left behind to complete destruction of all of his equipment " The column continued to move south until daylight and then holed up in the woods while its commander reconnoitered a further advance The column moved again that night, striking the 82d Airborne Division's outposts, and drawing some fire. During one of these episodes Major McCown escaped. Christmas Day he was back with his command

The capture of La Gleize on the 24th was almost an anticlimax An antitank gun held up the 119th elements driving from the west briefly and the fanatical Nazi rear guard attempted to rally at the church in the town By 10.40, however, the town was completely in American hands, and troops were cleaning out the slopes leading down to the river bank Capture of the town yielded 128 prisoners and released 170 Americans who had been held there The yield in matériel was enormous—39 tanks, 70 half-tracks, 33 guns, 30 other vehicles

The only pocket remaining north of the river now was in the wooded

[5]With 150 American prisoners on his hands, Colonel Peiper attempted to arrange an exchange whereby both the prisoners and the German wounded would be left behind, with the Germans to be returned to their own lines later Major McCown, who could of course give no assurance that the plan would be carried out, was in fact the only prisoner taken along He was to be returned to the American lines as soon as the German wounded had been delivered

area northeast of Trois Ponts Here the Germans made final counter-attacks twice on the morning of the 24th without success Twenty-five tanks were reported along the northeast bank of the river near Trois Ponts at noon but escaped across a ford farther east while artillery attempted unsuccessfully to hit them over the mask of the steep hillsides. The next day, December 25, the north bank of the river was completely cleared, as elements of all three regiments of the Division advanced easily to the water's edge To the south, enemy columns retreated southeast from Trois Ponts, harried by artillery and dive-bombers. Three days later the 18th Volksgrenadier Division was identified in the Division's sector.

*   *   *

Thus ended the ill-fated blitz of the 1st SS Panzer Division. By the time the *Leibstandarte Adolf Hitler* withdrew, it had lost two-thirds of its equipment and one-third of its fighting men Its known losses were 92 tanks, 23 truck-drawn artillery pieces, 7 self-propelled guns, 2 self-propelled rocket projectors, 95 half-tracks, several mounting 20mm cannon, one German-operated American tank destroyer; one German-operated American armored car; and 67 miscellaneous trucks At least 2,500 of its combat troops were dead

Actually, of course, the Germans lost a good deal more than the services of their crack panzer division in this eight-day struggle To understand the relation of the 30th's battle to the Ardennes battle as a whole, we must look around and see what was happening elsewhere.

Von Rundstedt attacked on December 16 Three days later, although up-to-date information was still lacking to the Allied commanders, the battle was beginning to assume a distinct form The north shoulder of the assault area, to which the 1st and 2d Infantry Divisions had rushed to help the 99th Division, was being vigorously defended generally along the German border to a point about as far south as Malmédy Here the 12th SS Panzer Division *Hitler-Jugend* was stopped. Its partner in I SS Panzer Corps, 1st SS Panzer Division, had driven 18 miles further west, only to run into Old Hickory. The 82d Airborne Division was pushing eastward toward the Salm River, turning back the advance guards of the *Leibstandarte's* southern column At St Vith, 11 miles south of Malmédy, the 7th Armored Division, cut off from supplies and all but intermittent radio communication with the rear, was waging a stubborn defense against frontal assault by the II SS Panzer Corps, while segments of three other divisions[8] under its control were losing

---

[8]A regiment each from the 28th and 106th Infantry Divisions and a Combat Command from the 9th Armored Division

the battle to keep Fifth Panzer Army's spearheads from slicing into its right rear and isolating it completely. That day enemy armor was reported at Hotton, 31 miles due west of St Vith The road center of Bastogne, farther south, was cut off on the north and being by-passed on the south

Thus the picture was one of German success Yet it must have seemed a strangely distorted one to Von Rundstedt's headquarters The fact was that the main effort had stalled almost completely, and, although vigorous efforts would be made to get it in motion again, it could not be depended upon Meanwhile, time and gasoline were running short. Liège and its vast supply dumps was getting no closer American control of the Malmédy–Stavelot sector blocked the quick route to Liège, and American control of St. Vith prevented use of one of the few major routes thereto. Faced with failure in the north, Von Rundstedt altered his plans, let his main effort sideslip to the left and follow the course of least resistance to the west as he searched for a place where he could turn north against Liège, and finally allowed his attention to be shifted to the "strategic wilderness" of Bastogne Hotton was no closer to the gasoline he had to capture than Malmédy. Bastogne, 27 miles almost due south of Stavelot, pointed up his problem even more sharply.

In moving straight west he was going in an indecisive direction, not toward his objective but increasingly at right angles to it. Worse still, he no longer had a breakthrough The first German attacks launched from the south toward Liège in the next few days, at Grandmesnil, Hotton, and several other road junctions, found the few Americans divisions coming into line almost as dispersed as the 30th had been, and these thrusts often were repelled or contained only by a great will to resist the Ardennes was a classic proving ground of American courage. But they *were* stopped, and, as the panzers regrouped for a new blow, the defenses facing them slowly grew stronger Von Rundstedt needed more troops[7] and more supplies With St. Vith still denied him, he needed Bastogne's roadnet, out of the way as it was, to support even the first attempts to break again into the clear.

December 20, Bastogne was encircled completely, and the 101st Airborne Division began its classic defense there against an angry circle of German tanks and infantry Meanwhile the German armor streamed into the vacuum to the west, by the next day it had reached Samrée, Laroche and Marcourt On the 22d the II Panzer Corps finally wrested St Vith from the 7th Armored Division, which then successfully withdrew back of the 82d Airborne Division The little pocket that the Sixth

---

[7]Especially towed artillery, which had been drastically "streamlined" out of the original plan for the operation

SS Panzer Army held as far west as La Gleize was now merged with the big one of Fifth Panzer Army *Das Reich* (2d SS Panzer Division) and *Hohenstaufen* (9th SS Panzer Division), blocked to the front, could slip south over the newly opened roadnet to join in the battle farther west.

But the tide was turning On the 23d, the 12th SS began falling back from its positions east of Malmédy, the American 4th Armored Division started its drive from the south to relieve Bastogne, and good weather filled the skies with Allied fighter-bombers descending on enemy columns. On Christmas Day the 2d Panzer Division, spearheading Manteuffel's drive, ran into the 2d Armored Division near Celles, five miles from the Meuse. There, almost out of gas, it was brutally mauled by the 30th's old partner. The 4th Armored Division was within a day of relieving the 101st Airborne Division in Bastogne It was apparent that the enemy was unable to advance farther, and that his supply problems were monstrous

Chapter XIV

ST. VITH COUNTEROFFENSIVE

The fighting in the Ardennes in December, 1944, was spectacular and tough. The Battle of the Bulge which followed in the next month was perhaps less spectacular, but it was definitely tougher The terrain was scarcely more rugged on the long haul south to St Vith than it had been along the north bank of the Amblève River But weather and ground conditions, bad enough in December, were at their worst in January, the first heavy snowfalls began after Christmas In December Old Hickory was on the offensive locally, in January it dragged itself forward on the attack over more than a dozen icy miles of hills and valleys For at least one of the regiments of the Division, the St Vith counteroffensive was the most exhausting operation it ever undertook

Two previous offensives had been launched in the Ardennes before the Battle of the Bulge took place In 1940 when the Germans made their main effort through these Belgian hills they had two factors in their favor, the attack was made in May, when terrain and weather conditions were at their best, and the French and Belgians were so convinced that the Ardennes were impassable that they didn't place many troops there The Germans were successful In December 1944, Von Rundstedt's attack had unfavorable natural conditions to face, but was favored by surprise There were few troops on hand to oppose him at first, and the Allies were less prepared than the Germans to cope with the problems of winter warfare in the hills The Germans were successful at first but then lost the battle when the Allies brought in sufficient troops to make a real defense The Battle of the Bulge, in which the Allies attacked to expel the Germans from Belgium, was made with both conditions unfavorable to the attacker Terrain and weather were at their worst The Germans massed in the Ardennes salient were still powerful and well aware of the possibility of an attack Yet this attack did succeed.

* * *

By the end of 1944, the enemy in the Ardennes had passed to the defensive During the last few days of the old year, he had attempted to drive north from Manhay toward Liège but had been stopped A large proportion of his power was engaged in counterattacks to contain the Third Army near Bastogne No longer attacking, Field Marshal Von Rundstedt had a new battle cry "We have succeeded in disrupting the enemy's planned winter offensive " He was quite right The thankless job of compressing the Germans back into the Siegfried Line

had to be completed before the Allies could strike hard into the Reich
The burning question for the Allied Expeditionary Forces was Can the
Ardennes debacle be converted into an asset?

The German bulge in the Ardennes was about the same size and shape
as the Falaise pocket. The comparison was a tempting one However,
the plan which finally emerged called for a general attack all along the
north flank of the bulge, beginning in the west, where British XXX Corps
and the American VII Corps were in line, then rippling eastward to
eventually involve all of the troops facing south along the flank of the
bulge The first objective was the road center of Houffalize, in the
center of the German salient, where Third Army troops advancing
from the south and First Army troops attacking from the north were
to meet St Vith, controlling the main roadnet in and out of the bulge,
would come later

On January 3 the drive for Houffalize from the north began, with the
2d and 3d Armored Divisions leading and the 83d and 84th Infantry
Divisions following up Progress was slow through snow and minefields and soon the order was reversed: the infantry divisions broke the
way and the armor followed Daily the advance inched forward On
January 6 the 117th Infantry and the 105th Engineer Battalion sneaked
bridges across the Amblève River just east of Trois Ponts, and the 112th
Infantry, resurrected from the ruins of the 28th Infantry Division after
Rundstedt's first onslaught, passed through to drive the enemy from
his weak positions along the high ground southwest of Stavelot toward
Grand Halleux and to join up with the attacking 82d Airborne Division
west of the Salm River By January 13—eleven days after it was launched
—the offensive had expanded far enough east along the battle line to
engage the 30th.

*   *   *

Geography was almost everything in the Ardennes The forest-covered hills rose 600 to 700 feet above the stream beds, every mile or two,
dominating the narrow valleys. There were some good roads, but they
were limited in number, mainly following the valleys. When they followed the valleys they could be easily blocked along the valley floor,
particularly in the ready-made fortifications of the Belgian villages.
Above them towered the hills. Whoever had the hills had observation
into the valleys and could bring down artillery fire on the roads Sometimes the hills were so steep that artillery could not cover all of the far
slopes, there were blind spots that even high-angle fire could not reach.
This hurt both sides, but it hurt the defenders less, for they could choose
their ground accordingly and set up where there would be no blind

spots through which the other side could attack When the roads wound up over the mountains they were equally vulnerable because they could be seen and shot at Here, too, the defender had the advantage It takes time and care to adjust artillery fire in rugged country The defender could register in advance and be ready for whatever came along

These were the all-year-around conditions imposed by terrain The bitter winter weather of January made some of these conditions more drastic and imposed new ones of its own The temperature hovered around the freezing point. Snow was deep, sometimes up to the armpits Snow and ice made the main roads slippery and often blocked cross-country or secondary-road vehicle movement completely Supply movements were concentrated on the principal roads, which broke down under the unexpectedly heavy·military traffic This was the big supply problem, the one that hampered the Germans in exploiting their breakthrough in December But there was another supply problem which was equally critical when the counteroffensive began in January This was the problem of the little units, the battalions and companies which needed ammunition and food and a way to get their wounded back to where they could be cared for There was the problem of getting weapons—tanks, tank destroyers, mortars, machine guns—up to where they could be used Some of these weapons were tiring when carried on the backs of infantrymen under even normal circumstances But hand-carrying, even marching itself, was an exhausting business in the hills and snowdrifts The way the hills broke up the ground into little compartments meant that the weapons had to be shifted more often than normally Often vehicles—the jeeps and light trucks that form the backbone of small unit supply—couldn't get forward at all This meant that manpower had to solve the problem. Sometimes weapons couldn't be moved to where they were needed. So infantrymen had to fight machine guns and 88s with what they could carry with them, without the aid they normally received from heavier accompanying weapons.

Perhaps the cruelest aspect of the situation was that the enemy had prepared for a winter campaign in the hills and we had not Winter fighting equipment—special mittens for riflemen, shoepacs, snow capes, heavy jackets—was not available in quantity to the Division until its part in the Ardennes battle was over And so the men improvised The 120th Infantry took salvaged blankets and had civilians sew crude slippers three layers thick which the men could put on at night in their foxholes—if they got the chance The Germans had white camouflage capes The 30th's fighting men made capes for themselves, out of sheets, curtains, mattress covers, anything white the civilians could give them. Tanks and cannons were painted white Crude sleds were constructed to carry back the wounded in place of litters The 105th Medical Battalion used some horse-drawn sleds for evacuation Division Artillery's pilots put skis on their light planes so that the air observation posts could function The engineers made up two-pound prescriptions of TNT so that infantrymen could blast out foxholes that would have required five hours to dig They built corduroy roads out of logs and constantly had to shovel gravel and dirt onto the main roads to keep them even barely passable Vehicles were always slipping off anyway Before a unit moved, the engineers came around to sweep the side roads into the area and cover them with dirt. Weapons were hard to keep in working order Later, after the offensive had started, a Reconnaissance Troop patrol and a German patrol met head on, the weapons of both groups were frozen and couldn't be fired

The 30th Division front broke down into two sectors Both were rugged On the west, the front lines were on the Amblève River until the 112th Infantry pushed them back over the patchwork of mountain forests and clearings By the time the 30th itself attacked, this area was someone else's responsibility On the east, stretching down from the front lines near Malmédy, the main road ran south to St Vith through three rows of hills The first series of elevations was north of the Amblève River, crowned by forests and dominating the open country between them and the American lines. The main road swung east from Malmédy and then twisted south through a deep, narrow pass between two of these hills, which rose 400 feet above the roadbed between them Along the low ground near the Amblève River, there were more clearings around the river towns, and then the ground rose in forests again These hills were slightly higher than those north of the river On the east edge of the Division sector they were linked by a saddle to the final ridge, also forested, which looked down the open slopes toward St Vith. The main road, after crossing the river, mounted the first of these two ridges, followed the high ground across to the second ridge, and then ran downhill to St Vith Between the two ridges was a clearing and the town of Recht

By the end of December, most of the front opposite the Division had been taken over from the 1st SS by the 18th Volksgrenadier Division, which had four battalions stretched from Trois Ponts as far east as the Malmédy–St Vith highway From Trois Ponts over to the junction of the Warche River with the Amblève, southeast of the Malmédy–Stavelot road, was the 294th Volksgrenadier Regiment This was the unit which the 112th Infantry drove off the ridge just south of the Amblève On the east, another German regiment, the 293d, had its main line of resistance along the hills facing Malmédy, with outposts in the little

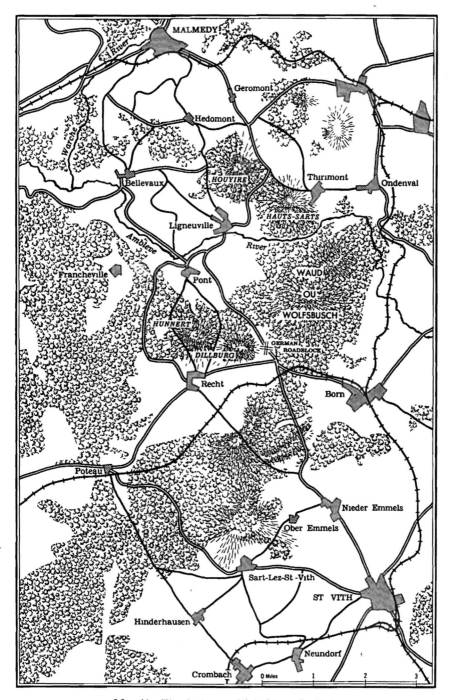

Map 11—The Ardennes Malmédy to St Vith

towns farther north One of these outposts, in the town of Chevefosse north of the Amblève and west of the Warche River, was a source of trouble to the 119th Infantry, which repeatedly tried to eliminate it, because artillery could not be used effectively over the mask of the steep hill. The reserve regiment was at first in Pont, on the Amblève River, but before the 30th jumped off was pulled out, committed and badly battered on the 82d Airborne Division front East of the Malmédy–St Vith highway was the 3d Parachute Division, a crack infantry outfit which was to hold the more open ground just east of the 30th's zone

This, then, was the situation that the Division developed as it sat in place, waiting for the signal to attack. Some of the information came from patrols which waded the icy waters of the Amblève River. Some came from the feints which a company of the 120th and a company of the 99th Infantry Battalion made on January 3, when the main assault was being launched far to the west The ground was difficult and the physical problem of moving ahead was full of quirks There was nothing to do but try to anticipate the difficulties and hope for the best If the terrain problem could be solved, the advance might be rapid Unsuccessful attempts were made to have the 1st Division attack alongside the 30th, to protect the left flank Finally, the order for Old Hickory to attack was received

*   *   *

The 30th jumped off at 6.00 A M on the 13th, with the initial task of reducing the enemy's main line of resistance along a six-kilometer front north of the Amblève River. The operation soon developed into a two-phased problem · that of maneuvering troops and weapons through the snow to positions from which they could reduce the weak but well-sited defenses of the 293d Volksgrenadier Regiment to the south, and that of securing the left flank uncovered as the Division moved south

The first phase of the problem was solved in two day's trudging and fighting. None of it was easy, mainly because of the terrain and the snow. These were even more consistently dangerous enemies than the cold, discouraged, louse-ridden Volksgrenadiers manning the enemy's machine guns and observation posts. During the first morning, a tank and then a wrecker were knocked out, blocking the main route of the right column, and several hours were consumed rerouting the tanks over an alternate route to support the renewal of the infantry assault Mines were everywhere, many of them evidently laid in December by the 1st SS Panzer Division's flank guards before the snows set in. These half-iced-in explosives were proof against mine detectors and often were detonated only after many vehicles had passed over them and worn down the protecting coat of ice. During the first three days of the attack 15 American tanks were disabled by mines. The town of Hedomont, on the open ridge-top commanding the center of the attack zone, was vigorously defended throughout January 13, despite two outflanking attempts by the attacking 3d Battalion, 119th Infantry. A company of infantry and a platoon of tanks from the regimental reserve advanced along a forest trail to the east to intervene but didn't arrive until after dark Hedomont, an initial objective, did not fall until a renewal of the attack at 11:30 P M., preceded by a heavy artillery preparation, induced the enemy to withdraw.

By nightfall of the first day, however, the infantry, tanks and tank destroyers of the 2d Battalion, 119th Infantry, were overlooking the Amblève River from the high ground back of Bellevaux, on the right flank of the attack. That night a patrol made its way down to the unde- fended town of Thioux, on the river bank. The next morning the bat- talion advanced in strength to the river bank, turned east along the valley to rout the enemy from Bellevaux and then crossed the river at Planche, where an eight-foot gap had been blown in the bridge. Oppo- sition was mainly from artillery, mortar and Nebelwerfers The in- fantry battalion command posts of the enemy were being overrun and his will to fight had declined considerably.

Somewhat similar opposition was encountered by two fresh battalions which joined the battle on January 14. The 1st Battalion of the 119th passed through the 3d Battalion at Hedomont to attack south at 7.00 A.M Some machine-gun and mortar fire were received as the battalion advanced over the brow of the hill, but it then continued to sweep slowly down to the river against light opposition. The 2d Battalion of the 117th Infantry, leading a column of battalions as its regiment joined the assault, moved through positions on Houyire Hill seized the previ- ous day by the 120th Infantry and closed in on the riverside town of Ligneuville. Here a jumble of disorganized troops was encountered and mopped up—rear echeloners of the 293d Regiment, and two re- serve companies of the 3d Parachute Division. The bridge over the Amblève River had been prepared for demolition but was not blown in time. Late in the afternoon elements of the battalion rushed across, by 6 35 P M two companies held a 300-yard-wide corridor on the south bank The 293d Volksgrenadier Regiment was, for all practical purposes, finished as a fighting organization With its other two regi- ments committed and decimated further west, the 18th Volksgrenadier Division itself was well nigh through as a factor to be seriously reckoned with Stage One of the attack was complete.

While its sister regiments were plowing south over the hills to the
Amblève River, the 120th Combat Team was locked in a bitter three-
day struggle for Thirimont, a ridge town which controlled the eastward entrance into the flank of the attack. Thirimont was the responsibility of paratroopers, eighteen to twenty-five years old and full of fire,
reckoned the best infantry in the German Army. Most of the 1st Battalion, 9th Parachute Regiment, was in the town, with another company
dug in atop Hauts-Sarts Hill, which commanded both Thirimont and
the Malmédy–St Vith highway. Besides, the paratroopers had plenty
of artillery support

The 120th attacked with two battalions abreast at 8:00 A.M on
January 13. The 3d Battalion, on the west, successfully drove through
the little towns of Geromont and Baugnez and on up to positions on
Houyire Hill, although the only route available for accompanying tanks
and tank destroyers proved impassable This was in the sector of the
293d Volksgrenadiers The 2d Battalion attacked on the left for Thirimont. The instructions were to keep moving as fast as possible. E and
F Companies were stopped in the open by heavy artillery and mortar
fire; late in the morning, G Company, which had kept on going, found
itself alone in the south part of the town with two by-passed enemy
strongpoints behind it

The enemy reaction was not long in coming. At 11:45 the Germans
still south of Thirimont struck G Company with about 100 men but
were driven back. At noon the regimental commander alerted his reserve battalion, the 1st, to be ready to attack for Thirimont, but the
attempt to secure the foothold in the town with the 2d Battalion continued through the afternoon. It was no go. The road from the north
into town was saturated with enemy artillery fire and reinforcement
that way was impossible. Attempts to work another company into town
from the west also proved fruitless. Meanwhile Company G was being
whittled down by fire in the town. At 6:00 P.M. the regimental commander ordered G to withdraw, because, even if successful, the 2d Battalion's new attack could not reach the town before 8:00 P.M. Just as
the company was preparing to infiltrate back, it was struck again by a
company of infantry and a company of tanks attacking from the east.
Total casualties for G Company that day, including attached machine
gunners from H Company, were approximately 100

Thirimont figured heavily in Division and Corps plans, and the
pressure was on General Hobbs attempted to have G Company ordered back into town but the company was out of communication.
Instead, the 1st Battalion, which had moved up to positions near Baugnez and Odimont, attacked a half hour after midnight. For four hours

the battalion moved slowly south along the main highway without contact, swinging east just north of the pass between Houyire and Hauts-Sarts Hills. The battalion's leading riflemen captured the ten western-most houses in Thirimont but were held up by strong small-arms and artillery fire, as were patrols which attempted to outflank the mutually supporting houses in the east part of town. Everything had to be hand-carried; the radios froze and communications depended on runners stumbling through the drifted snow During the night of the 13th-14th the 3d Battalion had attempted to cross a combat patrol from Houyire Hill to Hauts-Sarts Hill but had been driven back by strong fire. During the morning of the 14th the battalion attacked over the same route, up and down ground that rose 45 feet in every 100 yards of forward progress, but was stopped 500 yards short of its objective, with the enemy still looking down its throat

Meanwhile the 1st Battalion was being counterattacked vigorously The first thrust, by a tank and some 30 paratroopers early in the after-noon, was easily knocked back by artillery fire. The next attack, at dusk, was a heavyweight—a fresh battalion of paratroopers plus an assault gun battalion, which swept in in waves. American howitzers were soon firing at maximum rate on the area east of Thirimont, in-flicting heavy casualties, but the enemy troops kept on coming to within 50 yards of the American positions before they were stopped by the intensity of the fire being placed on them. Four enemy assault guns were destroyed in this action—two by bazookas, one by a minefield and one by artillery fire. Two hours later the enemy gathered enough strength to renew the assault with about two companies of infantry and five assault guns, but the attack was quickly spotted and neutralized by a torrent of artillery fire.

January 15, the next day, provided the climax of the battle Both sides planned early attacks, the German one jumped off first, at 6 00 A.M, with a mixed battalion representing all three regiments of the 3d Parachute Division and the 348th Assault Gun Battalion

Only driblets of American tank destroyers and tanks had been avail able for close-in work during the previous two days because of mine-fields and uncrossable terrain, one platoon of the 743d Tank Battalion, for example, had all of its tanks out of action at one time or another during the 14th By the morning of the 15th, however, the problems of getting tanks and self-propelled tank destroyers up into position to cope with the enemy strongpoints and assault guns was at least partially solved, and after absorbing the enemy assault the 1st Battalion and its attachments pressed slowly forward through the town while enemy ar-tillery fire rained in about them.

The unusual determination and fire power employed by the enemy in this action made it one of the fiercest in the Division's experience, and only by a high degree of teamwork were the Germans slowly driven out of their fortified houses. B Company of the 823d Tank Destroyer Battalion knocked out three and possibly four of the German assault guns, B Company of the 743d Tank Battalion destroyed two others and artillery fire probably knocked out another Then the tanks and tank destroyers went to work with the infantry on the Germans holed up in the houses By 1·30 P M. the town was completely cleared Most of the 11,000 rounds fired by Division Artillery on the 15th were directed at targets in the Thirimont area

The regiment's 3d Battalion also attacked early to clean out the company-strength garrison on Hauts-Sarts Hill which was delivering such deadly flanking fire into the 1st Battalion. But the battalion was too tired and hurt by the previous day's fighting to do much good in the heavy snow and steep terrain, against a well entrenched, dominantly sited enemy. K Company, which had a "foxhole strength" of only 63, gained its first objective but lost 14 dead and wounded trying to cross an open field farther on It was forced to pull back to cover L Company was first pinned down by machine-gun fire 1,000 yards away from its initial objective, and was able to reach that first goal mainly because of the heroism of Technical Sergeant Monte W Keener, killed while firing a Browning automatic rifle after he had knocked out two machine-gun nests with a bazooka, capturing 14 men Then Company L, too, was stalled.

This necessitated a change in plans The 2d Battalion, which was marching south to attack a hill south of the river, was recalled at 4 00 P M from its march column 500 yards from Ligneuville and instead ordered to join the 3d Battalion's attack, on the latter's right. At almost the same time that the 2d Battalion entered the fight, light tanks of the 743d finally succeeded in their all day struggle to get up the steep hill through the snow. Faced with this new strength, the enemy position quickly fell After this the Division left flank north of the Amblève was quiet And the 1st Division, which had attacked before dawn on the 15th, was moving slowly down to cover it.

The fight for Thirimont and for control of the vital highway to the south was won, but the cost had been high Total battle casualties for the 120th were 450 men. At dusk on the 15th the 3d Battalion had a fighting strength of only 150 men—less than that of a single full-strength company—in its three rifle companies The 2d Battalion, which had taken the brunt of the first day's action was only slightly better off G Company had only 53 men left The 1st Battalion, numerically

stronger, had just finished the toughest fight of its career and was critically tired. Everyone was cold, wet, miserable

South of the Ambléve River the battle was entering a new stage as
the 120th grappled with the paratroopers near Thirimont. With his
division in line virtually knocked out, the enemy no longer had hopes
of reestablishing a continuous line, but he had to hold open the St Vith
escape gap a few days longer For this purpose, he first used heavy artillery fire on the bridges and then scraps of infantry and armor locally
available Resistance took the form of roadblocks and counterattacks.

The first enemy countermeasures to the crossings of the Ambléve
River on January 14 were felt that night The 2d Battalion of the 119th
Infantry, advancing south toward Beaumont, found that town bitterly
defended by scrapings of infantry from the 294th Volksgrenadier Regiment and a few assault guns—evidently afraid that the attack would
branch out to the southwest. The main show, however, took place at
the 117th's main road crossing at Ligneuville.

Scarcely had the 2d Battalion taken up positions in the dark on the
south bank of the river when about a battalion of infantry and six tanks
struck from both east and west, headed by a 15-man combat patrol
which infiltrated to the bridge site, intent on destroying it. This patrol
was rounded up in the nick of time Prompt massed artillery fire broke
up the attack, though some of it had to be placed on the observer's own
position Staff Sergeant Rondeau of the 118th Field Artillery Battalion,
the man who directed the fire, had crossed with the 2d Battalion and
set up in a house about 50 yards from the bridge. During the counterattack the enemy occupied most of the first floor of the house, while
the forward observer party fled to the cellar. Rondeau called for fire,
whispering through a light infantry radio so that the enemy upstairs
could not hear him. The group then rushed upstairs and drove the
enemy out of the house before mounting to the second floor to recover
the artillery radio.

On January 15 the Division continued the motion southward, delayed mainly by snow, mines and temporary enemy positions The
119th Infantry's 1st Battalion circled around through the 117th's
Ligneuville bridgehead, being expanded uphill against negligible opposition, and captured the riverside town of Pont without major difficulty, while the 2d Battalion, farther west, drove through a roadblock
to the town of Francheville, with American tanks spraying fire as they
moved down the road, and ousted an enemy position about 1,000
yards farther south after a strong artillery preparation. The 1st Battalion swung southwest after taking Pont and headed down the paved

road toward Recht. The enemy artillery was still very much in the picture, hammering the forward· troops and the Ligneuville river crossing.

By the next day the enemy was better organized. His key position was in the defile just north of where the main Malmédy–St. Vith highway joined an eastward road connecting Recht with the good-sized town of Born, just east of the forested ridge. Possession of this area around the road junction was important, not only to block the route south to St Vith but to prevent our branching out eastward into the rear of the 3d Parachute Division's positions. This position, organized into two road-blocks about 500 yards apart, was set up with a battle group from the German 326th Infantry Division and about five assault guns In addition the two hilltops just west of the defile were defended with remnants of the 18th Volksgrenadier Division, and a couple of infantry roadblocks covered the paved road leading from Pont to Recht

Part of this position was reduced on the 16th. The 119th Infantry, working down the Pont–Recht road past a roadblock of 38 felled trees, made contact with the westernmost enemy positions and induced them to withdraw during the night. The 2d Battalion of the 117th Infantry finally took the more westerly of the two hills between the two roads, Hunnert Hill, by nightfall. The 3d Battalion of the 119th, attached to the 117th, swung far over to the eastern portions of the latter's sector to seize the towering 590-meter heights of Wolfsbusch, on the east of the Malmédy–St. Vith highway, and patrolled halfway down the hill toward the main enemy roadblocks before running into a fire fight with enemy patrols. The enemy's central positions covering the highway, however, held out. The positions on Dillburg Hill, overlooking the highway from the west, were taken in rear by the 1st Battalion, 117th Infantry's attack on the morning of the 17th, but attempts to expel the well knit infantry-tank team along the highway were unsuccessful.

On the 18th, the 120th Infantry, which had moved elements south of the river after a short rest in position following the gruelling fight for Thirimont, came back into the attack. The previous afternoon a 120th patrol had plodded south over the Wolfsbusch hill past the roadblock position, noting some enemy infantry moving in to reinforce it from the east and running into a short fire fight with an enemy patrol. On the following morning the regiment attacked south with the 1st and 3d Battalions, over the snow-cluttered trails its patrol had followed, reaching its objective southeast of the vital road junction by early after- - noon. The advance was almost entirely an exercise in movement under difficult conditions; two enemy patrols were gobbled up en route without disclosing the presence of the battalion and not until late afternoon did the enemy react, with a sudden counterattack from the south with six tanks and about 100 infantry. Artillery fire drove off the infantry, but the armored vehicles drove straight up the road into the middle of the 120th's lines before two tanks and a half-track were knocked out by bazooka fire. The confusion during the counterattack was increased as three enemy assault guns which had been at the crossroads roadblock fled south through the same area while the counterattack was still in progress.

Meanwhile the 117th was closing in on the roadblock farther north, with its tanks and tank destroyers channelized and held back by enemy assault gun fire and its infantrymen hampered in attempting to work bazooka teams forward. The chief accomplishment of the day was that of K Company, of the 119th, still under 117th control, which advanced through the woods down the hill on the east of the block and placed a minefield across the road south of the first roadblock, thus cutting off the route of escape of the assault guns there Three enemy assault guns, preceded by infantry to lift the mines, attempted to withdraw through this block, but K Company drove the enemy infantrymen back with rifle fire and the assault guns returned to their old positions Meanwhile supply for the two advance battalions of the 120th had to take place over the trails of the Wolfsbusch Hill.

Sleet and snow flurries slowed the advance on the following two days, but the enemy resistance deteriorated noticeably. On the night of the 18th-19th, most of the enemy garrison in shell-torn Recht pulled back, so that it was quickly taken the next morning by the 117th The last remnants of the twin roadblocks on the main road were finally reduced on the same day by the 117th Infantry, while the 120th expanded its positions on the last ridge before St. Vith The next day the 120th pushed farther to capture the little town of Nieder Emmelser Heide, at the south edge of woods along the main road to St. Vith, chasing a company of enemy infantry, three assault guns and a battery of horse-drawn artillery out into the open for the artillery to work over. St. Vith, only three and one-half miles away, was in sight.

By now the general American offensive further west was converging on the 30th's zone. New units opposing the Division were frequently units backing away from attacks from the northwest. Old Hickory had already taken over control of the 517th Parachute Battalion, which worked through the town of Poteau, southeast of Recht, and the 119th and 117th both advanced to positions on the ridge beside the 120th, slowed by snow, minefields, and occasional flurries of artillery and infantry fire Meanwhile the artillery was moving south to take up positions behind the newly won St Vith ridge.

To many of the participants in the battle, it seemed strange that St. Vith, already within light artillery range, still held much value for the retreating Germans Contact had been made between First and Third Armies near Houffalize on January 16 and progress in flattening the Bulge thereafter had been steady But the enemy was still concerned enough about St Vith to bring in a battalion of the 264th Infantry Division, from outside the Bulge, to counterattack the 30th's drive This attack, which was made on the morning of January 21, was beautifully planned, forming up in the woods east of the Division zone just north of St Vith, then moving up by a circuitous route so as to strike our positions in the flank along the axis of a firebreak through the woods Hidden by the woods, the attack was not disclosed until the enemy was practically in the positions of the 1st and 3d Battalions, 120th Infantry. A sharp hour-long fire fight finally drove back the enemy with over 50 per cent casualties, the fighting was too close in to use American artillery, so the infantry concentrated on separating the enemy infantry from the three assault guns supporting them while three American tanks and some infantry outflanked the attack, knocking out one of the assault guns. This was the last counterattack the enemy mounted during the operation.

The end for St. Vith was already in sight On January 20 the 7th Armored Division had passed through the 1st Division, which had made a gap for it down to the line of the Amblève River on the 30th Division's left flank, and was pressing south past Born. On the 22d both divisions continued to move south, and in the Old Hickory zone the enemy opposition showed increasing signs of chaos. Attacking into Sart-les-St -Vith with a very brief artillery preparation, the 117th swept into town so fast that one group of enemy soldiers were captured at the breakfast table. The 119th had similar success with Hinderhausen, while the 120th killed or captured most of the 250 German defenders in seizing Ober Emmels and then turning east to take Nieder Emmels The only hitch came in the latter town when friendly armor from the adjacent zone came into town without warning while the 120th was attacking. The enemy had the troops, mainly units withdrawing in the path of American attacks west of the 30th; the enemy still had assault guns and antitank guns, but organization was fast disintegrating

The same day the reason for the enemy's persistence in holding on to St Vith became apparent. The east-west roads through that ruined city provided Division Artillery's observers with the juiciest targets many of them had ever seen—roads packed with enemy troops of all types struggling eastward, with traffic snarled at several points The artillery vied with the Ninth Air Force's P-47s in slashing at these columns

On January 23, as 7th Armored Division tanks were triumphantly re-entering St. Vith, from which they had been ordered to retreat a month previously, the 30th continued its attack south, finally coming to a halt the following day along a river line about two miles south of St. Vith. There were still plenty of enemy groups in the vicinity, including ' armor, but their disorganization allowed of only sporadic and general-ly ineffectual resistance Enemy order of battle was of the laundry-list variety—a weird collection of lost, retreating segments.

Thus ended the active phase of the battle. Further pressure from the north was no longer necessary, Third Army's VIII Corps, advancing from the southwest, was, one by one, pinching out the First Army units which had participated in the January offensive to clean out the Bulge. The enemy's feverish struggle to pull back into the comparative safety of the Siegfried Line lost him 1,000 men a day in prisoners alone, and the massive Russian offensive toward Berlin had finally begun.

By midnight of January 27 VIII Corps troops had advanced all the way across the Division's front, cutting it off from direct contact with the enemy for the first time since the battle of the Ardennes began, and the troops moved back to an assembly area near Lierneux, 15 miles west of St. Vith The Division was badly in need of rest and warming up. Battle casualties had cost Old Hickory 1,390 men in infantry alone —the best part of three of its nine rifle battalions. Trench foot and frost-bite, which can be held down but not eliminated when men must fight and move and live in the open day after day, caused 463 more casual-ties—most of another infantry battalion The doughboys had been hardest hit by weather as well as bullets, despite the efforts of the regi-mental commanders to provide warm rooms where the men not fight-ing could be defrosted. The main reason why many line-company sol-diers kept fighting was to get themselves houses within which to bed down. But almost all of the Division had shared in the rigors of winter warfare—supply men wrestling their trucks over icy roads, engineers, signal construction men, artillery and antiaircraft cannoneers. The tank-ers grimly called their weapons "armored Frigidaires"; the tank de-stroyers might have said the same thing.

Part Five

THE BATTLE OF GERMANY

Chapter XV

ROER OFFENSIVE

The Battle of the Ardennes had been won There remained only to collect the fruits of victory Huddled back in its assembly area around Liernieux, attempting to find warmth and relaxation while it could, in the drafty buildings of villages shattered by Von Rundstedt's drive, the Division wondered about the future. The great northern drive to the Rhine, awaited so eagerly in the waning days of November, seemed remote indeed—certainly postponed, perhaps even abandoned Current plans called for Old Hickory to crack the Siegfried Line all over again, this time in the beetling forest-covered hills of the Eifel to the east, as soon as the 82d Airborne Division had worked its tortuous way through the snow-covered approaches to the first main line of log bunkers and obstacles.

Already reconnaissance parties were fighting their way through the long lines of trucks that clogged the twisting, treacherous and over-burdened roads to the front. The plan had been issued. The "Old Man" had gone forward to see General Gavin of the 82d—when on February 2 the reprieve came through. General Hobbs was to report to General McLain of XIX Corps without delay The 30th was to return to the "family"—to Ninth Army and XIX Corps The battle of the Cologne Plain, which the enemy had fought so desperately to avert, was soon to begin. And the 30th would play its part in it.

That night, lights blazing as they moved through what were now rear areas, the Division's trucks rolled northward to an assembly area just past Aachen. It was good to be back in the flatlands, to see the slag piles and neat miners' brick houses of the Dutch borderland, the even piles of ammunition which stretched for miles along almost every road.

The day after the Division arrived in its old stamping grounds in Germany, the Division command post, then set up in a ravaged apartment house in Aachen, received the plan for the assault to the Rhine The maneuver was direct and forceful. Ninth Army would remain under 21st Army Group, so that one commander, Field Marshal Montgomery, could control all of the drive toward the industrial Ruhr The Canadian First Army was to cross the Maas near its confluence with the Rhine and attack south, with the Rhine protecting its left flank Ninth Army, making the main effort, was to attack east across the Roer in the general direction of Cologne and then wheel northward along the west bank of the little Erft River, driving up toward the Canadians. British Second Army, sitting on the west bank of the Maas between the two striking arms of the pincers, was to wait for the time being, prepared to thrust across the river as the forces opposite it were pocketed The drive had two objectives to swallow up the German garrisons in the northern part of their western battle line, and to clean out to the Rhine opposite the rich Ruhr valley. Meanwhile on the south, U. S. First Army would attack alongside the Ninth, protecting the latter's flank against counterattack, and making the secondary drive toward Cologne

When the operation was first planned in late November, the German High Command had powerful armored and infantry reserves to throw into play behind the thin line of troops along the Roer. Now they were almost all gone—either still clutched in the painful mountain withdrawal east of the Ardennes, or like Sepp Dietrich's Sixth SS Panzer Army, consigned, still bleeding and bruised, to the shambles of the Eastern front. In this operation pressure would be maintained everywhere, so that the familiar German tactic of rushing waning mobile reserves from one critical point to another in succession would be voided by the sheer weight of the offensive. There would be too many fires to put out at once.

The Division had a difficult task. It faced the worst stretch of waterline along the entire front, between the two major highway crossings at Julich and Duren. In November the area had been considered unsuitable for crossing at all, and it had been planned to make only a feint there, with the Division actually crossing through Julich after a bridgehead had been established there. Now, to protect the flanks of the critical crossings on both sides of it, the Division was ordered to cross its forbidding stretch of river frontage and then swing north to take Steinstrass, which sat at the north end of a narrow corridor through the Hambach Forest guarding the main road from Cologne west toward Julich—the road down which a counterattack would most likely come

The operation was planned originally for February 10, three days after the Division had taken over control of 113th Cavalry Group, which was patrolling its part of the river front, and had moved the assault troops into forward assembly areas. It had been hoped that First Army troops, pushing in toward the great dams of the upper Roer, would be able to reach and control them by that date, but progress there was slow. Then, at midnight of February 8, the enemy blew the huge earthen Schwammenauel Dam's control sluices. This meant that the tons of water contained by the dam would empty out over a period of days. There would be no flash flood, as would follow destruction of the dam itself, but the lower Roer would be flooded slowly and effectively until the excess could drain off.

In the sixteen hours between 5:00 A.M. and 9:00 P.M. the river rose 13 inches in the division sector and was beginning to overflow its banks At 4:57 P.M on the 9th the operation was called off for the next day; twenty-four hours later, as the flood waters rose, it was called off indefinitely. The Canadians had jumped off on schedule on the 9th The Americans poised along the Roer would have to wait for days for the river to subside before the engineers could give the go signal

On the 13th the stream reached its peak stage of flooding, swelling to resemble a long lake and overrunning the canals and drainage ditches on either side to a width at some places of more than 600 yards The water receded slowly thereafter, leaving the approaches to the crossing sites boggy and the current still abnormally swift—more than six miles per hour in places

*   *   *

However unpleasant was this last fortnight of enforced delay and as much as it increased the engineer problem, the work done in this period contributed greatly to the speed with which the assault finally was made. There had been little time for reconnaissance and preparation before the original target date. It was known that the enemy's garrison on the far shore was weak, but his detailed dispositions were not known. During the waiting period commanders of all types of fighting units studied the crossing area with air photographs and from the artillery's Cub planes. Observations posts noted signs of the arrival of new enemy troops on the far shore, correctly diagnosed as a side-slipping of the enemy northward as the German 12th Infantry Division moved into line near Duren. Patrols crossing in the zone of the southern assault regiment, the 120th, had discovered a bridge site but were skeptical about the use of assault boats anywhere in the regimental sector, so swift was the current even then. In the northern sector, that of the 119th, the first patrols were unable to ford at the two appointed places because of the depth and the swiftness of the river. On the night of the 8th, however, patrols crossed successfully in both sectors, making contact with the German outposts.

Practically every night after the operation was postponed patrols moved down to the bogs—testing proposed crossing sites, checking for minefields and other danger spots on the far shore, seeking out the enemy outpost system. To be a member of these patrols proved danger- ous more than once, even when movement was executed so carefully that the enemy was unaware of their presence. Three engineers were swept downstream and drowned one night when their pneumatic boat capsized On another occasion three men were left struggling in the water when their boat was swept over by the current. Two were rescued after over an hour's work in the dark, but the third finally vanished downstream.

One Reconnaissance Troop patrol made the vital discovery that the Muhlenteich drainage ditch on the far side of the river was too deep and swift to be forded This information, obtained after two successive night's forays only forty-eight hours before the attack started, proved of prime importance in the operation itself Duckboard footbridges were built for the infantry to cross the canal. If they had not been available, the infantry crowded on the flat spit of land between the two waterways might have been smashed by artillery before crossing expedients could be brought up

The infantrymen who were to make the assault crossing practiced many times on the Inde River the techniques they would use on the Roer. Engineers not busy with reconnaissance and assault-boat practice constructed duckboard footbridges and carefully checked their equipment, while still other engineers worked on the unending process of repairing roads never built for heavy military traffic

If the two-week postponement gave the assault troops time to worry, it was also an uneasy fortnight for Von Rundstedt's headquarters German armies were in retreat all through the mountainous lower two-thirds of the Western Front The Canadian drive in the north had forced commitment of most of the skimpy armored reserves available to the German forces in the West The American armies along the Roer were probably making final preparations for an attack through the Cologne Plain, where the terrain was most suitable for armored thrusts once the river barrier was breached and where the stakes—Cologne itself and the Ruhr valley—were highest.

Elaborate precautions were therefore taken to mask the extent of the Ninth Army build-up north of Aachen, to keep the enemy from knowing that the 30th and the other divisions drawn to the Ardennes during the winter had returned. When the 30th left the Ardennes, shoulder patches and unit vehicular markings were removed or covered up on the Division's own initiative, for the first time on the Continent These precautions anticipated Ninth Army instructions to the same effect, received in the new area near Aachen New code names for road signs and telephone exchanges were set up. Camouflage was emphasized. The radios of the Division were silent, as was artillery until the last possible moment Troop movements were made at night.

One slip-up in the "blackout" scheme occurred when the 119th Infantry was assigned billets in Kohlscheid, a German border town which it had occupied previously, and where it was greeted enthusiastically despite its efforts to remain incognito The regiment's stay there was temporary, however, and no information seems to have leaked farther.

Thus, as it appeared after the attack, the German high command could guess at but did not know the plans. Daily the German radio's broadcasts in English bleated knowingly about the coming attack opposite Aachen Axis Sal, according to one account that made the rounds, talked about the 30th's return to the Aachen area Undoubtedly, some of the signs of renewed American activity back of the Roer were revealed to German aerial reconnaissance But if German information about the attack was any more specific, the German troops on line didn't hear of it.

German air was ominously active during the waiting period, with attacks on February 11, another by four or five planes on the night of the 14th and one by 10 to 12 planes the night of the 21st The biggest display of German planes, however, came on the 22d, the day before the assault. Six to eight separate attacks were made in the 30th's zone and similar actions took place along the entire three-corps Roer front Notable here was the prevalence, for the first time, of jet-propelled planes The 531st Antiaircraft Automatic Weapons Battalion claimed one plane totally destroyed and six planes damaged during this period.

*   *   *

The last great battle of the winter campaign, the Roer crossing, finally began during the pre-dawn hours of February 23 It was long overdue For almost three months American sentries had glared sourly and gloomily across the river from their outposts on the west bank. The attack had been postponed many times and it sometimes looked as though they would sit there forever Newly returned from the vicious fighting of the Ardennes, many of the assault troops worried about how successful their attack over that long-standing barrier, the Roer, would be. Weeks later, when a newspaper correspondent tried to coax some words of exultation out of some 30th infantrymen who had just assaulted across the Rhine, he found they preferred to talk about the Roer The Rhine battle was big and complicated and spectacular But the success of the Roer assault gave men proof that the long grinding winter battle was over, and hope that the end of the war, perhaps, was in sight.

First notice the enemy had of the attack came at 2:45 o'clock on the morning of the 23d, when all the cannoneers over a 25-mile stretch of river front, from south of Düren to north of Linnich, began a pounding that would last the forty-five minutes to H-hour. That monster barrage was the biggest ever fired on the Western Front in World War II On the 30th Division front alone, covering 8,000 yards of enemy front line, Division Artillery was reinforced by the three 18-piece battalions of 2d Armored Division's self-propelled artillery as well as Corps and Army battalions for a total of 246 tubes in action, or 1 for every 32 yards of front, in addition to 36 4.2 inch chemical mortars, firing high-explosive shells. The 823d Tank Destroyer Battalion's 36 guns also participated in the preparation.

Most of the Germans who remember that massing of artillery power didn't see it, for they took to the cellars as fast as possible From the American side of the river it was an almost unparalleled display—the glare of shell bursts to the east as far as the eye could see to right and left across that flat countryside, while the belch of the cannons to the rear broke windows and shook great slabs of plaster loose.

Even before the first volleys had whistled out, however, the real attack had begun, as the engineers hand-carried their heavy footbridges and boats, sometimes as far as 700 yards, down to the water's edge, setting the stage for the assault. At 1:30 A.M. 25 infantrymen were ferried across in the 119th sector to provide some protection for the men installing the footbridge. By 2 15 a group of engineers had crossed and was dragging through the water the assembled sections of duckboard which were to serve as footbridges over the Muhlenteich Canal. At 2.45, as the artillery crashed into the towns to the east, the first wave of 119th troops crossed in assault boats with almost complete success. One boat was swept downstream and grounded on a sandy spur in the river, but the occupants later were rescued. Construction of the 119th's footbridge started at 2:15 A.M. and progressed rapidly, although the original plan for placing the bridge in position had to be abandoned and the bridge reassembled in the water. Two men working in an assault boat were dumped in the river but they swam ashore and continued work. By 3:10 the bridge itself was in. Twenty minutes later the last job, that of placing luminous buttons along the guide posts on the bridge, was complete and the doughboys began to cross The first westbound crossing, by a consignment of 26 prisoners, was made at 4:00 o'clock. All of the 1st Battalion crossed in assault boats; subsequent battalions used the bridge.

A scattering of light artillery fire back from the western approaches to the crossing area was the only enemy reaction to the operation, as the leading riflemen of the 119th's 1st Battalion jogged over the Muhlenteich Canal duckboard bridges and headed for the little town of Selgersdorf, the regiment's first objective They entered the town by 3 45 and three-quarters of an hour later declared it clear. There had been some shooting in its darkened streets but not much, considering the fact that a reinforced enemy company was on hand there. So heavy had been

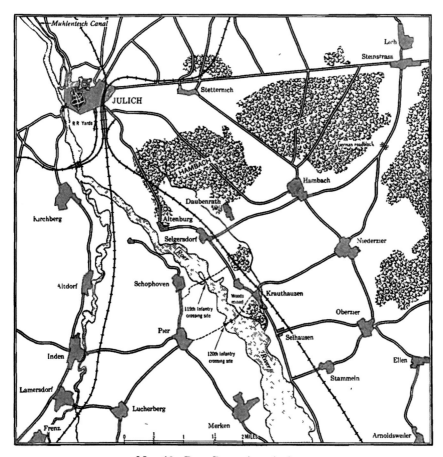

Map 12—Roer River Assault Area

the artillery fire and so rapid the advance of the infantry that most of the garrison had to be dragged out of cellars.

The enemy company in Altenburg, C Company's objective, was less passive, shooting machine guns from the edge of town and getting supporting fires from the woods to the East. Soon after dawn, however, the town was cleared

Down at the 120th's crossing sites, meanwhile, the battle with the river was not going well, and only the fact that several alternate schemes for crossing had been worked out in advance saved the regiment from stalling Two ferry sites and one footbridge site had been planned None of them worked At one of the ferry sites the initial attempt to cross an engineer party with a guide rope was unsuccessful. The second try upstream a short distance had better luck, and the rope, buoyed by wax-sealed floats improvised from hand-grenade cartons, was strung. But none of the three types of boats available could make the trip except at an estimated 50 per cent loss from swamping or overloading. At the second site the guide rope was in by 1:00 A M, but, loaded in the boat with only two men upstream so as to prevent swamping, the men were unable to hold on to the guide rope The first boat overturned just short of its destination, the men swimming ashore. The second boat jerked slowly across without mishap The third boat overturned almost as soon as it had left the near shore of the almost-half-mile-wide expanse of water. An experiment using wooden assault boats then was tried successfully. Some of the men from G Company, which was to lead, had meanwhile gotten across with difficulty in small pneumatic boats.

By this time, however, heavy mortar fire was crashing in on the west bank and into the stream and it was 3:30 o'clock—time for the attack. Only a fraction of one company was on the far shore Even if the mortar fire could be eliminated, the footbridge showed no signs of being ready in the near future, if at all; a round of artillery fire falling on the far shore had destroyed the result of hours of work by cutting the anchor line, crumbling the abutment and holdfast for the east end of the cable and puncturing the pneumatic boat. Two men were wounded

Huge awkward-looking "Alligators" (armored amphibious carriers) had been provided for just such an emergency, although they were earmarked for the Rhine crossing and not to be used unless absolutely necessary. F Company, which had been briefed on loading fast if they had to be used, was loaded on them and shuttled over, followed by most of the remainder of G Company. E Company and the rest of the battalion were rerouted to the 119th Infantry footbridge. While this problem was being straightened out, reports from the far shore told of further trouble. The woods just west of Krauthausen where F and G Companies were assembling were proving to be a "perfect hell" of booby traps and anti-personnel mines Seventy-five casualties were sustained in those woods and it looked for a time as though the 120th's assault battalion might still be disorganized and out of the battle when daylight came.

It was not F and G Company kept on going through the dark, mine-strewn woods. At 5 00 o'clock the 2d Battalion, unmindful of its losses, jumped off from its planned line of departure and went to work on Krauthausen and Selhausen Each of these towns, like the corresponding ones in the 119th sector, had company-strength garrisons, but here too resistance was fairly weak E and G Companies, closing in on Krauthausen from north and south respectively, found only one real strongpoint, at the railroad station, and F encountered no major difficulty in taking Selhausen. By 10 35 o'clock both towns had fallen. The first line of defense had been breached across the entire Division front

Had the elaborate precautions to cover up the presence of Old Hickory across the river been justified? According to the first sorry prisoners, prodded blinking from their cellar hideouts, yes Sure, they knew the Americans would attack sooner or later In fact, somebody had sent down a message two weeks previously warning of an attack. But those messages kept coming down all the time and nobody paid much attention to them. (Later it was discovered that German radio intelligence had learned of the attack at 2 45 o'clock, as the artillery barrage started —too late to warn the defenders)

This information might have been some consolation for many of the men who had seen, in the jet-propelled plane attacks of the previous day, strong proof that the Germans knew the score. It probably didn't make one man in Company D, 120th Infantry, feel much better. Fishing through his pockets in the early stages of the attack, he found an Old Hickory shoulder patch. He knew that it would be a certain giveaway if he were captured. Thrown away, it might fall into enemy hands. So he clapped it into his mouth and started munching

When he finally reached the company objective, the tough red and blue piece of fabric was no more and he told the story to his first sergeant He learned then that the Division had been taken off the secret list just before the attack started, that he could have worn the insignia on his shoulder

Both regiments now used their follow-up battalions to reduce the reserve positions along the slightly higher ground about 1,000 to 1,500 yards to the rear. The 2d Battalion, 119th Infantry, speeded in its getaway by its regiment's early success, pushed out at 7.30 o'clock to take the town of Daubenrath, which stood out like a spit from the south edge of the Hambach Forest, and a small farmstead to the south of there

Resistance was a little heavier here, for not only the reserve company but about 50 men from the German battalion headquarters, stationed in old emplacements in the edge of the woods, were in action By early afternoon, however, the job was being completed. The 120th's 3d Battalion, designated to take the reserve line, was across the river soon after dawn, and jumped off at 11:45. Its advance up the open slope was slowed by strong fire from the field emplacements it was to seize and from a high-velocity gun somewhere to the southeast, but by midafternoon its job, too, had been completed.

Only Hambach and Niederzier remained of the main strong points of the Roer Line in the Division sector. They didn't last the night. Jumping off at 11:00 P.M. in the dim light of distant searchlights and the burst of high explosive and white phosphorus shells that rained down in front of them, two fresh battalions, the 119th's 3d and the 120th's 1st, raced onto their objectives so close behind the artillery that preceded them that the battle was over almost before it had a chance to begin. Perhaps the defenders might have done better had the attack come the next morning. They never had an opportunity to prove it. Hambach was cleared by 1:30 A.M. Niederzier was slightly tougher; A Company spent an hour and a half working on a strongpoint north of the town. By 2:45, however, 1st Battalion and 3d Battalion, which had moved up an hour and a half after the 1st's jump-off to clean the northern part of the town, reported the objective taken, though burpgun and rifle fire was not entirely cleaned up before daybreak. The units took 168 prisoners.

*   *   *

While the assault units were methodically lopping off strongpoint after strongpoint in the enemy's prepared defenses, the battle of the river was being fought, with a great curtain of smoke masking the bridge construction. The unhappy platoon of engineers which had started on the 120th's footbridge before the attack began worked doggedly until 6:00 o'clock that night before its efforts were successful. The first guide rope emplaced had been cut by shell fire. The second snagged in debris and snapped. A third line was cut by a lucky enemy mortar shell, wounding three men On the fourth attempt the anchor had been put in place and 48 feet of bridge constructed before the river intervened again. The line snapped and the bridge broke. The fifth attempt worked.

The determination of this platoon was typical, though fortunately none of the other engineer teams had such a run of misfortune. If they had, the whole course of the operations might have been different, for success hinged directly on getting tanks, tank destroyers, artillery, and supplies across.

The engineers were lucky at that. Enemy artillery fire fell during the day but not accurately enough to aid the principal enemy—the river itself. The absence of the expected artillery reaction at the start resulted from several factors: the havoc wrought at enemy gun positions and along communications lines by the great barrage our own artillery had laid down, the lack of observation in the dark and sheer surprise. Serious bridging efforts at Duren and Julich were to be expected, certainly But not until it was too late, if then, did the Germans realize a bridge was being built opposite Schophoven.

The enemy never did get a chance to look at the 30th's bridges, either from the air or from the ridge which curved east just south of Julich, overlooking the river. For thirty-two hours the 50 generators of the 82d Smoke Generator Company poured out a screen 2,000 yards across, 3 to 4 miles long and 2,200 feet high Original plans called for only two hours of artificial fog Constant supervision, however, was necessary to keep the screen thick enough and yet not so dense or broad as to hinder our own troops working there or cut down our artillery observation of enemy positions.

And so the work went on—clearing debris, building bridge approaches across the bogs, working in the water. Not very glamorous, perhaps, but as important as anything that went on that day. Meanwhile other engineers went on to perform tasks that would keep them busy the rest of the operation—repairing roads, clearing the log obstacles that guarded each town, removing minefields.

Not all of the bridges were built by engineers. One hundred fifty prisoners, 20 American wounded and 35 German wounded were at a supply point being fed by Alligators crossing the Roer. The Alligators couldn't negotiate the canal, so a German-speaking lieutenant put a proposition to the prisoners something like this.

"Your wounded are badly in need of attention and it will take our engineers three hours to build a bridge so we can get them across How about pitching in and helping build a bridge now?"

They couldn't be forced to build a bridge and they knew it. But the appeal was successful, aided by German artillery and mortar shells falling nearby, and soon all 150 were busy carrying logs and planks. The bridge was built in 35 minutes One hundred and fifty yards away the fighting was still raging in Krauthausen.

*   *   *

The treadway bridge was completed by midnight of the 2d Thus, within twenty-four hours of the jump-off the critical stage of the operation had been reached. The engineers toiling in the muddy waters of the Roer had delivered the miracle of a vehicular bridge in twenty and one-half hours instead of the thirty-six hours estimated, and already the tanks and tank destroyers were lining up on the roads west of Schophoven waiting to cross The infantry, too, was well ahead of schedule. The two enemy battalions in line protecting the river had been broken— many of their men were already in the Division's prisoner-of-war cages Hambach and Niederzier, then being mopped up, constituted the enemy's divisional reserve line, occupied by a battalion of the German 363d Division's only remaining regiment, and the other battalion of that regiment was already located north of Julich where it would have its hands full Except for the scraps and pieces which could be flung together from its service troops, 363d Division was shattered, finished Now, unless the enemy was able to counterattack with enough success to reestablish a line, a breakthrough was imminent

But this was high-level stuff, to be pointed out by staff officers jabbing grease pencils at their maps in well lighted buildings Down on the ground, where the mopping up of the darkened houses of Hambach and Niederzier was going on, the fighting men had little time for such speculation. Perhaps the 363d Division was "kaput" But just the same, there were high-velocity guns shooting down at their new positions from somewhere in the woods or from the little farm buildings to the north and east.

The 24th brought the only real delay the enemy was able to inflict during the entire operation. The 117th Infantry, which had crossed the river while the other units were consolidating during the morning, was to attack next. It was held up, however, in getting off while the 120th was cleaning up two strongpoints supported by concrete-emplaced AA-AT guns and dug-in tanks past Niederzier When it did finally move through the two initial assault regiments it ran into trouble

Target for the day was Steinstrass, which lay at the end of the swath of road leading north through the forest from Hambach This was the last assigned objective for the Division and taking it and holding it would assure the XIX Corps commander that the ideal avenue of counterattack against his main bridgehead at Julich, over which the heavy supporting armor, artillery, and supplies would roll, was secured. The 29th Division, which had assaulted at Julich itself, had not been able to move as fast as the 30th, and VII Corps, on the south flank, was still tied up with bridge difficulties and the need to swing far around by a longer route to catch up with the wheeling flank of its northern neighbors The 30th was out in front

Prisoners taken the night before had spoken disparagingly of the garrison at Steinstrass, indicating that part of the 363d Division's replacement battalion and maybe some rear echelons were in town, and the regimental plan was to race down the road with a task force composed of a company of tanks carrying infantry and six tank destroyers, with six British flail tanks thrown in for good measure to detonate any minefields that might be encountered Meanwhile 2d Battalion on the left and 3d Battalion on the right would clean out the woods on either side of the road

The trouble was provided by 9th Panzer Division, which had responded to calls for help the previous night, and by the engineer battalion of the 363d Division, which had thoughtfully plastered the clearing astride the forest road with about 2,000 mines right where a log roadblock spanned the highway

The foot elements of the 117th made their way through the woods without too much difficulty and were just about opposite the roadblocks to south and west respectively on the outskirts of Steinstrass by midnight. Company L, operating with the task force, suddenly came upon three armored half-tracks carrying 20mm AA guns and protected by infantry. "We threw a paralyzing volume of fire at them with everything we could get our hands on—rifles, machine guns, bazookas and rifle grenades, and then made a bayonet charge," said the company commander The task force, however, though it also knocked out one 75mm antitank gun and other AA guns, was stopped cold by the roadblock. Three of the Shermans of B Company, 743d Tank Battalion, were disabled by mines when they attempted to work around the block, and one of the mine-detonating flail tanks was knocked out by a direct hit. At least two big enemy tanks were somewhere up along the road toward Steinstrass, and probably more antitank guns Even after the roadblock had been cleared and lanes made through the mine fields, the road corridor had little to recommend itself as an avenue of tank attack, at least until the tanks and antitank guns were taken care of.

The 119th jumped off at the same time as the 117th, spread out with battalions abreast to clean out the woods on the left Any long-standing fears that this might be another battle of the Hurtgen Forest was quickly dispelled The enemy artillery, that might have made the forest a hell with tree bursts, just wasn't shooting—some of its gun-tenders were already prisoners and the others were probably back across the Erft River by that time As for infantry opposition, there was some, yes But for the most part the 119th, like the120th—sitting in defense of the Division right flank till friendly units there could close in—spent the day mainly in cleaning up the wreckage of the 363d Division and the flak units which had been routed from their concrete gunpits. One wire team that day picked up 30 prisoners. The 119th captured a German regimental command post located in a chateau near the north side of the woods During the night 130 Germans wandered in thinking their command post was still functioning

The next morning the 1st Battalion, 119th Infantry, from its positions on the northern edge of the forest, had a field day shooting at the Germans retreating eastward across its front as the 29th Division advanced Meanwhile the 2d and 3d Battalions of the 119th were preparing their noon attack across the flats to Hollen and Rotengen, northwest of Steinstrass.

These two towns were considerably beyond friendly lines and the attack was met with fire, not only from the objectives but from tanks on both flanks of the advance. The leading infantry of both battalions nevertheless penetrated the settlements within an hour and a half after the jump-off, G Company, 119th Infantry, knocking out four tanks in Hollen. One Panther fell to a G Company private firing a bazooka for the first time; his platoon leader killed a German officer standing in the turret of the same tank flourishing a pistol Part of the 2d Battalion was pinned down in the open during the afternoon, but after nightfall the remaining infantry arrived, along with the new light tanks of the 744th, later to work with the 30th during the Rhine crossing, which contributed materially to the Division's advance during the rest of the Roer operation.

Steinstrass fell the same day in what was almost completely an infantry-artillery action. The 2d Battalion, 117th Infantry, attacking from the west at noon, started out with a platoon of 743d tanks which had worked up through the woods with it, but after two of the Shermans had been knocked out in rapid succession by an unlocated gun during the assault on a roadblock protecting the town, the infantry went on alone. By the time the remaining three tanks could be moved up without needless exposure the doughboys were in the town The 3d Battalion struck simultaneously from the east, its men jogging over 500 yards of exposed ground before they reached the outskirts of town The eastern edge of the village was seized two hours after the jump-off but determined house-to-house fighting further in delayed final capitulation another hour and a half During this fight five enemy tanks were chased out of town to the north and 80 prisoners were taken

The excitement there was not over, however; at dusk, while the weary soldiers were setting up defenses in their newly acquired positions, about a battalion of 9th Panzer Division's armored infantry came up in its half-tracks, supported by tanks, and attacked from the east along the h:ghway. In a matter of minutes artillery was lashing at them with huge concentrations of shells, but enough infantry penetrated into the town to yield 74 prisoners. Two enemy tanks and three half-tracks were knocked out.

To the south the roadblock in the woods which had held up the attack the previous day died a lingering death Engineers and infantrymen of the 117th's 1st Battalion cleared the minefields and took down the wooden barriers across the road by 3:00 o'clock in the morning, but there were still the tanks to worry about. One tank was completely destroyed by the 823d Tank Destroyer Battalion and the other was immobilized. All day that lone tank dominated the defile through the woods, though Division Artillery angrily rained concentrations of shells on it again and again. Finally, late in the day, the infantry worked its way up and completed the job.

With the capture of Steinstrass and the main supply route leading up to it from the south, the operation loosened up, and the technique of hopping from town to town so classically demonstrated in the drive to the Roer was given an encore—for the benefit of an increasingly miscellaneous collection of enemy soldiers In Kongishoven, one of the few remaining places defended with spirit and skill, a captured enemy battalion commander stated that the 119th's action there was the best example of effective infantry tactics he had seen in seventeen years of army life

There had never been any real question about continuing the advance northward after the first successes The Corps commander had phoned down, "Keep going," less than twenty-four hours after the attack had started So the Division leapfrogged its regiments and battalions forward almost as fast as the G-3 could get out instructions. A combat command of the 2d Armored Division moved in temporarily to protect the Division right flank east of Steinstrass

An organized defensive line no longer existed in the path of the Division—only haphazard town defenses manned by whatever troops and tanks the local commander could get his hands on. Often the last-minute battlefield marriages of armor and infantry didn't work too well, the prisoner-of-war cages echoed with the complaints of infantry commanders whose tanks had pulled out prematurely and without notice, and also with the recriminations of tankmen who felt they had been left holding the bag

Surprise played an important role in the lightning advance. Partly, it was achieved by the large-scale plan It was increasingly evident that the enemy didn't comprehend, until too late, that the main impetus was

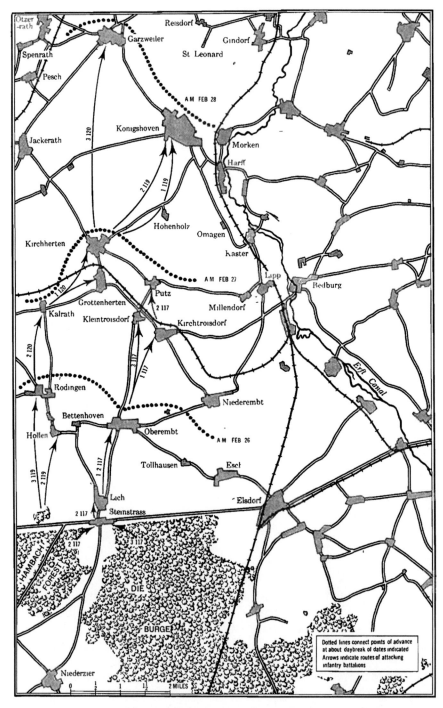

Map 13—Roer Assault Second Phase

north, toward Dusseldorf and the Ruhr Valley. He thought we wanted Cologne most of all. Thus, the armored infantry and tanks of 9th Panzer Division struggling to hold up Old Hickory's advance fell back to the east and tended to turn up in VII Corps' prisoner-of-war cages In turn, the 30th inherited—and to a considerable extent delivered to the Army Provost Marshal—the remnants of 11th Panzer Division and two infantry divisions which had drifted squarely across its front from that of XIII Corps and the 29th Infantry Division

The fighting men themselves, however, played a major part in fooling the enemy, by around-the-clock pressure and sheer aggressiveness The 117th, for example, collected 168 prisoners and knocked out a tank in a swiftly executed pre-dawn attack north to Oberembt on the 26th Prisoners stated that they themselves had arrived during the night and were feverishly setting up defenses against an attack *from the west* rather than from the south when the blow fell By 7:30 o'clock in the morning the victors were unconcernedly eating breakfast

It was at Oberembt that Company C collected the prize item in a long list of military booty gathered up during the operation. It was a monster 380mm. (15-inch) howitzer mounted on a heavy Royal Tiger tank chassis—the first one of that rare breed captured by Allied forces. When C Company's men moved in the gun was all ready to be fired, with one of its 770-pound shells in the chamber The entire crew was captured or killed

Even before the attack for Oberembt jumped off, there was some unexpected fighting to be done The attack was made from Lich, which the 2d Battalion had taken the same evening it helped capture Steinstrass To the outsider Lich would have seemed a mass of confusion at 2.45 o'clock that morning of the 26th. Seven tanks had been in the town when the 2d Battalion moved in. Five had fled, another had been knocked out—that last tank was still being tracked down in the dark Some of the 94 prisoners taken there were still being rounded up and evacuated. The 1st and 3d Battalions were moving up for their attack on Oberembt.

Soldiers of B and C Companies were waiting for tanks of the 743d Tank Battalion which they were to ride on the attack to Oberembt They heard tanks coming from their rear and sent out men to wave them down But they weren't American tanks they heard, they were German Mark Vs

"Move over," one German tank commander said to an open-mouthed C Company infantryman. Then the Germans quit talking and started shooting.

"I could have reached out and touched one of the tanks," one officer related, "when he swung that 'telephone pole' [an 88mm tank gun] around toward me."

The German armor, fighting to get out of a trap, ran through practically the whole surprised battalion before it was stopped. Two of the tanks and all of the half-tracks were knocked out A platoon of Company B, 117th Infantry, took care of 15 accompanying infantry

Most of the bounds forward from town to town were made by moonlight. The 117th, for example, consolidated Oberembt on the morning of the 26th, then waited until 10:30 P.M. before attacking Kirchtroisdorf and Kleintroisdorf with the 1st and 3d Battalions respectively. The two towns, side by side on the road, fell by midnight. Three hours later the 2d Battalion was passing through to take Putz, which fell before daylight in a short but stubborn battle. In the daytime, tanks and machine guns could lay down a deadly fire against troops attacking sometimes a mile or more at a time over the flat brown fields.

The reduced visibility which characterized night-fighting was the ideal answer for troops skilled enough to maneuver in the moonlight. These night attacks, following no definite time pattern, did much to keep the enemy off balance. The usual pattern was for infantry to ride the tank destroyers and tanks to the edge of town and then advance on foot as their armored "busses" provided assault fire.

Night attacks alone, however, didn't guarantee success. There was still plenty of fighting to be done. At Grottenherten and Kirchherten, assaulted simultaneously by the 1st Battalion, 120th Infantry, close to 10 enemy tanks were in action, including two that came out to meet the attackers in the fields, 88s and machine guns blazing and with burp gunners firing from the decks of the tanks. "The Krauts started shooting their machine guns into the ground, then slowly lifted their fire to sweep the ground," said one man. "They were shooting flares every two minutes and together with the fires we had started the place was as light as day." These tanks pulled back. In the town itself one tank was knocked out by a 175-yard bazooka shot, two Mark IVs were stopped by artillery and another was discovered intact in a farmyard.

Perhaps the best organized defenses uncovered were encountered by the 1st and 2d Battalions, 119th Infantry, on the 27th, during their three-mile daylight jump to Konigshoven. Halfway there from Grottenherten, the 1st Battalion, 119th Infantry, ran into field positions near the little town of Hohenholz and the woods nearby, with enemy tanks supporting the well coordinated infantry fires. One 743d tank was able to get within 50 yards of the little town before a high-velocity shell ripped into its armor, and the infantry found the going similarly tough. While the fight was raging in midafternoon, 12 enemy tanks moved up in two groups from the east and attempted to intervene The artillery forward observer swiftly called for a curtain of fire around the advancing American troops, however, and the tanks were forced to retreat. It turned out later, after the prisoners had been questioned, that the defenders were a battalion of panzer grenadiers from the 11th Panzer Division It was close to being the last stand that division ever made during World War II.

Konigshoven, too, presented difficulty, although the 119th's 2d Battalion hustled into town so fast that opposition was disorganized from the start But even disorganized die-hards can make trouble, especially when they are armed with 88s Six tanks of the 743d were hit during the Konigshoven assault, and five of them burned up One action, thus, accounted for half of the tank losses sustained by the battalion in the Roer offensive. Two self-propelled tank destroyers of the 823d were also disabled by enemy fire at Konigshoven

Three Mark V tanks were knocked out during the joint attack on the two towns

Meanwhile the 120th Infantry was hurrying to capture Garzweiler before nightfall It was a little more important than the other towns in the vicinity, though its civilian inhabitants probably didn't know that For one thing, it sat squarely on the main highway between Aachen and Dusseldorf For another, it was situated on a belt of trenches and anti-tank ditches that had been frantically constructed in the autumn of 1944 as a perimeter defense for the industrial towns of Munchen-Gladbach, Neuss, and Krefeld farther north By then the Germans knew that the main effort was northward The Canadians had pressed down south of Goch XIII Corps was pushing in on a continuation of the same defense line to the west There, if anywhere, was the place to hold a bridgehead opposite the Ruhr Valley. And, conversely, if the Germans could not hold there, that was the place for the Americans to shoot the armor through.

Thus, more or less, went the planning at Corps and Army Garzweiler itself, however, turned out to be slightly overrated. Two battalions of the 120th were sent up to capture the town Only the lead battalion, the 3d, was needed There were plenty of troops in town They had laid some mines They had weapons—AT guns, tanks, artillery But they lacked conviction During the approach march, some of them tried to leave town but they were promptly discouraged by artillery Within the town itself opposition was light except for a fight in the northwest corner where infantry and tanks teamed up for a struggle All in all, 216 prisoners, many of them city policemen only recently impressed into "Police Battalion Behrens," were captured, as well as three 105mm assault guns, three antitank guns, and four tanks One of the tanks, a Mark V, was intact That night the 2d Armored Division moved up and next morning rolled north toward the Rhine bridges at Dusseldorf

While the 2d Armored Division and then the 83d Infantry Division fanned out to the north to close to the Rhine opposite Dusseldorf, the men of the 30th set about "policing up" the eastern portion of its sector and protecting the right flank of XIX Corps while waiting for VII Corps units to close up on the far side of the Erft Canal By the end of the first day of March all of the territory west of the Canal was in American hands In most cases there was a little shooting, but not much, for the Germans were pulling back behind the water barrier of the Erft. One of the towns along the canal, Gustorf, was taken by the 120th in a fashion reminiscent of the August and September days in France and Belgium Reports came back from observers that white flags were flying in the town So a patrol was sent out—consisting of the 3d Battalion operations officer, the acting battalion intelligence officer, and a German-speaking private, decked out with captain's bars on his shoulder Eager civilians crowded around them, told them there were no German soldiers left in town and asked that the Americans move in The reconnaissance party, however, picked up 10 unhappy members of the *Wehr-macht* during their stay there and later, when the whole battalion moved in, nine more dejected *"landsers"* were apprehended Just as the patrol was leaving town they heard a deafening explosion marking the destruction of the bridge over the canal

The Germans weren't always so complaisant Until the drive northward on the far side of the Erft canal forced them to fall back, they resisted vigorously any efforts to cross And on the 2d of March one of the unit commanders of 11th Panzer Division, who had more of the old-school spirit than prudence, caused a half-day's worry farther north where the 83d Division was trying hard to get its troops up to the Rhine, and didn't have many to spare for protection of its long exposed right flank Rallying about seven tanks, some artillery, and a highly jumbled batch of infantry, the panzer commander struck across the Erft and succeeded in isolating one of the 83d's infantry companies in Kapellen, just north of the 120th's sector, capturing two platoons

The attack didn't last long Soon fighter-bombers came up and knocked out three German tanks And by the time the P-47s had finished and were starting home, Company A of the 120th, reinforced by a platoon of tanks from the 743d, was detrucking to clean up. When it mounted up in its trucks again it had knocked out a machine-gun nest, captured 15 prisoners and a half-track and reclaimed a 57mm. antitank gun which the Germans had wrested from the 83d Most of the enemy force didn't stay for the end of the action. Two Mark IV tanks were knocked out by artillery fire and two other tanks, noting with dismay the approach of American tanks and bazooka teams, backtracked across the river before they could be dealt with.

Meanwhile, the rest of the Division was taking its turn on guard, snapping up news of the fighting to north and east, and wrestling with the problems of military government West of the Roer there had been practically no civilians left in the battle-scarred towns, they had long since been evacuated by the Nazi Party East of the Roer, however, particularly in the last stages of the advance, the villages were crowded with refugees as well as the normal population

Finally on March 6, surrounded at last by friendly troops, Old Hickory moved out—back to the Belgian-Dutch-German borderland along the Maas for training, rest and rehabilitation It had been chosen to spearhead the Ninth Army's assault crossing over the Rhine

*   *   *

In many respects the Roer offensive had been the smoothest running operation the Division had ever undertaken The engineers had turned the difficult river crossing from a liability into an asset by providing a speedy crossing in strength where the enemy did not expect it A carefully worked out traffic-control plan, skillfully administered by the Military Police Platoon, using communications specially devised by the 30th Signal Company, kept traffic flowing smoothly over the bottlenecks at the river line This permitted Division Artillery to displace its battalions across the river in close support with notable speed Momentum was kept up by concurrent attacks on positions which could be mutually supporting and by constant leapfrogging of battalions This permitted units which had recently taken an objective an opportunity to reorganize and also automatically provided a defended base for the next jump The skill with which battalions on the ground performed these maneuvers, almost as much as their success in the actual fighting, kept the enemy constantly off balance. There was only one serious mishap, when four of the British flail tanks were knocked out one night by friendly tank fire while approaching unannounced Yet much of the movement took place by night, with strange units from different regiments occupying the same town The 119th attack on Konigshoven and the 120th attack on Garzweiler, for example, both took place on the same day from the same town, Kirchherten.

The artillery had also played an important role in the success, stopping at least two counterattacks north of Licht as well as the ones east of Steinstrass and south of Konigshoven

If any of the men doubted that they had done a good job, there were tangible proofs For most of the operation they had set the pace for the entire Ninth Army Two thousand nine hundred and eighty-six prisoners had passed through the Division cage. Twenty-nine tanks had been knocked out Some of these were evacuated by the enemy but at least 17 tanks, a few in good running order, had been abandoned or captured The troops had moved too fast to count all the booty, but even the incomplete list was impressive: 15 half-tracks, 19 150mm howitzers, 13 105mm howitzers, 15 88mm. guns, 15 20mm guns, 9 120mm mortars, 10 Nebelwerfers (multibarreled rocket projectors), 8 75mm. anti-tank guns, 13 80mm. mortars, and a crazy collection of vehicles, ammunition, small arms, and other military supplies

Further evidence was provided by a letter from Lieutenant General William H Simpson, the Ninth Army commander, on March 15, to the Division commander:

> It was a distinct pleasure for me last October when I learned that the 30th Infantry Division was being assigned to the Ninth Army, a pleasure all the more keenly felt because of the fact of my previous association as one-time commander of the Division I have been happy to share with you the pride of accomplishment that has characterized the history of your Division since the initiation of operations on the Continent
> The operation just concluded again furnished your Division with an opportunity to distinguish itself I scarcely need point out that this opportunity was accepted and completely exploited by the Division, thereby adding another glowing chapter to the record
> Particularly gratifying to me was the surprise which was achieved in your crossing the Roer River at an unsuitable site, and the ingenuity with which your organization overcame the difficulties of building up a bridgehead despite meager access and egress roads Your expeditious clearing of the Hambach Forest and the firm protection which you furnished the Army right flank, materially assisted the Army to successfully execute the maneuver by which the enemy was turned out of his positions and driven to retreat across his own line of communication
> It was characteristic of your Division that, with the original mission accomplished, you were ready and waiting to execute another mission—that of further securing the Army's right flank and facilitating the capture of the key strongpoint of Neuss
> It is with great personal pleasure that I acknowledge the splendid job performed by the 30th Infantry Division and express my commendation of the individual contribution made by every officer and man

Major General Raymond S. McLain, the XIX Corps commander, in forwarding General Simpson's letter, noted the Division's "thorough and rapid action by which the blow never lost its momentum and the enemy moves to check the advance were overrun before they got underway."

There were other reasons for high spirits when the troops pulled back to the Maas. Spring was at hand. They were back, perhaps for the last time during the European war, out of hostile territory and among people they liked. There were old friends to look up in the Dutch towns they had liberated to the south and new ones to find in the villages where they were billetted

Some of the reunions were more formal At Kerkrade, the citizens rededicated their public square on February 25, renaming it Old Hickory in memory of the troops who had fought to make it free again after four long years of Nazi oppression.

"For that freedom you gave us we will ever be grateful," Mayor Alphonse Habets told General Hobbs and Colonel Purdue of the 120th Infantry in a colorful ceremony "We will not forget and we do not intend our children shall forget."

An equally memorable ceremony took place March 11 at Maastricht, ancient capital of Limburg Province and chief city of the southern Netherlands This time the troops could be there—600 men from 2d Battalion, 117th Infantry, which had liberated the city along with men from the 743d Tank Battalion and the 823d Tank Destroyer Battalion on September 13, 1944 Packed into the public square along with thousands of joyous Netherlanders wearing the royal orange and waving their national colors, the troops heard the burgomeister express the gratitude of his people. Afterward each of the men was presented with a souvenir and entertained at a movie, a concert and a dance

"You see here only a part of the men who liberated Maastricht," Colonel Johnson of the 117th declared in acknowledgment "Many are left in the military cemetery east of the city. Will you remember us by remembering them on September 13 of each year?"

The ceremony was also attended by General Hobbs and by General Simpson of the Ninth Army

*   *   *

There was plenty of work to be done, too, back in the Echt area A secret planning room was set up at the Division command post at Echt and plans for the coming assault across the Rhine carefully developed The engineers cleared areas along the Maas of old German minefields and set up practice crossing sites All of the assault troops practiced there the jobs they were to do—loading into assault boats, use of the Navy-controlled larger landing craft, debarkation Finally, each of the assault units had a full dress rehearsal of the jobs it would do.

Chapter XVI

RHINE CROSSING

A month after the Roer offensive began, almost to the day, Old Hickory made its assault crossing of the Rhine During that month the German armies in the West lost heavily—150,000 men in prisoners alone The Roer drive had led to the stroke of luck at Remagen, First Army's three-corps bridgehead there was showing signs of breaking out of the circle of defenders flung around it Farther south General Patton had crushed the German Nineteenth Army in a savage drive to the Rhine On the eve of the 30th's assault Third Army troops had crossed south of Frankfurt and were beginning to exploit.

The enemy was in the unenviable position of trying to contain the two active threats in the south while husbanding his now meager resources against the attack he knew was coming in the north. The Ruhr was still the Number One target facing the Western Allies despite the spectacular developments farther south The last German rearguards had been driven east of the Rhine two weeks before the northern crossing took place In that fortnight the Germans had placed a shallow line of infantry and Volksgrenadier divisions along the river line and had frantically set up field works and barriers. Morale of the defenders was low Behind them were only two first-rate counterattacking divisions for the entire northern section of the front—the 116th Panzer Division and the 15th Panzer Grenadier Division

Thus, the Allied plan called for a Sunday punch in the north under 21st Army Group's Field Marshal Montgomery, an old hand at power plays Ninth Army, which held the west bank of the Rhine from south of Dusseldorf to the mouth of the Lippe River at Wesel, was to strike due east on a narrow front past the northern edge of the Ruhr cities to make contact with First Army and thus encircle the Ruhr. On Ninth Army's left, where the Rhine turns generally northwest, British Second Army was to attack on a broad front and strike to the northeast An Anglo-American airborne force would be dropped behind Wesel to fill in the gap between the two attacks

The 30th Infantry Division, under XVI Corps, was given the key role in the Ninth Army assault Its job was to assault across the Rhine with the Lippe River on its left flank, breaking through the enemy's defenses to permit exploitation eastward by the 8th Armored Division and later by XIX Corps, initially in Army reserve The 79th Division was to follow the 30th's attack with one of its own on Old Hickory's right, then turn south to contain the German troops in the Ruhr The

35th Division would follow and also peel off to the right on a containing
mission.   *   *   *

The Rhine was 1,100 feet wide in the 30th's crossing zone, thus providing an unusual technical problem of keeping men and matériel flowing across it Big and complicated as the crossing operation appeared,
however, it was less of a problem than the swollen, racing Roer had
been. The Rhine problem was one of size alone and could be solved by
sheer volume of equipment and organization.

Two major problems were involved in the crossing operation The
first was that of getting the assault troops across rapidly so as to minimize
the period in which they were vulnerable and non-effective on the water
This was to be solved by the use of motorized storm boats and assault
boats. The second problem was that of following up the assault waves
with an adequate and constant flow of heavy weapons, reinforcements
and supplies Bridging so wide a stream was expected to be a protracted
operation Therefore it was decided to use naval landing craft and amphibious engineer equipment until the bridges were completed This
decision created problems of its own in moving the special equipment
overland to the river bank and made necessary meticulous organization
of the shoreline However, the river itself was slow-moving and easy
to work in Most of the problems proved to be those of planning rather
than of operation

The supply situation was excellent Not only were the Navy craft
available for immediate support of the operation, but adequate bridging
material was on hand Ammunition was plentiful Large stocks of
gasoline were in rolling reserve, ready to be used in the exploitation
phase

The 30th Division's assault zone was approximately five miles wide,
extending south from the mouth of the Lippe Canal to Mehrum, where
the riverline of the Rhine extends eastward for approximately three
and one-half miles. Along the east bank of the river was a dike, but
behind it the ground was generally flat and open for two miles Then
two high railroad embankments crossed the sector from Wesel generally southeast toward the Ruhr, about 1,000 yards apart Behind them
the country gradually became wooded and more rugged About seven
miles inland a forested ridgeline faced westward, surmounted by an
incomplete *Autobahn* running north and south The rugged wooded
area, broken up by clearings, extended eastward as far as the Dorsten–
Osterfeld highway, approximately 14 miles inland

Good east-west roads, along the axis of the attack, were notably lacking One fair second-class road followed the southern edge of the Lippe

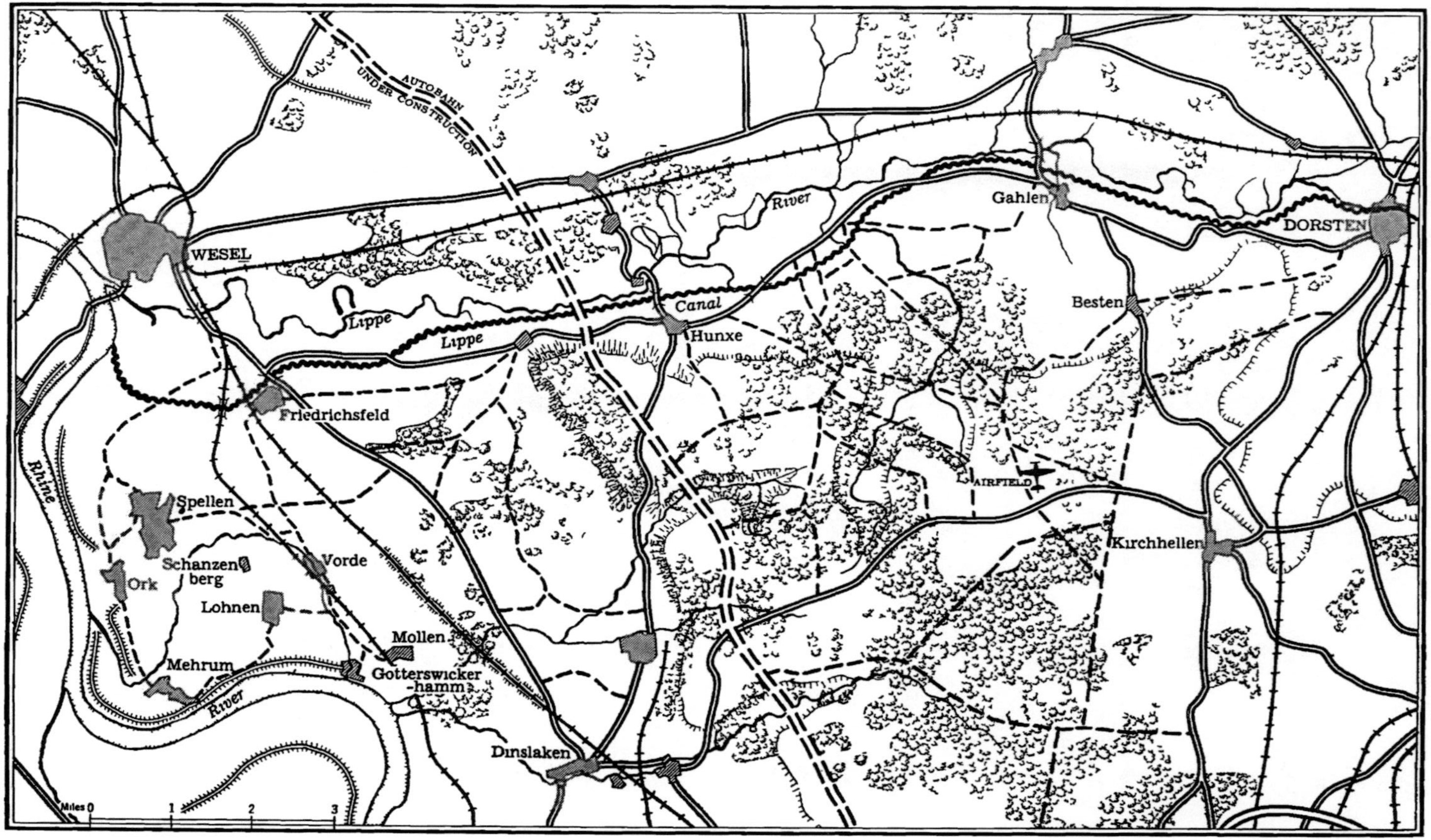

Map 14—Rhine River Assault Area

Canal and another road of the same caliber swung into the Division zone about 10 miles inland, going generally eastward thereupon Otherwise the east-west roads were poor forest trails The principal roads in the sector ran generally north and south Between Dorsten and the Rhine there were five major crossings of the Lippe River and Canal on the Division north flank.

The Division commander decided to attack with three regiments abreast, to obtain flexibility in crossing sites, with the 119th Infantry on the north being soon pinched out by the main effort 117th, which had a narrow sector in the center The 120th was to attack on the south Intelligence obtainable in the planning period indicated that the defending German 180th Division had only five infantry battalions available and had placed its main line of resistance along the dike, with local reserves in the towns just to the rear Permanent antiaircraft defenses guarding the Ruhr extended in depth through the Division attack corridor, but it appeared unlikely that many troops would be available to rally around these positions With only two panzer-type divisions available in reserve on the entire 21st Army Group front, large scale counterattack seemed unlikely. Thus, there were high hopes that the battle of the Rhine would be won within a few thousand yards of the riverline, and that once the railroad embankments and the ridgeline marked by the *Autobahn* had been secured, the armor could roll forward

Back near the Maas, the operation was planned and rehearsed with the usual attention to detail There the olive-drab-garbed sailors of the Navy's amphibious craft were available for instruction. All troops practiced the crossing operation, and each of the regiments had a full-dress night rehearsal Air photos and scale models were studied by the assault troops New defense data were obtained, first from the 75th Infantry Division, which patrolled the Rhine in the 30th's crossing area, then from the 30th Reconnaissance Troop, which set up observation posts on the river side Finally, a few days before the operation was to take place, the impatient regiments obtained permission to send their own patrols to check the far shore As in the Roer crossing, chief interest was in the physical condition of the banks and the location of obstacles and immediate defenses, rather than in enemy order of battle The important thing was to get troops ashore swiftly without mishap Artillery fire and speed and maneuver would take care of the defenses farther back.

Elaborate preparations were necessary even before the operation started The Signal Company, which had tried out various techniques for installing and maintaining wire circuits over the Rhine, laid and buried wire almost up to the water's edge, in at least one case using a plow and a jeep as wirelaying equipment It was believed necessary to bury the wire to avoid cutting of communication because of the heavy traffic or enemy shelling

Ninth Army was staking everything on success on a narrow front Thus it was essential that the enemy be kept ignorant of the crossing site. Special roads down to the crossing sites constructed by the engineers were duplicated as far south as the Dusseldorf area Patrolling was similarly duplicated, if a patrol went out in the assault area, similar patrols were sent out down the length of the Army river frontage The elaborate preparations necessary to make the attack an overwhelming success could not be hidden from the enemy; the point of assault could As later events proved, the deception plan was a considerable success

The 30th Division's reputation as a *Schwerpunkt* unit was also made use of The Division moved up from the Echt area to its assembly areas close to the Rhine March 16-21 with its vehicle markings obliterated and its shoulder patches removed At the same time a special group of troops and equipment marked with Old Hickory vehicle bumper markings and shoulder patches moved out from the same area to a point in the XIII Corps zone, directly opposite the Ruhr In addition, radio messages were sent indicating that the 30th Division was checking into the XIII Corps radio net Similar measures were taken with the veteran 79th Division, which was to assault on the 30th's right.

*   *   *

The great assault began the night of March 23-24. The cannonading commenced early in the evening, for the first British elements, far to the north, were to assault at 8 00 P M An hour later the assault at Emmerich began At 10:00 P.M. British commandos crossed silently just north of the 30th Division sector and lay in wait, 1,500 yards from Wesel, while more than 300 RAF Lancaster bombers pounded the city for fifteen minutes

At 1 00 A M approximately 200 tubes of 30th Division Artillery, reinforced, started an hour-long barrage which deposited more than 20,000 rounds of smoke and high explosive on the far shore. Backing up this monster artillery preparation were the heavy battalions of XVI Corps and XIX Corps artillery, firing at deeper targets

Meanwhile the west shore of the river was busy and crowded as the assault troops moved up, carrying their heavy assault and storm boats the 300 yards down to the water's edge, and as the massive trucks carrying the Navy's assault craft crawled up to the crossing sites and began unloading Troops of the 1153d Engineer Combat Group, in support of the Division, were busy setting up the ponton bridges they were to build in record time German artillery and mortar fire was falling sporadically.

At 2·00 A M the artillery fire shifted to deeper targets and the assault began It was a triumph of organization from the start Tracer bullets fired over the heads of the crossing troops indicated their landing places, later flashlights and luminous markers would be set up to mark them.

In the initial waves one group of boats became lost, with G Company of the 120th Infantry deposited in a spit of land almost a thousand yards away from the rest of the assaulting 2d Battalion Two power-driven assault boats in the 119th sector were knocked out Otherwise the initial crossings proceeded smoothly Each of the three assault battalions crossed in four waves. The engineer plan anticipated the need of bulldozers early in the operation to smooth a route over the dike They were not needed, however.

The striking echelons immediately went to work In the 119th sector, the 2d Battalion swept up to the dike and fanned out to take the locks at the mouth of the Lippe Canal on the north and a built-up area to the south In half an hour the first objective had been consolidated The 1st Battalion of the 117th had equally good going, sweeping up the riverside town of Ork within an hour and forty minutes Ork yielded 150 prisoners Smoke shells fired by chemical mortars and part of the screen already being placed over the crossing sites by a company and a half of chemical smoke generators had blinded the enemy defenders along the dike and the artillery had crippled them "There was no real fight to it," said one 117th company commander "The artillery had done the job for us" Despite the difficulty in getting G Company organized and in contact with the rest of the Battalion, the 2d Battalion of the 120th Infantry also attacked swiftly and successfully for its first objective, taking Mehrum at 4 25 A.M , then shoving north a mile in the next hour to capture a little settlement halfway to Schanzenberg

Meanwhile the supporting battalions were beginning to cross Two hours after the attack began, the 119th's 3d Battalion was attacking southeast from the 2d Battalion's newly won positions for Spellen The 117th's support battalion, the 2d, did not start across until Ork had been taken and was delayed en route A number of motors failed to function on the assault and storm boats and some of the boats lost direction despite the tracers and air bursts marking the crossing lanes Thus, not until 6·30 did the battalion cross the line of departure in Ork for its initial objective in the south part of Spellen The arrival of this battalion in the fight eased the pressure on the 3d Battalion, 119th In-

fantry, and it pressured its way through Spellen at 7.10, twenty minutes before the 117th's unit finished cleaning up its corner of the town
Not a man was lost in taking Spellen

While the 2d Battalion of the 120th Infantry was driving northeast
from the corner of the Division zone toward Schanzenberg, the 3d
Battalion was starting out on the most spectacular dash of the entire
operation All ashore by 4 00 A M , it started out half an hour later
from Mehrum toward Gotterswickerhamm, almost two miles due
east along the river bank Here opposition was markedly stronger than
that provided by the shaken-up and dispirited defenders along the river
bank to the west, because of the presence of a young Nazi lieutenant
in command of the town Not until the German commander had been
killed by Captain Harold P Plummer of K Company was the fight
won. The 100 men left of the garrison capitulated quickly after this
and by 8.40 the town was clear Already close to four miles east of the
30th's crossing sites the battalion reorganized and moved on to Mollen,
which straddled the first of the two railroad lines crossing the Division's
path By noon it had taken its objective.

The initial assaults had virtually wiped out the first line of defenses
Tanks, some of them amphibious, were coming ashore They could not
play a major role in the operation, however, until the two railroad embankments crossing the Division zone were taken, for the underpasses
under these embankments constituted formidable bottlenecks The
first railroad was reached and crossed during the morning The 119th
resumed its attack with the 2d Battalion on the north and the 3d Battalion on the south converging on the railroad embankment and the
cluster of buildings fronting it - Both underpasses were vigorously defended by small-arms fire and high-velocity shells, and one had three
enemy tanks in operation around it By 12:42, however, the coordinated
attack had overrun the underpasses

Spellen was just a way-station for the 2d Battalion of the 117th Infantry, which pushed on to the first railroad line just to the east Here
too, the underpass was defended by vigorous small-arms fire, backed up
by high velocity 40mm antiaircraft guns, but after a morning's work
the battalion had driven past the obstacle

Three huge craters in the roads near the underpasses were filled by
engineers under fire, so that the tanks and tank destroyers could advance

The 120th's zone was also cleared to the first embankment by early
afternoon. The 2d Battalion captured Schanzenberg at 9.30 and then
drove south to swallow up the larger town of Lohnen by 1.00 P M ,
in a stubbornly waged hour-long battle.

By early afternoon of the first day there was no longer an organized line of defense. The troops facing the 30th consisted of regimental and divisional headquarters and rear-echelon troops, only slightly augmented by Germans who had retreated from line positions Except at Gotterswickerhamm the enemy opposition had been half-hearted, already the prisoner-of-war estimates were swelling

The C-47 planes of the airborne attack passed over on schedule at 10.00 A M to drop the XVIII Airborne Corps northeast of Wesel Some of the planes were easy victims for fixed antiaircraft batteries which had survived the preliminary artillery blackout, but waves of planes kept on coming The airborne operation caused a slight let-up in some artillery fires because the 197th and other battalions could not fire without shooting into the mass of American planes However, during this brief period fire missions were transferred to other battalions that were able to shoot without endangering the airborne troops

Signs of enemy disintegration were strongest in the southern part of the Division zone. I Company, 120th Infantry, following instructions from Major Chris McCullough, the 3d Battalion commander, to go as far and as fast as possible, shoved a patrol out unopposed 800 yards beyond Mollen to the second railroad embankment, before Battalion ordered that forward motion be stopped because the battalion was getting too strung out The patrol reported that an objective a little over a thousand yards farther east, in the edge of the wooded area, was only thinly held.

The original plans had called for the reduction of built-up areas directly north of Mollen along the railroad embankments before this distant objective was taken, but Colonel Purdue, the regimental commander, felt that here was too good an opportunity to miss The 3d Battalion was given the go signal once again Led by K Company, mounted on a company of light tanks from the 744th Tank Battalion and two platoons of the 823d's tank destroyers, which had crossed on Navy landing craft during the morning, the 3d Battalion moved out along the road Probably convinced that no American armor was that far east, friendly artillery supporting the 79th Division hit at the column, but the attack soon became triumphant In some cases the advance was so rapid that enemy troops were machine gunned by enfilading fire into their trenches K Company's mechanized spearhead swept past the scattered farmhouses of the objective area to the next high ground, but was ordered to return because supporting artillery, still in position back of the Rhine waiting an opportunity to cross, could no longer support it By 5 30 P M the objective was clear of enemy

While the 3d Battalion was consolidating its positions far to the east, the 120th's 2d Battalion was continuing its own attack, driving from Lohnen to the settlement of Vorde, which nestled on the east side of the first railroad embankment. This set the stage for the 1st Battalion, which had been following close behind from Lohnen, waiting for a chance to go into action Attacking at 6 00 P M , the 1st Battalion passed through its sister unit and drove through another settlement along the second railroad track to a group of buildings on the far side, taking 114 prisoners.

The line of attack advanced almost as rapidly on the north. The 117th brought the 1st Battalion up for a new consolidated attack beside the 2d Battalion at 5 30 and by shortly after 10:00 P M the town of Holthausen, along the second railroad embankment, had fallen to the Americans. The 119th, bothered by small-arms and high-velocity antiaircraft gun fire from the island on its left flank between the Lippe Canal and River, sent G Company and then F Company to clean it out during the evening With the bulk of the 2d Battalion thus committed on a flank mission, the 1st Battalion was brought into the renewal of the attack eastward By 10 40 P M Friedrichsfeld, a town just past the second railroad line, was in our hands, as well as a factory area about 1,000 yards farther east The 3d Battalion reorganized and jumped off again for a patch of woods past the main Wesel–Dinslaken highway already cut at Friedrichsfeld Intense fire from a nest of 88mm and 20mm antiaircraft guns at the far edge of the woods it sought to take, however, held the battalion to a 2,000-yard gain in four hours and at 2:30 A M it held up for the night.

Thus within twenty-four hours the Division had driven more than six straight-line miles inland from its crossing sites—more than twice as far as it had gone on the brilliant first day of its Roer assault. More than 1,500 prisoners were streaming back to the rear. G Company of the 117th alone had taken 213 Germans into custody

*   *   *

All day long a great armada of Navy assault craft had churned back and forth across the Rhine under cover of small barrage balloons reminiscent of the Normandy beaches and a smoke screen skillfully maintained despite a shifting wind These craft brought over the tanks and tank destroyers, essential supplies and light support vehicles. By 4.00 P M the first treadway bridge, some 1,100 feet long, was in place Cautious staff officers had not dared count on a bridge's being constructed in less than thirty-six hours Preconstructed as much as possible, its installation carefully rehearsed, it was ready for business within nine hours The 118th Field Artillery was immediately hustled across, but further displacement of artillery was delayed another eight hours when a landing craft veered into the bridge By 2 00 A M. repairs had been rushed through and also a second bridge had been completed During the hours before daylight the bulk of the artillery directly supporting the Division moved into new positions east of the Rhine from which it could support the rapidly advancing assault troops.

On the first day of the attack, the speedy advance of the foot troops had been partially eclipsed by the triumph of matériel and organization over the imposing water barrier of the Rhine. During the morning of March 25 the Division gobbled up another four miles, completed its breakthrough of the enemy's 180th Division, and appeared to be ready for a spectacular dash eastward

The 117th was the first to renew the attack, bringing its 3d Battalion into action for the first time during the operation, on the left of the 1st Battalion at 2 30 A.M. An hour and a half's work sufficed to bring it to its objective, a built-up area just east of the woods the 119th had fought for the previous night The 119th, mopping up the woods soon after daylight close to the 117th's leading elements, captured 118 prisoners, eight 88mm dual purpose guns and several multiple-mount 20mm cannon

Then the 117th and 120th attacked simultaneously at 9 00 o'clock for objectives along the incomplete *Autobahn* atop the wooded ridge marking the western edge of the Bruckhauserheide The attack succeeded handsomely Part of the 117th's 1st Battalion moved around to the rear of the enemy positions and came up with 140 prisoners, including the commander of the 2d Battalion of the German 1221st Regiment of the 180th Division The 1st Battalion of the 120th, leading a column of battalions, used most of the tricks in the book to crush the enemy, with its leading elements on tanks, preceded by artillery fire and an air strike, and with its flank masked by smoke The enemy watched the attack develop and then actually came out to surrender, 200 men strong with surrender leaflets in hand Antiaircraft weapons were by this time the backbone of the defense, and it was evident that there was not enough flesh to make it a formidable one

The *Autobahn* was the corps intermediate objective. With a foothold obtained on the high ground and the opposition reduced to strongpoints of antiaircraft guns plus hasty collections of German infantrymen, the time for exploitation seemed ripe.

Two task forces were organized to crash ahead The 120th designated Lieutenant Colonel Hunt, commander of the 744th Light Tank Battalion, to lead his own unit, the regiment's 2d Battalion, and two companies of the 823d Tank Destroyer Battalion in the southern sector His ultimate objective was Kirchhellen, on the main road south from

Dorsten to the Ruhr cities, and about seven miles away. General Harrison, the assistant division commander, who was at the 117th Infantry, took charge of the other task force This consisted of the 2d Battalion of the 117th, most of the 743d Tank Battalion, and part of the 823d Tank Destroyer Battalion Its objective was Dorsten, which controlled a major crossing of the Lippe Canal Meanwhile the 1st Battalion of the 117th was to strike for Hunxe, another Lippe Canal crossing site The 119th had two battalions out on flank protection missions and its 1st Battalion prepared to attack north of the 117th for Gahlen, another canal crossing town The remaining two battalions of the 120th were to continue the attack on the flanks of Task Force Hunt

Two factors deprived the Division of the fruits of the breakthrough past the German 180th Infantry Division The first was bad terrain The second was the arrival, squarely in Old Hickory's path, of the 116th Panzer Division.

Task Force Hunt moved out through the 3d Battalion's old positions at 4:00 P.M , with infantrymen on the leading tanks. It soon ran into heavy resistance and was further slowed by the woods Enemy personnel losses were heavy and his matériel losses equally so, the task force knocked out or overran four half-tracks, five cannons and other pieces of equipment, but never was able to get past its first objective An enemy ammunition dump along the forest road before it was ablaze. Two friendly tanks had just been knocked out. Darkness was falling And the 3d Battalion, advancing on the right against heavy opposition, had just identified the 60th Panzer Grenadier Regiment of the 116th Panzer Division. After dark the 1st Battalion of the 120th came up alongside the task force on the north against sporadic but strong opposition

Task Force Harrison ran into difficulties with the roadnet even before its attack had begun. The 2d Battalion of the 117th Infantry, móving up to the line of departure in trucks, was snarled in traffic along the narrow chewed-up forest road available to it It was supposed to attack at the same time as Task Force Hunt, but arrived at the line of departure late and was then ordered to hold up after the 120th had identified the 116th Panzer Division It finally got moving at 10.45 P M on orders from Division, with the infantry advancing on foot alongside the tanks. At 1.15 A.M , after it had arrived at the road junction which was its first objective, approximately alongside the 120th, but still some distance north of that regiment, it took up defensive positions for the night. The 117th's 1st Battalion, tangled up at first in the task force column, had taken the Lippe Canal town of Hunxe before the task force finally attacked. The 119th Infantry elements along the Division's left rear contacted the British commandos who had taken Wesel.

The Division was on the attack again before dawn of March 26, still in hopes of shaking loose from the opposition and breaking into the clear, but the breakthrough was at least temporarily over with Before daybreak the 1st Battalion, 117th Infantry, captured five prisoners from the 156th Panzer Grenadier Regiment in advancing over rough ground to a knob about two miles southeast of Hunxe Both of the 116th Panzer's armored infantry regiments were now in action against the 30th It soon became clear that the entire division was committed against Old Hickory, with its reconnaissance battalion alone placed south of the 30th's zone, evidently in a flank protection role

*   *   *

There is reasonably good evidence that the enemy was deceived at least as to the date and the assault troops of the Ninth Army attack across the Rhine [1] However, the Germans in turn achieved notable surprise by their prompt commitment of the 116th Panzer Division, which moved in combat team formation on the night of March 24 from its assembly area on the Dutch-German border, across the entire British Second Army front to the south side of the Lippe. With only two first-rate enemy mobile divisions available for counterattack, it had been believed that the Germans would follow their usual practice of committing them piecemeal at widely separated points along the broad threatened front In fact, the other panzer type unit available, the 15th Panzer Grenadier Division, was so employed against the British bridgeheads.

There is no evidence of German insight in using the 116th Panzer Division in so unorthodox a fashion, except a statement of one officer prisoner that he had been told in the assembly area, by Major Guderian, its chief of staff, that the 116th was going to fight the 30th Division

[1] A German order-of battle map captured at the outset of the attack showed the 79th Division con siderably south of the assault area, placed the 94th Division where the 30th actually was and failed to locate the 30th Division at all All other American divisions north of Cologne were accurately marked on the map A captured order of German LXXXVI Corps, dated March 20, 1945, called for intensive preparation against attack at any time, but was not endorsed and forwarded to the line troops by the 180th Division's commander until March 22 The 180th commander then ordered reports on antiairborne preparations to be submitted by March 25 after which presumably he thought there would be time for correction and coordination Finally, although the Corps order warns against British Second Army's attack north of the Lippe River, Ninth Army's attack in the 30th's actual zone of operations, and airborne attacks in support of either ground assault, it discloses uncertainty as to whether either or both ground attacks will be carried out by stating that parachutists will be dropped along the Lippe Canal either to blow the bridges, safeguarding the British south flank or to hold the bridges for the use of Ninth Army Prisoners taken by the 30th, including battalion and regimental officers, unanimously stated they had been told to expect an attack from north to south across the Lippe, and not an attack from the west The enemy eventually blew all of the bridges across the Lippe River and Canal, evidently in furtherance of this idea

This was perhaps a compliment to Old Hickory's fighting ability
But it was one scarcely appreciated by Corps and Army, or by the fighting men, who had driven themselves hard to smash through one German
division only to find a fresh and powerful opponent confronting them

Insight or not, the German move placed Ninth Army in a delicate
position. Effectively, the Army possessed a one-division front, that of
the 30th Division. Two divisions were containing the Ruhr from the
north An entire corps was spread out along the west bank of the Rhine
The 8th Armored Division, slated to pass through the 30th as soon as
possible, and the Army's entire exploitation corps, the XIX, were
squeezing into the newly-won area east of the Rhine, waiting for a
chance to go to work.

Every other Allied army in the west was exploiting rapidly Ninth
Army, meanwhile would have to sit in place, until the 116th Panzer
Division could be chewed up enough to permit rapid expansion directly
eastward or be pushed back far enough from the Rhine for Ninth Army
to expand northward across the Lippe Canal without stumbling over
the British and airborne troops already there Thus, while higher echelons waited, Old Hickory's line troops drove ahead

The 1st Battalion of the 119th Infantry, which had moved steadily
through enemy roadblocks during the small hours of the morning, continued the advance during March 26 and made the best progress—
about three miles along the Division north flank to the edge of Gahlen
During this advance terrain was more of a delaying factor than the
enemy's successive roadblocks—in the woods about one-third of the way
to Gahlen the tanks with B Company bogged down completely. The
tanks with A Company were roadbound, could not maneuver, one of
them was knocked out by an enemy tank

The 117th Infantry was also slowed by a combination of bad terrain
and strong resistance centered around tanks and antiaircraft guns Eight
tanks and two tank destroyers with the 2d Battalion became mired along
the chopped-up muddy forest road Twenty minutes after the 2d Battalion jumped off the 3d Battalion attacked on its right The woods and
ridges ahead were full of machine guns and direct-fire weapons, which
became more deadly as the regiment approached the airport south of
Besten The 117th attack was aided by Lieutenant Alwyn D Conger,
a forward observer of the 113th Field Artillery Battalion, who brought
down deadly fire on a concentration of antiaircraft weapons guarding
the airport along the border between the two regiments and then
knocked out two machine guns, silencing one with his submachine gun
for the benefit of a 105mm self-propelled howitzer he led up to a firing

position In this last action 31 prisoners were taken and about 10 more enemy were killed The regiment advanced 4,000 yards during the day, with the 1st Battalion moving up to protect the left flank

When the 116th Panzer Division moved in, its leading battle group was organized around the 1st Battalion of the 60th Panzer Grenadier Regiment, on the south Thus the 120th Infantry had the roughest going on March 26 The 2d Battalion, attacking at 6:30 A M, advanced about a mile along the road through the woods and had reached the edge of a patch of woods, when the enemy attacked frontally with a company of infantry and about five tanks American artillery drove this attack back in disorder, but enemy resistance continued stiff Enemy artillery fire on the attack echelons and on key road junctions behind them was bitterly heavy and also hurt the 3d Battalion, which attacked on the right two hours after the 2d Battalion moved out Another source of confusion was the unannounced arrival of a company from the neighboring 35th Infantry Division on the battalion's right flank However the attack drove forward and by early afternoon both battalions had reached clearings in the woods Minefields had also caused vehicle casualties. The 2d Battalion's biggest immediate obstacle was a roadblock organized around a couple of houses at a crossroads along the main road at the edge of a 3,000-meter clearing toward the east Here the enemy used three dug-in tanks, finally routed after Private Raymond Butler of F Company maneuvered into the open to shoot three rifle grenades at one of them before he was killed

The 117th reached its objective at 11:00 A.M and was thus well ahead of the rest of the Division. The 3d Battalion was farthest forward because of the trouble the 2d Battalion on its right had had with the roads Consequently it received the brunt of the enemy fire. "We got into a lot of trouble on the objective," said one company commander "As we got to the edge of the woods we got fire from AA emplacements on the hill There were tanks in Besten and tanks in the woods The enemy was dug in and digging in on the high ground There were no enemy on the objective, but those that faced us were looking right down our throats."

The 120th's 1st Battalion was scheduled to pass through the 2d Battalion, 120th's positions at the edge of the woods and attack down the long exposed clearing toward the airport and the concrete emplaced antiaircraft defenses there, which were hammering at the 117th's leading troops. This attack was first slated for 1 45 P M., but was successively delayed to 5 00 P M and then to 8:30 German artillery was heavily shelling the routes of approach. Supporting weapons for the 2d Battalion still occupied most of the available space up forward and minefields were still being ferreted out with bayonets. Mine detectors didn't work against the wooden mines being encountered

Even with the protection of darkness the attack appeared risky to the regimental commander, who wanted to circle around and attack from the 117th's projecting salient to reduce the distance to be negotiated over open ground. His request was refused because such a maneuver would take too long, the 117th needed support as soon as possible. Enemy artillery fire had slackened when the attack at last began, but the battalion took no chances. As soon as the artillery preparation and the supporting fires from the 3d Battalion on the right opened up, the men of the two assault companies rushed forward for the first 400 yards; the reserve company lingered well behind the line of departure. This technique worked, when the enemy artillery responded it fell harmlessly on the deserted line of departure. Smoke was used to blanket the flanks of the assault, and in an hour the objective fell, without an American casualty

Meanwhile the 119th, which had committed its 3d Battalion at 5.30 P.M. through the 117th's lines, to aid the 1st Battalion at Gahlen, was engaged in a difficult struggle there. About 350 men—remnants of the German 180th Division stiffened by elements of the 156th Panzer Grenadier Regiment—held the town stubbornly to protect the important bridge crossing there, aided by five tanks and five assault guns. When a successful blitz attack to Dorsten had seemed possible the previous day, Gahlen had been given the code name "Hubert," after Sergeant Dick Wingate's *Stars and Stripes* cartoon character. In one cartoon, depicting Hubert and friends eating K rations in a bomb crater while a fiendish looking Nazi sniped at them, Hubert had blandly observed, "Let's ignore the bassar, maybe he'll go away." At 8:00 P.M. on the 26th, however, Colonel Russell A. Baker, the 119th's commander, mildly commented to the chief of staff that "Hubert" was somewhat of a misnomer. Gahlen could not be ignored

By the end of the 26th another delaying factor was making itself felt· sheer fatigue. The Division's assault troops had been on the attack day and night for three full days, demands of flank security and a broad front and the caliber of the enemy prevented the elaborate leapfrogging of battalions forward which had given the combat men some snatches of rest on the attack to the Roer, and on the later surge across it almost to the Rhine. They had had very little rest and no hot food in many cases since the attack across the Rhine had begun.

But there could be no letup for the time being, although the Division had already penetrated 12 miles in two days

At 5:00 P.M. on the 26th the XVI Corps commander informed Gen-

eral Hobbs that Army planned to pass the 8th Armored Division through
the 30th the next day or the day afterward, noting that "Army forced
this on us a little faster than we had expected " It was essential that the
30th, in that time, drive through the rest of the forest to give the armor
a springboard for rapid movement and if possible achieve at least a par-
tial breakthrough of the 116th Panzer Division, so that the mission assigned to the 8th Armored Division would be a suitable armored mission. Infantry makes the breakthrough, armor exploits Meanwhile a
combat team of the 75th Division was securing a crossing of the Lippe
Canal in the rear of the 30th at Hunxe.

So the weary 30th went back to work that night With the 119th
Infantry locked in battle at Gahlen and the 120th consolidating after
its successful evening attack, the 117th was the first to move again, attacking with its 2d and 3d Battalions at midnight A night attack had
been settled upon after the successful advance of the previous morning,
in order to cut down the advantage of observation which the enemy's
tanks, antitank guns and machine guns had from their hill positions to
the northeast. Even so, advance was difficult and slow The maps of the
area available failed to show all of the forest trails The 2d Battalion's
leading elements, advancing on the right, became lost in the thickets
at 3.00 o'clock in the morning and finally called for the artillery to
mark with smoke the crossroads which was their objective and then
fire smoke at the next crossroads There was the dangerous possibility
that the white phosphorus shells might have landed among the troops
but the trick succeeded and the advance continued By 4:45 A M both
battalions had moved up to the high ground near the road leading southeast from Gahlen. The 3d Battalion had a small fight at one settlement,
taking 80 prisoners When the fog lifted in the morning it found it had
pushed the enemy off of 20mm antiaircraft gun and 120mm mortar
positions.

Again the 117th was stuck out well in front of the rest of the Division,
and in consequence was subjected to the heavy fire of the 116th's panzer artillery. Roadblocks were strung out along the flanks of the salient.
Counterattacks were not long in coming At 5·00 A M. a two-man
patrol of E Company captured two enemy soldiers evidently on reconnaissance for an attack, for soon thereafter five tanks and 100 German
infantrymen showed up For an hour the battle raged, with heavy artillery fire from both German and American howitzers dominating
the scene. Most of the attack was driven back, but one tank and 20 ac-
campanying panzer grenadiers sideslipped and attempted to get past
a roadblock on the south flank Three of the infantry were taken prisoner and the others and the tank withdrew. The tank never got within

bazooka range "I'll give the artillery credit for keeping the remainder of the enemy from attacking," said one infantry officer there. G Company reported that the artillery and direct tank fire falling on it at 7:00 A M was the most intense it had ever encountered Miraculously there were only two casualties in the company Enemy tanks and infantry were active on the regimental front during the rest of the day, but constant artillery fire forced most of the enemy armor and infantry to keep its distance At 10.05 an enemy infantry-armor attack struck northeast toward the 2d Battalion while a simultaneous thrust with 200 men and two or three tanks southwest into the 3d Battalion's left flank was taking place Artillery knocked both attempts back, and the tanks, each accompanied by small groups of infantry for close-in protection, settled down to sniping with their cannons and attempting to infiltrate singly

The hottest battle was fought along the road leading southeast from Gahlen along the ridge Lieutenant Shaw's platoon of I Company mounted up on a platoon of tanks and two tank destroyers at 10 00 o'clock and made a "mad dash" for the road to cut it This move was a serious threat to the sizeable force still battling to hold Gahlen, and the enemy used about every weapon at his disposal to drive the little task force off its objective, pounding it incessantly for the next three and a half hours, from every direction The platoon suffered 24 casualties, lost two tanks and both tank destroyers, but held on grimly, although the position remained hot for the next forty-eight hours

The platoon's action was tied in with an attempt to seize Besten, farther north along the Gahlen road, but the rest of the attack was stopped dead by the intensity of the artillery and tank fire of the concurrent enemy counterattack Besten was shoved down on the schedule, to be attacked after nightfall

While the 117th was encountering the first of the enemy countermeasures around dawn, the 3d Battalion of the 120th Infantry was attacking to come up alongside the 1st Battalion positions near the airport By 7 35 it had reached the edge of the woods almost as far east as the 117th's leading troops. Principal opposition came from around the fixed concrete antiaircraft positions of the airport Captured in the attack were four huge 128mm antiaircraft guns and five flak wagons

The close-in fight for Gahlen which had begun the previous day continued through the early afternoon It was a straight street-fighting job against determined resistance, with the attack slowly moving ahead against heavy-machine gun and tank fire at close range which blanketed every American tank, tank destroyer, or infantry group that moved into the open.

Finally, however, the enemy line was cracked and the panzer grenadiers of the 116th Panzer Division withdrew from the town along the road to Dorsten, covered by tank fire from the hill to the east and leaving stragglers from other units in Gahlen During the afternoon the 119th fought its way forward approximately a mile to positions alongside the 117th.

By this time orders had been issued for the 8th Armored Division to pass through the 30th in the morning, although Old Hickory staff officers voiced scepticism that a predominantly armored unit could make much headway against the tanks and antitank guns still available to the 116th Panzer Division The Germans had lost most heavily in infantry And, although open ground had been reached, roads were still poor and fields muddy However, it appeared that the enemy would not put up strong defense forward of the north-south line through Dorsten

During the night both the 117th and the 120th moved forward to give the armor a better line of departure K Company of the 117th reduced Besten by moonlight before midnight In the 120th area, the edge of the woods was taken and cleaned out as a line of departure, and at 9:00 P.M., after an artillery preparation and with smoke shells laid down on the flanks and objective to screen the assault, the 2d Battalion attacked against strongpoints of the 60th Panzer Grenadier Regiment for the town of Holthausen, which covered the road leading eastward into the open By 3.00 A M the town had been cleared of enemy At 6:00 A M. the 8th Armored passed through the 30th and took up the attack. The 30th continued forward to new positions flanking the armor's routes of advance during the morning, but by nightfall was out of contact with the enemy For the first time in almost 100 hours the assault troops had a real chance to sit down and rest.

*   *   *

The Rhine crossing operation furnished a curious combination of success and disappointment Conceived in optimism, it had unfolded brilliantly at first During the three-and-one-half-day assault Old Hickory captured a rich bag of 3,500 prisoners and 33 antitank and artillery pieces, and for the first two days of the assault made the most rapid progress of any unit on the entire 21st Army Group front. Then terrain, new opposition and finally fatigue intervened, although the 116th Panzer Division had been shoved back and badly battered, it was still making skillful and tenacious use of its opportunities to delay when the 30th was ordered to drop out of the attack

Yet the enemy paid a high price for this local defensive success. By committing the 116th Panzer Division on a narrow front, the enemy neglected other weak points in his lines further north On March 30 the remnants of the 116th were still battling doggedly south of the Lippe Canal But by then Ninth Army's main effort had sideslipped to the north side of the Lippe, and its veteran 2d Armored Division was driving eastward without opposition

Chapter XVII

PURSUIT TO THE ELBE

When the 8th Armored Division passed through the 30th on March 28, Old Hickory's mission was to follow the armor in its old zone, mopping up by-passed pockets of resistance The XVI Corps commander told General Hobbs, March 27, that he thought the arrangement would allow the 30th's tired troops two or three days of rest, and that they probably would be completely motorized when they moved out

Both the Division mission and the Ninth Army main effort shifted, however, in the next few days As had been predicted, the combination of bad roads, fixed antiaircraft guns and the still determined opposition of the 116th Panzer Division made the 8th Armored Division's progress slow The key town of Dorsten, urgently wanted as a crossing site by Ninth Army, fell to the 8th Armored during the early morning of March 29, but Corps had already decided that the situation called for a predominantly infantry assault. A few hours after Dorsten fell, the 75th Infantry Division passed through the 8th Armored to take up the burden of the attack. The 30th, its place as the 8th Armored Division's partner taken by the 75th Division, was placed in XVI Corps reserve, earmarked for transfer to its old Corps, the XIX It passed to XIX Corps control the next morning at 6:00 o'clock

XIX Corps was to be employed north of the Lippe River and Canal, with its old' standby (and the 30th's favorite running mate), the 2d Armored Division, in the lead This division had been particularly restive waiting for a chance to go into action because of its long-standing rivalry with the 3d Armored Division, then spearheading First Army's spectacular advances At last, on March 30, the 2d Armored's tanks started out eastward, brushing past British tanks and trucks moving northeast through their zone toward Munster The 3d Armored Division, meanwhile, was almost up to Paderborn, 69 miles farther east.

The 30th wished its old partner well but watched it depart with regret that Old Hickory couldn't be in on the show At the time XIX Corps plans called for the fresh 83d Infantry Division to follow the 2d. Armored Just to the south the 30th was to follow the 8th Armored Division, about to be transferred to XIX Corps for operations north of the Lippe. But again plans changed At 10.00 P M on March 31 a XIX Corps staff officer phoned with a question: Could the 30th be ready to move before daylight—to follow the 2d Armored Division? It could and was At 4 00 A M on April 1, led by the 119th Infantry combat team, the Division jubilantly crossed the Lippe waterways at Hunxe

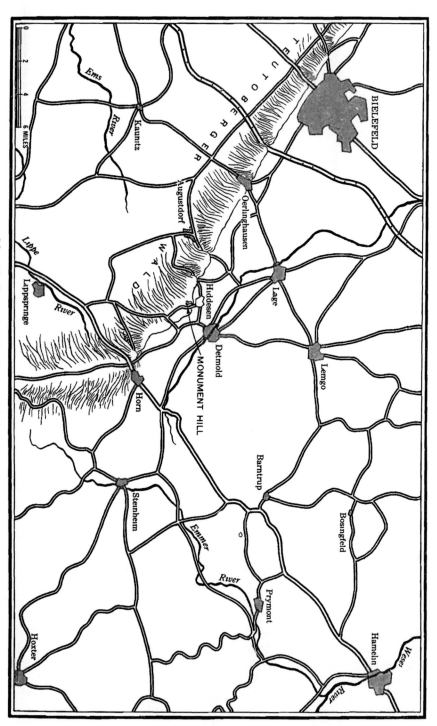

Map 15—From the Teutoberger Wald to Hameln

and started toward an assembly area near Drensteinfurt, 50 miles away

During the long advances of August and September, 1944, the speed of the Allied surge forward seemed to have outstripped the plans, and shortages of gasoline and other supplies held up progress This time was different Six attached quartermaster truck companies made the Division completely motorized The 30th started out with full gas tanks and a 40,000-gallon rolling fuel reserve Maps were issued covering a belt as far east as the Russian lines. Boundaries stretched almost as far east-ward The Division moved out in what was almost a carnival mood German resistance was cracking everywhere, if the radio could be be-lieved The 30th was to mop up by-passed resistance behind a division which would move as fast and as far as any division could The Corps objective was the southern portion of Berlin

*   *   *

The Division's last "ratrace," which was to take it 425 road miles from its initial point at Hunxe to the Elbe at Rogatz in 13 days, began as a simple road march The only notable incident during the first day's move was a preview of future problems the roads were filled with streams of liberated Allied prisoners of war wearing tattered uniforms of half a dozen countries and slave laborers newly escaped from their German masters Most of them walked with packs on their backs, some professionally neat, some makeshift. Some had bicycles, some had "req-uisitioned" horse carts Almost without exception, they were moving westward

Meanwhile the 2d Armored Division, 35 miles up ahead, had made contact with the 3d Armored Division near Lippstadt, thus completely encircling the Ruhr Valley At the same time, however, the tankers were having trouble at the passes through the high, heavily forested line of the Teutoberger Wald, which they had reached after a 25-mile ad-vance during the day This was the place where Hermann, the ancient Germanic tribal chieftain, had decisively defeated the invading Roman legions of Varus in 9 A D The ridgeline, rising sharply from the north German plain, dominated both the approaches from the west and the roads themselves as they passed through the narrow mountain defiles, and was a classic example of defensive terrain. No longer was there a cohesive German field force to defend there, but the *Wehrkreis,* or German military district, rallied to defend the passes This was the region that nurtured the Sixth SS Panzer Army, there was a tank training cen-ter near Augustdorf, on the near side of one of the passes, and another at Detmold, on the far side Thus there were some tanks available to support the makeshift infantry and antitank units that manned the heights and roadblocks covering the passes By the end of April 1, the western edges of one of the passes was forced but opposition was still bitter At 2·00 A M on April 2 the 119th Infantry was attached to the 2d Armored Division Forcing the passes was an infantry job.

The 30th jumped forward another 39 miles on April 2 and found more work waiting for it The 117th Infantry, which had been second in the long divisional column, arrived at 2 00 P M near Neuenkirchen, and split up, its 1st and 3d Battalions setting up roadblocks to protect the 2d Armored's main supply road near Kaunitz and the 2d Battalion moving north toward the major pass just south of Bielefeld, prepared to relieve armored units there The 125th Cavalry Squadron, with the 801st Tank Destroyer Battalion attached, patrolled the Division's left flank, not yet covered by XIII Corps The armor, aided by the 119th, had pushed through the northern passes but had not been able to break into the open because of the stubborn defense of the towns sitting on the eastern exits of the defiles Meanwhile enemy forces in the forests along the hills threatened to close in and recapture the passes

The 2d Armored's best progress had been along the *Autobahn* at the northern end of the joint divisional sector But the *Autobahn* wound north toward Hannover, out of the assigned zone of advance The proposed main supply road ran through Oerlinghausen, nestled in the east slope of the Teutoberger Wald Here resistance was fanatical, with 200 to 400 students from the Officer Candidate School at Detmold backing up some regular troops. The 119th Infantry and 2d Armored troops had little success with a frontal attack out of the pass until mid-afternoon, when at last tanks were negotiated around blown bridges on the northern route to threaten Oerlinghausen from the rear Meanwhile the 117th was relieving the troops protecting the mountain defiles and was mopping up slowly through the thick forest Artillery was handicapped in the ridge fighting—often the opposing troops were too close to open fire, and unobserved fire with map computations was out entirely because no large-scale maps were available

The 120th also went into action on the 3d, moving up its 1st Battalion through one of the southern passes in anticipation of instructions to clean out the southern part of the zone In this move C Company was suddenly hit while in the defile by strong small-arms and *Panzerfaust* (German bazooka) fire from well concealed positions to the north, and finally had to withdraw. The next day, on Division order, the 120th attacked in column of battalions to clean out as far east as Detmold

Meanwhile the 2d Armored Division was still having its troubles Two battalion-strength counterattacks struck to close the pass north of Augustdorf, between Oerlinghausen and the 120th's area, these were driven back with difficulty because of the enemy's tenacity On the far south, 2d Armored reconnaissance elements had a sharp fight with about 200 enemy dug in at the ridge line along the Paderborn–Hameln highway But by nightfall the enemy situation in the north disintegrated and the armored division's tanks raced 10 kilometers to Lage, and thus were in position to pressure Detmold from the north

The 120th's battle the next day was more with terrain than with the enemy, although an SS Battalion commander organized some stiff opposition on Monument Hill before ordering a retreat to Detmold The 1st Battalion, moving up a broad trail to a line of departure south of Monument Hill, on which Hermann's historic victory was commemorated, found the planned route impassable, and instead had to labor up and down Hill 393, just to the west, before engaging the company still on Monument Hill with marching fire while ascending About 50 enemy, some eager to quit and some still belligerent, were captured This action took all morning. Thereupon the 3d Battalion, which had moved up on the left while the 1st Battalion was advancing, attacked and seized the town of Hiddesen, on the east side of the ridge, breaking through a strong line on the edge of town and then encountering spotty opposition. Aided by the 2d Armored Division, which swept past the north side of Detmold, the 2d Battalion took that city during the evening without opposition except for snipers C Company, meanwhile, cleaned out the roadblock in the hills which had blocked it the previous day, with the aid of tank destroyers maneuvered up to within 200 yards of the enemy position.

With the opposition at the Teutoberger Wald crushed, the 2d Armored Division made rapid progress On April 5 it raced more than 25 miles forward to the outskirts of the fabled city of Hameln on the Weser River, against negligible opposition, and the next day, led by 119th Infantry troops, seized a bridgehead. Soon three bridges were operating, and 2d Armored swung north to gain crossings of the canal flanking Hameln on the south, consolidating its positions the next day. Meanwhile the 30th moved up behind, cleaning out pockets of resistance and maintaining flank security for the main supply road Organized opposition had ceased to exist, the caliber of the enemy resistance was entirely unpredictable Colonel Johnson of the 117th summarized on April 5 "The situation is very fluid. There are as many Germans behind the lines as there are in front—if you fire your pistol in the air a dozen Germans will come rushing in to be taken prisoner." Sometimes there were fights, usually ended by the appearance of an American tank or tank destroyer The Reconnaissance Troop captured 485 prisoners and ten 150mm howitzers that day, including one group of 280 men, in going about its assigned business of patrolling and making contact with the 84th Division on the left A couple of days later, however, in reconnoitering a town on the far side of the Weser, the troop lost two armored cars in an ambush which caught its patrol roadbound and unable to deploy.

The 2d Armored Division didn't want to fool with Hameln, so that picturesque old town was cleared in three hours on April 7 by the 117th, attacking from the south with its 1st and 3d Battalions, while the 2d Battalion sat in place on the west bank of the Weser opposite the city The next day, after the bulk of the Division had moved up to the Weser with its flanks apparently well covered, reports of enemy activity in the woods north of Lemgo, 24 miles to the rear, forced the dispatch of a task force of tanks, tank destroyers, cavalry and infantry under Lieutenant Colonel Ammons of 2d Battalion, 117th Infantry. Task Force Ammons moved back that evening and next day cleaned out a small force which had drifted down from the XIII Corps zone as the latter Corps' troops came up

The standing joke during this phase of the advance was a parody of the mine-clearance signs that the engineers posted along the highways—"Road clear of enemy to ditches " But mopping up the German soldiers off the main routes, which the armor ignored unless they caused trouble, in order to keep the advance speedy, was not the only problem of a follow-up division like the 30th Old Hickory was prepared to fight, but it also had to guard a wide variety of installations overrun—airports, ordnance shops, training camps, special research establishments The Division surgeon found himself in charge of close to 10,000 German soldiers in military hospitals, which Army was reluctant to take over until the last possible moment as the Division moved ahead K Company of the 117th took over control of a 9,000-man Allied prisoner-of-war camp west of the Teutoberger Wald on April 2 and remained there until April 7, as the rest of the Division raced far ahead of it. G-4 was already beginning to worry about food supply for Allied prisoner-of-war camps and displaced persons camps The policy of Supreme Headquarters Allied Expeditionary Forces was to hold both Allied prisoners of war and slave laborers in place temporarily, and although this policy was ignored by thousands of men, women and children clogging the roads, those that did comply had to be fed.

The 2d Armored Division pushed farther east on April 7 to the line of the Leine River south of Hannover At Schuleberg on the Leine the armor found a bridge intact and started crossing with tanks carrying 119th Infantry doughboys Three tanks had crossed and two more were on the bridge when the commander of the fourth tank shouted

"Cut that wire," pointing to smoke coming from the side of the bridge Sergeant Wilhelm O Jordan of E Company of the 119th scrambled off one of the tanks on the bridge and yanked at the wire, pulling the fuse cap away from the charge and detonating the fuse He was seriously wounded but he had saved an important bridge The fuse had been wired to approximately 1,000 pounds of explosives.

*   *   *

The line of the Leine River was the original boundary between the Russian and the Western Allied zones of occupation, so that it was designated a "no advance line" until April 9 By that time, however, necessary clearances had been obtained, and a new advance was ordered This time the 2d Armored Division, with the 119th Infantry still attached, was to drive straight east from newly captured Hildesheim to the Elbe River at Magdeburg The 30th Division was given a zone of advance of its own just to the north, with the mission of capturing the city of Brunswick and then continuing east to the Elbe near Tangermunde The only armed opposition was expected to come from *Wehrkreis* troops, who might attempt to delay at various places along the line and might even attempt to defend Brunswick Flanking Brunswick were a number of canals and ditches at right angles to the advance; these appeared to offer the greatest capability to delay the Division Phase lines were set up all the way to the Elbe The Division zone was divided between the 120th Infantry on the south and the 117th Infantry on the north. The attached 125th Cavalry was originally to sweep ahead of the motorized regimental columns It had one special piece of armament—the Division commander's armored car with a loudspeaker and German-speaking Lieutenant Henry Schmitz installed

It was hoped that Brunswick might be induced to surrender after the 117th Infantry had driven past the canals to the western outskirts of the city Dive bombers were alerted to demonstrate in support of a surrender ultimatum If the surrender negotiations were unsuccessful, the 117th would attack frontally while the 120th moved around to the south blocking the exits from the city.

The Division moved out the next day One battalion of the 120th Infantry was left in place because of lack of transportation, though many of the infantrymen were riding tanks and tank destroyers—Corps had ordered 170 trucks to haul ammunition Division Artillery borrowed 62 trucks from the 119th Field Artillery Group to replace those requisitioned to haul ammunition and thus was able to accompany the advance Also slowing the columns were some troops of the 2d Armored Division in the 30th zone and a convoy from the 5th Armored Division, operating on the north, which cut into the 30th Division zone During

Map 16—Brunswick and Vicinity

most of the day the cavalry ran into very scattered resistance which was quickly reduced, and the loudspeaker on the armored car was used effectively. By late afternoon the cavalry had reached the canal about three and a half miles west of Brunswick, where the bridge over the central route was blown. At the town of Vechelade nearby a German medical officer stated that the general commanding Brunswick was ready to surrender, and Private Solomon of the 125th Cavalry Squadron was guided through the lines to arrange a meeting, which was scheduled for 7.00 P.M. near the bridge. The leading troops closed up behind the canal and waited on the roads, while the rear elements continued to arrive. Meanwhile, unknown to the Americans, Germans were putting the final touches on bridge demolitions on the network of canals around Brunswick on the north and west.

The conference proved a waste of time. Lieutenant General Carl Veith, an antiaircraft artillery commander who had assumed the defense of Brunswick as the senior officer present, brought along with him two aides, an interpreter and a man who apparently represented the Nazi Party, though he, too, was in uniform. Veith rejected General Hobbs' unconditional surrender, proposing at first that he be allowed twenty-four hours to move his troops out of the city and thus save it from further damage. "The terms of the Allies are always unconditional surrender," General Hobbs replied.

The Germans were given five minutes to confer among themselves. Meanwhile General Hobbs and General Harrison, the 30th's assistant division commander, talked animatedly about ways and means of storming the city. Then General Veith made a new proposition: "Brunswick and vicinity will surrender unconditionally at 12:00 tomorrow. I will withdraw my troops before the town and those that are in the town."

"We don't care about the town. We want your troops," General Harrison snapped petulantly. The American position, based on the understanding that General Veith was prepared to surrender, was becoming more and more false. General Hobbs stated firmly, "I am not here to bicker. I want unconditional surrender." General Veith shrugged his shoulders and the American party started to leave The German interpreter asked how long the truce would last; after conferring with Lieutenant Colonel Stewart L. Hall, the Division G-2, General Hobbs announced that hostilities would be resumed in half an hour and then departed On the road leading west from the conference Colonel Johnson moved up and down the packed 117th Regimental Combat Team column announcing that there was going to be some shooting after all A group of enemy planes swept over the column but did not strafe.

The conference had been a liability. Witnesses do not agree on whether the bridges over the canal were blown during or before the conference, but blown they were.

The 2d Battalion of the 117th Infantry made two attempts to cross the canal the same evening, but were driven back by antitank, mortar, and small-arms fire Meanwhile the 120th Infantry moved up to Ufingen. During the night, the 3d Battalion of the 117th Infantry was substituted for the 2d in the assault role and at 9:30 A M after three unsuccessful attempts, forced a crossing of the canal, which was defended by three replacement battalions On the south two platoons of C Company, 120th Infantry, made a successful sneak crossing of the canal at 4:30 A.M , with the 3d Battalion of the same regiment following through at 7:00 o'clock.

The assault moved steadily ahead. By 12:30 the 117th had two battalions across, with the 2d Battalion waiting to move across the canal. At 4:30 Company A of the 105th Engineer Battalion had bridged the canal and tanks and tank destroyers were moving up to support the attack. Midnight found the 3d Battalion clearing up the center of the city, with the 2d Battalion past the antiaircraft defenses at the large airport in the southwest part of the city and the 1st Battalion clearing out small-arms resistance in the northwest portion of Brunswick. The chief problem was the lack of maps of the city; the new town plans available from Corps headquarters had not arrived in time to be used, and mopping up had to proceed by guess rather than by meticulously allotted sectors.

General Veith had fled; the burgomeister had committed suicide. A platoon leader of Company L, 117th Infantry, was sitting in a taxi office studying a street map of the city when a municipal functionary approached and said the acting burgomeister asked to see him.

Taking a runner with him, he followed the German to a huge underground office where several uniformed Germans were standing around. A secretary was writing out a long set of formal conditions of surrender. The tired platoon leader impatiently cut it down to two pages and agreed to take it to his commanding officer. Brunswick had fallen cheaply, though the British broadcasting system talked ponderously of heavy street fighting there.

The 3d Battalion of the 120th crossed a lock on the canal on foot early in the afternoon and pressed on 3,000 yards without opposition. When it reached the Oker River, which flows north through Brunswick, it found the road bridges blown but a railroad bridge intact, and this was used for a foot crossing. After reorganizing just before dark, the battalion moved northeast to establish road blocks on the southeast side of Brunswick In the vicinity of this roadblock Company L captured General Veith toward midnight

The motorized 2d Battalion came up from far to the rear and crossed a bridge over the canal which had been started by Company C of the 105th Engineer Battalion during the morning and finished at 6:25 P M. The battalion then circled down into the 2d Armored Division zone to cross the Oker River. As it continued the drive eastward the battalion ran into a roadblock, and its two leading quarter-ton trucks were knocked out by four enemy tanks dug in to support the roadblock. Friendly tanks were mired attempting to maneuver off the road At midnight the fight was still hot, by morning, however, the enemy had fled. Meanwhile, with the 2d Battalion held up, the 1st Battalion had mounted trucks during the night and had 'moved on up to the regimental objective near the 3d Battalion's position.

The eastern part of Brunswick had not been cleared by morning of April 12, but it was not worth waiting around for; the bulk of the garrison had fled The 117th Infantry left its 3d Battalion to clean out the rest of the city and then to guard the installations there, while the 3d Battalion of the 120th, without transportation, stayed in place, mopping up 236 prisoners The 125th Cavalry was still deadlocked in roadblocks along the canal crossing north of Brunswick, but the rest of the Division streaked another 35 miles eastward, with the two regimental columns led by the 30th Reconnaissance Troop. Resistance consisted mainly of scattered roadblocks defended by small-arms fire and *Panzerfausts*. Usually the towns themselves were undefended, or swiftly cowed with the aid of machine guns, tank destroyers or tanks. In one town which civilians declared clear of enemy soldiers, however, two Americans were shot in the back. The angry doughboys then rounded up 100 uniformed Germans The 117th Infantry during this day's drive secured, intact, crossings over the Weser–Ems Canal against light small-arms fire at Calvorde Except for the thick woods ahead, which would require considerable effort to clear, the next delaying position available to the Germans was the Elbe River. A record 2,500 prisoners were taken during the day, 280 of them by the two Reconnaissance Troop platoons spearheading the 120th's advance.

The next day, April 13, the Division reached the Elbe, with the prospect that it would soon cross it, either by direct assault or on a bridgehead two armored infantry battalions of the 2d Armored Division and the 2d and 3d Battalions, 119th Infantry, then held south of Magdeburg. The original plan of driving almost due east for the Elbe was changed, because the 5th Armored Division had swung south slightly to take the riverside city of Tangermunde, originally in the 30th sector When the new instructions were received from Corps the regiments were on the road, still advancing in three columns, with the 120th on the south, the 117th in the center and the 125th Cavalry Squadron lagging on the north as it skirted enemy opposition in the woods and town to its left The new division boundaries were being changed and were as yet unknown. The Division command post was split up in two echelons along the road. Thus, when the columns turned southeast in the Letzlinger woods there was no real assurance that the area had been cleared of opposition; regimental boundaries did not exist. Another 2,000 prisoners were rounded up during the day as the small unit convoys moved ahead. Along one forest road the bodies of murdered political prisoners, still wearing their striped prison garments, were strewn The 120th's leading elements caught up with a column of 15 trucks and cars in retreat; this column was thoroughly battered by armored cars and tanks carrying E Company. At Colbitz a camp containing 2,000 Allied prisoners, most of them British and American, was overrun, as was a column of British and American prisoners being marched westward away from the erupting Russian front The Division command group moved blithely through its prospective command post location at Colbitz to Wolmirstedt without protection except from its own armament The 117th drove down to the Elbe at Rogatz during the evening, with opposition bitter, at first, against the 2d Battalion's attack. The 1st Battalion, following, went on to the town of Loitsche, and obtained the surrender of the town by threatening to destroy it if the natives did not surrender the enemy soldiers prepared to defend there The 120th moved down to Barleben, on the outskirts of Magdeburg, only to receive mortar and small-arms fire Magdeburg had been reported taken by the 2d Armored Division. It very clearly was not Another battle took place at roadblocks which the enemy set up to cover the approaches to the autobahn crossing the Elbe Signs along the autobahn read *"Berliner Ring 87 km"*

Tankers of the 743d, entering the town of Farsleben, came upon a tragic scene—a train crowded with 2,400 political prisoners: men, women and children, most of them Jews, being transported away from their concentration camp. The guards fled; some were later captured. The prisoners had gone for days without food and were weakened by exhaustion, hunger and disease Several had already died of typhus. Under the supervision of the 823d Tank Destroyer Battalion, which took over the town, these derelicts were housed in the village and the burgomeister was ordered to run the bakery all night and slaughter sheep and cattle to provide food for them. Later the Division's Military Government detachment moved them to barracks.

Plans continued indefinite for the next few days, while rear areas were cleared out and positions consolidated. The Reconnaissance Troop, sent on reconnaissance along the new main supply road, captured 270 prisoners at Hillersleben, which proved to contain a principal German ordnance proving grounds, comparable to the American Aberdeen Proving Grounds More than 2,000 artillery pieces, vehicles of all kinds, signal and radar equipment, and miscellaneous military items were found there The 120th Infantry cleaned out the woods near Glindenberg The great Letzlinger Forest to the north was still swarming with enemy bands, including sabotage teams sent out from an engineer school east of the Elbe, and remained dangerous to small convoys for days 'afterward Meanwhile, as signs of enemy preparations to defend the east bank of the Elbe River began to be noticed, the 2d Armored Division's bridgehead was driven back across the river. Approximately 60 men of the 119th's 3d Battalion were missing in action. Unable to get friendly armor across the river for close support, the force holding the bridgehead had been struck sharply by infantry and tanks. Still farther south, however, the 83d Division held an expanding bridgehead

The plan to cross the Elbe died somewhere in higher echelons, with the Russians already on the attack in the Berlin area. Instead the elimination of the German bridgehead across the Elbe at Magdeburg became the center of attention, although as late as the 16th the 3d Battalion of the 120th Infantry practiced river crossings in case of an order to assault across the river.

Magdeburg at first appeared to be a fairly easy objective to take, and the 120th Infantry was actually alerted on the morning of April 16, soon after the job had been plunked in the 30th's lap, to attack the city alone from the north, while the 2d Armored Division, still controlling the 119th Infantry, contained the rest of the city's perimeter

There was some hope that the garrison could be induced to surrender, and a party led by the regimental intelligence officer went forward to the enemy outposts to see about it The attempt was unsuccessful. The surrender party, flying white flags on its vehicles, was stopped at an enemy roadblock and, after some phoning, two of the party were blindfolded and driven to the headquarters of the Magdeburg commander. This they correctly judged to be on the island in the Elbe. At the garrison headquarters they were met by the commanding general's chief of staff, who informed them that his general was not empowered to discuss surrender terms The American representatives sensed that many of the Germans wished to surrender, but the German colonel's reply was supported by evidence of strong roadblocks around the perimeter and the presence of SS troops among those guarding the city's perimeter

Plans were changed; instead of one regiment, both the 30th and the

2d Armored Divisions would attack. The ground assault was to be preceded by a heavy bombing by 11 groups of medium bombers Meanwhile the 117th Infantry was moving into positions on the 120th's right and the artillery was shifting so as to be able to support the attack The 119th Infantry, which had occupied the northern part of the 2d Armored Division sector, reverted to 30th Division control at midnight

Magdeburg was cleared in twenty-four hours. The three-and-one-half-hour air preparation which preceded the ground attack appeared to have little effect, probably because it was aimed at the already well bombed center of town, while the defensive positions were generally scattered in a deep belt around the outskirts of the built-up area The ground attack, which began at 3:15 P M., ran into troublesome but not intense opposition. The enemy defenses had not been completed before the assault began; gangs constructing antitank ditches and roadblocks were overrun in the heart of the city. The enemy defended with what he had—roadblocks built around machine guns and antitank guns, and snipers hidden in the rubble, bearing rifles and *Panzerfausts* Trolley cars, wagons filled with dirt and other makeshifts were used to physically block the roads Mopping up, combing through the rubble, searching large apartment houses room by room, took time. Artillery, which showered the city heavily in the early phases of the operation, could not be used effectively in the close-quarter fighting which characterized the action, and it was difficult to maneuver tanks and tank destroyers to assist Small units had to change direction frequently because the axis of the attack often did not conform to the axis of the streets. Mortars were the most effective supporting weapons

The attack held up at nightfall, and resumed the next morning at 6 30 The division pressed steadily down to the river, only to have the bridges over the Elbe blown by the Germans at almost the last moment, leaving rear guards to be taken prisoner.

Even before the fighting came to an end early in the afternoon of April 18, civilians were getting in the way, their presence interfering with movement of troops and even sometimes obstructing fields of fire By the time the town was completely cleared, what had started as a problem in street fighting had become a policeman's headache The streets were thronged with civilians. There was no opposition to the Americans from them, but mob looting started in many places, particularly at food warehouses. Germans and displaced persons alike fought impersonally to get at the booty. In one case only a shot fired over the head of the crowd sufficed to break up the looting. Platoons, squads, individual sentries, were ordered out as rapidly as possible to liquor stores, butcher shops, clothing stores, and a host of other establishments.

They were often difficult to locate because town plans of Magdeburg were not available in quantity.

With the capture of Magdeburg on April 18, the 30th's fighting career in Europe came to a conclusion For the next few days the river front was active as patrols crossed to the island in the Elbe at Magdeburg to obtain surrender of the enemy troops still there. Division Artillery managed to find targets to shoot at as late as May 2. But every day the position of the Germans still fighting became more hopeless The enemy troops still along the east bank of the Elbe were menaced from the rear by the Russians advancing through Berlin, and the signs of their disintegration and panic were increasingly evident

The fighting was over, but there were other chores to perform. During the three weeks between the fall of Magdeburg and the cessation of hostilities in Europe, the Division captured 7,468 prisoners—as many as it had taken in its first three months of fighting in 1944—and could have taken many others. Some of the prisoners were individually ferretted out; others gave themselves up in compliance with military government proclamations The largest number, however, came from east of the Elbe, crossing the broken bridges or in boats to escape capture by the oncoming Russians

So large a number of prisoners was difficult to feed, handle and evacuate. Ninth Army confessed on May 5 that it was unable to accept any more prisoners for the time being, although it could not formally authorize refusal to accept their surrender In the meantime makeshift solutions had been worked out along the riverfront Some groups wishing to surrender were sent back after their kitchen facilities and food stocks before they were accepted Others were simply refused passage across the Elbe, although it was increasingly evident that the flow of would-be prisoners could not be entirely stopped without gunfire One of these prisoners was Lieutenant General Kurt Dittmar, the German General Staff radio spokesman, who crossed the Elbe by boat on April 25, under a white flag He came, he said, to arrange aid for the German wounded on the east bank of the Elbe and the evacuation into American-held territory of the civilians there It developed that he commanded no troops and had crossed without the knowledge of the German sector commander. Dittmar was offered a chance to surrender himself, at first refusing and then changing his mind on the way down to the riverside. His son and an artillery major surrendered with him

Displaced persons and allied prisoners of war created similar problems. An accurate figure on the number of persons in these categories handled by the Division between April 18 and May 8 is not available, but some idea of the magnitude of the problem may be gained from the fact that the 30th evacuated 2,207 Allied prisoners of war and 4,719 displaced persons from Western Europe in the first eight days of May and on the 8th had 47,690 displaced persons and 15,926 Allied prisoners of war on its hands Capture of *Wehrmacht* food stores in Magdeburg partially alleviated the problem of feeding this group—approximately four times the normal strength of the Division—but there was still the problem of evacuating them to the rear. At the time the Division's ration train had to make a two-day round trip to the Army quartermaster supply points, which meant doubling the normal number of trucks used to haul the Division's own food. However, ammunition was not needed, and ammunition trucks constituted most of the pool of 75 trucks set up within the Division to haul displaced persons and Allied prisoners.

At the time most of the line elements of the Division were split up on guard details Magdeburg, in particular, was cluttered with installations to guard—food warehouses, *Wehrmacht* and Nazi Party headquarters, liquor stores, industrial establishments, even a bank with a vaultful of German currency. Outside of Magdeburg were mines converted into storehouses and factories, airports, the vast proving grounds at Hillersleben, and many others. Much of the work of military government was farmed out to the units, which were assigned zones of responsibility; the typical platoon leader of the Division celebrated VE-day as a burgomeister, with his feet placed firmly on top of the biggest desk in town. Down along the Elbe, the observation posts still functioned, reporting minor movements of enemy across the river and setting up rumors about the approach of the Russians Reports of clouds of dust in the distance, of the sound of cannon fire, would bring everyone running with field glasses, until the game had lost its allure. On April 25 the Red Army made contact with American troops at Torgau, far to the south, and thereafter new contacts were reported daily. But the Russians seemed to be in no hurry to reach the Magdeburg section. At last, during the night of May 4-5, 10 days after the first meeting of the two allies, the Red Army quietly reached the Elbe near Grunewald, south of Magdeburg. Contact was officially made there by Company G, 119th Infantry, at 6:30 P.M. At 10:10 a Russian truck and motorcycle drove up to the Elbe opposite the 117th's positions in Magdeburg, and later in the morning Company L, 120th Infantry, sighted Red Army soldiers on its front and made arrangements for the 3d Battalion, 120th Infantry, commander to cross in an assault boat in midafternoon to participate in the rites of greeting. Two days later General Hobbs had lunch with General Bagilevsky, commanding general of the Russian 370th Infantry Division at the 117th's command post in Madgeburg, which made it official. On the morning of the same day a teletypewriter message had announced the end of the war.

V-E Day was an emotional disappointment. By the middle of May 7 virtually everyone knew that hostilities would officially cease at midnight that night and that the official day for celebrating would begin a full twenty-four hours later, on May 8. But the war had been over for Old Hickory for many days. On May 8 the 120th Infantry was moving to its new occupation area in the edge of the Hartz Mountains. The Division as a whole was busy with military government of an area forty miles wide along the bank of the Elbe and approximately forty miles deep—about one square mile for every ten men in the Division. And everyone had the same question: What comes next?

Appendix 1

AFTER VE-DAY

The story of the 30th Infantry Division following VE-day is, for the most part, a record of moving or waiting to move The Division remained temporarily as an occupation unit at first, continuing to function in the Madgeburg area until relieved by British units on May 27, and then assuming control of six *Landkreise* in Thuringia, between Saalfeld, south of Weimar, and the Czechoslovakian border near Plauen The Division command post was at Possneck

By the end of June, however, Old Hickory had been designated for redeployment through the United States to the then still active Pacific battlefields and had started the long trek homeward In the last three days of the month most of the old-timers of the Division, eligible for discharge under the point system, were transferred to the 76th Infantry Division and to other units, being replaced by low-point men, mainly from the 76th Approximately 550 officers, three-quarters of the Division complement, and 4,500 enlisted men departed in this wholesale exchange

Two months after VE-day the reconstituted 30th was reentering France on its way from a week-long halt around Heppenheim, on the Rhine plain south of Frankfurt The Division remained for most of July at Camp Oklahoma City, near Sissone, France, turning in vehicles and other equipment, preparing for the long voyage home, and sending men to Paris and Reims on pass July 29 it moved by train to Camp Lucky Strike, a staging camp for the Le Havre Port of Embarkation

On August 2 the entire Division, except for the 119th Infantry, crossed the English Channel to Southhampton on the USS *Exchequer* and the USS *Marine Wold,* there to wait for the *Queen Mary,* returning to its old berth in Southhampton for the first time in four years On August 16 Old Hickory boarded the *Queen Mary* and on the next day steamed out of the harbor The 119th Infantry was then five days at sea, having sailed from Le Havre August 12 on the Coast Guard transport USS *General Black*

The 119th Infantry landed first, at Boston on August 19 Two days later, steaming up the North River in the dark, the rest of the Division, aboard the *Queen Mary,* was receiving a tumultuous welcome from New York City

The war over, the 30th was scheduled for deactivation At least two-thirds of its men did not rejoin the Division following the 45-day leaves given them as soon as they returned to the United States Others were sent out again on furlough or transferred to other units when they did report back to Fort Jackson, South Carolina, where the Division's advance detachment had-been functioning since September 3 Orders for the Division's deactivation were received at Fort Jackson on October 19 Deactivation was completed November 25, 1945

Final tribute to the work of the 30th had previously been paid by the four states from which the Division had entered Federal service in 1940 and by General Jacob L Devers, Commanding General of Army Ground Forces The governors of Georgia, North and South Carolina and Tennessee joined in proclaiming October 30 "Old Hickory Day" within their states, and marked the occasion with appropriate ceremonies at the state capitals and with a special radio program General Devers, in a letter to the 30th's commanding general dated September 21, stated

The inactivation of the 30th Infantry Division brings to a close a brilliant chapter in American history The officers and men of the Old Hickory Division, which was formed from National Guard units of North Carolina, South

Carolina, Georgia and Tennessee, have maintained the highest standards of our infantry from the federalization of the unit on September 16, 1940, to the present

Your division landed in France in June 1945 and during the rest of the war performed, often spectacularly, in an efficient, destructive manner After spearheading the memorable St Lô breakthrough, your troops were called upon to repel the German attempt to split the American First and Third Armies at Avranches In one of the most decisive battles of the war, the 30th crushed the enemy assault and held open the vital corridor to the south

`At Aachen, through Belgium, Holland and on into Germany, you continued the offense As a result of the terrific mauling you gave to some of the *Wehrmacht's* best troops, the enemy dubbed you "Roosevelt's SS Troops" The final weeks of the war found your men engaged in the drive which encircled the Ruhr and bagged thousands of German prisoners

Your Division is now being inactivated, but many of your men must remain in the service, while the national security demands their retention Until they can be released, I am sure they will continue to carry out their assignments with loyalty and vigor

The 30th has fought courageously and relentlessly, in keeping with the finest traditions of our country I am proud that, on behalf of your fellow countrymen, I have this opportunity to commend your officers and men for their devotion and self-sacrifice in the victory over tyranny

Appendix 2

NOTES ON ORGANIZATION

"The infantry division is the basis of organization of the field forces It is the smallest unit that is composed of all of the essential ground arms and services and which can conduct, by its own means, operations of general importance   The combat value of the infantry division derives from its ability to combine the actions of the various arms and services to maintain combat over a considerable period of time " Par 1010, FM 100-5, *Field Service Regulations, Operations,* 1944

Particularly in the early days of the war, a good many writers tended to single out a particular arm as the key to victory Immediately after the German blitz through the Low Countries and France in 1940, the emphasis was on armor The seizure of Crete illustrated the important capabilities of airborne troops Later, the more enthusiastic exponents of air power talked and wrote as though bombs alone could assure success in warfare Finally, after Cassino, the infantryman, who has—by and large—the nastiest and most dangerous job in combat, began to achieve public recognition

The fact of the matter is, of course, that battles are won by teams composed of all arms and services, and winning so big a thing as a war itself is an achievement shared from the front lines all the way back to the factories of the homeland Some assignments are more dangerous or more unpleasant than others Some are more colorful But success in battle depends upon the driver of the ammunition truck, upon the telephone linesman, as well as on the doughboy It depends, too, in large measure on how well their efforts are coordinated.

A running narrative of combat cannot convey adequately a balanced picture of the actions and relationships of all the 16,000-plus men who fought and worked simultaneously with the 30th Infantry Division in the field The following notes on who was in the 30th and how they worked together may assist the reader in obtaining that picture

The standard infantry division which made up the bulk of the American fighting forces in Europe in 1944-45 was a highly complex mechanism, somewhat smaller in size than its World War I precursor but possessed of much greater fire power and variety of means In addition to the traditional infantry-artillery team, the infantry division possessed its own resources in tanks, tank destroyers, and antiaircraft artillery It had a cavalry troop of its own Fighter-bombers were normally available to the division and an Air Corps representative was permanently stationed with it to control them Each of the combat units had its own supply, signal, and maintenance personnel Backing them up as part of the permanent division team were whole units of specialists—engineers, signal corps men, medical, ordnance and quartermaster troops, military policemen, and, at division headquarters, administrative and intelligence specialists (The organization of the 30th Infantry Division is shown in Diagram 1)

Infantry, of course, provided the backbone and the *raison d'etre* of the entire organization Out of the divisional strength of approximately 16,000 (including normal attachments), approximately 9,000 men were divided equally among the three infantry regiments, the 117th, 119th and 120th Each regiment consisted of three rifle battalions, a cannon company (six 105mm infantry howitzers), an antitank company (nine 57mm AT guns), and headquarters and service companies The rifle battalion, with a combat strength normally of about 500 men, is the yardstick of fighting requirements up to approximately army level, regiments and divisions are important, principally, as convenient mechanisms for controlling and supporting, with fire and supplies, the fighting battalions Each rifle battalion has three rifle companies and a heavy-weapons company, in addition to a head-quarters company The rifle company, with a normal strength of 189 men, includes three 40-man rifle platoons and a weapons platoon containing two light machine guns and three 60mm mortars, in addition to a command group, and is armed with rifles, antitank rocket launchers (bazookas), Browning automatic rifles (the heavy weapons of the three 12-man squads in a platoon) The companies are lettered consecutively In the 1st Battalion of a regiment, Companies A, B and C, are rifle companies, while Company D is a heavy-weapons company armed with eight heavy machine guns and six 81mm mortars In the 2d Battalion, E, F, and G are rifle companies, and H a heavy-weapons company In the 3rd Battalion, I, K, and L are rifle companies and M a heavy-weapons company

Division Artillery consisted of four field artillery battalions, each armed with twelve howitzers as well as individual arms for local protection Three battalions, the 118th, 197th and 230th, were equipped with the 105mm howitzer, which fires a 35-pound shell up to approximately 10,000 yards The 113th's 155mm howitzers could fire a 95-pound projectile about 14,000 yards Normally, additional artillery was placed under Division Artillery control, while still other battalions of Corps and Army artillery fired on deeper targets Some of the artillery units attached to the 30th were almost permanent fixtures, fighting as part of the 30th throughout most of the campaign They were the 70th Field Artillery Battalion (105mm howitzer), the 203d Field Artillery Battalion (155mm howitzer) and the 119th Field Artillery Group (normally controlling two 155mm howitzer and one 155mm gun ["Long Tom"] battalions) The artillery was notable for its relative wealth of wire and radio communications and for this reason frequently provided the fastest means of communication with the front Each of the three firing batteries within the battalion sent out forward observers, and the light (105mm howitzer) battalions each possessed three liaison sections stationed with the battalion headquarters of the infantry regiment each normally supported Each battalion and Division Artillery headquarters also possessed two light liaison-type airplanes for observing fire These planes were normally based together at a single field and their advantages thus pooled

The 30th Cavalry Reconnaissance Troop was designed primarily for mounted patrolling and was entirely motorized The patrolling team consisted of two quarter-ton trucks and one armored car with radio and light cannon The Troop's normal missions were those of contact and security patrolling between scattered infantry elements of the Division or between the 30th and an adjacent division, and maintenance of roadblocks In static situations it furnished reconnaissance patrols into enemy territory and set up observation posts In long sweeps forward it often operated under control of a cavalry squadron attached to the Division Although almost as strong in numbers as a rifle company, the Troop rarely was used as infantry, because of its specialized abilities and because so many men in it were tied down to vehicles and radios

The 105th Engineer Combat Battalion performed a variety of duties Its principal function was the maintenance of roads and bridges, often through actual construction and repair of vehicular routes but mainly through prompt clearance of mines and obstacles from roads needed by the supporting vehicles of the assault troops Thus, the engineers generally operated well forward Equipped with wooden assault boats and small pneumatic boats, and prepared to construct foot-bridges, the Battalion was a key part of the team in river crossings Heavier bridges were obtained from attached engineer units, although the 105th Engineer Battalion was often called upon for aid in installation An important piece of equipment pressed into service by the Battalion was the bulldozer In defensive situations the Battalion set up minefields, barriers and roadblocks It was occasionally employed as infantry

Three units which were not organic to the 30th but were attached for the entire campaign greatly augmented the Division's power

The 531st Antiaircraft Artillery Battalion, equipped with thirty-two 40mm automatic AA guns and with multiple-mount caliber 50 machine guns, furnished protection against low-flying enemy planes both while in position and on the move It normally protected Division Artillery's gun positions, although it sometimes furnished AA protection to stream-crossing sites pending the arrival of Corps and Army AA installations On occasion it furnished direct high-velocity fire in support of the infantry

The 743d Tank Battalion, with three medium-tank companies and a light-tank company, put 77 tanks and assault guns at the 30th's disposal, as well as a self-propelled 81mm mortar platoon Fifty-four of the tanks were M4 Sherman mediums The 743d always worked with infantry, which sometimes rode into action on the tanks

The 823d Tank Destroyer Battalion, with its 36 three-inch or 76mm antitank guns, possessed fire power equivalent to that of an artillery battalion in each of its three line companies Its towed guns were replaced by self-propelled armored carriers beginning in December 1944 The 823d held the United States Army record for tanks destroyed by a TD battalion between June 6, 1944 and May 8, 1945, on the Continent, knocking out 111 tanks in addition to armored cars, self-propelled guns, and a variety of other items In addition to its primary purpose and mission, the battalion furnished close support to the infantry against non-armored targets, especially after it became self-propelled One company (twelve guns) was often used by Division Artillery for long-range night interdiction missions

The combat elements of the Division constituted about ninety percent of its strength, though it should be remembered that these units contained supply, evacuation, communications, maintenance, and headquarters personnel of their own Backing them up were the service units of the Division Their roles are briefly summarized below

The 30th Signal Company was charged with maintaining wire, radio, and messenger communication between Division headquarters and lower units Organized into wire, radio and message center sections, it normally maintained wire and radio teams with each of the regiments

The 105th Medical Battalion was organized into three collecting companies which normally set up collecting stations immediately in rear of the three infantry regiments on a combat team basis, and a clearing company (Company D) which established a clearing station for processing wounded received from the collecting stations before their removal out of the Division area to evacuation hospitals In addition to medical battalion personnel, Medical Corps soldiers were assigned to medical detachments with the troops, with aid men stationed in the line companies and artillery batteries and small aid stations set up at battalion and regimental level Casualties were evacuated direct from the battalion aid station to the collecting station

The 30th Quartermaster Company was charged with supply from Army trucks or railheads of food, gasoline and motor oil, and such items as clothing and light equipment not needed on a daily basis An attached graves registration detachment administered the Division cemetery Quartermaster was also charged with obtaining laundry and bath facilities, either locally or through mobile units The trucks of the Quartermaster Company furnished the immediate reserve of transportation within the Division, to be used in motorizing infantry, handling prisoners, etc

The 730th Ordnance Company was primarily a maintenance unit, although it was also responsible for supplying the guns, tanks, and trucks it repaired The Division Ordnance Officer controlled the supply of ammunition within the Division, but the ammunition trains of the units physically drew their ammunition from Army supply points The light maintenance company organic to the Division was normally supported by a medium maintenance company established in close proximity

The 30th Military Police Platoon, under the Division Provost Marshal, was charged with physical control of traffic, evacuation of prisoners, and maintenance of order

In addition to the General Staff sections charged with aiding the commanding general in formulation and issue of orders, the Division staff contained a number of specialists, commissioned and enlisted The Finance Section, for example, handled a monthly payroll of one million dollars The Adjutant General's Section handled the Division's records and personnel system and ran a post office with a business equivalent to that of a city of 50,000 population in the United States The Counterintelligence Corps detachment had important functions Additional staff specialists included the Judge Advocate, Inspector General, Surgeon, and the Chemical Warfare Officer A Military Government detachment had its headquarters with the Division and representatives at each of the three regiments

The stable character of the Division's fighting team created advantages of long familiarity and mutual confidence, not only among the commanders concerned but among the troops

These advantages were also realized in the grouping of combat elements within the Division, through the medium of combat team organization

The term "regimental combat team," specifically refers to the regiment itself, plus troops which are under regimental control (i e , attached) when the infantry regiment is in march formation or dispatched on an independent mission—both occasions when close divisional control is out of the question However, the combat team allocation of troops was normally used even when a regiment did not have actual control of all the troops working with it (Normal combat team formations are illustrated in Diagram 2)

The best and clearest example is that of the light artillery The 118th Field Artillery Battalion, for example, always was emplaced so as to assist the 117th Infantry Regiment, whether the battalion was directly under the 117th's orders, or whether it was under Division Artillery control The 197th Field Artillery Battalion always supported the 119th Infantry Regiment as long as that regiment was on the battle line When a 230th Field Artillery Battalion man referred to "his" infantry, he meant the 120th Infantry Regiment At the same time, the

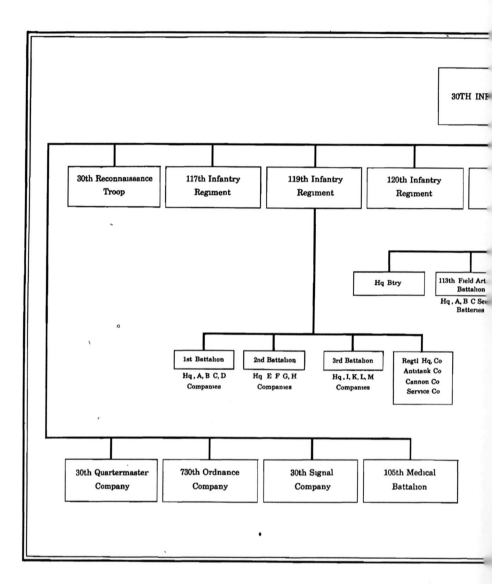

30TH INF

30th Reconnaissance Troop

117th Infantry Regiment

119th Infantry Regiment

120th Infantry Regiment

Hq Btry

113th Field Art Battalion

Hq, A, B C Ser Batteries

1st Battalion

Hq, A, B C, D Companies

2nd Battalion

Hq E F G, H Companies

3rd Battalion

Hq, I, K, L, M Companies

Regtl Hq, Co Antitank Co Cannon Co Service Co

30th Quartermaster Company

730th Ordnance Company

30th Signal Company

105th Medical Battalion

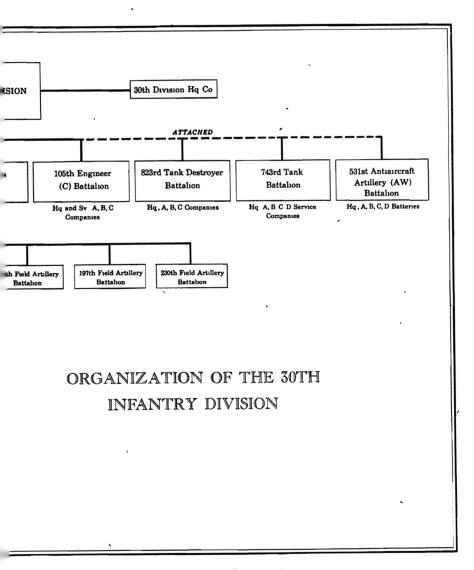

SION ────── 30th Division Hq Co

ATTACHED

| 105th Engineer (C) Battalion | 823rd Tank Destroyer Battalion | 743rd Tank Battalion | 531st Antiaircraft Artillery (AW) Battalion |

Hq and Sv A, B, C Companies

Hq, A, B, C Companies

Hq A, B C D Service Companies

Hq, A, B, C, D Batteries

| th Field Artillery Battalion | 197th Field Artillery Battalion | 230th Field Artillery Battalion |

ORGANIZATION OF THE 30TH
INFANTRY DIVISION

Diagram 1

infantry cannon company was usually placed under the control of the regiment's combat team artillery partner as a six-gun firing battery

Except on rare occasions, the 531st Antiaircraft Artillery Battalion was split up among the four artillery battalions of the division Battery D of the 531st, for example, moved with the 230th Field Artillery Battalion, protected its positions, and considered itself a part of that unit as well as of the 531st

Other arrangements were somewhat less rigidly permanent but were standard enough to warrant mention The 105th Engineer Combat Battalion's three "line" companies worked in the zones of specific regiments unless the situation called for a concentration of engineer resources at a particular place The 823d Tank Destroyer Battalion normally sent a company to each of the infantry regiments—and the same company each time The 743d Tank Battalion, of all of the supporting arms, was least regular in its infantry affiliations The tanks needed infantry as much as the infantry needed tanks—which was normally a good deal—but the individual companies of the battalion were assigned according to the situation—the possibilities for tank action in various sectors of the Division zone, the location of the main effort, the presence of additional armor to help the division

Control of so heterogeneous a fighting team as the infantry commander usually had at his disposal demands, of course, good communications

The most elaborate system for coordination was maintained by the artillery In addition to close cooperation with regiment by direct support artillery battalion headquarters, the latter stationed a liaison officer and his party with each of the regiment's three rifle battalion command posts These officers were prepared to adjust fires, but their primary mission was to stay with the infantry battalion commander and arrange for artillery concentrations he needed, both before and during an action Each field artillery battalion sent out about six forward observers during a fight These observers usually operated in the areas of the assault companies and thus were directly available to a company or platoon commander who needed fire Infantry mortar observers "tied in" with artillery communications under standing operating procedure and on many occasions directed artillery fire Artillery representatives with the infantry were equipped with both telephones and radios The infantry used sound-powered telephones and short range light radios for their own control, while tanks and tank destroyers had radio contact with their company and battalion headquarters Both the tank and tank destroyer battalions normally maintained a representative at the command post of the regiments they were supporting and frequently merged command posts

*   *   *

When the motor of a two-and-a-half-ton Army cargo truck is worn or damaged beyond repair, mechanics take out the old motor and install a new one. When the entire truck is destroyed, Ordnance issues a new one to take its place

The Army tries to do the same thing with men When a division needs, let us say, 400 men to replace casualties, they are ordered from a reinforcement depot by military occupation specialty number, the way one orders from a mail order catalogue, a rifleman is a "745," a machine gunner is a "605," and there is a "spec number" for every job One rifleman or machine gunner or tank driver or radio man is supposed to be as good as another Actually, it's not quite as simple as that. Despite all the efforts of the army to make training of replacements uniform, there are marked variations in the finished product This was especially noticeable when "retreads" brought in from other arms and services were received as infantry

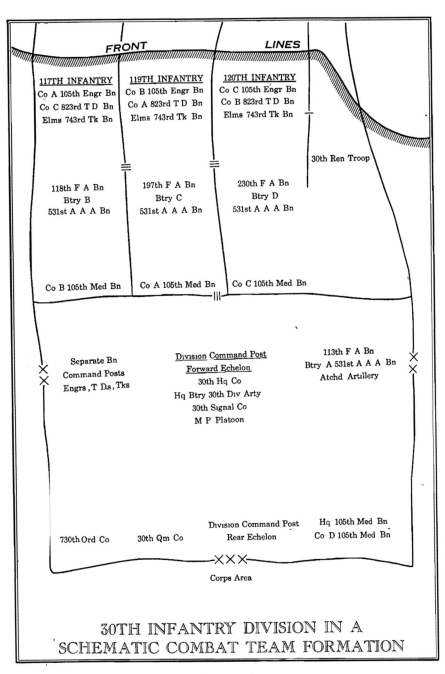

FRONT   **LINES**

117TH INFANTRY	119TH INFANTRY	120TH INFANTRY
Co A 105th Engr Bn	Co B 105th Engr Bn	Co C 105th Engr Bn
Co C 823rd T D Bn	Co A 823rd T D Bn	Co B 823rd T D Bn
Elms 743rd Tk Bn	Elms 743rd Tk Bn	Elms 743rd Tk Bn

30th Ren Troop

118th F A Bn	197th F A Bn	230th F A Bn
Btry B	Btry C	Btry D
531st A A A Bn	531st A A A Bn	531st A A A Bn

Co B 105th Med Bn   Co A 105th Med Bn   Co C 105th Med Bn

Separate Bn
Command Posts
Engrs , T Ds , Tks

Division Command Post
Forward Echelon
30th Hq Co
Hq Btry 30th Div Arty
30th Signal Co
M P Platoon

113th F A Bn
Btry A 531st A A A Bn
Atchd Artillery

730th Ord Co   30th Qm Co   Division Command Post
Rear Echelon

Hq 105th Med Bn
Co D 105th Med Bn

Corps Area

30TH INFANTRY DIVISION IN A
SCHEMATIC COMBAT TEAM FORMATION

Diagram 2

replacements Furthermore, the most rigorous and standardized training cannot do away with the need of acquainting new men with the men they are to work with and with the localized techniques of getting things done It is impossible to completely standardize the way an army fights, even at squad or platoon level

These points are worth noting because of the high rate of turnover within the basic fighting arm—the infantry Each of the three infantry regiments of the 30th had combat losses in eleven months of fighting equivalent to approximately twice their table-of-organization strength Losses were, of course, most severe in the rifle companies, which had an even higher turnover rate Line company men who hit the beach with the Division in June 1944 and were still with their companies on VE-day were almost non-existent as a class, although a few officers and men originally in rifle companies remained with their regiments in safer positions at battalion or regimental level The turnover in platoon leaders and company commanders was especially high mainly because these officers had to expose themselves to maintain control of their units The same sort of changes in personnel were going on, but at a slow rate, among the other elements of the infantry regiment, the tankers, tank destroyer men, and forward observer and liaison teams of the artillery

Thus the line-up within the small unit team varied tremendously from one major operation to the next The companies, platoons, and squads which fought the battles of the Siegfried Line and the Aachen Gap were almost entirely different in make-up from those which had fought in Normandy And, in many companies, those who had fought in October and November would have had difficulty in finding many old faces on Old Hickory's return from the Ardennes Newspaper references to "veteran troops" were frequently a mockery of the truth

Despite the continuous change in the fighting personnel of the 30th, however, the Division did retain its character as a fighting organization This is not to say that new men joining the Division somehow underwent a spiritual transformation which suddenly made them skilled warriors resolved to do or die for Old Hickory It does mean that the Division was not noticeably weakened for having a high proportion of new men in it at any given time, and that except sometimes at the small-unit level, the lessons of previous battles were cumulative and did not have to be relearned over and over again

If replacements were received during quiet periods the problem of their assimilation was, of course, greatly reduced, for during such periods there was time for rehearsal of small-unit problems and instructions in the use of weapons During the Division's major battles, however, reinforcements came up to the line without opportunity for learning their duties and getting acquainted with their teammates away from the urgency of battle One by-product of this state of affairs is revealing The first sergeant of a company is supposed to report casualties daily It soon became apparent that the only report that a first sergeant could be expected to make was a simple roster of the men on hand The company clerk, sitting at his desk at the regimental rear echelon, figured out who was missing or wounded or dead The first sergeant could find out, from the platoon leaders, who was present for duty But even a squad leader couldn't be expected to remember the names of all of the twelve men who had been under his command twenty-four hours previously

Relative stability in the chain of command upwards from battalion level played an important role in maintenance and development of the Division's combat efficiency Turnover of battalion commanders was confined almost entirely to the infantry The only other unit to undergo a change was the Engineer Battalion, which was taken over by the executive for three months while its commander recovered from wounds The nine infantry battalions of the Division had, on the average, two and one-half commanders during eleven months of combat Two battalions, the 1st and 3d of the 117th Infantry, had the same commanding officers throughout The 1st Battalion of the 120th Infantry also had only two commanders during the entire period, save for the first week in October 1944, when two other officers were temporarily in charge of it Four other battalions, the 2d of the 117th, the 2d and 3d of the 119th, and the 2d of the 120th each had three different combat leaders The 3d Battalion of the 120th Infantry had four different commanders

Control of the three infantry regiments and of Division Artillery changed hands less frequently When Brigadier General Raymond S McLain left Division Artillery to assume command of the 90th Infantry Division (and later of XIX Corps) on July 26, 1944, his successor, Brigadier General James M Lewis, remained for the rest of the campaign Colonel Henry E Kelly of the 117th Infantry left the Division because of physical reasons late in July, 1944, just before the Mortain–St Barthelmy battle, and was succeeded by the regimental executive, Colonel Walter M Johnson Colonel Branner P Purdue succeeded Colonel Hammond D Birks October 7, 1944, when the latter left to become assistant division commander of the 9th Infantry Division The 119th Infantry had three commanding officers, Colonel Alfred V Ednie, who was succeeded by Colonel Edwin M Sutherland on July 15, 1944, and Colonel Russell A Baker, who took over command on December 27, 1944

At Division level there was no significant change in the tactical staff which had existed prior to the 1943 maneuvers Major General Leland S Hobbs had commanded the 30th since September 12, 1942 The assistant division commander, Brigadier General William K Harrison, had been with the Division since November of the same year Colonel Richard W Stephens, formerly the G-3 (Operations Officer), had been chief of staff since August, 1943 The G-4 (Supply Officer), Lieutenant Colonel Walter L Frankland, assumed that position back in the spring of 1942 The G-3, Lieutenant Colonel Harold E Hassenfelt, came to the job in the summer of 1943, and the G-1 (Personnel Officer) and the G-2 (Intelligence Officer), Lieutenant Colonels John W Dandridge and Stewart L Hall respectively, had both served in those positions during the 1943 fall maneuvers in Tennessee

* * *

Another relationship is worthy of note, that with the XIX Corps, which took over control of the 30th soon after its arrival in England and under which Old Hickory served approximately half the time it was in combat on the Continent Relations with XIX Corps were exceptionally close and cordial, not only between the two headquarters but between Corps Artillery and Division Artillery and in other less centralized relationships Although it fought under five other Corps, the 30th tended to regard itself as a XIX Corps unit This cordiality extended to the 2d Armored Division, which normally furnished the armored element in XIX Corps

A particularly happy relationship of mutual trust and esteem also existed with Ninth Army Headquarters, under which the 30th served from October 22, 1944 until VE-day, except for its month-and-a-half service with First Army in the Ardennes Here the confidence engendered during working relations was buttressed by old friendships Lieutenant General William H Simpson, the Ninth Army's commanding general, and Major General James E Moore, his chief of staff had immediately preceded General Hobbs and Colonel Stephens in corresponding positions with the 30th

Appendix 3

UNITS CITED IN WAR DEPARTMENT GENERAL ORDERS IN THE NAME OF THE PRESIDENT

UNIT	ACTION FOR WHICH CITED	DATES
1st Battalion, 117th Infantry	Defense at St Barthelmy, France	August 7, 1944
Company E 117th Infantry	Diversionary attack in Battle of Aachen Gap	October 16, 1944
1st Battalion 119th Infantry (attached Company C, 740th Tank Battalion and 2d Platoon, Company A, 823d Tank Destroyer Battalion)	Battle with 1st SS at Lorce Chevron and Stoumont, Belgium	December 18 21, 1944
2d Battalion, 120th Infantry	Defense of Hill 314, near Mortain, France	August 6 12, 1944
Company K, 120th Infantry	Defense of Hill 314, near Mortain, France	August 6 12, 1944
1st & 2d Platoons, Antitank Company, 120th Infantry	Defense of roadblocks near Mortain, France	August 7-12, 1944
1st Battalion, 120th Infantry	Attack on Bardenberg, Germany	October 8 12, 1944
3d Platoon Company B, 105th Engineer Battalion	Vire River crossing	July 7, 1944
Companies A & B, 823d Tank Destroyer Battalion	Defensive action near Mortain, France	August 6 12, 1944
743d Tank Battalion	D Day action on Omaha Beach	June 6, 1944

The 30th Infantry Division as a whole (including the 743d Tank Battalion, 823d Tank Destroyer Battalion, and 531st AAA AW Battalion) was awarded the Fourragere of Belgium in a Belgian Decree, No 1393, dated November 20, 1945, for its part in Belgian liberation between September 4 and 10, 1944, and for its actions in the Ardennes fighting between December 17, 1944 and January 25, 1945

INDIVIDUALS DECORATED
FOR SERVICE WITH THE 30th INFANTRY DIVISION

Key

BS—Bronze Star (U S)
DFC—Distinguished Flying Cross (U S)
DSC—Distinguished Service Cross (U S)
DSM—Distinguished Service Medal (U S)
LM—Legion of Merit (U S)
CMH—(Congressional) Medal of Honor
SS—Silver Star (U S)
AM—Air Medal (U S)
SM—Soldier's Medal (U S)

Key

OLC—Oak Leaf Cluster (equivalent to second award of a decoration)
C d'G—Croix de Guerre (French)
LH—Legion d'Honneur (French)
DSO—Distinguished Service Order (British)
GFM—Grand Flag Medal (USSR)
MM—Military Medal (British)
MC—Military Cross (British)

Approximately 20,000 Purple Hearts were conferred on members of the 30th Infantry Division Many of these awards were made by evacuation hospitals and other installations outside the Division A record of such awards was not available within the Division files and therefore Purple Heart awards have not been included in the following list '

1st Lt Kenneth H Aamodt, 119 Inf, BS
Capt Ernest I Aas, 743 Tnk, SS
T/5 Joe Abata, 823 TD, BS
1st Lt Henry C Abbes, 117 Inf, SS w/OLC BS
T/Sgt George E Abbot, 743 Tk, BS w/OLC
S/sgt Glenn L Abbott, 120 Inf, SS w/OLC
Sgt Max Abercrombie, 118 FA, BS
CWO Robert L Able, 730 Ord, BS
Pfc James A Abner, 120 Inf, BS
S/Sgt John D Abernethy, 105 Eng, BS w/OLC
T/4 Paul Abraham, 118 FA, BS
Pfc Edward Abramczyk, 119 Inf, BS
T/4 William Acker, 117 Inf, BS
Capt Jasper D Ackerman, Hq 30, BS w/OLC
T/Sgt Robert F Ackerman, 117 Inf, SS BS
Pvt David P Acosta, 230 FA, BS
T/5 John Acosta, 119 Inf, BS
1st Lt Alexander P Adams, 117 Inf, BS
Pfc Arlon L Adams, 119 Inf SS BS
Cpl Forest E Adams, 117 Inf BS
Sgt Harold D Adams, 743 Tk, SS C d'G
Pfc Hillard E Adams 120 Inf BS
Pfc Jackson C Adams, 120 Inf, BS
T/5 James G Adams, 105 Eng, BS
1st Lt Otis L Adams 730 Ord, BS
Pfc Paul H Adams, 119 Inf BS
T/5 Tice C Adams, 736 Tk SS
Pfc Walter L Adams, 117 Inf, BS
T/Sgt William T Adams, 113 FA, BS —
S/Sgt Elmer J Adamson, 118 FA, BS
S/Sgt Maurice E Adcock, 119 Inf, SS
T/5 Vaudre Addison, 230 FA, BS
S/Sgt Steadman Adelung, 92 Chem, BS
Pvt Curtis Adkins, 105 Eng, SS
Pfc Edwin Adkins, 105 Eng, SS BS
Pfc Larence Adkins, 120 Inf. BS
Capt Lloyd J Adkins, 743 Tk, BS
S/Sgt Raymond C Adkins, 197 FA, BS
2d Lt Theodore B Adkinson 743 Tk, SS w/OLC
S/Sgt Edward M Adlesic, 119 Inf SS
Cpl George H Adolphson, 120 Inf, BS
Pfc John Adoro, 119 Inf SS
Pfc Paul P Aguirre, 120 Inf, BS
Pfc Edward W Aherns 119 Inf BS
Cpl Walter O Ahinger 119 Inf, BS
Sgt Herman W Ahrlich 105 Eng, SS
T/Sgt Banaba Ahyo, 120 Inf SS
Pfc Aubrey W Aiken 117 Inf BS
T/4 Ralph C Aiken, 105 Eng, BS
S/Sgt Robert A Aitken 117 Inf, SS
Pfc George F Aker, 117 Inf, BS w/OLC
T/5 James M Akin, 117 Inf BS
Cpl Giovanni Albani, 823 TD, SS

1st Lt Edward A Albano, 105 Eng, SS
Pfc Arthur D Albertson, 30 Rcn, BS
T/5 James G Albright, 30 Sig, BS
1st Lt Robert C Aldern, 203 FA, SS
2d Lt Thomas C Alderson, 743 Tk, BS
Cpl Paul Aldmon, 120 Inf, BS
Cpl Harley S Alred, 120 Inf, BS
T/5 Alfred D Aldrich, 119 Inf, BS
T/5 George E Aldridge, 113 FA, BS
Capt William J Aldridge, 120 Inf, BS
Pfc Vincent J Aleo, 117 Inf SS w/OLC
S/Sgt Jerome H Alex, 120 Inf SS
T/5 Franzel E Alexander, 117 Inf, SS BS
Pvt Irvin F Alexander, 105 Eng, BS
Capt Merrill S Alexander, 230 FA, SS BS
Pfc R D Alexander, 120 Inf, BS
Cpl Robert S Alexander, 118 FA, BS
Pvt Samual J Alexander, 120 Inf, BS
Sgt Charles L Alexandria, 86 Chem, BS
Pfc Franklin T Algard 119 Inf, SS
T/5 Dan W Allard, 30 Sig BS
Sgt Frank J Allegretti, 743 Tk, SS
1st Lt Andrew W Allen Jr, 117 Inf, SS w/OLC BS
Sgt Chester B Allen, 117 Inf, BS w/OLC
Pfc Clifford J Allen, 119 Inf, BS
Capt Eugene N Allen, 743 Tk, BS
T/5 Harold F Allen, 118 FA, BS
Sgt John F Allen, 744 Tk, SS
Pfc Kenneth Allen, 30 Rcn BS
Pfc Lester Allen 120 Inf, SS
Sgt Marcel J Allen, 120 Inf, BS
M/Sgt Melville H Allen, 119 Inf, BS
T/4 Robert Allen, 117 Inf, BS
S/Sgt Robert R Allen, 119 Inf, BS
Pfc Walter Allen, 120 Inf, BS
T/Sgt William W Allen 117 Inf, BS
1st Lt John E Allensworth, 823 TD, BS
Sgt L D Alley 117 Inf, BS
Pvt William W Alley, 119 Inf BS
Pfc Francis R Allison 119 Inf, BS
Maj John A Allison, 105 Eng SS BS w/OLC
Pfc Franklin C Alloway, 117 Inf, BS w/OLC
Capt Robert Y Allred, 119 Inf, BS w/OLC
Pfc Octavio Almodovar 120 Inf, BS
Pfc Jonah M Almond, 120 Inf, BS
Pfc Fred R Aloisio, 117 Inf, BS w/OLC
Sgt Jacob Altergott, 743 Tk, SS BS
Cpl David L Alther, 230 FA, BS
T/5 Michael S Altieri, 120 Inf BS
T/Sgt Arthur F Altree Hq 30 Div, BS
T/5 James B Alvis Jr 119 Inf, BS
Capt Allen L Amend, 730 Ord BS

Pvt Howard L Amlingmeyer, 30 MP, BS
T/5 Carlo A Ammirati, 119 Inf, BS
Lt Col Benjamin T Ammons, 117 Inf,
     SS w/OLC BS w/3 OLC
S/Sgt Claude V Ammons, 30 Sig, BS
S/Sgt Neil A Ammons, 120 Inf, BS
1st Lt Elbert V Amos, 730 Ord, BS
Pfc Henry H Amparan, 117 Inf, BS
2d Lt Harlan J Amundson, 743 Tk, BS
2d Lt Alfonso A Anaya, 119 Inf, BS
Pfc John W Ancil, 119 Inf, BS w/OLC
S/Sgt Albert Anderson, 119 Inf, BS
T/5 Albert G Anderson, 105 Eng, BS
Pfc Albert O Anderson, 120 Inf, BS
Pfc Charles B Anderson, 117 Inf, BS
T/3 Charles L Anderson, 117 Inf, BS
Pvt Duane R Anderson, 119 Inf, BS
T/Sgt Glen W Anderson, 531 AAA, BS
Pfc Hubert E Anderson Sr, 120 Inf,
     BS w/2 OLC
S/Sgt James E Anderson, 120 Inf, BS
Sgt James L Anderson, 119 Inf, BS w/2 OLC
T/4 James S Anderson, 743 Tk, BS
S/Sgt Lawrence E Anderson, 119 Inf, BS
S/Sgt Melvin R Anderson, 119 Inf, SS BS
T/5 Lester Anderson, 113 FA, BS —
Pfc Robert D Anderson, 743 Tk BS
1st Lt Robert P Anderson, 531 AAA, BS
T/4 Roy L Anderson, 105 Eng, SS BS w/OLC
Cpl William H Anderson, 118 FA, BS
Pfc William M Anderson, 119 Inf, SS
Pvt Michael E Andrea, 105 Eng, BS
Pvt Arthur T Andrew, 117 Inf, SS
1st Lt Tom E H Andrew, 120 Inf SS
Sgt Edward E Andrews 120 Inf, SS
T/5 Lyle M Andrews, 531 AAA, BS
Pfc Phillip M Andrews, 120 Inf, BS
Pfc Robert G Andrews, 743 Tk, BS
S/Sgt William J Andrews, 119 Inf, BS
Pvt Francis Andruski, 120 Inf, BS
Pfc Victor M Andruskiewiez, 117 Inf, BS
Pvt Clemens R Andrzetkowicz, 117 Inf, BS
S/Sgt Edward J Anenen, 120 Inf BS w/OLC
Pfc Pasquale Angarano, 117 Inf, BS
Pvt Francis E Angell 117 Inf, BS
Capt Richard B Angell, 105 Med, BS
Cpl Albert J Angotti, 120 Inf, BS
Pfc Robert C Angus, 120 Inf, BS
Sgt Phillip Annexstein 119 Inf, BS
Pfc Alfred L Annis, 120 Inf, SS
Capt John I Ansbro, 119 Inf, BS
1st Lt Alfred J Ansejus, 119 Inf, BS
T/Sgt Glenn W Ansley 120 Inf, BS
Pfc James N Anthow, 117 Inf, BS
Pfc Alexander H Antoniewiez 119 Inf, BS
Pvt Alvin T Apple, 119 Inf, BS
Pfc Walter E Apple, 120 Inf, BS
T/Sgt William Aralle, 120 Inf, BS
T/5 Alfred E Arbuckle, 117 Inf, BS
Pfc Francis T Arcand, 119 Inf, BS
Sgt Riccardo Arcaro, 117 Inf, BS w/OLC
T/3 James J Archambeault Div Arty, BS
T/4 Causey W Archer 197 FA, BS
Sgt Cleon Archer, 120 Inf BS
S/Sgt Lawrence Arent 120 Inf BS
Pvt Clyde L Archie, 120 Inf, BS
T/4 Ben F August, 30 Sig, BS
Sgt Dominic W Armato, 531 AAA BS
T/5 Leonard L Armato, 117 Inf, BS
Pfc Edward J Armentrout, 120 Inf, BS
Pfc Patrick J Armes 117 Inf, BS
Pfc Roy D Armstead, 117 Inf, BS
S/Sgt Arthur Armstrong, 230 FA BS
Pfc Elmer Armstrong, 119 Inf, BS w/OLC
1st Lt Frank H Armstrong, 283 FA, BS
Capt John E Armstrong, Hq 30 Div, BS
T/Sgt Leon Armstrong, 117 Inf, BS
Pfc Mason H Armstrong, 119 Inf, BS
1st Lt Edward C Arn, 119 Inf, SS w/OLC
Pfc Franklin T Arner, 119 Inf BS
Pfc LaMoine N Arnett, 117 Inf, BS
Sgt Clare E Arnold, 120 Inf, BS
Sgt Herman F Arnold 119 Inf BS
2d Lt Richard C Arnold, 230 FA, SS

T/5 William E Arnold, Div Arty, BS
Cpl Edwin Arps, Div Arty, BS
T/4 Dennis F Arrington, 118 FA, BS
Sgt James H Airowood, 120 Inf BS
S/Sgt Larry C Arrington, 120 Inf, BS
S/Sgt William G Arrington, 119 Inf, BS
Pfc John S Arruda, 197 FA, BS
S/Sgt William Arruda, 30 MP, BS w/OLC
1st Lt Paul Arst, 120 Inf, BS
Pvt Ralph Arthur, 117 Inf, BS
S/Sgt Roy B Arthur, 117 Inf, BS
T/4 Alexander M Arzoumanian, 118 FA, BS
2d Lt Roy W Asbury, 531 AAA, BS
S/Sgt Joseph C Ashby, 119 Inf, SS
T/5 James A Ashley, 19 Inf, BS
Cpl Richard Ashliman Jr 117 Inf, BS w/OLC
Pfc Torrise Ashurst, 30 MP, BS
Pfc William A Ashworth, 119 Inf, SS
2d Lt Clair F Askew, 119 Inf, SS
Pfc Wilton W Askew, 117 Inf, BS
Sgt Vincent J Asselin, 119 Inf, BS
Sgt Wilson M Atchison, 117 Inf, BS
Capt Athas Athanasopoulou, 92 Chem,
     BS w/2 OLC
Pvt Woodrow P Atkins, 120 Inf, BS
Pfc Hardy T Atkinson, 105 Med, BS
Pvt Nissin Attas, 230 FA, SS
Sgt Harry R Attebery Jr, 230 FA, SS BS
T/Sgt William D Atwell, 120 Inf, BS w/OLC
T/5 Walter L Auclair, 119 Inf, BS
Pfc Roland P Aucoin, 117 Inf, SS
Pfc George A Auer, 117 Inf, SS w/OLC
Cpl James Aughinbaugh Jr, 118 FA, BS w/OLC
T/5 Clifford J August, 117 Inf, BS
T/5 Lee Auliso, 119 Inf, BS
Sgt Lendell A Austermiller, 119 Inf, SS
Pfc Edward A Austin, 120 Inf, BS
2d Lt Kenneth F Austin, 119 Inf, SS
Sgt Lawrence E Austin, 120 Inf, BS
WOJG Lester B Austin, 105 Eng, BS
T/5 Milton C Austin, 105 Med, BS w/2 OLC
Pfc Ned Austin Jr, 662 QM, SS
Sgt Robert S Autry Jr, 120 Inf, BS
S/Sgt Ernest L Avellar, 117 Int, BS
2d Lt Herbert I Avery, 117 Inf, SS BS w/OLC
T/5 Willie L Avery, 105 Eng, SS
Pfc Milton Avol, 117 Inf, BS w/OLC
Sgt Ralph M Avery, Hq 30 Div, BS
2d Lt Edwon W Ayers, 197 FA, SS
Pvt Joseph H Ayers, 120 Inf, BS w/OLC
S/Sgt Lawrence H Ayers, 120 Inf, SS
S/Sgt Jay F Aykens, 119 Inf, SS BS w/OLC
S/Sgt John R Ayscue, 197 FA, BS w/OLC
T/Sgt Donald D Babcock, 120 Inf, SS BS
Cpl Richard E Babin, 30 Rcn Trp, SS
T/5 Russell A Baber, 117 Inf, BS
1st Lt Frederick F Babo, 120 Inf, BS
Pfc Benjamin Baca, 120 Inf, BS
Pfc Frank Baccaire, 119 Inf BS
Pfc Zoltan P Bachey, 117 Inf, BS
Cpl Ralph H Backes, 743 Tnk, BS
Pfc William C Backett, 743 Tnk, BS
T/5 Howard O Backhaus, 120 Inf, BS
Pfc Victor W Backhaus 117 Inf, BS
Pfc Harold A Bacon, 119 Inf, SS
Sgt Robert F Bacon, 119 Inf, BS
2d Lt Harris E Baer, 230 FA AM BS w/OLC
Sgt Harry L Baer, 230 FA BS
T/3 Martin A Baer, 119 Inf, BS
Pvt Daniel Baffaro, 105 Eng, BS
1st Lt Frederick D Bagford, 117 Inf, SS
S/Sgt Clayton E Baggett, 119 Inf, BS w/OLC
T/4 William L Baggett, 30 Sig, BS
Pvt Charles D Bagshaw 119 Inf, BS
1st Lt Edward M Bahoric 747 Tnk BS
T/Sgt Burnice Bahr, 120 Inf SS BS
T/5 Joseph Bahr, 120 Inf, BS
Sgt George H Bales, 119 Inf BS
T/5 Clarence P Bailey, 120 Inf, SS
Pvt David R Bailey, 30 QM BS
S/Sgt John A Bailey, 30 Div Arty, BS
T/Sgt Ted Bailey, 120 Inf, BS
1st Lt Vernon M Bailey, 83 Chem, BS
S/Sgt William E Bailey, 197 FA, BS

T/5 Caryl R Baird, 119 Inf, BS
2d Lt James R Baird, 105 Eng, SS BS w/OLC
S/Sgt Robert J Baird, 120 Inf, BS
S/Sgt Silas L Baird, 120 Inf, SS BS w/OLC
Pfc Newton R Baittinger, 119 Inf, BS
Cpl Matthew Bajcar, 120 Inf, SS BS
Maj Alonzo N Baker, 30 Div Hq, BS
Pfc Andy Baker, 117 Inf, BS
Pfc Clifton E Baker, 117 Inf, BS w/OLC
Pfc Don Baker, 120 Inf, BS
Sgt Edmund W Baker, 747 Tnk, BS
S/Sgt Elwood E Baker, 117 Inf, SS
1st Lt George D Baker, 119 Inf, SS
T/4 James M Baker, 113 FA, BS —
Pfc John R Baker, 120 Inf, BS
T/5 Millard E Baker, 230 FA, BS
S/Sgt Onnie R Baker, 120 Inf, BS
T/5 Paul A Baker, 105 Eng, BS
Sgt Paul E Baker, 120 Inf, BS
Col Russell A Baker, 119 Inf,
     LM SS BS w/2 OLC
Pvt Walter E Baker, 120 Inf, BS
Pfc Wayne Baker, 117 Inf, BS
T/Sgt Glenn M Bakken, 120 Inf, BS
Pfc Michael Balak, 117 Inf, BS
Pfc Nello J Baldacci, 119 Inf, BS
Pfc George J Baldone, 120 Inf, BS w/OLC
T/5 Marvin E Bales, 743 Tnk, BS
T/5 Elmer C Ball, 117 Inf, BS
Pfc Prentice W Ball 117 Inf SS
1st Lt John J Ballentine, 118 FA, SS w/OLC BS
S/Sgt James R Ballard, 120 Inf, BS w/OLC
T/3 Percy G Ballentine, 117 Inf, BS
Pfc Pilar Ballestero, 120 Inf, SS
S/Sgt Stewart K Ballinger, 117 Inf, BS
Pfc Anthony J Baltruses, 30 Div Arty, BS
T/4 Stanlev J Banach, 119 Inf, BS
Pfc Albert F Banda, 105 Eng, BS
Cpl Hy Bander, 113 FA, BS —
Sgt John Bandise 120 Inf, BS
Pfc Kenneth W Bandy, 118 FA, BS
S/Sgt Donald A Banes, 119 Inf, BS
Sgt Charles H Baniewski 197 FA, BS
Sgt George D Banks, 113 FA, BS —
Pfc Grover Banks, 117 Inf, BS
T/Sgt Francis R Banner, 117 Inf, BS w/OLC
Capt Donald B Bannerman, 119 Inf, BS w/OLC
T/5 Shirley D Bannister 119 Inf, BS
Sgt Alvy G Banzhoff, 120 Inf, SS
1st Lt John D Barabasz 117 Inf, BS w/OLC
2d Lt Michael Baran, 117 Inf, BS
Capt Lester J Baranoy, 823 TD, BS
S/Sgt Daniel Barbarito, 119 Inf, BS
Pfc Robert E Barbee, 117 Inf, BS
Pfc Floyd A Barber, 120 Inf, BS
Pvt Robert Barber, 30 Div Arty, SS
1st Lt Samuel K Barber, 531 AAA, BS
S/Sgt Cullen J Barbier, 30 Div Hq BS
Sgt Salvatore E Barbieri, 117 Inf, SS BS w/OLC
T/Sgt Daniel Barbuzi, 120 Inf, SS BS
1st Sgt James E Barclay, 117 Inf, BS
Sgt John A Bard, 117 Inf, BS
S/Sgt Jessie O Barefoot, 119 Inf, BS
1st Lt William P Barenkamp, 120 Inf,
     SS BS w/2OLC
1st Sgt Noah W Barfield, Hq Co 30 Div, BS
T/Sgt Watson L Bargeron, 118 FA, BS
S/Sgt James H Bargy, 117 Inf, BS
S/Sgt Joseph L Baril, 120 Inf, SS BS
Pfc Dominic A Barile, 120 Inf BS
Pfc Bruno F Barilla, 120 Inf, BS
Sgt George E Barker, 120 Inf, BS
Cpl Harry H Barker 113 FA, BS —
Pfc James L Barker, 119 Inf, SS
1st Lt Thelbert J Barker, 119 Inf, SS BS w/OLC
T/5 Willie Barker, 120 Inf BS
Cpl Ivan A Barkus 743 TD BS
Pfc Ward L Barlow, 105 Eng BS
T/Sgt Milton J Barna, 119 Inf BS
Pfc Carl N Barnard, 119 Inf SS
Pfc Sterling J Barndt, 105 Eng BS
Pfc Donald G Barnes, 120 Inf BS
Pfc John T Barnes 117 Inf, SS
Pvt Leroy W Barnes, 117 Inf, BS

2d Lt Charles M Barnett, 120 Inf, SS BS
Capt James J Barnett Jr, 119 Inf, BS
Pfc Earl W Barnhart, 120 Inf, BS
Pfc Harry L Barnum Jr, 120 Inf, BS w/OLC
Pfc Salvatore F Barone, 119 Inf, BS
Pfc Paul M Barquin, 120 Inf, BS
S/Sgt James V Bair 119 Inf. BS
T/5 John D Barr, 120 Inf, BS
Pfc Esteban Barraza, 120 Inf, BS
Pfc Santos S Barrera, 120 Inf, BS
Pfc James R Barrett, 117 Inf BS
Pfc John F Barrett, 230 FA, BS
T/5 James H Barrington, 105 Med, BS
S/Sgt Donald G Barron, 113 FA BS —
1st Sgt Euphus M Barron, 117 Inf, BS
1st Lt John E Barron, 823 TD, BS
S/Sgt Charles R Barry, 119 Inf, BS
Pfc Robert B Barry, 119 Inf, BS w/OLC
T/4 Robert W Barth, 117 Inf, BS
Pfc Wilbert D Barth, 120 Inf, BS w/OLC
1st Lt Gene A Barthelme, 230 FA, SS
S/Sgt Edward K Bartholomew, Hq 30 Div, BS
Sgt Wayne H Bartholomew, 743 TK, BS
Pfc Michael J Bartolomeo, 117 Inf, BS
Sgt Leon C Barton, 823 TD, BS
Pfc Frank Bartonek, 119 Inf, BS
Sgt Marlyn H Bartsch, 743 TK, BS
T/5 John Bartunek, 30 Sig BS
Sgt Frank Bartuska, 743 TK, BS
1st Lt Charles A Bartz, 230 FA, SS
Pfc Clovis C Basden, 119 Inf, BS
T/5 Charles A Basil, 730 Ord, BS
Cpl Michael E Basile, 747 Tnk, BS
T/Sgt Raymond L Basinger, 119 Inf, BS
Pfc Charles E Basnaw, 119 Inf, BS
Pfc Lance E Bass, 120 Inf, BS
T/5 Sidney Bass, 120 Inf, BS
Pfc Joseph Bass, 120 Inf, BS
T/5 William D Bassett, 117 Inf BS w/OLC
Pfc Robert B Bassing, 117 Inf, BS w/OLC
Pfc William J Batchelor, 120 Inf, BS
S/Sgt Guy C Bates, 119 Inf, SS
Pfc Harvey K Bates, 119 Inf, BS
1st Lt James L Bates, 747 Tnk, BS
S/Sgt Robert L Bates, 117 Inf, BS
S/Sgt Robert W Bates, 119 Inf, BS w/OLC
Pfc Joseph J Batesky, 117 Inf, BS
Capt Richard T Batson, 105 Eng, BS
Pfc Anthony Battistini, 120 Inf, SS
Capt Joseph M Battle, 117 Inf, BS w/OLC
S/Sgt Ernest J Bauer, 400 FA, SS
Pvt William C Bauer, 120 Inf, BS
Cpl John J Baum, 823 TD, SS
T/5 Raymond E Baum, 120 Inf, BS
Sgt Daniel R Baumberger, 120 Inf, BS
Pvt Alvin J Baumgardner, 230 FA, BS
T/5 Ray Baumgartner, 118 FA BS
Sgt Arbuth Baumgarner, 120 Inf, BS
Pfc Donald J Baxter, 120 Inf, BS
Sgt Merle E Baxter, 531 AAA, BS
Pfc Norman E Baxter, 120 Inf BS
T/Sgt Batiste L Bayhylle 120 Inf, SS
T/Sgt Richard C Beam, 119 Inf, BS
T/Sgt Jerry H Beamon, 120 Inf, SS BS
Pvt David E Bean, 117 Inf BS
Sgt John T Beane, 117 Inf BS
Pfc Lewis Beard, 105 Eng, BS
S/Sgt Louis K Beard, 105 Eng, SS
Pfc Lawrence Beardslee, 105 Eng, BS
S/Sgt Jack R Beatty, 119 Inf, SS
S/Sgt Leon C Beaudette 119 Inf SS BS
S/Sgt Edward F Beaudoin, 119 Inf, SS
1st Lt Raymond O Beaudoin 119 Inf, CMH BS
Pvt Pershing C Beaudre, 117 Inf, BS
Sgt Horace Beaulieu 117 Inf, SS
S/Sgt Leo M Beaulieu, 117 Inf, SS BS
Sgt Rene W Beaulieu, 119 Inf, SS
Sgt Chester E Beayon, 117 Inf, BS
Pfc Theodore V Beben, 120 Inf, SS
Pvt Harry F Bechtold, 119 Inf, BS
S/Sgt George N Beck, 119 Inf, BS
Sgt Edward J Becker, 120 Inf BS
1st Sgt Meldrim R Becker, 118 FA BS
Capt Ralph E Becker, Hq 30 Div, BS

Pfc Ruford Beckett, 119 Inf, BS
Pfc William C Beckett, 743 TK, BS
2d Lt Everett Beckham, 117 Inf, BS w/OLC
T/Sgt Marion B Beckham, 743 TK, BS
Cpl William H Backham, 740 Tnk, SS
T/Sgt Arthur J Beckingham, 531 AAA, BS
Maj Edward C Beckley, Div Arty, BS
Sgt George L Beckwith, 113 Cav, BS
S/Sgt Warren E Beckwith, 197 FA, BS
1st Sgt Claude J Bedenbaugh, 119 Inf, BS
S/Sgt Joseph J Bednarczyk, 117 Inf, SS
Sgt Joseph P Bednarz, 105 Eng, BS
S/Sgt Robert K Bee, 743 Tnk, BS
T/5 Blain H Beebe, 823 TD, SS
Pvt John L Beeler, 120 Inf, BS
Sgt Lloyd W Beerbower, 118 FA, BS
Pvt Lewis H Beers, 119 Inf, BS
Pfc Bernard L Beesley, 120 Inf, BS
Pfc William G Beetlestone, 119 Inf, BS w/OLC
Pfc Robert E Beffa, 117 Inf, BS w/OLC
T/4 John L Begnaud, Hq 30 Div, BS
1st Lt Warren E Behrens, 119 Inf, BS
Pvt Denver E Belford, 117 Inf, BS
Pfc Marcel G Belisle, 120 Inf, BS w/OLC
Pfc Thomas P Belka, 119 Inf, SS
Pfc Charles N Bell, 120 Inf, SS
Pfc Earl J Bell, 117 Inf, BS
Capt Ernest W Bell, 120 Inf, SS
T/5 Harry E Bell, 168 Sig, BS
T/4 Howard L Bell, 743 TK, BS
Pfc James M Bell, 119 Inf, SS BS
Pvt R A Bell, 119 Inf BS
T/4 Walter H Bell, 120 Inf, BS
Pfc Rene J Bellavance, 117 Inf, BS
Pfc John S Belleza, 120 Inf, BS
T/5 Adam J Belowski Jr, 120 Inf, SS
T/5 Preston J Belt, 118 FA, BS
Pfc Clarence A Bench, 120 Inf, BS
Sgt Chester P Bender, 117 Inf, BS
S/Sgt Charles M Beneke, 120 Inf, SS
Pfc Andrew J Benish, 120 Inf, BS
Sgt George P Benish, 117 Inf BS
Maj Clarence L Benjamin, 743 Tnk,
    BS w/OLC
T/5 Fred H Benjamin, 197 FA, BS
Pvt Reginald H Benner, 117 Inf, BS
S/Sgt Brian H Bennerr, 119 Inf, SS
Sgt Claude P Bennett, 117 Inf BS
1st Lt Ernest R Bennett, 30 Div Arty,
    BS w/OLC
Pvt James L Bennett, 117 Inf, BS
Sgt Robert D Bennett, 743 Tnk, BS
Capt Robert W Bennett, 119 Inf, BS
Sgt Robert W Bennett, 743 Tnk, BS
Sgt Wayne G Bennett, 120 Inf, BS
Sgt Charles D Bennington, 823 TD, BS w/OLC
Pfc Gerard Benoit, 120 Inf, BS
Pfc Lester Benoit, 119 Inf, BS
Sgt Minus J Benoit, 120 Inf, BS
Pvt Louis W Benore, 120 Inf, BS
Pfc Esterino A Benso, 30 Rcn, SS
Sgt Howard M Benson, 230 FA, BS
Sgt Julian Benson, 823 TD, BS
Pfc Lawrence J Benson, 119 Inf, BS
2d Lt Leo W Benson, 120 Inf, BS
T/4 Marshal T Benthal, 119 Inf, BS
Pfc James Bentis, 119 Inf SS BS
T/5 Marion H Bentley, 120 Inf, BS
Pfc Howard L Benz, 117 Inf BS
T/5 Charles L Beranek, 117 Inf, BS
Sgt Herbert H Beireis, 743 Tnk, BS
Sgt Charles F Berding, 117 Inf, BS
Sgt William F Berek, 120 Inf, SS
1st Lt James H Berg, 30 Rcn Trp, BS w/OLC
S/Sgt Lester R Berg, 30 Div Arty, BS
Pfc Henry W Berger, 120 Inf, BS
Cpl Milton N Berk 30 MP, BS
Cpl Leroy J Berkel, 119 Inf, BS
Pfc Gerald Berman, 119 Inf, BS
Pfc Junior T Berkley, 120 Inf BS
1st Lt Charles H Bernard, 117 Inf BS
Pfc Wesley M Bernard, 120 Inf, SS
T/4 Arthur A Berndt, 197 FA, BS
T/Sgt Vincent F Bernier, 120 Inf, BS w/OLC

T/Sgt Benjamin B Berry, 117 Inf, BS w/OLC
Sgt Clifton E Berry, 119 Inf, BS w/OLC
Capt James D Berry, 740 Tnk SS
Pvt Joseph J Berry, 119 Inf, SS
T/5 Kenneth L Berry, 105 Med, BS
Pfc Robert F Berry, 117 Inf, BS
CWO William J Berry, 230 FA, BS
T/5 Joseph Bersick, 120 Inf, BS
Sgt Neal M Bertelsen, 119 Inf, SS BS w/OLC
Pfc Maurice R Bertrand, 105 Med, BS
2d Lt Simon J Bertulis, 120 Inf, SS
T/Sgt Joseph T Bettencourt, 119 Inf, BS
S/Sgt Roy A Bettes, 117 Inf, SS
T/5 Sante Bianchi, 118 Inf, SS BS
S/Sgt Lawrence M Bianconi, 117 Inf,
    BS w/OLC
T/5 Jack Bickler, 119 Inf, BS
1st Lt James Bickley, 120 Inf, BS w/2OLC
Pfc Herman S Biddle, 119 Inf, SS
Col William S Biddle, 113 Cav, BS
1st Sgt Fred C Biddy, 120 Inf, BS
Pvt William A Bidwell, 120 Inf, BS w/OLC
Pfc Herbert W Bieber, 120 Inf, BS
2d Lt Melvin H Bieber, 743 Tnk, DSC
T/5 Irvan H Bieck, 117 Inf, BS
Pfc Norman F Biehl, 119 Inf, BS w/OLC
T/5 Theodore J Bielefeld, 119 Inf, BS
S/Sgt Kermit W Biertz, 743 Tnk, SS
Pfc William C Bigham, 117 Inf, BS w/OLC
Pfc Adolph J Bigos, 119 Inf, BS
T/4 Donald F Bigwood, 197 FA, BS
Pfc Claud Bilbrey, 86 Chem, BS
Pvt Joseph Bilis, 105 Eng, BS
T/Sgt Barney J Billa, 119 Inf, SS
Pfc Lake D Biller, 117 Inf, BS
S/Sgt Richard W Biller, 119 Inf SS BS
Sgt William Billets, 105 Eng, BS w/OLC
T/4 Bohmir V Bily, 117 Inf BS
T/5 Charles E Binckley, 120 Inf, BS
S/Sgt Robert L Binfoeld 117 Inf, BS
Pfc John W Bingham, 117 Inf SS BS
Pfc John T Binkley, 117 Inf, BS
Capt Richard J Binnicker Jr 113 FA, BS
Sgt Andrew Bird in Ground, 120 Inf, BS
Col Hammond D Birks 120 Inf SS
Sgt Timothy L Birt, 117 Inf SS
T/5 Robert J Bishe, 30 Sig, BS
T/4 Robert E Bishir, 30 Rcn, BS
S/Sgt Charles E Bishop, 119 Inf, BS
Pvt James Bishop, 117 Inf, BS
Pfc Joseph Bishop, 117 Inf, BS
Pfc Roy V Bishop, 120 Inf SS
Cpl Troy E Bishop, 823 TD, BS
S/Sgt James C Bissette 120 Inf, BS
Pfc Edward Bissonnette, 119 Inf, BS
2d Lt Thomas E Bivins 117 Inf SS
T/5 Raymond Bixler, 197 FA SS
Capt Hyman M Bizzell, 113 FA BS
S/Sgt Charles W Black, 117 Inf, BS
Pfc Chester F Black 118 FA, BS
1st Lt David C Black, 70 FA, 2d OLC to AM
T/5 Edward R Black, 118 FA BS
Pfc Ephram E Black, 119 Inf BS
T/5 Jere Black Jr, 744 Tnk, BS
T/5 Morris L Black, 120 Inf, BS
S/Sgt William T Blackburn, 120 Inf, BS
Pfc Jack B Blackett, 117 Inf, BS
Pfc Caleb L Blackwelder, 117 Inf, BS
Pfc Edward C Blaesius, 120 Inf, BS
Sgt Edward J Blaha, 120 Inf, SS
Sgt Raymond A Blaha, 118 FA BS
Sgt Henry Blaida, 120 Inf, SS
1st Lt Donald C Blair, 120 Inf, BS
T/4 Willis N Blake, 230 FA, SS
T/5 James L Blankenship, 30 Div Hq, BS
Pfc Jean M Blanchetts, 743 Tnk, SS
Capt Harry R Blanck, 531 AAA, BS
Capt George H Bland, 230 FA, BS
Pfc Mathew E Blanford, 119 Inf, BS
T/4 Henry Blank, 117 Inf, BS
S/Sgt Snow H Blalock, 117 Inf, BS
Pvt Leonard C Blankenship, 119 Inf, SS BS
T/Sgt Benjamin T Blanton, 119 Inf, DSC

T/Sgt Richard M Blatchford, 117 Inf,
  SS w/OLC
Sgt Walter F Blazonis, 120 Inf, BS
Pfc Kindred T Bledsoe, 230 FA, BS
Pfc William J Bledsoe, 105 Med, BS
Pfc Gordon O Blegan, 30 Div Hq, SS
Pfc Martin Blessant, 120 Inf, SS
Pfc William V Blocker, 230 FA, BS
Capt Charles N Blodgett, 119 Inf, BS w/OLC
Maj Jack Blohm, 30 Div Arty, SS AM w/5 OLC
T/5 Robert M Blosser, 743 Tnk, BS w/OLC
Maj John W Blount, 30 Div Hq, BS
Cpl Frank Blovsky, 119 Inf, SS
S/Sgt Donald L Bloyd, 117 Inf, BS w/OLC
Sgt Pete E Bludis, 230 FA, BS
Pfc William H Blum, 119 Inf, BS w/OLC
Pfc James V Blundo, 117 Inf, BS
Cpl Wallace H Blunkall, 119 Inf, SS
T/Sgt Franklin Boaz, 730 Ord, BS
Sgt George Boazzo, 230 FA, BS
1st Lt Woodrow W Bobo, 736 Tnk, BS
T/5 George J Bock, 730 Ord, BS
Pfc Paul B Bock, 119 Inf, DSC SS
Pfc William A Bocklet, 105 Med, BS w/OLC
1st Lt Richard M Bode, 117 Inf, BS w/OLC
T/Sgt Evar E Bodeen, 120 Inf, BS
Pfc Andrew J Bodnar, 120 Inf, BS
Pfc John J Bodnar, 117 Inf, BS w/OLC
Sgt Alfred F Bodsford, 117 Inf, BS
Pvt Ernest F Boeck, 117 Inf, BS
T/5 Werner H Boehl, 119 Inf, BS
1st Lt Bennie R Boehm, 117 Inf,
  SS w/OLC BS w/OLC
Pfc Kenneth A Boel, 119 Inf, BS w/OLC
Sgt Edwin F Boelsen, 258 FA, BS
Pvt Orman J Botamy, 117 Inf, SS
Pfc Hiram M Bogart, 119 Inf, BS
Pfc Verne W Bogart, 120 Inf, SS BS
T/5 Norman J Boger, 117 Inf, BS
Pfc Edward W Bogner, 120 Inf, BS
Capt Robert M Bogue, 105 Med, BS
T/Sgt William A Bogue, 117 Inf, SS
Pfc Farmer W Bohannon, 119 Inf, BS
Pfc Walter D Bohard, 117 Inf, BS
S/Sgt Arthur W Bohn, 531 AAA, BS
Pfc Harold R Bohn, 120 Inf, BS w/OLC
Pfc William L Bohn, 117 Inf, BS
Pfc Earl L Bohrer, 120 Inf, BS
Pfc Ervin L Boicourt, 120 Inf, BS
Pfc Wilfred Boissonneault, 117 Inf, BS
Pfc Gerard H Boivin, 119 Inf, SS
1st Lt Arnold W Bokesch, 117 Inf, BS w/2OLC
S/Sgt Charles E Boland, 120 Inf BS
Pfc Edward L Boland, 119 Inf, BS
1st Lt James Boland Jr, 197 FA, SS AM w/7OLC
Pfc Roy F Boland, 120 Inf, BS
Sgt Paul L Bolden, 120 Inf, SS BS w/OLC
Pfc Elmo T Boles, 30 Sig, BS
Pfc Everett W Boles, 117 Inf, BS
Maj James E Bolin, 30 Div Hq, BS
Pfc Alfred E Bollenger, 120 Inf, SS w/2OLC
2d Lt Ellsworth E Bolles, 117 Inf BS
M/Sgt Jesse L Bolling, 120 Inf, BS w/OLC
Sgt Gerald M Bolt, 743 TD, BS
Pfc Barnie E Bolton, 119 Inf, BS
Sgt Wilbur R Bond, 120 Inf, BS
Pfc Harvey J Bonds, 120 Inf, SS   -
T/Sgt Robert C Bondurant, 120 Inf, BS w/OLC
Pfc Elmer R Bongiorno, 117 Inf, BS
Pfc Richard Bongiovanni, 120 Inf, BS
Pfc Peter Bonilla, 119 Inf BS
Pfc Alphonse J Bonk, 119 Inf, BS
Pvt Pasquale Bonnanzio, 119 Inf SS
1st Lt Ferdinand Bons, 119 Inf SS BS
T/5 Bontje J Bontjes, 120 Inf, BS w/OLC
Pfc Joseph Boochever, 117 Inf, BS
Sgt Ray G Boocher, 120 Inf, BS w/OLC
T/4 Stanley A Booker Jr, 117 Inf, BS
Cpl Andrew R Boomhower, 117 Inf, BS
S/Sgt Buren L Boone, 119 Inf BS
T/Sgt Ottoway B Boone 120 Inf, BS
T/5 Charles D Booth, 117 Inf, BS
Pvt Gilchrist Booth 743 Tnk, SS
Pfc Samuel L Booth 120 Inf, BS

Pfc Duane W Boothe, 119 Inf, BS
1st Lt John Boots, 119 Inf, BS
Pfc George Booz, 119 Inf, SS
1st Lt James R Boozer, 120 Inf, SS BS
Sgt Clyde Border, 120 Inf, BS
Pfc Ralph Borghese, 105 Eng, BS
T/5 Refugio Borjas, 30 Sig, BS w/OLC
Cpl Harry J Born, 743 Tnk, BS
T/5 Anthony S Bordone, 105 Eng, SS
T/Sgt John E Borstdorf, 531 AAA, BS
1st Lt Don A Borton, 117 Inf, SS BS
Pfc Mile Borus, 119 Inf, SS
1st Lt Edward J Bosch, 113 FA, BS
S/Sgt Wayne L Bosler, 120 Inf, BS BS
T/5 Sidney Bosofsky, 119 Inf, SS BS
S/Sgt Charles F Boss, 119 Inf, BS
Sgt Joseph Bossa, 120 Inf, BS
Pfc Bernard Bossert, 197 FA, SS
T/5 Joseph R Bost, 117 Inf, BS
Pfc George B Boston, 119 Inf, BS
Pfc Leo D Bouknight, 120 Inf, BS
S/Sgt Frank J Boswell, 197 FA, SS
Pvt Wally O Bosworth, 119 Inf, SS
Pvt Camillo A Bosco, 291 Eng, BS
Pfc Joseph A Bosco, 119 Inf, SS
Pfc Edward Boteilho, 117 Inf, BS w/OLC
Sgt John W Botkin, 120 Inf, BS
Sgt Clarence C Botsford, 117 Inf, BS
Sgt Donovan R Bottorff, 30 Sig, BS w/OLC
Sgt George W Bouchard, 803 TD, SS
Pfc Joseph D Boucher, 120 Inf, BS
Capt Michael S Bouchlas, 230 FA, DSC BS
Pfc Joseph B Boudreaux, 117 Inf, BS
Pfc Percy G Boudreaux, 120 Inf, BS
T/5 Raymond L Boulanger, 117 Inf, BS w/OLC
Pvt Leo J Boulard, 197 FA, SS
S/Sgt Wilfred F Bourassa, 120 Inf, BS
Sgt Harry W Boures, 120 Inf, SS BS MM
Pfc Bernard L Bourgeois, 120 Inf, BS
Pfc Milton D Bourgeois, 120 Inf, BS
T/5 Ernest L Bourke, 30 Sig, BS
Sgt James G Boustead, 120 Inf, BS
Pfc John D Boutin, 120 Inf, SS w/OLC
Capt Allie V Boutwell, 120 Inf, BS
Pfc Clayton M Boutwell, 99 Inf, BS
1st Lt Howard W Bowden, 120 Inf, BS
Maj Haygood S Bowden, 118 FA, BS w/OLC
Pfc Lacy Bowen, 119 FA, SS
Sgt Orbie D Bowen, 119 FA, BS
Pfc James A Bower, 120 Inf, BS
1st Lt Earl C Bowers, 119 Inf, SS
S/Sgt Glen L Bowers, 117 Inf, BS
T/5 John H Bowers, 120 Inf, BS
Pfc Max R Bowers, 120 Inf, BS
1st Lt Walter M Bowers, 120 Inf, SS BS
S/Sgt Harry O Bowersox, 120 Inf, SS
Pfc Robert K Bowes, 119 Inf, BS
Sgt Clarence W Bowick, CWS, BS
1st Lt Don K Bowles, 531 AAA BS
Sgt Raymond C Bowling, 117 Inf, BS w/2OLC
Pvt Thomas C Bowling, 117 Inf, BS
1st Lt Albert H Bowman, 105 Med BS
S/Sgt Elmer L Bowman, 117 Inf, BS w/OLC
Sgt Frederick J Boyd, 120 Inf, BS
Pfc Jerry R Boyd, 117 Inf, BS
T/Sgt John A Boyd, 119 Inf, SS
1st Lt John L Boyd, 120 Inf, BS w/OLC
T/Sgt Lewis M Boyd, 30 Div Arty, SS BS
Sgt John V Boyer, 105 Eng SS
CWO James A Boykin, 30 Div Hq, BS
Pfc Virgil C Boyle, 120 Inf BS
Pfc Jim A Bradford, 117 Inf BS
Lt Col William S Bradford, 120 Inf, SS BS
Pfc Felix F Bradley, 743 Tnk, BS
T/4 James J Bradley, 117 Inf, BS
T/5 John W Bradley, 119 Inf, BS
Capt Ralph H Bradley, 230 FA, SS BS
1st Lt Roger I Bradley, 119 Inf, BS
Pfc James E Bradshaw, 117 Inf, BS
1st Lt Edward T Bradt, 531 AAA, BS
Sgt Hugh E Brady, 120 Inf, BS
T/4 James I Brady, 120 Inf BS
Sgt John J Brady Jr, 117 Inf, BS
Pfc Roland W Brady, 105 Med, BS

Pfc Beecher L Bragg, 120 Inf, BS
Pfc Herman N Bragg, 119 Inf, BS
Sgt Frank C Brakefield, 117 Inf, SS
1st Lt Frank E Braker Jr, 120 Inf, BS
Cpl Woodrow W Bramblett, 120 Inf, BS
Pfc Harry Bramson, 120 Inf, SS
Pvt Anthony Branchini, 230 FA, BS
S/Sgt Henry F Brand, 117 Inf, SS
Capt Ernest L Brandis, 120 Inf, BS
S/Sgt Charles F Branton, 113 FA BS
Pfc Charley S Brandon, 120 Inf, BS
T/5 Clifton A Brandon, 113 FA, BS w/OLC
1st Lt Robert W Brandon, 823 TD, BS
Sgt Darit K Branson, 117 Inf, BS
Pfc Allen L Brasel, 120 Inf, BS
T/Sgt Roy L Brantley, 120 Inf, BS w/2OLC
S/Sgt Joe H Bratten, 105 Eng, SS
Pvt Oscar W Bratz, 230 FA, BS
Pfc Emil J Braun, 117 Inf, BS
Pfc Harry J Braun, 105 Eng, BS
Capt Robert F Braun, Ad C, BS
T/5 Robert W Braun, 743 Tnk, BS
1st Lt Leo A Brausch, 117 Inf, SS BS w/OLC
S/Sgt William J Brazeau, 119 Inf, SS BS
Sgt LaVern F Brazil, 823 TD, BS
1st Lt Raymond P Brazil, 120 Inf, SS BS
Pfc Frank W Breach, 117 Inf, BS
S/Sgt Michael Breazzano, 120 Inf, BS
2d Lt Ethelbert L D Breckenridge, 275 FA, BS
Cpl Albert C Breed, 823 TD, SS
T/5 Allen E Breed, 526 Armd Inf, BS
Pfc Albert M Breeding, 117 Inf, BS
S/Sgt Donald W Breeding, 117 Inf, SS
WOJG James R Breedlove, 105 Med, BS
S/Sgt Nolan C Breedlove, 118 FA, BS
Pfc Frank P Brellis, 117 Inf, BS
T/5 Thomas J Brennen, 120 Inf, SS BS
T/Sgt George A Brentzel, 105 Eng, BS
Pvt Albert D Bresler, 119 Inf, BS w/OLC
Pfc Paul L Bretz Jr, 120 Inf BS
Pfc Carl J Brewer, 117 Inf, BS
Pfc Charles D Brewer, 120 Inf, BS
Maj Paul L Brewer, 203 FA, BS
Sgt Travis J Brewer, 823 TD, BS
Pfc Samuel A Breyer, 119 Inf, SS
Sgt Jay H Bricker, 531 AAA, BS
T/5 James O Bridges, 119 Inf, BS
T/5 Windell Bridges, 117 Inf, BS
Pfc Lloyd E Briese, 120 Inf, BS
S/Sgt Paul K Briggs, 119 Inf, BS
Pfc John H Bright, 117 Inf, BS
T/5 Hyman W Brill, 117 Inf, BS w/OLC
1st Sgt Andrew L Brindamour, 120 Inf, BS
T/3 Douglas P Brindley, 117 Inf, BS
S/Sgt Robert L Bringle, 230 FA, BS
Pfc Jerome H Brink, 120 Inf, SS BS
S/Sgt Paul E Brinkley, 120 Inf, BS
2d Lt Paul A Brinkman, 117 Inf, BS
1st Lt Robert W Brinkmeyer, 117 Inf, SS BS
Pfc Harold J Brisk, 117 Inf, BS w/OLC
Pfc Leo D Brissette, 120 Inf, BS
Pfc Raoul L Brister, 120 Inf, BS w/OLC
Pvt Loy E Britcher, 120 Inf, BS
Capt Clarence H Brittain, 803 TD, BS
Pfc Rands A Brittain, 119 Inf, BS
S/Sgt Robert O Britton, 30 Div Arty, BS w/OLC
Pfc Marvin Broadway, 197 FA, BS
T/Sgt Harry W Brocki, 30 Sig, BS
Pvt William W Brockmeyer, 117 Inf, BS
Sgt John E Brodell, 230 FA BS
T/5 John H Broderick, 120 Inf, SS
Pfc Joseph M Broderick, 117 Inf, BS w/OLC
Pvt Anthony J Brogus, 119 Inf, BS
Pvt Paul Vanden Brook, 119 Inf, BS w/OLC
T/5 Carl F Brooks, 120 Inf, SS
Pfc Edwin S Brooks, 531 AAA, BS
Cpl Floyd E Brooks 230 FA, BS
T/4 Robert Brooks, 230 FA, BS
1st Lt T F Brooks Jr, 119 Inf, BS
Pfc Walter R Brooks 117 Inf, BS
Sgt Ben R Brothers 744 Tnk, BS
Pfc George R Brouillette, 117 Inf, BS
Capt Edward C Broussard, 120 Inf,
    SS BS w/2 OLC

Pvt Nicholas O Broutzilo, 119 Inf, BS
Sgt Alvah L Brown Jr, 120 Inf, BS
Pfc Benjamin H Brown, 117 Inf, BS
Capt Charles H Brown, 30 Div Hq, BS
Lt Col Courtney P Brown, 119 Inf,
    SS BS w/OLC C d'G
Cpl Curtis L Brown, 117 Inf, BS w/OLC
Cpl Edwin Brown, 120 Inf, BS
T/Sgt Francis J Brown, 117 Inf, BS
2d Lt Frank R Brown, 120 Inf, SS
Pfc Fred A Brown, 117 Inf, SS
WOJG Fred W Brown, 105 Med, BS
Pfc Gill H Brown, 120 Inf, BS
Capt Gordon W Brown, 105 Eng, SS BS
Pfc Harold J Brown, 120 Inf, BS
T/Sgt Harold V Brown, 119 Inf, SS BS w/3 OLC
1st Lt Herbert W Brown Jr, 119 Inf, SS
T/5 Howard C Brown, 120 Inf, BS
S/Sgt Jack E Brown, 823 TD, BS
Pfc Jimmie M Brown, 120 Inf, BS
Cpl John K Brown, 113 FA, SS
Sgt Joseph E Brown, 117 Inf, BS w/OLC
Capt Joseph E Brown Jr, 120 Inf, SS
1st Lt Joseph E Brown, 120 Inf, BS w/3 OLC
Pvt Leslie L Brown, 119 Inf, BS w/OLC
Sgt Milo H Brown, 119 Inf, BS
Pfc Monford Brown, 117 Inf, BS
Pfc Paton C Brown, 117 Inf, BS
T/Sgt Ray Brown, 120 Inf, SS BS
Pvt Robert H Brown, 105 Eng, BS
Pfc Robert S Brown, 30 MP, BS
Pvt Robert T Brown, 119 Inf, BS
Sgt Rufus O Brown, 117 Inf, SS
Pfc Russell E Brown, 120 Inf, BS
Pfc Samuel H Brown, 117 Inf, BS
T/5 Seymour Brown, 105 Eng. BS
Pvt Staley A Brown, 117 Inf, BS
Capt William J Brown, Hq 30 Div, BS
2d Lt Willie D Brown, 744 Tnk, SS
S/Sgt Delbert H Browning, 119 Inf, BS
Pfc Frank S Bruce, 823 TD, BS
Pfc Ralph Bruce, 105 Eng, SS
Cpl Russell A Bruchu, 531 AAA SS
Pvt John F Brugalette, 120 Inf, BS
T/4 Louis Brukets 117 Inf, BS
Pfc Joseph R Brunacini, 120 Inf, BS
1st Lt Ervin M Bruner, 120 Inf, BS w/OLC
T/5 Jack H Bruner, Sp Sv, BS
S/Sgt James O Bruney, 117 Inf, BS w/3 OLC
Pfc John R Brush, 105 Eng, BS
1st Lt Joe H Bruton, 823 TD, BS
M/Sgt Roy L Bruton 30 Sig, BS
Pvt Earl W Bryan, 117 Inf, BS w/OLC
Pfc Edward T Bryan, 119 Inf BS
1st Lt Alvesta Bryant, 120 Inf BS w/OLC
Pvt Charles L Bryant, 117 Inf, BS
1st Lt John T Bryant, Hq 30 Div, SS
S/Sgt Carroll Bryla, 120 Inf, BS w/OLC
S/Sgt Arthur C Bryson, 119 Inf, SS
Pfc Alex R Bub, 120 Inf, BS
Pvt Anthony F Bucci, 120 Inf, BS
T/4 Greene D Buchanan, 30 Sig BS
Pfc Hayle Buchanan, 119 Inf, BS
Pfc Lawrence W Buchanan 30 Sig, BS w/OLC
Pfc Twyman Buchanan, 823 TD, SS
Pvt Peter E Buchman, 119 Inf, BS
T/3 James C Buchner, 120 Inf BS
T/5 George L Buck, 117 Inf BS
Pfc Lewis H Buck, 120 Inf BS
1st Lt Taylor S Buck, 118 FA, SS AM w/8 OLC
T/4 Alvin H Buckalew 105 Eng BS
Pfc Frank M Buckingham, 117 Inf, BS w/OLC
Pfc Halden T Buckingham, 117 Inf BS
Pvt Frederick J Buckley, 120 Inf SS
1st Lt Robert M Buckley, 117 Inf BS w/OLC
Capt William A Buckley 117 Inf BS w/OLC
T/5 David O Buckner, 117 Inf, BS
Pfc Carl F Budde, 117 Inf, BS
Pfc Raymond S Budzinski 119 Inf, BS
Sgt Stanley E Budzisz, 105 Eng, BS
Pfc Ervin G Buehner, 119 Inf BS
Pfc Clifford O Buelow, 119 Inf, BS
Sgt John Bueno, 105 Eng, DSC BS

Pfc Wilfred C Buerge, 119 Inf, BS
T/5 Richard P Buettner, 197 FA, BS
Pvt George W Buford, 117 Inf, BS
T/Sgt Graham W Buford, 30 Div Band, BS
Pvt Jack Buford, 120 Inf, BS
Pfc Herman G Bulau, 119 Inf, BS
Sgt Robert T Bulger, 120 Inf, BS
Capt Richard Bulkan, 743 Tnk, BS
1st Lt Sidney C Bulla, 531 AAA, BS
Pfc Johnnie N Bullock, 117 Inf, SS
Pvt Kenneth D Bulson, 117 Inf, BS
T/Sgt Joe T Bumgarner 120 Inf, SS
CWO Adam Z Bunch, 30 Div Sig, BS w/OLC
Pfc Stanton L Bunker, 119 Inf, BS
Pfc James B Bunnell, 120 Inf, BS
S/Sgt Norman H Bunnells, 117 Inf, BS
T/5 James W T Buntyn, 120 Inf, SS w/OLC
S/Sgt Richard S Buracker, 117 Inf, SS
Sgt Russell L Burdg, 823 TD, BS
T/5 Frank L Burdine, 117 Inf, BS
T/5 Raymond M Burg, 117 Inf, BS
Capt Albert F Burgess, 30 Sig, BS
1st Sgt Charles E Burgess, 120 Inf, BS
S/Sgt Donald F Burgess, 105 Eng, BS
S/Sgt Garland O Burgess, 117 Inf, BS
S/Sgt James E Burgess, 117 Inf, SS
Pvt John C Burgess, 117 Inf, BS
S/Sgt Eugene E Burgoyne, 203 FA, BS
S/Sgt James E Burke, 119 Inf, BS
1st Lt Robert C Burke, 118 FA,
   DSC SS w/OLC BS
Pvt Stanton L Burke, 113 FA, BS w/OLC
T/5 William O Burke, 119 Inf, BS
Pfc Dempsey Burkeen, 120 Inf, SS
S/Sgt Jerome E Burkett, 117 Inf, SS
Pfc Robert H Burkhardt, 119 Inf, SS
T/5 James R Burkholder, 283 FA, BS
Pvt Arne G Burkman, 30 Div MP, SS
T/5 Adam F Burko, 105 Eng, DSC BS
T/Sgt Julius F Burleson, 120 Inf, BS
S/Sgt Eugene R Burner, 120 Inf, SM
Pfc Kenny Burner, 119 Inf, BS
Sgt Charles B Burnette, 117 Inf, BS
Capt Elijah Burnett, 744 Tnk, BS
T/4 Carlton G Burnette, 113 FA, BS
T/Sgt Eugene G Burnette, 117 Inf, BS w/OLC
Sgt Harold Burney, 230 FA, SS w/OLC BS
Pvt Lanis K Burns, 118 FA, BS
S/Sgt Lloyd M Burns, 118 FA, BS
1st Lt Olin L Burnsed, Hq Co 30 Div, BS
Capt Albert D Buron, 117 Inf, BS w/OLC
Pfc Thomas J Burr, 119 Inf, SS
Pfc William R Burrie, 119 Inf, BS
Pfc Derral H Burright, 117 Inf, BS
S/Sgt James F Burris, 117 Inf, BS
T/Sgt Charles W Burroughs, 120 Inf, BS
S/Sgt Walter G Burroughs, 119 Inf, BS
T/5 Robert T Burruss, 120 Inf, BS
1st Lt Charles S Burton, 105 Eng,
   SS BS w/2 OLC
T/5 Fred P Burton, 117 Inf, BS w/OLC
Pfc James F Burton, 119 Inf, BS
Pvt Joe R Burton 117 Inf, BS
Pfc Robert P Burton, 120 Inf BS
Pfc Thomas W Burton, 823 TD, BS
CWO Rayford O Busby 117 Inf, BS
Sgt Benjamin H Bush, 117 Inf, BS
Pfc Dean L Bush, 119 Inf, BS
1st Lt Frank H Bush, 119 Inf, BS
Capt James A Bush 117 Inf BS w/OLC
Sgt J L Bushnell, 230 FA, SS
S/Sgt Carl E Bussabanger, 119 Inf, BS
Pfc James W Busse 117 Inf BS
Pfc Herman D Butcher 120 Inf SS
Sgt Louis B Butcher, 120 Inf, BS w/OLC
Sgt Robert O Butcher, 30 Div Rcn,
   SS BS C d'G
Pfc Albert Butler, 120 Inf, BS
Lt Col Bradford Butler Jr, 258 FA, SS
Pvt Dave A Butler, 744 Tnk, BS
S/Sgt Edward M Butler 119 Inf BS
Sgt Ellis J Butler, 197 FA, BS
Sgt Harmon W Butler, 119 Inf, SS

2d Lt James J Butler, 120 Inf, BS w/OLC
Sgt John E Butler, 119 Inf, BS
1st Sgt Robert H Butler, 117 Inf, BS w/OLC
Pvt William F Butler, 113 FA, BS
Pfc Ben B Buton, 117 Inf, BS
Capt William P Buttler, 117 Inf, BS w/OLC
Pfc Harry A Butts, 117 Inf, BS
T/Sgt John A Butts, 117 Inf, BS
Pfc Raymond O Butts, 119 Inf, DSC
Pfc Clifford W Buzzard, 117 Inf, DSC C d'G
S/Sgt Morris E Buzzell, 120 Inf, BS
Sgt DeForest H Byce Jr, 30 MP, BS
WOJG Dougan W Byers, 30 Div Arty, BS
Pfc Henry Byers, 119 Inf, BS w/OLC
Maj James J Bynum, 120 Inf, BS
Capt Delmont K Byrn, 120 Inf, DSC SS BS
Pfc James E Byrne, 117 Inf, BS
Pfc Matthew M Byrne Jr, 119 Inf, BS
Cpl John J Byrnes, 119 Inf, BS
Pvt Edgar F Byrns, 120 Inf, SS
Pfc Sterling Caddell, 117 Inf, BS
1st Lt Billy V Cade, 105 Eng, SS
Pvt Clifford A Cade, 120 Inf, BS
Pfc William P Cadematori, 117 Inf, BS
Sgt William W Cadwallader, 120 Inf, SS
Sgt John A Cafaro, 119 Inf, BS
Pfc Arthur A Cain, 120 Inf, BS
T/5 Harry M Cain, 117 Inf, BS
T/5 Oscar M Cain, Div Arty, BS
Pfc Thomas W Cain, 117 Inf, BS
Sgt Virgil G Cain, 117 Inf, BS
2d Lt Francesco Calabrese, 120 Inf, SS BS
S/Sgt John Calaganis, 743 Tk, BS
Cpl Leo Calderon, 230 FA, BS
Pfc Charles E Calderwood, 117 Inf, BS
Pfc Anthony G Cale, 120 Inf, BS
T/4 Matthew N Caldwell, Div Hq, BS
Capt Robert E Caldwell, 117 Inf, BS w/2 OLC
Sgt Robert V Caldwell, 119 Inf, SS
S/Sgt R C Colhoun, 120 Inf, BS
Pfc James Caliguiri, 117 Inf, BS
Sgt Harry M Call, 117 Inf, SS
Sgt William J Callahan, 119 Inf, BS
1st Lt William H Callaway, 120 Inf, DSC
2d Lt John E Calloway, 740 Tk, SS
T/4 William Calvert, 105 Med, BS
Pvt Charles W Cameron, 117 Inf, BS
Pfc Mariano J Camerota, 119 Inf, BS
Cpl Ashley L Camp Jr, 743 Tk, BS
Lt Col Elbert L Camp, 30 Sig, SS
Pfc Lewis F Camp, 117 Inf, BS
Pfc Robert O Camp, 117 Inf, BS
S/Sgt Arthur E Campbell, 823 TD, SS
Pfc Austin B Campbell, 120 Inf, SS BS
Pfc Calvin L Campbell, 120 Inf BS
Pfc Edward C Campbell 119 Inf, BS
Pfc Dairl L Campbell, 120 Inf, BS
WOJG Harry T Campbell 118 FA, BS
S/Sgt Jack Campbell, 117 Inf, BS w/2 OLC
Pfc James T Campbell, 105 Eng, BS
Pfc Jess W Campbell, 117 Inf, BS w/OLC
T/5 Joe R Campbell, 120 Inf, BS
S/Sgt John C Campbell 92 Chem, BS
Pfc Leroy Campbell, 117 Inf BS
Pfc Leroy F Campbell 119 Inf, BS
Cpl Lonnie A Campbell 117 Inf, BS
Sgt Ralph O Campbell 120 Inf BS
T/5 Robert F Campbell, 119 Inf BS
2d Lt William P Campbell 119 Inf, BS
1st Sgt Louis C Campo, 120 Inf, SM
T/3 William T Candler, Div Hq BS
Sgt Samuel L Canerday 119 Inf, BS
Pfc Sam Cannella 119 Inf BS
S/Sgt Charles D Cannon, 120 Inf, BS
Cpl Ernest E Cannons, 119 Inf BS
Pfc James E Canter, 118 FA BS
Lt Col James W Cantey, 120 Inf
   SS w/2 OLC BS w/OLC, C d'G
Lt Col James L Cantrell 70 FA, BS
T/5 Robert C Cantrell, 119 Inf, BS
S/Sgt John A Capaul, 823 TD, BS
Pfc Joseph Capitelli 105 Eng BS
Pfc Charles W Capp 120 Inf BS w/OLC
Sgt Alfred Cappy, 119 Inf, SS

Major John P Carbin, Div Hq, BS
S/Sgt Lester A Carbonneau, 120 Inf, SS
Pfc Carmen D Cardarelli, 119 Inf, BS
Pfc Hobert Carder, 119 Inf, SS
S/Sgt Antonio Cardinale, 120 Inf, SS w/OLC
S/Sgt Mario D Cardosi, 119 Inf, SS
T/3 Cecil D Cardwell, 120 Inf, BS w/OLC
Pfc Daniel Carey, 105 Eng, BS
S/Sgt Leo P Carey, 120 Inf, BS
Pfc Roy S Cargal, 744 Tk, BS
Pvt Patrick J Carito, 120 Inf, BS
Pfc John R Carleton, 120 Inf, SS
Pfc Leno Carletti, 119 Inf, BS
Sgt Raymond Carlew, 105 Eng, SS
T/Sgt Jesse J Carline, 117 Inf, BS
Pfc Hollis D Carlisle, 120 Inf, BS
Pfc Ora E Carlisle, 117 Inf, BS
Sgt Richard W Carlisle, 118 FA, BS w/OLC
Pfc Hubert E Carlock, 119 Inf, BS
Pvt Clarence C Carlos, 113 FA, BS —
T/4 Clarence W Carlson, 743 Tk, BS
1st Lt Lester W Carlson, 99 Chem, BS
S/Sgt Oscar A Carlson, 531 AAA, BS
T/4 Roy E Carlson, 120 Inf, BS
Pfc Verland E Carlson, 117 Inf, BS
Capt William B Carlton, 113 FA, BS w/OLC —
Pfc John P Carman, 230 FA, BS
Pfc Roland L Carmichael, 117 Inf, BS
S/Sgt Delton J Carnley, 120 Inf, BS
Pfc Nicholas Caroccia, 119 Inf, SS BS
Pfc Joseph Carol, 119 Inf, BS
Pfc Christopher C Caros, 117 Inf, BS
Pfc Burtis R Carpenter, 117 Inf, BS
Pfc David I Carpenter, 120 Inf, BS w/OLC
Pfc Emmit J Carpenter, 105 Eng SS BS w/OLC
T/5 Frank L Carpenter, 119 Inf, BS
S/Sgt Herbert F Carpenter, 120 Inf, BS
Pfc Kenneth I Carpenter, 119 Inf, BS
S/Sgt William E Carpenter, 120 Inf, BS
Sgt William J Carpenter, 117 Inf, BS
Pfc Edward F Carr, 117 Inf, BS
1st Lt James R Carr, 119 Inf, BS
Capt Kenneth G Carr, 119 Inf, BS w/OLC
Pfc Paul O Carr, 119 Inf, BS
Pvt Ralph E Carr, 120 Inf, SS
Pfc John Carrabino, 120 Inf, BS
Pfc Wilbert J Carriers, 119 Inf, BS
Pfc Frank A Carrillo, 120 Inf, BS   -
T/4 Willie M Carrillo, 119 Inf, BS
S/Sgt Harley E Carson, 119 Inf. SS BS
Capt John R Carson, 258 Eng, BS
Pfc Eugene Carter, 117 Inf, BS
Lt Col George T Carter, 295 Eng. BS w/OLC
S/Sgt John W Carter, 105 Med, BS
1st Sgt Robert W Carter, 120 Inf BS
Pfc Thomas F Carter, 120 Inf, BS
S/Sgt Travis C Carter, 117 Inf, BS
Pvt Willie M Carter, 105 Eng, BS
T/5 Frank C Carvalho, 230 FA, SS
Pfc Emmet W Carver, 120 Inf, SS
Cpl James H Carver, 113 FA, BS ⟵
S/Sgt Louis D Carver, 117 Inf, SS
Pfc Walter S Carver, 120 Inf, BS
Pfc Salvatore V Cascone, 120 Inf BS
2d Lt Horace A Case, 230 FA, AM BS
S/Sgt James B Case, 119 Inf, SS BS
Pfc Roger P Casey, 119 Inf, BS
2d Lt John S Cash, 117 Inf, BS
Pfc Clifton W Cashion, 120 Inf SS
S/Sgt Francis J Cashman, 117 Inf, BS
Pfc John A Cashman, 119 Inf BS w/OLC
Pfc Andrew E Casimiro, 117 Inf, SS BS
Pvt Samuel N Cass, 117 Inf, BS
Sgt Charles L Cassar, 105 Eng, BS
Pvt Robert E Casselbury, 117 Inf, SS
Pfc Gilbert S Castaneda, 117 Inf, SS BS w/OLC
Cpl Ettore J Castellante Jr 118 FA, BS
Pfc Andrew Castillo 120 Inf BS
S/Sgt Billie M Castleberry, 120 Inf, BS
Pfc Garland M Castleberry, 120 Inf, BS
Pfc John D Castro, 120 Inf, BS
Pfc Peter Castronova, 119 Inf, BS
T/4 William C Castrovinci, 119 Inf, BS
S/Sgt John P Cataline, 117 Inf, SS

Cpl John F Catenacci, 197 FA, BS
T/4 Lester R Cates, 120 Inf, BS
T/Sgt Robert S Catlett, 105 Med BS
Pvt Raymond L Caton, 117 Inf, BS
Capt John M Caughlin, 3508 Ord, BS
Sgt Bernie H Caughran, 119 Inf, BS
1st Lt Martin F Caulfield 531 AAA, BS w/OLC
Pfc Johnny P Causby, 120 Inf, BS
Cpl Ernest G Causton, 105 Eng, BS
S/Sgt Frederick S Cavanaugh, 117 Inf,
    BS w/2 OLC
S/Sgt Mario A Cavanna, 743 Tk, BS
Pfc Edward Cavill, 119 Inf, BS
S/Sgt Joseph P Cawley, 117 Inf, BS w/OLC
T/Sgt James C Caylor, 117 Inf, BS
Pfc Russell C Caywood, 105 Eng, BS
S/Sgt Edward E Ceccatti, 117 Inf, BS
Pfc John S Celis, 117 Inf, BS
M/Sgt William R Cely Jr, 197 FA, BS
S/Sgt Joseph H Cenertich, 117 Inf, BS
T/5 Ivan F Cenkovich, 119 Inf, BS
Pfc Sylvio J Censullo, 105 Eng, BS
Pfc Emil Cepak, 118 FA, BS
T/4 Daniel P Cerasuolo, 30 Sig, BS
Capt Russell A Chabaud, 119 Inf, SS BS
Pfc Peter P Chackan, 117 Inf, BS w/OLC
Pfc Cecil J Chadwick, 120 Inf, BS
Pfc Wayne M Chardwick, 119 Inf, SS
T/5 Amos M Chaffin, 118 FA, BS
Sgt Ralph M Chafin, 120 Inf, SS BS
Pvt William Chaiken, 105 Eng, BS
Pfc John P Chalone, 117 Inf, BS w/OLC
T/3 Albert H Chamberlain, 30 Sig, BS
Pfc Edward F Chamberlin, 119 Inf, SS
T/5 Harold K Chamberlin, 117 Inf, BS
T/Sgt Norman J Chambers, 119 Inf, BS
Pfc Verling Chambers, 120 Inf, BS
Pfc Ernest L Champagne, 117 Inf, BS
Capt Charles B Chandler, 197 FA, BS w/OLC
Cpl Gordon W Chandler, 743 Tk, BS
Capt Philip M Chandler, 120 Inf, BS w/OLC
Sgt Thomas J Chandler, 119 Inf, BS w/OLC
Sgt Collier E Chaney, 119 Inf, SS
Cpl Clarence Chang, 119 Inf, BS
Pfc Robert M Channell, 30 MP, BS
T/5 Frank D Chapin, 120 Inf, BS
S/Sgt Robert W Chapin, 119 Inf, SS
1st Lt Nick Chapis, 803 TD, BS
Pfc Charles P Chapman, 117 Inf, SS
Cpl Clarence J Chapman, 120 Inf, SS
S/Sgt Edward J Chapman, 30 Band, BS
Pvt Foster D Chapman, 30 Rcn, BS
Pfc Harvey C Chapman, 120 Inf, BS
Lt Warren H Charleston, 120 Inf,
    SS w/OLC BS w/OLC
T/5 James A Charron, 117 Inf, BS
S/Sgt Edgar A Chase, 120 Inf, BS
1st Lt Murray Chase, 119 Inf, BS
S/Sgt Thomas L Chason, 119 Inf, BS
Pfc Estanislao C Chavana, 823 TD, SS
Pfc Jesus Chavez, 119 Inf, BS
Pfc Claude W Chavis, 117 Inf, BS
Sgt Robert D Checketts, 823 TD, BS
T/Sgt Marvin E Cheek, 120 Inf, BS
Pfc Paul B Cheffer, 120 Inf, BS
Pvt Albert Chelli, 120 Inf, BS
Pfc Hal H Cherry Jr, 117 Inf BS
T/5 John R Cherry, 117 Inf, BS
Cpl Charles Chesler, 119 Inf, BS
Pfc Robert J Childers, 117 Inf, BS
T/5 J L Cheshir, 118 FA, SS BS
S/Sgt James R Chester, 30 Rcn, BS
1st Lt Charlie D Chewning, 531 AAA, BS
Pfc Jerome Chiappise, 120 Inf, BS
T/5 Joseph J Chikla, 230 FA, SS BS
T/Sgt James C Chieco, 120 Inf, BS
T/5 Thomas Chidester, 293 FA, BS
Cpl Ralph L Childress, 120 Inf, BS
Pvt Tom S Childress, 120 Inf, BS
Pfc Walter E Childs, 120 Inf, BS
Pfc George A Chilton, 230 FA, BS
1st Lt John C Chisholm, 30 QM BS
T/Sgt Carlo Chislaghi, 119 Inf BS
Pvt Raymond H Chittwood, 120 Inf, SS

Sgt George D Conley, 119 Inf, SS BS
T/5 Kenneth R Connaher, 113 FA, BS
T/5 James J Connell, 117 Inf, BS
Cpl Regis D Connell, 117 Inf, BS
Pfc Donald O Connelly, 105 Med, BS
T/5 Ronald H Connolly, 117 Inf, BS
1st Lt Herbert O Connor, 197 FA,
   BS AM w/OLC
Sgt Horace C Conquest, 197 FA, BS
Capt Jacob D Conrad, XIX Corps, BS
T/5 Warren O Conrad, 30 Rcn, BS
Pvt Edward E Conrey, 120 Inf, BS
Pfc Marion A Conrey, 119 Inf, BS
Pfc Francis A Conroy, 120 Inf, BS SM
Pfc Joseph A Consiglio, 120 Inf, BS
Pfc Biton P Constantine, 120 Inf, BS
S/Sgt Valdo J Conte, 30 Band, BS
1st Lt James F Conti, 105 Eng, BS
Cpl Louis S Conti, 119 Inf, BS
Sgt Vincent J Conti, 105 Eng, SS
1st Lt Donald J Conway, 119 Inf, SS
Pfc Wilfred G Conway, 120 Inf, BS
Pfc Tommie J Coogle, 30 MP, BS
Sgt Charles F Cook, 30 QM, BS
Pvt Eastman R Cook, 743 Tk, BS w/OLC
T/Sgt Edgbert P Cook, 117 Inf, BS
1st Lt Eugene Cook, 119 Inf, SS w/OLC
Pfc George E Cook, 118 FA, BS w/2 OLC
Pfc George J Cook, 118 FA, BS
Pfc Guy R Cook 117 Inf, BS
T/5 James A Cook, 120 Inf, BS w/OLC
1st Lt Joseph W Cook, 120 Inf, BS w/OLC
T/Sgt Julian F Cook, 120 Inf, BS
Pfc Kenneth E Cook, 117 Inf, BS
T/4 S T C Cook, 743 Tk, SS BS
Pvt Carl T Cooley, 117 Inf, BS
Cpl Glen E Coombs, 120 Inf, BS
Pfc Herbert W Coombs Jr, 119 Inf, BS
S/Sgt Kenneth R Coon, 120 Inf, SS BS w/OLC
T/5 Donald E Coons, 823 TD, BS w/OLC
Pvt Robert N Coons, Div Hq, SS
S/Sgt Fred H Cooper, 120 Inf, SS
T/5 Joseph Cooper, 118 FA, BS
2d Lt Leroy C Cooper, 120 Inf, SS
Pfc Robert F Cooper, 117 Inf, BS
T/4 Robert W Cooper, 117 Inf, SS w/OLC BS
1st Lt Stanley W Cooper, 117 Inf,
   SS BS w/OLC C d'G
M/Sgt Stephenson A Cooper, Div Hq, BS
Pfc Wayne H Cooper, 119 Inf, BS
Cpl William C Cooper, 113 FA, BS
Pfc William E Cooper, 230 FA, BS
Pvt Yancey M Cooper, 119 Inf, BS
Pfc Nathan Cooperstein, 119 Inf, SS
1st Lt Edward H Cope, 117 Inf, SS
Cpl William J Cope, 119 Inf, BS
S/Sgt Arthur J Copeland, 117 Inf, BS
Pvt Marvin L Copher, 117 Inf, BS
T/4 Dale S Copper, 743 Tk, SS
Pvt George Coppola 197 FA, BS
Pfc Clarence Corbellow, 70 FA, SS
Pfc Hildrie Corbin, 743 Tk, SS
T/Sgt Francis M Cordle, 119 Inf, SS BS
T/4 George W Corf, 823 TD, BS
M/Sgt Michele Corhan, 119 Inf, BS
Pfc Fred D Corl, 105 Med, BS
Sgt Leslie E Corlis, 117 Inf, BS
T/3 George W Corn, 30 Sig, BS
S/Sgt John L Corn, 230 FA, SS
Capt Kenneth C Cornelius, 30 Rcn, SS
Pvt Harold J Cornwell, 120 Inf, BS
Capt Joseph D Cornwell, 119 Inf, SS
T/4 Earl C Cornfield, 117 Inf, BS
S/Sgt Arthur B Correll, 117 Inf, BS
2d Lt Edward C Correll, 747 Tk, BS
Pvt Robert D Corrigan, 119 Inf, BS
Sgt William B Corrigan, 119 Inf, BS
Pfc Anthony J Corsi, 120 Inf, SS BS
T/4 Andrew C Corsino, 119 Inf, BS
Pvt Anthony M Cortese, 117 Inf, SS
Pfc Joseph M Cortese, 120 Inf, BS
Pfc Clifford B Coryer, 119 Inf, BS
1st Sgt Rufus V Cosby, 531 AAA, BS
T/4 Frank Cosharek, 30 Sig, BS

Pfc Lewis D Cosmano, 117 Inf, SS
Pfc Lawrence J Cosmo, 120 Inf, BS
Pfc Dick Cosper, 117 Inf, BS
Pvt Arnold R Cossin, Div Arty, BS
Pvt Domenic Costa, 113 FA, BS
Pfc Joseph E Costanza, 120 Inf, BS
Sgt Henry J Costello, 230 FA, SS w/OLC
Capt James P Costello, 197 FA, BS w/OLC
Pfc Raymond O Costello, 117 Inf, BS
Maj Edward A Costomiris, 823 TD, BS
Pfc Clarence J Cote, 120 Inf, BS
S/Sgt Emile F Cote, 119 Inf, BS
Pfc Robert M Cottrell, 119 Inf, BS
1st Lt Robert E Coulson, 531 AAA, BS
2d Lt Bayard V Coulter, 120 Inf, BS
Pfc Thomas R Coulter, 120 Inf, BS w/OLC
2d Lt Robert E Counseller, 120 Inf, SS
1st Sgt Donald G Counts, 531 AAA, BS
1st Lt Joseph A Couri, 743 Tk, BS w/OLC
T/5 Jay C Courter, 119 Inf, BS
Pfc John E Courtney, 120 Inf, BS
Sgt Raymond W Courtney, 743 Tk, BS
Lt Col John B Cousar, 105 Med, BS C d'G
Cpl Edward L Couture, 120 Inf, BS
Pfc William R Couvillion, 120 Inf, BS
Pfc Hyman D Coverman, 120 Inf, BS w/OLC
Pvt Marvin R Covey, 117 Inf, BS
Pfc Curvin M Covington, 119 Inf, SS
Pfc Cecil V Cowan, 117 Inf, SS
Capt Kenneth R Cowan, 743 Tk, BS
Pvt Alexander Cowart, 119 Inf, BS
1st Lt John C Cowden Jr, 117 Inf, BS
T/Sgt Wilbur R Cowell, 230 FA, SS
Capt Stuart H Cowen, 118 FA, BS w/OLC
S/Sgt Francis D Cowles, 120 Inf, BS
Pfc Alfred Cox, 105 Eng, BS
T/4 Cecil B Cox, 119 Inf, BS
S/Sgt Clifford J Cox, 118 FA, BS
S/Sgt Elmer M Cox, 113 FA, BS
Pfc Everett F. Cox, 119 Inf, BS
Pfc Francis L Cox, 119 Inf, SS
Pfc Francis X Cox, 117 Inf, BS
2d Lt Grover C Cox Jr, 120 Inf, SS w/OLC BS
S/Sgt Henry J Cox, 230 FA, BS w/OLC
Pfc Herbert Cox Jr, 117 Inf, BS
Pfc James M Cox, 744 Tk, BS
T/5 Junior L Cox, 105 Eng, BS
T/4 Kermit W Cox, 113 FA, BS w/OLC
Lt Col William C Cox, 119 Inf, SS
1st Lt Edward J Coyle, 92 Chem, BS
Pvt John F Coyle, 120 Inf, BS
Pfc John J Crabal, 113 FA, BS
S/Sgt John M Crabbs, 119 Inf, BS
T/4 Harold D Crabtree, 120 Inf, SS BS
S/Sgt William H Crabtree, 119 Inf, DSC SS
T/5 Nicholas A Cracker, 117 Inf, BS w/OLC
Pfc Melvin L Craft, 120 Inf, BS
Capt John A Crago, 118 FA, SS BS w/OLC
S/Sgt Claude C Graham, 119 Inf, SS
Pfc Clinton F Craig, 117 Inf, BS w/OLC
Capt Frank B Craig, Div Hq, BS
T/Sgt James E Craig, 117 Inf, SS
Pfc John W Craig, 119 Inf, BS
Maj John W Craig, Div Hq, BS w/OLC C d'G
Pfc Robert Craig, 117 Inf, BS
Sgt Murlin W Cramer, 197 FA, BS
T/Sgt Billy B Cranberry, Div Hq, BS
S/Sgt Johnie R Crandell, 113 FA, BS
Sgt Joseph A Crane, 120 Inf BS
1st Lt Robert M Crane, 531 AAA, BS
1st Lt Chauncey G Cravens, 117 Inf, SS
S/Sgt Louis D Craver, 117 Inf, SS
Pfc Carl R Crawford, 117 Inf BS
1st Lt Elzie L Crawford, 117 Inf, BS
2d Lt Henry V Crawford, 197 FA, SS
1st Sgt Howard C Crawford, 119 Inf, BS
Pvt William M Crawford, 117 Inf, BS
Pfc William M Crawford, 120 Inf, BS
T/Sgt Levey P Creech, 113 FA BS
T/4 Leland C Creel, 117 Inf, BS
Capt Wylie F Creel, 105 Med, BS
T/Sgt Claude L Creighton, 117 Inf,
   SS w/OLC C d'G
1st Lt Charles P Crepeau, 120 Inf, SS

WOJG Deward B Cress, 117 Inf, BS
T/5 Robert R Cresswell, 30 Sig, BS
2d Lt Arthur J Crews, 120 Inf, BS
T/4 Howard L Crews, 117 Inf, BS
Cpl Arthur A Crick, 118 FA, BS
T/Sgt Abram B Criddle, 531 AAA, BS
S/Sgt James E Crisp, 823 TD, BS
Capt Bruce A Crissinger, 823 TD, SS BS
S/Sgt Kenneth G Crist, 823 TD, BS
Pfc Peter D Crivelli, 119 Inf, BS w/OLC
Sgt Lloyd L Crockett, 120 Inf, BS w/OLC
Sgt Ernest Cronin, 119 Inf, SS
1st Sgt Jeremiah J Cronin Sr, 119 Inf,
   BS w/OLC
Pfc William E Crook, 117 Inf, BS w/OLC
S/Sgt Clayton B Cross, 117 Inf, BS
S/Sgt Jearld H Cross, 117 Inf, BS
Pfc Roy V Crosslin, 120 Inf, BS
Pfc Arthur F Croteau, 120 Inf, BS
S/Sgt Arthur D Crowe, 197 FA, BS
Pfc Fred W Crowe, 120 Inf, BS
S/Sgt Miles E Crowe, 120 Inf, SS
Cpl Osborn M Crowe, 197 FA, SS
Sgt Amos S Crumbine, 120 Inf, SS
T/5 David J Crump, 119 Inf, BS
Sgt Hollis Crump, 120 Inf, BS
S/Sgt Henry B Crumpler, 113 FA, BS —
Pfc Clarence B Crymes, 117 Inf, BS
T/3 Bennie P Cucchiara, 823 TD, BS
Pfc Walter W Cudworth, 120 Inf, BS
Pfc Samuel G Cuellar, 117 Inf, BS w/OLC
Pfc Salvatore J Cuippa, 119 Inf, BS
Pvt Tommie Culberhouse, 117 Inf, BS
Maj R Jerald Culhane, 117 Inf, SS
Pfc Louis J Cullen, 119 Inf, SS BS
Pfc James A Culler, 117 Inf, BS
Pfc Ernest S Cullums, 120 Inf, BS
Pfc Carlos A Culp, 120 Inf, BS
T/5 Jess P Culp, 30 Sig, BS w/OLC
Capt Wayne R Culp, 117 Inf, SS BS
T/Sgt Ryley L Culpeper, 120 Inf, BS
Pvt James H Culver, 119 Inf, BS
T/4 James Cumming, Div Hq, BS
Pfc Daniel J Cummings, 119 Inf, BS
Pfc Howard A Cummings, 117 Inf, BS
S/Sgt William E Cummings, 92 Chem, BS
Sgt Clifford J Cummings, 117 Inf, BS
Pfc David C Cunliffe, 30 Sig, BS
1st Lt Chipman W Cunningham, 119 Inf,
   BS w/OLC
Pvt George W Cunningham, 120 Inf, BS
Sgt Harry B Cunningham, 823 TD, BS
Pfc Jack C Cunningham, 117 Inf, DSC
T/4 William S Cunningham, 117 Inf, BS
Pfc Alvin C Curl, 117 Inf, BS
Pfc Charles W Curl, 119 Inf, BS
Cpl Francis J Curran, 230 FA, BS
Pfc Patrick F Curran, 119 Inf, SS
Capt Paul R Currer, 105 Med, BS
T/Sgt Francis S Currey, 120 Inf, CMH SS
1st Lt John J Currey, 30 Sig, BS w/OLC
Cpl John O Curry, 197 FA, BS
Pfc Palmer Curry, 119 Inf, BS
Sgt Byron D Curtis, 120 Inf, BS
S/Sgt Charles Curtis Jr, 119 Inf, BS w/OLC
1st Lt Claude W Curtis Jr, 120 Inf, BS
T/Sgt Earl R Curtis, 117 Inf, DSC
Capt Elbert R Curtis, 823 TD, BS
Pfc John P Curtis, 117 Inf, BS
1st Lt Robert E Curtis, 120 Inf, SS
T/3 Watt C Curtis, 117 Inf, BS
Pfc Mitchell A Curylo, 30 Sig, BS MM
1st Lt Harold R Cushing 803 TD, BS
Pfc Marion D Cushing Jr, 119 Inf, BS
1st Lt Robert P Cushman, 117 Inf, SS
Pvt Victor D Cutsinger, 117 Inf, BS
Pvt John C Cwik, 230 FA, BS
S/Sgt Fred E Cyr, 120 Inf, BS
Sgt Louis G Cyrus 113 FA, BS —
S/Sgt Maultis M Cyrus, 113 FA, SS
Pfc Joseph S Cyzio, 119 Inf, BS
T/4 John J Czachura, 119 Inf, BS
2d Lt Walter J Czarnecki, 531 AAA, SS
Pfc Jeffry W Czerniawski, 120 Inf, BS

S/Sgt Edward J Dabrowski, 30 Sig, BS
S/Sgt Henry Dachinger, 117 Inf, BS
Pfc Robert J Dackerman, 117 Inf, BS
Cpl George D Acy, 120 Inf, BS
S/Sgt Vincent J Daddino, 117 Inf, BS w/OLC
1st Lt Elwood G Daddow, 117 Inf, BS
Pfc Norman D Dague, 120 Inf, BS
2d Lt George Dail, 117 Inf, DSC BS
T/4 Howard W Dale, 117 Inf, BS
T/5 Martin M Dale, 99 Inf, BS w/OLC
Cpl Perry E Dale, 30 Rcn, BS
S/Sgt Woodrow W Dale, 105 Med, BS
T/5 Nicholas J Dalia, 120 Inf, BS
Pfc Walter J Dalida, 119 Inf, BS
Sgt Joseph K Dalke, 119 Inf, BS
Pfc Howard G Dallas, 230 FA, BS
Lt Col Thomas S Dallas, 116 Inf, SS
Lt Col John C Dalrymple, 82 Eng, BS w/OLC
Capt Robert W Dalrymple, 1153 Eng, BS
Sgt Joseph H Dalsant, 823 TD, BS
Cpl Artis E Dalton, 117 Inf, BS
Pfc Estal B Dalton, 120 Inf, BS
Capt Oscar D Dalton, 119 Inf, SS
S/Sgt Thomas W Dalton, 120 Inf, BS w/OLC
T/4 Willard T Dalton, 119 Inf, BS
T/5 Joseph R Daly, 117 Inf, BS
Cpl Milton J Daly Jr, 823 TD, BS
T/5 Frank R Damato, 230 FA, SS
S/Sgt Ralph M D'Ambrosio, 120 Inf, SS C d'G
Capt John D'Amico, 120 Inf, SS w/OLC BS
Pvt Albert H Damore, 120 Inf, SS
Pfc Russell A Damos, 105 Eng, BS
S/Sgt Alex A Damsen, 119 Inf, BS w/OLC
2d Lt Merrill D Dan, 120 Inf, SS
Pvt Albert F Dancause, 120 Inf, BS
Pfc Leonard Danczak, 197 FA, BS
Lt Col John W Dandridge, Div Hq, BS C d'G
1st Lt Ralph C Daniel, 117 Inf, SS BS MC
Sgt Thomas E Daniel Jr, ECAD, BS
1st Sgt Jan Danielek, 119 Inf, BS
S/Sgt Nathan Daniels, 119 Inf, BS
Pfc Max Dannenberg, 117 Inf, BS
T/4 Floyd E Danner, 120 Inf, BS
Sgt Vernee V Darby, Hq 30 Div, BS
S/Sgt George Darden, 197 FA, BS
Cpl Stanley A Dare, 743 Tk, BS
S/Sgt Alvio J Darin, 117 Inf, BS
Pvt Garrett Darland, 117 Inf, BS
Pfc Kenneth F Darling, 118 FA, BS w/2 OLC
T/5 Max L Darling, 531 AAA, BS
T/5 Donald B Darnell, 117 Inf, BS
Cpl Lloyd N Darnell, 117 Inf, SS
T/Sgt Vernon Darnold, 117 Inf, BS
2d Lt Don J D'Auben, 120 Inf, BS w/OLC
1st Lt Charles E Darwent, 117 Inf, SS BS
Pvt Donald D Darwin, 120 Inf, SS
Sgt Leonard V Daugherty, 117 Inf, BS
1st Lt Louis A Daugherty, 119 Inf, BS SS
Pfc Meredith L Daugherty, 119 Inf, BS
Sgt Nelson O Daugherty, 120 Inf, BS
T/5 Willard C Daugherty, 120 Inf, BS
Sgt James R Daughty, 117 Inf, BS
T/4 Daniel C Daunt, 117 Inf, BS
Pvt Raymond J Dauterive, 832 TD, SS
Pfc Louis J Dauterman, 120 Inf, BS
Pvt Joe P Davenport, 744 Tk, SS
Cpl John G David 120 Inf, BS
S/Sgt Charlie W Davidson, 119 Inf, BS
Capt Donald T Davidson, 531 AAA, BS
S/Sgt Herman A Davidson, 119 Inf, BS
Pfc Joseph O Davidson Jr, 117 Inf, BS w/OLC
T/Sgt Mansel J Davidson, 117 Inf, SS BS
Pfc William E Davidson, 119 Inf, BS
Cpl William L Davidson, 117 Inf, BS
Sgt Alfred H Davis, 119 Inf, BS
Pfc Barney Davis, 120 Inf, BS
T/4 Baxter J Davis, 117 Inf, BS
T/Sgt Bill Davis, 105 Eng, BS
Sgt Cecil L Davis, 743 Tk, SS BS w/OLC
1st Sgt Charles H Davis, 119 Inf, SS
Pfc Charles J Davis, 117 Inf, BS
Sgt Charles R Davis, 120 Inf, SS BS
T/5 Frank E Davis, 119 Inf, BS
Cpl Frank S Davis, 120 Inf, BS

Pvt George Davis, 823 TD, BS
Pfc Hiram L Davis, 120 Inf, BS
1st Lt Hubert W. Davis, 86 Chem, BS
S/Sgt Huey Davis, 119 Inf, BS
Sgt Jasper D Davis Jr, Div Hq, BS
Capt John R Davis, 82 Eng, BS
1st Lt John W Davis, 120 Inf, SS
Pfc Joseph Davis, 117 Inf, BS
Capt Lawrence A Davis, 117 Inf, BS
Pfc Lloyd A Davis, 105 Eng, BS
S/Sgt Louis L Davis, 117 Inf, BS
Pfc Lucious C Davis, 120 Inf, BS
S/Sgt Marcus T Davis, 119 Inf, SS
Sgt Martin F Davis, 119 Inf, BS
Sgt Oscar J Davis, 119 Inf, BS
Pfc Oscar P Davis, 117 Inf, BS
Sgt Paul Davis, 117 Inf, BS
Pfc Quentin Davis, 117 Inf, SS
T/5 Raymond A Davis, 823 TD, BS
Sgt Richard C Davis, 120 Inf, SS
Cpl Richard E Davis, 743 Tk, SS
Sgt William B Davis, 120 Inf, BS w/OLC
T/Sgt William M Davis, 119 Inf, BS
T/4 Willie J Davis, 120 Inf, BS
Pfc Zenon A Davis, 117 Inf, BS w/OLC
Pfc Herbert W Dawson, 119 Inf, SS
Pvt Raymond W Dawson, 117 Inf, SS BS
Pfc Aubrey L Day, 117 Inf, BS
1st Sgt George R Day, 119 Inf, BS w/OLC
Pvt John E Day, 118 FA, BS
Pvt Norman N Day, 117 Inf, BS
Capt Albert Dakin, 197 Inf, SS w/OLC
T/Sgt Howard E Deadman, 120 Inf,
    SS w/OLC C d'G MM
S/Sgt James D Deal, Div Arty, BS
T/4 Emery Deak Hq 30 Div, BS
Pfc George B Dean, 117 Inf, BS
Pfc Nicholas DeAndrea, 117 Inf, BS w/OLC
Pfc Herbert H Deans, 117 Inf, SS
Sgt Lloyd Dearman, 120 Inf, SS BS
T/Sgt Ashley R Deaton, 120 Inf, BS w/OLC
Pfc James C Deaton, 119 Inf, BS w/OLC
Cpl Frank G DeBartolo, 105 Eng, BS
Pfc Frank M Debor, 117 Inf, BS
T/4 Clayton E DeVord, 119 Inf, BS
T/5 Franklin Debuskey, 823 TD, BS
T/5 Benito de Campos, 117 Inf, BS
Pfc Sebastian A Dechiaro, 119 Inf, SS
Pfc Louis DeChristopher, 118 FA, SS
Pfc Walter A Decker, 105 Med, BS
Pfc George DeCosta, 119 Inf, BS
Pfc Dante DeDomineco, 105 Eng, BS
S/Sgt Edwin J Deedrick, 30 Rcn, BS
Pvt Frank J Deegan, 119 Inf, BS
Capt James S Deehan, 105 Med, BS w/OLC
T/4 Henry W Dees, 117 Inf, BS
Pfc J C Dees 120 Inf, BS
Sgt Hollis G Degenhardt, 120 Inf, BS,
Pfc Joseph DeGeorge, 744 Tk, SS
Pvt John DeGiacomo, BS
T/5 Guido DeGregorio, 118 FA, BS
T/4 Joseph J DeHope, 119 Inf, BS
Sgt Bernard J Dekalich, 197 FA, BS
T/5 Charles E Delancey, 120 Inf, BS w/OLC
Pfc Donald A Delaney, 120 Inf, BS w/OLC
Pfc John L Delay, 120 Inf, BS
Capt Francis J DelBena, 119 Inf, SS
Pvt Richard Delbrook, 119 Inf, SS
Pfc Arthur C DeLeon, 823 TD, BS
T/4 Richard E Delfs, 743 Tk, BS
T/4 James J D'Elia, 30 Sig, BS
Sgt Salvatore A Delise, 105 Med, BS
S/Sgt Edward J Dell, 120 Inf SS
Pfc Harold H Dellinger, 197 FA, BS w/OLC
T/5 George H Dells, 105 Eng, BS w/OLC
Sgt Harris E DeLoach, 117 Inf, BS
Pfc Robert W Delorey, 119 Inf, BS
Pfc Giovanno DeLuca, 120 Inf, BS
Pfc Edward J Devlin, 30 MP, BS
S/Sgt Mike G Demarkos, 120 Inf, BS w/OLC
Pfc Carlo F DeMarchil, 117 Inf, BS w/OLC
WOJG Robert J Dematio, 118 FA,BS
2d Lt Frank A DeMichele, 230 FA, BS
T/Sgt Dana B Deming, 117 Inf, BS

Lt Col James C Dempsey, Hq 30 Div, BS
T/5 Lloyd J. Dempsey, 117 Inf, BS w/OLC
Pfc Peddus Dempsey, 120 Inf, BS
WOJG Percy E Dempsey, 120 Inf, BS w/OLC
T/4 Weldon B Dempsey, 105 Med, BS
Pfc Simon A. Denaro, 120 Inf, SS BS
Pfc Franklin W. Denius, FA, SS w/2 OLC
Pfc Donald A Denker, 120 Inf, BS
2d Lt Richard G. Denlinger, CIC, BS
Pfc Benjamin F Denney, 117 Inf, BS
S/Sgt William E Denney, 119 Inf, BS
T/4 Arthur J Dennis, 120 Inf, BS
Cpl Herbert T Dennis, 120 Inf, BS
Pfc David W Denny, 117 Inf, SS w/OLC BS
Maj Robert M Denny, 30 QM, BS w/OLC
Pfc Charles R Denton, 119 Inf, BS
1st Lt George D Denton, 30 MP, BS w/2 OLC
1st Lt James W Denton, 283 FA, BS
T/5 Chester W DePerry, 105 Eng, BS
Pfc Natale A DePietropoalo, 99 Inf, SS
T/4 Charles J DeRaedt, 119 Inf, BS
Capt Robert S Derby, 743 TD, BS
Maj Walker C DeRenne, 234 Eng, BS
Cpl Gordon W Deringer, 118 FA, BS
2d Lt Jerry F DeRoss, 823 TD, BS
Cpl Cecil O Derr, 823 TD, SS BS
T/5 Lewis Derrick, 117 Inf, BS
Pfc John T Derry, 119 Inf, BS w/OLC
Pvt Ralph B Derry, 117 Inf, BS
Pvt Theodore S Derucki, 30 MP, BS
Sgt Jesse DeSoto, 120 Inf, SS BS
Sgt Ralph A Desposito, 230 FA, BS
Pfc Harry S Despotopulos, 119 Inf, BS
S/Sgt Elias L Dettelbach, Hq 30 Div, BS
Lt Col Stanley Dettmer, 823 TD SS BS C d'G
1st Lt Frank E. Deupree, 823 TD, BS
Sgt Nathan H Devine, 120 Inf, BS w/OLC
Pfc Thomas DeVito, 117 Inf, BS w/OLC
Pfc Ralph A DeVitto, 120 Inf, BS
Sgt John DeVries, 105 Eng, BS
Capt James A DeWeerd, 120 Inf, SS
1st Lt Helmer H Dewey, 120 Inf, SS
S/Sgt Roscoe W DeWitt, 118 FA, BS
Cpl Andre P Dewulf, 105 Eng, BS
Maj Robert Dexheimer, 92 Chem, BS
Pfc Walton Deyette, 120 Inf, BS
1st Lt Burrell H DeYoung, 117 Inf, BS w/OLC
1st Lt Joseph A Dezman, 120 Inf, BS w/OLC
Pfc James L Diamond, 120 Inf, BS
Pfc Jesse F Diaz, 823 TD, SS
Cpl Victoriano E Diaz, 117 Inf, BS w/OLC
T/Sgt Joseph A DiBiase, 118 FA, BS w/OLC
Pfc Trent J Dibiasi, 120 Inf, BS
S/Sgt Lester C Dickens, 120 Inf, BS
S/Sgt Charles Dickey, 119 Inf, BS
Pfc Lawrence W Dickey, 119 Inf, SS BS
Pfc Gene Dickie, 119 Inf, BS
Sgt Roy E Dickson, 120 Inf, BS
Pfc Melvin T Didelot, 120 Inf, SS BS
Sgt Louis V Didier, 120 Inf, BS
Pfc Eugene DiDio, 117 Inf, BS
Pfc Anthony DiDonato Jr, 119 Inf, SS
Pfc Dominic C Diego, 117 Inf, SS
1st Lt George F Dieser, 743 Tk, BS
T/3 Daniel J Dieter, Div Arty, BS
Capt Donald G Dieter, 197 FA, BS
Pfc Hugh B Dietrich, 120 Inf, BS
Pfc Joseph Dilger, 105 Eng, BS
Pvt Raymond A Diliberto, 120 Inf, BS
T/Sgt Albert A Dill, 828 TD, BS
Pfc Edmon Y Dill, 120 Inf BS
T/5 Frank A Dill, 30 Sig, BS
Pfc Andrew DiMaio 120 Inf, BS
Cpl Anthony T Di Marco, 258 FA, BS
1st Lt John M DiMarco, 105 Eng, SS w/OLC
Pfc Anthony J DiMaria, 117 Inf BS
1st Sgt Mike E Dimas, 119 Inf, SS BS
Pvt Carmen A DiMatteo, 119 Inf, BS
Pvt Clair W Dinger, 120 Inf, BS
S/Sgt John C Dinwiddie, 120 Inf, BS
1st Lt Wilkes H Dinwiddie, 118 FA, BS w/OLC
Pvt Patsy E DiPietro, 30 MP, BS
Pvt Joseph J Disalvo, 120 Inf, SS
Cpl Robert G Discher, 120 Inf, BS

S/Sgt Louis Diskin, 197 FA, BS
Pfc Louie Dittmer Jr, 117 Inf, BS
Pfc Armand Di Vincenzo, 117 Inf, BS
Pfc Carlo A DiVirgilio, 105 Med, BS
Pfc Lorenzo E DiVitto, 117 Inf, SS
S/Sgt Amos H Dixon, 117 Inf, SS
T/3 Harold M Dixon, 117 Inf, DSC BS w/OLC
Pfc Harry C Dixon, 113 FA, BS
T/5 Lawrence E Dixon, 120 Inf, BS
Pfc Thomas L Dixon, 117 Inf, BS
Pfc Walter S Dixon, 120 Inf, BS
T/5 John L Dlugopolski, 230 FA, BS
Sgt John J Doane, 743 Tk, SS
Pfc Felix N Deckery, 117 Inf, BS
T/4 Charles F Dockhorn, 117 Inf, BS
Pfc Johnnie P Dockray, 119 Inf BS w/OLC
S/Sgt Eugene P Dodge, 117 Inf, BS w/OLC
Pfc George C Dodson, 120 Inf, BS
S/Sgt Wilfred R Doeron, 120 Inf, BS
2d Lt Joseph F Dogle, 119 Inf, BS
Cpl Joseph F Doherty, 113 FA,
    SS w/OLC BS w/OLC
Pvt Wilfred D Doiren, 120 Inf, BS
Pfc Albert J Dolan, 119 Inf, SS
T/5 Philip B Dolan, 120 Inf, BS
Pfc Philip Delcemascolo, 117 Inf, SS BS
Cpl Casimer J Domaleck, 105 Eng, BS
T/5 Anthony J Dombroso, 117 Inf, BS w/OLC
Pvt Edward M Dominick, 197 FA, BS
Cpl Isadore P Domenicone, 120 Inf, BS w/OLC
T/3 Joseph F Dominik, Div Hq, BS
Sgt John E Donahue, 197 FA, BS
2d Lt John R Donahue, 105 Eng, BS w/OLC
Cpl Arthur E Donaldson, 105 Eng, BS
Cpl Harbert B Donegan, Div Arty, BS
S/Sgt Ottis M Dinegan, 117 Inf, BS
Capt Thomas F Donelon, 117 Inf, BS w/OLC
T/Sgt Thomas J Donnells, 119 Inf, BS
T/5 Harry W Donnelly, 120 Inf, BS
Pfc Samuel Donofire, 117 Inf, BS
Pfc Albert D'Onofrio, 120 Inf, BS w/2 OLC
Pfc Gilbert D Donogoe, 119 Inf, SS
Sgt Voyd J Donoway, 120 Inf, BS
T/5 Darrel H Dooley, 119 Inf, BS
Pfc Otis B Dooley, 117 Inf, BS w/OLC
Pfc William J Dooley, 30 Sig, BS
T/4 Hyman, L Doolittle, 823 TD, BS
T/4 Abraham Doomchin 120 Inf, BS w/OLC
Capt Robert H Dopp, 283 FA, BS
Lt Col John G Doran, 203 FA, BS
Cpl Francis M Dorer, 743 Tk, BS
Pfc Charles Dorfman, 119 Inf, BS
T/Sgt James G Dorsey, 531 AAA, BS
Capt Joseph F Dostie, 203 FA, BS
Pfc William Dote, 105 Eng, BS
T/5 Carter Dotson, 120 Inf, BS w/OLC
S/Sgt Armand Doucette, 117 Inf, SS
Pfc Byrl R Dougan, 116 Inf, BS w/OLC
Sgt Edward J Dougherty, 117 Inf, BS
Pfc Francis J Dougherty, 117 Inf, BS
1st Lt Gale E Dougherty, 117 Inf, BS
Pvt Clarence E Douglas, 113 FA, BS —
Pfc John P Douglass, 743 Tk, SS BS
Sgt Leon W Dow, 119 Inf, SS
Pvt Lawrence E Dowd, 30 MP, BS
S/Sgt Willard H Dowden, 117 Inf, BS w/OLC
S/Sgt James Dowdle, 117 Inf, BS
T/5 Neil R Dowdy, 117 Inf, BS w/OLC
- Pvt Lewis L Dower, Div Hq, BS
S/Sgt Harold D Dowler, 120 Inf, BS
T/5 Francis L Downey, 120 Inf, BS
1st Lt Doyle B Downing, 117 Inf, BS
Pfc Myron J Downing 120 Inf BS
Pfc James F Doxey, 119 Inf, BS
1st Lt James R Doyle, 531 AAA, BS
1st Lt John A Doyle, 120 Inf, SS BS
1st Lt John F Doyle, 117 Inf, SS
Cpl Michael J Doyle, 120 Inf, BS
Capt William T Dozier, Hq 30 Div, BS
Pfc Steve J Drag, 120 Inf BS
T/4 John F Dragan 30 QM BS
S/Sgt James H Drake, 230 FA, BS
Pfc Luther W Drake, 230 FA, SS BS
T/5 John E Draper, 230 Inf, SS

S/Sgt Purnie W Draper, 120 Inf, BS
T/4 Louis E Draves, 744 Tk, BS
T/4 Alvin V Dreier, 230 FA, SS w/OLC BS
S/Sgt Isidore F Dreitzer, 258 FA, BS
Capt Guy Drennan, 119 Inf, BS
T/4 Herbert W Dresser, 120 Inf, BS
T/5 Henry E Drewett, 120 Inf, BS
Sgt Harold P Driscoll, 120 Inf, BS
S/Sgt Michael Drotter, 119 Inf, BS
Capt William W Druckenmiller, 117 Inf,
    SS w/OLC
T/5 Robert J Drury, 119 Inf, BS
Sgt Stephen Drysielski, 117 Inf, BS w/OLC
1st Lt Grover Q Duck, 117 Inf, BS
S/Sgt Harry U Duckett, 120 Inf, BS w/OLC
Pfc John P Duddy, 119 Inf, BS w/OLC
Cpl Mike A Dudek, 230 FA, SS
S/Sgt Grover C Dudley, 117 Inf, BS w/OLC
Sgt Ray E Ducley, 823 TD, SS
T/5 Fredrick A Duebler, 117 Inf, BS
Pvt John F Duffy, 120 Inf SS
Pvt Roley J Dufrene, 120 Inf, BS
Sgt Emmett Dugan, 119 Inf, BS
1st Lt James A Dugan Jr, 119 Inf, BS w/OLC
Pfc John J Duggan, 117 Inf, BS
Pvt Raymond G Duggan, 120 Inf, BS
T/Sgt Roy B Duggan, 117 Inf, BS w/OLC
S/Sgt James M Duggins, 120 Inf, BS
T/3 Nathan H Duggins, 105 Med, BS
S/Sgt Leo Duhamel, 120 Inf, BS
T/4 John Duke, 113 FA, BS
Pfc Namon C Duke, 120 Inf, BS
Sgt Ray M Duke, 823 TD, SS
2d Lt Hubert R Dull, Div Hq, BS
Pfc Arthur A Dumond, 119 Inf, BS
T/4 Lucius V Dunagan, 120 Inf, BS
Pfc James J Duncan, 117 Inf BS
Lt Col William D Duncan, 743 Tk,
    SS BS w/2 OLC C d'G
1st Lt William L Duncan, 168 Sig, BS
Pfc William P Duncan, 119 Inf, SS BS
Pfc William R Duncan, 120 Inf, BS
Sgt Aloysius F Dundas 119 Inf, BS
Pfc Milton J Dunlop, 120 Inf, BS
Lt Col Carrol H Dunn, 105 Eng
    SS BS w/2 OLC C d'G
Pfc Clifford C Dunn, 117 Inf, BS
S/Sgt James P Dunn 117 Inf, SS
Pfc Lewis W Dunn, 120 Inf, SS
Pfc Michael J Dunn, 117 Inf, BS
T/5 Raymond N Dunn, 120 Inf BS
T/Sgt Richard J Dunn, 119 Inf, BS
S/Sgt Thomas A Dunn, 119 Inf, BS
T/Sgt Walter H Dunn, 119 Inf, BS
Pvt Robert G Dunnam, 823 TD, SS
T/5 Henry Dupuis, 119 Inf BS
Cpl Jessie M Dupuis, 823 TD, BS
Pfc Roland A Dupre, 120 Inf, BS
Pfc Ernest L Durbin, 117 Inf, BS
Cpl Fredrick Durcholz, 230 FA, BS
Pvt Douglas E Durfee, 117 Inf, BS SM
T/5 Edmund M Durham, 823 TD, SS
Pfc John P Durkin, 117 Inf, BS
Sgt James J Dusek, 119 Inf BS
Pfc Harry L Dust, 120 Inf, SS BS
S/Sgt Sidney H Dutcher, 119 Inf, BS
T/5 William J Dutcher, Sp Trps, BS
Pfc Richard E Dutter, 117 Inf, BS
Pfc George E Duval, 105 Med, SS
S/Sgt Cecil Duval, 119 Inf SS BS
Col Philip R Dwyer 116 Inf, SS
Pfc Dale A Dyer, 119 Inf, BS
T/5 Hugh C Dyer, 105 Eng, BS
Pfc John A Dyke, 119 Inf, BS
Pfc Harold R Dymond, 117 Inf, BS w/OLC
Pfc James W Dyer, 117 Inf, BS
Pfc Theodore J Dziezic, 30 Rcn, BS
T/5 Stanley J Dzwilewski, 30 Rcn, BS
T/3 Maurice E Eagle, 119 Inf, BS
T/4 Frank L Earlage, 197 FA, BS w/OLC
1st Lt Richard W Earll, 119 Inf, BS
Pvt Malcolm C Earls, 117 Inf, BS

S/Sgt John W Fargis, 120 Inf, BS
Sgt Junior J Farhatt, 120 Inf, BS w/OLC
Capt John L Faris, 119 Inf, SS w/2 OLC
2d Lt Clair F Farley, 823 TD, BS w/OLC
T/5 Raymond J Farley, 258 FA, BS
S/Sgt Clyde G Farmer, 120 Inf, BS w/OLC
T/Sgt Kenneth M Farmer, 117 Inf, SS C d'G
T/4 Samuel D Farmer, 105 Med, BS
S/Sgt Harold Farnsworth, 120 Inf, BS
T/5 James C Farr, 117 Inf, BS w/OLC
1st Sgt Welcome G Farr, 230 FA, BS
T/5 J O Farrar, 117 Inf, BS
T/4 Howard T Farrell, 197 FA, BS
Cpl James Farrell, 197 FA, SS BS
1st Lt Joseph T Farrelly, 119 Inf, BS
T/Sgt Harry C Farrington, 117 Inf,
          BS w/2 OLC
Sgt Vincent Fassi, 119 Inf, BS
S/Sgt James W Fassmann, 119 Inf,
          SS BS w/OLC
T/4 Robert R Faucheau, 120 Inf, BS
Pfc Owen Faughey, 120 Inf, BS
Pfc James O Faulkner, 119 Inf, BS
Cpl Shelby H Faulkner, 120 Inf, BS
S/Sgt Roland J Fauteaux, 119 Inf, SS BS
1st Lt William D Fauver, 197 FA, BS
Sgt Frank Favata, 197 FA, BS
Pvt Roy A Favorite, 117 Inf, SS
Cpl Lloyd F Favret, Div Arty, BS
Cpl Wayne W Fawcett, 743 Tk, SS BS
1st Lt Earl A Fay, 119 Inf,
          SS w/OLC BS w/OLC
S/Sgt Edward R Fay Jr, Spec Tr, BS
Capt Norman F Fay, Div Arty, BS AM
S/Sgt Robert J Faye, 117 Inf, BS
Cpl Natale R Fazio, 118 FA, SS
Pfc Peter A Fazio, 117 Inf, BS w/OLC
T/5 Herman M Fedderson, 118 FA, BS
Cpl Frank Fedolphi, 105 Eng, BS
S/Sgt Sam Fedowicz, 119 Inf, BS
T/4 Michael S Feffer, 119 Inf, BS
Pfc Jack L Feibush, 117 Inf, BS w/OLC
Pvt Daniel J Feldman, 119 Inf, BS
S/Sgt Louis Feiertag, 117 Inf, BS
S/Sgt Horace W Feimster Jr, 120 Inf, BS
S/Sgt Martin H Feldt, 120 Inf, BS
Cpl Thomas R Felion, 197 FA, SS
Capt Donald R Fell, 119 Inf, SS
Pfc Marvin A Feller, 117 Inf SS
1st Lt Malcolm A Fellman, 197 FA, BS
Pfc Amos J Felton, 117 Inf, BS
Pfc Charles J Felz, 120 Inf, BS
S/Sgt Charles R Fender, 119 Inf, BS w/OLC
Capt David G Ferguson, 197 FA,
          BS AM w/5 OLC
T/5 James E Ferguson 743 Tk BS
Pfc Joe G Ferguson, 117 Inf, BS
T/5 Richard D Ferguson, 30 Sig, BS
Pvt Ernest S Fergusson, 117 Inf, BS
T/4 Loys G Fernald 30 Sig, BS
Cpl Enrique Fernandez, 117 Inf, BS
Sgt Ivan Fernberg, 119 Inf, BS
1st Lt Roy J Fernding, 117 Inf, BS w/OLC
Sgt Adolph Ferrara, 119 Inf SS w/OLC
Capt Phillip K Ferrier, 119 Inf, SS BS
1st Lt James F Ferris, 120 Inf, BS w/2 OLC
Pfc Roland Ferris, 119 Inf, BS
T/4 William J Ferriter, 230 FA BS
Sgt Ishmael M Ferry 743 Tk BS
Pvt Willard C Fessler, 823 TD, BS
Pfc Joseph M Fichtner, 30 Sig, BS
Pfc Benjamin Fiedler, 117 Inf, BS
Sgt Edward W Field, 117 Inf, BS
Cpl John H Fieldgrove 119 Inf BS
Sgt Fred Fielding, 105 Eng, SS BS
Pvt Herbert L Fielding 823 TD, BS
Pvt Charles F Fields 117 Inf BS
Pvt Gale E Fields, 105 Eng BS
Sgt Marshall E Fields 743 Tk BS
T/4 Leslie E Fiferlick, 119 Inf, BS
T/4 William V Figge 168 Sig, BS
1st Lt San Dominic Filippo, 117 Inf, BS
Pfc Walter J Filler, 120 Inf BS
S/Sgt Clifford R. Finch, 823 TD, BS

S/Sgt James T Finch, Med, BS
Pfc Chester C Finck, 117 Inf, BS w/OLC
Sgt Marion E Fink, 117 Inf, SS
Pfc Stephen J Fink, 197 FA, BS w/OLC
T/4 Jacob M Finkelstein, 117 Inf, BS
S/Sgt Frank T Fiorica, 120 Inf, BS
Sgt Herman A Fischer, 120 Inf, DSC
Pfc George M Fish, 117 Inf, BS
T/Sgt Bower P Fisher, 117 Inf, BS
1st Lt Charles Fisher, 105 Med, BS
Pfc Charles V Fisher, 117 Inf, BS
Sgt Frank I Fisher, 120 Inf, BS w/OLC
T/4 Fredric A Fisher, 230 FA, BS w/OLC
T/5 Myron J Fisher, 743 Tk, BS
1st Lt Harold D Fayette, 119 Inf, BS w/OLC
T/Sgt Stanley J Fisher, 119 Inf, BS
T/Sgt Toy T Fisher, 117 Inf, SS
Capt William T Fisher, 105 Med, BS
Sgt Richard J Fitscher, 120 Inf, BS
Pfc Thomas H Fitzgerald, 120 Inf, BS
1st Lt Clifton Fitzgibbons, 743 Tk, SS
Sgt William A Fitzhenry, 117 Inf, BS w/OLC
Cpl Robert J Fitzmyer, 283 FA, BS
Pvt Henry S Fitzpatrick, 119 Inf, BS
T/5 Patrick J Fitzpatrick, 531 AAA, BS w/OLC
T/5 John Fjarlie, 99 Inf, BS
1st Lt Maurice Flack, 117 Inf, BS w/OLC
S/Sgt Robert J Flaherty, 117 Inf, BS w/OLC
Pfc James H Flake, 117 Inf, BS
Cpl Harvey B Flammer, 823 TD, BS
Sgt Arvel Flanagan, 120 Inf, BS w/OLC
T/4 James J Flanagan, 30 Sig, BS
Pfc Raymond A Flanagan, 823 TD, BS
T/5 Lewis B Flanigan, 120 Inf, BS C d'G
1st Lt Raymond L Flanner, 30 Rcn, SS C d'G
2d Lt Joseph M Flannigan, 531 AAA, SS
S/Sgt Edwin P Flansburg, 117 Inf, BS
Pfc Bernard J Fleischer, 119 Inf, BS
Sgt Arthur W Fleischmann, 120 Inf, SS BS
Capt Lawrence Fleischmann, 119 Inf, BS
Pvt David E Fleishman, 120 Inf, SS
Sgt Martin Fleischner 113 FA, BS —
Sgt Alton N Fleming, 740 Tk, BS
1st Lt James C Fleming, 743 Tk, BS
Capt James P Fleming, 105 Eng, BS w/OLC
Pfc Leo G Fleming, 119 Inf BS
Pfc William H Fleming, 119 Inf, SS
T/5 James R Flener 30 Sig, BS
T/5 Clyde B Fletcher, 120 Inf, BS
Pfc Lily V Flinn, 117 Inf, BS
Pvt Earl L Flint, 105 Eng, SS
Pfc Harrison L Flint, 120 Inf, BS
S/Sgt Douglas J Flippence, 119 Inf, BS
T/4 Bernon B Flippo, 823 TD BS
S/Sgt John E Flores, 120 Inf, SS
S/Sgt Claude L Flow Jr, 117 Inf, BS w/OLC
T/Sgt Thomas H Flowere, 117 Inf, BS w/OLC
1st Lt Charles A Flowers Div Arty, BS
Cpl Frank L Flowers, 118 FA, BS
T/5 James E Flowers 740 Tk, BS
Pvt Robert W Flowers 119 Inf, BS
T/4 Willie Flowers, 120 Inf, BS
S/Sgt Arthur H Floyd, 119 Inf, BS
Pfc Silas E Floyd, 119 Inf SS
Pfc Thomas A Floyd, 119 Inf, BS
S/Sgt William P Flye, 113 FA, SS —
Cpl Dale F Fochtman 531 AAA, BS
T/5 George J Foerst Jr, 113 FA, BS —
Capt Daniel B Fogarty 691 FA, BS
T/5 Edward E Fogg 120 Inf BS
T/Sgt Thomas W Fogli, 120 Inf, SS w/OLC
Sgt John D Foley 120 Inf, BS
1st Lt Orlyn H Folkestad, 743 Tk, BS w/OLC
Pfc Hollis H Folsom, 117 Inf, BS
Cpl Harry J Folts, 118 FA, BS w/2 OLC
T/4 Wilbur R Foltz, 117 Inf BS w/OLC
Capt Donald V Foncellino, 258 FA SS
Pfc York G G Fong, 30 Div Hq, BS
Pvt Paul J Fontaine, 120 Inf, BS
Cpl Joseph D Fontenot, 823 TD, SS
Pfc Joseph F Fontenot, 119 Inf BS
T/4 Hilman F Fookes, 113 FA, BS w/OLC —
2d Lt Theodore V Foote 117 Inf SS BS
S/Sgt Richard Forbey, 120 Inf, BS

Capt Harley M Force Jr, 197 FA, BS w/OLC
T/5 Dallas H Ford, 117 Inf, BS
T/4 Everett O Ford Jr, 743 Tk, BS
Pfc George L Ford, 117 Inf, BS
Maj Gerald W Ford, Hq 30 Div, BS
Pfc Leroi M Ford, 117 Inf, BS
Pfc Wayne H Ford, 117 Inf, BS
Pfc Gerald C Forde, Hq 30 Div, BS
1st Lt David L Foresman, 119 Inf, SS
S/Sgt Gilbert Forget, 120 Inf, BS
Pfc Louis C Forrester, 120 Inf, BS
Sgt Robert A Forrester, 30 MP, BS
Cpl Harold C Forsberg, 743 Tk, BS
S/Sgt Armand J Fortier, 119 Inf, BS
Cpl Carl G Foster, 105 Eng, BS
2d Lt Charles B Foster, 117 Inf, BS w/2 OLC
Pfc Charles K Foster, 119 Inf, BS
Pfc Henry Foster, 119 Inf, BS
Pfc J B Foster, 230 FA, BS
Sgt John R Foster, 117 Inf, BS
T/4 Max P Foster, 120 Inf, SM
Pfc Wyman C Foster, 119 Inf, BS
M/Sgt Andrew A Fountain Jr, Div Arty, BS
S/Sgt Leslie T Fowdin, 113 FA, BS w/OLC
T/4 James A Fowler, 117 Inf, BS
Cpl James B Fowler, 120 Inf, SS
Sgt Shannon L Fowler, 120 Inf, BS
M/Sgt Darrel H Fox, 105 Eng, BS
Pfc John Fox Jr, 743 Tk, BS
T/3 Ross E Fox, 119 Inf, BS w/OLC
Capt Warren L Fox, 119 Inf, SS
Pfc Stephen D Foyle, 119 Inf, BS
Pfc Francisco H Fragosa, 119 Inf, BS w/OLC
T/5 Bunch Braley, 119 Inf, BS
Capt Gordon R Franceshina 531 AAA, BS
2d Lt Lino N Francescon, 400 FA, SS
T/4 Eugene P Francis, 117 Inf, BS
S/Sgt Marvin R Francisco, 117 Inf, BS
Pfc Edward F Franczewski, 120 Inf BS
1st Lt Peter R Frank, 823 TD, SS
Lt Col Robert E Frankland, 117 Inf,
    DSC SS BS w/3 OLC C d'G
Lt Col Walter L Frankland, G-4,
    LM, BS w/2 OLC C d'G
1st Lt Edwin J Franklin, 120 Inf, SS BS w/OLC
T/5 John C Franklin, 743 Tk, BS
Pvt John L Franklin, 531 AAA, BS
Capt Oliver W Franklin, 119 Inf, BS
Pfc Omer W Franklin, 120 Inf SS
S/Sgt Walter R Franklin Jr 120 Inf, BS
Pfc George Franko, 105 Med, BS w/OLC
1st Lt Emmitt A Frantz Jr, 117 Inf, BS
Pfc John A Franz, 119 Inf, BS
Pfc Mervin M Franz, 119 Inf, BS
Cpl Anthony E Franzo, 119 Inf, BS
Pfc Glenn A Frazier, 117 Inf, BS w/2 OLC
Sgt James C Frazier 30 QM, BS
Cpl Ollie M Frazier, 113 FA, BS
Cpl Robert L Frazier, 197 FA, BS
T/Sgt Charles W Fredrick, 120 Inf, BS
Sgt John E Frederick, 119 Inf BS w/OLC
T/5 William C Frederick, 105 Eng, BS
Pfc Arnold Freed 117 Inf, SS
Capt Clifford W Freeman, 117 Inf, BS w/OLC
S/Sgt Ferdie L Freeman, 120 Inf, BS
Pvt Floyd E Freeman, 119 Inf, BS
T/3 John D Freeman, Hq 30 Div, BS
Pfc William V Freeman, 119 Inf, BS
Pvt Elbert M Freeze, 120 Inf, BS
Pfc Frederick J Friedman, 120 Inf, BS
Pfc Otto Freimund, 120 Inf, SS
T/4 Frank J Freitas, 117 Inf, BS
Maj John O Frerics, 197 FA, SS BS
S/Sgt James H Frey, 117 Inf, BS
T/5 William O Frick, 119 Inf, BS
Cpl William J Friddle 117 Inf, BS
T/Sgt John L Friedrich, 120 Inf, BS
T/4 Vern Friend 117 Inf BS
Lt Col Stuary G, Fries, 747 Tk, BS w/OLC
1st Lt Curtis D Friesner, 120 Inf, SS BS
S/Sgt Louis D Frinchi, 803 TD, BS
T/4 William R Frink, 743 Tk BS
T/Sgt Jon C Frisby, CIC, BS
Capt Donato P Frischetti, 531 AAA, BS w/OLC

Pvt Charles A Fritts, 117 Inf, BS
Sgt Delbert A Fritz, 120 Inf, BS
1st Lt William M Frizell, Hq 30 Div, BS
T/4 John H Froberg, 743 Tk, BS
Sgt John C Frodgue, 117 Inf, BS w/OLC
S/Sgt Angelo L Frole, 117 Inf, BS
1st Lt Bernard W Fruhwirth, 743 Tk, SS
S/Sgt Leo W Fry, 119 Inf, BS
T/5 Lewis C Frye, 119 Inf, BS
Lt Col Arthur H Fuller, 117 Inf, DSC C d'G
S/Sgt Darrell E Fuller, 120 Inf, SS BS
Pfc Edwin W Fuller, 117 Inf, BS
Capt James E Fuller, Hq 30 Div, BS
S/Sgt William E Fuller, 197 FA, BS
1st Lt William R Fuller, 113 FA, BS
S/Sgt Morley L Fultz, 120 Inf, BS
Cpl Benjamin W Funfinn, 118 FA, BS
S/Sgt Dale E Funk, 119 Inf, SS
CWO Harry W Funk, 531 AAA, BS
Maj Joseph Funk, Div Arty, SS
Pfc Joseph Funk, 120 Inf, SS
Pfc Sigmund H Funk, 117 Inf, SS BS w/OLC
Sgt Phillip E Furnari, 120 Inf, BS
Capt Louis J Furrer, 117 Inf, SS
Pfc John A Furst, 117 Inf, BS
Cpl Shelby E Gaar, 117 Inf, BS
Cpl Joseph F Gaavinese, 119 Inf, BS
Pfc Eugene B Gablehouse, 119 Inf, SS
Pfc Frank G Gaboardi, 743 Tk, BS
Cpl Steve A Gagajewski, 120 Inf BS
Capt Lawrence J Gagliano, 119 Inf, BS w/OLC
T/5 Roland F Gagnon, 197 Inf, BS
T/Sgt George D Gailey, 119 Inf, BS
S/Sgt Mortimer B Gaines, 30 Rcn, BS
S/Sgt John V Gainey, 120 Inf, BS
M/Sgt Paul W Gaither, Div Hq, BS
Pfc Frank D Galbraith, 197 FA, BS
Pfc Gordon D Galbraith, 113 FA, BS
T/Sgt Emil J Galka, 119 Inf, BS
S/Sgt Louis G Gall, 120 Inf BS
Pfc James C Gallagher, 117 Inf, BS
Cpl Ramon Gallegos, 120 Inf BS
T/4 Robert W Gallenstein, 119 Inf, BS
Pfc John E Galli, 117 Inf, BS
T/5 Louis Gallio, 120 Inf, SS
Sgt John A Galligher, 30 Sig, BS
Sgt Joseph M Gallo, 117 Inf BS
Pfc Dude J Galmer, 120 Inf BS
Pfc Henry A Galongo, 119 Inf, BS
Sgt Michael Gambert, 119 Inf, BS
T/5 John F Gamble, 117 Inf BS
S/Sgt John B Gandini, 531 AAA, BS
Pfc Gerald J Ganley, 113 Rcn, SS
Sgt Melvin H Garber, 120 Inf, SS
Pvt Harry O Garbrick, 120 Inf, BS
S/Sgt Angel M Garcia, 120 Inf, SS
Pfc Edmond G Garcia, 119 Inf, BS
Pfc Soferino A Garcia, 120 Inf, SS
S/Sgt Arthur F Gardner 823 TD, BS
T/5 Edwin R Gardner, 119 Inf, BS
Pfc Frank Gardner Jr, 120 Inf, BS
Pfc George L Gardner, 119 Inf, BS
Pfc Vernon W Gardner, 117 Inf, SS w/OLC
T/5 Walter H Gardner, 117 Inf, BS w/OLC
Sgt Paul S Gargas, 117 Inf, BS
1st Lt Paul E Garhart 119 Inf, SS
T/3 Charles Garizas, 30 Sig, BS
Maj James E Garland, 1153 Eng, BS
T/4 Richard W Garland Jr, 119 Inf, BS
Pfc Jack R Garlow, 117 Inf, BS
T/5 Alphues F Garman, 120 Inf, BS
Pfc Weldon R Garman, 119 Inf BS
S/Sgt Bennie E Garnand, 117 Inf, BS w/2 OLC
Pvt Boyd O Garner, 119 Inf SS
M/Sgt Elvin Garner, 119 Inf, BS
Pfc Emerson L Garner, 117 Inf, BS
Pfc Nolan Garner, 118 FA, BS
1st Lt Thomas R Garner, 120 Inf, BS
Cpl Alexander G Garofalo, 117 Inf, BS
T/5 Robert J Garon, 230 FA, SS w/OLC
Sgt Walter B Garr, 30 QM, BS
Pfc Charles T Garrison, 119 Inf BS
Sgt Clarence Garrison, 120 Inf, BS
S/Sgt Ellis R Garrison, 120 Inf, BS

Pfc Herbert W Garrison, 119 Inf, BS
Pfc Louis H Garrison, 119 Inf, SS
S/Sgt Robert C Garrison, 113 FA, BS
Cpl Dan C Garrott, 230 FA, SS C d'G
T/Sgt Hayden D Garrett, 120 Inf, SS BS
Pfc John G Garstka 119 Inf, BS
Sgt M L Garten, 823 TD, SS BS
Cpl Hugh J Gartland 230 FA, BS
Pfc Jasper W Garton, 117 Inf, BS
S/Sgt Edward B Garwood, 117 Inf, BS
Pfc George C Gary, 120 Inf, SS
S/Sgt Anthony Casillo, 531 AAA, BS
Pfc David L Gaskill, 117 Inf, BS
Pfc Joseph Gaspard, 117 Inf BS
Sgt Frederick M Gassen, 120 Inf, BS
Pfc William E Gast, 743 Tk SS
Sgt Roy E Gates, 120 Inf, SS
1st Lt Everett L Gatlin, 823 TD, BS
Pfc Fred M Gatto, 119 Inf, BS
Cpl Edward J Gatz, 118 FA, BS
Sgt Darrell A Gaudet, 120 Inf, SS
Pvt Walter J Gauger, 117 Inf, BS
Cpl Richard M Gault, 736 Tk, SS
Pfc Joseph E Gauthier, 120 Inf, BS
2d Lt Francis J Gavell, 117 Inf, BS w/2 OLC
Capt Charles G Gavin Jr, 117 Inf, BS
Sgt Eugene A Gavin, 230 FA, BS
T/Sgt George A Gay, 117 Inf, BS
Pfc George J Gayda, 120 Inf, BS
Pvt Vincent L Gaydoes, 120 Inf, SS
T/6 Eugene Gayhart, 118 FA, BS
Sgt Richard W Gaylord, 113 FA, SS BS –
T/5 Charles H Gaynor, 117 Inf, BS
1st Lt Sam F Gaziano, 117 Inf, BS w/OLC
Pvt Victor G Gazowsky, 105 Med, BS
Pfc Jack E Gebert, 119 Inf, DSC
T/Sgt Raymond D Gebhart, 120 Inf, BS
Sgt Neville G Geesin, 119 Inf, BS
Sgt Vincent A Geglia, 120 Inf, BS
Sgt Samuel L Gehris, 119 Inf, BS
T/5 Warren J Gehrke, 30 Sig, BS
Pfc William J Geiger, 119 Inf, BS
Cpl George L Geisler, 743 Tk, SS BS
Pfc John Gelardi, 120 Inf, SS
Cpl Howard L Gelfer, 230 FA, SS BS w/OLC
Pvt Louis D Gena, 119 Inf, SS w/OLC
Pvt Joseph Gendel, 119 Inf, BS
Sgt Abram R Gennet, 120 Inf, BS w/OLC
Pvt Albert Gentile, 823 TD, SS
Sgt Clyde B Gentry, 823 TD, SS
Sgt Hubert Gentry, 117 Inf, SS BS
Cpl John W Gentry, 119 Inf, BS
Sgt Vernon A Gentz, 743 Tk, BS
T/4 Frederick F Georg, 117 Inf, BS
Sgt Frank P George, 119 Inf, SS
T/5 John P George, 119 Inf, BS
S/Sgt Raymond E Geppner, 119 Inf, BS
T/5 Ray Geralds, 120 Inf, BS w/2 OLC
Capt Thomas H Geraty, 118 FA, BS w/OLC
Cpl Louis J Gerber, 531 AAA, SS
Pfc Kenneth W Gerboth, 120 Inf, BS
2d Lt John G Gerl, 120 Inf,
          SS w/OLC BS w/OLC
S/Sgt Robert S German, 119 Inf, SS
Pfc James J Germanos, 120 Inf, BS
Pvt Charles N Gerrard, 823 TD, SS
Pfc Herman Gershon, 120 Inf, SS BS
Pfc Albert Gerstein, 120 Inf, BS
2d Lt Marshall D Gerth, 120 Inf, SS
Capt Eric G Gesell, 120 Inf, BS w/2 OLC
Pfc Max W Getz, 823 TD, SS BS
T/Sgt Peter Giaimo, 118 FA, BS
S/Sgt Joseph J Gialdini, 120 Inf, BS
Pfc Paul A Giallombardo, 117 Inf, BS
2d Lt Crawford D Gibbes, 119 Inf, BS
Cpl Otis Gibbons, 120 Inf BS
T/5 Patrick Gibbons, 30 Rcn, BS w/OLC
Pfc Benjamin W Gibbs, 117 Inf, BS w/OLC
S/Sgt Grady B Gibbs, 120 Inf, SS BS C d'G
Sgt Harold M Gibbs 743 Tk, SS BS
1st Lt Thomas R Giblin, 119 Inf, BS w/OLC
T/5 Edward M Gibson 823 TD BS
Pvt James R Gibson, 120 Inf BS
Pfc Russell E Gibson, 117 Inf, BS

Pfc William D Gibson, 117 Inf, SS
S/Sgt Eugene E Gick, 117 Inf, BS
Capt Robert R Giebink, 120 Inf, BS w/OLC
Cpl Frederick G Giesz, 120 Inf, BS
Cpl Alcide Giguere, 117 Inf, BS w/OLC
Sgt Charles L Gilbert, 120 Inf, BS
Pfc Harold L Gilbert, 119 Inf, SS
Pfc William R Gilbert, 117 Inf, BS
Pfc Curtis L Gilbertson, 120 Inf, SS
Pfc James C Gildea, 120 Inf, SS
T/5 Victor J Giles, 117 Inf, BS
Maj Warren C Giles, 117 Inf, BS w/OLC
Sgt Donald R Gill, 30 Rcn, BS w/OLC
Pvt Aaron G Gillespie, 120 Inf, BS
T/Sgt Marshall Gillespie, 30 QM, BS
Sgt Harold A Gilley, 120 Inf, SS BS
Pfc James A Gilliam, 119 Inf, BS
Pvt John F Gilligan, 119 Inf, BS
S/Sgt Leo J Gilligan, 120 Inf, SS
Sgt Warren G Gillum, 119 Inf, BS w/OLC
S/Sgt John T Gilmer, 119 Inf; BS
Pfc Charles E Gilmore, 119 Inf, SS
S/Sgt Richard J Gilmore, 230 FA, BS
S/Sgt George C Ginsberg, 120 Inf, BS
1st Lt Robert E Ginter, 744 Tk, BS
T/5 Albert Giocomo, 105 Eng, BS
Pvt James J Gioias, 117 Inf, BS
S/Sgt Albert Girardi, 117 Inf, BS
Pfc William F Girardi, 119 Inf, BS
T/5 James W Gish, 197 FA, SS
T/Sgt Richard J Giudici, 117 Inf, BS
Pfc Americo Giusti, 117 Inf, BS
Sgt David M Givens, 120 Inf, BS
Pfc Clyde W Gladson, 120 Inf, BS
1st Lt Millard A Glantz, 743 Tk, SS BS –
Cpl Thomas H Glasby, Div Arty, BS
1st Lt Herman L Glass, 117 Inf, BS w/OLC
Pfc Daniel J Glasscock, 120 Inf, BS
Sgt Frank C Glataska Jr, 120 Inf SS
Maj Ezekial L Glazier, 120 Inf, BS w/OLC
S/Sgt Kenneth I Gleason, 120 Inf, SS w/3 OLC
T/5 Wayne B Glenn, 117 Inf, BS
Pfc Elmer H Glenz, 119 Inf, SS
T/5 Hubert H Glisson, Div Arty, BS
T/Sgt Boyd M Gloveer, 113 FA, BS –
Cpl Francis B Glowacki, 113 FA, BS –
Sgt Lane E Gluba, 119 Inf, BS
Cpl William S Gnann, 30 MP, BS
Pfc Carl S Goad, 120 Inf BS
Sgt Garnett Godbee, 118 FA, BS
Pfc Willie C Godfrey, 117 Inf, SS BS
Pfc William T Godwin, 117 Inf, BS
S/ Sgt George J Goebel, 120 Inf, BS
Pfc Joseph I Goebel, 118 FA, BS
T/5 Edward J Goedde, 30 Sig, BS
S/Sgt Werner Goertz, 120 Inf, SS
Pfc Donald R Goff 120 Inf, BS
T/5 Wilford R Goff Jr, 105 Eng, BS
Pvt William S Goforth, 120 Inf SS
Pfc Chester J Gogel, 120 Inf, BS
Pfc James W Goings, 117 Inf, BS w/2 OLC
S/Sgt Everette Goins, 120 Inf, BS
T/5 Walter F Golas, 120 Inf, BS
Pvt Howard L Gold, 118 FA, BS
Sgt Lawrence H Gold, 823 TD, BS
1st Lt Edward L Goldberg, 744 Tk SS
T/Sgt Sol Goldberg, 117 Inf, BS w/OLC
T/5 Melvin L Goldblatt, 120 Inf, BS
T/4 Sherman Goldstein, 230 FA, SS w/3 OLC
Pvt Aaron Goldstein, 743 Tk, BS
Pvt Julius J Goldworm, 743 Tk, BS
1st Lt Jack W Gollust, 120 Inf, BS
Sgt Daniel A Golman, Div Hq, BS
Pfc John Goloback, 120 Inf, BS
1st Lt Frank J Golojuch, 117 Inf, DSC
S/Sgt Milton S Golowski, 117 Inf SS BS
1st Lt Mylous T Colson, 118 FA, SS BS
Sgt Stephen M Gonda, 119 Inf, BS
1st Lt Fred N Gonder, 120 Inf, SS
Pfc Joseph T Gontarsky, 117 Inf, BS
Pvt Pablo B Gonzales, 823 TD, SS
Sgt Salvador Gonzales 120 Inf, SS
Pfc Herbert A Gonsalves, 105 Eng, BS
Capt Henry A Goodall, Div Hq BS

1st Lt John L Goode, 119 Inf, BS
T/Sgt Lawrence T Goode, 119 Inf, BS
Pfc Herbert A Goodman, 105 Eng, BS
Pfc Hyman L Goodman, 823 TD, BS
Pvt Frank E Grabosky, 117 Inf, BS
S/Sgt James W Goodman, 120 Inf, SS C d'G
T/5 Samuel J Goodman, 197 FA, BS
T/4 Walter A Goodman, 119 Inf, BS
1st Lt Walter J Goodman, 119 Inf, BS
Pfc Merlyn Goodmanson, 120 Inf, BS
S/Sgt Frederick W Goods, 120 Inf, BS w/OLC
Cpl Cecil B Goodwin, 105 Eng BS
S/Sgt Chester L Goodwin, 120 Inf, SS BS
Sgt J B Goodwin, 744 Tk, BS
Pfc Morris H Goodwin, 117 Inf, BS w/OLC
T/5 Raymond H Goodworth, 119 Inf, BS
T/4 Forrest A Goosetree, 117 Inf BS w/OLC
1st Lt Alvan H Gordon, 120 Inf, SS w/OLC
Pfc David A Gorden, 119 Inf, BS
Pfc Ralph G Gordon, 30 Rcn, BS
T/4 James D Gore, 113 FA, BS w/OLC —
Sgt Frank J Gorecki, 117 Inf, BS w/ OLC
Cpl William H Gorlitz, 400 FA, SS
1st Lt James F Gorman, 117 Inf, SS BS w/OLC
1st Lt Joseph G Gorman, 120 Inf, BS
Pvt Joseph J Gorman, 743 Inf, BS
Pfc Albert Gorneault, 119 Inf, BS
Pfc Verner J Gosney, 117 Inf, BS
Pfc Robert D Goss, 30 MP, BS
T/5 William P Goss, 117 Inf, BS
Pfc James E Gossa, 113 FA, BS
1st Lt Thomas E Gossard, 120 Inf SS
Pfc Douglas B Gossett, 119 Inf, BS w/OLC
S/Sgt Robert G Gossett, 120 Inf, BS w/OLC
Pfc Thomas B Gossman, 120 Inf, BS
Pfc Louis A Gouge, 120 Inf, BS
Pfc Vern L Gough, 119 Inf, SS
Pfc Raymond W Gould, 120 Inf, SS w/OLC
Pfc Arthur Govoni, 119 Inf BS
T/5 Roy W Gowler, 531 AAA, BS
T/4 Lawrence Graber, 120 Inf, BS
S/Sgt Walter H Grabert, 119 Inf, BS
2d Lt Clarence C Graeser, 117 Inf, BS w/OLC
Pvt Carl R Graham, 230 FA SS
Pfc Clarence J Graham, 120 Inf SS
S/Sgt Claude C Graham, 119 Inf, BS
T/4 Francis C Graham, 117 Inf, BS
Sgt Hollis Graham, 117 Inf BS
Pfc James G Graham, 120 Inf, BS
1st Lt Richard G Graham, 117 Inf,
    SS BS w/OLC
Pfc Robert W Graham, 120 Inf, BS w/OLC
Pvt Warren G Graham 117 Inf, BS w/OLC
Pfc Arthur T Grant, 120 Inf, BS
1st Lt Brian M Grant, 400 FA, SS
M/Sgt Gerald J Grant, 230 FA, BS
Pfc James W Grant, 823 TD, BS
Pfc Norman Grant, 120 Inf BS
T/3 Richard M Grant Jr, 743 Tk, BS
Cpl Ted L Grant, 117 Inf, BS
Pfc Louis S Grasich, 117 Inf, SS
Sgt James R Gratto, 230 FA, BS
Pfc Paul L Gravenstein Jr, 120 Inf BS w/OLC
Cpl Arthurs S Graves, 743 Tk, SS BS w/OLC
Pvt Charles C Graves, 120 Inf, BS
S/Sgt Clarence W Graves 117 Inf, BS
Sgt Ivan B Graves, 119 Inf, BS
T/4 Ivan E Gray, 117 Inf, BS
S/Sgt James F Gray Jr, 117 Inf, BS w/OLC
T/Sgt John L Gray, 117 Inf, SS
Pfc Karl W Gray, 230 FA, BS
Pfc Kenneth G Gray, 119 Inf BS w/OLC
T/5 Robert R Gray, 117 Inf BS
Pvt Seymour Gray, 119 Inf SS
Pvt Salvatore Graziano, 117 Inf, BS
1st Lt Sam F Graziano, 117 Inf BS
Pfc Charles V Green, 120 Inf, SS
Pvt Delmar F Green, 120 Inf, BS
Sgt George S Green 743 Tk, BS
S/Sgt Jack M Green 117 Inf, BS
Maj John H Green 30 Sig, BS w/OLC
Pvt Paul J Green, 117 Inf, BS
Cpl William C Green, 743 Tk, BS
Pfc William G Green, 119 Inf, BS

Pfc John T Greenawalt, 117 Inf, SS
S/Sgt James T Greene, 120 Inf, BS
1st Lt Jefferson F Greene, 118 FA, BS
1st Lt Londole Greene, 117 Inf, SS w/OLC BS
S/Sgt Rupert E Greene, 113 FA, BS —
Pfc Oswald P Greenland, 119 Inf, BS
Sgt David C Greenway, 30 MP, BS
S/Sgt Thomas D Greenway, 230 FA, BS
Sgt Clifford N Greenwood, 120 Inf, BS
T/5 Francis A Greenwood, 105 Med, BS
Maj Howard W Greer, 120 Inf,
    DSC SS w/OLC BS w/OLC
Pfc William T Greer, 117 Inf, BS
2d Lt John P Gregory, 117 Inf, BS
T/4 Stanley A Grenda, 823 TD, BS
S/Sgt Robert K Grenfell, 119 Inf, BS
T/Sgt Armand J Grenier, 119 Inf, BS w/2 OLC
Pfc Edwin N Gresh, 119 Inf, BS
1st Lt Michael Gretsky, 117 Inf, BS w/OLC
T/5 Ernest A Greunke, 105 Med, BS
S/Sgt C L Griffin, 117 Inf, SS w/OLC
T/4 Charles A Griffin, 230 FA, SS
S/Sgt Clarence W Griffin, 119 Inf, BS
Lt Col Edward F Griffin, 113 FA, BS w/OLC —
Pfc Hill L Griffin, 117 Inf, BS
Pfc James D Griffin, 120 Inf, BS
1st Sgt Louie J Griffin, Div Hq, BS
2d Lt Paul E Griffin, 113 FA, SS AM w/6 OLC ∽
T/Sgt Reginald E Griffin, 117 Inf, BS
S/Sgt Roy W. Griffin, 120 Inf, BS
Pvt William Griffin, 120 Inf, BS
S/Sgt William F Griffin, 197 FA, BS
Maj Lyle R Griffis, 120 Inf, BS
Maj Harold S Griffith, 120 Inf, BS
Pfc James P Griffith, 119 Inf, BS
Pfc Paul H Griffith, 117 Inf, BS
Sgt Seabron J Griffith, 230 FA, BS
Pfc Frederick D Griffiths, 119 Inf, BS
T/5 Emmett D Griggs, 168 Sig Pho, BS
S/Sgt Herbert T Griggs, 120 Inf, SS
Cpl Glenn Grigsby, 105 Eng, BS
Pfc Joseph E Grill, 120 Inf, BS
Pvt Frank Grimes, 117 Inf, BS
Sgt George J Grimm, 743 Tk SS
1st Lt Jack S Grimshaw, 120 Inf, BS
S/Sgt Carl B Grinder, 117 Inf, BS
T/3 James S Grisco, 120 Inf, BS
2d Lt James R Grist, 113 FA, BS w/OLC
1st Lt Everett C Groe, 105 Eng, BS w/OLC
Pfc Kenneth J Grogan, 120 Inf, BS
S/Sgt Lawrence J Grogan 120 Inf, BS w/2 OLC
1st Lt William G Grohne, 283 FA, BS
Pfc Harland E Groot 117 Inf, BS
Pfc Frank J Gross, 120 Inf, BS
Pvt Chester J Grosskopf, 230 FA, BS
Cpl Walter L Grothe, 120 Inf, BS
Sgt Francis X Grove, 119 Inf, BS
T/5 Carl E Groves, 120 Inf, BS
Sgt Lonnie N Groves, 120 Inf, SS
Pfc Archie L Grow, 119 Inf, BS
2d Lt Howard B Grubb, 120 Inf, SS
Pfc Kenneth L Grubb, 120 Inf, BS
T/4 Lawrence Grudzinski 118 FA, SS BS
Pvt Amos S Grumbine, 120 Inf, SS
T/5 Keve Grunin, 117 Inf, BS
Pfc John M Guerrero, 105 Eng, BS
S/Sgt Robert F Guest, 120 Inf, BS w/OLC
Pfc Thomas R Guess, 119 Inf, BS
Pvt Dominick E Guido, 120 Inf, BS
S/Sgt Victor F Guillemette 120 Inf, SS
Pvt Adrien E Gulette, 117 Inf, BS w/OLC
Pfc Gene G Guilyard 117 Inf, SS
Cpl Alfred O Guimond, 230 FA, SS
Pfc Lezime Guimond, 119 Inf, BS
Pvt John J Guiton Jr, 120 Inf, BS
Pvt Robert W Gulick, 113 FA, BS —
Pvt Aubrey M Gulledge, 743 Tk, BS
Sgt Robert C Gum 230 FA, BS
Pfc Gordon W Gunderson 120 Inf, BS
Pfc Randall B Gunderson, 120 Inf, SS
S/Sgt Doyle L Gunn 117 Inf SS
Pvt Farnham A Gunter, 118 FA, BS
T/4 John E Gunter, 120 Inf, BS
Cpl Fred W Gupton, 118 FA, BS

Pfc Malcolm E Harris, 119 Inf, BS
Pfc Mathews R Harris, 30 Div Arty, BS
Cpl Merlin D Harris, 743 Tnk, BS
S/Sgt Reid A Harris, 118 FA, BS
Pfc Samuel J Harris, 117 Inf, BS
1st Sgt Taylor J Harris, 117 Inf, BS
Pvt Thomas H Harris, 117 Inf, BS
T/5 Alvin M Harrison, 119 Inf, BS
Sgt Harry G Harrison, 230 FA, BS
Pfc Raleigh S Harrison, 117 Inf, BS
Brig Gen William K Harrison, 30 Div Hq, DSC
    DSM LM SS BS w/OLC DSO LH C d'G GFM
Pfc Donald E Harrod, 117 Inf, BS
T/4 Raymond W Harrop, 823 TD, BS
T/5 Benjamin W Hart Jr, 120 Inf, BS
Pfc Charles T Hart, 120 Inf, BS
Capt Corby L Hart, 119 Inf, BS
Pfc Hubert C Hart, 117 Inf, BS w/3 OLC
WOJG Jesse O Hart, 117 Inf, BS
1st Lt Theodore W Hart, 117 Inf, SS BS
Pfc Dale R Harter, 120 Inf, BS
Capt Harold J Hartley, 531 AAA BS
Cpl Oscar Hartley, 113 FA, BS w/OLC
Cpl Loman Hartline, 120 Inf, BS
Pfc Franklin S Hartman, 120 Inf, SS
Pfc Jonas D Hartman, 119 Inf, BS
Pfc Mason E Hartman, 119 Inf, BS
Major Paul Hartman, 283 FA, BS
1st Lt Wilbert E Hartman, 117 Inf,
    SS BS w/2 OLC
2d Lt Eddie J Hartsfield, 197 FA, AM w/7 OLC
Pfc Carl W Hartwell, 117 Inf, BS
S/Sgt Walter Hartwig, 119 Inf, BS
Pfc Alexander K Harvey, 119 Inf, BS w/OLC
S/Sgt Luther Q Harvey, 119 Inf, BS
Sgt Jay R Haselwood, Hq 30 Div, BS
Capt Jerome B Hasemeier, 118 FA,
    SS BS w/OLC
T/5 Ray L Haserodt, 119 Inf, BS
T/4 Richard L Haskett, 197 FA, SS
Pfc Robert E Haslam, 120 Inf, SS
Pfc James K Haslet, 120 Inf, BS
Lt Col Harold E Hassenfelt, 30 Div Hq,
    LM BS w/2 OLC C d'G
Pfc Clifford Hatch, 119 Inf, BS
Sgt Kenneth E Hatfield, 117 Inf, BS w/2 OLC
T/4 Lee B Hatfield, 118 FA, SS BS w/OLC
Pfc Albert J Hathern, 118 FA, BS
Sgt Fred O Hatley, 117 Inf, BS
T/4 James Hatley, 120 Inf, BS
T/5 Herman L Hatton, 117 Inf, BS
1st Lt James F Hatton, 234 Eng, BS
S/Sgt Robert L Haufe, 736 Tnk, BS
S/Sgt Cecil C Haun, 531 AAA, BS
Pfc Howard W Haupt, 120 Inf, BS
T/3 Robert B Hauser, 168 Sig BS
T/5 Walter H Hauser, 743 Tnk, BS
Pfc Eugene H Hausleiter, 117 Inf, BS
T/3 Eldon Havel, 120 Inf, SS BS
T/4 Harland C Haver, 118 FA, BS
Pfc Judas L Havird, 120 Inf, BS
2d Lt Walter R Hawbaker 118 FA, SS
Pfc Herman A Hawker, 119 Inf, BS
1st Sgt Woodrow W Hawkins, 119 Inf, BS
T/Sgt Fay F Hawley, 119 Inf, BS
Cpl Gerald J Hawn, 118 FA, SS
Pfc Glenn M Haws, 120 Inf, BS
Cpl Henry D Hawsey, 119 Inf, SS
1st Lt Max M Hayden, 119 Inf, BS
Capt Oakes M Hayden, 105 Eng SS BS w/OLC
T/5 Roland E Hayden, 120 Inf BS
Pfc Teddy K Hayek, 117 Inf, BS
Pfc Clayton A Hayes, 117 Inf, SS
1st Lt Daniel E Hayes, 743 Tnk, BS
T/Sgt Hobdy W Hayles, 119 Inf, SS w/OLC
T/Sgt Charles O Haymons, 117 Inf, SS BS
Pfc John D Haynes, 120 Inf, BS
Pfc Victor W Hayward, 117 Inf, BS
Pfc Reginald Hazen, 119 Inf, BS
S/Sgt John D Healy, 119 Inf, SS BS
Cpl Michael J Healy, 105 Eng, BS w/OLC
T/Sgt Lavern E Heap, 531 AAA, BS
Pvt William V Heaps, 117 Inf, BS
T/5 Carlton H Hearn, 117 Inf, BS

Cpl Claude S Heath, 283 FA, BS
Pfc D P Heath, 105 Eng, SS
Pfc Charles E Heathcoat, 105 Eng, BS
Cpl Samuel W Heathcock, 30 QM, BS
Sgt Phayne E Heathman, 531 AAA, BS
Pfc Joseph F Heaton, 120 Inf, SS
T/5 Willis A Heaton, 230 FA, BS
1st Lt Thomas C Harvey 30 Cav, SS
T/5 Loy T Heavner, 120 Inf, BS
Sgt Andrew J Heban, 119 Inf, BS
1st Lt George F Heberer, 119 Inf, BS w/OLC
Pfc Hector G Hebert, 113 FA, BS
Pfc Kenneth J Heckman, 120 Inf, BS
S/Sgt Roger A Hedgbeth, 117 Inf, BS
Pfc Raymond F Hedinger, 117 Inf, BS
Pfc Anthony J Hedyka, 120 Inf, BS
Capt Van K Heely, 113 FA, BS
Capt Marvin P Heery, 118 FA,
    SS BS w/OLC C d'G
S/Sgt Daniel J Hefferman, 117 Inf, SS
Pfc Charles A Hegwood, 119 Inf, BS
Pfc Harry H Heidt, 120 Inf, BS
Cpl Marin M Heilbrunn, 197 FA, BS
Pfc John S Heilman, 117 Inf, BS
Pfc Paul D Heilman, 117 Inf, BS
Sgt John Heinemeier Jr, 120 Inf, BS
T/5 Haskell A Heinrichy, 120 Inf, SS
Maj Edward J Heinze, 280 Eng, BS
Pfc Otto E Heinze, 120 Inf, SS
T/Sgt Donald W Heiserman, 119 Inf, BS
T/4 John C Heisey, 30 Div Hq, BS
T/4 Harry M Heiskell, 117 Inf, BS
Sgt Vernon T Heitkoetter, 119 Inf, SS
Pvt Julius M Helder, 743 Tnk, BS
Pfc Roy E Helein, 117 Inf, BS
S/Sgt Merville E Helle, 117 Inf, BS
Pfc Robert R Hellen, 117 Inf, BS
Sgt Charles Z Heller, 120 Inf, BS
Sgt Herman Heller, 117 Inf, BS
T/Sgt Donald J Helmly, 118 FA, BS
1st Lt James L Helms, 119 Inf, SS w/OLC BS
Sgt Kenneth O Helsabeck, 119 Inf, BS
Pfc Ralf R Hemke, 743 Tnk, BS
T/5 Rufus W Hemphil, 823 TD, BS
Pfc Paul C Hemple, 119 Inf, BS
Pvt Earl W Henderson, 119 Inf, BS w/OLC
T/5 Herbert A Henderson, 197 FA, BS
T/5 Norris D Henderson, 30 Div Hq, BS
1st Lt Peter L Henderson, 743 Tnk, SS BS
S/Sgt Richard P Henderson, 119 Inf, BS
Pfc William J Henderson, 120 Inf SS BS
Pfc Harold C Hendrick, 117 Inf, BS
S/Sgt Lyle J Hendricks, 120 Inf, BS
1st Lt Paul E Hendricks, 70 FA, AM w/OLC
T/5 Aldrick E Hendrickson, 197 FA, SS
Capt Fredolph A Hendrickson, 117 Inf SS
S/Sgt Henry J Hendrickson, 117 Inf, BS
T/Sgt Buck Hendrix, 119 Inf, BS
Pfc John G Hendrix, 105 Med, BS
2d Lt Samuel W Hendrix, 119 Inf, SS
Capt Robert J Henglein, 119 Inf, DSC
Sgt Claude F Henley, 117 Inf, BS
S/Sgt Lenard W Henry, 119 Inf, SS w/OLC BS
Sgt Melvin R Henry, 531 AAA, BS
T/Sgt Donald F Henshaw, 117 Inf, BS
Capt Frederick L Hensler, 105 Eng, BS w/2 OLC
Pfc Kyle Hensley 197 FA, BS
Pfc Talmage F Hensley, 117 Inf, BS w/OLC
T/3 Elmer I Henson, 30 Div Hq, BS
Pfc Ralph Henson, 113 FA, SS
1st Lt John H Henterly, 120 Inf BS
Pfc Ralph N Hentges, 117 Inf BS
1st Lt Francis L Herbert, 120 Inf, SS w/OLC
1st Lt Fred Herbolzheimer, 105 Eng, BS
T/Sgt Vernon Herche, 119 Inf, SS w/OLC
Sgt Henry J Herchel, 119 Inf SS
Pfc Damel J Herd, 119 Inf, BS
Pfc Steve Herko, 120 Inf, BS
Lt Col Robert H Herlong, 119 Inf,
    SS w/3 OLC BS w/OLC
S/Sgt George A Hernandez, 113 FA, BS
Pfc Nasario Hernandez, 119 Inf, BS
S/Sgt Thomas Hernandez, 230 FA, BS
Pfc Glenwood Hernert, 120 Inf, BS

T/5 Abraham D Herrera, 803 TD, BS
Pfc Mariano M Herrero, 119 Inf, BS
Pfc Cletus M Herrig, 119 Inf, BS
Pfc James O Herring, 105 Med, BS w/OLC
Pvt LeRoy Herrmann, 118 FA, BS
Pfc James C Herron, 119 Inf, BS
T/5 Harold R Hershberger, 105 Eng, BS
Capt Stephen W Herthel, 30 QM, BS
Pfc Frank L Herzig, 120 Inf, BS
Pfc Thomas J Heslip, 230 FA, BS
S/Sgt Louis L Hespe, 117 Inf, BS
Capt Carl M Hess, 30 Div Hq, BS
Capt James K Hess, 105 Eng, BS
S/Sgt Lawrence J Hess, 117 Inf, BS
Pfc William C Hess, 119 Inf, BS
Cpl William A Hesse, 823 TD BS
Capt Carl A Hessel, 30 Div QM, BS
2d Lt William A Hester, 120 Inf, SS BS w/OLC
1st Lt Henry L Hetherman, 105 Eng, BS
S/Sgt Frank J Heumiller, 117 Inf, BS
Sgt Roy C Heusohn, 744 Tnk, SS
Capt Armand P W Hewett, 105 Eng, BS
Pfc Cecil E Hewitt, 120 Inf, BS
Maj Robert L Hewitt, 30 Div Hq, BS
T/5 Bernard M Hiatt, 105 Eng, BS
Pfc Herbert L Hibbs, 120 Inf, BS
Pfc Clyde J Hickey, 120 Inf, BS
2d Lt William Hickman Jr, 117 Inf, BS w/OLC
Pfc Alfred Hicks, 117 Inf, BS
Pfc Arkley F Hicks, 117 Inf, BS
Pvt Frank S Hicks, 119 Inf, BS
1st Lt Gordon D Hicks, 120 Inf, BS w/OLC
S/Sgt Jack C Hicks, 30 Sig, BS
Pfc John N Hicks, 117 Inf, SS
Sgt Paul J Hicks, 120 Inf, SS BS w/2 OLC
S/Sgt Ralph B Hicks, 531 AAA, BS
Pfc Theodore A Heibrzydoski, 119 Inf, BS
Pfc Dean Higbee, 117 Inf, BS
Pvt John T Higgins, 113 FA, SS —
Cpl Raymond S Higgins, 744 Tnk, SS
S/Sgt William E Higgins, 823 TD, BS
T/5 William F Higgins, 119 Inf, BS
Sgt Eugene M High, 120 Inf, BS
Pvt Charles E Hildebrand, 120 Inf, BS
Capt Shelby J Hildebrand, 118 FA, BS
Pfc Robert F Hilderbrand, 120 Inf, BS
T/4 John H Hileman, 120 Inf, BS
Capt Edward M Hill, 120 Inf, SS BS w/4 OLC
Pvt Kenneth W Hill, 120 Inf, BS
Sgt Martin L Hill, 117 Inf, SS
Pvt Ray H Hill, 117 Inf, SS
T/4 Warren L Hill, 743 Tnk, BS
T/4 William F Hill Jr, 117 Inf, BS
Pvt John T Hillard, 117 Inf, SS C d'G
Sgt Cecil R Hiller, 119 Inf, BS w/OLC
T/4 Ralph E Hilleren, 743 Tnk BS
Pfc Fred A Hillerich, 30 Div Hq BS
Pvt Harold Himmelstein, 117 Inf, BS w/OLC
1st Sgt James Hincemen, 105 Eng, BS
T/5 Joseph W Hinebaugh, 117 Inf BS
S/Sgt Bowman E Hinely, Hq 30 Div, BS
Sgt Cecil F Hines, 119 Inf, BS
Lt Col John B R Hines, 25 FA, BS
Pfc Phil Hines, 120 Inf, BS
T/5 William A Hines Jr, 30 Rcn, SS
T/5 Robert T Hingston, 120 Inf, BS
Cpl Jack E Hinton, 30 MP, BS
T/5 Michael F Hintzel, 120 Inf BS
Pfc Donald A Hipple, 117 Inf, BS
Pfc Myer J Hirsh, 743 Tnk, BS
Sgt William B Hirst, 120 Inf, BS
Pfc Levin G Hitch, 120 Inf, BS w/OLC
T/5 Amos A Hite, 30 Rcn, BS
Pfc Earl H Hite, 117 Inf, SS BS
1st Sgt Robert L Hoagland 117 Inf, BS
Pfc English Hobbs, 120 Inf, BS
Maj Gen Leland S Hobbs, 30 Div,
          DSM SS w/OLC BS w/2 OLC LH C d'G
Pfc Ralph C Hobbs, 117 Inf, BS
Capt Robert M Habgood, 120 Inf, SS
Pfc Miles R Hadson, 120 Inf, BS
T/Sgt Charles E Hoburg, 119 Inf, BS
Cpl Anthony F Hocever, 197 FA, BS
S/Sgt Charles L Hocter, 119 Inf, SS BS

T/4 Harold E Hodel, 105 Eng, SS BS
Pfc Cecil E Hodge, 120 Inf, SS
Pvt Edward C Hodge, 117 Inf, SS
Pfc Russell Hodge, 119 Inf, SS BS
Pvt David L Hodges, 117 Inf, SS
Sgt Francis O Hodges, 197 FA, BS
Col George H Hodges Jr, 1115 Eng, BS
Pfc Percy L Hodges, 119 Inf, BS
Pfc Miles R Hodson, 120 Inf, BS
Pfc Anthony J Hodyka, 120 Inf, BS w/2 OLC
S/Sgt John E Hoffarth, 119 Inf, BS
S/Sgt Marion E Hoffer, 120 Inf, SS BS
Sgt Edgar L Hoffman, 119 Inf, BS
T/5 Fred R Hoffman, 120 Inf, BS
Pfc Frederick J Hoffman, 119 Inf, BS
2d Lt Raymond E Hoffman, 105 Eng, BS w/OLC
S/Sgt Stanley Hoffman, 120 Inf, SS
Sgt Thomas R Hoffman, 119 Inf, BS
Cpl Forrest L Hoffmaster, 113 Cav, SS
Sgt Elijah J Hogan, 823 TD, BS
T/5 Hebert P Hogan, 117 Inf, BS
1st Sgt Thomas F Hogan, 118 FA, BS
T/Sgt William E Hogan, 119 Inf, BS
Sgt John B Hogarth, 117 Inf, BS
Sgt Alexander Hogg Jr, 120 Inf, SS BS
Sgt Nollie E Hoggard, 105 Med, BS
T/Sgt Marshall A Hogins, 117 Inf, SS
1st Lt Guy O Hogle, 120 Inf, SS w/OLC BS
Pfc John W Hogue, 258 FA, BS
Pvt John G Hohman, 119 Inf, BS
Pfc August A Hehmann, 117 Inf, SS BS
1st Lt Robert G Holbrook, 120 Inf, BS
1st Lt Eldon D Holcomb, 531 AAA, BS
Sgt Bernard J Holda, 117 Inf, BS
1st Lt John M Holden, 120 Inf, BS
Pfc Guy M Holder, 117 Inf, SS
Pvt Knox C Holder, 117 Inf, BS
Sgt Alfred S Holland, 1 ECAC, BS
Sgt William H Holland, 117 Inf, BS
Pvt George R Holliday, 823 TD, SS
S/Sgt John Hollingsworth, 119 Inf, SS
Sgt Robert L Holloman, 113 FA, BS —
Pfc Robert W Hollopeter, 119 Inf, BS
Sgt Charles B Holloway, 117 Inf, SS
S/Sgt Lynn A Holmes, 119 Inf, BS
M/Sgt Sidney F Holmes, 113 FA, BS —
1st Lt Roy W Holmquist, 120 Inf, BS
T/4 Ernest Holms Jr, 120 Inf, BS
Pfc Leslie Holst, 117 Inf, BS
Pfc James T Holt Jr, 119 Inf, BS
Pfc John D Holt, 119 Inf, BS
Pvt Kenneth B Holt, 117 Inf, BS
Pfc Melvin R Holt, 117 Inf, BS
Pfc Oliver D Holt, 117 Inf, SS BS
Pfc Robert W Holt, 120 Inf, SS
Pvt Walter A Holt, 105 Eng, BS
S/Sgt Alvin O Holtan, 117 Inf, BS w/OLC
Pfc Clinton O Holter, 119 Inf, SS
Cpl James J Holtaus, 119 Inf, BS
Pfc Joseph G Holtz, 120 Inf, BS
1st Lt Harold L Holycross, 119 Inf, BS w/OLC
1st Lt Vincent C Homand, 117 Inf BS
Sgt Russell W Hominger 119 Inf, SS
1st Lt Jose M Homs, 117 Inf, BS w/OLC
T/5 Thomas N Honey, 119 Inf, BS
Sgt Donald L Honeycutt, 117 Inf, BS
T/4 Ardis R Honsowetz, 743 Tnk, SS BS
Sgt Virgil J Hoon, 120 Inf, BS
CWO Al Z Hooper, 120 Inf, BS w/OLC
T/5 Ralph E Hooper, 105 Eng, BS
Pvt Richard W Hooper, 117 Inf, BS
Capt Thomas F Hooper, 120 Inf, SS BS w/OLC
T/5 John D Hoover, 743 Tnk, BS
Capt Harry J Hopcraft, 119 Inf, SS w/OLC BS
Sgt Eric W Hope, 119 Inf, BS
2d Lt Richard K Hopermann, 118 FA,
          SS w/OLC
Sgt James A Hopkins, 531 AAA, BS
Pfc Robert J Hopkins, 117 Inf, BS
Capt Harold F Hoppe, 117 Inf, SS w/OLC
Pfc John E Hoppe, 119 Inf, BS
Pfc William P Hoppe, 117 Inf, BS
Pfc Clyde W Hopper, 125 Cav Rcn, BS
1st Lt Edward P Horahan, 117 Inf, BS

1st Lt Walter J Horan, 30 Div Arty, BS
Pfc Allen M Horldt, 119 Inf, BS w/OLC
Pvt Bernard D Horn, 117 Inf, SS
1st Lt Samuel H Horn, 120 Inf, BS
Sgt James C Horne, 119 Inf, BS
Pfc Freeman V Horner, 119 Inf, BS
Capt Harold Horner, 113 FS, BS
Sgt Andrew Horton, 119 Inf, SS
Pfc Ceyral C Horton, 197 FA, BS
T/4 James S Horton, 30 Div Arty, BS
T/5 John W Horton, 120 Inf, BS
Cpl Joseph C Horvath Jr, 117 Inf, BS
Pfc Robert E Hosler, 120 Inf, BS
Pvt Robert F Hott, 105 Eng, BS
Cpl Wayne H Houchen, 119 Inf, BS
Pfc Arthur T Houck, 120 Inf, BS
Pfc James L Hough, 117 Inf, BS
Pvt William V House, 117 Inf, BS
S/Sgt William L Horvath, 743 Tnk, BS
Pvt Chester C Howard, 120 Inf, BS
Sgt Floyd Howard, 117 Inf, BS w/2 OLC
T/5 Guy Howard, 120 Inf, BS
S/Sgt John L Howard, 120 Inf, SS
Sgt John L Howard, 120 Inf, SS BS
Sgt Leverne E Howard, 86 Chem, BS
Pfc Paul L Howard, 119 Inf, SS
Pvt James A Howden, 117 Inf, SS
M/Sgt Andrew B Howe, 118 FA, BS
T/5 Everett F Howe, 197 FA, BS
Cpl Frank J Howe, 119 Inf, BS
1st Sgt Harold L Howerter, 118 FA, BS
T/5 William Howerton Jr, 117 Inf, BS
T/5 Rufus G Howlett, 113 FA, BS
1st Lt Robert R Howling, 119 Inf, SS
Pvt Paul L Howrie, 119 Inf, BS
S/Sgt Melvin L Hoy, 117 Inf, BS
S/Sgt Franklin E Hoyle, 120 Inf, BS
Pfc Merlyn J Hoyt, 119 Inf, BS
Pfc Stanley R Hribar, 117 Inf, SS
Pfc Matt Hrinko, 117 Inf, BS
Pfc Chester A Hrydriusko, 117 Inf, BS
Capt Allen S Hubbard, 119 Inf, BS
Pfc James H Hubbard, 120 Inf, BS
Sgt Charles F Huber, 117 Inf, BS w/2 OLC
Cpl Henry E Huber, 197 FA, SS BS w/OLC
Pfc Kenneth L Huber, 117 Inf, BS w/OLC
Pfc Cyril H Huber, 119 Inf, BS
S/Sgt Lacy M Huckabee, 120 Inf, BS
T/5 Michael Hudak, 197 FA, SS
Pvt Glenn Huddleston, 120 Inf, BS
Pfc Floyd C Hudgene, 117 Inf, BS
Pfc Macrus E Hudgins, 105 Eng, BS
Sgt Clyde Hudiburg, 120 Inf, BS
Pfc James C Hudman Jr, 117 Inf, BS
Pfc Elmo Hudnall, 117 Inf, BS w/OLC
T/5 Jack Hudnall, 197 FA, BS
S/Sgt Claude A Hudson, 117 Inf, SS w/OLC
Pvt Erle W Hudson Sr, 117 Inf, BS
Pfc Milburn D Hudspeth, 119 Inf, SS
Cpl Charles B Huesman, 119 Inf, BS w/OLC
Capt Rufus D Huff, 30 Div Hq, BS w/OLC
T/Sgt George W Huffman, 119 Inf, BS
Sgt Howard J Huffman, 119 Inf, SS BS w/OLC
Sgt Martin C Hug, 743 Tnk, BS
Pvt Donald A Hughes, 119 Inf, BS
Pfc Francis H Hughes, 743 Tnk, BS
Sgt LaVern R Hughes, 743 Tnk, BS
Cpl John J Hughes, 119 Inf, BS
S/Sgt Wade Hughes, 120 Inf, SS
S/Sgt William F Hughes, 119 Inf, SS
T/3 William A Hulet, IPW BS
Pfc Arthur M Huling, 119 Inf, BS
Pfc Kenneth W Hull, 197 FA, SS
T/4 Richard M Hull, 30 Div Arty, BS
Cpl Ronald N Hull, 119 Inf, BS
Capt James Hume Jr, 30 Rcn, SS BS
Sgt Michael S Humenik, 117 Inf, BS w/OLC
Pfc Vincent Humeumptewa, 119 Inf, BS
Pvt Earl F Humiston, 119 Inf, BS
T/5 Grady B Humphrey, 117 Inf, BS w/OLC
Pfc Joe H Humphrey, 230 FA, SS
T/5 Ralph F Humphrey, 30 Sig, BS
Pfc Fred H Humphreys, 120 Inf, BS w/OLC
Sgt Joe W Humphries, 119 Inf, SS

S/Sgt John D Humphries, 119 Inf, BS
Pfc Edwin E Hundertmark, 119 Inf, SS
1st Lt Edward W Hunn, 120 Inf, SS BS
Sgt Lewis A Hunnewell, 119 Inf, SS BS
S/Sgt George L Hunsick, 120 Inf, SS BS
1st Lt Harold E Hunt, 113 FA, BS w/OLC
Pfc Hugh T Hunt, 119 Inf, SS
1st Lt Gordon Hunt, 117 Inf, BS w/OLC
1st Lt Max A Hunt, 230 FA, BS w/OLC
Cpl Odel Hunt, 117 Inf, SS
Lt Col Richard J Hunt, 744 Tnk, SS OLC to BS
T/5 Arvel W Hunter, 120 Inf, BS
T/5 Frank E Hunter, 117 Inf, BS
1st Lt Hilburn A Hunter, 197 FA, BS
2d Lt Laurin C Hunter, 117 Inf, SS
1st Lt Oliver Hunter, 197 FA, BS
Pfc Rance V Hunter, 120 Inf, BS
T/5 Robert G Hunter, 119 Inf, BS
S/Sgt Robert H Hunter, 120 Inf, SS
Sgt Zane G Hunter, 230 FA, BS
1st Lt Wendell L Huntzinger, 105 Eng, BS
S/Sgt George R Hurd, 197 FA, BS
Pfc Frank J Hurley, 120 Inf, BS
T/5 George Hurley, 119 Inf, BS
1st Lt John S Hurley, 120 Inf, BS
1st Lt Charles W Hurst, 30 Div MP, BS
Pvt Joseph E Hurst, 736 Tnk, SS
Pfc Thomas Husar Jr, 119 Inf, BS
S/Sgt Christian O Husing, 117 Inf, BS
Pfc Cornelius L Husky, 120 Inf, BS
Pfc Saleen Y Husni Jr, 105 Eng, BS
1st Lt Harold H Huston, 119 Inf, BS w/OLC
1st Lt Kenneth R Hutcherson, 119 Inf, BS w/OLC
Cpl Francis E Hutchinson, 117 Inf, BS
T/4 D L Hutson, 197 FA, AM w/6 OLC
Col Carl I Hutton, 2 Armd Div, 3d OLC to BS
Pfc Edward J Huyser, 117 Inf, BS
Pfc Wallace J Huziak, 230 FA, BS
S/Sgt Erving Hyatt, 743 Tnk, BS
Pfc Harry J Hyder, 117 Inf, BS w/OLC
S/Sgt Theodore A Hyla, 120 Inf, BS
T/Sgt I Hyland, 743 Tnk, BS
Cpl Jerome Hyman, 117 Inf, SS
Sgt Valentine Iacoli, 105 Eng, BS w/OLC
Sgt Louis A Iaeck, 119 Inf, BS
T/Sgt Dale H Iler, 119 Inf, BS
Pfc John F Iles, 291 Eng, BS
Pfc William G Ilse, 120 Inf, BS
Pfc Andrew J Imro Jr, 119 Inf, SS
Sgt Earl E Ingram, 117 Inf, SS
1st Lt James E Ingram, Div Arty, BS
T/Sgt Carthel Inman, 117 Inf, BS
2d Lt Charles P Inman, 119 Inf, SS w/OLC
Sgt Everett J Inman 30 Sig, BS
Pfc Lester A Inman 120 Inf BS
Pfc Loren D Inman, 117 Inf BS
S/Sgt Samuel Inoff, 117 Inf BS w/OLC
Pfc James A Insalaco, 117 Inf, BS
Pfc Alva B Insko, 120 Inf, BS
Capt Willie B Irby, 120 Inf, SS BS
Pvt Ralph E Irelan, 119 Inf, BS
Sgt Frank E Irish, 823 TD, BS
Pfc Paul Irvin 117 Inf, BS
Pfc Edward W Irving, 117 Inf, BS
Lt Col Carlisle J Irwin, 526 Arm Inf, BS
Capt Wallace G Irwin, 118 FA BS
2d Lt Joseph E Isbell 230 FA, SS
Pfc Nicola Isidore, 117 Inf BS
S/Sgt Eric Isler, 30 QM, BS
Pfc Charles A Islip, 117 Inf, BS w/OLC
S/Sgt Edwin O Iszler, 120 Inf SS BS w/OLC
Pfc Henry E Iverson 117 Inf, BS
Sgt Carl V Ivey, 120 Inf, SS
T/4 Attilio Izri Jr 119 Inf, BS
Pfc Joseph Jachymczuk, 113 FA, BS
Pfc Merton A Jackman, 197 FA BS
Pfc Calder W Jackson, 117 Inf BS
2d Lt Eugene V Jackson, 823 TD, BS
Capt Harry L Jackson 120 Inf, BS
Sgt James H Jackson, 117 Inf BS
Pfc Leonard E Jackson, 105 Eng, BS
S/Sgt Norwood J Jackson, 120 Inf BS
S/Sgt Paul T Jackson, 743 TD, SS BS

T/5 Terrell Jackson, 823 TD, BS
Maj William H R Jackson, Hq 30 Div, BS
Cpl Willard R Jackson, 117 Inf, BS
Sgt Michael W Jacob, 120 Inf, BS w/2 OLC
Pfc Marvin W Jacobi, 119 Inf, BS
Pfc Burnett Q Jacobs, 117 Inf, BS
1st Lt John Jacobs, 230 FA, SS w/OLC
S/Sgt Mike Jacobs Jr, 120 Inf, BS
Sgt Ronald H Jacobs, 120 Inf, SS BS
Capt John N Jacobsen, 120 Inf,
    SS w/2 OLC BS w/OLC
T/4 Merle W Jacobsen, 117 Inf, BS
S/Sgt Nard D Jacobson, 823 TD, BS
T/5 Merle N Jacques, 203 FA, SS
Pvt Gerald M Jacquot, 30 Rcn, SS
Pvt Albert J Jaeger, 531 AAA, SS
Sgt Tony R Jaegers, 743 Tk, BS
Pvt Curley P Jagneaux, 119 Inf, SS
Pfc Elmer W Jahn, 120 Inf, SS
Sgt Harold G Jahnke, 117 Inf, BS
Pfc William M Jakovec, 120 Inf, SS BS
Sgt Francis A Jamell, 743 Tk, BS
T/4 Grover R James, 120 Inf, BS
S/Sgt Howard D Jamison, 30 Sig, BS
Sgt George Jana, 119 Inf, BS
Pfc John J Janco, 117 Inf, SS BS
Pvt Norman L Jandreau, 117 Inf, BS
1st Lt Jarol H Jansen, 117 Inf, BS
Pfc Roman J Jansen, 258 FA, BS
Cpl Leonard J Janssen, 283 FA, BS
T/4 Phillip L Janssen, 117 Inf, BS
Pfc Harold G Jantzen, 120 Inf, SS
T/5 Stanley C Jarmula, 105 Eng, SS BS
1st Lt James F Jarrell Jr, 119 Inf, SS BS
S/Sgt Frank E Jarrett, 117 Inf, BS
T/5 George Jarrett, 120 Inf, BS
Cpl Robert C Jarvis, 743 Tk BS w/2 OLC
1st Lt Frank S Jarzabek, 120 Inf, BS w/2 OLC
Pvt Franklin J Jasensky, 105 Med, SS
Pvt Francis W Jaudon, 300 MP, BS
S/Sgt Sam J Javitch, 120 Inf, BS w/OLC
T/Sgt Alvis E Jay, 119 Inf, BS
Cpl Robert K Jay, 743 Tk, BS
T/Sgt Peter P Jazdowski, 120 Inf, BS
Pfc Louis Jazdzyk, 105 Eng, BS
T/5 Henry J Jedra, 120 Inf, BS
Pfc Carl Jefferson, 119 Inf, BS
Cpl Richard V Jelinski, 113 FA, BS ⌐
Pfc Clifford L Jenkins, 117 Inf, SS BS w/OLC
1st Lt Floyd M Jenkins, 743 Tk, BS
Sgt George W Jenkins, 118 FA, BS
S/Sgt Irby A Jenkins, 230 FA, BS
S/Sgt Otto K Jenkins, 119 Inf, BS
T/5 Ronald H Jenkins, 120 Inf, BS
Pfc Thomas C Jenkins, 119 Inf, BS
Pvt Vincent H Jenkins, 119 Inf, BS
Pfc Wesley Jenkins, 120 Inf, BS
1st Lt William J Jenkins, 531 AAA, BS
Maj Alexander T Jennette, Hq 30 Div, BS C d'G
Pfc Wesley E Jennings, 117 Inf, BS
T/5 William P Jennings 120 Inf BS
S/Sgt Nels P Jensen, 117 Inf, BS
Pfc Arthur H Jentsch 117 Inf, SS
Pvt Noland D Jerls, 120 Inf, BS
WOJG Robert L Jerome, 105 Eng, BS
Pfc Daniel R Jesionowski, 120 Inf, SS
Pfc Richard L Jespen, 120 Inf, BS
Sgt James R Jesse, 120 Inf BS
T/5 Parker Jesse 120 Inf SS BS w/OLC
Pfc Vincent Jimenez, Div Hq, BS
Pfc James R Jimison, 119 Inf, SS
T/5 Frank Jirkovsky, 120 Inf, BS
Pfc Raymond C Joarnt, 119 Inf, BS
T/4 Vernon J Jochman, 230 FA, SS
T/5 Albert H Jodoin, 117 Inf, SS
Cpl Joseph A Joel, 120 Inf, SS
Pfc Gunnar G Johannessen, 99 Inf, BS
Capt Clarence A Johanson, 118 FA, BS
Pfc Roy C Johnk, 120 Inf, SS
T/5 Ellsworth W Johns, 117 Inf, BS
1st Lt Albert E Johnson, 105 Med, SS
S/Sgt Alfred F Johnson, 823 TD, BS w/OLC
1st Lt Alfred W Johnson, Div Arty,
    DFC AM w/2 OLC C d'G

Pvt Arthur Johnson, 120 Inf, BS
Pfc Calvin M Johnson, 119 Inf, BS
S/Sgt Charles A Johnson, 120 Inf, BS
Sgt Chester A Johnson, 117 Inf, BS
1st Lt Clarence J Johnson, 117 Inf,
    SS BS w/OLC
T/5 Clinton M Johnson, 119 Inf, BS
Cpl Dale C Johnson, 117 Inf, BS
T/Sgt Earl D Johnson, 120 Inf, SS BS w/OLC
Pfc Earl R Johnson, 113 FA, BS
Pfc Edward Johnson, 120 Inf, SS
T/Sgt Elmer S Johnson, 117 Inf, BS
1st Lt Eric A Johnson, 119 Inf, BS
Pfc Everet M Johnson, 119 Inf, BS
Pvt Floyd S Johnson, 120 Inf BS
Pfc Francis E Johnson, 105 Eng, BS
Sgt Gene W Johnson, 743 Tk, BS
Pfc George A Johnson, 120 Inf, SS BS w/2 OLC
Sgt George M Johnson, 118 FA, BS
Pvt George W Johnson, 823 TD, SS
Pvt Gorden L Johnson, 113 FA BS ⌐
S/Sgt Harland J Johnson, 117 Inf, BS w/OLC
S/Sgt Harold F Johnson, 730 Ord, BS
Pfc Harold L Johnson, 119 Inf, BS
Pfc Herman C Johnson, 118 FA, BS
S/Sgt Leonard Johnson, 120 Inf, BS w/OLC
Pfc Leonard E Johnson, 120 Inf, SS
Pfc Louis E Johnson, 120 Inf, BS
S/Sgt Merlin C Johnson, 119 Inf, BS
Pvt Orville Johnson, 118 FA, BS
Pfc Orville R Johnson, 823 TD, BS
Sgt Phillip E Johnson, 120 Inf. BS
T/5 Richard W Johnson, 119 Inf, BS
Sgt Ronald C Johnson, 117 Inf SS
T/4 Rudolph Johnson, 30 Rcn BS w/OLC
S/Sgt Rufus B Johnson, 120 Inf, BS
T/4 Theron E Johnson, 117 Inf, BS
Col Walter M Johnson, 117 Inf,
    SS w/2 OLC BS w/3 OLC C d'G
2d Lt Walter T Johnson, 120 Inf, BS
Pvt Wilbur A Johnson, 119 Inf, BS
T/4 Willie Johnson, 744 Tk, BS
Pfc W L Johnson 120 Inf, SS
T/Sgt Albert H Johnston, 117 Inf, BS
1st Sgt Harold L Johnston, 119 Inf, BS
Pfc John B Johnston II, 119 Inf, BS
T/4 John W Johnston, 30 Rcn, BS
Pvt Joseph O Johnston, 120 Inf, BS
Pfc Orvil R Johnston, 119 Inf, SS BS w/OLC
Pfc Robert A Johnston, 117 Inf BS w/OLC
T/4 Robert R J Johnston, 118 FA, BS
2d Lt Thomas J Johnston, 743 Tk, SS
Cpl William O Johnston, 119 Inf, BS
1st Lt Robert H Johnstone, 117 Inf, SS
T/5 Edwin M Jokinen, 117 Inf, BS
S/Sgt Dorence R John, 120 Inf, BS
Pfc Joseph J Jolivette, 119 Inf, BS
Pfc James E Jolley, 117 Inf, BS
Pfc Bernard L Jones, 120 Inf, BS
Sgt Aaron M Jones, 105 Eng, BS
Pfc Bryine Jones, 117 Inf BS
Pfc Calvin T Jones, 119 Inf, SS
S/Sgt Clarence R Jones, 117 Inf, BS
T/5 Clyde L Jones, 117 Inf SS
T/5 Edward E Jones, 120 Inf, SS BS w/OLC
T/5 Frederick Z Jones, 117 Inf, BS
Sgt Harold C Jones 119 Inf, SS
Pvt Harold E Jones 120 Inf, BS
Pfc Harry C Jones, 117 Inf, BS
Pfc Harvey H Jones 119 Inf, BS
Sgt Henry C Jones, 117 Inf BS
Capt Henry W Jones, 743 Tk BS
S/Sgt Hershel D Jones, 117 Inf BS
2d Lt Hobert C Jones, 743 Tk SS
S/Sgt Hugh S Jones 120 Inf BS
Sgt Ivey E Jones, 120 Inf BS
S/Sgt Jack A Jones, 117 Inf, BS
S/Sgt James P Jones, 119 Inf BS
Pfc Jimmie J Jones, 117 Inf, SS
S/Sgt John W Jones, 119 Inf, BS
S/Sgt Joseph B Jones 30 QM, BS
Sgt Larry L Jones 119 Inf, BS
Pvt Lee B Jones, 120 Inf, SM
Pfc Leroy J Jones, 117 Inf, BS

Sgt Stanley J. Kielbowicz, 119 Inf, BS
Pfc John F Kieurance, 117 Inf, SS
Pvt John H Kiker, 117 Inf, BS w/OLC
T/Sgt Glenn L Kilborn, 730 Ord, BS
1st Lt Lew J Kilburn, Div Hq, BS
Sgt James F Kiley, 120 Inf, BS
Pfc Ernest K Kill, 117 Inf, BS
S/Sgt William M Killingsworth, 117 Inf, BS w/OLC
1st Lt Clair H Kilton, 117 Inf, SS
1st Lt Frederick V Kimball, 823 TD, BS
2d Lt James R Kimball, 117 Inf,SS w/OLC, BS
Sgt Roy T Kimbel, 117 Inf, BS
T/4 Homer W Kimpton, 823 TD, BS
T/5 John D Kimrey, 120 Inf, BS
Pfc James F Kinahan, 119 Inf, BS
1st Lt Charles M Kincaid, Div Arty, BS AM
Maj Joel R Kincaid Jr, 70 FA, LM
S/Sgt Elmer I Kincer, 117 Inf, BS
S/Sgt Wilbur W Kindschi, Div Hq, BS
Pvt Harold G Kiner, 117 Inf, CMH
Pfc Alvin King, 119 Inf, SS
Pfc Bryan D King, Div Hq, BS
Pfc Dayne L King, 120 Inf, BS
S/Sgt Ernest H King, 119 Inf, SS
Cpl Fred A King, Div Arty, BS
Pvt J M King, 119 Inf, BS
2d Lt Jesse McA King, 119 Inf, SS
T/5 Joseph A King, 120 Inf, BS
S/Sgt Michael King, 120 Inf, SS w/2 OLC
Capt Richard M King Jr, 119 Inf, SS BS
S/Sgt Robert H King, 119 Inf, BS
Pfc Robert W King, 105 Eng, SS
1st Lt Roy N King, 120 Inf, BS
T/5 Wayne W King, 119 Inf, BS
Pvt William B King, 119 Inf, BS
Pfc Herbert K Kinman, 119 Inf, BS
T/Sgt Chester S Kinne, 120 Inf, BS
Pfc Charles M Kinnon, 117 Inf, BS
T/5 Joseph F Kinnon, 117 Inf, BS
Sgt James H Kinsland, 119 Inf, BS
Pvt Robert G Kinsmann, 117 Inf, BS w/OLC
1st Sgt Joseph C Kirby, 119 Inf, BS w/OLC
S/Sgt Lee R Kirby, 120 Inf, BS w/OLC BS
Pvt Robert L Kirch, 117 Inf, SS
T/Sgt Robert C Kircher, 120 Inf, SS
S/Sgt Howard E Kirian, 120 Inf, SS BS
Pfc Owens L Kirk, 120 Inf, DSC
S/Sgt Raymond G Kirk, 120 Inf, SS
Pfc Thomas E Kirk, 119 Inf, BS
1st Sgt Thomas H Kirkman, 119 Inf, BS
T/5 Marion E Kirkpatrick, 120 Inf, BS
Pfc Raymond Kirkpatrick, 119 Inf, BS
Sgt Earnest L Kirksey, 743 Tk, DSC
Cpl Lonnie H Kirksey Jr, Div Arty, BS
Sgt Leon W Kirschner, 105 Eng, BS
Pfc Walter J Kisiel, 120 Inf, BS
Pfc Henry P Kisielewski, 120 Inf, BS
Pfc Adrian T Kiss, 117 Inf, BS
Sgt Ray Kisselbach Jr, 119 Inf, BS
T/5 Norman Kitamura, 30 Sig, BS
T/Sgt Elmer Kitchell, 120 Inf, SS BS
Pfc Jack E Kittell, Div Hq, SS
T/5 Howard M Kittle, Div Hq, BS
T/5 Walter Kittle, 105 Eng SS BS
Cpl Henry C Klander, 119 Inf, SS BS
Pfc Wallace A Klang, 30 Rcn, BS
S/Sgt Joe H Klebba, 117 Inf, BS
Pvt Robert G Klees, 117 Inf, BS w/OLC
Pfc Joseph K Klein 197 FA, BS
Pfc Sam Klein, 120 Inf SS BS
Pfc William Klein, 120 Inf, BS
Lt Col Anthony F Kleitz, 125 Cav, BS
T/4 Hilbert A Klem, 120 Inf, BS w/OLC
Pfc Lester Klepoch, 117 Inf, BS w/OLC
Cpl Joseph W Klimczak, 197 FA, BS
Pfc John A Klimek, 120 Inf, BS
Sgt Clarence H Kline, 119 Inf BS
Pfc John W Kline, 117 Inf, BS
Sgt Raymond F Kline 120 Inf, BS MM
Capt Robert J Kline, Div Hq, BS
Pfc Donald T Klinger, 120 Inf, BS
S/Sgt Jerre C Klingermand, 119-Inf, BS
T/5 Tony N Klipfel, 743 Tk, BS

Pfc Andrew D Kloke, 119 Inf, SS
Pfc Paul J Klopf, 119 Inf, BS
T/5 John P Kloppenborg, 120 Inf, BS
Pfc Joseph A Kloskie, 119 Inf, BS
1st Sgt Albert W Klossner, 117 Inf, SS
2d Lt Fred Kluge, Div Hq, BS
S/Sgt Michael C Kmech, 119 Inf, BS
Maj William E Knaus, 120 Inf, BS w/2 OLC
Sgt Norman G Knapp, 117 Inf, BS
WOJG Ralph E Knapp, 118 FA, BS
Pfc Virgil O Knapp, 119 Inf, BS
Pfc Charles F Knauft, 119 Inf, SS
Pfc Luther K Knechtly, 120 Inf, BS
T/4 Alfred J Knight, 120 Inf, BS
1st Lt Ancil W Knight, 400 FA, AM
Pfc Donald T Knight, 197 FA, SS
Cpl Herman L Knight, 230 FA, SS
Cpl Joseph B Knight, Div Arty, BS
T/5 Orie L Knight, 120 Inf, BS
S/Sgt Robert H Knight, 117 Inf, BS
T/5 Edward J Knize, 230 FA, BS
Pfc Franklin F Knott, 120 Inf, BS
1st Lt Kenneth R Knowe, 119 Inf, SS
1st Lt David F Knox, 119 Inf, SS w/OLC BS w/OLC
Pfc John B Knox, 117 Inf, BS w/OLC
1st Lt Wallace N Knutsen, 99 Inf, BS
T/5 Helmut P Kobrak, 117 Inf, BS
Cpl Willard C Koch, 119 Inf, BS
Pfc Robert L Kochanowicz, 119 Inf, BS w/OLC
S/Sgt Thomas E Koehler, 119 Inf, BS
T/4 Chester G Kochmit, 105 Med, BS
T/5 John A Kock, 120 Inf, BS
Pvt George P Kocotis, 119 Inf, SS
T/4 Peter T Koenig, 743 Tk, BS
Capt John A Koenigshoff, 117 Inf, BS
Pfc Joseph F Koerner, 118 FA, SS
Pfc Carl Kofton, 117 Inf, BS w/OLC
Pfc John G Kokinakis, Div Arty, BS
1st Lt Wade S Kolb, 113 FA, BS
Pfc Joseph E Koledziejczak, 117 Inf, BS
T/4 Louis Kolesarich, 117 Inf, BS
Sgt Alexander R Kolsky, 120 Inf, BS w/OLC
Pfc Michael Komko, 105 Eng, BS
T/5 Ralph W Konitshek, 117 Inf, BS w/OLC
Sgt Kinter K Koontz, 120 Inf, SS
1st Lt John L Koop, 531 AAA, BS
Sgt Albert J Kopaska, 230 FA, BS
Pfc Richard J Koop, 120 Inf, SS
Pfc David L Koreal, 117 Inf, BS
T/4 Edward J Kordas, 117 Inf, BS
S/Sgt Toivo A Korhonen, 117 Inf, SS
Capt Joseph T Kornegay, Div Arty, BS w/2 OLC
Capt Ambrose B Kores, 119 Inf, BS
Capt David W Korrison, 743 Tk, SS
S/Sgt Walter C Kos, 119 Inf, BS
Capt Frank J Koschir, 120 Inf, SS BS w/3 OLC
Pvt Edward J Koshak, 117 Inf, BS w/OLC
Cpl Stanley J Kosierowski, 119 Inf, BS
Pfc Raymond E Koski, 117 Inf, BS
Capt Harold F Kothenbeutel, 120 Inf SS BS
S/Sgt Leo J Kowalski, 120 Inf, BS
T/4 William Kowynia, 119 Inf, BS
T/5 Chester R Koza Div Hq, BS
Pfc Paul P Koza, 117 Inf BS
Pfc Joseph A Kozak, 230 FA, BS
T/Sgt Joseph L Kozei, 120 Inf, SS BS
Pvt Chester L Kozubal, 119 Inf, BS
Pfc Daniel Krachuk, 117 Inf, BS
Sgt Arthur A Kraft, 120 Inf, BS
Pfc Robert W Kraft, 117 Inf, BS
Pvt Michael J Kralic, 117 Inf, BS
Capt Howard L Krall, 113 FA, BS w/OLC
Pfc Donald Kramer, 119 Inf, BS
Pfc Wilbert M Kramer, 119 Inf, SS
Sgt Robert S Krankeola, 531 AAA, BS
Pvt Junious B Krantz, 105 Eng, BS
Pfc Edward R Kranz, 120 Inf, BS
S/Sgt John F Kraus, 119 Inf, BS
Pfc John J Kraus, 117 Inf, SS
1st Lt Leonard J Kraus, 119 Inf, SS w/2 OLC BS C d'G
Pvt Edward Krauss, 119 Inf, SS

Cpl John J Krawec, 117 Inf, BS
Pfc Joseph S Krawets, 120 Inf, BS
Pfc Royal O Kretschmer, 197 FA, BS
Pfc Walter T Krieger, 105 Eng, BS
Sgt Leo C Krimmelbein Jr, 30 Sig, BS w/OLC
Pfc William Kripps, 119 Inf, SS
Pfc Holger Kristoffersen, 120 Inf, SS w/OLC
S/Sgt Frank Krivosucky, 823 TD, SS
Pfc James J Kriz, 117 Inf, BS w/OLC
T/5 George A Kroehling, 120 Inf, BS
T/5 Raymond R Kroells, 117 Inf, BS
Pvt Benedict J Kroll, 823 TD, BS
Pfc Max O Kroll, 117 Inf, BS
T/Sgt Charles Kronk Jr, 117 Inf, SS w/OLC
Sgt Rolland C Krouse, 117 Inf, BS
T/Sgt Arthur J Krueck, 120 Inf, SS BS
Capt Eugene F Krueger, 120 Inf, BS
2d Lt Marcus Kruke, 117 Inf, SS
Sgt William J Krull, 119 Inf, BS
T/Sgt Michael Krupnick, 117 Inf, BS
Pfc Michael Kryka, 117 Inf, BS
T/4 Paul Kubik, 117 Inf, BS
S/Sgt Edward Kucharski, 120 Inf, BS
1st Lt Dan R Kuchenrither, 120 Inf, SS
Pfc John E Kuehna, 119 Inf, SS BS
Sgt Walter C W Kuehner Jr, Div Hq, BS
WOJG Quentin D Kuenzli, 119 Inf, BS
Sgt John E Kulbatski, 105 Eng, BS
Pvt Alex Kulik, 117 Inf, BS
T/3 Harold S Kulp, 105 Med, BS
Pvt Carie T Kumpe, 119 Inf, BS
Pfc John R Kunce, 117 Inf, BS
Pvt George M Kunic, 117 Inf, BS w/OLC
Pfc Harry Kunkiewicz, 119 Inf, BS
Capt Ronald A Kunz, Div Arty, BS
T/4 Hans I Kunze, 119 Inf, SS
1st Lt Jack Kupfer, 118 FA, BS
Pfc John Kuprasch, 119 Inf, SS
Sgt John Kurch, 119 Inf, BS
Sgt Stanley Kurek, 120 Inf, BS
Pfc Walter Kures, 117 Inf, BS
Cpl Michael S Kurpaska, 117 Inf, BS
Capt Hanns G Kurth, 117 Inf, BS
Pfc Kenneth W Kurth, 30 Rcn, BS
Pvt Chester J Kusek, 119 Inf, BS
Sgt Charles Kussy, 117 Inf, BS
T/4 Leroy D Kutz, 119 Inf, BS
Sgt Joseph L Kuszaj, 120 Inf, SS BS
T/4 Joseph Kuzio, 120 Inf, BS
Pvt Frank P Kuzma, 119 Inf, BS
T/5 William J Kwapil 531 AAA, BS
T/4 Russell S Kyle, 118 FA, BS
S/Sgt William A Labenz, 119 Inf, SS BS
Cpl Stephen J Labuda, 113 FA, SS —
Pfc Anthony LaCagnina, 120 Inf, BS w/OLC
Pfc Lewis H Lacefield, 119 Inf, BS
Sgt Cruz La Cerda, 823 TD, BS
Pfc Richard H Lacey, 120 Inf, BS w/3 OLC
Pfc Cletus H Lackey, 119 Inf, BS
2d Lt Frank H Ladd, 120 Inf, BS
Pfc Lawrence E Ladnier, 117 Inf, BS
Pfc Louis L Laemmerhirt, 120 Inf, BS
Pfc Rolf Laerm, 120 Inf, BS
Pfc Lou W LaFever, 119 Inf, BS
Sgt Robert W Lafitte, 197 FA, BS
S/Sgt Leon J Larfican, 117 Inf, BS
Pfc Garland W SaGrone, 823 TD, BS
Pfc Earl S Laird, 117 Inf, BS
Pfc Joseph M LaJone, 119 Inf, BS
T/5 Herman A LaKamp, 117 Inf, SS
T/Sgt Alexander E Lakatos, Div Arty, BS
S/Sgt Curtis D Lake 120 Inf, BS
S/Sgt Edward P Lake, 119 Inf, BS w/OLC
2d Lt Koloman S Lalka, 117 Inf, BS w/OLC
Pvt Michael Lallich, 117 Inf, BS MM
Sgt Charles D Lamb, 744 Tk, SS
T/4 Edward F Lamb, 197 FA, BS
Pfc Robert M Lamb, 119 Inf, BS
Pfc Vernon L Lamb 119 Inf, BS
Pfc William H Lamb, 230 FA BS
Maj Leland L Lambe, 120 Inf, BS
Pvt Elton Lambert, 119 Inf, BS
1st Lt Frederick E Lambert, 120 Inf, BS
Pfc Ferdinando A Lambiase, 120 Inf, BS

Pfc Joseph J Lamke, 119 Inf, BS
Pfc Wiley F Lamm, 120 Inf, BS
Pfc Harvey D Lamon, 120 Inf, BS
T/5 Harold L Lampkin, 105 Inf, BS
Sgt Carroll D Lamson, 117 Inf, BS
T/5 Elmer G Lancaster, 531 AAA, BS
T/4 Frank O Lancaster, 743 Tk, BS
Pvt William J Lance Jr, 119 Inf, BS w/OLC
Sgt Elridge H Land, 105 Med, BS
Pfc Hugh L Land, 117 Inf, BS
2d Lt John L Land, 117 Inf, SS
T/5 Roy T Land, 120 Inf, BS
Pfc Donald V Landin, 119 Inf, BS
T/5 Robert E Landis, 744 Tk, BS
S/Sgt Walter W Landis, 120 Inf, BS w/OLC
Pfc Henry L Landry, 117 Inf, BS
Sgt Merlin C Landry, 823 TD, BS
Pfc Wesley H Landswork, 120 Inf, SS w/OLC
1st Sgt Ernest M Lane, 30 Sig, BS
S/Sgt Harry E Lane, 117 Inf, BS
Pfc John E Lane, 119 Inf, SS BS
Capt Lawrence G Lane, Hq 30 Div, BS
Pfc Paul G Lane, 120 Inf, BS
Maj Nathaniel J Laney Jr, 119 Inf, BS w/OLC
1st Lt Thomas P Laney, 230 FA, SS
T/Sgt Downs B Lanford, 117 Inf, BS
Pfc Phillip N Lang, 105 Eng, BS
Pfc William J Lang, 119 Inf, BS
T/5 Harold W Langevin, 105 Med, BS
Sgt John M Langland, 119 Inf, BS
Pvt Harold J Langler, 531 AAA, BS
Pfc Arthur L Langlois, 119 Inf, BS
Sgt Lloyd G Languis, 531 AAA, BS
Pfc George M Lanser, 743 Tk, SS
Pfc Charles T Lantz, 120 Inf, BS
Pfc Ralph E Lanum, 120 Inf, BS
Pvt Gino D Lanzi, 105 Eng, BS
Pfc John C Laracy, 117 Inf, BS
Sgt Bernard M Lardy, 743 Tk, BS
Sgt Kenneth C Largess, 105 Med, BS
Pfc Bernard E Larios, 119 Inf, BS
Pvt Haakon A Larsen, 99 Inf, BS
1st Lt Carnot C Larson Jr, BS w/2 OLC
Pfc Charles E Larson, 120 Inf, BS
T/4 Gillard L Larson, 743 Tk, BS
Pfc Sam W Larson, 119 Inf, BS
Pfc William J Larter, 120 Inf, BS
Pfc James W Lasater, 119 Inf, BS
1st Lt John A Lasch Jr, 119 Inf, BS w/3 OLC
T/5 Garner L Lasher, 120 Inf, BS
Sgt Carl C Lassen Jr, 744 Tk, BS
Pfc Walter Lassila, 120 Inf, BS
1st Lt Theodore Lassoff, 117 Inf, BS w/OLC
Pfc Forrest B Lathbury, 120 Inf, BS
T/5 Adolph J Latka, 119 Inf, BS
Pfc Thomas W Lauderdale, 119 Inf, BS
Pvt Willie L Laudordale, 119 Inf, BS
Sgt Edward G Laughney, 105 Med, BS
Pfc Andy Lauko, 120 Inf, BS
Pfc Bertrand G Laverdiere, 117 Inf, BS
S/Sgt John J Lavery, 119 Inf, BS
Pfc Donat J Lavoie, 120 Inf, BS w/OLC
T/5 Waverly C Law, 120 Inf, BS
Pfc Newell A Lawley, 230 FA, BS
Pvt Dudley J Lawrence, 230 FA SS BS
Sgt Otho W Lawrence, 117 Inf, BS w/OLC
Pvt Vernon D Lawrence, 197 FA, BS
Pfc Warren G Lawrence, 120 Inf, BS
S/Sgt Silas C Lawson, 117 Inf, SS MM
Pfc Oscar C Lawton Sr, 120 Inf, BS
Pfc Harrison N Lax, 119 Inf, BS
S/Sgt Arthur E Lay, 119 Inf, BS
CWO Harry W Lay Jr, Hq 30 Div, BS
Pfc Howard M Layne, 119 Inf, BS
Pfc Boleslaus Lazdowski, 119 Inf, BS
Pfc William L Lazenby, 120 Inf, SS BS C d'G
1st Sgt Raymond C Leahey, 120 Inf, SS BS
Cpl James F Leahy, 105 Med, BS
Pfc Max W Leake, 120 Inf, SS w/OLC
S/Sgt Robert L Leary, 118 FA, BS
Cpl Elwyn J Leatherman, 526 AAA, BS
T/5 Richard T Leatherman, 119 Inf, BS
Sgt Oscar J LeBaron, 823 TD, BS
Pfc Henry D LeBlanc, 119 BS

Pfc Jacinto Lecodet, 117 Inf, BS
Sgt Harold W. Ledbetter, 120 Inf, BS w/OLC
Pfc William J. Leddin, 120 Inf, BS
T/5 Warren Lederhos, 531 AAA, BS
Pfc Arthur E Lee, 120 Inf, BS
S/Sgt Ayden H Lee, 113 FA, AM w/6 OLC
Sgt Berry W Lee, 117 Inf, BS
1st Lt Clarence J Lee, 120 Inf, BS
M/Sgt Clarence M Lee, 197 FA, BS
Pvt Felix J Lee, 117 Inf, BS
S/Sgt Forrest H Lee, 117 Inf, BS
Pfc Fred W Lee, 119 Inf, BS
Pfc Frederick H Lee, 30 MP, BS
Sgt Harold M Lee, 230 FA, SS BS
S/Sgt James E Lee, 117 Inf, BS w/2 OLC
Pvt James T Lee, 105 Eng, BS
Pfc John L Lee, 120 Inf, BS
Pfc Leo W Lee, 120 Inf, BS
1st Lt Robert S Lee, 117 Inf, BS w/2 OLC
Pfc Roy P Lee, 117 Inf, BS
Pvt Tollie C Lee, 117 Inf, BS
Pvt Walter L Lee, 117 Inf, BS
T/5 William J Lee, 119 Inf, BS
Sgt William T Lee, 119 Inf, BS
Cpl Robert P Leen, 743 Tk, BS w/OLC
1st Lt Agnew C Lefevre, 119 Inf, BS w/OLC
S/Sgt Michael Lefko, 117 Inf, BS
Pfc Anthony Leger, 119 Inf, SS
Sgt Ilfred Leger, 823 TD, BS
Pfc Albert P Legere, 117 Inf, SS BS
M/Sgt Earl L Leggett, Hq 30 Div, BS
S/Sgt McMillard Leggette Jr, 113 FA, BS
Pfc Edward G Lehman, 113 FA, BS
Pfc Ernest C Lehmann, 120 Inf, BS
T/5 John C Lehnen, 743 Tk, BS
1st Lt John V Lehnerd, 119 Inf, SS
Sgt Norbert J Lehnert, 118 FA, SS w/OLC
Pfc Martin L Lehrer, 120 Inf, BS
S/Sgt Theodor H Lehrmann, 117 Inf, SS
Pfc Aarne A Lehtonen, 120 Inf, BS
Pfc Sidney Leib, 119 Inf, BS
Capt Thomas C Leinback, 203 FA, BS
Pfc John Leinen, 119 Inf, DSC BS
S/Sgt Jack D Leisenring, 119 Inf, BS
Cpl Stanley E Lelito, 105 Eng, SS
Pfc Francis G Lema, 117 Inf, BS
Pfc Tom Lemarr, 119 Inf, BS
Pfc Louis G Lenkay, 119 Inf, BS
T/4 Thomas J Lennon, 117 Inf, BS
2d Lt Fred C Leno, 117 Inf, SS BS
Pfc Albert C Lenroot, 119 Inf, BS
Pfc Arthur H Lentz, 119 Inf, BS
Pfc David J Leo, 119 Inf, SS
Cpl James S Leo, 120 Inf, BS
Sgt Orest Leon, 120 Inf, SS
Pfc Alfred J Leonard, 119 Inf, BS
Sgt Jasper E Leonard, 743 Tk, BS
T/4 Josephus Leonard, 197 FA, SS
Pfc Anthony D Leone, 120 Inf, SS
Pvt Pablo S Leos, 105 Eng, BS
1st Lt Jean LePage, 120 Inf, BS w/OLC SS
Pfc Lawrence L Lepak, 120 Inf, BS
Pfc George J Lepine, 120 Inf, BS
Capt Bernard Lerner, 30 Div Hq, BS w/OLC
Pfc Lawrence Lerner, Div Arty, BS
T/5 Joe F Lesiewski, 823 TD, SS
Pvt Ervin N Lesser, 119 Inf, BS
Pfc Nicholas Lessick, 119 Inf, BS
Pfc David W Lester, 105 Eng, BS
Pvt Fred Lester, 117 Inf, BS
Pfc Garnet Lester, 105 Med, BS
T/4 Wilson Lester, 743 Tk, BS
1st Sgt Walter O Letbetter, 197 FA, BS
Pfc John J Letko, 119 Inf, SS
Pfc Claude W Letson, 117 Inf, BS
S/Sgt Charles F Leusner, 117 Inf, SS
2d Lt Raymond E Levan, 120 Inf,
     SS w/OLC BS w/2 OLC
Pfc Joseph C Leve, 119 Inf, BS
Pfc Henry J Leveille, 105 Eng, BS
Pfc Charles J Leveque, 743 Tk, BS
Pfc Gordon C Levere, 119 Inf, BS
T/Sgt Harold J Leverson, 120 Inf, BS
Pfc Louis J Levesque, 117 Inf, BS

Sgt Henry Levine, 823 TD, BS
Pfc Herbert S LeVine, 120 Inf, BS
T/Sgt Bernard S Leviton, 743 Tk, SS
Capt Bernard J Levy, 113 FA, BS
S/Sgt Alphonse J Lewandowski, 117 Inf,
     SS w/2 OLC BS
T/5 Theodore E Lewellen, 117 Inf, BS
Cpl Edward Lewis, 119 Inf, BS
Pvt Frank P Lewis, 230 FA, BS
S/Sgt Galen Lewis, 119 Inf, BS
T/5 Gerald M Lewis, 120 Inf, BS
Brig Gen James M Lewis, Commd Arty,
     LM BS w/OLC LH C d'G
1st Sgt Joe D Lewis, 823 TD, BS
S/Sgt John D Lewis, 120 Inf, SS w/OLC
S Sgt Joseph C Lewis, 120 Inf, BS
Sgt Milford L Lewis, 117 Inf, BS
Pfc Millard C Lewis, 117 Inf, BS
Pfc Milton A Lewis, 105 Eng, BS w/OLC
Pfc Noah Lewis, 119 Inf, BS
Pfc Paul Lewis, 230 FA, BS
Pvt Preston G Lewis, 117 Inf, BS
S/Sgt Raymond F Lewis, 120 Inf, BS
S/Sgt Richard J Lewis, 120 Inf, BS
S/Sgt Robert F Lewis, 120 Inf, BS
Pfc Vernon E Lewis, 119 Inf, BS
T/5 Wilbour T Lewis, 118 FA, SS BS w/OLC
S/Sgt William E Lewis, 119 Inf, BS
Sgt Winston E Lewis, 197 FA, BS
1st Lt Richard J Lewman, 120 Inf, BS
T/5 Clarence F Leyk, 531 AAA, BS
Pvt Roland L -L'Henreux, 119 Inf, BS w/OLC
Pfc Matthew A Liberowski, 120 Inf BS
T/4 Charles Licata, 230 FA, SS w/OLC
Pfc Bert Liberman, 119 Inf, SS BS
Pfc Robert L Liel, 105 Eng, SS
Cpl Clayton A Liester, 119 Inf, BS
Pfc John F Lieurance, 117 Inf, SS
Cpl Earl P Likens, 823 TD, BS
CWO James B Liles, 120 Inf, BS w/OLC
T/3 William B Liles, 113 FA, BS
1st Lt Trumen I Lillie, 203 FA, BS
Sgt Frederick A Lilley, 92 Chem, BS
Cpl Raymond E Lilly, 230 FA, BS
T/5 Manuel A Lima, 119 Inf, BS
Capt Philip W Limburg, 105 Med, BS
T/5 William F Linck, 117 Inf, BS
2d Lt William B Lindberg, 118 FA, SS C d'G
T/4 Victor H Lindemann, 119 Inf, BS
Pfc Richard T Linden, 119 Inf, BS
1st Lt David E Lindenau, 120 Inf, SS
Pfc William L Lindquist, 119 Inf, SS
S/Sgt William L Lindquist, 743 Tk, BS
Capt Samuel M Lindsay, 125 Cav, BS
S/Sgt Henry C Lindsey, 117 Inf, BS w/OLC
Pfc Oliver A Lindsey, 119 Inf, BS w/OLC
Pfc John V Linebaugh, 117 Inf BS
Pfc Ralph W Lineberger, 119 Inf, BS
Pfc Joseph P Linehan, 120 Inf, BS
S/Sgt Richard O Linehan, 119 Inf, BS
T/4 Hamit Lingo, 119 Inf, BS
Pfc Jess L Lininger, 117 Inf, BS
Pfc Howard A Linker 120 Inf, SS BS
S/Sgt Joe H Lintner, 531 AAA, BS
T/4 John J Linville, 117 Inf, BS
Sgt Walter W Lippert, 120 Inf, BS w/OLC
Pfc Gregorio G Lira, 120 Inf, BS w/2 OLC
Pfc Joseph Liscia, 117 Inf, SS
Pfc Edward F Liszewski, 120 Inf BS
S/Sgt James A Litchford, 117 Inf, BS
Sgt Jack L Litinsky, 117 Inf, BS
S/Sgt John Litteral, 117 Inf, BS
S/Sgt John W Little, 120 Inf, BS
Pfc Melvin E Litzau, 117 Inf, BS
Cpl William Livedalen, 203 FA, BS
S/Sgt Carl E Livingston, 119 Inf, BS
Pfc Ervin L Livingston, 119 Inf, BS w/OLC
Pfc Melvin A Livingston, 117 Inf, BS
Cpl Willard R Lizzotte, 743 Tk, BS
Capt Joseph A Llewellyn, 105 Med, BS w/OLC
1st Lt John R Lloyd 230 FA, BS
Pfc Wilmer W Lloyd 120 Inf, BS
Pfc Otto Loccisano, 105 Med, BS
Sgt Deen D Locke, 120 Inf, BS

T/4 Jasper L Locke, 117 Inf, BS
T/5 Ralph Locke, 113 FA, BS —
Cpl Raymond W Locke, 743 Tk, SS
1st Lt William L Locke, 117 Inf, SS
Col James W Lockett, 117 Inf, SS
Pfc Robert J Locklear, 117 Inf, SS
1st Lt Bendix Loewenthal, 105 Eng, BS w/OLC
S/Sgt Belton R Loftis, 120 Inf, SS
Pvt Delbert R Logan, 105 Med, BS
1st Lt Carl V Loggans, 197 FA, BS
Pfc Hick F Loggins, 119 Inf, BS
Pfc Karl K Lohne, 99 Inf, BS
Pfc Clarence Lohr, 119 Inf, BS
Pfc Charles W Lomis, 117 Inf, BS
1st Lt Adrian K Long, 105 Eng, BS
T/Sgt Fred S Long Jr, 120 Inf, BS
Pfc Frederick H Long, 119 Inf, SS
Cpl Glen V Long, 105 Eng, BS
S/Sgt Guy D Long, 120 Inf, BS
Pfc Jean M Long, 113 FA, BS ←
1st Lt Joyce W Long, 105 Eng, BS w/OLC
Maj Lyndon A Long, 531 AAA, BS
Pvt Richard E Long, 105 Med, SS BS
Pfc Ellwood C Longendyke, 117 Inf, BS w/OLC
Sgt Jacob P Longino, 113 FA, BS —
T/4 Daniel J Longworth, Div Arty, BS
Pfc Robert E Look, 119 Inf, BS
S/Sgt Charlie W Loopey, 740 Tk, SS BS
Sgt Jacob Loos, 531 AAA, BS
Pfc Alfred G Lopas, 120 Inf, BS
Pfc Clarence Loper, 119 Inf, BS
Cpl Lee Lopez Jr, 823 TD, BS
Cpl Santiago Lopez, 117 Inf, BS
Pfc Santiago R Lopez, 119 Inf, BS
Sgt Leodore Lord, 119 Inf, BS
Pfc William T Lord, 119 Inf, SS
Pvt Joseph M Lorence, 120 Inf, SS
Pfc Robert J Lorenz, 119 Inf, BS
Pfc Hubert J Lorenzen, 117 Inf, BS
Pfc Angelo Lorenzo, 120 Inf, BS
T/3 Rupert A Lorimor, 117 Inf, BS
Sgt Joseph W Lormand, 823 TD, BS
T/4 Clifford L Losh, 120 Inf, SS BS
1st Lt Gilbert R Loshek, 120 Inf, BS
Cpl James E Lothrop, 120 Inf, BS
T/Sgt Alvin C Lotshaw, 119 Inf, SS BS
S/Sgt Clyde Lott, 119 Inf, BS
Capt James V Lott, 120 Inf, BS
Pfc James W Lott, 117 Inf, BS w/OLC
T/5 Eston E Lough, 230 FA, SS
T/5 Glenn A Louis, 230 FA, BS w/OLC
Pfc Lawrence J Louis, 117 Inf, BS
Maj James E Love, 531 AAA, BS
Sgt Ben J Lovato, 117 Inf, BS
Pfc Glynn F Lovelace, 119 Inf, SS
Pvt Glen O Loveland, 117 Inf, BS
Sgt Herbert L Loveland, 120 Inf, BS
Sgt William P Loveland, Hq 30 Div, BS
Pfc Frank W Lovell, 119 Inf, BS
Pfc James C Lovett, 119 Inf, BS
S/Sgt James F Lovette, 120 Inf, BS
T/5 Christy J Lovrovich, 119 Inf, BS
Sgt Robert P Lovvorn, 117 Inf, BS
S/Sgt La Verne P Lowe, 119 Inf, BS
Maj Vivien F Lowell, 30 Div Hq, BS
M/Sgt Wayne F Loyer, 105 Eng, BS
Pfc Tony Lubin, 119 Inf, BS
CWO Astor C Lucas, 113 FA, BS —
T/4 Calvin S Lucas, 117 Inf, BS
Pvt Edwin E Lucas, 117 Inf, SS
Pfc Fred Lucas, 120 Inf, SS
T/Sgt Paul A Lucas, 119 Inf, BS
2d Lt Thomas I Lucci, 743 Tk, BS
T/5 Frank J Luce, 744 Tk, BS
Pfc Adam Lucero, 120 Inf, SS w/OLC
Pvt Paul Luchynsky, 120 Inf, SS
Sgt Fransisco Lucio, 113 Cav, SS
T/4 William C Luckett, 743 Tk, BS
Pfc Ernest W Ludwig, 120 Inf, BS
Cpl Basil L Lugenbeel, 531 AAA, SS
T/5 Charles J Lugenbuhl, Div Arty, BS
Cpl Benny J Lukaszewski, 203 FA, BS
T/4 Hubert B Luker, 119 Inf BS
T/4 John Lukins, 743 Tk, SS BS

Pfc Gerald R Luksa, 120 Inf, BS
T/4 Kenneth W Lumbley, 117 Inf, BS
T/Sgt James O Lumpkins, 117 Inf, BS w/OLC
S/Sgt Sam Lund, 120 Inf, BS
2d Lt Walter R Lund, 99 Inf, BS
Pfc Donald V Lundin, 119 Inf, BS
T/5 Michael J Lundy, 30 Rcn, BS
T/Sgt Rex Lunsford, 119 Inf, SS
Pfc Paul E Lunt, 119 Inf, BS
Pfc Arne A Luoma, 120 Inf, SS
Pfc Samuel F Lupinacci, 119 Inf, BS
Pfc Charles E Luskleet, 197 FA, BS
Pfc John E Lust, 119 Inf, BS
Pfc Clifton W Luther, 117 Inf, SS
T/5 Leonard D Lutts, 743 Tk, BS
T/5 William P Lutz, 105 Eng, BS
Cpl Edward J Luzwick, 119 Inf, BS
S/Sgt Clem Lyhes, 118 FA, BS
Pfc George R Lyles, 119 Inf, BS w/OLC
1st Lt William J Lyman Jr, 117 Inf, BS w/OLC
Pfc John R Lynch, 230 FA, BS
Pfc Woodrow Lynch, 119 Inf, SS
T/5 Walter G Lyon, 120 Inf, SS
Pfc Edward B Lyons, 120 Inf, BS
Pic Gerald J Lyons, 119 Inf, BS
Maj Robert J Lytle, 1153 Eng, BS
Cpl Earl H Lytton, 119 Inf, BS
S/Sgt Ray A Lytton, 120 Inf, BS
Pfc Eugene E Maag, 120 Inf, SS
Pfc Winford Mabie, 743 Tk, BS
Pvt Rex H Mabry, 117 Inf, SS
1st Lt Robert J MacCulley, 120 Inf, SS BS
Sgt James MacCune, 120 Inf,
        SS w/OLC BS w/2 OLC
Pfc Arthur J MacDonald, 119 Inf, BS
Sgt Francis D MacDonald, 119 Inf, SS BS
2d Lt Winslow H Macdonald, 119 Inf, SS BS
S/Sgt Donald R Mace, 119 Inf, BS
Lt Col Rector T Mace, 531 AAA, BS C d'G
Pfc Joseph J Macera, 105 Eng, BS
T/5 Donald R MacGregor, 105 Eng, SS BS
Pfc Anton R Machovec, 117 Inf, SS
1st Lt Walter D Macht, 743 TD, SS BS
Maj Edward J Mackay, 119 Inf, BS w/OLC
T/Sgt James E Mackey Jr, Div Hq, BS
Cpl James L MacVean, 120 Inf, SS BS w/OLC
Sgt Robert W Macys, 117 Inf, BS
Maj Edward M Maddock 258 Eng, BS
Sgt Charles C Maddox, 230 FA, BS
Pfc Herman S Maddox, 117 Inf, BS
Pfc Christian F Madsen, 120 Inf, BS
T/5 Ivan B Madsen, 823 TD, SS BS
Sgt Richard M Maes, 531 AAA, BS
Pfc Ignacio R Maestas, 120 Inf, BS
Pfc George V Maganelli, 119 Inf, BS
T/3 Lawrence L Maggiano, 118 FA, BS
Cpl Vincent N Maggio, 118 FA, BS
T/5 John J Maginnis, 120 Inf, SS BS
S/Sgt Joseph F Magriby, 120 Inf, BS
Pfc William A Magruder, 117 Inf, BS
Sgt William L Mahaney, 120 Inf, BS
Cpl Hubert E Maharg, 117 Inf, BS
Pfc Frederick J Maher, 119 Inf, BS
Pvt James P Maher, 120 Inf, BS
Pvt John J Maher, 105 Eng, BS w/OLC
Pfc Jens H Mahler, 117 Inf, BS
Pvt Jerr J Mahoney, 30 Sig, BS
T/Sgt Jesse A Mahoney, 119 Inf, BS
Pfc Joseph W Mahoney, 120 Inf, BS
S/Sgt Martin Maier, Div Hq, BS
S/Sgt Ray K Maiden, 120 Inf, BS
Cpl Ben H Maikotter, 823 TD, BS
Pfc William S Mailander, 117 Inf, BS
Pfc Irvin Mailshander, 283 FA, BS
Pfc Phillip Maine Jr, 120 Inf, BS
Pfc John R Mainland, 823 TD, BS
Lt Col Hugh I Mainord, 120 Inf, SS BS
Pfc Howard E Mains 117 Inf, SS BS
T/4 LeMont R Mair, 30 Rcn, BS
Sgt Jesse B Maird, 120 Inf, BS
Pfc Elbert H Majors, 117 Inf, SS
Pfc Charles L Malatesta, 113 FA, BS w/OLC ←
1st Lt William H Malcomson, 823 TD, SS
Cpl Louis J Malfer, 117 Inf, BS w/OLC

Sgt Steve Malich, 736 Tk, BS
M/Sgt Sam M Mallison, 197 FA, BS
T/Sgt Charles G Malloy, 120 Inf, BS
S/Sgt Hubert H Malone, 119 Inf, BS
Pfc Furlon L Maloney, 119 Inf, BS
1st Lt John M Maloney, 117 Inf, SS
S/Sgt Melvin J Maloney, 117 Inf, BS
Pfc William W Maloney, 120 Inf, BS w/2 OLC
Pfc Bertrand J Mandeville, 119 Inf, SS
Pvt George Mandigo, 120 Inf, SS
T/Sgt Wilmer C Mandrup, 531 AAA, BS
T/5 Jewell F Maness, 117 Inf, BS
WOJG Howard S Maney, 113 FA, BS
Sgt John F Mangan, 117 Inf, BS
Pfc Lorenzo Mangicapro, 118 FA, BS
Pfc Carmen Mangini, 120 Inf, BS
Sgt Frederick A Maniccia, 117 Inf, BS
S/Sgt Francis S Mankowski, 105 Eng, BS
Pfc James G Manley, 117 Inf, SS
1st Lt Jay Manley, 117 Inf, SS
Pfc Delmar F Mann, 30 Rcn, BS
Pfc John J Mann, 120 Inf, BS
Maj Romulus M Mann, 119 Inf, SS BS
Pfc Carmelo A Manna, 120 Inf, SS BS
1st Lt James I Manning, 119 Inf, SS BS
T/5 John F Manning, 105 Eng, BS
Sgt Walter R Mansfield, 105 Eng, BS
T/4 Theodore F Manus, 743 Tk, BS
Pfc Daniel B Mapel, 120 Inf, BS
T/5 Wade E Maple, 105 Med, BS
T/4 Norbert W Marback, 230 FA, SS
Pfc Anthony J Marchetta, 117 Inf, BS
M/Sgt Charles R Marco, 531 AAA, BS
Pvt John M Marcone, 117 Inf, SS BS
Pfc Francis L Marcotte, 118 FA, BS
Sgt Francis L Marcotte, 119 Inf, BS
T/5 Edward J Marek, 117 Inf, BS
Pfc Albert Marello, 120 Inf, BS
T/5 Alvin Margolian, 118 FA, BS
T/5 Joseph F Mariano, 105 Eng, BS w/OLC
T/5 Joseph R Marino, 197 FA, BS
T/4 Albert A Marinucci, 230 FA, SS BS
Pfc William R Marion, 119 Inf, BS
T/4 Cecil O Markham, 730 Ord, BS
Pfc Edward Markinson, 120 Inf, BS
T/Sgt George E Markland, 117 Inf, SS
Sgt Neal S Markle, 120 Inf, BS
S/Sgt Ralph E Markley, 119 Inf, SS BS
Pfc Mark J Markuson Jr, 117 Inf, BS
Pvt Guy R Marlar, 117 Inf, SS
S/Sgt Elmo F Marley, 203 FA, BS
Cpl Dwight R Marlin, 117 Inf, BS
Pfc Champ C Marlow, 120 Inf, BS
T/5 Ernest W Marlow, 230 FA, SS BS
T/4 Albert E Marquardt, 743 Tk, BS
Sgt Lloyd W Marquardt, 531 AAA, BS
Pfc Richard W Marquette, 120 Inf, BS
T/4 Wayne H Marquis, 120 Inf, BS
S/Sgt Henry J Marrama, 120 Inf, BS
Pfc Albert Marrello, 120 Inf, BS
M/Sgt James W Marsh, 117 Inf, BS
Maj Shirley R Marsh, Div Hq, BS
Pfc William Marsh, 117 Inf, BS
Pfc Alfred O Marshall 30 Sig, BS
T/5 Harry W Marshall Jr, 120 Inf SS BS
T/4 Robert E Marshall, 119 Inf, BS
Sgt Ulisse Marsili, 120 Inf, BS
S/Sgt Curtiss A Martell, 119 Inf, SS
S/Sgt Arnold Martin, 117 Inf, SS w/OLC
Sgt Charles D Martin, 823 TD, BS
S/Sgt Chester Y Martin 117 Inf, SS
Sgt Edward Martin, 120 Inf, BS
Pfc Edward G Martin, 118 FA, BS
Pfc Eldon E Martin, 119 Inf, SS
Pvt Francis H Martin, 120 Inf, BS
T/5 Frankie E Martin, 119 Inf, BS
Pfc Grady C Martin, 105 Eng, BS
S/Sgt John D Martin, 230 FA, BS w/OLC
S/Sgt John E Martin, Div Hq, BS
Pvt Leo R Martin, 743 Tk, BS
M/Sgt Lester E Martin, 117 Inf, SS BS C d'G
Pfc Horace Martin, 119 Inf, BS
S/Sgt Joseph G Martin, 197 FA, BS
T/5 Ralph S Martin, 119 Inf, BS

S/Sgt Raymond C Martin, 117 Inf, BS w/OLC
S/Sgt Robert C Martin, 117 Inf, BS
Lt Col Ronald L Martin, 92 Chem, BS
Pfc Stanley J Martin, 119 Inf, BS
Cpl Thomas J Martin, 197 FA, SS
S/Sgt William B Martin, 197 FA, BS
Pfc William E Martin, 119 Inf, BS
T/5 Willie A Martin, 117 Inf, BS
Pfc Willis Martin, 113 FA, BS
Pfc Anthony Martinelli, 117 Inf, BS
Pvt Henry A Martinelli, 117 Inf, BS
Pfc Hector D Martinez, 119 Inf, BS
Pfc Jose A Martinez, 117 Inf, BS
Pfc Sam G Martinez, 119 Inf, BS
S/Sgt Victor P Martinez, 92 Chem, BS
Sgt Joseph A Martini, 117 Inf, SS
S/Sgt Vincent Martinilli, 117 Inf, BS
Pvt Benjamin O Martiniz, 117 Inf, BS
T/4 Rocco D Marzilli, 30 QM, BS
S/Sgt Joseph Mascari, 119 Inf, BS
Pfc George Masef, 117 Inf, BS
2d Lt Donald L Mason, 743 Tk, SS BS
Pfc Henry C Mason, 119 Inf, BS
T/Sgt Leo H Mason, 230 FA, BS
1st Lt Noel N Mason, 119 Inf, BS
T/4 Marshall F Massey, 30 Rcn, BS
Cpl John R Massing, 119 Inf, BS
T/5 Robert L Massingill, 117 Inf, SS
Pfc Homer L Master, 117 Inf, SS
Pfc George Mastovich, 119 Inf, BS
T/4 Amelio D Mastrogiovanni, 120 Inf,
    BS w/OLC
Pfc Alfred T Matacena, 105 Med, BS
Pfc Joseph E Matava, 105 Eng, BS
S/Sgt Robert I Mater, 117 Inf, SS
Pfc Carl E Mathas, 197 FA BS
T/5 Arnold R Mather, 117 Inf, BS
M/Sgt James P Mather, 117 Inf, BS
Pvt Leonard C Mathis, 120 Inf, BS
Sgt DeVerne N Mathison, 99 Inf, BS
Capt Robert J Mathwig, 117 Inf, BS w/2 OLC
Pfc Vester V Matlock, 117 Inf, BS
T/Sgt Gerald E Matney, 119 Inf, BS
T/3 Norman C Mattern, Div Hq, BS
Sgt John H Mattes, 119 Inf, BS
1st Lt Joel S Matteson, 743 Tk, BS
Pfc Everett F Matthews, 120 Inf, BS
T/4 Thomas G Matthews, Div Arty, BS
Pvt Edgar L Mattix, Jr, 117 Inf, BS
S/Sgt John F Maturi, 120 Inf BS w/OLC
1st Lt Carl E Maukonen, 230 FA, SS BS
2d Lt Paul H Maupin, 117 Inf, BS w/OLC
1st Lt John E Maus, 118 FA, SS
T/5 Willie F Mawson Jr, 120 Inf, SS
Pfc Herbert T Max, 119 Inf, BS
T/5 James C Maxey, 120 Inf, SS
Pfc Russell Maxey, 117 Inf, BS
Sgt Allen D Maxwell, 30 Rcn, SS
1st Sgt Reginald W Maybee, 120 Inf, SS BS
Lt Col Richard H Mayer, 118 FA, BS w/2 OLC
S/Sgt Raymond J Mayfield, 117 Inf, BS
S/Sgt Lawrence H Maylin, 117 Inf, BS
Pfc Harlan R Maymon, 120 Inf, BS
Sgt Donald A Maze, 230 FA SS BS
S/Sgt Frank Mazzucchelli, 120 Inf, SS
Pvt Jack G McCanless, 120 Inf, SS
Pfc John A McGlone, 120 Inf, BS
T/3 Manning V McWhorter, 119 Inf, BS
Sgt Earl T Mead, 117 Inf, SS
1st Lt Lynn H Mead Jr, 117 Inf, SS BS
Capt James R Meador, 120 Inf, BS
Pfc Albert H Meadows, 120 Inf, BS
Pfc Dean Meadows, 120 Inf, BS
T/Sgt Raiford J Meadows, 197 FA, BS
Sgt Thornton W Means Jr, 30 MP, BS
Pfc Jack W Mears, 118 FA, BS
Pvt Woodfred L Mears, 119 Inf, BS
Sgt Austin L Mecham, 823 TD, BS
S/Sgt Olis L Medcalf, 119 Inf, SS
Pfc Manuel S Medeiros, 117 Inf, BS
Pfc John E Medes, 120 Inf, BS
Sgt Eduardo Medina, 119 Inf, BS w/2 OLC
T/5 John H Medley, 120 Inf, BS
Pfc Ralph M Medley, 120 Inf, SS

T/5 Arthur F Medlin, 119 Inf, BS
T/4 Thomas A Meehan, 119 Inf, SS
S/Sgt Bernard D Meeker, 117 Inf, SS
S/Sgt Denzil Z Meeks, 117 Inf, BS
T/5 Earl Meeks, 119 Inf, SS
T/5 Richard T Meeks, 30 Rcn, BS
Pvt Joseph P Mehelich, 119 Inf, SS
Pfc Olin E Mehrer, 117 Inf, BS
Capt Carl O Meier, 1r8 FA, SS BS w/OLC
Sgt Edward Meier, 117 Inf, BS
T/Sgt Ralph H Meierotto, 743 Tk, BS
Cpl Ford R Meister, Div Arty, BS
Pfc Joseph A Melchiore, 230 FA, BS
Sgt Andrew S Melendrez, 120 Inf, SS
Capt Herbert C Melin, 99 Inf, BS
Pvt Howard J Melker, 120 Inf, BS
Pfc Antone C Mello, 30 Rcn, BS
1st Lt Harry Melnick, 117 Inf, BS w/2 OLC
M/Sgt Dominick L Meloni, 105 Eng, BS
Sgt Ralph J Melphy, 531 AAA, BS
Pfc David E Melton, 120 Inf, BS
T/5 James E Melton, 117 Inf, BS
1st Sgt Max P Melton, 230 FA, BS
Pfc Maurice J Melvin, 117 Inf, BS w/OLC
Pfc Alfred Melzer, 105 Eng, BS
Pfc Herman J Melzer, 119 Inf, BS
Pvt Laurence V Mena, 120 Inf, BS
Pfc Frank Menendez, 823 TD, BS
Pfc Donald R Menery, 117 Inf, SS
Pfc Theodore J Mercik, 117 Inf, BS
Pfc Michael A Mercurio, 120 Inf, SS
1st Lt Julius F Merkel, 730 Ord, BS
Pfc William B Merkel, 120 Inf, SS BS
T/5 Frederick S Meron, 117 Inf, BS
T/4 Jesse N Merriman, 120 Inf, BS
T/Sgt Lloyd E Merritt, 119 Inf, BS w/OLC
Pfc John G Merrow, 117 Inf, BS
Pfc Eugene F Merschman, 119 Inf, SS BS
CWO Russell E Mersereau, 823 TD, BS
Pfc Elmer L Mertens, 30 MP, BS
Pfc Oscar C Mertz, 117 Inf, BS
Sgt Harold R Merz, 119 Inf, BS
Capt Herbert E Meshekow, 105 Med, BS
T/5 Allen B Messer, 117 Inf, DSC
1st Sgt Jappie G Messer, 120 Inf, SS
Pvt Earl R Messerly, 117 Inf, SS
Pvt Albert Mestas, 117 Inf, SS BS
T/5 Anthony J Mette, 120 Inf, BS
Pfc Ernest R Metz, 120 Inf, SS
Cpl Herman G Metz, 113 FA SS −
Capt John M Metzger, 197 FA, BS
Pfc Adolph E Meyer, 119 Inf, BS w/OLC
Pfc Erwin W Meyer, 119 Inf, BS w/OLC
Cpl Howard L Meyer, 120 Inf, SS BS
T/4 Leroy B Meyer, 743 Tk, BS
1st Sgt William C Meyer, 197 FA, BS
Sgt Nicholas W Meyers 120 Inf BS w/OLC
Pfc Steve M Meyers, 119 Inf, BS
Pfc Jasper Michael Jr, 119 Inf, BS
Pfc Henry T Michaelsen, 230 FA, SS
T/5 Walter V Michalski, 119 Inf, BS
S/Sgt Francis N Michels, 117 Inf, BS
T/4 William A Michelsen, Div Hq, BS
T/5 Hubert Michiels, 119 Inf, BS
Pvt Carl J Michini, 117 Inf, BS w/2 OLC
T/5 Gordon B Mickelson, 113 FA, BS −
2d Lt Edwin J Mickevicz, 117 Inf, BS
Pfc Charlie J Middleton, 105 Med, SS BS
S/Sgt Clyde C Middleton, 117 Inf, BS
1st Lt Edward H Middleton, 730 Ord, BS
Pfc Lowell E Middleton 119 Inf, BS
T/4 Julian E Midgett, 120 Inf, BS
Pfc Gerald W Miedema, 119 Inf, BS w/OLC
S/Sgt Charles A Miezis, 117 Inf, SS
Pvt Walter P Mikieta, 117 Inf, BS
S/Sgt Henry H Mikula, 117 Inf, BS
Pfc Louis P Mikulenka, 117 Inf, BS
Pfc Elmer D Miles, 119 Inf, BS
Sgt Virgle W Miles, 120 Inf BS w/OLC MM
Pfc Arthur T Milewski, 120 Inf, BS
Pfc Ross Milhanti, 120 Inf, BS
Pfc Norman D Millage, 120 Inf, BS
Pfc Floyd R Millard, 117 Inf, BS
Pvt George E Millard, 120 Inf, BS

Pfc Clyde W Millard, 120 Inf, BS
Pfc Aaron Miller, 117 Inf, SS
Sgt Allan Miller, 117 Inf, BS
Pfc Archie B Miller, 119 Inf, BS
T/4 Clair G Miller, Div Hq, BS
T/4 Donald A Miller, 119 Inf, BS
Capt Edward D Miller, 743 Tk, BS w/OLC
1st Lt Garfield Miller, Div Hq, BS
Sgt George L Miller, 743 Tk, BS
Pfc Glenn W Miller, 119 Inf, BS
Sgt Harold D Miller, 117 Inf, BS
Pfc Harry A Miller, 119 Inf, BS
2d Lt Henry N Miller, 118 FA, SS BS
Pfc Hershel Miller, 119 Inf, BS
Cpl Jack W Miller, 105 Eng, BS
Pvt James E Miller, 119 Inf, BS
Pfc John A Miller, 119 Inf, BS
T/Sgt John E Miller, 120 Inf, BS w/OLC
T/4 John T Miller, 743 Tk, BS w/OLC
T/4 Lawrence N Miller, 105 Eng, SS BS
Pfc Leo Miller, 120 Inf, SS
Sgt Lewis M Miller, 119 Inf, BS
Sgt Melvin C Miller, 119 Inf, BS
Sgt Minor L Miller, 120 Inf, SS
Cpl Paul D Miller, 823 TD, SS
Pfc Raymond J Miller, 117 Inf, BS w/OLC
Pfc Robert R Miller, 120 Inf, BS
Pfc Wade R Miller, 117 Inf, BS
S/Sgt Wallace J Miller, 120 Inf, BS w/OLC
Pfc William C Miller, 119 Inf, BS w/OLC
1st Lt William J Miller, 117 Inf, BS w/OLC
S/Sgt William M Miller, 120 Inf, BS
Pfc Donald L Millerin, 230 FA, BS
Pfc James L Millet, 120 Inf, SS
Pfc Ervin Millhollen, 113 FA, BS −
Maj Raymond W Millican, 118 FA,
        SS BS w/OLC
Capt John S Milligan Jr, 197 FA, DSC
T/4 David F Milliron, 105 Eng, BS
1st Lt Donald C Mills, 230 FA, DSC SS
Sgt Cardell Mills, 105 Eng, BS
T/5 Francis E Mills, 120 Inf, SS
Pvt Roy J Mills, 117 Inf, SS
T/4 Joseph M Milner, Div Hq, BS
1st Lt Leonard J Mimoni, 743 Tk, BS
S/Sgt Larry A Minalga, 117 Inf, SS BS
Cpl Roy M Minch, 230 FA, BS
Sgt Carl A Minervini 125 Cav, BS
Capt Sidney Minkoff, 120 Inf, SS BS
Pfc Walter L Minnick, 119 Inf, SS
Pvt Stephen J Minta, 119 Inf, BS
S/Sgt Percy W Minton, 197 FA, BS
Pfc Andrew J Minyard Jr, 119 Inf, BS
2d Lt Robert L Minyard, 120 Inf, BS
Capt Francis Miraglia, 117 Inf, BS w/OLC
Pvt Charles E Mirick, 119 Inf, BS
Pfc Adolph R Mirra, 119 Inf, SS BS
Pfc Joseph A Miscerri, 119 Inf, DSC
Pvt Stephen J Mish, 120 Inf, BS
T/5 Raymond P Miskiewicz, 119 Inf, BS
S/Sgt Eugene Mitchell, 197 FA, BS w/OLC
1st Lt Floyd Mitchell Jr 743 Tk, BS
S/Sgt Floyd Mitchell, 823 TD, BS
Pfc Fred F Mitchell, 230 FA, BS
S/Sgt Homer C Mitchell, 119 Inf, SS
T/5 James I Mitchell Jr 30 Rcn, BS
S/Sgt Ray A Mitchell, 823 TD, BS
T/Sgt Van J Mitchell, 117 Inf, SS
T/5 Wallace E Mitchell, Div Arty BS
Maj William P Mitchell, 230 FA, SS BS w/OLC
Pfc Robert A Mitchem, 743 Tk, BS
Pfc John Mitzko, 117 Inf, BS
1st Sgt Horace R Mixson,, 118 FA, SS
Pfc Doyle Mizell, 823 TD, SS w/OLC
Pfc Edward C Mlyner, 117 Inf BS
T/Sgt Herbert W Mobley, 118 FA, BS
1st Sgt James R Mobley, 113 FA, BS −
Pfc Eril R Mock, 119 Inf, SM
Sgt Thomas J Mock, 120 Inf, BS w/2 OLC
Sgt Clarence H Mockbee Jr, 117 inf,
        BS w/2 OLC
T/Sgt W Mocniak, 120 Inf, BS w/OLC
Pfc James C Modlin, 105 Eng, BS
S/Sgt Max D Moeller, 117 Inf, BS

T/5 Wilbur S Mohr, 119 Inf, BS
Pvt Adam J Mokszycki, 120 Inf BS
Sgt James M Molgaard, 120 Inf, BS w/2 OLC
Sgt Ernest W Molnar, 119 Inf, SS BS w/OLC
S/Sgt Paul A Molters, 30 Sig, BS
Pvt James G Monahan, 120 Inf, BS
Pvt Sam Monceaux, 230 FA, BS
Capt Charles W Moncrieff, 120 Inf,
    SS w/OLC BS
Pfc Elmer L D Moncus, 119 Inf, BS w/OLC
T/5 Clyde B Money, 119 Inf, BS
Pfc Donald A Mongeon, 120 Inf, BS
Pvt Harold A Mongin, 117 Inf, BS
Pfc Frank S Moniz, 119 Inf, SS BS
Pvt George Monks, 120 Inf, BS
Sgt Robert E Monsarrat, 117 Inf, BS
2d Lt Paul J Monson, Div Hq, BS
T/5 Ivan Montague, 117 Inf, BS
Pfc Peter D Montalbano, 120 Inf, BS
Pfc Lazarus C Montalvo, 119 Inf, BS
S/Sgt John C Monteith, 203 FA, BS
T/Sgt Floyd M Montgomery, 120 Inf, SS
Pfc John H Montgomery, 117 Inf, BS
Pfc Antonio Montoya, 117 Inf, BS
Pfc George R Montoya, 119 Inf, BS
Pfc Salvadore Montoya, 120 Inf, BS
Sgt Earl F W Moody, 113 FA BS
Pfc Hagop J Mooradian, 117 Inf, BS
Cpl Benjamin J Moore, 117 Inf, BS
Pfc Charles W Moore, 117 Inf, BS
Pfc Cloyd Moore, 120 Inf, SS
Pvt David M Moore, 120 Inf, BS
Pfc Dempsey R Moore, 105 Eng, BS w/OLC
Cpl Everett D Moore, 118 FA, BS
T/4 George W Moore, 119 Inf, BS
Pfc Hardin Moore, 119 Inf, SS BS
T/4 Herbert H Moore, 117 Inf, SS
Sgt Hollis G Moore, 197 FA, BS
T/Sgt Ishmael N Moore, Div Hq, BS
2d Lt James A Moore, 118 FA, SS BS w/OLC
Pfc John M Moore, 117 Inf, BS
Pfc John W Moore, 117 Inf, BS
Pfc Linwood P Moore, 119 Inf, BS
T/Sgt Malcolm Moore, 117 Inf, BS w/OLC
Pfc Manuel Moore, 120 Inf, BS
1st Lt Norvel Q Moore, 744 Tk, BS
Pfc Ray A Moore, 117 Inf, SS
Pvt Raymond W Moore, 117 Inf, BS
1st Lt Robert L Moore, 120 Inf, BS
S/Sgt Robert L Moore 120 Inf, BS
Pfc Roy C Moore, 119 Inf, BS
Pfc Rufe A Moore, 105 Med, BS
Cpl Stephen L Moore Jr, 119 Inf, BS
Pfc Willis F Moore, 117 Inf, SS
Pfc Bernardino D Mora, 120 Inf, BS w/OLC
Sgt Agapito B Morales, 119 Inf, SS
Pfc Antoine Moran, 105 Eng, BS
Sgt Thomas J Moran, 120 Inf, BS
Pvt Guerrino T Morell, 117 Inf, BS
Pfc Leon R Moreno, 117 Inf, BS
S/Sgt Frederick R Morey, 743 Tk, SS BS
S/Sgt Aaron L Morgan, 117 Inf, SS
1st Lt David W Morgan, 117 Inf, SS BS
Pfc G R Philmore Morgan, 119 Inf, BS
Pfc Harley V Morgan, 120 Inf, BS
Pfc Henry G Morgan, 30 Sig, BS
Pvt Homer J C Morgan, 117 Inf, SS
S/Sgt Kenneth V Morgan, 119 Inf, BS
S/Sgt Lawrence E Morgan, 230 FA, BS
M/Sgt Robert A Morgan Jr, Div Hq, BS
Sgt William R Morgan, 823 TD, BS
Pvt Daniel G Morgenthaler, 119 Int, BS
Pfc Louis P Morin, 120 Inf, BS
T/4 Joseph P Morisoli, 119 Inf, BS w/OLC
S/Sgt Delbert J Moritz, 230 FA, BS
T/5 Edwin A Morken, 117 Inf, BS
Sgt John Morocco, 120 Inf, BS
T/5 Clifford J Morris, 117 Inf, SS BS
S/Sgt Curtis M Morris, 119 Inf, BS w/OLC
Pfc Enoch W Morris, 119 Inf, BS
T/Sgt George E Morris, 117 Inf, SS
T/4 Herbert S Morris, 119 Inf, BS
Cpl Jean H Morris, 113 FA SS BS w/OLC
Pfc John R Morris Jr, 117 Inf, BS

Pfc John T Morris, 120 Inf, BS w/OLC
Pfc John T Morris, 119 Inf, BS
S/Sgt Johnnie Morris Jr, 117 Inf, BS
Pvt Melvin E Morris, 117 Inf, BS w/OLC
Pfc Pat A Morris, 197 FA, BS w/OLC
S/Sgt Randolph B Morris, 119 Inf, BS
2d Lt Silvas V Morris, 117 Inf, SS
T/5 Thomas A Morris, 117 Inf,
    SS w/OLC BS w/OLC
Sgt Harvey Morrison, 119 Inf, BS
S/Sgt James E Morrison, 118 FA, BS
Pvt James S Morrison, 119 Inf, BS
Sgt Ralph E Morrison, 120 Inf, BS
S/Sgt Robert V Morrison, 120 Inf, SS
2d Lt Carl N Morrow, 117 Inf, SS w/OLC
T/4 Clyde O Morrow, 117 Inf, BS
Pfc John C Morrow, 120 Inf, BS
T/4 Murphy J Morrow, 119 Inf, BS
T/Sgt Rother P Morrow, 120 Inf, SS BS
S/Sgt Samuel H Morrow, 117 Inf, BS w/OLC
1st Sgt Urban W Morrow, 531 AAA, BS
S/Sgt Earl Morse, 117 Inf, SM
T/Sgt Theodore E Morse, 531 AAA, BS
Pvt Santo J Mortellaro, 120 Inf, BS
T/4 Joe B Morton, 230 FA, SS
Pvt Malcolm F Morton, 117 Inf, BS
S/Sgt William J Morton, 743 Tk, BS
Pvt Theodore T Morus, 105 Eng, BS
1st Lt Eugene G Mosbacher, 105 Eng, BS
1st Lt James L Mosby, 120 Inf,
    DSC BS w/2 OLC
2d Lt Antonio C Moschetta, 230 FA, SS
T/4 Joseph Moschetta, 230 FA, BS
T/4 Emil L Moses, 743 Tk, BS
Pvt William L Moses, 119 Inf, BS
Cpl Raymond E Mosher, 105 Eng, BS
S/Sgt John H Mosley, 120 Inf, BS w/2 OLC
S/Sgt Henry R Moss, 117 Inf, BS
Pvt James K Moss, 120 Inf, BS
S/Sgt Jesse Moss, 117 Inf, BS
2d Lt Jack Motes, 118 FA, SS w/OLC
Pfc Delmar J Motlik, 120 Inf, BS
1st Lt Edward E Mottern, 117 Inf, SS
Lt Col George E Motz, Div Hq, BS
Pvt James J Moudry, 120 Inf, BS
Pfc Charles E Mould, 105 Eng BS
Pvt Woodrow W Mountjoy, 119 Inf, BS
1st Lt Forrest K Mountz, 120 Inf, SS
Pfc William W Mountz, 823 TD, SS
Pfc Gehard H Mousel, 117 Inf, BS
S/Sgt Arthur W Moushon, 119 Inf, BS w/OLC
Pfc Andrew A Mousin, 119 Inf, BS
Pfc Jack T Mowat, 105 Eng, BS
Pfc Clifford F Moyland, 119 Inf, BS
S/Sgt Thomas J Moyland, 119 Inf, BS
T/5 William T Moyland, 119 Inf, BS
Pfc Joseph C Mrugala, 120 Inf, BS
Pfc Nicholas Mucci, 30 Rcn, SS
Pfc Mike M Mucciante, 119 Inf, BS
S/Sgt George Mudd, 125 Cav, BS
T/4 Joseph Mudra, Div Hq, BS
T/5 Edward A Mufich, 230 FA, BS
T/4 Charles P Mulder, 30 Sig, BS
Pfc Royal F Mulder, 117 Inf, BS
T/5 Clyde D Mulkey, 117 Inf, BS
Pfc Albert Mull, 117 Inf, BS
Pvt Harold E Mull, 120 Inf BS
Cpl Paul M Mull, 119 Inf, BS
Pfc Beverly C Mullaniz, 117 Inf, BS
Pfc Joseph W Mullany, 119 Inf, BS
Pfc Raymond O Mullen, 743 Tk BS
Pvt Gideon E Mueller, 120 Inf, BS
T/Sgt Ira S Mullins, 120 Inf, BS w/OLC
Sgt Guy W Mullis, 197 FA, BS
Pvt Walter F Mulvaney, 105 Eng, BS
Pfc Wayne E Mumma, 120 Inf, BS
T/Sgt John D Munn, 120 Inf, BS
Sgt Julian E Munoz, 119 Inf, BS
S/Sgt Thomas Munoz, 120 Inf, SS
Pfc Anthony F Muraco, 117 Inf, BS
S/Sgt Raymond H Murdock, 117 Inf, BS w/OLC
1st Lt Charles E Murello, 531 AAA, BS
1st Lt William B Murnigham, 230 FA, SS BS
Cpl Milton Murphey, 113 FA, BS

Pfc Charles Murphy, 117 Inf, BS
T/5 Edward J Murphy, 120 Inf, BS
Pfc George J Murphy, 120 Inf, BS
Sgt John B Murphy, 119 Inf, BS w/OLC
Pfc Leron A Murphy, 120 Inf, BS
S/Sgt Louis J Murphy, 119 Inf, BS
Sgt Olin W Murphy, 119 Inf, BS
Pfc Paul J Murphy, 117 Inf, BS
Sgt Paul S Murphy, 120 Inf, BS
S/Sgt William R Murphy, 120 Inf, BS
Cpl Allen E Murphy, 120 Inf, BS
Sgt Clarence S Murray, 117 Inf, BS
Cpl Elwood L Murray, 113 FA, BS —
1st Lt Robert O Murray, 117 Inf, SS BS
Pfc William J Murray, 117 Inf, BS
T/5 Lynford P Murri, 105 Eng, BS
Pvt Enrico Musatti, 119 Inf, BS
T/5 Joseph R Muskey, 230 FA, BS
Cpl Charles Musselwhite, 113 FA, BS—
Cpl John L Musser, 105 Eng, BS
Pvt William H Mustard, 120 Inf, BS
S/Sgt Walter B Mustian, 120 Inf, BS
Pfc Mike Mustradi, 30 Sig, BS
Pvt Blair L Mutimer, 119 Inf, BS
T/5 David W Myers, 117 Inf, BS w/OLC
Pfc Dorwin J Myers, 823 TD, BS
T/4 Everette L Myers, 743 Tk, BS
T/5 Joseph E Myers, 117 Inf, BS
Sgt Luther G Myers, 120 Inf BS
T/Sgt Walter E Myers, 230 FA, BS
T/5 Marvin Mygrant, 120 Inf, BS
Pfc Kenneth F Myhre, 120 Inf, BS
Capt James E McAdams, 17 Eng, BS
Pfc Gleason N McAdoo, 743 Tnk, BS
Cpl Carey McAfee, Hq 30 Div, BS
1st Lt Leo E McAlpine, 117 Inf, BS
Capt Edward J McArdle, 230 FA, SS BS
Pfc Delos U McArthur, 117 Inf, BS w/OLC
1st Lt Myrl N McArthur, 117 Inf BS
S/Sgt Bernard L D McBay, 117 Inf,
    BS w/2 OLC
T/4 Milton McBee, 230 FA, BS
Capt Edward E J McBride, 119 Inf, SS
Pfc Edwin S McBlain, 197 FA, BS
T/5 Jim F McBride, 117 Inf, BS
Capt George W McBurney, 30 Div Hq, BS
Pfc James B McCain, 118 FA, SS
Cpl John A McCall, 30 Div MP, SS
Maj Samuel L McCall, 113 FA, BS —
Cpl William J McCall, 117 Inf, BS
S/Sgt Jack W McCalligan, 119 Inf, BS w/OLC
Pfc George T McCann, 119 Inf, BS
Pfc Robert J McCann, 120 Inf, BS
S/Sgt Glenn E McCarl, 120 Inf BS
Pfc Bernard McCarthy, 30 Sig, BS
Sgt William C McCarthy, 117 Inf, SS
T/5 Henry F McCartney, 117 Inf, BS w/2 OLC
Pfc Joseph J McCaskey, 117 Inf, BS
Capt James R McCauley, 230 FA, SS BS
Pvt William J McCauley, 120 Inf, BS
Cpl Marion J McCaulley 743 Tnk, BS
Cpl Bruce B McCay, 120 Inf, BS
Cpl Clifford McClain, 230 FA, SS BS
Sgt George J McClain, 119 Inf, SS
Capt Ralph E McClain, 120 Inf, BS
1st Lt George L McClanahan, 117 Inf,
    SS w/OLC BS w/OLC
Cpl Robert L McClanahan, 230 FA, BS w/OLC
Pfc Otis H McClary, 117 Inf SS
Pfc Gail E McCleary, 120 Inf, BS
Cpl Samuel M McClellan, 119 Inf, BS w/OLC
Pfc Roy C McCloud, 117 Inf, BS
Sgt Donald F McClure, 120 Inf, BS
T/5 Everett McClure, 117 Inf, BS w/2 OLC
Lt Col Paul W McCollum, 120 Inf, DSC SS
Pfc Leland N McConnell 117 Inf, SS
Pfc William T McConnell, 119 Inf, SS
Cpl Hardman B McCool, 197 FA, BS w/OLC
T/Sgt Ezra M McCord, 30 QM, BS
S/Sgt William R McCorkindale, 117 Inf, SS
T/5 Elmer I McCormick, 105 Eng, BS
2d Lt Marvin McCormick, 118 FA, SS BS
Lt Col Hal D McCown, 119 Inf,
    SS w/OLC BS w/OLC

Capt John C McCoy, 743 Tnk, BS w/OLC
Cpl Orville L McCoy, 120 Inf, BS
Pfc Roy McCoy, 30 Div MP, BS
Sgt Lawrence L McCracken, 119 Inf,
    SS BS w/OLC
S/Sgt Richard D McCracken, 743 Tnk, SS
S/Sgt Leon B McCrary, 117 Inf, BS
1st Lt Lawrence D McCrea, 230 FA, SS BS
Pfc Daniel O McCuller, 113 FA, BS
T/Sgt Charles E McCullough, 120 Inf,
    SS w/OLC
Maj Chris McCullough, 120 Inf, SS w/OLC BS
Pvt Felix E McCullough, 119 Inf, BS
Sgt Thomas E McCullough, 117 Inf, SS
S/Sgt John A McDaniel, 117 Inf, BS w/OLC
Sgt Robert R McDaniel, 119 Inf, BS
Sgt Neill A McDiarmid, 119 Inf, BS
Pfc Albert E McDonald, 105 Eng, SS
Pfc Clinton McDonald, 117 Inf, BS
1st Lt Dan M McDonald, 119 Inf, BS
S/Sgt Frederick W McDonald, 203 FA, BS
Pfc George E McDonald, 117 Inf, SS BS w/OLC
Pfc George J McDonald, 119 Inf, BS
Lt Col Hugh McDonald, 283 FA, BS
Pfc Joseph H L McDonald, 119 Inf, BS
Pfc Sheldon E McDonald, 117 Inf, SS
Capt Edward P McDonough, 258 Eng, BS
1st Lt Charles E McDowell, 105 Med, BS
Lt Col Samuel T McDowell, 117 Inf,
    SS w/2 OLC BS w/3 OLC
T/Sgt Carl D McDuffie, 30 Div Arty, SS
T/5 Clarence E McDuffie, 118 FA, BS
Cpl Conrad R McEachern, 823 TD, BS
T/5 Garner F McElroy, 743 Tnk, BS
Pfc Waldon G McElroy, 119 Inf, BS w/OLC
Pvt Allen B McFadden, 117 Inf, SS BS
S/Sgt Charles M McFadden, 119 Inf, BS
Sgt Turner D McFarland, 117 Inf, SS
Pfc Lawrence E McGahan, 119 Inf, SS
T/5 Edward R McGaw, 30 Sig, BS
Sgt Kenneth E McGaughey, 531 AAA, BS
1st Lt John F McGee, 117 Inf, BS w/2 OLC
T/5 Joseph F McGee, 30 Sig, BS
Pvt William McGee, 119 Inf, BS
T/4 Charles L McGhie, 119 Inf, BS
Pfc William T McGilton, 118 FA, BS
S/Sgt Elmo H McGinnis, 743 Tnk, BS
Pfc James M McGough, 30 Div MP, BS
Pfc Donald J McGourty, 117 Inf, BS
Pvt Frank C McGovern, 230 FA, BS
1st Lt Frank A McGowan, 117 Inf, BS
Capt Gordon W McGowan, 105 Med, BS
Sgt Max E McGowan, 119 Inf, SS
Pfc Lawrence E McGahan, 119 Inf, BS
S/Sgt Alan D McGraw, 120 Inf, SS
S/Sgt George T McGraw, 117 Inf, SS w/OLC BS
T/Sgt Arthur J McGuire, 736 Tnk, BS
T/4 James M McGuire, 120 Inf, BS w/2 OLC
Pfc Paul G McHale, 119 Inf, BS w/2 OLC
T/5 Robert W McHenry, Div Hq, BS
Col Harry D McHugh, 30 Div Hq, SS BS w/OLC
2d Lt Joe E McInerney, 118 Inf, SS w/OLC
Capt Ellis W McInnis, 823 TD, SS BS
T/5 Charles E McIsaac, 117 Inf, BS
T/4 Ralph L McKain, 105 Eng, BS
Sgt Elmer S McKay, 119 Inf, BS
Cpl James A McKenna, 117 Inf, BS
Cpl John T McKenna, 117 Inf, BS
Cpl Archie P McKenry, 117 Inf, BS
1st Lt William E McKenzie, 119 Inf, SS
S/Sgt James L McKeon, 105 Eng, SS BS
Pfc Alexander B McKeveny, 736 Tnk, SS
Pfc Norman S McKewen, 117 Inf, BS
Pvt Arthur E McKinley, 117 Inf, BS
1st Sgt Hugh F McKinley, 117 Inf, BS
Pfc David A McKinney, 120 Inf, BS
Pfc Herbert A McKitrick, 119 Inf, BS
T/Sgt Roger W McKnight, 117 Inf, BS
Pfc John F McLacken, 119 Inf, SS BS
T/4 Cecil F McLane 120 Inf, BS
Pfc John D McLaughlin, 119 Inf, BS
Pfc Norman J McLaughlin, 119 Inf, BS
1st Lt Robert C McLaughlin, 118 FA,
    SS w/OLC BS

Pfc William A McLaughlin, 117 Inf, BS
T/Sgt Charles S McLean, 117 Inf, BS
S/Sgt Everett V McLemore, 119 Inf, BS
T/Sgt Donald McLeod, 120 Inf, BS
T/4 John McLeod, 117 Inf, SS
Pvt John C McLeod, 113 FA, BS
S/Sgt Rovert E McLeod, 119 Inf, BS w/OLC
T/Sgt Melvin L McLester, 119 Inf, BS
Pfc Hugh McMahon, 118 FA, SS BS
T/Sgt James McManaman, 120 Inf, SS
S/Sgt John F McManamin, 120 Inf, BS
Pvt Edward J McManus, 119 Inf, BS
Cpl Frederick J McMichael, 117 Inf,
        BS w/3 OLC
Pfc James K McMillan, 30 Div MP, BS
M/Sgt Thomas H McMillan, Div Hq, BS
Capt James A McMillan Jr, 119 Inf, BS
Pfc Edwin T McMinds, 30 Div Rcn, BS
1st Lt Edward L McMullen, 113 FA,
        SS BS w/OLC
Pvt William B McNamara, 120 Inf, SS BS
T/5 Paul McNeely, 120 Inf, BS
1st Sgt Grady McNeil, 117 Inf, BS
Pfc Roscoe J McNemar, 119 Inf, SS BS
1st Sgt Gerard T McNulty, 117 Inf, BS
S/Sgt Warner R McNulty, 230 FA, BS
Pfc Alfred R McNutt, 117 Inf, SS
Pfc Stanley R McPhee, 117 Inf, BS w/OLC
S/Sgt Ray J McPherson, 119 Inf, BS
Pfc Orville J McQueen, 117 Inf, BS
Lt Col Dwight L McReynolds, 117 Inf,
        BS w/2 OLC
Sgt Jack D McRoberts, 823 TD, BS
Pfc John J McShane, 230 FA, SS
Pfc Lester A McTire, 823 TD, SS
T/5 Clifford McVey, 117 Inf, BS
S/Sgt Max C McWhorter, 120 Inf, SS BS
T/5 Robert S McWilliams, 119 Inf, BS w/OLC
T/5 William R Nace, 125 Cav, BS
Pfc Leopold Nadeau, 117 Inf, BS
Pvt Lionel A Nadeau, 119 Inf, BS
T/4 Lawrence Nammings, 118 FA, BS
Sgt Robert A Nance, 120 Inf, BS
T/5 Clyde M Nanney, 119 Inf, BS
Pvt Edward J Nannery, 120 Inf, SS w/OLC
T/5 Joseph F Naples, 117 Inf, SS
Sgt LeRoy E Napp, 119 Inf, SS BS
T/Sgt John P Narodowski, 117 Inf, BS
Sgt Bernard E Narow, 531 AAA, BS
Capt Louis Nash, 120 Inf, BS
2d Lt Wallis C Nash, 120 Inf, SS
T/3 James Nassar, 230 FA, BS
Cpl William L Nassau, 743 Tk, BS
Pfc Nicodemus R Natale 117 Inf, BS
S/Sgt Louis Nathan, 117 Inf, BS
Sgt Lawrence Naymik, 120 Inf, BS w/OLC
T/5 Victor Nayone, 119 Inf, BS
Pvt Fred T Nazimiec, 120 Inf. BS
S/Sgt Robert E Neahr, 120 Inf, SS
1st Lt Charlie L Neal 117 Inf, SS
T/5 Lester E Neal, 117 Inf, BS w/OLC
T/5 Raymond F Neal, 120 Inf, BS
Pfc Billie Neel, 120 Inf, BS
Sgt James D Neel, 117 Inf, BS
1st Lt Leon L Neel, 823 TD, SS w/OLC C d'G
T/4 Ryan R Neely, 120 Inf, BS
Pfc George E Neidhardt, 117 Inf, SS
1st Lt Charles G Neighbor, 117 Inf, BS
Pfc Morten W Neilsen, 120 Inf, BS
Capt Allen C Neiswander, 120 Inf, BS w/2 OLC
S/Sgt Charles W Nelson, 117 Inf, SS
Pfc Clyde N Nelson, 117 Inf, SS BS
Pfc Frank O Nelson, 119 Inf, BS
T/3 Harlan M Nelson, 531 AAA, BS
2d Lt Harold D Nelson, 120 Inf, BS w/OLC
Cpl John O Nelson, 105 Eng, BS
Pfc John W Nelson, 120 Inf, BS
1st Lt Kenneth R Nelson 120 Inf, DSC
Pvt Leonard Nelson, 105 Eng, BS
Pfc Lucien D Nelson, 117 Inf, BS w/OLC
1st Lt Ralph G Nelson, 119 Inf, BS
Pfc Robert W Nelson, 120 Inf, BS
Pfc Urho I Nelson, 743 Tk, BS
Pfc Joe V Nemec, 743 Tk, BS

T/4 Oswald G Nencioni, 113 FA, BS —
T/4 Leo J Nerone, 30 Sig, BS
Pfc George Nesky, 30 Sig, BS
Pfc Alfred Ness, 120 Inf, BS
Cpl Howard L Ness, 119 Inf, BS
Capt Arthur T Neumann, 120 Inf, BS
Pfc Robert G Neumann, 113 FA, SS —
Sgt Lorenzo C Nevarez, 823 TD, SS
Pfc Walter L Newcomb, 197 FA, BS
1st Lt Forest P Newman, 120 Inf, SS BS
Cpl Philip S Newman, 197 FA, BS
S/Sgt William H Newnich, 740 Tk, BS
S/Sgt Harold J Newton, 117 Inf, BS
Pfc James E Newton, 120 Inf, SS
1st Lt Otis D Newton, 120 Inf, SS w/OLC BS
S/Sgt Hugh D Newsome, 119 Inf, BS
Pvt John W Newton, 120 Inf. BS
T/5 Herald J Nibel, 743 Tk, BS MM
Pfc Howard E Nicholls Jr, 117 Inf, BS
T/5 Kenneth L Nicholas, 119 Inf, BS
S/Sgt David C Nichols, 117 Inf, SS
T/5 Leonard F Nichols, 230 FA, BS
Pfc Patrick H Nichols, 117 Inf, BS
Capt Robert G Nichols, 120 Inf, BS
Lt Col William H Nicholas, Hq 30 Div, BS
T/4 William L Nichols, 120 Inf, BS w/OLC
S/Sgt Willard P Nichols, 119 Inf, BS w/OLC
T/4 Vollie W Nicholson, 230 FA, SS
T/Sgt William Nicholson, 117 Inf, SS
1st Lt Jack C Nickolai, 30 MP, BS w/3 OLC
Capt Arne Nielsen, 117 Inf, SS BS w/OLC
Pfc Morten W Nielsen, 120 Inf, BS
1st Sgt Richard E Nielsen, 117 Inf, BS
Pfc Risto M Niemi, 117 Inf, SS
Pfc John A Nigro, 117 Inf, BS
Pfc Willebaldo Nila, 30 Rcn, SS
Pvt Paul Niosi 105 Eng, BS
Cpl Humberto Nival, 117 Inf, BS
T/5 Barney E Nixon, 230 FA, SS
Pfc Donald K Noble, 119 Inf, BS
Pfc George D Noble, 117 Inf, SS
Pfc Edward S Nobles, 119 Inf, BS
Pfc Johnie J Nobles, 105 Med, BS
1st Lt Ervil R Noel, 30 Sig, BS w/OLC
Pfc Roy G Noel, 120 Inf, BS
Pfc Paul W Noglow, 117 Inf, BS
T/5 Raymond J Nohner, 531 AAA, BS
T/Sgt John M Nolan, 119 Inf, BS w/OLC
Sgt Roy E Noland, 120 Inf, BS
Pfc Sam J Nole, 743 Tk, BS
Pfc Charles M Noonan, 743 Tk, BS
S/Sgt Donald M Norgaard, 119 Inf, BS
Pfc Edison Norman, 119 Inf, BS
Sgt Loyal T Norman, 105 Eng, BS
Pvt Donald L Norris, 120 Inf, BS
T/Sgt Marcus L North, 120 Inf, SS
Pfc Woodrow W Northcutt, 120 Inf, BS
Pfc Edward J Northrop, 117 Inf, BS
Pfc Martin J Norton, 117 Inf, BS
S/Sgt William Norton, 117 Inf, SS
Capt York Norwood, 120 Inf, BS
Cpl Frank J Novak, 117 Inf, BS
Pfc Fred H Novak, 117 Inf, BS
Sgt Victor L Novickie, 119 Inf, BS
T/4 Daniel T Novitsky, 197 FA, BS
1st Lt James J Nowicki, 119 Inf, BS w/OLC
Pfc Maland C Nowland 30 Rcn, BS w/OLC
Pfc Daniel J Noyes, 119 Inf SS BS
Pfc William W Nuckols, 117 Inf, BS w/OLC
S/Sgt Andrew A Nudge Jr, 117 Inf, BS
Sgt Malery Nunn, 823 TD, SS
Capt William L Nusbaum, 120 Inf, BS
Pfc Melvin J Nutt, 120 Inf, BS
Pfc Donald E Nyberg, 120 Inf, BS
Pfc John J Nyhan, 120 Inf, BS
Pfc George L Nyland, 120 Inf, SS
Sgt Harold E Nyland, 119 Inf, SS
T/5 Arnt M Nysetvold, 30 Sig, BS
Pvt Gordon H Oakes, 113 FA, SS —
2d Lt John H Oakes, 119 Inf, SS BS
T/4 Dale W Oakley, 30 Rcn, BS
Cpl William L Oakley, 120 Inf, SS BS
Sgt Russell L Oates, 117 Inf, BS
Pfc Edward F Obremski, 117 Inf, BS w/OLC

S/Sgt Charles J Obrenski, 120 Inf, BS
S/Sgt Robert W O'Briant, 117 Inf, BS
Pfc Edward J O'Brien, 120 Inf, BS
Pfc James A O'Brien, 119 Inf, SS BS
Pfc James D O'Brien, 117 Inf, BS
1st Lt John J O'Brien, 743 Tk, SS
Pfc John K O'Brien, 120 Inf, BS
T/5 William J. O'Brien, Div Hq, BS
Pvt Howard W Ochiltree, 30 Rcn, SS
1st Sgt James R Ochtel, 119 Inf, SS
T/5 Gene F Ochwat, 230 FA, SS
Pfc John N O'Connell, 119 Inf, BS
T/Sgt Raymond R J O'Connor, 120 Inf, BS
Pfc Gerald J Odegaard, 117 Inf, BS
S/Sgt Albert B Odle, 743 Tk, BS w/OLC
Pfc Willie J Odom, 117 Inf, BS
1st Lt Edwin T O'Donnell, 105 Eng, BS
Cpl William J O'Donnell, 117 Inf, BS
Pfc George A Oestreicher, 120 Inf, SS
Pvt Dean E Oetjen, 117 Inf, BS w/OLC
Cpl Robert J Offord, 117 Inf, BS
Sgt Charles L Ogburn, 117 Inf, SS
Sgt Alexander W Ogilvie, 118 FA, BS
T/5 Hiram W Ogilvie, Hq 30 Div, BS
Pfc Edward R Ogle, 119 Inf, SS
1st Lt David Oglensky, 740 Tk, SS
M/Sgt Thomas B Oglesby, 120 Inf, BS
Sgt Jesse A Ognosky, 823 TD, SS
Pvt John J O'Grady, 113 FA, BS—
Cpl John J Ogulin, 120 Inf, BS
Pfc John P O'Hare, 117 Inf, SS
Cpl Richard C O'Hare, 120 Inf, BS w/OLC
Pfc James F Ohler, 120 Inf, BS w/OLC
T/5 Herman O Oistad, 117 Inf, SS
S/Sgt Daniel E O'Keefe, 117 Inf, BS
Pfc Theodore A Okrzesik, 119 Inf, BS w/OLC
T/Sgt Edwin H Oland, 119 Inf, SS
S/Sgt Fred A Oldenl, 117 Inf, SS
T/5 Edward E Oldendorf, 120 Inf, BS
Pvt Leonard G Oldfield, 117 Inf, SS
S/Sgt Robert Oldham, 120 Inf, SS
Pvt John A Olesh, 118 FA, BS
Sgt Wilson R Olive, 117 Inf, BS
Pvt Allie J Oliver, 120 Inf, BS
Sgt Harold B Oliver, 197 FA, SS
Pvt Harry C Oliver, 118 FA, BS
Pfc James U Oliver, 117 Inf, BS
Sgt Robert G Oliver, 120 Inf, SS
T/4 Frank J Oliverio, 119 Inf, BS
Capt Arthur K Olsen, Hq 30 Div, BS
Pvt Barney B Olsen, 105 Eng, BS
Sgt Erling C Olsen, Hq 30 Div, BS
Pfc George A Olsen, 119 Inf, BS
Pfc Johnny J Olsen, 105 Eng, BS
Sgt Daniel S Olshefski, 113 FA, BS w/OLC —
S/Sgt Lester W Olson, 119 Inf, BS
S/Sgt Orville R Olson, 119 Inf, BS
T/4 Rudolph Olson, 743 Tk, BS
Cpl Warren I Olson, 113 FA, BS —
Sgt Joseph S Olszak, 119 Inf, BS
Sgt George O'Malley, 119 Inf, BS
1st Lt George C Onderdonk, 531 AAA, BS w/OLC
Capt Joseph J Ondre, 743 Tk, BS
Pfc Edward E O'Neal, 113 FA, BS —
Sgt John L O'Neill, 117 Inf, BS
1st Lt William J O'Neill, 117 Inf, SS w/OLC
Pfc Emil Opaiser, 120 Inf, BS
Pfc August P Oppedisano, 119 Inf, BS
Pfc Robert E Orban, 119 Inf, BS
Pvt Stanley T Orczyk, 120 Inf, BS w/OLC
Cpl Arthur H Ordung, 119 Inf, BS
T/Sgt John J O'Reilly, 119 Inf, SS
Pfc Ramiro J Orena, 120 Inf BS
Pfc Richard F Orf, 117 Inf, BS
Pfc Rudy Oritz, 117 Inf, SS
Pfc Frank D Orlando, 119 Inf, SS
Maj Eric C Orme, 105 Eng, BS
Pfc Cormack J O'Rourke, 117 Inf, BS
1st Lt Victor B Ortega, 119 Inf, BS
T/5 Lloyd V Ortgieson, 119 Inf, BS
Cpl Oscar A Oritz, 105 Med, BS
S/Sgt Jack R Osborn, 531 AAA, BS
T/Sgt Lynn H Osborn, 119 Inf, BS

Pfc John P Osborn, 119 Inf, BS
Pvt Charles E Osborne, 531 AAA, SS
T/Sgt Raymon E Osborne, 117 Inf, BS
S/Sgt Edgar M Ose, 105 Eng, BS
Pfc Daniel T Oseak, 120 Inf, SS
Capt Donald W Osgood, 117 Inf, BS w/2 OLC
Pvt Gilbert A O'Shea, 119 Inf, BS
Pfc Joseph T. O'Shea, 119 Inf, BS
1st Lt Norman O'Shea, 120 Inf, BS SM
S/Sgt Alexander Oski, 743 Tk, SS
Sgt Warren G Osman, 117 Inf, BS w/OLC
Pfc Jesse J Osment, 119 Inf, BS
T/5 Clifford W Osterhoudt, 30 Sig, BS
2d Lt Norbert V Osterland, 119 Inf, BS
Pfc William M Ostrander, 119 Inf, BS
T/5 Eugene J Ostrom, 197 FA, BS
T/4 Charles R Ottino, 197 FA, BS
Pfc Earl A Otto, 120 Inf, BS
Pvt Wildo A Ouellette, 117 Inf, BS
T/4 Taylor H Overcash, 120 Inf, BS
T/Sgt John H Overman, 119 Inf, SS BS
Sgt William R Overman, 120 Inf, SS
Pfc James H Overstreet, 120 Inf, SS
S/Sgt Douglas T Overton, 105 Eng, BS
2d Lt Joseph H Owen, 117 Inf, BS w/OLC
T/Sgt Larry D Owen, 120 Inf, SS
Pfc William L Owen, 119 Inf, BS
T/4 William T Owen, 120 Inf, SS
Pfc David Owens, 120 Inf, SS
S/Sgt Frank H Owens, 119 Inf, SS BS
1st Sgt Fred Owens, 120 Inf, BS
Sgt James E Owens, 105 Eng, BS w/OLC
2d Lt Thomas L Owens, 531 AAA, BS
Pfc Wallace W Owens, 117 Inf, BS
1st Lt William H Owens, 531 AAA, BS
Sgt Toivo V Paavola, 117 Inf, BS
1st Sgt Janadus S Pace, 113 FA, BS
T/5 Frank E Pachoor, 117 Inf, BS
S/Sgt Mike Pachuta, 119 Inf, BS
T/4 Edward F Padar, 117 Inf, BS
Pvt Jack Padgett, 105 Eng, BS
T/5 Edwin W Page, 119 BS
S/Sgt James L Page, 119 Inf, BS w/OLC
Pfc Henry A Pakrul, 119 Inf, BS
Pfc Ervin F Pakulski, 119 Inf, BS
Pvt James W Pal, 120 Inf, BS
T/4 Frank E Palco Jr, 120 Inf, DSC SM
Pfc Carl Palermo, 120 Inf, BS w/OLC
Pfc Charles C Palmer, 119 Inf, BS
Pfc Frank J Palmer, 120 Inf, BS
Pfc Homer W Palmer, 120 Inf, BS
Pfc Eugene D Palmisano, 119 Inf, BS
S/Sgt Thomas G Palomino, 120 Inf, SS
Sgt Matthew R Pankowski, 113 FA, BS —
M/Sgt George A Pannal, 118 FA, BS
Pfc Michael Panno, 119 Inf BS w/OLC
Pfc Joseph Pantisamo, 120 Inf, SS
Pfc Leonello J Paolette, 117 Inf, BS
Pvt Charles C Papesh, 105 Eng, BS
Cpl George J Papesh, 197 FA, BS
Pvt Joseph Pappalardo, 117 Inf, BS
2d Lt Eric W Pappas, 230 FA, SS w/OLC BS
Pfc Harry Pappas, 744 Tnk, SS
Pfc William C Pappert, 119 Inf, BS
Pfc Norman J Paquette 119 Inf, BS w/OLC
Pfc Joseph P Paradis, 30 Div Rcn BS w/OLC
Cpl Albert G Paramore 113 FA, BS —
Pfc Joseph L Pardini, 120 Inf, BS
1st Lt Frank W Parent, 120 Inf, BS
Pvt Anthony J Parento, 743 Tnk, SS
T/5 William H Parham, 30 Sig BS w/OLC
Pfc Milton C Parke, 120 Inf, BS w/OLC
Cpl Charlie H Parker 197 FA BS
Pfc Earl W Parker 117 Inf, BS w/OLC
2d Lt Fay M Parker, 117 Inf, SS
T/5 Herman O Parker, 117 Inf, BS
T/4 Kenneth C Parker, 120 Inf, BS w/2 OLC
2d Lt Marvin R Parker, 531 AAA, BS w/OLC
T/5 Milford H Parker, 120 Inf, BS
Pfc Roy D Parker 120 Inf BS
T/4 Samuel S Parker 105 Eng, BS
Sgt Sylvester Parker 743 Tnk BS
S/Sgt Tom Parker 120 Inf SS
Capt Warne R Parker, 119 Inf, SS

1st Sgt William R Parker Jr, 119 Inf, BS
Pfc Clifford G Parkinson, 119 Inf, SS
M/Sgt Norman Parkinson, 30 Div Hq, BS
Pfc Socrates J Parkis, 119 Inf, BS
T/5 Henry A Parkman, 119 Inf, BS
T/Sgt J W Parks, 117 Inf, DSC C d'G
Sgt Lloyd T Parks, 119 Inf, BS
Pfc Marvin E Parks, 117 Inf, BS
1st Lt Milton J Parks, 119 Inf, BS
T/5 Raymond W Parks, 120 Inf, BS
Capt Frank Parlavecchia, 119 Inf, SS
Sgt John W Parmenter, 119 Inf, SS
Pfc Metro Paroskie, 105 Eng, BS
Pfc Donald J Parr, 120 Inf, BS
S/Sgt George E Parr, 117 Inf, BS
T/5 Henry Parra, 120 Inf, BS
1st Lt James F Parramore, 119 Inf,
    SS BS w/OLC
Maj Jesse J Parrish, 30 Div Arty, BS w/2 OLC
T/5 William L Parsley, 30 Div Rcn, BS
Pvt Curtis E Parsons, 105 Eng, SS
Pfc Henry J Parsons, 117 Inf, BS
T/Sgt Charles R Partridge, 117 Inf, BS
Sgt Clarence A Partridge, 119 Inf, SS BS
S/Sgt Anthony Pascale, 117 Inf, SS
S/Sgt Guy Pascale, 30 Div Arty, BS
Cpl John A Pasierb, 105 Eng, BS w/OLC
Pfc Manuel Pasquinucci, 120 Inf, BS
Pfc Charles V Passenau, 120 Inf, BS
Sgt Taras Pastuf, 117 Inf, BS
S/Sgt Peter P Patalano, 117 Inf, SS BS w/OLC
Pfc Bertram D Patch, 120 Inf, SS
S/Sgt Carson P Pate, 30 Sig, BS
1st Lt Isaiah S Pate, 117 Inf, BS w/OLC
Sgt Edwin O Patterson, 119 Inf, BS
Maj Fred G Patterson, 117 Inf SS BS
Lt Col George D Patterson, Sp Trps,
    BS w/2 OLC C d'G
Cpl J B Patterson, 823 TD, BS w/OLC
T/4 John B Patterson, 743 Tnk, BS w/OLC
S/Sgt Paul L Patterson, 743 Tnk, SS
Sgt Robert B Patterson, 120 Inf, SS
Pfc Edward P Patton, 120 Inf, BS C d'G
Pfc Hugh Patton, 117 Inf, BS
Cpl James C Patty, 230 FA, BS
Pfc Frank J Patullo, 117 Inf, BS
Sgt Rudolph Paukoucek, 120 Inf BS w/OLC
Cpl Edward P Paul, 743 Tnk, BS w/OLC
1st Sgt Philip L Paul, 113 FA, BS w/OLC
S/Sgt William L Paulick 120 Inf SS BS
Pfc Harry C Paulsen, 119 Inf, BS
Pfc Lou W Paulsen, 119 Inf, SS
Sgt Stanley A Pauly, 120 Inf, SS
Pfc Anthony Pavlidis, 119 Inf, BS
Pfc Anthony J Pavlik, 119 Inf BS
Sgt Alfred J Pawlick, 119 Inf, BS
T/Sgt Harley D Paxton, 119 Inf SS BS w/OLC
T/Sgt Clarence J Payne, 117 Inf, BS w/OLC
1st Lt Henry C Payne, 117 Inf, SS
Sgt James L Payne 230 FA BS
Pfc John W Payne Jr Div Hq, BS
T/5 Ralph Payne, 120 Inf, BS
T/5 William K Payne, 119 Inf, BS
S/Sgt Alva M Payton 531 AAA BS
Pfc Arthur L Peach 119 Inf, BS
WOJG Ele W Pearce 117 Inf, BS w/OLC
Pvt Jim A Pearce, 743 Tnk, SS
Pvt William A Pearce 117 Inf SS BS
1st Lt Albert F Pearsall, 608 QM, BS
Pfc Arthur L Pearson, 119 Inf BS
Pfc Charles W Pearson 120 Inf, BS
Pfc Delbert I Pearson, 117 Inf, BS
T/5 Elmer V Pearson, 743 Tnk, BS
1st Lt Frank O Pearson, 119 Inf, BS
Pfc Glenn L Pearson, 117 Inf BS
Pvt Glenn R Pearson, 119 Inf BS
T/5 Merlyn W Pearson, 120 Inf, BS
Cpl George J Pechmann, 743 Tnk, BS
Pvt James H Peck 119 Inf, BS
T/3 Thomas D Peck Spec Trps, BS
T/4 Peder B Pedersen, 105 Eng, BS
Pfc Edward B Peek, 105 Eng, BS
T/Sgt Clarence L Pegram, 120 Inf, BS
T/5 Franklin J Pehl, 743 Tnk, BS

1st Lt John V Pehovic, 526 Eng, BS
S/Sgt Glen E Peifer, 117 Inf, BS
Cpl Robert Peiffer, 120 Inf, BS
S/Sgt Stephen J Peine, 120 Inf, BS
T/4 John A Pekala, 120 Inf, BS
T/5 Joseph Pekar, 230 FA, BS w/OLC
WOJG Frank Pasquinucci, 120 Inf, BS
T/5 Frank B Pelkey Jr, 120 Inf, SS
Pvt Ralph L Pelky, 105 Eng BS
S/Sgt Harry S Peloquin, 119 Inf, BS
Cpl Lewis A Pelton, 120 Inf, BS
T/4 Berlie Pemberton, 119 Inf, BS
Pfc Stephen Pembroke, 119 Inf, BS
Sgt Tilford S Pence, 120 Inf, BS
Pfc Jack J Pendleton, 120 Inf, CMH
Pfc James C Pendleton, 119 Inf, BS
T/5 Dean F Penewit, 230 FA, SS BS
T/5 Dean F Penewit, 230 FA, SS BS
T/5 Lewis P Penn, 230 FA, BS
T/5 Edward E Pennington, 117 Inf, BS
S/Sgt Avery G Peoples, 113 FA, BS
Sgt Salvatore Pepe, 119 Inf, DSC
T/Sgt Rodney B Pepper, 30 Sig, BS
Sgt Wayne H Perdue, 120 Inf, SS
T/5 John Perez, 120 Inf, BS
Pfc Johnnie M Perez, 119 Inf, BS
S/Sgt Santos Perez, 117 Inf, BS
Lt Col David E Pergrin, 291 Eng, SS
Sgt Joseph Perko, 120 Inf, BS
Pfc Charles F Perkins, 120 Inf, SS w/OLC BS
T/5 Freeland J Perkins, 120 Inf, BS
Pfc Lincoln Perkins, 117 Inf, SS
Sgt Robert F Perlett, 30 QM, BS
S/Sgt Cecil M Permenter, 120 Inf, BS
Sgt Louis Perella, 119 Inf, SS
T/4 John C Perren, 823 TD, SS
2d Lt Arvel H Perry, 120 Inf, SS
T/Sgt Frank S Perry, 119 Inf, BS
M/Sgt Johnnie S Perry, 120 Inf, BS
Sgt Joseph E Perry, 120 Inf, BS
S/Sgt Joseph F Perry, 120 Inf, BS
Pfc Robert S Perry, 30 Sig, BS
Pfc Robert T Perry, 117 Inf, BS
1st Lt William T Perry, 117 Inf, BS
1st Lt Glyn N Persons, 120 Inf, BS
T/5 Wesley G Persons, 105 Med, BS
S/Sgt Francis W Perucki, 119 Inf, BS
Pfc Michael Perucki, 119 Inf, BS
Sgt Joseph E Pesak, 823 TD, SS
Sgt John G Pesola, 119 Inf, BS
1st Sgt George Petcoff, 119 Inf, BS
S/Sgt George Pete, 120 Inf, BS
Pfc Cloyd M Peters, 120 Inf, BS
2d Lt Harry R Peters, 120 Inf, BS w/3 OLC
Pfc Jack W Peters, 119 Inf, SS BS
Sgt James E Peters, 118 FA, SS w/OLC
Sgt Joseph E Peters, 30 MP, BS
S/Sgt Raymond W Peters, 105 Eng, BS
1st Lt Robert A Peters, 117 Inf, SS w/OLC
Pvt Donald E Petersen, 105 Eng, BS
S/Sgt Daniel W Peterson, 119 Inf, BS w/OLC
T/4 Edward W Peterson, Div Arty, BS
1st Lt Edwin R Peterson, 119 Inf, BS
T/5 Ehrmel G Peterson, 823 TD, SS
Pvt Evert E Peterson, 119 Inf, BS
T/Sgt Howard B Peterson, Hq 30 Div, BS
T/4 Leonard Peterson, 743 Tk, BS
Pvt Louis H Peterson, 120 Inf, SS
T/4 Richard K Peterson, 117 Inf, BS
Sgt William Peterson, 120 Inf, SS
S/Sgt William J Peterson, 119 Inf SS
Pfc Theodore H Peterworth, 105 Eng, BS
Sgt James A Peth, 120 Inf, BS
1st Lt Salvatore F Petinga, 120 Inf, BS w/OLC
M/Sgt Ashley L Petit, Div Hq, BS w/OLC
Pfc Jack L Petitt, 120 Inf, BS
Pfc Lawery Petitt, 120 Inf, SS
Sgt Bruno Petri, 197 FA, BS
Sgt Joseph M Petrik, 120 Inf, BS
Cpl Angelo S Petrina, 117 Inf, BS
T/5 Charles J Petro, 117 Inf, BS
Cpl Raymond W Petrosky, 197 FA, BS
T/5 Rocco D Petruzzi, 105 Eng, BS
M/Sgt Hugh E Pettigrew, 117 Inf, BS w/OLC

Pfc Daniel L Pettus, 119 Inf, BS
Pvt Raymond H Petty, 823 TD, BS
Sgt Roland D Peveto, 823 TD, BS
1st Lt Warren R Pfaff, 823 TD, SS BS
Pfc Bernard Pfeffer, 119 Inf, BS
Sgt John D Pfeifer, 120 Inf, BS
2d Lt William A Pfeil, 230 FA, AM w/3 OLC
Maj Vodra C Philips, 743 Tk, BS w/OLC
Pvt Fred Phillipp Jr, 117 Inf, BS
Pfc Charles F Phillips, 105 Med, BS
T/5 Edward Phillips, 117 Inf, BS
T/5 Francis H Phillips, 117 Inf, BS
Pvt Henry M Phillips, 117 Inf, BS
Sgt Henry O Phillips Jr, 230 FA, BS
T/Sgt Jeryl B Phillips, 117 Inf, BS
Sgt Jimmie F Phillips, 120 Inf, SS
S/Sgt Joe R Phillips, 119 Inf, BS
T/5 Paul H Phillips, 743 Tk, BS
Sgt Thomas J Phillips, 197 FA, BS
Pfc Troy H Phillips, 119 Inf, BS
Pfc Webster E Phillips, 117, Inf, BS w/2 OLC
Maj William T Phillips, 117 Inf, BS
Pfc Lorimer H Phillis, 119 Inf, BS
Pfc Robert V Phipps, 120 Inf, BS w/OLC
2d Lt Guy O Phleger, 230 FA, SS AM w/6 OLC
Pfc Robert E Phyfer, 119 Inf, BS w/OLC
Cpl William I Piatt, 743 Tk, BS
S/Sgt Dale G Pick, 120 Inf, SS BS
Pfc Walter L Pickard, 117 Inf, BS
Pfc Edward C Pickering, 30 MP, BS
S/Sgt William L Pickette, 119 Inf, DSC SS
S/Sgt Warren G H Pickler, 230 FA, BS
Pfc Chester A Piedzewich, 117 Inf, BS
Sgt Buell C Pieper, 117 Inf, BS
T/4 Henry B Pierce, Div Hq, BS
T/5 Keith W Pierce, 30 Rcn, BS
S/Sgt Mack W Pierce, 117 Inf, BS
Pfc Robert M Pierce, 105 Eng, BS w/OLC
T/Sgt William W Pierce, 119 Inf, BS
M/Sgt James E Piercy, 531 AAA, BS
Sgt Charles C Pierson, 120 Inf, BS
Pfc Glenn W Pierson, 120 Inf, SS
Pfc Julius C Piersch, 120 Inf, BS
Pfc Edward S Pierug, 119 Inf, SS
Pfc Stanley Pietras, 119 Inf, BS
1st Lt Charles B Pike, 120 Inf, SS
Pfc Donald G Pike, 119 Inf, SS
Pfc Fred Pike, 113 FA, BS
Pfc Joseph F Pillsbury, 120 Inf, BS
Pfc Elmer G Pilz, 117 Inf, BS w/OLC
Pvt Richard W Pimley, 120 Inf, BS
Capt Wilbur S Pinchbeck, Div Hq, BS w/OLC
S/Sgt Charles B Pinkston, 120 Inf, BS
Sgt Joseph S Pinnell, 113 FA, BS —
T/5 Roman J Pioter, 823 TD, BS
Pfc Frank S Piovek, 117 Inf, BS
S/Sgt Henry Pirth, 105 Med BS
T/Sgt Joseph J Pisciotta, 119 Inf, BS w/OLC
1st Lt Archie J Piscitello, 120 Inf, SS
Pvt Anthony F Pistilli, 119 Inf, DSC
Sgt William E Pitney, 120 Inf, BS
Cpl Joseph D Pitre, 197 FA, BS
Capt Harold M Pitt, 86 Chem, BS w/OLC
S/Sgt Jack A Pittman, 120 Inf, BS
Pfc Preston H Pittman, 117 Inf, BS
Cpl Joseph V Pitzer, 113 FA, BS —
Pfc John W Pivanik, 120 Inf, BS
T/Sgt George Placko, 119 Inf, BS w/OLC
Pfc Clarence J Placzek 105 Eng, BS
Pfc Carmen Plant, 117 Inf BS
Pfc Harold H Plasky, 743 Tk, BS
Pfc Richard S Platts, 117 Inf, BS
Pvt John H Playdon, 823 TD BS
T/5 Willard F Fletcher, 118 FA, SS
S/Sgt Ernest M Pletz 117 Inf, BS
CWO Gordon A Pleuthner 119 Inf, BS
T/4 Alfred J Plewes, 823 TD, BS
Capt Adolph C Ploehn, 125 Rcn, BS w/OLC
M/Sgt Wayne L Plott, 30 Sig, BS w/OLC
Pfc Francis Plourde, 120 Inf, BS
Capt Harold P Plummer, 120 Inf, BS
Sgt Carl W Plyler, 120 Inf, BS w/OLC
T/5 Victor J Poahllo, 119 Inf, BS
Pvt Anthony M Pocaro, 117 Inf, SS

T/4 Frank Podlesnik, 197 FA, BS
Pfc Joseph S Podrasky, 105 Med, BS
Pfc Leon Podrove, 120 Inf, BS
Pfc Edward L Poffi, 117 Inf, BS w/OLC
Pfc Bernard A Pogensky, 119 Inf, SS
Capt Bernard S Pogorel, 117 Inf, SS BS w/OLC
Pfc Clarence W Pohren, 105 Eng, BS
Pvt Thomas Poidomani, 117 Inf, BS
Pvt Vincent Poidomani, 230 FA, SS BS
S/Sgt William D Poindexter, 105 Med, BS
Sgt Oliver G Pointer, 105 Eng, SS
T/4 Ernest A Pokel, 117 Inf, BS w/OLC
T/5 Joseph P Pohorny, 743 Tk, BS SS
T/5 Maurice I Poland, 118 FA, BS
Pfc Louis P Polasek, 117 Inf, BS
Pvt Aldrich A Polehna, 117 Inf, BS
S/Sgt Micardy M Polick, 119 Inf, BS
T/5 Hurley M Poling, 119 Inf, BS
S/Sgt Andrew Polishuk, 120 Inf, BS
Pfc Charles E Politano, 119 Inf, BS
Pvt Salvatore A Polito, 117 Inf, BS
Pvt Joseph Pollack, 119 Inf, SS BS
T/5 Howard F Pollard, 117 Inf, BS
Capt Ray H Pollom, 119 Inf BS
Pvt John Polowchak, 120 Inf, SS
Pfc John J Polselli, 120 Inf, BS
S/Sgt Cecil P Polston, 117 Inf, BS
Pfc Albert J Polyansky, 120 Inf, BS
T/5 James S Pomeroy, 743 Tk, BS
Sgt Charles E Pomper, 120 Inf, BS
Pfc Stephen L Pomykala, 117 Inf, BS w/2 OLC
Pfc Ralph W Poncelet, 120 Inf, BS
Sgt Joseph S Poniatowski, 117 Inf, BS
Pvt Donald L Pontius, 117 Inf, BS
S/Sgt Marvin Poole, 730 Ord BS
1st Lt Herbert G Poppe, 117 Inf SS BS
T/4 Joe Poremba, 117 Inf, BS
T/3 Alexander H Porter, Finance, BS
T/Sgt James W Porter, 120 Inf, BS
T/5 Lester J Porter, 120 Inf, BS
S/Sgt Thomas B Porter, 197 FA, BS
T/Sgt Raymond J Posch, 117 Inf, BS
Pfc Jesse A Posey, 117 Inf, BS
Capt Gerald E Posner, 119 Inf, SS w/OLC BS
Pvt Chester I Poss, 117 Inf, BS
Cpl John J Pothoff, 120 Inf, BS
Pfc Raymond L Potter, 117 Inf, BS
Pfc William J Potter, 105 Eng, BS
Sgt George L Potts, 119 Inf, SS BS w/OLC
Pfc Ernest H Pouhot, 117 Inf, SS BS
S/Sgt Gregg N Pouliot, 743 Tk, BS
T/5 Daniel R Poutas, 120 Inf, SS BS w/OLC
1st Lt Harold D Powe, 117 Inf, BS
Sgt Cecil C Powell, 117 Inf, SS
Sgt Charles E Powell, 118 FA, BS w/OLC
T/4 Delaware M Powell, 230 FA, SS BS
Pfc Fulton Powell, 119 Inf, BS
Pfc James Powell, 197 FA, BS
Cpl Raymond T Powell, 117 Inf, BS
Capt Richard L Powell, 197 FA, BS
Sgt William A Powell, 119 Inf, BS
S/Sgt William R Powell Jr, 197 FA, BS w/OLC
2d Lt Charles B Powers, 740 Tk, SS
Maj James P Powers Jr, Div Hq, BS w/OLC
T/5 Samuel J Powvall, 119 Inf, BS
T/5 Heimmo H Poykko, 743 Tk BS
Pfc Gilbert W Poynter, 119 Inf, BS
S/Sgt Elroy F Prample, 120 Inf, BS
Pfc Michael S Prascak, 117 Inf, BS w/OLC
Capt Charles A Prater, 744 Tk, BS
Sgt Bernard S Pratt, 120 Inf, SS BS
Pfc James W Pratt, 120 Inf, BS
T/5 Walter H Pratt 117 Inf BS
Pvt George Preble 743 Tk, BS
S/Sgt Turner W Preddy 119 Inf BS
Cpl Henry L Prejean, 743 Tk, BS
Capt John E Prejean, 117 Inf, SS BS
Pfc David E Prendergast '117 Inf, BS
Sgt Henry B Prenger, 120 Inf SS w/OLC
1st Lt Chester H Prentice, 30 Rcn,
      SS BS w/2 OLC
Pvt Peter Preslipskv, 117 Inf, DSC C d'G
1st Sgt William G Presnell, 120 Inf BS
S/Sgt James T Pressnell, 119 Inf, BS

Sgt Roy G Preston, 823 TD, BS w/OLC
T/5 Francis S Previtali 30 Div Arty, BS
T/5 Benjamin H Prewitte, 120 Inf, SS
M/Sgt Otto E Pribram, Div Hq, BS
S/Sgt Calvin C Price, 113 FA, BS —
T/5 Emrose E Price, 743 Tk, BS
Sgt Henry F Price, 120 Inf, SS
Pfc James R Price, 120 Inf, BS
Pvt John W Price, 119 Inf, BS
Sgt Joseph E Price, 119 Inf, SS
Pfc J W Price, 105 Med, BS
Pfc Melvin T Price, 119 Inf, BS w/OLC
S/Sgt Ralph R Price Jr, 120 Inf, BS
S/Sgt William H Price, 120 Inf, BS
Pfc Philip Priemazon, 120 Inf, BS w/2 OLC
Pvt Ralph E Prier, 230 FA, BS
Pfc Walter G Prieve, 99 Inf, BS
S/Sgt Charles S Prince, 119 Inf, BS w/2 OLC
Cpl Arthur L Prior, 119 Inf, BS
T/5 Michael C Prisco, 120 Inf, BS
Capt Charles E Pritchard, 120 Inf, SS BS
Pfc James M Pritchard, 119 Inf, BS w/OLC
Pvt Mac D Pritchard, 117 Inf, BS
1st Sgt Roy M Pritchard, 30 QM, BS
S/Sgt Clyde V Proby, 119 Inf, SS
Pfc Charles L Prochaska, 117 Inf, BS
T/5 Robert L Proctor, 105 Eng, SS BS
Sgt Bavil Proffitt, 120 Inf, BS
T/5 Alfred T Proulx, 105 Eng, BS
T/3 Irving J Proulx, 30 Sig, BS
Cpl William F Prucha, 120 Inf, BS
T/4 James H Pruette, 691 FA, BS w/2 OLC
S/Sgt Frank H Pruitt, 120 Inf, BS
Cpl Tommie S Pruitt, 120 Inf, SS
S/Sgt Steven Psiliopoulos, 119 Inf, BS
Pfc John A Pszenny, 117 Inf, BS
1st Lt Andrew T Pucalik, 230 FA, BS
Sgt Francis G Puckett, 117 Inf, BS w/OLC
Sgt Paul Pudelka, 120 Inf, SS w/OLC
Pfc Donald Pudney, 119 Inf, SS
Pvt Emmett W Pugh Jr, 117 Inf, BS
Cpl Benjamin P Pugliese, 105 Eng, BS w/OLC
S/Sgt Michael F Pugliese, 119 Inf, BS
Sgt Steve J Puhalla, 119 Inf, SS BS MM
Pfc Charles N Pullen, 119 Inf, BS w/OLC
Pfc John J Pullin, 119 Inf, SS
Pfc James M Pulley, 117 Inf, BS
Pvt Elmo D Pulver, 119 Inf BS
1st Lt Murray S Pulver, 120 Inf,
        DSC SS BS w/OLC
Sgt James Purcell 120 Inf BS
Col Branner P Purdue, 120 Inf,
        LM SS w/2 OLC BS w/OLC C d'G
1st Lt John F Purdum, Div Hq, BS
Capt John A Purvis, 197 FA, BS
Sgt Carl E Putt, 117 Inf, BS
Pfc Ben H Quarles, 117 Inf, BS
Pvt James D Quarles 117 Inf, BS w/OLC
Pfc Norman Queler, 25 FA, BS
Sgt Karl E Quesenberry 119 Inf, BS w/OLC
Pfc Mike Quezada, 117 Inf, BS
Sgt John F Quick, 118 FA BS
Sgt Charles O Quimley, 117 Inf BS
Pfc Daniel R Quinn, 119 Inf, BS
Lt Col Daniel W Quinn, 119 Inf, SS
S/Sgt John J Quinn, 120 Inf, BS
S/Sgt John Rabreau, 120 Inf, DSC
Pfc Vern D Race, 113 FA, BS —
Pfc Gaston J Racette, 120 Inf, BS
Pfc Hubert H Racette, 120 Inf, BS
Pfc Dennis V Raciot, 117 Inf, BS w/OLC
Cpl Samuel C Racina, 119 Inf, BS
Sgt Lawrence E Radcliff, 119 Inf, BS
Sgt Robert W Radcliffe 120 Inf, BS w/OLC
Pfc David I Rae, 119 Inf, SS
S/Sgt Francis E Rafferty, 120 Inf, BS
Sgt Vincent J Rafferty, 119 Inf, SS BS
Pfc Floyd E Ragan, 120 Inf, BS
Pfc Orville R Ragan, 119 Inf, BS
S/Sgt Jess J Ragucci, 117 Inf, BS
S/Sgt Andrew P Rahart, 119 Inf, SS
Pfc Thomas J Raia, 119 Inf, SS w/OLC
T/Sgt Richard E Raimes, 119 Inf, BS

Pfc Edmund Raimbolt, 119 Inf, BS
Cpl William A Rainbolt, 230 FA, SS
Pfc Albert T Raith Jr, 117 Inf, SS
Pfc George J Rajher, 283 FA, BS
S/Sgt William L Ralston, 120 Inf, BS
S/Sgt Howard E Ramaley, 120 Inf, BS
2d Lt Robert J Ramberg, 230 FA, SS w/OLC
Sgt Joseph C Ramholz, 119 Inf, BS
Pfc Alfredo Ramirez, 120 Inf, BS w/OLC
Pfc John Ramos, 117 Inf, BS
Pfc George E Ramoth, 117 Inf, BS
T/4 Robert J Ramsay, 117 Inf, SS
Maj Jay O Rand, 691 FA, BS
Sgt Woodrow C Randolph, 117 Inf, BS
1st Lt Thompson L Raney, 823 TD, SS BS
Pfc Louis R Rangel, 120 Inf, BS w/OLC
Pfc James L Rapin, 120 Inf, BS
S/Sgt Albert A Rapini, 120 Inf, SS BS
T/3 Elton E Rapp, Hq 30 Div, BS
T/4 Clarence A Rasmusson, 743 Tk, SS BS
T/4 Victor J Rassier, 743 Tk, BS
Pfc William T Rath, 823 TD, BS
T/Sgt Milton E Ratliff, 117 Inf, BS
Sgt William L Ratliff, 30 QM, BS
S/Sgt Kenneth R Rau, 117 Inf, BS
T/4 Alex L Rasmussen, 531 AAA, BS
Pfc Remo Ravera, 119 Inf, BS
1st Lt Gilbert M Ray, 105 Eng, SS
Pfc James B Ray, 120 Inf, BS
1st Sgt James C Ray, 120 Inf, BS
Pfc Robert L Rayhon, 117 Inf, BS
Sgt Arthur J Raymond, 117 Inf, BS
S/Sgt Robert L Reagan, 118 FA, BS
T/4 Perry W Reams, 743 Tk, SS BS
Capt Joseph C Reaser, 120 Inf, DSC SS BS C d'G
S/Sgt Ferdinand Rebechini, 119 Inf, BS
Sgt Maximilian R Recher, Div Arty, BS
Pfc Ira C Recs, 117 Inf, SS
Pvt Richard H Reddinger, 119 Inf, BS
Sgt Robert E Reddington, 117 Inf, BS
T/5 Marvin W Redick, 30 Rcn, BS
Cpl Nolan W Redington, 120 Inf, BS
S/Sgt James J Redmond, 117 Inf, BS
Pfc Robert W Redshaw, 117 Inf, BS
Pfc Wesley W Redwine, 117 Inf BS
S/Sgt William B Redwine, 119 Inf, SS
Sgt Claude C Reed, 120 Inf, BS
Sgt Clayton H Reed, 117 Inf, BS
Pfc David E Reed, 197 FA, BS
Pvt David I Reed, 117 Inf, BS
S/Sgt George A Reed 117 Inf BS
T/5 James M Reed, 117 Inf, BS
T/4 Keith E Reed 743 Tk, BS
Pvt Lester L Reed. 119 Inf, BS
1st Sgt Orville Reed, 119 Inf, BS
Pfc Ralph C Reed, 119 Inf, BS
Pfc Robert R Reed, 120 Inf, SS
T/Sgt Charles H Reese, 117 Inf, BS
Pfc Glen W Reese, 119 Inf, BS
Pfc James D Reese, 120 Inf, BS
Pfc Joe Reese, 119 Inf, BS
1st Lt John H Reese, 119 Inf, BS
T/3 Roy B Reese, 730 Ord, BS
Pvt Henry W Reeveas, 823 TD SS
1st Lt George R Reeves, 120 Inf, SS w/2 OLC
S/Sgt Lewis A Reeves, 117 Inf BS
1st Lt Whitney O Refvem, 117 Inf,
        SS BS w/OLC
Pfc Charles H Regal, 105 Eng, BS
Sgt Arthur J Regan, 117 Inf, BS w/OLC
Sgt Frank D Regan, Div Arty, BS
Pfc Mario T Reghitto, 117 Inf, BS
Pfc Harvey A Rehder, 120 Inf, BS
Capt George D Rehkopf, 119 Inf, BS
S/Sgt Ted Reid, 120 Inf, BS
T/Sgt John T Reidy, Hq 30 Div, BS
Pfc Junior Reif, 120 Inf, BS
Pfc Eugene C Reigel, 120 Inf, BS
2d Lt Elmer V Reilly, 117 Inf, BS
T/5 Clyde D Reimler, 119 Inf, BS w/OLC
Capt Allen P Reininger, 92 Chem, BS
T/4 Bernhard Reitstetter, 117 Inf, BS
T/Sgt Edward R Reitz, 119 Inf, BS
S/Sgt Donald B Releford, 119 Inf, BS

Cpl Joseph W Rembisz, 105 Eng, BS
Pfc Paul E Remwolt, 119 Inf, SS
T/5 Kenneth L Remy, Hq 30 Div, BS
Sgt Maurice D Reney, 117 Inf, BS w/OLC
Pfc Marshall H Renfro, 823 TD, BS
Pfc William B Renfroe, 120 Inf, BS
Sgt Albert L Renner, 120 Inf, SS
T/Sgt John Rescigno, 120 Inf, SS
Cpl John W Restad, 743 Tk, BS
Capt Clinton E Restamayer, 118 FA, SS BS
Capt Gordon E Reupke, 118 FA,
    SS BS w/3 OLC
Pvt Simon Revak, 119 Inf, BS
T/Sgt Abbie Reviere, 117 Inf, SS w/OLC BS
S/Sgt Arion Revis, 823 TD, SS
T/5 Walter S Revis, 197 FA, BS
Pvt Cecil L Rewis, 120 Inf, BS
Pfc Oscar R Reyes, 119 Inf, BS
Pfc James C Reynolds, 119 Inf, BS
S/Sgt Alton R Reynolds, 118 FA, BS
Cpl Charles L Reynolds, 743 Tk, BS
1st Lt John W Reynolds, 117 Inf, SS w/OLC
Lt Col Joseph H Reynolds, 120 Inf, BS
Pvt Raymond E Reynolds, 120 Inf, BS
Pvt Varnon D Reynolds, 119 Inf, SS BS
Cpl Claude Rhame, 117 Inf, BS
S/Sgt Howard W Rhein, 117 Inf, BS
Pfc Howard R Rhine, 117 Inf, BS
Pfc Daniel L Rhoades, 119 Inf, BS
T/3 Harold H Rhodes, Hq 30 Div, BS
S/Sgt Roy W Rhoten, 119 Inf, SS
T/Sgt Jacob M Rhyne, 120 Inf, BS w/OLC
Pfc Michael Ricciardi, 119 Inf, BS
Pfc Alfred V Riccio, 117 Inf, SS
T/4 Arthur L Rice, Hq 30 Div, BS
Capt James F Rice, 105 Eng,
    SS w/OLC BS w/OLC
T/5 William M Rice, 113 FA, BS
T/4 Wilson E Rice, Hq 30 Div, BS
2d Lt Barney K Rich, 230 FA, BS
Capt Charles F Rich, Div Arty, BS
2d Lt Jesse W Rich, 119 Inf, BS w/2 OLC
Sgt Murray Rich, 119 Inf BS
S/Sgt Julian P Richard, 823 TD, BS
Sgt Clifford A Richards, 113 FA, SS BS
Pvt Donald S Richards, 120 Inf, BS
Pfc Earl V Richards, 120 Inf, SS
Sgt Eli N Richards, 823 TD, BS
Sgt Harold R Richards, 113 Cav, SS
Pfc James Richards Jr, 117 Inf, BS
Pfc Mearl E Richards, 117 Inf, BS
1st Lt William F Richards, 117 Inf, SS BS
Pfc Cecil C Richardson, 120 Inf, SS
Pfc Cleo W Richardson, 120 Inf, BS
S/Sgt Harold A Richardson, 119 Inf BS
S/Sgt Leon O Richardson, 119 Inf, BS
Sgt Lowell L Richardson, 105 Eng,
    SS BS w/OLC
Pfc Marion R Richardson, 120 Inf, SS
T/3 Ralph R Richardson, 120 Inf, BS
Pfc Raymond E Richardson, 119 Inf, BS
Pfc Hans Richert, 119 Inf, SS
Pfc Edmondo Richiedei, 119 Inf SS
Pvt Ralph B Richey, 105 Eng, BS
Pfc William W Richey, 118 FA, BS
Pfc Sterling J Richner, 531 AAA, BS
S/Sgt Bergie J Rickard, 119 Inf, SS
Pfc Paul K Rickenbaugh, 120 Inf, BS w/OLC
Pfc Leonard L Rickert, 119 Inf, BS
Pvt Carl N Riddle, 117 Inf, BS
T/Sgt Edward N Rider, 119 Inf, BS
T/5 Vernon W Rider, 117 Inf, BS
1st Sgt Robert J Ridings, 117 Inf, SS BS
Capt Edward L Rieff, 531 AAA BS
Pfc William J Rieger, 117 Inf, BS
Pfc Carl P Ries, 197 FA, BS
1st Lt Melvin L Riesch, 119 Inf, SS
Pfc Raymond L Riffle, 117 Inf, SS
Sgt James E Riggan, 120 Inf BS w/OLC
M/Sgt John W Riggan 105 Med BS
T/4 Finis G Riggins, 117 Inf BS
Pfc David L Riggle 823 TD, BS
S/Sgt Kalorvo R Rikalva, 120 Inf, SS
Pfc Earl R Riley, 119 Inf, BS

S/Sgt Francis J Riley, 120 Inf, SS
Pvt Warren N Riley, 120 Inf, BS
Pfc William E Riley, 117 Inf, BS
Pfc Gerald S Rinaca, 119 Inf, BS
Pfc Beyrl B Rinard, 120 Inf, SS
Pvt Walter G Rine, 119 Inf, BS
T/5 Frank D Rinella, 105 Med, BS
Pfc Emery W Ring, 117 Inf, BS
Sgt Herbert C Ringheim, 743 Tk, BS
Pfc Salvatore A Rini, 117 Inf, BS
Pfc Frederick E Rinker, 120 Inf, BS
Pvt Cosmo L Riozzi, 120 Inf, BS
T/5 Moderille J Ripley, 113 FA, BS
T/4 Albert A Risaliti, 105 Med, BS
T/Sgt Walter L Risinger, 197 FA, BS
Capt Richard A Risser, 105 Med, BS
M/Sgt Haran R Ritchie, 230 FA, BS
Pfc James F Ritter, 120 Inf, SS
Pfc Cruz B Rivera, 119 Inf, BS
S/Sgt Furney M Rivers, 120 Inf, BS w/OLC
Pfc Joseph A Riviello, 117 Inf, SS
T/3 Harold E Rix, Div Arty, BS
Pfc Joseph N Rizzo, 823 TD, BS
S/Sgt Louis R Rizzo, 120 Inf, BS
Cpl Matale S Rizzotte, 105 Eng, SS
Pfc Charles E Roach, 117 Inf, BS
S/Sgt James F Roach, 120 Inf, BS
T/4 Simeon A Roach, 823 TD, BS
2d Lt Quentin W H Robb, 117 Inf, BS
S/Sgt Harris Robbe, 531 AAA, BS w/OLC
Capt Lee D Robbins, 531 AAA, BS
Sgt Robert C Robbins, 120 Inf, BS
T/Sgt Lambert J Roberson, 117 Inf, SS
Pfc Robert A Roberson, 117 Inf, SS BS
1st Lt Allen E Roberts, 117 Inf, BS w/OLC
S/Sgt Edwin A Roberts, 120 Inf, BS
Pfc Francis F Roberts, 117 Inf, SS
Pfc George J Roberts, 117 Inf, BS
Pfc Harry W Roberts, 117 Inf, BS w/OLC
S/Sgt Homer D Roberts, 30 Rcn, BS
Pfc James A Roberts, 119 Inf, BS
S/Sgt Eugene B Roberts, 119 Inf, BS
T/Sgt John S Roberts, 117 Inf, SS
Pfc Joseph A Roberts, 105 Med, BS
S/Sgt Lester Roberts, 119 Inf, SS
Capt Wendell A Roberts, Div Arty, BS
S/Sgt Wesley R Roberts, 117 Inf, BS
2d Lt Ervin E Robertson, 118 FA, BS w/OLC
T/3 George G Robertson, 120 Inf, BS
Pvt George O Robertson, 275 Armd FA, BS
1st Lt Gordon H Robertson Jr, 117 Inf, BS
T/Sgt Guy E Robertson, 119 Inf, SS
T/5 Guy R Robertson, 743 Tk, SS BS
Sgt Joseph L Robertson, 30 Rcn, BS w/OLC
Pvt William G Robertson, 120 Inf, SS
Sgt Herman Robinette, 730 Ord, BS
T/5 Alfred Robino, 117 Inf, SS
Pfc Anthony Robino, 117 Inf, SS
Pvt Carl E Robinson, 105 Eng, BS
Sgt Clyde R Robinson, 119 Inf, BS
1st Sgt Frank E Robinson, 117 Inf, BS
1st Lt Glen L Robinson, 120 Inf, BS
S/Sgt Harry L Robinson, 119 Inf, BS
T/Sgt Henry Robinson, 30 Sig, BS
S/Sgt Henry D Robinson, 730 Ord, BS
S/Sgt Rawl O Robinson, 117 Inf, BS
Sgt Raymond J Robinson, 119 Inf BS
Capt Theodore K Robinson, 30 QM, BS w/OLC
Sgt James H Robison, 119 Inf, SS
Pfc Joseph F Robrecht, 120 Inf, SS BS
Pfc Everett T Robson, 120 Inf SS
1st Lt Richard B Roche, 230 FA, SS BS
2d Lt George J Rochelle, French Army, BS
Maj Julius Rock, 105 Med, BS
Pfc Eldon R Rockafello, 120 Inf, BS
T/Sgt Cornelius E Rockenstyre, 117 Inf,
    BS w/OLC
S/Sgt Richard W Rockett, 823 TD, BS
S/Sgt Gilbert A Rockhold, 117 Inf, BS
1st Lt Dudley N Rockwell, 117 Inf, BS w/OLC
T/5 Donald C Roddy, 119 Inf, BS
Pfc Joseph S Roddy, 117 Inf, BS
T/5 David B Rodger, 113 FA, BS
T/Sgt Duane O Rodgers, 119 Inf, BS w/OLC

Maj Wesley L Rogerson, 119 Inf, BS
Pfc Ray N Rodman, 117 Inf, BS
Maj Wiley C Rodman Jr, 113 FA, BS
T/5 Alfred P Rodoni, 119 Inf, BS
Capt Exor M Rodriquez, 105 Eng, BS
Pfc John A Roffi, 117 Inf, BS
Pvt Cecil E Rogers, 258 FA, BS
S/Sgt Cecil W Rogers, 119 Inf, BS
1st Lt Frank A Rogers, 120 Inf, SS
S/Sgt Fred A Rogers, 117 Inf, BS
S/Sgt Garland W Rogers, 105 Eng, BS
T/5 James D Rogers, 197 FA, BS w/OLC
T/Sgt Marshall B Rogers, 120 Inf, BS w/OLC
T/Sgt Max Q Rogers, 30 Sig, BS
Pfc Philip J Rogers, 119 Inf, BS
Pfc Robert S Rogers, 117 Inf, BS
2d Lt Wilford O Rogers, 744 Tk, BS
Sgt William W Rogers, 197 FA, BS
T/5 Alvin V Roggenkamp, Div Arty, BS
Pfc Joseph J Rogowski, 105 Eng, BS
Sgt Joseph D Roguski, 744 Tk, BS
2d Lt Eugene F Rohatsch, 823 Tk, BS w/OLC
Pfc Aubrey L Roher Jr, 105 Eng, BS
1st Lt Elmer C Rohmiller, 120 Inf, SS BS
Maj Ernest B Roland, 1153 Eng, BS
Pfc Arthur D Rolfe, 117 Inf, BS
Pvt Charles E Rolland, 118 FA, SS
Sgt William E Rolland Jr, 120 Inf, SS
S/Sgt Clarence C Rollins, 117 Inf, BS
1st Lt Samuel S Rolph, 197 FA, BS
Cpl Arthur Romano, 118 FA, BS
Pfc Bolaiz C Romero, 117 Inf, BS
Pfc Edward P Romero, Div Arty, BS
Pfc Jean L Romero, 119 Inf, BS
Sgt Michael Rominyk, 105 Med, BS
Pfc Benny J Ronciglione, 113 FA, SS
T/4 Claude E Rondeau, 118 FA,
      SS w/OLC BS w/OLC
T/5 Thomas W Rondina, 117 Inf, BS
Sgt Maurice D Roney, 117 Inf, BS
T/Sgt Myron H Ronnberg, 743 Tk, BS
Pvt Bethel A Rood, 120 Inf, BS
Pfc Carl V Rook, 30 Sig, BS
Pfc Stephen L Ropko, 117 Inf, BS w/OLC
Pfc Hallie A Rorrer, 119 Inf, BS
S/Sgt Anthony J Rosa, 119 Inf, BS
Pfc Dominic N Rosa, 120 Inf, BS
Cpl David C Rose, 120 Inf, BS
M/Sgt Elliot E Rose, 120 Inf, BS w/OLC
Pfc Elmer Rose, 117 Inf BS
Pvt Elmer G Rose, 120 Inf, BS
T/5 Frederick M Rose, 743 Tk, SS
1st Sgt James K Rose, 113 FA, BS
Pvt Norman M Rose, 119 Inf, BS
1st Lt Ray R Rose, 117 Inf, SS
Pvt Robert Rose, 117 Inf, SS
Pvt Waymon D Rose, 119 Inf, BS
Pfc Norman D Rosenberg, 119 Inf, BS w/OLC
2d Lt Elmer G Rosenberger, 113 FA,
      AM w/3 OLC
Pfc Louis Rosenfeld, 120 Inf BS
Pfc Karl G Rosenquist, 120 Inf BS
Pfc Alexander Rosenthal 117 Inf, BS
Pvt John E Rosich, 30 MP, BS
S/Sgt Louis Rosolia, 119 Inf, BS
Pfc Charles D Ross, 119 Inf, BS
T/5 Clifford G Ross, 120 Inf, BS
S/Sgt Frank J Ross 119 Inf, BS
S/Sgt Raymond W Ross, 119 Inf, BS
T/5 William F Rosselot, 117 Inf, BS
T/4 Ernest A Rossi, 105 Eng, BS
T/4 Garnett W Rosson, 120 Inf, BS w/OLC
Sgt Howard W Roszell, 743 Tk, BS
Pvt Anton J Rotchadl, 119 Inf, SS
S/Sgt Ray A Rothaar, 120 Inf, BS w/OLC
Sgt Raymond Rotondo, 823 TD BS w/OLC
Cpl Lawrence R Rouden, 119 Inf, BS
Pfc Gus Rouff, 120 Inf, BS
Pfc Charles W Rountree Jr, 120 Inf, BS
S/Sgt Vernon E Roush, 117 Inf, BS
S/Sgt Garnett M Rowden 119 Inf, BS w/OLC
Pfc Willard F Rowe, 119 Inf, BS
Pfc Edward J Rowland, 117 Inf, BS
Pfc Granville W Rowland, 117 Inf, BS w/OLC

1st Lt Hugh G Rowland, 736 Tk, BS
Pfc Kenneth E Rowley, 120 Inf, SS, BS
Pvt Roy G Rowton, 531 AAA, BS
Pfc Frank J Roy, 743 Tk, BS
Capt Lester D Royalty, 117 Inf, BS w/OLC
Cpl Norman W Roylance, 743 Tk, BS
Lt Col George K Rubel, 740 Tk, BS
T/5 Bennett Rubenstein, 113 FA, BS
Pfc Anthony F Rubino, 117 Inf, BS w/OLC
Pfc Felix R Rubio, 119 Inf, BS
S/Sgt Woodrow Rucker, 119 Inf, SS BS
Pfc Raleigh W Rudd, 120 Inf, BS
Capt Richard S Rude, 117 Inf, BS
1st Lt Robert C Rudell, 117 Inf, BS
T/5 Andrew V Ruder, 197 FA, BS
T/5 Frank J Ruditys, 119 Inf, BS
Sgt Lawrenson C Rue, 30 Div Hq, BS
Capt Edwin Rufenacht, 119 Inf, SS BS
T/4 Socrates Ruffus, 120 Inf, BS
Pfc Joseph J Ruggiero, 119 Inf, BS
Pfc Louis Ruiz, 120 Inf, BS
2d Lt Harold C Ruland, 747 Tk, BS
Pfc Alva W Rule, 117 Inf, BS
Sgt Nelson L Ruling, 120 Inf, BS w/OLC
Sgt John R Rumble, 120 Inf, BS
Sgt Hurchial G Runnels, 119 Inf, SS
T/5 Arthur C Ruse, 113 Cav BS
T/4 George A Rushing, 113 FA, BS
Sgt Donald E Russ, 743 TD, SS
T/4 Tomlinson R Russ, 118 FA, SS
Capt Archie E Russell, 531 AAA, BS
T/5 Arthur A Russell, 119 Inf, BS
1st Lt Curtis L Russell, 197 FA, BS
Pfc Elsie L Russell, 120 Inf, BS
Pfc John B Russell, 120 Inf, BS
1st Sgt Joseph E Rullell, 230 FA, BS w/OLC
WOJG Leon Russell, 743 Tk, BS
Pfc Lewis W Russell, 117 Inf, BS
S/Sgt Albert L Russo, 30 MP, BS
T/5 Henry P Russo, 120 Inf, BS
Sgt Sebastian M Russo, 30 QM, BS
T/5 Thomas W Russum, 117 Inf, BS w/OLC
Pfc Allen D Rust, 119 Inf, BS
Pfc Willis V Ruth, 119 Inf, BS
T/3 Calvin R Rutherford, 120 Inf, BS
S/Sgt Albert Rutman, 120 Inf, SS
T/5 Denzil W Ruyle, 118 FA, BS
Capt James F Ryan, 197 FA, BS
Capt James W Ryan, 120 Inf, SS
S/Sgt Thomas J Ryan, 120 Inf, BS
Pfc Chester W Rybak, 105 Eng, BS
Pfc Stanley R Rychnovsky, 120 Inf, BS
T/5 Richard L Ryder, 117 Inf, BS
Pfc Chester L Rymszewicz, 119 Inf, BS
Pfc Thomas E Rynn, 117 Inf BS
1st Lt Arthur J Saalfield, 120 Inf,
      SS w/OLC BS
S/Sgt Siegfried S Sabarsky, 119 Inf, BS
Sgt William C Sabella, 105 Eng, BS
Sgt Joseph E Sabith, 119 Inf, BS
Pfc Louis A Saccomanno, 119 Inf, SS BS
T/5 Joseph A Saccon, 120 Inf, BS
Capt Elias A Sadallah, 119 Inf, SS
Pvt George A Saddig, 113 FA, BS
Cpl Wilbur H Sadler, 230 FA, SS BS
S/Sgt Milo R Safar, 119 Inf, BS
Pfc Ivan N Sager, 119 Inf, BS w/OLC
Pfc Paul L Sager, 119 Inf, BS
T/4 John B Salaga, 120 Inf, BS w/OLC
Capt Victor Salem, 117 Inf, SS w/2 OLC BS
Pfc Joseph J Salkowski, 120 Inf, BS
Cpl Grady Salmons, 120 Inf, SS
Pvt Thomas L Salmons, 117 Inf, BS
Sgt Kenneth F Saltsgaver, 531 AAA, BS
Pvt Ross S Salve, 117 Inf, BS
Sgt Michael Sammaciccia, 120 Inf, BS
Sgt Gino J Sammaritano, 117 Inf, BS
S/Sgt Michael G Sampieri, 117 Inf, SS w/OLC
Pfc David J Samples, 119 Inf, SS
T/4 Emil H Samuels, 117 Inf, BS
Sgt Francisco D Sanchez, 120 Inf, BS w/OLC
Pfc Salvador M Sanchez, 531 AAA, BS
Capt Robert K Sandager, 531 AAA, BS w/OLC
Pfc Huston A Sandel, 823 TD, BS

1st Lt Dewey J Sandell Jr, 823 TD, SS
Cpl Claude L Sanders, 230 FA, BS
Pfc John W Sanders, 119 Inf, SS
Sgt Thomas D Sanders, 119 Inf, SS
Pvt William D Sanders, 117 Inf, SS
Pvt Frank A Sandillo, 119 Inf, BS
T/5 Martin Sandolino, 118 FA, BS
S/Sgt Erick Sandor, 230 FA, BS w/2 OLC
1st Sgt Charlie B Sandoval, 823 TD, BS
Pfc Phillip Sandoval, 119 Inf, SS
1st Lt Dominic San Filippo, 117 Inf, BS
T/5 Angelo J Santangelo, 117 Inf, BS
Pfc Joseph J Santangelo, 120 Inf, BS
Sgt Donald J Santella, 120 Inf, DSC
Sgt Jesse Santanna, 120 Inf, BS
Pfc Nestore S Santini, 30 Sig, BS
T/5 Pasquale N Santivasci, 118 FA, SS BS
T/3 Graef J Santmier, 117 Inf, BS
T/4 George A Santos, 120 Inf BS
T/4 Louis A Santucci, 120 Inf, BS
Pvt Louis A Saporito, 113 FA, SS
S/Sgt George W Sapp, 119 Inf, BS
Maj John D Sapp, 283 FA, BS
Pfc Raymond S Sarnowski, 120 Inf, BS
Pfc Joseph Sartorio, 117 Inf, BS w/OLC
S/Sgt Charles G Sasher, 119 Inf, BS
T/4 Armon A Sasser, 230 FA, SS BS
Pfc Sverre O Satre, 99 Inf, SS
1st Lt Irvin Sattler, 119 Inf, BS
Pfc Paul M Saucier, 118 FA, BS
Pfc Harold V Sauer, 119 Inf, BS
Sgt James H Sauer, 119 Inf, BS
Sgt Joseph W Saur, 119 Inf, BS
Pfc Norris A Savage, 117 Inf, BS
T/4 Carl E Savard, 118 FA, BS w/OLC
Pvt Tony Sawicky, 119 Inf, SS w/OLC
S/Sgt Frederick O Sawyer, 120 Inf, DSC BS
Maj James L Sawyer, Div Hq, BS
Capt Kenneth T Sawyer, 295 Eng, BS
Pfc Vernon L Sawyer, 120 Inf, SS
Sgt Allan E Sawyers, 120 Inf, BS
Pfc Sherman Sayer, 117 Inf BS
2d Lt Warren C Sayers, 118 FA,
      SS AM w/5 OLC
Sgt George W Saylors, 120 Inf, BS
Sgt Gerald E Sayre, 119 Inf, BS w/OLC
Pfc Louis R Sberna, 230 FA, BS w/OLC
S/Sgt Alvin A Scallion, 117 Inf, BS
1st Lt Jerome E Scanlon, 400 FA, AM
Cpl Walter Scarborough, 119 Inf SS BS
Sgt Elno M Schacher, 743 Tk, BS
T/Sgt Edwin J Schaeffer, 119 Inf, SS BS
Pvt Gerald Schafer, 119 Inf, BS
T/Sgt Bernard Schaffer, 120 Inf, BS
Pvt Herbert F Schain, 120 Inf, SS BS w/OLC
T/4 Stephen N Schanzer, 105 Med, BS
Sgt Carl C Schaudt, 117 Inf, SS
Pfc Lawrence Scheel, 120 Inf, SS
S/Sgt Joseph A Scheiwe, 119 Inf, BS
S/Sgt Donald R Schemensky, 119 Inf, SS
Pfc John E Scheep, 119 Inf, BS
S/Sgt Philip H Scherb, 120 Inf, SS BS
Pvt George F Scheufel, 105 Eng, BS
1st Lt Raymond B Scheuring, 119 Inf SS BS
1st Lt Frederick A Schieferstein, 120 Inf,
      BS w/OLC
2d Lt Max E Schifferdecker, 119 Inf, SS BS
T/4 Henry J Schiks, 743 Tk, SS BS w/OLC
Cpl George J Schiler, 823 TD, BS
Pfc Harry H Schilling, 119 Inf, BS
Pfc Shepard R Schimel, 119 Inf, BS
Cpl Clarence A Schlegel, Div Hq BS
Pfc George C Schlegel, 120 Inf, BS
Capt Henry E Schlegel, 119 Inf, SS BS w/OLC
M/Sgt Henry G Schleich, Div Hq, BS
Pfc Ralph W Schlemme, 105 Eng, BS
Sgt Kenneth A Schlessinger, 120 Inf, BS
Pfc Lloyd L Schlichting 119 Inf, BS
Sgt Nicholas Schmer, 119 Inf, SS
T/5 Harry W Schmeyer, 120 Inf, BS
Pfc John A Schmidmeister, 117 Inf BS
Pfc Clarence F Schmidt, 117 Inf, BS
Pfc Donald J Schmidt, 119 Inf, BS
T/4 Edward L Schmidt, 120 Inf, BS

Pfc Harvey H Schmidt, 117 Inf, BS
Sgt Herman A Schmidt, 743 Tk, BS
1st Lt Leland C Schmidt, 117 Inf, BS
Sgt Leo J Schmidt, 531 AAA, BS
Pfc Louis J Schmidt, 30 Sig, BS
1st Lt Henry Schmitz, 117 Inf, BS
Pfc Earl J Schneider, 105 Eng, BS
Sgt James H Schneider, 120 Inf, BS
Sgt Harry G Schniering, 119 Inf, BS
Pvt Russell E Schober, 743 Tk, SS
1st Lt Vernon H Schock, 117 Inf, SS
Sgt William Schoener, 117 Inf, SS
Pvt Jack Schoenmann, 99 Inf, BS
S/Sgt Sam D Schofield, 117 Inf, BS w/OLC
Sgt Darrell H Schooley, 120 Inf, BS w/OLC
Pfc James F Schooley, 30 Sig, BS
S/Sgt Walter C Schrader, 120 Inf, BS
Pfc Emil Schrag, 120 Inf, BS
Cpl Robert C Schrage, 117 Inf, SS BS
Sgt Lawrence Schreiber, 117 Inf, BS
WOJG Richard C Schreiber, 197 FA, BS
T/Sgt Joseph J Schreiner, 743 Tk, BS
Cpl Walter H Schubert, 120 Inf, BS
Capt Melvin J Schueller, 823 TD, BS
Pfc Donald J Schuh, 119 Inf, BS
S/Sgt Willis P Schuler, 197 FA, BS
1st Lt William Schulman, 258 FA, BS
Sgt Arthur W Schultz, 119 Inf, SS BS
Pvt Charles H Schultz, 118 FA, BS
T/Sgt Clarence E Schultz, 117 Inf, BS
Pfc Fernly R Schultz, 117 Inf, BS w/OLC
T/4 Philip M Schultz, 117 Inf, BS w/OLC
Pfc Roy A Schuman, 119 Inf, BS
S/Sgt Paul M Schunk, 120 Inf, BS
Pfc Lawrence H Schuster, 117 Inf, BS
1st Lt David G Schwager, 30 QM, BS
S/Sgt Heinz K Schwartz, 119 Inf, SS BS
T/5 Fred E Schwarz, 197 FA, BS
M/Sgt Carl J Schwedler, Div Hq, BS
Capt Frank E L Schweissing, 120 Inf, SS BS
Sgt Mark Schwendiman, 119 Inf, SS BS
S/Sgt Edwin C Schwenke, 119 Inf, BS
Pfc Peter A Sciarra, 105 Eng, BS
Pfc Salvatore Scifo, 105 Eng, BS w/OLC
Pfc Gene B Scoggins, 120 Inf, BS
Pfc Dominic J Scolaro, 531 AAA, BS
Maj William C Sconyers, Div Hq, BS
S/Sgt Claude H Scott, 117 Inf SS
S/Sgt Elton A Scott, 119 Inf, BS w/OLC
S/Sgt Francis E Scott 30 Rcn, SS BS
Sgt Harold R Scott, 105 Eng BS
Cpl Joseph F Scott, 120 Inf, BS
Pfc Joseph L Scott, 117 Inf, SS
S/Sgt Leo C Scott, 105 Eng BS
Capt Malcolm F Scott, 119 Inf, BS
Capt Richard A Scott, 531 AAA, BS
Pfc Roger O Scott, 119 Inf, SS BS
Pfc Samuel L Scott Jr, 531 AAA, SM
M/Sgt Walter L Scott, 283 FA, BS
S/Sgt Watson G Scott Jr 117 Inf, BS
Pfc William L Scott, 120 Inf, BS
Sgt Winfield D Scott, 119 Inf, BS
S/Sgt Robert Scriven, 120 Inf, BS w/OLC
Sgt Ernest V Scudder, 120 Inf BS
1st Lt Vincent S Scurria, 119 Inf, SS BS
Sgt Dominick Scutella, 120 Inf BS
Sgt Walter L Seagren, 119 Inf, BS
Cpl Paul W Sealy, 117 Inf, BS
1st Sgt Weldon B Seamons, 120 Inf, BS
S/Sgt Seldon Sear, 117 Inf, BS
T/Sgt George F Sears, Div Hq, BS
Pfc Joseph Sears, 117 Inf, BS
Lt Col Patrick E Seawright, 197 FA,
      BS w/2 OLC
T/5 Daniel M Seay, 119 Inf, SS
T/5 Jack F Secaur 120 Inf, BS w/OLC
Pfc Paul D Secor, 117 Inf SS
Pfc Frank Sedita, 120 Inf, SS
Sgt Roman J Sedmidubsky, 117 Inf, BS
S/Sgt Arthur F See, 105 Eng, BS
Capt Harold F Seeber, 119 Inf BS
Pfc Franklin H Seeberger, 230 FA SS
T/5 Vincent E Seeman, 531 AAA, BS
Pfc George W Sehren, 823 TD, BS

Pvt George E Seidler, 119 Inf, BS
T/5 Benedict Seidman, 120 Inf, BS
T/5 Paul C Seiler, 30 Rcn, BS
T/5 Walter C Selfridge, 119 Inf, SS
S/Sgt Willmer E Sellers, 120 Inf, BS
T/Sgt Carleton L Sells, 117 Inf, BS
Cpl Raymond K Sells, 119 Inf, SS
Capt Louis F Sency, 119 Inf, BS
Pfc Wayne E Senft, 117 Inf, BS
Pic John A D Senger, 117 Inf, SS
Cpl Joseph R Senica, 118 FA, BS
S/Sgt Benjamin C Sensing, 117 Inf, BS
Pfc Clyde S Sentell, 119 Inf, SS
Pvt Henry G Sentell, 117 Inf, BS
T/5 Gerald W Senter, 120 Inf, BS
T/4 Joseph M Serena, 105 Eng, BS
Capt Oscar Serlin, 105 Med, BS w/OLC
Cpl Jesse P Serrano, 119 Inf, BS
T/Sgt Robert W Serviss, 119 Inf, SS w/OLC
Pfc John C Settoon, 117 Inf, BS
T/5 Keith J Severin, 120 Inf, BS
Sgt Donovan K Seymour, 120 Inf, BS
Capt Cornelius Shaffer, 120 Inf, SS
T/5 Daniel G Shager, 30 Sig, BS
Sgt Fred E Shagner, 120 Inf, BS
T/4 Benton L Shahan, 117 Inf, BS
S/Sgt Clarence W Shahan, 117 Inf,
    SS BS w/OLC
Maj William B Shanahan, 197 FA BS w/2 OLC
1st Lt Robert B Shane, 117 Inf, BS
Pvt Harold E Sharp, 30 Sig BS
S/Sgt Robert R Sharp, 119 Inf, BS
1st Lt Ernest F Sharps, 120 Inf, BS w/OLC
Pfc Bernard C Shaut, 117 Inf, BS
Pfc John R Shaver, 230 FA, BS
Capt Charles R Shaw, 120 Inf, SS w/OLC BS
Sgt Melvin Shaw, 117 Inf, BS
T/4 Carroll E Shay, 743 Tk, BS
Sgt Theodore Shayer, 120 Inf BS
Pfc Millard J Shea, 117 Inf, BS
2d Lt Robert J Shea, 120 Inf, SS
T/5 Arthur B Shearin, 119 Inf, BS
Pfc Elmer G Sheeder, 119 Inf, BS
1st Lt Merle Sheen 120 Inf SS BS
1st Lt Seymour Shefrin, 119 Inf, SS BS
Pfc James B Sheil, 120 Inf, BS
Pvt William Shelby, 120 Inf,
    SS w/OLC BS w/OLC
T/5 Leo R Shellehamer, 120 Inf, BS
Sgt Robert D Shellito, 105 Eng, SS
Pvt Andrew J Shelton, 119 Inf, BS
T/5 Jack D Shelton, 117 Inf, BS
P'c Jack M Shelton, 120 Inf, SS BS
WOJG Marvin V Shelton, Div Hq, BS
Pfc Robert N Shelton, 117 Inf, BS
S/Sgt Sherman C Shelton, 119 Inf, SS
CWO Merritt M Shenk, 113 FA, BS —
Lt Col Frederick C Shepard, Div Arty, BS
T/3 Edward J Shepaum, 117 Inf BS
T/5 Carvel A Shepherd, 105 Med BS
S/Sgt David C Shepherd, 120 Inf, SS w/2 OLC
Cpl Buel C Sheridan, 823 TD, SS
Pvt Bernard S Sherman, 117 Inf, BS
Pfc Morris G Sherman, 120 Inf, BS
T/4 Willard W Sherrill, 119 Inf, BS
1st Lt Sylvester Shetter, 119 Inf, SS
Pfc Elmer W Shewmake, 117 Inf, BS
Cpl Harvey B Shick, 113 FA, SS —
S/Sgt Lewis W Shields, 120 Inf, BS
Pfc Lynden A Shiets, 120 Inf BS
1st Lt Joseph M Shifalo, 203 FA, BS
T/Sgt Elbert C Shiflett, 119 Inf, SS
Sgt James L Shikles, 531 AAA, BS
Sgt Richard G Shingleton, 119 Inf, BS
2d Lt Benjamin H Shipley, 119 Inf BS
Pfc Joe O Shipley, 120 Inf, SS C d'G
Pfc John E Shipley, 119 Inf, SS
S/Sgt Woodrow W Shirah, 119 Inf, SS
T/4 Raymond L Shively, 743 Tk, BS
Pfc Scottie Z Shiverdecker, 117 Inf, BS
Pfc Edward W Shoemake 117 Inf, BS
Pfc Joseph N Shore, Div Hq, BS
T/5 Edwin A Short, 736 Tk, BS
T/4 Norman A Short, 105 Eng, BS

T/Sgt Ralph P Short, 119 Inf BS
Pfc Kenneth B Shotwell, 117 Inf, BS
S/Sgt James H Shouse, 119 Inf, BS
Pfc James M Shroyer, 120 Inf, SS
1st Sgt Joseph Shtundel, 120 Inf, BS w/OLC
1st Lt Leo Shufrin, 531 AAA, BS
Pvt William E Shula, 120 Inf, BS
1st Sgt Edwin W Shuler, 823 TD, BS
1st Lt Alfred M Shull, 117 Inf, BS
Sgt James D Shull, 117 Inf, BS
Pfc Newton Shultis, 117 Inf, BS
Pfc John D Shumway, 117 Inf, SS
S/Sgt Calvin Shupert, 120 Inf, BS
Sgt Warren N Shurtleff, 823 TD, SS
Pfc William Shusman, 120 Inf, BS
T/5 John S Siarnicki, 30 Sig, BS
Capt George H Sibbald, 117 Inf, SS w/OLC BS
Cpl Earnest S Sibby, 113 FA, BS w/OLC—
Cpl Nicholas A Siea, 230 FA, SS
Cpl James Siciliano, 120 Inf, BS
Pvt Vernon J Sidenbender Jr, 230 FA, BS
Pfc Ralph L Sides, 117 Inf, BS
Sgt John J Siebel, 120 Inf, BS
T/4 John R Sieg, 823 TD, BS
Pvt George K Siegle Jr, 105 Eng, BS
Pfc Raymond F Sielewicki, 117 Inf, BS
Sgt George G Sigl, 119 Inf, BS
Pfc Argil D Sigley, 119 Inf, BS
Pfc Isaac S Sigley Jr, 119 Inf, BS
Pfc Erwin Sikkema, 119 Inf, BS
1st Lt Andrew J Sikorsky, 120 Inf BS
Pfc Domingos F Silva, 117 Inf BS
S/Sgt Edwin G Silva, 120 Inf, SS
S/Sgt Edgar S Silver, 743 Tk, BS
T/5 Louis Silvestri, 118 FA, SS
Pfc Joseph A Simmance, 120 Inf, BS
Sgt Oscar N Simmen Jr, 119 Inf, BS
Maj Gardner M Simes, 120 Inf, SS
1st Lt Alex J Simmons, 197 FA, BS w/OLC
T/Sgt Buster M Simmons, 120 Inf, BS
S/Sgt Herbert B Simmons, 118 FA, BS
Pfc Jack W Simmons, 119 Inf, BS
T/4 James W Simmons, 120 Inf, BS
Capt Ross Y Simmons, 119 Inf, SS BS MC C d'G
1st Lt Walter F Simmons, 117 Inf, BS w/2 OLC
S/Sgt Willie C Simmons, 117 Inf, BS
T/4 Fred D Simon, 117 Inf, BS
Pfc Howard C Simon, 117 Inf, BS
S/Sgt Hyman Simon, 197 FA, BS
M/Sgt Robert E Simon, Div Hq, BS
S/Sgt Andrew Simone, 119 Inf SS BS
2d Lt George A Simons, 258 FA, BS
Pfc Rolf W Simonsen, 99 Inf, SS
S/Sgt Edgar T Simpers, 119 Inf, BS
Pfc Leroy Simpkins, 120 Inf, BS
Pfc Trujillo Simplicio, 119 Inf, SS
Pfc Fidus G Simpson, 743 Tk, BS
T/Sgt Howard J Simpson, 113 FA, BS
T/4 Wayman P Simpson, 743 Tk, BS
S/Sgt William F Simpson, 117 Inf BS
Pfc Kenneth I Sinclair, 117 Inf, BS
Pfc Irving Sinensky, 117 Inf, SS
Pfc Jacob Singer, 117 Inf, BS
Sgt John C Singer, 120 Inf, BS
S/Sgt George L Singleton, 119 Inf, BS
Pfc Hugh T Singleton, 119 Inf, SS
Maj Julius Singleton, 117 Inf, BS w/OLC
T/4 Lowell W Singleton, 119 Inf, BS
1st Lt Luther G Sink, 119 Inf, BS
T/5 Harold E Sipes, 120 Inf, BS
Sgt William T Sipola, 117 Inf, DSC
1st Lt Matthew F Siranovich, 117 Inf, BS
Pfc Marvin Sirotkin, 117 Inf, SS BS
1st Sgt Peter A Sirtoli, Div Hq, BS
Sgt Robert L Sisk, 105 Eng, SS
2d Lt Paul K Sisson, 105 Eng, SS
Pfc Edward J Sitar, 119 Inf BS
1st Lt Stephen B Sitar, 117 Inf, BS w/2 OLC
T/5 Stephen P Sitarik, 120 Inf, BS
Capt George W Sitz, 823 TD, BS
2d Lt August G Sitzman 400 FA, BS
Sgt Charles Sizemore, 120 Inf, BS
T/5 Jack H Sizemore, 119 Inf, BS
S/Sgt Vernon D Skaggs, 743 Tk, BS w/OLC

Pfc Zigmund Skarbek, 117 Inf, BS
T/5 John H Skeen, 30 Sig, BS
Pfc Ernest H Skenandore, 120 Inf, SS
Sgt Vincent P Skenyon, 120 Inf, BS
Pfc Alex O Skinner, 120 Inf, BS
Pvt Charles H Skinner Jr, 117 Inf, BS
Cpl Joseph F Skipp, 120 Inf, BS
S/Sgt Norman E Skiver, 120 Inf, SS BS
S/Sgt Emil J Skodon, 119 Inf, BS
Pfc Edgar C Skuzie, 119 Inf, BS
Capt Charles R Slager, 230 FA, BS w/OLC
T/5 Robert C Slane, 197 FA, BS
Pfc Rolf Slang, 99 Inf, BS
S/Sgt Gerard J Slania, 120 Inf, SS BS
Sgt William C Slappey, 30 Rcn, SS
Sgt Roscoe Slater 531 AAA, BS
Sgt Carl J Slattebo, 803 TD, BS
Pfc Herbert J Slepicka, 119 Inf, BS
WOJG Vernon M Slichter, 531 AAA, BS
S/Sgt Charles E Sliger, 531 AAA, BS
Pfc Bernard L Slimp, 119 Inf, BS
CWO Robert L Sloan, Div Hq, BS
Pvt Robert M Slobodnik, 117 Inf, SS
2d Lt Edward G L Slonaker, 120 Inf, BS
Sgt John H Slone, 120 Inf, SS
Cpl Sylvester E Slotten, 197 FA, BS w/OLC
Pfc Joseph Sluserczyk, 120 Inf, SS
T/4 Donald J Small, 120 Inf BS
Pvt James A Smallwood, 117 Inf, SS BS
T/5 Ralph E Smart, 197 FA, BS
1st Lt Willard F Smart, 117 Inf, SS
2d Lt Rufus E Smather 119 Inf, SS w/OLC
Pvt Samuel Smedley, 120 Inf, BS
Sgt Spencer J Smiley, 119 Inf, SS
1st Lt Albert A Smith, 120 Inf, SS w/OLC
1st Lt Albert L Smith, 105 Eng, SS
T/5 Albert W Smith, 120 Inf, BS
WOJG Angus T Smith, 120 Inf, SS BS
Pfc Atlas H Smith, 119 Inf BS
Pfc Burton R Smith, 105 Eng, SS BS
S/Sgt Carl A Smith, 526 Armd Inf, SS
T/4 Carl E Smith, 117 Inf BS
T/5 Carl H Smith, 119 Inf, BS
S/Sgt Charles Smith Jr 120 Inf, BS w/OLC
S/Sgt Charles H Smith, 120 Inf, BS
1st Lt Charles I Smith, 119 Inf, SS BS
Pfc Charles W Smith 119 Inf BS w/OLC
Pfc Claude D Smith, 117 Inf, BS
T/5 Clifton M Smith, 823 TD, BS
Pfc Clyde W Smith, 117 Inf, BS
Pvt Curtis M Smith, 743 Tk, SS BS
Pfc Daniel D Smith, 117 Inf, SS BS
Pfc Donald I Smith, 117 Inf, BS
T/5 Drudy L Smith, 105 Med, BS
S/Sgt Edward M Smith 230 FA SS
T/Sgt Edwin E Smith, 119 Inf, BS
Pvt Elisha V Smith, 30 Rcn, SS
1st Lt Elmer H Smith, 119 Inf, BS
Pfc Elmer W Smith Jr, 120 Inf SS w/OLC
1st Lt Francis H Smith, 120 Inf, SS
S/Sgt Francis P Smith, 119 Inf, SS BS w/OLC
T/4 Frank P Smith 117 Inf BS
Capt Frank W Smith 203 FA BS
T/5 Frederick L Smith, 400 FA, BS
S/Sgt George E Smith, 120 Inf BS
Sgt Harvey E Smith, 117 Inf, BS
1st Lt Henry V Smith, 119 Inf, BS
T/4 Howard L Smith, 117 Inf, BS
Pfc Howard P Smith, 117 Inf BS
S/Sgt Izadore C Smith, 120 Inf, SS
Pfc J D Smith 119 Inf BS
Pfc Jack L Smith, 119 Inf, BS
Pvt Jack R Smith, 120 Inf, BS w/OLC
Pfc James E Smith 120 Inf, BS
T/Sgt James G Smith, 117 Inf, SS
Pvt James H Smith, 119 Inf BS
Pvt Jessie J Smith, 30 Sig, BS
T/5 John R Smith 117 Inf, BS
Pfc John W W Smith, 117 Inf, BS
Pfc Joseph H Smith, 117 Inf, BS
Cpl Kelly Smith 30 MP BS
T/5 Kenneth C Smith, 113 Cav, SS –
Pvt Kenneth R Smith, 117 Inf, BS
Pfc L N Smith, 120 Inf, BS

Pfc L T Smith, 120 Inf, SS
T/4 Louis C Smith, 120 Inf, BS
S/Sgt Merlin R Smith, 119 Inf, SS BS
1st Lt Milton Smith, 120 Inf, SS
Cpl Monroe Smith, 105 Eng, SS
Pvt Palmer G Smith, 197 FA, BS
S/Sgt Paul H Smith, 118 FA, BS
1st Sgt Raymond C Smith, 120 Inf BS
Capt Raymond W Smith, 119 Inf, BS
2d Lt Reginald U Smith, 117 Inf, SS
S/Sgt Robert E Smith, 120 Inf, SS w/OLC
Pfc Robert H Smith, 120 Inf, BS
Pfc Thomas C Smith, 120 Inf, BS
2d Lt Thomas E Smith 119 Inf, BS
Sgt Travis L Smith, 823 TD, SS BS
1st Sgt Vance D Smith, 823 TD, BS
T/5 Wesley H Smith, 230 FA, BS
T/Sgt William A Smith, 120 Inf, SS
Pfc William C Smith, 117 Inf, BS w/OLC
Pfc William L Smith, 118 FA, BS
Maj Charles G Smither, 119 Inf, SS BS
T/Sgt Robert L Smitherman, 120 Inf, BS
T/5 John E Smithson, 743 Tk, SS
Pfc James H Smoak, 119 Inf, BS
Capt Odell W Smothers, 120 Inf, BS
Pvt Adelbert C Snell, 823 TD, BS
S/Sgt Warren G Snell, 119 Inf, BS
1st Lt William M Sneller, 105 Med, BS
Cpl Elmer S Sniff, 120 Inf, SS
Sgt Russell N Snoad, 120 Inf, DSC BS
S/Sgt Robert J Snodgrass, 117 Inf, BS
Sgt Gordon L Snorgrass, 531 AAA, BS
S/Sgt Henry A Snotherly, 120 Inf, SS BS
1st Lt Arthur L Snow, 120 Inf, SS BS w/OLC
S/Sgt Archie K Snow, 105 Eng, SS
Sgt Cecil J Snow, 120 Inf, BS SS
Pfc Harvey D Snow, 117 Inf, BS w/OLC
Sgt Raymond P Snow Jr, 120 Inf, BS
T/3 Vance J Snow, 119 Inf, BS
2d Lt Arnold L Snyder, 120 Inf, SS w/2 OLC BS
T/4 Edward J Snyder, Div Hq, BS
Sgt John E Snyder, 117 Inf, BS
Cpl Simon Snyder, 120 Inf, BS
Pfc Theryn E Snyder, 117 Inf, BS
T/5 Walter A Snyder, 120 Inf, BS
Pfc Joseph P Sobleskie, 119 Inf, BS
Pfc Chester Sobkiewicz, 743 Tk, SS BS
T/5 Carl Sohn, 113 FA, BS
Sgt Stanley Soileau, 531 AAA, BS
Sgt Leslie L Soland, 743 Tk, BS
Pfc Frank S Solano, 120 Inf, BS
Pfc Ernest E Solis, 30 MP, BS
S/Sgt Salvador B Solis, 119 Inf, SS BS
Sgt Albert L Soli, 120 Inf, BS
Pvt Hubert A Solmonson, 120 Inf, BS
Cpl Bernard Solomon, 113 Cav, BS –
1st Lt Harold Solomon, 120 Inf, SS BS
1st Lt Saul Solow, 120 Inf, BS w/OLC
WOJG Benjamin F Somers, 105 Eng, BS
1st Lt Albert P Sommers, 117 Inf, SS BS
Cpl Joseph J Sommers Jr, 119 Inf, BS
Pfc Sidney Sonenblum, 117 Inf, BS
Pfc Yuksue Soo Hoo, 119 Inf, BS
Cpl Joseph E Sopel, 119 Inf, BS
S/Sgt Eugene J Sopenski, 119 Inf, SS
T/5 Dale E Soper, 117 Inf, BS
1st Lt Don W Soper, 120 Inf, SS
T/5 James B Soper, 117 Inf, BS
Cpl Gordon L Sordahl, 743 Tk BS
T/5 Einar Sorenson, 743 Tk, SS BS
Pvt Wiley R Sorrel, 119 Inf, BS
T/5 Eugene Sosinski, 120 Inf, BS
Pfc Bernardo G Sotelo 120 Inf, BS
T/4 Lionel G Soucy, 117 Inf BS
T/4 Lawrence Sourwine, 531 AAA, BS
S/Sgt Ancil L Southern, 117 Inf BS
T/5 LeRoy Southmayd Jr, 531 AAA, BS
Pvt Harold E Southwick 743 Tk, BS
Pfc Lawrence L Southwick 117 Inf, SS
Sgt Frederick E Southworth, 117 Inf, BS
2d Lt Virgil T Sowers, 119 Inf SS BS
T/5 Gilbert F Spahn, 120 Inf BS
T/4 Charles O Spahr Jr, 120 Inf, BS
T/4 Ernest S Spain Jr, 113 FA, BS –

Cpl Glen V Spangler, 105 Eng, BS w/2 OLC
Pvt William E Spangler, 117 Inf, BS
Sgt Alexander Spann Jr, 117 Inf, BS
Pfc Anthony Sparacio, 30 MP, BS
S/Sgt Howard J Sparks, 119 Inf BS
Pfc Robert D Sparks, 118 FA, BS
S/Sgt William L Sparks, 120 Inf,
    SS w/OLC BS w/2 OLC
S/Sgt William Spatafore, 117 Inf, BS
Sgt Lyman E Spaulding, 105 Eng, SS
Pfc Homer I Spearman, 120 Inf, BS
1st Lt Jean M Spector, 119 Inf, SS w/OLC
1st Lt Leon Spector, 118 FA, BS w/OLC
T/Sgt John W Speed, 120 Inf, BS
1st Lt Raymond L Speer, 120 Inf, SS BS
Sgt Walter H Spence, 30 Sig, BS w/OLC
Sgt Edward L Spencer, 117 Inf, BS
2d Lt Marshall E Spencer, 120 Inf, BS
1st Lt William Spencer, 258 Eng, SS BS
2d Lt Bob M Spicer, 113 FA, SS AM w/6 OLC
2d Lt Cyril B Spicer, 117 Inf,
    SS w/OLC BS w/OLC
Sgt William M Spicer, 117 Inf, SS C d'G
Sgt Joseph J Spidaletto, 120 Inf, BS
1st Lt Aaron I Spiegel, 400 FA, AM
S/Sgt Hubert M Spielman, 120 Inf, BS
Sgt Loren L Speilman, 531 AAA, SS
S/Sgt Angelo Spieres, 117 Inf, BS
Capt Robert C Spiker, 117 Inf, SS C d'G
Cpl Cornelius V Spillane, 30 Rcn, BS
Capt Ernest Spillinger, 117 Inf, BS w/OLC
1st Lt Claude M Spilman, 117 Inf,
    SS BS w/OLC
T/4 Anello J Spina, 120 Inf, BS
S/Sgt Patrick J Spinarelli, 119 Inf, SS BS
Pfc Matha Spires, 117 Inf, BS
Pfc Glen A Spitler, 120 Inf, BS
Sgt Charles Spohr, 823 TD, SS
Pfc Warren S Spoor, 119 Inf, BS
T/5 Oreste Sposato, 120 Inf, SS
Pfc Claud J Sprague, 120 Inf, BS
1st Lt Edward L Sprague, Div Arty,
    SS AM w/OLC
1st Lt Frank A Spraker, 119 Inf, BS
Pfc Harold G Sprankle, 119 Inf, BS
S/Sgt Paul E Spratt, 117 Inf, BS
S/Sgt Baney E Sprawls, 119 Inf, SS
Capt George R Springer, 113 FA, BS w/2 OLC
1st Lt Thomas Springfield, 823 TD, SS BS C d'G
S/Sgt Roy H Spruill, 105 Med, BS
Cpl Foy Spurlin, 117 Inf, BS
Capt Floyd B Spurlock, 120 Inf, SS BS
Sgt Frank J Stabile, 119 Inf, BS
Pfc Thomas J Stabile, 197 FA, BS
Pfc Michael Stack, 117 Inf, BS w/OLC
Cpl John M Stadnik, 743 Tk, SS
1st Lt Raymond G Staffilena, 743 Tk, BS
S/Sgt Ira U Stafford, 117 Inf, BS
Pfc John Stafura, 119 Inf, SS
Pfc Arnold B Stalder, 119 Inf, BS
Pfc Earl E Stallings, 120 Inf, BS
S/Sgt Joseph E Stalls, 113 FA, BS
T/5 Dorsey J Stalnaker, 30 Sig, BS w/OLC
Sgt Dean F Stamey, 105 Eng, BS
Pfc George Stampley, 120 Inf, BS
T/4 Joseph E Stan, Div Hq, BS
Sgt Sol G Standberry 117 Inf, BS
Pfc Gustave T Standfuss, 119 Inf, BS
Pfc Clyde E Standridge, 743 Tk, BS
Cpl George M Stanfield, 119 Inf, SS
Capt Robert S Stanfield, 119 Inf, BS
Capt Leslie E Stanford, 119 Inf, SS BS
Pfc Joseph Stanko 119 Inf, SS
Pfc James S Stanley, 117 Inf, BS
Pfc Paul L Stanley, 119 Inf, BS
Capt Robert B Stanlev 105 Med BS
1st Lt Thomas E Stanley Jr, 117 Inf,
    BS w/2 OLC C d'G
T/5 William S Stanley, 823 TD, BS
T/5 John J Stanton, 230 FA, SS
Pfc Ervin C Stapels, 120 Inf, BS
Capt Charles D Stapleton, 117 Inf, DSC
S/Sgt Stafford L Starcher, 120 Inf, BS
Sgt Dennis C Stark, 120 Inf, BS

Pfc Harry L Stark, 119 Inf, BS
Capt Jack W Starling, 120 Inf, BS w/OLC
Pfc Melon H Starnes, 117 Inf, BS
T/Sgt Walter Stasko, 117 Inf, SS
Pfc Joseph Staszak, 117 Inf, BS
Pfc John F Stavonet, 744 Tk, SS
Sgt Benjamin F St Clair, 105 Med, BS
Pfc Earl W Stearn, 117 Inf, BS w/OLC
T/4 Benedict R Sterns, 105 Med, BS
Sgt Warren B Steed, 117 Inf, BS
T/4 Ercel H Steele, 120 Inf, BS
Pfc Howard J Steele, 119 Inf, SS
Pfc Lester J Steele, 119 Inf, BS
S/Sgt Thomas E Steele, 119 Inf, SS BS
T/Sgt Fred D Steelman, 119 Inf, DSC
Pfc Robert H Steeves, 120 Inf, BS w/OLC
Pfc George C Stegall, 119 Inf, BS
2d Lt Bernard R Stegeman, 113 FA, SS
Pvt William H Stegeman, 30 Sig, BS
S/Sgt George F Steigleman, 120 Inf, BS
S/Sgt Henry H Stein, 823 TD, BS
Cpl Gerard J Steinbach, 117 Inf, BS w/OLC
Pfc Robert Stein, 743 Tk, BS
2d Lt Adolf Steiner, 120 Inf, BS
T/5 Jerrold C Steiner, 823 TD, BS
Sgt Harry S Steinfeld, 119 Inf, BS
Sgt Norman H Steinkritz, 119 Inf, BS
S/Sgt Robert W Stell, 120 Inf, BS
T/4 Robert Stelter, 743 Tk, BS
S/Sgt John W Stempkoski, 117 Inf, BS w/OLC
Sgt Arnold B Stene, 743 Tk, BS
Pfc Frank J Stenger, 119 Inf, SS
Capt Fred H Stenstrom, Div Hq, BS
S/Sgt Frank M Stepanek, 120 Inf, BS
Pfc John W Stepnowski, 120 Inf, BS
Sgt Benjamin A Stephens, 113 FA, BS
Pfc Charles Stephens, 119 Inf, BS w/OLC
T/5 George E Stephens, 117 Inf, BS
Col Richard W Stephens, Div Hq,
    LM BS w/2 OLC LH C d'G DSM
T/5 Austin L Stepheny, 197 FA, BS
Sgt William E Stephenson, 120 Inf, BS
Sgt Carlos Stepp, 120 Inf, BS
Maj Antonin M Sterba, 105 Eng, SS BS w/OLC
Pfc Vincent N Sterba, 105 Eng, BS
T/Sgt Harold V Sterling, 117 Inf,
    DSC SS BS C d'G
Capt Bruce D Stern, 230 FA, BS
Pvt Clyde F Sternberg, 120 Inf, SS
Pfc Clarence W Sterner, 230 FA, BS
Pfc Stanley N Stetson, 30 Sig, BS
Lt Col Earle M Stevens, 30 Sig,
    BS w/3 OLC C d'G
S/Sgt Edwin C Stevens, 119 Inf, BS w/OLC
Cpl Gordon A Stevens, 113 FA, BS
S/Sgt Henry Q Stevens, 119 Inf, BS
Sgt Robert A Stevenson, 119 Inf, SS
S/Sgt William K Stevenson, 117 Inf, BS
Pfc Charles D Stewart, 119 Inf BS
1st Lt Charles M Stewart, 120 Inf, SS
T/5 Edgar R Stewart, 230 FA, BS
Capt Frederick C Stewart, Div Hq, BS
2d Lt George A Stewart, 120 Inf, BS w/OLC
Pfc Owen J Stewart, 119 Inf, BS
Sgt Richard S Stewart, 120 Inf, SS
Capt Robert P Stewart, 230 FA, BS w/OLC
Sgt Robert W Stewart, 119 Inf, BS
Sgt Roy S Stewart, 117 Inf, BS
1st Lt Russell D Stewart, 113 FA, BS
S/Sgt Thomas E Stewart Jr, 120 Inf, SS
T/5 James N St Germain, 117 Inf, BS
T/5 Irvin Stiber, 120 Inf, SS
Pfc Francis B Stidfole, 117 Inf BS
2d Lt Stewart A Stidham, 119 Inf,
    SS w/OLC BS
Sgt James T Stikoleather, 119 Inf, BS w/OLC
S/Sgt Roger B Stiles, 119 Inf, SS
Pfc Vernon D Stiles, 117 Inf, BS
Sgt Carmelo Stillittano, 117 Inf, BS w/OLC
2d Lt Adam N Stillo, 117 Inf, SS w/OLC BS
Cpl John S Stilwell, 30 Rcn, BS
Pfc Maurice A Stimpson, 120 Inf, SS
Pvt John A Stimson, 119 Inf BS w/OLC
Sgt William T Stinnett, 823 TD, SS

Pfc Alvin L Stinson, 120 Inf, SS
Pfc John A Stimson, 119 Inf, BS
Pfc William B Stinson, 117 Inf, BS
1st Lt Raymond J Stock, 197 FA, BS
Pfc Ralph B Stoerger, 120 Inf, BS
Sgt Milford Stofer, 119 Inf, BS
Capt Morris A Stoffer, 117 Inf, SS
Pfc Adam Stoichick, 117 Inf, BS
Pvt Granville M Stokes, 117 Inf, BS
Pfc Ralph E Stokes, 117 Inf, BS
Pfc William R Stokes, 119 Inf, BS
T/4 Jack Stollak, 120 Inf, BS
Pvt Lowell L Stomm, 119 Inf, SS
1st Lt David B Stone, 119 Inf, BS
S/Sgt Ronald J Stone, 119 Inf, SS
Sgt Todd C Stone, 119 Inf, BS
Sgt Tommy Stone, 30 Sig, BS
Pfc Junior F Stoneham, 117 Inf, BS
1st Lt Robert H Stoner, 120 Inf, BS
Maj Oscar S Stonesifer, 119 Inf, BS w/OLC
2d Lt Jack T Storm, 120 Inf, BS w/OLC
S/Sgt Robert E Stough, 117 Inf, BS
Pfc Harry O Stout, 117 Inf, BS
S/Sgt Wayne E Stout, 117 Inf, BS
T/5 Clifton W Stovall, 120 Inf, BS
CWO George E Stovall, Div Hq, BS
Pfc George R Stovall, 120 Inf, BS
M/Sgt Earl E Stover, Div Hq, BS
M/Sgt Larkin B Stowe, 30 Sig, BS w/OLC
Pfc Walter K Stowell, 120 Inf, SS
Sgt Tyler E Stratton, 118 FA, BS w/2 OLC
T/Sgt Warren D Stratton, 117 Inf, SS
T/5 Delbert H Street, 117 Inf, BS
Pvt Thomas E Street, 120 Inf, BS
Pfc Walter L Streit, 120 Inf, BS
Pfc Eugene Strickland, 117 Inf, BS
Pfc Harold W Strickland, 119 Inf, BS w/3 OLC
T/4 George E Strickler 30 Rcn, BS
Sgt J B Strickler, 823 TD, BS
Pfc Thomas J Stringfello Jr, 230 FA, BS
S/Sgt Victor E Strobel, 120 Inf, SS w/OLC BS
Pvt Adolphe P Strojny, 119 Inf, BS
Sgt George Strollo, 120 Inf, BS
1st Lt Norman G Stroud, 113 FA, AM w/7 OLC
Pvt Joseph S Strucki, 117 Inf, SS BS
Pfc John T Stuart, 117 Inf, BS
1st Sgt Louis C Stuart, 30 Rcn, BS
Pfc George A Stulb, 119 Inf, BS
1st Lt John C Stull, 531 AAA, BS
Pfc James W Stump, 119 Inf, BS
Pfc Joseph M Stumpo, 120 Inf, BS
Pfc Roy D Sturdivan, 119 Inf, BS
Pfc John E Sturgeon, 120 Inf SS
Pfc Ray W Sturm, 119 Inf, BS
T/5 Elmer C Sturms, 120 Inf, BS
Pfc Lee V Styles, 119 Inf, BS
Pfc George L Suchomel, 120 Inf, SS
Pfc Stanley C Suffridge, 120 Inf, BS
Pfc Harold C Suit, 120 Inf, SS
Pfc Fred Sullins, 744 Tk, BS
Pfc Adrian D Sullivan, 230 FA, SS
2d Lt Charles F Sullivan Jr, 117 Inf, SS
T/4 Charles H Sullivan Jr, BS w/OLC
T/5 Cloyd V Sullivan, 230 FA, BS
Pfc Francis D Sullivan, 119 Inf, BS
Pfc Herbert L Sullivan, 197 FA, BS
T/5 James M Sullivan, 105 Eng, BS
T/5 John D Sullivan, 105 Med, BS
Pfc John J Sullivan, 30 MP, BS
Cpl John L Sullivan, Div Hq, SS
Pfc John L Sullivan, 120 Inf, BS
T/5 Robert L Sullivan, 117 Inf, BS
M/Sgt Warren P Sullivan 730 Ord, BS
T/5 William J Sullivan 120 Inf, BS w/OLC
Pfc Billey Sullivent, 119 Inf, BS
2d Lt Joseph P Sultan, 120 Inf, SS BS
2d Lt Leroy Summer, 117 Inf, BS w/2 OLC
Pfc Grover S Summerlin Jr, 119 Inf, BS
Pfc Carleton L Summers, 120 Inf, SS
T/4 P L Summers, 119 Inf, BS
1st Lt Willard S Summers, 197 FA, BS
Pfc Emerson D Summerville, 105 Med,
   BS w/OLC
T/5 Roland V Sumner, 119 Inf, BS

1st Sgt Herbert L Summey, 105 Eng, BS
Sgt Hugh A Sumrell, 113 FA, BS —
Pfc Dennis L Sunderland, 119 Inf, BS w/OLC
Pfc Donald H Sunkel, 117 Inf, SS
T/5 James J Susens, 113 FA, BS w/OLC
T/5 Robert M Susner, 118 FA, BS
Pfc Elmer Sussman, 120 Inf, BS
Pfc Donald Sutherland, 119 Inf, BS
Col Edwin M Sutherland, 119 Inf, SS C d'G
S/Sgt Thomas M Sutherland, 119 Inf, BS
Pfc William K Sutlive Jr 119 Inf, BS
Pfc Harry E Sutton, 117 Inf, BS
Pfc William E Sutton, 119 Inf, BS
Pfc Andrew E Svetlovics, 117 Inf, BS
T/4 Robert E Swain, 117 Inf, BS
Pvt William S Swallow Jr, 275 Armd FA, BS
Sgt William C Swanner, 119 Inf, SS
Cpl Clarence E Swanson, 117 Inf, BS
Capt Samuel D Swanson, 823 TD, BS
Pfc Henry A Swartz, 113 FA, BS —
S/Sgt Raymond H Swartzback, 117 Inf, BS
Capt Knut Swee, 99 Inf, BS
T/5 Edward G Sweeney, 230 FA, BS
T/4 Paul J Sweeney, 230 FA, BS
Pfc Ray G Sweet, 120 Inf, BS
Pfc Elmer P Sweet, 105 Med, BS
Pfc John J Sweeten, 744 Tk, BS
T/5 George D Sweeting, 120 Inf, BS w/OLC
T/5 Noralf O Swennes, 30 Rcn, BS
Sgt Andrew Swiake, 105 Eng, BS w/OLC
T/4 Hyman Swidler, 120 Inf, SS BS
2d Lt Charles W Swienty, 230 FA, BS
Pfc Harry R Swiger, 119 Inf, BS
1st Lt Harrison D Swillev, 823 TD, BS
Pfc Harry W Swim, 120 Inf, BS
Pfc Arthur C Swinarski, 119 Inf, BS
S/Sgt Pete Swingle, 119 Inf, BS
S/Sgt Bronislaw A Swistak, 120 Inf, BS
Sgt Howard F Swope, 823 TD, BS
Pfc Keith L Sy, 119 Inf, BS w/OLC
S/Sgt Michael Sydoryk, 117 Inf, BS w/OLC
S/Sgt James E Sykes, 30 QM, BS
Pfc Joseph W Sykora, 117 Inf, BS
Pfc Stephen Syrnick, 119 Inf, BS
T/5 Walter S Szczepaniak, 119 Inf, BS
S/Sgt Joseph A Szostak, 531 AAA, BS
Pfc Francis A Szukics, 120 Inf, BS
Cpl Edmund L Szulczynski, 117 Inf, BS
1st Sgt Roy L Tabor, 117 Inf, SS BS
S/Sgt William O Tabor, 744 Tk, BS
Pfc Calvin L Tabucchi, 119 Inf, BS
Pfc Edmund W Tacey, 117 Inf, BS
2d Lt Jack H Tafeen, 230 FA AM w/OLC
T/Sgt Fred C Taff, 120 Inf, SS
Pfc Clifton Tager, 113 FA, BS w/OLC —
S/Sgt Benjamin E Tagg, 119 Inf SS
T/5 Tomas B Talamante Jr 823 TD, BS
Pvt George F Talarico, 120 Inf, SS BS
Sgt Gustav J Tallaksen 99 Inf BS
T/5 William T Tally, 117 Inf BS
Pfc Harley Tangen, 747 Tk, BS
Sgt Chester E Tanner, 119 Inf, BS
1st Lt Hubert E Tansey, 117 Inf BS
Pfc Arthur J Tanzella, 119 Inf, BS
1st Lt Frank A Tarbutton, Div Hq, BS
Capt Carl F Tarlowski, 743 Tk, SS
Pfc Dominic A Tarquinio, 117 Inf, SS
S/Sgt Jimmy H Tarkington, 30 Band, BS
S/Sgt Fred Tarver, 119 Inf, BS
Pfc Mike Tatalovich 119 Inf, BS
T/Sgt Bruce W Tate, 120 Inf, SS BS
S/Sgt Charles L Tate, 120 Inf, DSC
S/Sgt James H Tate, 120 Inf, BS
1st Sgt John C. Tate, 117 Inf, BS
Pfc Clifford W Tatman, 117 Inf, BS
S/Sgt Costanzo D Tatta, 119 Inf SS w/OLC
Sgt Charles A Tatum, 119 Inf, BS
Sgt Clay Taylor, 105 Eng, SS BS
Pvt Clifford L Taylor, 230 FA, BS
Pfc Clofus Taylor, 120 Inf, BS
Pfc Donald R Taylor, 120 Inf, BS
Pfc Elmer P Taylor, 120 Inf, BS
1st Lt Elvie G Taylor, 117 Inf, SS
Pfc George B Taylor, 118 FA, BS

Pfc Granville Taylor, 120 Inf, BS
Capt Harry A Taylor, 258 FA, BS
T/Sgt Herbert R Taylor, 120 Inf, SS
S/Sgt Iry T Taylor, 117 Inf, BS
Pfc Jack L Taylor, 120 Inf, BS
Pfc James B Taylor, 823 TD, SS
Capt James C Taylor, 119 Inf, BS
Sgt Jasper H Taylor, 119 Inf, BS
Pvt John E Taylor, 119 Inf, BS
T/5 John F Taylor, 743 Tk, SS
S/Sgt Lonnie R Taylor, 117 Inf, SS BS w/OLC
Pfc Ralph F Taylor, 117 Inf, BS
Pfc Roscoe L Taylor, 526 Inf, BS
T/5 Sam R Taylor, 117 Inf, BS
T/5 Wiley E Taylor, 120 Inf, BS w/OLC
Sgt Bayne C Teague, 119 Inf, SS
Pvt Russell R Teague, 119 Inf, BS
T/4 Charles O Tebeau, Hq 30 Div, BS
T/4 Lawrence H Teed, 117 Inf, BS
Sgt Philip N Tedschi, 531 AAA, BS
T/5 William J Teetsell, 230 FA, BS
1st Lt Ralph G Teich, 197 FA, BS w/OLC
Capt Gunnar J Teilman Jr, 120 Inf, SS
1st Sgt Henry J Teja, 119 Inf, SS
S/Sgt Anthony A Tempesta, 743 Tk, DSC
Pfc Howard W Temple, 117 Inf, BS
S/Sgt Jesse R Temple, 120 Inf, BS
Pfc Lloyd J Temple, 117 Inf, SS
Cpl Homer E Ten Cate, 120 Inf, BS
Pfc Aristides S Tentas, 30 MP, BS
T/5 John Teplica Jr, 105 Eng, BS
T/5 Candido Terone, 197 FA, BS
Sgt James W Terral, 105 Eng, BS
Pfc Edgar E Terrell, 119 Inf, BS
Cpl Delmar L Terrill, 743 Tk, BS
Pfc Claude W Terry, 119 Inf, BS
1st Lt George W Terry, 120 Inf, SS BS w/3 OLC
Pfc George H Tessier, 120 Inf, BS w/2 OLC
1st Lt Thomas Tetreau Jr, 120 Inf, SS BS
Pvt Lloyd C Texel, 230 FA, BS
Pfc Elton M Thaggard, 120 Inf, BS
S/Sgt John M Tharp Jr, 120 Inf, BS w/OLC
Pfc Ogwin S Tharp, 120 Inf, SS BS
Pfc Kenneth A Thayer, 119 Inf, BS
Pfc Kenneth C Thayer, 119 Inf, DSC
Pfc Lavein R Theesfeld, 119 Inf, BS
Pfc Leonard J Thibeault, 119 Inf, BS
Pfc Arthur M Thibedau, 120 Inf, SS BS
T/5 Wilfred R Thibodeau, 119 Inf, BS
1st Lt Dalton J Thibodeaux, 117 Inf, SS
Pfc Frank Thiel Jr, 119 Inf, BS w/OLC
1st Lt Robert C Thiele, 119 Inf, BS w/OLC
Pvt Harold A Thigpen, 30 QM, BS
T/5 Arthur R Thomas, 743 Tk, SS BS
S/Sgt Carl Thomas, 119 Inf, BS
Pfc Carmen J Thomas, 120 Inf, BS w/OLC
S/Sgt Clyde A Thomas, 120 Inf SS
1st Lt Edwin Thomas, 120 Inf BS w/OLC
S/Sgt Edwin R Thomas, 117 Inf, SS
S/Sgt Elias D Thomas, 120 Inf, BS
Maj Eugene H Thomas, 120 Inf, BS w/OLC
Pfc Gordon S Thomas, 743 Tk, BS
S/Sgt James Thomas, 119 Inf, BS
T/5 Lynn B Thomas, 230 FA, SS
Pfc Norman H Thomas, 119 Inf, SS
Pvt Ople B Thomas, 117 Inf, SS
1st Lt Paul C Thomas, 117 Inf, SS
Pfc Paul J Thomas, 117 Inf, BS
Pfc Roy W Thomas, 120 Inf, BS
Sgt Sammie C Thomas, 117 Inf, BS
Pfc Stanley E Thomas, 119 Inf, BS
Capt William H Thomas, 117 Inf, BS w/OLC
T/5 Atherman W Thomason, 105 Med, BS
T/5 Austin Thomason, Div Hq, BS
Cpl Alvis B Thompson, 743 Tk, SS
T/Sgt Benjamin O Thompson, 823 TD, BS
Cpl Billy J Thompson, 119 Inf, SS BS w/OLC
Pfc Clifford P Thompson, 120 Inf BS
1st Lt Ford L Thompson Jr, 118 FA,
BS AM w/5 OLC
1st Lt George E Thompson, 117 Inf, BS
1st Sgt Gordon K Thompson, 743 Tk, BS
Pfc James H Thompson, 117 Inf, BS
T/5 John Thompson, 105 Eng, SS

T/4 John F Thompson Jr, 30 Sig, BS
Pfc Marvin C Thompson, 120 Inf, BS
S/Sgt Roy D Thompson, 119 Inf, BS w/OLC
Sgt Victor C Thompson, 119 Inf, BS
T/5 Oge Thomsen, 117 Inf, BS
T/Sgt Alan C Thomson, 120 Inf, SS
Cpl Forrest P Thornburg, 743 Tk, BS
Pfc Stanley J Thornbury, 120 Inf, BS
Pfc Clarence L Thorne, 743 Tk, BS w/2 OLC
T/4 Walter G Thorne, 117 Inf, BS
2d Lt Clyde S Thornell, 743 Tk, SS BS w/OLC
T/4 Doyle R Thornton, 105 Med, BS
Pvt Elwin E Thornton, 117 Inf, BS
2d Lt Marcel Thouviot, French Army, BS
Pfc Robert W Thun, 118 FA, BS
Pfc Vito M Tibollo, 119 Inf, BS
Pfc Elmer C Tidwell, 117 Inf, BS
Sgt Robert W Tietz, 823 TD, BS
Pfc Samuel T Tilford, 119 Inf, BS
S/Sgt Vernon L Tillotson, 120 Inf, SS BS
1st Lt Richard C Timpe, 117 Inf, SS '
T/5 Melvin C Tingley, 823 TD, BS
T/Sgt Lawton E Tinley, 117 Inf, BS
Sgt Charles A Tinnin, 118 FA, BS
T/Sgt Louis W Tippit, 120 Inf, BS
Pfc Dorsey E Tipton, 743 Tk, BS
T/4 Donald Tisher, 119 Inf, BS
S/Sgt Alvin R Tisland, 743 Tk, SS BS
Pfc Michael Tkach, 119 Inf, BS
Pvt Ivan L Tock, 117 Inf, SS
Sgt Ralph T Todd, 117 Inf, BS
Pfc John A Toepfer, 117 Inf, BS
Pvt Raymond Tolbert, 117 Inf, BS w/OLC
Pfc Richard A Tolbert, 117 Inf, BS
Pfc Jacob W Tollefsen, 99 Inf, BS
Capt Buford C Toler, 119 Inf, BS
T/5 Edward J Tomasetti, 30 Sig, BS
Pfc Albert R Tomasunas, 120 Inf, BS
S/Sgt John C Tomczyk, 117 Inf, BS
Pfc Robert E Tomlinson, 119 Inf, BS
Pvt William C Tomlinson, 230 FA, BS
S/Sgt William T Tomlinson, 120 Inf, BS
T/4 Mario Tommasone, 113 FA, BS w/OLC
S/Sgt Hiram T Tomozak, 120 Inf, BS
T/5 Henry F Tompkins, 823 TD, BS
Sgt Michael A Tontsch, 105 Eng, BS w/OLC
Pfc Kenneth A Toothman, 117 Inf, BS
T/5 Milton W Topel, 105 Eng, BS
Cpl Allen E Toppila, 105 Eng, BS
T/5 Albert M Torino, 113 FA, BS
T/5 Thomas F J Tormey, Div Hq, BS
Capt Egedio E F Torreti, 105 Eng, BS w/OLC
Pfc George T Torrey, 117 Inf, BS
S/Sgt Frank J Torrissi, 117 Inf, BS
Cpl Frank E Toth 117 Inf, BS
Pfc Joseph M Totora, 120 Inf, BS
Pfc Leonard E Totten, 117 Inf, BS
Pvt Charles S Tourtellot, 230 FA, BS
T/4 John J Tower, Hq 30 Div, BS
1st Lt Frank W Towers, 120 Inf, BS
Pfc Robert E Towne, 117 Inf, BS
Sgt David D Townsend, 230 FA, SS
Pvt Robert J Townsend, 119 Inf, SS
Capt Rodman Townsend, 744 Tk, BS
Pfc Tad R Tragasz, 117 Inf, BS
Cpl Morris W Trammell, 230 FA, BS
S/Sgt Will N Trammel, 119 Inf, SS BS
T/4 Buford C Trantham, 230 FA, BS
Sgt Oliver C Trantham Jr, 120 Inf, BS
Sgt Ernest R Trapp, 119 Inf BS
Capt Richard P T Trauth, 230 FA,
SS BS w/OLC
Pfc James F Travis, 119 Inf, BS
Pfc Jerry C Travison, 120 Inf, BS
Sgt Lee H Traywick, 118 FA, BS
T/Sgt Bernard J Treacy, 119 Inf, BS
Pfc Michael J F Treacy, 230 FA, BS
Capt Albert Trearse, Hq 30 Div BS w/OLC
Pvt Alfred Treffiletti, 119 Inf, SS
Lt Col Alfred J Treherne, Div Surg,
BS w/2 OLC C d'G
S/Sgt Charles P Tremaine, 117 Inf BS
S/Sgt Paul E Tremmel, 119 Inf, SS BS
T/5 Virgil L Trennepohl, 113 FA, BS

T/4 Eldred E Trent, 120 Inf, SS BS
Pfc Vincent Trento, 197 FA, BS
Pfc George J Tressel, 120 Inf, BS
2d Lt Thomas M Tressler, 120 Inf, BS
Pfc Willis A Trettin, 117 Inf, BS
Lt Col Ward R Treverton, 730 Ord, BS
1st Lt Robert E Trigg, 197 FA,
    AM w/7 OLC C d'G
S/Sgt Thomas V Triggs, 120 Inf, BS
T/5 William C Trilli, 823 TD, BS
Pvt Achille J Troiani, 119 Inf, BS
Cpl Robert V Troiani, 744 Tk, SS
Pfc Leonard P Trombetta, 105 Eng, BS
S/Sgt William R Trombley, 120 Inf, SS BS
1st Lt Clarence A Trosvig, 99 Inf, SS
Sgt William F Trowbridge, Hq 30 Div, BS
Pvt Willis M True Jr, 120 Inf, SS BS w/3 OLC
T/5 Jim R Truett, 823 TD, BS w/OLC
Pvt Ira T Truitt, 119 Inf, BS
T/5 Paul R Truitt, 120 Inf, BS
Pfc Manuel B Trujillo, 105 Med, BS
M/Sgt Seledon E Trujillo, 823 TD, BS
Pfc Simplicio Trujillo, 119 Inf, SS
T/4 George G Truman, 117 Inf, BS
Pfc Ignatius Trzeciak, 119 Inf, SS
Pfc Donald B Tucker, 120 Inf, BS
Sgt Embra A Tucker, 105 Eng, BS
S/Sgt Eugene Tucker, 119 Inf, BS
1st Lt Thomas E Tucker, 120 Inf, BS
Pfc James A Tucker, 120 Inf, BS
Sgt Ray Tuckett, 119 Inf, SS
Pvt Irvin J Tudor, 105 Eng, BS
Pfc John L Tudor, 117 Inf, BS
S/Sgt Thomas R Tuell, 117 Inf, BS
Pfc Richard Tull, 120 Inf, BS
1st Lt John E Tullbane, 119 Inf, SS BS
S/Sgt Ernest W Tullis, 117 Inf, SS
Cpl Bill Turanyi, 120 Inf, BS
Pfc John C Turco, 120 Inf, BS
Sgt Edgar M Turnbaugh, 105 Eng, BS w/2 OLC
1st Lt James H Turner, 197 FA, BS w/OLC
1st Lt James K Turner, 105 Eng, BS w/2 OLC
Cpl Ruel J Turner, 30 QM, BS
T/5 Rufus B Turner, 30 QM, BS
Pfc Wayne E Turner, 119 Inf, BS
S/Sgt Ewell M Turns, 119 Inf, BS
T/4 Edgar H Tutterow, 117 Inf, BS
S/Sgt Edward Tuttle, Hq 30 Div, BS
Capt Paul R Tuttle, 120 Inf, BS w/OLC
1st Lt Grover C Twiner, 117 Inf, BS w/OLC
1st Lt William A Twohig, 105 Eng,
    SS w/OLC BS
Pfc John E Twomey, 119 Inf, BS
M/Sgt Howard W Tyler, 117 Inf, BS
Pfc John W Tyler, 119 Inf, BS
1st Lt Robert A Tyler, 120 Inf, SS
Pfc Robert L Tyler 120 Inf, BS
T/4 Lee R Tyner Jr, 30 Rcn, BS
2d Lt Alexander H Tyrity, 744 Tk, BS
1st Lt Jean M Ubbes, 743 Tk, SS BS
S/Sgt Stephen Uhring, 120 Inf, BS
T/4 Albert Ujcich, 120 Inf, BS w/OLC
Cpl Joseph Uliano, 120 Inf BS
Cpl Jose C Ulibarri, 823 TD, SS
Pfc Gerhard M Umlauf, 743 Tk, BS w/OLC
Pfc Walter L Underahl, 117 Inf, BS
Sgt Walter E Underhill, 823 TD, SS
Pfc Billie Underwood, 531 AAA, SS
S/Sgt Don A Underwood, 120 Inf, SS
T/Sgt Joseph B Underwood, 117 Inf, BS w/OLC
S/Sgt Thomas J Underwood, 117 Inf, BS
2d Lt Frederick W Unger, 119 Inf,
    DSC SS BS C d'G
T/4 Max P Uniglicht, 117 Inf BS
T/5 Leonard L Uphaus, 120 Inf, BS
Pfc Clyde R Upright, 120 Inf, BS
1st Lt Elbert R Upshaw, 117 Inf, SS
S/Sgt Badger V Upton Jr, 120 Inf, BS
Sgt Michael Urban, 119 Inf, SS BS
Pfc Frank S Urbanski, 119 Inf, BS
Pfc Leonard G Urbansky, 743 Tk, BS
Pfc Anthony B Vabolis, 120 Inf, BS
Cpl Peter J Vaccaro, 105 Eng, SS
Sgt Theodore A Vacura, 117 Inf, SS

1st Lt Joseph H Vaden, 531 AAA, BS
Sgt William P Vafeas, 120 Inf, BS w/OLC
Pfc Julius M Vajda, 119 Inf, BS
T/Sgt William A Valdes, 30 Div Hq, BS
T/4 Epifanio Valdez Jr, 743 Tk, BS
1st Lt Isidro S Valdez, 70 FA, AM
T/3 Dominic R Valente, Div Hq, BS
Pvt Thomas A Valles, 113 FA, BS
T/Sgt Walter G Van Cleave, 117 Inf, BS
Pfc William J Vandenberg, 117 Inf, SS
Pvt Paul Vandenbrook, 119 Inf, BS
Sgt John Van Der Kamp, 120 Inf, DSC BS
Pfc Levi H Van Der Kolk, 117 Inf,
    SS BS w/2 OLC
2d Lt Neal Van Der Kooy, 119 Inf, BS
Pfc Francis G Vander Voort, 117 Inf, SS
T/5 William S Vanee, 117 Inf, BS w/OLC
T/3 Ray Van Epps, Div Hq, BS
T/4 Delmar J Van Gundy, 105 Med, BS
1st Lt Adrian A Van Hook, 113 FA, SS BS
T/4 Merrill F Van Horn, 823 TD, BS
Cpl George R Van Horne, 113 FA, BS
T/4 Thomas L Van Houten, 118 FA, SS BS
Cpl William Van Leuven, 743 Tk, BS
Pfc Floyd A Van Loan, 117 Inf, BS
Pfc Roy E Vann, 117 Inf, BS
S/Sgt Joseph L Van Meter, 117 Inf, BS
Pvt Mickey M Van Natta, 105 Eng, BS
Pfc William K Vannell, 120 Inf, SS
S/Sgt Daniel B Vannice, 119 Inf, SS BS
Lt Col Thomas E Van Noppen, Div Hq,
    BS C d'G
S/Sgt John C Van Pelt, 105 Eng, BS
Capt Arthur R Van Sistine, 99 Inf, BS
Pfc Raymond E Van Treese 105 Med BS
Sgt James R Van Winkle, 117 Inf,
    SS BS w/2 OLC
Sgt John Van Wyk, 120 Inf, SS
Cpl Richard Varela, 743 Tk, BS w/OLC
Pfc Robert H Varnell, 117 Inf, BS
Sgt Fred F Varva 117 Inf BS
Cpl Bert W Vaughn, 119 Inf, BS
S/Sgt William R Vaughn, 119 Inf, BS
Cpl Henry J Vecchio, 397 FA, BS
Pfc Luigi G Vece, 119 Inf, BS
S/Sgt Joseph P Veenstra, 119 Inf, BS
Pvt Martin Vega, 105 Eng, BS
Pfc Fred J Veleta, 120 Inf, SS
Pfc Joseph N Velino, 117 Inf, BS w/OLC
Cpl Theodore Veltman, 230 FA, SS
Pfc Albert Venditti, 117 Inf, BS
Pfc Fred H Vendt, 117 Inf, SS
S/Sgt Anthony Venzon, 230 FA, BS
Pfc Elmer L Vercammen, 117 Inf BS
1st Lt James R Vareen, 230 FA, BS
S/Sgt Harry L Vernon, 117 Inf, BS
Sgt Philias J Verrette, 119 Inf, SS
Pfc Mario J Vertucci, 120 Inf, BS
S/Sgt Matthew G Vesel, 120 Inf, SS
S/Sgt Arthur Vest, 117 Inf, BS
T/4 Clarence A Vest, 120 Inf, BS
T/5 Charles Vestal Jr, 120 Inf BS
S/Sgt William P Veteto, 120 Inf BS w/OLC
T/Sgt Adrian F Vetter, 119 Inf, BS
Sgt Cecil S Via, 105 Eng BS
Pvt Eldred Viard, 119 Inf, SS
T/5 Winnie L Viatore Jr, 118 FA, SS BS
Pfc Graydon M Vickery, 120 Inf, BS
Pfc William Victor, 117 Inf, BS
Lt Col Lewis D Vieman, 230 FA,
    SS BS w/2 OLC
Pfc Bruno C Viertel, 117 Inf, BS
Sgt Alvin J Vig, 118 FA, BS
Pfc Philip A Vigeant, 117 Inf, BS
S/Sgt Anthony P Viggiano, 119 Inf SS
T/4 Alexander J Vilcsek, 119 Inf BS
T/Sgt Barney J Villa, 119 Inf BS
Sgt Jimmie G Villa 119 Inf, SS
T/4 Thomas Villalovas, 117 Inf, SS
Pfc Gennaro J Villano, 119 Inf, BS
Sgt John A Villar, 730 Ord, BS
T/3 Anthony J Villardi, Div Arty, BS
T/4 R G Vincent, 105 Eng, BS
Cpl Dominic S Vincenzo, 30 Rcn, SS

S/Sgt John M Vinson, 120 Inf, SS
WOJG Wiley S Vinson, 119 Inf, BS
1st Lt William K Virgin, 117 Inf, BS w/OLC
Pfc Frank A Vit, 119 Inf, BS
T/5 Albert A Vitale, 120 Inf, BS
Cpl Michael Vitale, 119 Inf, BS
Sgt Philip J Vitale, 120 Inf, SS
Pvt Pasquale J Vitalone, 117 Inf, SS BS
Pfc Raymond W Vogan, 120 Inf, BS
S/Sgt Charles C Vogel, Div Hq, BS
Sgt Peter J Vogels, 120 Inf, BS w/OLC
T/5 Rollin M Volkers, 120 Inf, BS
Pfc Junior R Vollmar, 120 Inf, BS
Pfc Joseph L Volmer, 117 Inf, BS
Pfc Rocco V Volonino, 105 Med, BS
Pfc John S Volpe, 117 Inf, BS
Pfc Frank Vomacka, 117 Inf, BS
Pfc Camille Vonck, 120 Inf, BS
T/5 Thurston Von Der Tenn, 120 Inf, BS
1st Lt Thomas K Voorhis, 120 Inf, SS
Sgt Frank H Vore, 120 Inf, SS BS
Sgt Burvel Voss, 823 TD, BS
Pfc Joseph Vukelich, 117 Inf, BS
Sgt John W Vye, 823 TD, BS
1st Lt Henry T Waddell, 119 Inf, SS BS w/OLC
1st Lt Jack W Waggoner, 117 Inf, BS
S/Sgt August G Wagner, 120 Inf, BS w/OLC
Pfc Eugene R Wagner, 119 Inf, BS w/OLC
Pfc Gilbert L Wagner, 119 Inf, BS w/OLC
Pfc Glenn L Wagner, 120 Inf, BS
Pvt Henry L Wagner, 119 Inf, BS
Pfc John E Wagner, 119 Inf, BS
Pfc Thomas M Wagner, 117 Inf, SS
Sgt Wilfred D Wagner, 117 Inf, BS
Capt George E Wagoner, 747 Tk, SS
Sgt Willard L Waid, 119 Inf, BS
S/Sgt Victor G Waldahl, 119 Inf, BS w/2 OLC
Pfc Albert L Walden, 120 Inf, BS
S/Sgt Henry C Walden, 197 FA, SS
Pfc Bruce Waldman, 120 Inf, BS w/OLC
Pfc James H Waldron, 743 Tk, BS
Pfc Jethro Waldron, 120 Inf, SS
T/Sgt James H Waldrop, 117 Inf, BS
Pfc Franklin E Walker, 120 Inf, BS
Sgt Harry L Walker, 120 Inf, BS w/OLC
Pvt Herman E Walker, 117 Inf, BS
Pfc Joseph H Walker, 119 Inf, BS
T/Sgt Marvin F Walker, Hq 30 Div, BS
T/5 Oscar P Walker, 113 FA, BS
Pfc Rhea H Walker, 117 Inf, BS
S/Sgt Robert L Walker, 119 Inf, BS
Sgt Roy C Walker, 30 Sig, BS
Sgt Thomas E Walker, 117 Inf, BS
Sgt Warren P Walker, 117 Inf, BS
S/Sgt Edward F Wall, 117 Inf, BS
T/Sgt Joe T Wall, 120 Inf, BS
T/Sgt Lewis Wall, 120 Inf, BS
Col David C Wallace, 1153 Eng, BS
Sgt John T Wallace, 117 Inf, BS
2d Lt Richard T Wallace, 118 FA, SS BS
1st Lt Thomas S Wallace, Hq 30 Div, BS
Pvt William O Wallace, 113 FA, BS
CWO Jack E Wallen, Hq 30 Div, BS
Pvt Aaron K Waller, 117 Inf, BS w/OLC
T/4 Norman Waller, 113 FA, BS
S/Sgt Richard R Waller, 119 Inf, BS
S/Sgt William W Waller, 118 FA, BS
1st Lt Robert M Wallin, 120 Inf, BS
Cpl Finis E Walls, 119 Inf, BS
1st Lt Francis J Walsh Jr, 117 Inf, BS
Pfc Ralph J Walsh, 117 Inf, BS
Sgt Archie W Walstrom, 119 Inf, BS
1st Lt Frederick J Walter, 119 Inf, BS
1st Lt Nelson M Walter 119 Inf BS
T/4 Albert O Walters, 119 Inf, BS
T/Sgt Charles E Walters, 120 Inf, BS
T/5 Edward A Walters, 117 Inf, BS
S/Sgt William A Walters, 118 FA, BS
Cpl Mark P Walthers, 30 Rcn, BS
T/4 Elmer J Waltzing, 743 Tk BS
Sgt Joseph M Wanczowski, 119 Inf, BS
Cpl John A Wanderski, 117 Inf, BS
Sgt Joseph M Wanczowski, 119 Inf, BS
Pfc Richard L Wanex, 119 Inf, BS

Cpl Wilson O Wanner, 743 Tk, BS
Sgt Irwin Wanshek, 120 Inf, BS
Pfc William P Warburton, 119 Inf, SS
S/Sgt Carl W Ward, 117 Inf, SS
1st Lt Donald A Ward, 119 Inf, SS
S/Sgt Harold M Ward, 230 FA, SS
Pfc Lawrence A Ward, 105 Med, BS
Pfc Norris O Ward, 117 Inf, BS
Lt Col Peter O Ward, 120 Inf, BS w/2 OLC
Pfc Robert T Ward, 117 Inf, SS w/OLC BS
Pfc Ronald L Ward 117 Inf, BS w/OLC
Pfc Vance Ward, 120 Inf, BS
Pfc Walter S Ward, 119 Inf, BS
S/Sgt William R Ward Sr, 119 Inf, SS
T/4 Patrick M Warden, 823 TD, BS
Pfc William C Ware, 119 Inf, BS w/OLC
Pvt Joseph C Wargo, 119 Inf, BS
Pfc Bertrand C Waring, 119 Inf, BS
Capt Sterlin W Wark 203 FA, BS
Cpl Arthur L Warner, 105 Eng, BS
1st Lt David M Warner, 117 Inf, BS w/2 OLC
Pfc James R Warner, 99 Inf, BS
Sgt Mason R Warner, 119 Inf, BS
1st Lt Robert S Warnich, 120 Inf, SS BS w/OLC
2d Lt Frank Warnock, 117 Inf, DSC
Pfc Alfred A Warren, 120 Inf, BS
Pfc Luther R Warren, 119 Inf, BS
Sgt Ralph C Warren, 120 Inf, BS
Capt Sam F Warren, 973 FA, SS
Sgt Michael Waryha, 117 Inf, BS
1st Lt Richard Washburn, 803 TD, BS
Pfc John Wassel, 119 Inf, BS
Pvt Michael W Wasserman, 117 Inf, BS
T/Sgt Richard E Wasson, 119 Inf, BS
T/Sgt Arthur H Waters, 120 Inf, BS
S/Sgt Joseph C Wathen, 120 Inf, BS
1st Lt Jack C Watkins, 118 FA, SS BS w/OLC
T/5 James C Watkinson, 117 Inf, BS
T/Sgt John W Watlington, 117 Inf, BS
Sgt Floyd C Watson, 117 Inf, BS
1st Sgt Gene A Watson, 117 Inf, BS
S/Sgt Grant G Watson, 105 Eng, BS
T/4 John M Watson, Div Hq, BS
Pvt Morgan S Watson, 117 Inf, BS
Pfc Ralph E Watson, 117 Inf, BS
Capt Randolph C Watson, 119 Inf, BS
Cpl Raymond L Watson, 120 Inf, BS
CWO Walter L Watson, 105 Eng, BS
Pvt Warren G Watson, 526 Armd Inf, SS
S/Sgt Edwin B Watt, 119 Inf, BS
Pfc Hobson Watts, 119 Inf, BS
Pfc Lawrence C Watts, 119 Inf, BS
Pvt Wesley J Watts, 119 Inf, SS
T/4 Albert J Wawrkiewicz, 119 Inf, BS
Pfc Frank W Way, 119 Inf, SS
Pvt Harlen W Way, 117 Inf, DSC
T/4 Loyd Q Way, 120 Inf, BS
1st Lt Norman J Wayman, 120 Inf, BS
Capt Clayborn P Wayne, 119 Inf, SS BS
S/Sgt Ralph H Weagel, 120 Inf, BS w/OLC
Pvt Frank M Weagley Jr, 105 Med, BS
T/Sgt Frank L Wease, 119 Inf, DSC BS
Maj Abbott C Weatherly, 197 FA, BS w/OLC
Pfc Jack B Weatherly, 120 Inf, BS
Capt J T Weatherspoon, 117 Inf, BS w/OLC
T/5 Buster J Weaver, 531 AAA, BS
1st Sgt Hubert H Weaver, 119 Inf, BS
Sgt Willie L Weaver, 105 Med, SS
Pvt Calvin J Webb, 117 Inf, BS
S/Sgt Joseph M Webb Jr, 120 Inf, BS
CWO Lloyd P Webb, 30 Div Band, BS
1st Lt Russell H Webber, 117 Inf, SS
1st Lt Clarence W Weber, 105 Eng, SS
S/Sgt Donald P Wedberg, 119 Inf, SS
Capt Paul R Weed, 118 FA,
 SS w/OLC BS w/OLC
Pfc John F Weekley 120 Inf, SS BS
1st Sgt Thomas M Weems, 120 Inf,
 SS BS w/OLC
S/Sgt Jack C Weeren, 119 Inf, BS
Sgt Edward W Wehrle Jr, 117 Inf, BS
1st Sgt Alexander J Weiler, 117 Inf, BS
Sgt Grant W Weiler, 120 Inf, BS
1st Lt Raymond W Weiler, 120 Inf, BS

Cpl William F Weiler, 744 Tk, BS
T/5 Rodney J Weinand, 118 FA, BS
Pvt Harry Weinberg, 117 Inf, BS
S/Sgt Jack I Weinblatt, 113 FA, BS w/OLC
Pfc Melvin Weiner, 120 Inf, BS
Pfc Alvin N Weinstein, 119 Inf, BS
Pvt Myron H Weisbart, 117 Inf, BS
2d Lt Robert T Weisberg, 120 Inf, SS
Pvt John J Weisgerger, 117 Inf, SS
Pfc Floyd J Weishaar, 117 Inf, BS
Sgt Sam Weisman, 117 Inf, BS
Cpl Frederick C Weiss, Div Arty, BS
Pfc Meyer Weiss, 120 Inf, BS
1st Lt Robert L Weiss, 230 FA, SS C d'G
S/Sgt Elbert G Weitman, Hq 30 Div, BS
S/Sgt Francis E Welch, 120 Inf, SS
Pfc Marion A Welch, 120 Inf, BS
Capt Raymond Welch, 120 Inf, BS w/OLC
Pvt Robert W Welch, 30 Sig, BS
Pfc William J Welch, 119 Inf, SS
Cpl Guye E Welford, 119 Inf, BS
Pfc Charles D Wells, 117 Inf, BS
S/Sgt Edward R Wells Jr, 120 Inf, BS
 Pfc John B Wells 120 Inf, BS
S/Sgt John W Wells, 113 FA, BS
S/Sgt Martin S Wells, 113 FA, BS
Pfc Richard C Wells, Hq 30 Div, BS
T/5 Raymond W Welsh 105 Eng, BS
Capt Rodney C Welsh, ECAD, SS
T/4 Paul A Welter, 119 Inf, BS
Pfc Herbert W Wendelken, 119 Inf, BS
Pfc Edward J Wenert, 120 Inf, BS
Cpl L Wennell, 120 Inf, BS
Sgt Waldo P Wennerberg, 743 Tk, BS w/OLC
Pfc Chester A Wenning, 120 Inf, BS
T/Sgt George J Wenzel, 117 Inf, BS w/OLC
1st Lt Walter A Wert, 120 Inf, SS w/2 OLC BS
Sgt Harry D West 119 Inf, BS
S/Sgt Homer L West, 117 Inf, BS
Cpl James C West, 743 Tk, SS
Cpl Leo West, 197 FA, BS
Pfc Russell L West, 117 Inf, BS
Pvt August B Westberg, 117 Inf, SS w/OLC
1st Lt Charles A Westbrook, 120 Inf BS w/OLC
Pfc Thomas G Westbrook 119 Inf, BS
Sgt Don W Wester, 117 Inf, BS
Sgt Frank M Westerberg, 117 Inf, BS
Pvt Louis K Westerfield, 120 Inf, BS
Sgt Willard Westfall, 30 Sig, BS
2d Lt Alton L Westman, 743 Tk BS
Pfc Eugene C Wetherill, 119 Inf, BS
Sgt Charles F Weyant, 117 Inf, BS
S/Sgt Lawrence F Weyer, 117 Inf, SS BS
Sgt Ralph R Weyh, 120 Inf SS
1st Lt Will B Wharton, 120 Inf, SS MC
Pfc Cecil E Whatley, 117 Inf, BS
S/Sgt Robert E Wheat, 120 Inf, BS
T/5 Norman J Wheel, 118 FA, BS
Pfc Alfred E Wheeler, 119 Inf, SS
Pfc Arthur F Wheeler, 117 Inf, BS
T/5 Edward E Wheeler, 105 Eng SS
T/5 Henry W Wheeler, 117 Inf, BS
Pvt Roy C Wheeler, 117 Inf, BS
Sgt Elbert B Whisnant, 119 Inf SS w/OLC
Pfc Martin L Whitaker, 117 Inf BS
Cpl Harlan Whitcomb, 743 Tk, BS
Pfc Dale G White, 117 Inf, BS
Pfc Francis L White, 119 Inf, BS
Pfc Franklin F White, 119 Inf, BS w/OLC
T/4 Harley White 119 Inf BS
Pfc Harold P White, 823 TD, SS
S/Sgt Herbert F White, 119 Inf, BS
Cpl James A White, 120 Inf, BS
Capt James B White, 230 FA, BS
2d Lt James R White 120 Inf, BS w/OLC
Sgt John White, 119 Inf, BS
S/Sgt Marion S White, 117 Inf SS
S/Sgt Owen R White, 120 Inf, BS
Pvt Payson D White 119 Inf, BS
S/Sgt Raymond P White 117 Inf, SS BS w/OLC
Pfc Richard J White, 119 Inf, BS
Pfc William J White, 119 Inf, BS
T/5 Darwin E Whitenight, 117 Inf, BS
Pfc Herbert J Whiting, 117 Inf, BS

1st Sgt James R Whiting, 823 TD, BS
Pvt Evan F Whitis, 119 Inf, SS
1st Sgt Guy A Whitley, 117 Inf, BS w/OLC
Pfc Monroe J Whitley, 823 TD, SS
1st Lt Clarence R Whitlock, 117 Inf, SS BS
S/Sgt Ralph D Whitt, 119 Inf, BS
1st Lt David S Whittaker, 119 Inf, SS w/OLC
Pfc Francis J Wiatrowski, 119 Inf, BS
S/Sgt George H Wichterich Jr, 823 TD, BS
Cpl Raymond J Wick, 30 MP, BS
Sgt Charles E Wicklund 117 Inf, BS
T/5 Charles T Widdop, 823 TD, BS
S/Sgt William J Widener, 119 Inf, DSC SS BS
1st Lt Warren L Wieber, 120 Inf, BS w/OLC
T/4 Werner Wiebelt, 120 Inf, BS
Pvt Frank B Wieczorek, 743 Inf, BS
Pfc Joseph J Wiedmayer, 283 FA, BS
Pfc Julius Wiener, 119 Inf, BS
Sgt Alfred M Wiesemann, 120 Inf, BS
2d Lt Lambert V Wieser, 743 Tk,
        SS w/2 OLC BS
S/Sgt Burnie H Wiggins, 120 Inf, SS BS
S/Sgt Russell W Wike, 117 Inf, SS
Pfc Kenneth A Wiker, 119 Inf, SS
Capt Daniel W Wilbur, 105 Med, BS
Cpl William J Wilburn, 743 Tk, BS
Pfc Harry Wild, 119 Inf, BS
Sgt Edward M Wildeber, 119 Inf, BS
Sgt Thomas W Wilder, 117 Inf, BS
Sgt Willard A Wilder, 197 FA, BS
T/Sgt Arthur P Wiley, 120 Inf, BS w/OLC
S/Sgt John W Wiley, 743 Tk, BS
T/Sgt Jack B Wilhelm, 120 Inf, BS
T/3 Leonard L Wilhelm, 30 Sig, BS
Sgt Donald L Wilhere, 119 Inf, BS w/OLC
Pvt Dude Wilderson, 117 Inf, BS
Pfc Lavoy Wilkerson, 117 Inf, BS
T/4 Freeman Wilkins, Hq 30 Div, SS
Pfc Raymond L Wilkins, 119 Inf, BS
WOJG Robert J Wilkins, 120 Inf, BS
Pfc Marion E Wilkinson, 743 Tk BS
Cpl Marvin O Wilkinson, 113 Cav, SS
Pvt Clifford A Willeat, 120 Inf, BS
Sgt John R Willette, 203 FA, BS
Lt Col Adrian W Williams, 258 Eng, BS
Capt Alfred H Williams Jr, 743 Tk, BS
Cpl Carl E Williams, 197 FA, SS
Pvt Carl E Williams, 119 Inf, SS
S/Sgt Carl H Williams, 120 Inf, BS
Pfc Carl H Williams, 117 Inf, BS
Pvt D J Williams, 120 Inf BS
Capt Wilbur D Williams, 120 Inf, BS
Cpl Elmer G Williams, 823 TD, SS
1st Lt Elmo T Williams, 120 Inf, BS w/OLC
Pfc Emmett L Williams, 117 Inf, BS
Capt George E Williams Jr SS BS
Pfc George V Williams, 117 Inf, BS
T/Sgt Gerald D Williams, 117 Inf, BS
S/Sgt James D Williams, 119 Inf, BS
T/5 James E Williams, 823 TD, BS
Pfc John C Williams, 117 Inf BS
2d Lt John M Williams, 117 Inf, BS
Cpl John V Williams, 283 FA BS
Pfc John W Williams, 120 Inf, BS
Pvt John W Williams, 120 Inf, BS w/OLC
Cpl June E Williams, 117 Inf, BS
2d Lt Norlie W Williams, 119 Inf, SS BS w/OLC
Sgt Otis P Williams, 120 Inf, BS
Cpl Paul R Williams, 119 Inf, BS
Pfc Raymond A Williams, 117 Inf BS
1st Sgt Robert L Williams 119 Inf, BS
Pfc Ross B Williams, 119 Inf, BS
S/Sgt Roy J Williams, 119 Inf, SS BS
Pvt Shirley A Williams, 120 Inf BS
Pfc Travis L Williams 117 Inf, BS
S/Sgt Truman C Williams, 117 Inf BS
Cpl Verlon A Williams, 230 FA, SS
S/Sgt Vernon O Williams, 117 Inf, BS
Pfc Warren L Williams, 119 Inf, BS
S/Sgt Wiley Williams, 120 Inf BS
Pfc Wilfred H Williams, 230 FA, BS
S/Sgt William E Williams, 531 AAA BS
S/Sgt William H Williams, 743 Tk, SS

S/Sgt Edward G York, 120 Inf, SS
T/5 Willie D York, 119 Inf, BS
S/Sgt Ernest Yost, 120 Inf,
    SS w/OLC BS w/OLC
T/5 Benjamin E Youmans, 197 FA, SS
1st Lt Scott A Youmans, 119 Inf, SS
T/4 Arthur N Young Jr, 119 Inf, BS
Capt Edward L Young, Div Arty, SS
Pfc Francis J Young, 117 Inf, BS w/OLC
Sgt James H Young, 117 Inf, BS
Maj Joseph A Young, 119 Inf, SS BS
Pfc Lloyd W Young, 120 Inf, SS
Pfc Luther A Young, 120 Inf, BS
Pfc Marion D Young, 119 Inf, BS
T/5 Marvin M Young, 113 Rcn, BS
2d Lt Roy V Young, 120 Inf, SS w/OLC
S/Sgt Vester C Young, 119 Inf, BS
1st Sgt William H Young, 730 Ord, BS
Pfc Walter H Young, 120 Inf, BS
S/Sgt Jerome A Younger, Div Hq, BS
Pfc Louis Yurkevicz, 117 Inf, SS BS
Sgt Martin J Zabicki, 120 Inf,
Cpl Jesse W Zadroga, 113 FA, BS
Pfc Edward A Zaidins, 120 Inf, BS
Cpl P Zak, 119 Inf, BS w/OLC
Pfc Walter E Zakrison, 105 Eng, BS
Pfc Casimir J Zalucki, 119 Inf, BS w/OLC
Pvt Walter J Zamjoski, 119 Inf, BS
T/5 Andrew M Zampella, 117 Inf BS w/OLC
S/Sgt Peter J Zanella, 119 Inf, SS BS
1st Lt Robert H Zankl, 730 Ord, BS

Sgt Joseph Zaraza, 120 Inf, SS BS
T/5 Edward Zareski, 117 Inf, BS
Pvt Steven Zarkovich, 230 FA, BS
Pfc John Zasadni, 120 Inf, BS
Pfc Edward G Zdnowski, 119 Inf, BS
Capt Joseph E Zehner, 117 Inf, BS w/OLC
S/Sgt Richard W Zeigler, 120 Inf, BS
1st Lt Leroy E Zieschang, 3695 QM, BS w/OLC
Sgt Steve V Zelip, 117 Inf, BS
Sgt Ramon R Zepeda, 120 Inf, BS w/OLC
Pfc Paul V Zero, 117 Inf, BS
Capt Clement T Ziegler, 113 FA, SS
Capt William M Ziegler, 117 Inf, BS
Pvt Edwin F Zielinski, 105 Eng, BS
T/Sgt Raymond H Zielinski, 117 Inf, BS
Pfc William Zilinek, 120 Inf, BS
T/Sgt Alfred Zimkin, 119 Inf, BS
Pfc Lawrence Zinman, 119 Inf, BS
Pfc Leon B Ziolkowski, 117 Inf, BS
1st Sgt Hugh W Zittrauer, 230 FA, BS
S/Sgt John G Zizzo, 119 Inf, BS w/OLC
S/Sgt Milton L Zofi, Div Hq, BS
Pfc Thomas F Zontini, 120 Inf, BS
Pfc John J Zorena, 119 Inf, BS w/OLC
T/Sgt Harold Zornes, 105 Med, BS
T/Sgt John A Zuidema, 120 Inf, BS
S/Sgt Marvin E Zumwalt, 119 Inf, SS BS
Pfc John J Zurack, 117 Inf, BS w/OLC
Sgt Anthony J Zuvella, 105 Eng, SS BS w/OLC
Pfc Edward W Zweifel, 117 Inf, BS
S/Sgt Joseph R Zywiec, 803 TD, BS

Appendix 5

GERMAN PRISONERS TAKEN

117th Infantry	15,893
119th Infantry	16,096
120th Infantry	13,242
Division Artillery	1,450
105th Engineer Battalion	410
531st Antiaircraft Battalion	649
743d Tank Battalion	2
823d Tank Destroyer Battalion	1,342
30th Reconnaissance Troop	3,504
30th Division Headquarters Company	111
30th Signal Company	149
30th Quartermaster Company	157
730th Ordnance Company	18
TOTAL	53,023[1]

[1]50,774 prisoners were processed by 30th Division Military Police and 105th Medical Battalion Others were turned in at prisoner of war inclosures run by other units Approximately 12,000 wounded German soldiers, captured when their hospitals were overrun, are not included in above totals

MEMBERS OF THE 30th INFANTRY DIVISION KILLED
IN ACTION OR MISSING IN ACTION

Joseph Abad, 120 Inf
Thomas Abel, 119 Inf
Leonard E Abernathy, 117 Inf
Thomas E Abernathy, 117 Inf
Glenn L Abbott, 120 Inf
Edmond Abomczvk, 119 Inf
Lyle C Abrahamson, 120 Inf
Isadore J Accardi, 119 Inf
Rabon F Acred, 120 Inf
Jacob Acton, 119 Inf
Baudra Addison, 230 FA
Alces P Adams, 119 Inf
Arlon L Adams, 119 Inf
Carl Adams, 119 Inf
Frank L Adams, 119 Inf
Horace H Adams, 119 Inf
Leslie W Adams 117 Inf
Ruben Adams, 120 Inf
William E Adams, 117 Inf
Chester J Adamski, 119 Inf
William Adkins, 119 Inf
Robert G Adkisson, 120 Inf
Lloyd E Agney, 119 Inf
Morris W Ahern, 119 Inf
Floyd E Akerley, 119 Inf
Benjamin Akers, 119 Inf
Sam L Albert, 120 Inf
Albert J Albertson, 105 Eng
Giovanni L Albini, 120 Inf
Guadalupe R Alcantar, 119 Inf
Dominick J Alco, 120 Inf
Austin O Alcorn, 120 Inf
Earl C Alcorn, 117 Inf
Rudulfo A Aldana, 117 Inf
Hershel F Alexander, 119 Inf
M C Alexander, 117 Inf
Louis M Aliperto, 120 Inf
Joseph S Allen, 120 Inf
Willard J Allen, 120 Inf
Lewis L Alley, 120 Inf
William W Alley, 119 Inf
Albert Q Aligood, 119 Inf
Norman P Alston, 120 Inf
Christ F Alt, 119 Inf
Michael W Altamari, 120 Inf
Alvin T Althage, 119 Inf
Clifford F Althoff, 117 Inf
Mathew American Horse, 117 Inf
Robert L Amiel, 117 Inf
Vernus Amis, 120 Inf
Joseph Amodio, 117 Inf
Beecher L Anderson, 119 Inf
Floyd J Anderson, 120 Inf
France H Anderson, 120 Inf
Harold L Anderson, 120 Inf
James R Anderson, 119 Inf
John A Anderson, 120 Inf
Lloyd G Anderson, 120 Inf
Nels M Anderson, 117 Inf
Robert J Anderson, 117 Inf
William A Anderson, 120 Inf
Joseph A. Andrade, 119 Inf
Arthur T Andrew, 117 Inf
Tom J Andrew, 120 Inf
Steve J Andrews, 119 Inf
Joseph A Andrulewicz, 120 Inf
Clyde T Angel, 117 Inf
Harry Angelo, 120 Inf
Alfred L Annis, 120 Inf
Jildo M Antonelli, 119 Inf
Raymond L Antonelli, 120 Inf
Harry E Appel, 120 Inf
James J Archambeault, 113 FA

Clyde L Archie, 120 Inf
Arthur F Archuleta, 119 Inf
Salvatore S Arcidiacone, 117 Inf
Nathan H Arenson, 120 Inf
Lawrence Arent, 120 Inf
Ralph Armitage, 117 Inf
Elmer Armstrong, 119 Inf
Leon Armstrong, 117 Inf
Zeagle C Arnett, 119 Inf
Harold M Arney, 119 Inf
Richard C Arnold, 230 FA
Ernest J Arsenault, 119 Inf
Vernon W Arvin, 120 Inf
Albert J Ash, 119 Inf
Willis E Asher, 117 Inf
James L Ashmore, 120 Inf
Clyde E Ashworth, 119 Inf
Claire F Askew, 119 Inf
Frank J Astemborski, 119 Inf
Fred H Atkinson, 117 Inf
Nissim Attas, 230 FA
David O Atwood, 117 Inf
William G Aubut, 119 Inf
Roland P Aucoin, 117 Inf
James A Ault, 119 Inf
Dan Austin, 120 Inf
Junior D Austin, 120 Inf
Cecil A Autry, 117 Inf
Earl L Autry, 117 Inf
Julius T Autry, 117 Inf
Harold E Avery, 120 Inf
Emmet M Ayers, 120 Inf
Lawrence H Ayers, 120 Inf
Lloyd W Ayers, 120 Inf
McClure R Ayscue, 117 Inf
Demetrio Baca, 117 Inf
Franklin P Bachelder, 119 Inf
Floyd R Bachtel, 117 Inf
Hazil L F Backus, 120 Inf
Curtis B Baber, 119 Inf
Richard E Babin, 30 Rcn Tr
Henry A Baecker, 105 Eng
Aaron Baer, 120 Inf
Clayton E Baggett, 119 Inf
Grover C Baggett, 117 Inf
Dennis Bahem, 117 Inf
Maxsdll L Bail, 119 Inf
Aubrey C Bailey, 119 Inf
David W Bailey, 119 Inf
James W Bailey, 119 Inf
Willis E Bain, 117 Inf
Carl L Bair, 119 Inf
Robert J Baird, 120 Inf
Broughton A Baker, 117 Inf
Donald W Baker, 120 Inf
Millard E Baker, 197 FA
Pete F Baker, 117 Inf
Robert S Baker, 119 Inf
Robert G Baker, 120 Inf
Samuel W Baker, 117 Inf
Vernon T Baker, 117 Inf
Walter V Bakewicz, 117 Inf
Glenn M Bakken, 120 Inf
Stewart E Bakken, 117 Inf.
Joe Balaski, 119 Inf
John M Balaska, 120 Inf
Lawrence R Baldy, 117 Inf
Wayne E Baldwin, 119 Inf
Nathan Balick, 120 Inf
Henry J Balk, 120 Inf
Gordon W Ballam, 120 Inf.
Donald Ballard, 117 Inf
Edward C Ballard, 119 Inf

Morris Bobrow, 119 Inf
Walter A Bobzin, 119 Inf
Joseph Boccanfuso, 119 Inf
Roy L Bocher, 119 Inf
David R Bodkin, 105 Eng
Orman J Bofamy, 117 Inf
Stuart F S Bogey, 117 Inf
Carl T Boggs, 120 Inf
Kent E Boggs, 117 Inf
Earl L Bohrer, 120 Inf
Raymond J Boker, 120 Inf
Bernard H Boland, 120 Inf
Sylvester Bolick, 119 Inf
Henry J Boltshauser, 119 Inf
Boyd M Bond, 117 Inf
John W Bonnetti, 120 Inf
Earle C Bood, 120 Inf
John C Book, 117 Inf
Buren L Bone, 119 Inf
James Booth, 117 Inf
Pat Booth Jr, 117 Inf
Robert Booth, 119 Inf
John Boots, 119 Inf
Raymond J Borcjman, 117 Inf
Antonio S Borges, 119 Inf
John A Borkenhagen, 117 Inf
John F Bormann, 119 Inf
Irving Bornstein, 117 Inf
Rosario J Bosco, 120 Inf
Glen G Bosman, 119 Inf
John E Bosnek, 120 Inf
Edward C Bottoms, 120 Inf
Roy W Bottom, 120 Inf
Antoine J Boucher, 117 Inf
Walter L Boughter, 120 Inf
Wilfred F Bourasso, 120 Inf
Francis O Bousky, 117 Inf
Roman W Bovy, 119 Inf
Earle C Bowers, 119 Inf
Edward J Bowers, 120 Inf
Everett D Bowers, 119 Inf
Harry O Bowersox, 120 Inf
James O Bowles, 117 Inf
Charles E Bowley, 119 Inf
Carter Bowling, 120 Inf
Thomas E Bowling Jr, 117 Inf
Reynolds V Bowser, 119 Inf
Cecil W Boyd, 120 Inf
Herbert L Boyle Jr, 117 Inf
Louis S Bozzay, 120 Inf
Elmer H Bracken, 117 Inf
Theodus Braddock, 117 Inf
Alton L Bradford, 117 Inf
Everett J Bradford, 117 Inf
Travis L Bradford, 120 Inf
Alfred R Bradley, 120 Inf
Lee R Bradley, 119 Inf
Palmer L Bradley, 120 Inf
Ruhel W Bradley, 120 Inf
Charles Bradshaw, 120 Inf
William H Braford, 119 Inf
Boyd Bragg, 120 Inf
Elbert N Bradley, 119 Inf
Claude O Bramlet, 119 Inf
Vernon Bramlette, 117 Inf
William H Brammer, 119 Inf
Hugh P Brandon, 120 Inf
Leon F Brann, 117 Inf
Vilas A Brannon, 120 Inf
Allen L Brasel, 120 Inf
Clarence C Brautigam, 119 Inf
Raymond A Bray, 117 Inf
Raymond P Brazil, 120 Inf
Irving J Brean, 117 Inf
Harry G Bredenberg, 119 Inf
Leslie B Bremer, 120 Inf
Walter T Brenning, 117 Inf
Kurt W Brieltgens, 119 Inf
Raymond E Briggs, 120 Inf
William J Briggs, 117 Inf
Dollard H Brisette, 120 Inf

Willard E Brister, 117 Inf
George Britch, 120 Inf
Eulus B Britt, 117 Inf
Russell L Brittingham, 119 Inf
Carl D Brizendine, 117 Inf
Edward E Brock, 117 Inf
Norman M Brock, 120 Inf
Robert R Brodbeck, 119 Inf
Archiliow Brodon, 105 Eng
Paul L Brookhart, 120 Inf
Bill J Brooks, 119 Inf
Edward C Brooks, 119 Inf
Robert N Brooks, 120 Inf
Robert F Brottmiller, 120 Inf
Arthur H Brouillard, 120 Inf
George R Brouillehe, 117 Inf
Harry E Brousseau, 120 Inf
Clarence J Brown, 117 Inf
George R Brown, 120 Inf
Horace C Brown, 117 Inf
Kenneth C Brown, 120 Inf
Meletious B Brown, 117 Inf
Oran W Brown, 117 Inf
Paul H Brown, 119 Inf
Raymond H Brown, 117 Inf
Robert J Brown, 119 Inf
Robert L Brown, 117 Inf
William C Brown, 117 Inf
John P Browning, 117 Inf
Kenneth E Brownlee, 117 Inf
Raymond L Broyles, 119 Inf
Kershel V Bruce, 120 Inf
Martin P Bruckerhoff, 119 Inf
Fred Bruner, 120 Inf
William E Bruner, 120 Inf
Leopold A Bryaert, 119 Inf
Charles A Bryant, 120 Inf
Paul B Bryant, 119 Inf
Walter Bryden, 120 Inf
Atigelo R Bucci, 120 Inf
Joseph Buchanan, 120 Inf
Henry W Bucholz, 119 Inf
Earl C Buckey, 120 Inf
Cleaver F Buckler, 119 Inf
Jay B Buckner, 105 Eng
Joseph E Bud, 120 Inf
Stephen Bukovina, 119 Inf
Calvin T Bullard, 120 Inf
John C Bulson, 120 Inf
Walter A Bunch, 120 Inf
Kenneth F Bunker, 119 Inf
Charles E Bunn, 120 Inf
James T W Buntyn, 120 Inf
Michael H Burchell, 119 Inf
Hubert A Burgess, 119 Inf
James E Burgess, 117 Inf
Phillip Burgess, 117 Inf
Dempsey Burkeen, 120 Inf
Leroy D Burkett, 120 Inf
Robert R Burkhardt, 120 Inf
Herman J Burkhart, 119 Inf
James F Burleigh, 117 Inf
Bernie E Burleson, 119 Inf
Charlie F Burnette, 119 Inf
Kenneth Burns, 117 Inf
Kennon C Burns, 119 Inf
Thomas J Burr, 119 Inf
Robert T Burruss, 120 Inf
Joe R Burton, 117 Inf
Leonard A Bury, 120 Inf
J L Bushnell, 197 FA
Fred Van Buskirk, 120 Inf
Carl E Bussabarger, 119 Inf
Elton E Bussewitz, 119 Inf
Arsene H Busslere, 117 Inf.
Nelson H Bustin, 120 Inf
John E Butcher, 117 Inf
Leslie M Butcher, 117 Inf.
Harold O Butler, 120 Inf
Richard S Buvacker, 117 Inf.
Wilburn A Byers, 120 Inf.

Donald E Byers, 120 Inf
Thomas R Byers, 119 Inf
James J Bynum, 120 Inf
John Cabral, 117 Inf
Manuel Cabral, 120 Inf
Joe H Cagle, 120 Inf
Edward Cahill, 120 Inf
Virgil G Cain, 117 Inf
Pasquale M Calabrese, 117 Inf
Earl Caldwell, 117 Inf
Jesse R Caldwell, 120 Inf
Richard D Caldwell, 117 Inf
John Caligary, 120 Inf
Bruno G Calka, 117 Inf
Howard E Callaway, 120 Inf
John J Callos, 117 Inf
Jack M Calloway, 119 Inf
Frank Calvelli, 119 Inf
Roy L Calvert, 120 Inf
Henry K Camaacho, 120 Inf
Charles Cammardta, 117 Inf
Elza O Camp, 120 Inf
Nicholas A Campagna, 119 Inf
Charles J Campbell, 117 Inf
Furman B Campbell, 117 Inf
Joseph B Campbell, 117 Inf
Joseph E Campbell, 120 Inf
Kenneth K Campbell, 120 Inf
Leroy F Campbell, 119 Inf
John G Canavera, 120 Inf
John C Cantley, 119 Inf
Abner O Cantrell, 117 Inf
Joseph W Cantrell, 119 Inf
Hank Cantrell, 117 Inf
Robert D Capelli, 117 Inf
Tony A Capetanakis, 120 Inf
Frank J Capozzi, 117 Inf
Edward F Capps, 117 Inf
Clifford H Capshaw, 119 Inf
Cleo E Card, 117 Inf
Robert J Cardner, 117 Inf
Mario D Cardosi, 119 Inf
Russell A Carey, 117 Inf
Robert B Carlson, 117 Inf
Adelard G Caron, 120 Inf
Wilfred C Caron, 117 Inf
James M Carothers, 119 Inf
George W Carmack, 117 Inf
Charles L Carpenter, 119 Inf
Clyde Carpenter, 119 Inf
Homer W Carpenter, 117 Inf
Joseph P Cardtenuto, 117 Inf
Patrick J Carito, 120 Inf
John R Carleton, 120 Inf
John A Carr, 119 Inf
Russell Carrico, 120 Inf
Bernard V Carroll, 120 Inf
Jesse Carroll, 120 Inf
John Carroll, 119 Inf
Leonard E Carroll, 120 Inf
Price W Carroll, 105 Eng
Steve W Carroll, 113 Inf
Harley Carson, 119 Inf
Burley Carte, 117 Inf
Dan W Carter, 120 Inf
Eugene Carter, 117 Inf
Johnnie V Carter, 119 Inf
Walton L Carter, 120 Inf
Wilbur M Carter, 119 Inf
Stanley P Carty, 117 Inf
Bleton R Carver, 119 Inf
Edward K Carver, 120 Inf
Emmett W Carver, 120 Inf
James E Carver, 119 Inf
John F Casanova, 117 Inf
Paul W Casas, 120 Inf
Roscoe E Case, 119 Inf
James W Cash, 120 Inf
Walter L Cassell, 119 Inf
Gerhlot Casselli, 117 Inf
Andrew Cassels, 117 Inf

Anthony T Cassese, 120 Inf
Raymond F Castay, 117 Inf
Jose A Castenade, 119 Inf
Arlando O Casterton, 117 Inf
Frank T Castiglia, 117 Inf
Isabel U Castillo, 119 Inf
Merlyn C Castner, 30 Rcn Tn
Roy R Casto, 117 Inf
Tony A Castruita, 117 Inf
Robert E Catino, 120 Inf
James R Carlett, 120 Inf
Floyd A Caul, 119 Inf
Wilfred B Causey, 117 Inf
John Cavato, 117 Inf
Edward W Cavill, 119 Inf
Raymond E Cejka, 119 Inf
Albert J Cella, 119 Inf
Daniel G Cellucci, 117 Inf
Salvatore Cennami, 120 Inf
James Centers, 120 Inf
Joseph Cernich, 119 Inf
Lawrence E Chadd, 120 Inf
Cecil J Chadwick, 120 Inf
Lawrence J Chadwick, 117 Inf
Neal H Chaffee, 117 Inf
Thomas H Chaffin, 117 Inf
Ola R Chamberlain, 117 Inf
Kenneth E Chambers, 119 Inf
Monroe Chambliss, 119 Inf
Robert V Champion, 120 Inf
Jack E Chandler, 120 Inf
Thomas E Chandler, 119 Inf
Thomas W Chandler, 117 Inf
Bueford L Chanellor, 120 Inf
Robert W Chapin, 119 Inf
Silas E Chapman, 120 Inf
Lewis E Chapman, 120 Inf
Cubie C Chappell, 119 Inf
Ira E Chappell, 120 Inf
John A Chappell, 119 Inf
Robert G Chappell, 117 Inf
Dan E Chason, 119 Inf
George J Check, 120 Inf
Evans H Cheney, 120 Inf
Joseph D Chestnutwood, 119 Inf
David I Chew, 117 Inf
Gennaro Chiappetta, 120 Inf
Jack M Chilton, 120 Inf
Sam Chimento, 117 Inf
Michael J Chiollo, 117 Inf
William F Chisolm, 120 Inf
Carl M Chittum, 117 Inf
Raymond H Chittwood, 120 Inf
Robert M Chrisman, 120 Inf
Floyd Christensen, 117 Inf
Jeroy Christianson, 117 Inf
Martin Christopher, 120 Inf.
Ralph L Christy, 120 Inf
Granvel S Church, 117 Inf
Joseph J Ciccarelli, 117 Inf
Dominick Cide, 105 Eng
John H Cieszkowski, 119 Inf
Tillman R Clara, 117 Inf
Bernard W Clark, 120 Inf
Donald L Clark, 120 Inf
Edward J Clark, 120 Inf
George H Clark, 120 Inf
Howard M Clark, 119 Inf
James E Clark Jr, 113 FA
Marvin E Clark, 119 Inf
Preston C Clark, 113 FA
R Clause Jr, 117 Inf
James G Claypool, 120 Inf
Felix R Clemente, 119 Inf
Virgil Cleland, 120 Inf
Robert H Cline, 119 Inf
Claude W Clampit, 120 Inf
Larry B Clancy, 119 Inf
Merrill J Clum, 120 Inf
Francis X Coady, 120 Inf
James L Coalburn, 120 Inf

Charles E Cobbey, 117 Inf
Charles E Coble, 119 Inf
Walter D Coburn, 119 Inf
Albert W Cochran, 120 Inf
Russell L Cochran, 120 Inf
Joe E Cockerill, 117 Inf
Clifford C Cody, 119 Inf
Jesse J Cody, 120 Inf
Stanley Coffman, 119 Inf
Abram R Cohen, 120 Inf
Joe C P Cohey, 120 Inf
Anthony Colavecchio, 119 Inf
Frederick R Coldicott, 120 Inf
Arthur Cole, 119 Inf
Berwyn G Cole, 119 Inf
Charles H Cole, 117 Inf
Charles G Coleman, 120 Inf.
Harry W Coleman, 120 Inf
Lawrence E Coleman, 119 Inf
Jack C Colley, 119 Inf
James B Collier, 113 FA
Ernest W Collins, 119 Inf
Joe M Collison, 119 Inf
Julian M Collison, 119 Inf
Joseph S Collura, 119 Inf
Lawrence V Colson, 120 Inf
Donald W Colvin, 120 Inf
Robert H Colvin, 119 Inf
Dante A Comastri, 120 Inf
Forrest M Combs, 117 Inf
Harold M Combs, 117 Inf
Hubert Combs, 117 Inf
Richard D Combs, 120 Inf
Virgil C Combs, 119 Inf
Louis F Commander, 117 Inf
Fabior Compannucci, 117 Inf
Harry C Compton, 119 Inf
Wiley M Compton, 119 Inf
Joseph E Concillo, 117 Inf
Earnest Conkin, 120 Inf
Francis T Connelly, 119 Inf
Cletus J Connolly, 120 Inf
Floyd T Connor, 117 Inf
Wilbert W Conover, 120 Inf
Raymond H Conway, 119 Inf.
Stephen L Conroy, 120 Inf
Leonard S Conselletti, 117 Inf.
Joseph A Consiglio, 120 Inf
Nick Consiglio, 120 Inf
Biton P Constantine, 120 Inf
Wilfred G Conway, 119 Inf
Herman G T Coogins, 113 FA
Albert S Cook, 117 Inf
Andrew S Cook, 117 Inf
Arnold H Cook, 120 Inf
Charles B Cook, 117 Inf
John M Cook, 120 Inf
Lester R Cook, 119 Inf
William J Cook, 119 Inf
John J Cooke, 117 Inf
Thomas H Cooke, 105 Eng
Jack Cooley, 117 Inf
John W Coon, 119 Inf
Vito P Coope, 119 Inf
Billy C Cooper, 119 Inf
David T Cooper, 120 Inf
Fred H Cooper, 120 Inf
Robert W Cooper, 119 Inf
Edward W Copes, 120 Inf
Dexter A Corbin, 119 Inf
John L Corn, 230 FA
Joseph P Cormier, 119 Inf
Charles M Cornell, 119 Inf
Duane C Cornell, 197 FA
Daniel Corral, 117 Inf
Anthony M Cortese, 117 Inf
Joseph A Cortrel, 117 Inf
Mario S Coscia, 120 Inf
Joseph Costa, 119 Inf
Joseph Costa, 120 Inf
John J Cota, 119 Inf

Emile P Cote, 119 Inf
Joseph Cotterell, 120 Inf
Huston G Coulliette, 120 Inf
Ray C Counts, 117 Inf
Percy H Couey, 120 Inf
Jack B Coursey, 117 Inf
John J Courtis, 117 Inf
Cecil V Cowan, 117 Inf
Lewis Cowperthevait, 117 Inf
Charles L Cox, 120 Inf
Glenn E Cox, 119 Inf
Henry J Cox Jr, 120 Inf
Hilton Cox, 119 Inf
James C Cox, 119 Inf
James W Cox, 120 Inf
Joe W Cox, 120 Inf
Wilbur Cox, 120 Inf
Delbert J Coy, 119 Inf
William I Cozzens, 120 Inf
Lenvil Crabtree, 120 Inf
Ira Q Craft, 117 Inf
Robert E Craig, 119 Inf
William H Cramer, 119 Inf
Howard B Craven, 117 Inf
Albert J Cravens, 117 Inf
Earl W Crawford, 120 Inf
Henry I Crawford, 119 Inf
Henry V Crawford, 197 FA
Howard G Crawford, 117 Inf
Roy R Creamer, 119 Inf
Edward J Cribb, 119 Inf
Isom D Cribbs, 119 Inf
Rocci J Cricca, 120 Inf
Joseph A Criden, 117 Inf
Merton B Crisman, 120 Inf
John J Criste, 117 Inf
Paul J Criswell, 117 Inf
William H Croddy, 119 Inf
James J Cronin, 105 Eng
Joseph P Cronin, 119 Inf
Kenneth L Cross, 120 Inf
Delmer E Crouch, 119 Inf
Fred W Crowe, 120 Inf
Roland R Crum Jr, 120 Inf
Boughton B Crumley, 120 Inf
Marion P Crutchfield, 117 Inf
James B Cruzen, 117 Inf
Aton Cubnetti, 117 Inf
Tom Culberhouse, 117 Inf
John J Culbertson, 119 Inf
Raymond P Culbertson, 119 Inf
Francis Cullen, 120 Inf
Reece W Cummings, 119 Inf
Cecil V Cunningham, 119 Inf.
Richard W Cunningham, 119 Inf
Donald H Currie, 120 Inf
Roland Curriveau, 117 Inf
Cornelius E Curtin, 119 Inf
Earl R Curtis, 117 Inf
Raymand L Custer, 117 Inf
Harry C Cutler, 117 Inf
John D Cutler, 119 Inf
John J Cynkar, 120 Inf
Bernard J Cyr, 120 Inf
Stanley J Czaja, 119 Inf
Julius P Czechowicz, 120 Inf
Henry J Czujak, 117 Inf
Julius J Dabros, 117 Inf
Merton J Dalaba, 120 Inf
Clarence E Dale, 120 Inf
Perry E Dale, 30 Rcn Tr
John V Dalesic, 117 Inf
Richard E Daley, 120 Inf
George H Dalimonte, 119 Inf
Charles E Dalinsky, 117 Inf
Joseph K Dalke, 119 Inf
Lando L Dallas, 117 Inf
John R Dalon, 117 Inf
Berkeley P Dalton, 120 Inf
Holland P Dalton, 115 Inf
James M Dalton, 120 Inf

William N Dalton, 117 **Inf**
John O Daly, 119 **Inf**
James P D'Ambrosio, 119 **Inf**
John N D'Amico, 117 **Inf**
Adger M Daniel, 119 **Inf**
Joseph R Daniel, 119 **Inf**
Robert W Daniel, 119 **Inf**
Francisco P Daniels, 120 **Inf**
Garon J Daniels, 117 **Inf**
Sigmond J Danielczyk, 105 **Eng**
Natoli D'anna, 120 **Inf**
Charles S Danner, 119 **Inf**
Jack B Daugherty, 120 **Inf**
Shelley H Davant, 120 **Inf**
Arthur Davis, 117 **Inf**
Earl J Davis, 120 **Inf**
Ed C Davis, 119 **Inf**
James D Davis, 119 **Inf**
James S Davis, 113 **FA**
John P Davis, 117 **Inf**
Mortimer Davis, 120 **Inf**
Robert T Davis, 117 **Inf**
Starling J Davis, 120 **Inf**
Homer E Davison, 120 **Inf**
James J Deacy, 157 **FA**
Howard E Deadman, 120 **Inf**
Fletch Deaton, 119 **Inf**
Michael J DeBeire, 119 **Inf**
John A Debelak, 119 **Inf**
Robert De Beradinis, 120 **Inf**
R DeChenne, 117 **Inf**
James A Decore, 117 **Inf**
Louis J DeFede, 119 **Inf**
Joseph A DeFillipo, 119 **Inf**
Jose Y Degado, 120 **Inf**
Hollis G Degenhardt, 120 **Inf**
Roland A Deguise, 119 **Inf**
Wade T Deitz, 117 **Inf**
Warren L Delcamp, 119 **Inf**
Theodore Delgadillo, 119 **Inf**
George G Delistle, 120 **Inf**
Giovanno N Del Luca, 120 **Inf**
James W DeLong, 119 **Inf**
John J Deluca, 120 **Inf**
Lawrence J Del Priore, 120 **Inf**
Arthur T Del Santo, 117 **Inf**
Alphonse A Demars, 120 **Inf**
Vincent J De Matteo, 120 **Inf**
George Demyanchik, 119 **Inf**
Walter R Denkeler, 119 **Inf**
Robert F Denn, 119 **Inf**
William E Denney, 119 **Inf**
Walter E Dennis, 30 **Rcn Tr**
David C Denson, 120 **Inf**
Charles DePalma, 117 **Inf**
Roger M DePontbraind, 117 **Inf**
Virgil W Dermon Sr, 117 **Inf**
Roy C Derr, 117 **Inf**
Steve L Desecki, 117 **Inf**
Edward A Devine, 119 **Inf**
Joseph A DeVito, 120 **Inf**
James F Devlin, 117 **Inf**
William L De Vorl, 119 **Inf**
Helmer H Dewey, 120 **Inf**
John DeYoung, 119 **Inf**
Manuel S Diaz, 117 **Inf**
Eval F Dickens, 117 **Inf**
Leon H Dickens, 119 **Inf**
Earl Dickerson, 230 **FA**
Gervis R Dickerson, 117 **Inf**
Anthony Di Daneto, 119 **Inf**
Melvin T Didelot, 120 **Inf**
Dominic C Diego, 117 **Inf**
Arthur J Diehl, 120 **Inf**
Ernest G Dierks, 119 **Inf**
Arthur W Diers, 117 **Inf**
John L Dietsch, 119 **Inf**
Benjamin F Diffenderfer, 117 **Inf**
Angelo Di Giuseppe, 117 **Inf**
Andrew R Di John, 117 **Inf**
Horilo D Dillard, 117 **Inf**

Joseph R Dillman, 120 **Inf**
Anthony J Di Maria, 117 **Inf**
John D Dimartino, 117 **Inf**
William F Dingevan, 119 **Inf**
Dominic J Dinnielli, 105 **Eng**
Scipione D Di Pierro, 120 **Inf**
Carmen P Di Pietro, 120 **Inf**
Achillo Di Scuillo, 119 **Inf**
Antonio DiVeglio, 119 **Inf**
Clarence J Dixon, 119 **Inf**
Rush C Dixon, 117 **Inf**
James O Dobbs, 120 **Inf**
Jack M Dodge, 105 **Eng**
John J Dogostino, 120 **Inf**
Harold L Dolan, 120 **Inf**
Thurston T Dolph, 120 **Inf**
George V Domarcus, 117 **Inf**
Edward P Dombkowski, 30 **Rcn Tr**
Harry F Dombroski, 119 **Inf**
Clebert J Dominique, 120 **Inf**
Thomas B Donnelly, 117 **Inf**
John P Donohue, 119 **Inf**
Boyd J Donoway, 120 **Inf**
Bernard Dorfman, 120 **Inf**
Steve Dornich, 117 **Inf**
Willard G Dossett, 119 **Inf**
Gene W Dost, 119 **Inf**
John F Dotson, 120 **Inf**
Robert O Dotson, 117 **Inf**
Charles H Dotts, 119 **Inf**
John H Doty, 120 **Inf**
Bernard D Doucette, 30 **Rcn Tr**
Eldon D Douglas, 120 **Inf**
Jesse C Douglas, 120 **Inf**
Harold D Dowler, 120 **Inf**
Harold V Downing, 117 **Inf**
Leo I Downs, 119 **Inf**
Louis A Doyle, 30 **Sig Corps**
Frederick Durchholtz, 230 **FA**
Roy W Drake, 117 **Inf**
William Draves, 119 **Inf**
Joe L Duba, 117 **Inf**
Kurt F Dubel, 119 **Inf**
James K Dubose, 117 **Inf**
Henry T Duch, 120 **Inf**
Gustave A Duchane, 120 **Inf**
James P Dudley, 117 **Inf**
Ralph R Duey, 119 **Inf**
Patrick H Duffy, 117 **Inf**
Clifton M Duke, 119 **Inf**
Namon C Duke, 120 **Inf**
Roy L Duke, 117 **Inf**
Eugene Dunavent, 120 **Inf**
James F Dunbar, 119 **Inf**
Harry A Duncan, 120 **Inf**
Allen B Dungan, 120 **Inf**
George E Dunger, 120 **Inf**
Thomas D Dunlap, 117 **Inf**
Ermon A Dunn, 117 **Inf**
Gaston Dunn, 119 **Inf**
Henry L Dunn, 117 **Inf**
James P Dunn, 117 **Inf**
John E Dunn, 120 **Inf**
Lewis W Dunn, 120 **Inf**
Roger E Dunn, 119 **Inf**
Joseph E Duntuch, 119 **Inf**
Alfred J Dupee, 120 **Inf**
John K Dupuis, 120 **Inf**
Julius G Durham, 119 **Inf**
Clifford G Dusano, 120 **Inf**
James E Dusek, 119 **Inf**
Alfred P Dutresne, 119 **Inf**
James Dye, 119 **Inf**
Richard S Dye, 120 **Inf**
Donald Dykema, 117 **Inf**
Joseph E Dzurka, 117 **Inf**
Edward Dzwierzynski, 119 **Inf**
Kenneth E Early, 117 **Inf**
Robert M Eaglesome, 119 **Inf**
Herbert V Eastham, 120 **Inf**
Norman E Eastman, 119 **Inf**

Harold E Eaves, 120 Inf
Roy J Eckert, 119 Inf
Frederick T Eckhoff, 120 Inf
Etheridge F Edgeworth, 120 Inf
Clarence M Edwards, 105 Eng
Donald B Edwards, 105 Eng
Donald L Edwards, 120 Inf
Henry H Edwards, 120 Inf
Herman R Edwards, 117 Inf
Isaac L Edwards, 117 Inf
Norris L Edwards, 120 Inf
Robert L Edwards, 120 Inf
Howard B Efferen, 120 Inf
Christian A Eicker, 117 Inf
John K Eigo, 117 Inf
Isadore Eisenberg, 120 Inf
John P Eisenberger, 120 Inf
Herman W Elders, 119 Inf
Elton B Eldidge, 119 Inf
Louis J Elia, 119 Inf
John B Ellenburg, 119 Inf
George R Elliot, 120 Inf
Clarence A Ellis, 120 Inf
Dale H Ellis, 120 Inf
George W Ellis, 119 Inf
Lawrence H Ellis, 119 Inf
Mark A Ellis, 119 Inf
Milton Ellison, 120 Inf
Willard J Ellison, 119 Inf
Thomas C Englehart, 120 Inf
Joseph E English, 119 Inf
Lyndon W English, 117 Inf
John D Ent, 119 Inf
Victor L Ephrem, 119 Inf
Loren M Erb, 119 Inf
William J Erb, 120 Inf
Ed G Erickson, 120 Inf
Axel I Erikson, 117 Inf
Thomas D Ervin, 119 Inf
Thurston E Eskelin, 119 Inf
Fernando R Espinosa, 117 Inf
Rudy N Esposito, 117 Inf
Ralph W Estevez, 120 Inf
Harold W Etheridge, 117 Inf
Thermon E Etheridge, 119 Inf
Lacey W Eury, 105 Med
Aaron L Evans, 119 Inf
Charles D Evans, 120 Inf
Clarence R Evans, 119 Inf
Henry E Evans, 117 Inf
John W Evans, 120 Inf
Oliver R Evans, 119 Inf
Raymond L Evans, 119 Inf
Robert Evans, 117 Inf
Frances M Eversole, 120 Inf.
Rudy G Ewert, 120 Inf
Doyle C Ezzell, 120 Inf
Sheldon B Fabian, 120 Inf
Frank Faison, 119 Inf
Darrell K Fallina, 117 Inf
Archie L Falor, 119 Inf
Frank M Famiglietti, 117 Inf
Orlando A Fantuzzi, 119 Inf
Adam Farias, 119 Inf
Charles H Farley, 119 Inf
James D Farlso, 120 Inf
George R Farmer, 119 Inf
Fred C Farris, 120 Inf
Thomas W Farris, 113 FA
Lee N Fasken, 117 Inf
James W Fassman, 119 Inf.
James O Faulkner, 119 Inf
Shelby M Faulkner, 120 Inf
Jacob Faust, 120 Inf
Frank S Faustina, 119 Inf
Virgil E Fauver, 119 Inf
John J Feeney, 119 Inf
Horace W Feimster Jr, 120 Inf
Philip Feldman, 119 Inf
Charles R Felix, 119 Inf
Leonardo G Felix, 117 Inf

Lawrence I Felluie, 119 Inf
Herbert Felsman, 119 Inf
John A Fender, 117 Inf
Lane Fenstermacher, 119 Inf
Thomas L Fentress, 117 Inf
Estelle E Fenwick, 117 Inf
John H I Ferguson, 119 Inf
Ivan Fernberg, 119 Inf
Joseph M Ferrari, 119 Inf
Arthur C Ferrell Jr, 117 Inf
Fernando J Ferreria, 119 Inf
Melvin H Ferris, 120 Inf
Wayne R Fessler, 120 Inf
Alexander Fetchik, 119 Inf
Russell K Fett, 30 Rcn Tr
Clarence J Fezette, 119 Inf
Jess J Fiddler, 119 Inf
Lewis W Fidler, 117 Inf
Steve F Fieder, 119 Inf
Wayne C Fields, 117 Inf
Paul J Fiehl, 117 Inf
Austin P Finch, 117 Inf
Jerome L Finkelstein, 117 Inf
Sol Finkelstein, 120 Inf
John J Finn, 119 Inf
Arthur Finnegan, 117 Inf
George A Fischer, 119 Inf
Robert Fischer, 120 Inf
Garold W Fish, 119 Inf
Charles Fishei, 105 Med
Clarence E Fisher, 117 Inf
John E Fisher, 120 Inf
Thomas C Fisher, 117 Inf
Joseph M Fitchner, 30 Sig Corps
Richard H Fite, 120 Inf
William A Fitzgerald, 120 Inf
Charles E Fitzpatrick, 119 Inf
Oscar B Fix, 117 Inf
John J Flaherty, 117 Inf
Mitchell E Flak, 117 Inf
Richard H Flanagan, 119 Inf
Lester G Flanigan, 117 Inf
Lewis R Flanigan, 120 Inf
Carl P Flannery, 117 Inf
Glen B Flanning, 120 Inf
Jack Fleming, 117 Inf
Douglas C Fleury, 119 Inf
William F Foehl, 120 Inf
Daniel Fogel, 117 Inf
Edward Folkersman, 119 Inf
Marvin J Foltz, 120 Inf
Rex T Ford, 117 Inf*
Walter A Ford, 117 Inf
Edward B Fordham, 119 Inf
Harry W Foreman, 117 Inf
Ellis Forest, 117 Inf
Dominic F Forino, 119 Inf
Armand J Fortier, 119 Inf
Wyman C Foster, 119 Inf
Glenn F Fox, 117 Inf
Warren L Fox, 119 Inf
Ralph Fragnito, 117 Inf
Ralph E Francis, 117 Inf
Merton Frandel, 119 Inf
Robert A Frank, 117 Inf
Joe A Franklin, 117 Inf
Leo J Franklin, 117 Inf
Downey T Frazier, 120 Inf
Ernest E Frazier, 117 Inf
James M Frazier, 117 Inf
Alfonso Freda, 119 Inf
Ralph E Frederick, 117 Inf
Thomas C Freeman, 119 Inf
Tom Freeman, 119 Inf
Herbert Frankel, 117 Inf
Arnold Friedman, 120 Inf
Curtis D Friesner, 120 Inf
Ray F Frisbee, 117 Inf
Gilbert P Frisco, 120 Inf
Charles A Fritts, 117 Inf
Deane E Froning, 119 Inf

George W Frost, 117 Inf
Kelley G Frost, 117 Inf
John R Frusch, 119 Inf
Leo W Fry, 119 Inf
Allan L Fuller, 119 Inf
Edwin W Fuller, 117 Inf
Reuben G Funderbruk, 117 Inf
Dale E Funk, 119 Inf
Joseph Funk, Hq Div Arty
John D Furgerson, 117 Inf
Joseph L Fury, 119 Inf
Eugene Gabarini, 119 Inf
Thomas Gacek, 119 Inf
Daniel R Gaddy, 117 Inf
John V Gagliano, 119 Inf
John V Gainey, 120 Inf
Alphonse R Galatas, 117 Inf
William M Gallaher Jr, 117 Inf
Daniel T Gallagher, 120 Inf
Edward A Gallagher, 119 Inf
William A Gallman, 119 Inf
Dude J Galmer, 120 Inf
Henry S Galuppo, 120 Inf
Robert L Gamble, 120 Inf
Gurle Gammel, 120 Inf
Adolph B Gansarski, 120 Inf
John F Gantt, 119 Inf
John C Garcia, 120 Inf
Tony M Garcia, 120 Inf
Matthew S Gardner, 119 Inf
Robert W Gardner, 120 Inf
Raymond F Gardtlausen, 117 Inf
Jack R Garlow, 117 Inf
Weldon R Garman, 119 Inf
Fred N Garner, 120 Inf
James S Garner, 117 Inf
Daniel A Garnice, 120 Inf
Willis Garren Jr, 120 Inf
Clois W Garrett, 119 Inf
Henry M Garrett, 119 Inf
Howard L Garrett, 120 Inf
Fulton E Garrick, 117 Inf
Herbert W Garrison, 119 Inf
Julio Garza, 119 Inf
Lauren A Gates Jr, 119 Inf
Wildred O Gates, 120 Inf
Attilio Gatt, 117 Inf
Calvin J Gatzman, 119 Inf
Charles J Gauthier, 117 Inf
Raymond A Gawkowski, 105 Eng
Vincent L Gaydos, 120 Inf
William J Geary, 117'Inf
Charles Gebhardt Jr, 119 Inf
Lyle M Gebo, 120 Inf
William J Geddes, 119 Inf
Neville G Geesin, 119 Inf
Robert W Geiger, 117 Inf
Joseph L Geise, 120 Inf
Leroy W Geiser, 119 Inf
Joseph M George, 119 Inf
Constantin Georgeson, 120 Inf
Michael Gerazunis, 119 Inf
Jack E Gerbert, 119 Inf
William T Gerke, 117 Inf
Billy J Gerkin, 120 Inf
Walden J Germain, 119 Inf
Robert S German, 119 Inf
Anthony Germano, 119 Inf
John A Gersomovic, 120 Inf
Albert Gerstein, 120 Inf
Marshall D Gerth, 120 Inf
Theodore Gettman, 117 Inf
Mario J Giancini, 117 Inf
John N Giandonato, 120 Inf
Joseph Giardino, 120 Inf
Robert L Gibbens, 119 Inf
Robert L Gibbs, 105 Eng
George G Gibson, 120 Inf
James R Gibson, 120 Inf
Olen C Gilbert, 105 Eng
George L Gilbreath, 120 Inf

John P Gilkey, 119 Inf
Andrew P Gilia, 117 Inf
Donald R Gill, 30 Rcn Tr
William D Gill, 117 Inf
Everette Gillam, 120 Inf
Rayburn Gillespie, 119 Inf
Donald A Gillie, 119 Inf
John J Gilson, 120 Inf
Henry Ginder, 120 Inf
James J Gioia, 117 Inf
Roy R Giometti, 117 Inf
Aley Given, 117 Inf
Michael J Givliani, 120 Inf
Clyde W Gladson, 120 Inf
John C Glasbee, 117 Inf
Werlie L Gleason, 117 Inf
Howard L Glefer, 230 FA
Paul Glick, 105 Eng
Bruno E Glonke, 120 Inf
Elbert L Glosson, 120 Inf
James C Glover, 117 Inf
Steve L Gluhan, 120 Inf
Clyde E Glumm, 120 Inf
John L Glynn, 117 Inf
Edward J Godleski, 119 Inf
Hugh C Godwin, 105 Eng
Warren R Goetz, 120 Inf
Alvin P Goertz, 119 Inf
Donald R Goff, 120 Inf
Alvin L Gohr, 117 Inf
Everette Goins, 120 Inf
James W Golden, 117 Inf
Robert W Golden, 120 Inf
Donald F Goldsmith, 117 Inf
Aldysius A Golimowski, 120 Inf
Fred N Gonder, 120 Inf
Edward J Gonet, 119 Inf
Julio Gonzelez, 117 Inf
Frederick Good, 120 Inf
Irving Good, 120 Inf
Lowell A Goode, 119 Inf
Luther Goodman, 119 Inf
Merlyn Goodmanson, 120 Inf
Lawson Goodner, 119 Inf
James R Googe, 120 Inf
Arthur L Goolsbe, 119 Inf
Harry L Gordan, 120 Inf
Elmer E Gordon, 117 Inf
Fred D Gordon, 117 Inf
John T Gordon, 120 Inf
Percy H Gordon, 120 Inf
Robert Gordon, 119 Inf
Leo C Gores, 120 Inf
Wilson N Gorham, 117 Inf
Edward R Gorman, 117 Inf
Steve W Gorta, 119 Inf
Milton H Goshien, 120 Inf
Robert W Goss, 119 Inf
Herbert A Goueia, 117 Inf
Howard S Gouin, 120 Inf
Raymond W Gould, 120 Inf
Walter Grabiec, 117 Inf
Roy C Graddy, 117 Inf
Richard Grady, 117 Inf
Steve S Grahal, 120 Inf
Claude C Graham, 117 Inf
James P Graham, 117 Inf
William C Graham, 120 Inf
William P Graham, 117 Inf
Charles C Graves, 120 Inf
Everett O Graves, 119 Inf
Joe P Graves, 120 Inf
Johnnie O Graves, 120 Inf
John L Gray, 117 Inf
William Gray, 117 Inf
Albert M Green, 119 Inf
Delmar F Green, 120 Inf
Grover M Green, 117 Inf
Herbert S Green, 119 Inf
Julius W Green, 105 Eng.
Merrill M Green, 119 Inf

Robert Green, 117 Inf
William L Green, 120 Inf
Hyman Greenberg, 197 FA
James T Greene, 120 Inf
Merwyn H Greene, 120 Inf
Arthur K Greeno, 120 Inf
Clifford N Greenwood, 120 Inf
Salvator J Grego, 119 Inf
Frank C Gregory, 117 Inf
Sylvester N Grembos, 117 Inf
Fred E Grenke, 119 Inf
France R Gricoskie, 117 Inf
Leonard Griffee, 119 Inf
Sammie Griffin, 119 Inf
Donald V Griffith, 120 Inf
Harold F Griffith, 120 Inf
Herbert B Grimes, 119 Inf
Johnnie G Grimes, 120 Inf
Patrick Grimes, 119 Inf
Jack S Grimshaw, 120 Inf
Salvatore M Grinaldi, 120 Inf
Edward P Grindrod, 117 Inf
John N Griner, 119 Inf
Albert L Grishom, 117 Inf
Earnest W Grisson, 120 Inf
James L Grittis, 117 Inf
Lawrence W Gritz, 120 Inf
Paul W Gritzmacher, 119 Inf
John T Groce, 120 Inf
Benjamin F Groff, 120 Inf
James H Grogan, 119 Inf
Kenneth J Grogan, 120 Inf
Richard A Gross, 117 Inf
Harry Grossman, 119 Inf
Martin Grossman, 120 Inf
Morris Grossman, 117 Inf
John F Grote, 119 Inf
Bion J Grover Jr, 120 Inf
Benjamin Gudatis, 197 FA
Earl M Guessford, 119 Inf
Peter H Guest, 120 Inf
Robert J Guest, 120 Inf
John J Guidorizzi, 120 Inf
Alfred Guimond, 197 FA
George S Gulick, 120 Inf
Robert C Gum, 197 FA
Anderson Gupton, 117 Inf
Charles P Gurien, 119 Inf
Herbert Gutkuhn, 119 Inf
Walter Gumen, 119 Inf
Edward H Haake, 117 Inf
Charles F Haas, 117 Inf
John A Hackett, 117 Inf
Paul M Hackett, 119 Inf
Charles W Hagel, 119 Inf
Earl Hagen, 120 Inf
Warren L Hagner, 120 Inf
Russell W Hague, 120 Inf
Edward E Hairfield, 120 Inf
Edward F Hajec, 119 Inf
George O Halbrook, 120 Inf
Frederick L - Haldiman, 30 Rcn **Tr**
Clarence C Hale, 117 Inf
Roland E Hale, 117 Inf
Robert Hales, 119 Inf
Cleatus E Hall, 120 Inf
Dean F Hall, 120 Inf
Garland R Hall, 119 Inf
Herbert Hall, 119 Inf
Otis G Hall, 113 FA
Robert J Hall, 120 Inf
Wesley C Hall, 119 Inf
Glenn W Halverson, 117 Inf
Eugene L Hamby, 117 Inf
Alva D Hamilton, 120 Inf
Chauncey J Hamme, 119 Inf.
Allen C Hammers Jr, 117 Inf
Howard L Hamsher, 119 Inf
James E Hancock, 120 Inf
Louis S Handley, 117 Inf
Alvin K Haney, 119 Inf

Rex A Hanis, 105 Eng
Roger N Hanks, 120 Inf
Thomas J Hanley, 119 Inf
William J Hanley, 105 Eng
Frank Hanna, 120 Inf
Henry E Hause, 117 Inf
Elmert Hansen, 120 Inf
Harold J Hansen, 119 Inf
Henry E Hansen, 120 Inf
Odell S Hanson, 119 Inf
Raymond Hanson, 117 Inf
Claude A Harbit, 119 Inf
Vaughn L Hardacker, 117 Inf
Charles F Hardegree, 117 Inf
Carl C Harden, 120 Inf
Carnation B Harden, 117 Inf
Vernon P Hardison, 197 FA
Leopold Hardy, 120 Inf
Chester L M Hargrove, 120 Inf
Harry T Harmon, 119 Inf
Gilbert W Harper, 117 Inf
Norman W Harper, 120 Inf
Walter B Harper, 117 Inf
Haywood S Harrell, 119 Inf
Charles E Harrill, 117 Inf
Albert A Harris, 120 Inf
Emmett L Harris, 120 Inf
Raymond H Harris, 117 Inf
Russell H Harris, 119 Inf
Samuel B Harris, 119 Inf
William J Harris, 120 Inf
Henry O Harrison, 117 Inf
Leroy C Harste, 119 Inf
Harold W Hart, 117 Inf
Roy W Hart, 117 Inf
Floyd H Hartbecke, 117 Inf
Elmer F Hartwig, 117 Inf
Elvin E Hartman, 120 Inf
James H Hartman, 120 Inf
Robert Z Hartness, 120 Inf
Bernard A Harvey, 117 Inf
John E M Haskins, 120 Inf
Robert E Haslam, 120 Inf
Vernon H Hass, 117 Inf
Martin J Hasson, 117 Inf
Elmer A Hastings, 117 Inf
Eugene G Hatch, 119 Inf
Lawrence J Haught, 120 Inf
Barry Haviland, 120 Inf
Grady W Hawley, 120 Inf
Robert S Haws, 119 Inf
Teddy K Hayek, 117 Inf
Turner J Hayes, 117 Inf
Carl H Haynes, 117 Inf
Forrest G Haynes, 119 Inf
William G Haynes, 119 Inf
Arthur Hazlett, 120 Inf
Anton J Hazlinger, 119 Inf
Carl R Heagy, 120 Inf
Linwood E Heath, 230 FA
Virgie Heatherly, 119 Inf
Percy L Hedgepath, 120 Inf
David A Hedland, 115 Inf
Monroe Hedrick, 117 Inf
Carl C Heflin, 119 Inf
Ira M Hegarty, 117 Inf
Dewey R Heichel, 120 Inf
Oscar F Heinzman, 30 MP Plat.
Marvin H Helbert, 117 Inf
Homer L Hehe, 120 Inf
Merville E Helle 117 Inf
Herman Heller, 117 Inf
Robert F Heller, 117 Inf
Roy E Heller, 119 Inf
Cleo R Helm, 119 Inf
James L Helms, 119 Inf
Samuel Helman, 197 FA
Guy Henderson, 117 Inf
Richard P Henderson, 119 Inf
George A Hendley, 119 Inf
Floyd J Henley, 120 Inf

Wilfred M Henley, 119 Inf
Vernie L Henning, 120 Inf
David L Henry, 119 Inf
Joe P Henry, 119 Inf
Earl R Hensel, 119 Inf
Freeman Henson, 117 Inf
Orville R Herl, 120 Inf
Norman Hermann, 119 Inf
John B Herndon, 117 Inf
Donald H Hermann, 120 Inf
Joseph Herring, 119 Inf
Kenneth C Hersey, 119 Inf
Lawrence J Hess, 117 Inf
Clarence W Hettrick, 119 Inf
Walter Hibbard Jr, 120 Inf
John G Hickey, 119 Inf
Gordon D Hicks, 120 Inf
Karl K Hicks, 120 Inf
Wendell W Higgins, 119 Inf
Shelby J Hildebrand, 118 FA
Carl J Hiljer, 117 Inf
Cecil E Hill, 119 Inf
James P Hill, 117 Inf
Martin L Hill, 117 Inf
Roy A Hill, 117 Inf
Rollis Hines, 120 Inf
William A Hines Jr, 30 Rcn Trp
Robert T Hingston, 120 Inf
Eldon W Hinton, 119 Inf
Jake L Hinton, 119 Inf
William B Hirst, 120 Inf
Charles T Hise, 120 Inf
Charles E Hissom, 119 Inf
John W Hobday, 120 Inf
Robert M Hobgood, 120 Inf
Ralph L Hockridge, 120 Inf
Arthur N Hodges, 117 Inf
David L Hodges, 117 Inf.
Morton J Hodges, 119 Inf
Marion E Hoffer, 120 Inf
Joseph M Hoffman, 120 Inf
Leonard J Hoffman, 117 Inf
Thomas R Hoffman, 119 Inf
Lawrence W Hogan, 120 Inf
Marshall Hogins, 117 Inf
Charles J Hohn, 120 Inf
Hilary P Hohn, 120 Inf
Stanley J Hojnacki, 119 Inf
William B Holden, 119 Inf
Baxter M Holder, 119 Inf
Fred Holdsworth, 119 Inf
Dallas H Hopkins, 105 Eng
Clifford W Holland, 120 Inf
Maxwell L Holler, 120 Inf
William Holleran, 117 Inf
A J Holley 119 Inf
Milton Hollingsworth, 120 Inf
Charles R Holloway, 117 Inf
John R Holum, 120 Inf
David M Holste, 117 Inf
Harold J Holtz, 119 Inf
Arthur W Homberg, 119 Inf
Wilbert Honeck, 120 Inf
Bernard A Honeychuck, 120 Inf.
Junior Hood, 117 Inf
Charles Hooker, 120 Inf
Herbert A Hoover, 120 Inf
Charles E Hoover, 117 Inf
Charles L Hoover, 120 Inf
Isaac D Hornbeck, 117 Inf
Jess O Horner, 119 Inf
Arthur L Horntredt, 120 Inf
Floyd W Horsley, 120 Inf
George W Horton, 119 Inf
Joe B Horton, 119 Inf
Wallace J Horton, 119 Inf
Peter J Hospit, 120 Inf
Walter C Houk, 119 Inf
Thomas P Houlnan, 120 Inf
James H Hounshell, 117 Inf
Arthur B Houston, 117 Inf

Belle G Houston, 117 Inf
Leonard L Hoven, 119 Inf
Alfred Hovland, 120 Inf
Bennie F Howard, 120 Inf
Green V Howard, 119 Inf
Julian L Howard, 120 Inf
Earle S Howe, 120 Inf
John S Howe, 115 Inf
Amos Howell, 120 Inf
Lawrence D Howell, 119 Inf
James E Howington, 120 Inf
Paul L Howrie, 119 Inf
Lawrence J Huard, 120 Inf
Cyril H Huber, 119 Inf
Levi L Hubert, 117 Inf
Glenn Huddleston, 120 Inf
Joseph L Huddy, 117 Inf
Floyd C Hudgens, 117 Inf
Curtis L Hudgins 120 Inf
Charles W Hudson, 117 Inf
John E Hudspeth, 119 Inf
Ralph C Huerta, 120 Inf
Earl W Huff, 105 Eng
Phillip A Huffman, 120 Inf
William R Huffman, 119 Inf
James G Huggins, 117 Inf
Hubert L Hughes, 117 Inf
Nicholas J Huha, 119 Inf
Roy E Hultien 120 Inf
Gert Humbert, 117 Inf
John B Humphiey, 117 Inf
Charles B Hunigan, 117 Inf
Maurice Hunley, 117 Inf
Delmar Hunsinger 117 Inf
Edward Hunt, 120 Inf
Odell Hunt, 117 Inf
Hilburn A Hunter, 197 FA
Robert H Hunter, 120 Inf
Gordon R Huntley, 119 Inf
Herbert Hupp 119 Inf
Odell Hupp 117 Inf
Weiner J Hurbig, 105 Eng
Charles A Hurley, 119 Inf
Frank J Hurley, 120 Inf
William B Hurley, 120 Inf
John A Hussli, 113 FA
John H Hutchins, 117 Inf
Francis L Hutchinson, 119 Inf
Randolph L Hutchinson, 117 Inf
Walter A Huth, 120 Inf
James J Hrabik, 120 Inf
Nicholas Hvaszta, 197 FA
Carl C Hyde, 117 Inf
Jerome Hyman, 117 Inf
Francis J Ianni, 120 Inf
Luigi Iannucci, 230 FA
John Iannuzzo, 120 Inf
Raymond A Ive, 119 Inf
Anthony Imprudente, 119 Inf
Andrew J Imro, 119 Inf
Charles S Indzwiak, 119 Inf
Richard D Ingalsbe, 119 Inf
Jacob E Ingle, 117 Inf
Earle R Innis, 119 Inf
Maron J Innuse, 119 Inf
Anthony J Iozzo, 119 Inf
Elden C Irwin, 120 Inf
Hubert M Irwin, 120 Inf
Eugene Isaac, 120 Inf
Odia Isaacs, 119 Inf
Charles A Islip, 117 Inf
Henry E Iverson, 117 Inf
Jesse E Ivy, 120 Inf
Cosimir D Jablonski, 117 Inf
Daniel B Jackowski, 117 Inf
Allison H Jackson, 119 Inf
Lewis W Jackson, 120 Inf
Ronald H Jacobs, 120 Inf
Gerald M Jacquot, 30 Rcn Tr
Joseph G Jagla, 117 Inf
Howard D Jahnke, 117 Inf

Edward J Jakubdzak, 120 Inf
Leonard T James, 119 Inf
Lester L James, 117 Inf
Walter E James, 120 Inf
Stanley Jamraz, 120 Inf
John J Janco, 117 Inf
Norman L Jandreau, 117 Inf
Howard E Japs, 120 Inf
Aloysius S Jara, 119 Inf
Walter W Jarrad, 119 Inf
Uennerm Jarrett, 120 Inf
Marwood A Jarriett, 120 Inf
George H Jarvis, 117 Inf
Walter J Jasinski, 117 Inf
Henry J Jaskwricze, 117 Inf
Eda F Jaszczak, 117 Inf
John B Jauch, 119 Inf
Walter J Jaworski, 117 Inf
Gilbert R Jazwinski, 117 Inf
James R Jefferson, 117 Inf
William C Jeffries, 119 Inf
Edmund S Jendris, 117 Inf
Luther C Jenkins, 117 Inf
Marvin L Jenkins, 117 Inf
Samuel T Jenkins, 117 Inf
Ernest R Jennings, 120 Inf
Nels P Jensen 117 Inf
Willis W Jernigan, 120 Inf
Jerome L Jerome, 117 Inf
Maynard M Jerome, 119 Inf.
William Jerzembeck, 120 Inf
Thomas H Jessman, 120 Inf
Arthur Jivery, 117 Inf
Leon M Johns, 117 Inf
Allen A Johnson, 117 Inf
Carl H Johnson, 117 Inf
Elwood E Johnson, 119 Inf
Jack B Johnson, 120 Inf
Leonard D Johnson, 120 Inf
Oliver P Johnson Jr, 117 Inf
Ralph F Johnson, 119 Inf
Raymond D Johnson, 117 Inf
Raymonse Johnson, 119 Inf
Roy D Johnson, 117 Inf
Thomas L Johnson, 119 Inf
Vince P Johnson, 119 Inf
Willard C Johnston 117 Inf
Mark R Jolly, 119 Inf
Aubrey A Jones, 120 Inf
Calvin T Jones, 119 Inf
Charles I Jones, 120 Inf
Coy G Jones, 120 Inf
Herbert C Jones, 120 Inf
Hugo W Jones, 120 Inf
Hubert T Jones, 119 Inf
Jack A Jones, 117 Inf
James D Jones, 119 Inf
Jim M Jones, 120 Inf
Lawrence S Jones, 117 Inf
Pink D Jones, 119 Inf
Richard D Jones, 119 Inf
Richard H Jones, 120 Inf
William E Jones, 120 Inf
John T Jordan, 117 Inf
Johnie E Jordan, 120 Inf
Martin W Jordan, 120 Inf
Melvin R Jorgenson, 120 Inf
Nassia G Joseph, 120 Inf
Henry O Josephson, 117 Inf
Eleck Jubera, 117 Inf
Norman G Juedes, 120 Inf
John Jukas, 117 Inf
Joseph P Julian, 105 Eng
Harold J Junga, 120 Inf
Alphonse R Juodzevich, 119 Inf
Robert E Jurca, 119 Inf
George Jurebie, 119 Inf
Louis Kahn, 105 Eng
Raymond M Kaiser, 105 Eng
Harold W Kalaba, 119 Inf
Sabba A Kaliff, 120 Inf

Bruno J Kalinauskas, 120 Inf
Michael Kandracs, 120 Inf
Thomas P Kane, 119 Inf
Merrill A Kanline, 119 Inf
Paul R Kannan, 120 Inf
Edmund Kanses, 119 Inf
William A Karrer, 117 Inf
Robert L Karriker, 120 Inf
Lester J Karroll, 119 Inf
Rayute E Karvin, 117 Inf
Frank A Karwel, 119 Inf
Sam Katz, 117 Inf
Sidney Katz, 119 Inf
John E Kaucher, 105 Eng
Joel Kaufman, 119 Inf
John Kavaney, 119 Inf
David H Kay, 117 Inf
Finis M Keaster Jr, 120 Inf
Louis W Kee, 105 Eng
Robert F Kee, 119 Inf
Phillip J Keegan, 119 Inf
Paul T Keenan, 117 Inf
Monte W Keener, 120 Inf
Herman L Keesee, 119 Inf
Donald D Keesling, 119 Inf
Ray S Kegley, 120 Inf
Charles W Kehl, 117 Inf
Jesse J Keith, 120 Inf
Richard H Keith 119 Inf
Earl D Keller, 117 Inf
Edward J Kelley, 117 Inf
James L Kelley 120 Inf
Newman C Kelln, 120 Inf
Carl G Kelly 120 Inf
Charles J Kelly, 119 Inf
John G Kelly, 117 Inf
Simon A Kelly, 120 Inf
John R Keltner, 120 Inf
Earl Kemp, 119 Inf
Elwyn M Kemp 120 Inf
Franklin L Kemp, 119 Inf
Houston D Kemper, 119 Inf
Daniel M Kendall, 120 Inf
Edward S Kendall, 119 Inf
Forrest L Kendrick, 120 Inf
William Kendrick, 117 Inf
Francis X Kenlon, 117 Inf
Everett F Kennedy, 117 Inf
Gerald E Kennedy, 119 Inf
Robert J Kennedy, 117 Inf
Herbert W Kenyon, 120 Inf
Delroy L Kern, 119 Inf
William F Kerstetter, 117 Inf
Clarence W Ketterer, 120 Inf
Myron D Kidd, 105 Eng
Robert E Kidd, 119 Inf
Sammie H Kidd, 117 Inf
Robert R Kiefman, 117 Inf
Thadius J Kielbasinski, 120 Inf
Stanley J Kielbowicz, 119 Inf
Joseph R Kietzman, 120 Inf
Ernest W Kill, 117 Inf
Maurice H Kimball, 30 Rcn Tr
Roy T Kimbel, 117 Inf
Francis C Kimmel, 120 Inf
Claur K Kimmerer, 120 Inf
Richard A Kindig, 119 Inf
Harold G Kiner, 117 Inf
Howard E King, 117 Inf
James D King, 120 Inf
John N King Jr, 120 Inf
Orwell L King, 120 Inf
Robert H King, 119 Inf
Dennis R Kingery, 120 Inf
Johnie Kingore, 117 Inf
R J Kinman Jr, 120 Inf
John J Kinney, 119 Inf
Joseph F Kinnon, 117 Inf
Louis Kinsey, 119 Inf
Charles F Kiragis, 119 Inf
Donald T Kirby, 119 Inf

Owen L Kirk, 120 Inf
Homer E Kirkland, 117 Inf
James G Kirkwood, 120 Inf
Edwin F Kirschman, 119 Inf
Walter G Kiser, 119 Inf
Roy Kisselback, 119 Inf
Milton W Kleckner, 117 Inf
Stanley J Kleczkowski, 120 Inf
Lloyd E Kleinman, 119 Inf
Dale A Klieforth, 119 Inf
Andrew D Kloke, 119 Inf
Robert H Klose, 117 Inf
Joseph A Kloskie, 119 Inf
Julius V Klostermann, 117 Inf
Sam Klotz, 120 Inf
Jacob J Kluch, 117 Inf
Ress C Knapton, 120 Inf
Casper Knazynski, 120 Inf
Howard E Kneak, 117 Inf
Henry A Knecht, 119 Inf
Herman L Knight, 230 FA
James A Knight, 120 Inf
Kenneth R Knowe, 119 Inf
Leslie F Knzi, 117 Inf
Alvin W Koehn, 120 Inf
Harry S Koeppel, 119 Inf
Harold J Koettel, 117 Inf
Stephen Kofton, 117 Inf
Alex F Kojelowicz, 119 Inf
Stanley A Kohto, 117 Inf
Joseph D Koller, 105 Med
Andrew S Konder, 117 Inf
Russell B Koon, 117 Inf
Steve J Kopec, 119 Inf
Thaddeus L Koperniak, 120 Inf
Fred Kopp, 119 Inf
Raymond E Koski, 117 Inf
James Kotakis, 119 Inf
Thomas M Kotrba, 119 Inf
Ralph A Kovs, 117 Inf
Alexander Kowalczyk, 117 Inf
Leo J Kowalski, 120 Inf
Theodore Kowalski, 119 Inf
Joseph E Kozen, 119 Inf
Joseph J Kozera, 120 Inf
Ralph D Kozlowski, 119 Inf
Donald Kramer, 119 Inf
Raymond E Kramer, 119 Inf
Robert M Kramer, 119 Inf
Edward J Krasinakas, 230 FA
Nathan Krassak, 118 FA
Bernard Krause, 119 Inf
Leo J Krebsbach, 119 Inf
Herbert Koreker, 120 Inf
Karl A Krone, 117 Inf
John Kronik, 117 Inf
Charles Kronk, 117 Inf
William A Kropf, 117 Inf
Gerald B Krout, 119 Inf
Walter D Kruger, 119 Inf
Walter J Kruszynski, 117 Inf
Frank J Krzeszowski, 119 Inf
Florian O Kucera, 119 Inf
Dan R Kuchenrither, 120 Inf
Charles S Kuester, 120 Inf
James E Kuhfahl, 119 Inf
Donald E Kuhn, 120 Inf
Gail C Kuhn, 119 Inf
Victor J Kuinius, 117 Inf
John J Kull, 30 Rcn Tr
George I Kulp, 120 Inf
Ralph D Kuney, 119 Inf
Franklin C Kunkle, 120 Inf
Lyle L Kunselman, 117 Inf
Michael Kuten, 117 Inf
Henry C Kwiatkowski, 117 Inf.
Frank J Labelle, 120 Inf
Edward La Bier, 119 Inf
Mario J Lacedonia, 119 Inf
Ellsworth N Lacy, 117 Inf
Lonnie La Favers, 119 Inf

Joseph R La Frenier, 120 Inf
Peter A Lalooses, 119 Inf
Carl Lamb, 120 Inf
John H Lambe, 120 Inf
Leland L Lambe, 120 Inf
Frederick Lambert, 120 Inf
Wendell C Landtroop, 117 Inf
John Lane, 117 Inf
Harry Lander, 120 Inf
Thomas P Laney, 230 FA
John C La Padulo, 120 Inf
Dewey A Lappin, 117 Inf
Thomas Lares, 119 Inf
Raymond L Large, 119 Inf
Walter F Large, 120 Inf
Normand O Lariviere, 119 Inf
Stanley V Larocca, 120 Inf
Richard Larock, 119 Inf
John G La Rouche, 120 Inf
Norman L Larson, 119 Inf
George H Lassiter, 117 Inf
J G Latham, 119 Inf
Forrest R Lathbury, 120 Inf
Willie L Lauderdale, 119 Inf
Donald A La Vanway, 119 Inf
George J La Vere, 120 Inf
Rene J Lavimodiere, 120 Inf
William T Lawrence, 119 Inf
Waymon R Lawhorn, 119 Inf
James A Lawler, 119 Inf
Johnson H Lawrence 120 Inf
Gilbert D Lawson, 119 Inf
Lucious R Lawson, 120 Inf
Theodore Laycock, 120 Inf
Gregorio A Lazcano, 119 Inf
William L Lazenby, 120 Inf
Gray L Lea, 120 Inf
Richard T Leatherman, 119 Inf
Henry D LeBlanc, 119 Inf
Donald A Lee 119 Inf
John T Lee, 117 Inf
Lewe F Lee, 117 Inf
Murray Lee, 120 Inf
Tollie C Lee, 117 Inf
George R Lemire, 120 Inf
Charles J Lemoine Jr, 120 Inf
James J Lemon Jr, 120 Inf
William W Lemoreaux, 117 Inf
James S Leo, 120 Inf
Salvador T Leon, 117 Inf
George E Leonard, 117 Inf
Anthony LePanto, 119 Inf
Walter B Leppek, 119 Inf
Dwayne D Lester, 117 Inf
Everette E Letz, 119 Inf
Gordon Levere, 119 Inf
Henry R Levesque, 117 Inf
Kenneth A Levett, 119 Inf
Hyman Levine, 120 Inf
John S Levy, 120 Inf
Robert Lewelly, 119 Inf
Richard J Lewingdon, 117 Inf
Hinton C Lewis, 120 Inf
Joseph C Lewis, 120 Inf
Leonard T Lewis, 119 Inf
Paul J Lewis, 120 Inf
Robert F Lewis, 120 Inf
Thomas R Lewis, 117 Inf
William R Lewis, 120 Inf
John J Lewoxz, 119 Inf
James Lichille, 120 Inf
Gerald A Lichtle, 119 Inf
William Lickfield, 119 Inf
Robert L Liel, 105 Eng
Herschel G Likens, 117 Inf
Dean T Lill, 119 Inf
Stephen Limyansky, 119 Inf
Franklin J Lindemuth, 119 Inf
William V Linder, 119 Inf
Robert C Lindgren, 120 Inf
Ralph W Lineberger, 119 Inf

Richard O Linehan, 119 Inf
Donald Lingo, 120 Inf
Raymond J Linich, 119 Inf
Donald E Link, 119 Inf
George J Linscott, 119 Inf
Irvin F Linton, 119 Inf
Roy C Lippard, 120 Inf
Leonard J Lippert, 117 Inf
Marshal E Lipscomb, 120 Inf
Harry Lipson, 117 Inf
George W Lipstreu, 119 Inf
Patsy A Liscio, 117 Inf
Emmett D Littleton, 117 Inf
William F Lizor, 120 Inf
Edward D Lloyd, 120 Inf
Thomas M Lloyd Jr, 117 Inf
George E Loader, 119 Inf
Dean D Locke, 120 Inf
William C Lockett, 120 Inf
Belton A Loftis, 120 Inf
Jesse C Lohr, 119 Inf
Anthony J Lonczyski, 119 Inf
Benjamin F Long, 120 Inf
Robert E Look, 119 Inf
Bobby S Lookabill, 119 Inf
John J Lopez, 120 Inf
Manuel Lopez, 119 Inf
Herbert E Lord, 120 Inf
Joseph M Lorence, 120 Inf
Guenter W Lorenz, 119 Inf
Alben W Loring, 120 Inf
Michael A Losacco, 119 Inf
James V Lott, 120 Inf
Wilhem A Loudermilk, 117 Inf
Robert W Loudfoot, 119 Inf
Johnnie Louiem, 119 Inf
Michael Loupe, 105 Eng
Robert M Loveless, 117 Inf
LaVerne F Lowe, 119 Inf
Miles M Lowell, 119 Inf
Leonard Lowery, 117 Inf
William J Lowery, 120 Inf
Carl R Lowry, 119 Inf
Tony Lubin, 119 Inf
George E Lucas, 120 Inf
Patrick R Lucey, 120 Inf
Lester G Ludeman, 119 Inf
Leofas V Lugo, 120 Inf
Ambrose Luketic, 119 Inf
John M Lunsford, 120 Inf
George J Lustro, 119 Inf
John J Luteman, 120 Inf
Clifton W Luther, 117 Inf
James T Luther, 117 Inf
Matthew Lutzkivich, 120 Inf
Richard Lyeznski, 30 Rcn Tr
Harold Lynch, 119 Inf
Robert A Lynch, 119 Inf
Charles S Lyme, 119 Inf
Donald E Lyons, 120 Inf
James J Lyons, 120 Inf
Benjamin F Mabry, 120 Inf
Donald G Macbain, 119 Inf
Joseph J Macera, 105 Eng
Anton R Machovec, 117 Inf
Joseph J Maciejewski, 117 Inf
Albert A Mackie, 117 Inf
Edward J Madaj, 119 Inf
Andrew L Madden, 117 Inf
Francis J Madden, 120 Inf
John W Maddox Jr, 117 Inf
Andres A Madrid, 117 Inf
John J Maginnis, 120 Inf
Joseph J Mahoney, 120 Inf
David I Maile, 117 Inf
Michael Maksim, 120 Inf
Charles J Malandra, 119 Inf
Frank G Malandro, 117 Inf
John R Malay, 119 Inf
Manuel Maldonado, 120 Inf
Arthur S Malena, 119 Inf

Robert A Malm, 119 Inf
Raymond Malone, 119 Inf
Richard J Malone, 119 Inf
Robert O Mance, 117 Inf
Matie M Mancebo, 117 Inf
Stanley A Mankiewicz, 120 Inf
Frank Mankin, 120 Inf
William A Manuel, 119 Inf
William E Mapin, 117 Inf
Burnest Maples, 105 Eng
Peter Marchitello, 117 Inf
John O Marcone, 117 Inf
Dominic J Marconi, 120 Inf
Ernest G Margharito, 119 Inf
Milton Mark, 119 Inf
Armsin P Marinelli, 117 Inf
Edward Markinson, 120 Inf
George E Markland, 117 Inf
Neals Markle, 120 Inf
Charles W Marks, 117 Inf
George J Marks, 105 Eng
Joseph J Marks, 30 Sig Corps
Guy R Marlar, 117 Inf
Charles Marple, 119 Inf
Dominick Marrone, 119 Inf
Rubert C Marsh, 120 Inf
Herbert J Marshall, 117 Inf
Jacob G Marshall, 113 FA
Leo G Martel, 119 Inf
Russell D Martens, 119 Inf
Arnold Martin, 117 Inf
Ernest R Martin, 119 Inf
Hugh D Martin, 117 Inf
John W Martin, 113 FA
Joseph P Martin, 117 Inf
Samuel C Martin, 105 Eng
Solen H Martin, 120 Inf
Roy W Martindale, 117 Inf
Felizando C Martinez, 117 Inf
Jesse C Martinez, 120 Inf
John R Martinez, 120 Inf
Jose C Martinez, 119 Inf
Manuel Martinez, 120 Inf
Ray S Martinez, 119 Inf
Frank D Marzano, 120 Inf
Arthur E Mason 119 Inf
Jesse A Mason, 120 Inf
Robert M Mason, 119 Inf
Joe Masterbray, 120 Inf
Fiore D Mastraci, 120 Inf
Daniel L Mastronardi, 120 Inf
Constantine Matausch 120 Inf
Ben D Mathews, 119 Inf
Francis E Mathews, 119 Inf
Leonard Mathis, 120 Inf
Ralph F Matirko, 117 Inf
John P Matt, 117 Inf
Robert M Matthews, 120 Inf
William Matthews, 120 Inf
Albert J Maudice, 117 Inf
Henry Maul Jr, 117 Inf
Edward C Maurer, 119 Inf
Howard May Jr, 119 Inf
Carle E Mayle, 119 Inf
Alvin L McBride, 117 Inf
James B McCain, 118 FA
Mack McCall, 120 Inf
Robert F McCarthy, 119 Inf
Thomas F McCarthy, 119 Inf
Gail R McCleary, 120 Inf
Charles McClendon, 117 Inf
Ellis P McClenney, 120 Inf
John McClure, 119 Inf
John C McClure, 105 Eng
Sheldon A McClure, 30 Rcn Tr
Paul G McClurkan, 120 Inf
Waymon R McClurkan, 117 Inf
Charles E McCollough, 120 Inf
Paul W McCollum, 119 Inf
Bertis C McConnell, 117 Inf
Glenn H McConnell, 119 Inf

Peter S McConnell, 120 Inf
George W McCorkle, 119 Inf
William J McCormick, 119 Inf
Frederick L McCoy, 117 Inf
Russell L McCracken, 117 Inf
Francis J McCrann, 119 Inf
Felix E McCullough, 119 Inf
Seth McCurry, 120 Inf
Russell J McDaniel, 117 Inf
Victor V McDaniel, 120 Inf
Albert C McDeavitt, 120 Inf
Dennis J McDonald, 117 Inf
Porter A McDonald, 117 Inf
Joseph J McDonough, 117 Inf
Francis E McElliott, 117 Inf
Patrick E McFadden, 119 Inf
Frank R McGarry, 119 Inf
Bernard H McGovern, 119 Inf
Edward P McGovern, 120 Inf
Frank C McGovern, 230 FA
John T McGrath, 117 Inf
Henry M McGregor, 117 Inf
Charles McGroarty, 120 Inf
Bernard E McGuire, 117 Inf
Donald K McIntosh, 197 FA
Ferd McIntosh, 117 Inf
Warren C McIntosh, 120 Inf
Thomas M McIver, 120 Inf
James F McKay, 117 Inf
James L McKeen, 105 Eng
Norman J McKendry, 119 Inf
Leonard J McKenzie, 119 Inf
James B McKeon, 120 Inf
Edward B McKelvy, 120 Inf
Albert L McKinley, 117 Inf
Clarence McKinney, 119 Inf
Claude W McKinney, 120 Inf
Jerden J McKinney, 120 Inf
John M McKinney, 119 Inf
Karl E McKinney, 119 Inf
Durward B McKinnon, 117 Inf
Herbert A McKitrick, 119 Inf
Warren K McLaughlin, 117 Inf
Cecil E McLendon, 113 FA
Harry McMahon, 117 Inf
Walter McMahon, 119 Inf
Leo B McMullen, 117 Inf
Wilfred L McNamar, 120 Inf
George P McNamara 117 Inf
Carl C McNew, 117 Inf
Charles McPherson, 119 Inf
Joseph A McPortland, 117 Inf
Robert M McTigue, 120 Inf
Allen R Mead, 119 Inf
Daniel A Meade, 119 Inf
Joseph B Meador, 119 Inf
Melvin P Meadows, 117 Inf
James C Mears, 119 Inf
Leroy Medders, 119 Inf
Charles Medeiros, 120 Inf
Lewis V Medeiros, 119 Inf
Raymond M Medina, 117 Inf
J C Medlin, 120 Inf
R L Meek, 117 Inf
Bernard D Meeker, 117 Inf
Robert L Meetin, 117 Inf
Marvin D Meils, 120 Inf
David W Meinders, 119 Inf
John B Meixner, 117 Inf
Peter F Mele, 117 Inf
John Melovoitz, 119 Inf
James S Melton, 117 Inf
Harlan Melvin, 120 Inf
Lawrence V Mena, 120 Inf
Donald R Menary, 117 Inf
Stanley F Mendenhall, 120 Inf
Jess Mendoza, 230 FA
Galvin P Merchant, 117 Inf
Norman J Mercier, 117 Inf
Michael S Mereantante, 117 Inf
Alfred J Merlino, 119 Inf

Harold R Merz, 119 Inf
Jack E Messer, 30 Sig Corps
Jappie G Messer, 120 Inf
Willie L Messer, 120 Inf
Metrus F Messina, 120 Inf
Waldemar D Metcalf, 117 Inf
Arnold R Metque, 117 Inf
Francis Metz, 119 Inf
Raymond Metzker, 117 Inf
Charles A Mew, 120 Inf
Lemuel J Mewborne 120 Inf
Rolland R Meyer, 120 Inf
Richard M Meyers, 120 Inf
Alois J Mica, 119 Inf
Joseph A Micceri, 119 Inf
Arthur Michels, 120 Inf
Staislaus J Michon, 119 Inf
Joseph Mickna, 119 Inf
Charles A Miczis, 117 Inf
Carmaine Middei, 120 Inf
Donald F Middleton, 117 Inf
Richard J Mikesell, 120 Inf
Floyd J Mikula, 119 Inf
Edward F Milarch, 119 Inf
Stanley Milewski, 120 Inf
Denzil F Milfs, 117 Inf
Donald Milks, 119 Inf
Charles A Miller, 117 Inf
Darrell E Miller, 117 Inf
Donald Miller, 119 Inf
Edward G Miller, 120 Inf.
Eugene W Miller, 117 Inf
Howard M Miller, 117 Inf
James D Miller, 120 Inf
Jim K Miller, 120 Inf
John M Miller, 119 Inf
Louis Miller, 117 Inf
Marvin J Miller, 117 Inf
Milace H Miller, 120 Inf
Oliver V Miller, 120 Inf
Paul H Miller, 120 Inf
Paul W Miller, 119 Inf
Nathaniel T Miller, 119 Inf
Sidney W Miller, 119 Inf
Stanley J Miller, 119 Inf
William Miller, 120 Inf
William H Miller, 119 Inf
James B Millhorn, 120 Inf
John J Milligan, 197 FA
Roy J Mills, 117 Inf
Walter W Mills, 119 Inf
Acie V Milner, 117 Inf
Johnnie J Milten, 117 Inf
Blane Minix, 119 Inf
John Mink, 117 Inf
Alfred L Minton, 119 Inf
Morton Minton, 119 Inf
Edward A Miskiewicz, 119 Inf
Raymond P Miskiewicz, 119 Inf
Peter A Miskow, 119 Inf
Floyd N Mistler, 117 Inf
Eugene Mitchell, 197 FA
Leon R Mitchell, 119 Inf
Van J Mitchell, 117 Inf
Norman L Mitdrell, 120 Inf
Mike Mitrus, 119 Inf
Harold R Mitten, 119 Inf
Robert C Mitten, 120 Inf
David Mixsell, 119 Inf
Horace R Mixson, 118 FA
Leonard H Mobley, 120 Inf
Eril R Mock, 119 Inf
Frank J Mole, 119 Inf
Vincent J Molinaio, 120 Inf
George D Moll, 117 Inf
Roy V Molyneaux, 119 Inf
Edward S Moniak, 117 Inf
Gerald J Monahan, 117 Inf
Sam Monceau, 230 FA
Donald A Mongeon, 120 Inf
Stanley F Moniuszko, 113 FA

Alvin Monlezun, 119 Inf
Charles F Monroe, 120 Inf
James E Monroe, 117 Inf
Thomas A Montalband, 117 Inf
Girolome P Montalione, 120 Inf
Salvatore Montanino, 119 Inf
Gabino Montiel, 120 Inf
Peter Montour, 117 Inf
James F. Moody, 117 Inf
Wayman J Moon, 119 Inf
Hugh W Mooney, 117 Inf
Herbert H Moor, 117 Inf
Clayton G Moore, 120 Inf
Glen D Moore, 120 Inf
Hardin Moore, 119 Inf
Herbert A Moore, 120 Inf
Herbert E Moore, 117 Inf
John W Moore Jr, 117 Inf
Kenneth H Moore, 119 Inf
Robert L Moore, 120 Inf
Wayne Moore, 120 Inf
Leo H Mootz, 105 Eng
Bernard D Mora, 120 Inf
Raymond F Moran, 120 Inf
Thomas J Moran, 120 Inf
Herman J Mordenhaus, 120 Inf
George C Morehead, 120 Inf
Carl J Morgan, 120 Inf
Charles E Morgan, 120 Inf
Virgil V Morgan, 120 Inf
Theodore Morgenou, 117 Inf
Grady Morris, 117 Inf
Henry N Morris, 117 Inf
Robert A Morris, 119 Inf
William H Morris, 120 Inf
Robert V Morrison, 120 Inf
Roy E Morrison, 120 Inf
Anthony V Morroney 117 Inf
James J Morse, 120 Inf
John Morton, 120 Inf
Jack W Moser, 120 Inf
Kendrick B Moser, 117 Inf
John W Moses, 117 Inf
Mario Mosquedo, 120 Inf
Arthur D Moss, 117 Inf
Jack H Moss, 117 Inf
John D Mosso, 120 Inf
Aaron Mostel, 117 Inf
Jerome J Mottingh, 117 Inf
Woodrow W Mountjoy, 119 Inf
Jay A Mowery, 120 Inf
Wils M Moxheim, 117 Inf
Joseph T Mrowca, 120 Inf
Joseph C Mrugale, 120 Inf
James A Mucci, 119 Inf
Nicholas Mucci, 30 Rcn Tr
Vincent J Mucci, 120 Inf
Anthony J Muldoon, 117 Inf
Harold E Mull, 120 Inf
Leland C Mull, 117 Inf
Bobby B Mullen, 119 Inf
John H Mullen, 119 Inf
Thomas R Mullina, 120 Inf
John H Mullins, 119 Inf
John P Mulvey, 120 Inf
Roberto Q Muno, 119 Inf
William B Murningham, 230 FA
Borbert G Murphy, 119 Inf
Brian J Murphy, 119 Inf
Carl E Murphy, 120 Inf
Edward V Murphy, 119 Inf
Herschel E Murphy, 117 Inf
John E Murphy, 120 Inf
Silby Murphy, 120 Inf
Clarence P Murray, 117 Inf
Howard G Murray, 117 Inf
John A Murray, 120 Inf
William A Murray, 119 Inf
Harry P Murrell, 117 Inf
James M Murry, 117 Inf
Joseph R Muskey, 230 FA

John Mureus 120 Inf
Charles A Myers, 120 Inf
Edgar R Myers, 117 Inf
Hugh A Myers, 120 Inf
Lawrence N Myers 117 Inf
Henry C Nadeau, 120 Inf
Claus G Nagel, 117 Inf
Otis W Nall, 117 Inf
Edward J Nannery, 120 Inf
Edward H Napper, 119 Inf
Wldon A Nash, 117 Inf
Ben Nasheldky, 117 Inf
Michael Naso, 117 Inf
Dominic Nastri, 117 Inf
George A Natter, 117 Inf
Robert E Neahr, 120 Inf
Jack Neely, 120 Inf
Theodore J Nega, 119 Inf
Paul K Nehrkorn, 120 Inf
Darrel M Neil, 120 Inf
John E Nelms Jr, 113 FA
Arthur O Nelson, 117 Inf
Bennie G Nelson, 119 Inf
Cavern W Nelson, 120 Inf
Harold R Nelson, 119 Inf
James J Nelson, 117 Inf
Kenneth R Nelson, 120 Inf
Robert L Nelson, 120 Inf
Robert W Nelson Jr, 120 Inf
Roger W Nelson, 117 Inf
Alfred Ness, 120 Inf
George M Nettles, 119 Inf
Dewey M New, 119 Inf
Robert E New, 120 Inf
Charles W Newcomb, 117 Inf
Earl F Newman, 119 Inf
Nathan Newman, 117 Inf
Lamar H Newsome, 120 Inf
John F Newton, 117 Inf
John W Nicas, 117 Inf
Peter G Nicholas, 117 Inf
John C Nichols, 119 Inf
Marvin D Nichols, 120 Inf
Remus O Nichols, 119 Inf
Andrew Nick, 117 Inf
Carmine P Nicosia, 119 Inf
Harold E Nielson, 119 Inf
Theodore Niewiedowski, 120 Inf
Louis G Nikmeyer, 117 Inf
Willebaldo Nila, 30 Rcn Tr
Winfield Niles, 117 Inf
Stanley N Nissen, 119 Inf
Theodore A Noak, 117 Inf
Claude H Nodurft, 120 Inf
Ralph F Nodurft, 120 Inf
Floyd L Now, 120 Inf
Leonard Noel, 119 Inf
Roy G Noel, 120 Inf
James F Nolan, 119 Inf
Hesschel H Nolen, 117 Inf
Lester L Norman, 117 Inf
William E Norman, 119 Inf
Donnie M Norris, 117 Inf
Richard E Norton, 119 Inf
Willie E Norton, 117 Inf
Case Noteboom, 120 Inf
Mike Noto, 119 Inf
Victor L Novickio, 119 Inf
Casimer H Nowakowski, 117 Inf
Edward W Noyes, 120 Inf
Andrew A Nudge, 117 Inf
James A Null, 119 Inf
Roy Numez, 119 Inf
Donald E Nyberg, 120 Inf
John H Oakes, 119 Inf
Vernon L Oakley, 117 Inf
Clinton L Oakes, 119 Inf
Edward S Obal 120 Inf
Charles E Obenour, 30 Rcn Tr
Kenneth Oberlin, 119 Inf
Alexander O'Brien, 119 Inf

Edward J O'Brien, 117 Inf
Francis J O'Brien, 119 Inf
James T Ochsenschlager, 119 Inf
Michael J O'Connor, 119 Inf
Michael P O'Connor, 120 Inf
Kenneth M O'Dell, 119 Inf
Edward R Ogle, 119 Inf
James E Ogle, 117 Inf
Joseph J Okolo, 120 Inf
Robert Oldham, 120 Inf
Frank O'Leary, 119 Inf
Allie J Oliver, 120 Inf
Harold B Oliver, 197 FA
James R Oliver, 117 Inf
Phillip T Ollenburg, 120 Inf
Leonard G Olofield, 117 Inf
Norman Olsen, 117 Inf
Richard C Olsen, 117 Inf
Robert F Olsen, 119 Inf
Wayne C Olson, 117 Inf
Allen M Oltz, 117 Inf
John P Olvany, 119 Inf
Robert J O'Malley, 117 Inf
James O'Neal, 117 Inf
Rowland O'Neal, 117 Inf
John P O'Neill, 117 Inf
Generino W Ordille, 117 Inf
Florencio V Ordonez, 120 Inf
Frank C Orecchio, 120 Inf
Curtis E Orkins, 117 Inf
Toros Ornadzian 119 Inf
George Orosz, 117 Inf
Joe P Ortiz, 120 Inf
Ruben C Ortiz, 119 Inf
Albert S Osborn, 120 Inf
Clifton C Osborn, 120 Inf
Marvin S Osborne, 120 Inf
Keith Ose, 120 Inf
Anthony W Oshensky, 120 Inf
Paul L Osterhold, 117 Inf
Steve S Ostrowski, 119 Inf
Ralph V Oswalt, 120 Inf
Arthur J Ott, 117 Inf
Arthur L Otto, 120 Inf
Henry L Otto, 119 Inf
Albert A Overbeck, 117 Inf
Everette F Overcash, 119 Inf
William H Overcasher, 120 Inf
William R Overman, 120 Inf
Clarence R Overton, 119 Inf
James Overy, 119 Inf
Harold N Ownes, 117 Inf
Edward F Padar 117 Inf
Isable Padilla, 120 Inf
John Pagliarallo, 120 Inf
Walter H Paige Jr, 120 Inf
Charles H Painter, 119 Inf
Clarence A Painter, 120 Inf
Howard M Painton, 120 Inf
Anthony F Palermo, 120 Inf
Jerry C Palmento, 117 Inf
Harry R Palmer, 120 Inf
Ellis H Palmertree, 117 Inf
Nicholas M Palmiotti, 119 Inf
Peter C Panicali, 120 Inf
Fred F Panko, 117 Inf
Frank A Pape, 119 Inf
Stephen J Papes Jr, 120 Inf
Jesse T Parido, 119 Inf
Simone Paristi, 119 Inf
Charles H Parker, 187 FA
Frank J Parker, 117 Inf
Jimmie Parker, 117 Inf
Rolland E Parkins, 117 Inf
Raymond E Parks, 117 Inf
Frank J Parlvaecchia, 120 Inf
Lewis E Parris, 117 Inf
Duel R Parrish, 119 Inf
Thomas C Parrot, 119 Inf
Curtis Parson, 105 Eng
Charles H Paschal, 120 Inf

Charles J Pascik, 120 Inf
Michael Pasko, 119 Inf
Robert W Pastor, 120 Inf
Paul J Pastva, 120 Inf
Raymond J Paquette, 187 FA
Luigi L Patalano, 119 Inf
George Patrician, 120 Inf
Louis L Patrick, 120 Inf
Floyd J Pattigrew, 120 Inf
Gino J Pauletto, 120 Inf
Paul H Pauley, 120 Inf
Clarence Paulson, 117 Inf
James Paulton, 120 Inf
Joseph Pavusko, 120 Inf
Frank P Pawlik, 120 Inf
Earl Paxton, 117 Inf
Duane W Payne, 117 Inf
Orville Payne, 117 Inf
Oscar R Payne, 117 Inf
Walter C Paynter, 117 Inf
Allen A Payton, 119 Inf
Howard N Pearce, 119 Inf
Marvin R Pearce, 120 Inf
Daniel Pearson Jr, 119 Inf
Glenn R Pearson, 119 Inf
Merlyn W Pearson, 120 Inf
William A Pearce Jr, 117 Inf
Alfred Pearson, 117 Inf
Richard E Pearson, 117 Inf
Robert G Pearson, 117 Inf
Winfred A Pearson, 119 Inf
Foster S Pease, 120 Inf
Ralph A Peay, 119 Inf
Joseph P Pechacek, 119 Inf
Edward B Peck, 105 Eng
Raymond H Peck, 120 Inf
Robert J Peck, 120 Inf
Albert P Peckus, 119 Inf
Arthur W Peeples, 117 Inf
Fred J Peltier, 117 Inf
Kenneth W Pence, 120 Inf
Jack J Pendleton, 120 Inf
William F Penn, 120 Inf
Harold W Pennington, 120 Inf
William T Pentecost, 120 Inf
Corbett L Penton, 119 Inf
Elmo Penton, 119 Inf
Allen L Peoples, 120 Inf
Raymond V Peplinski, 120 Inf
Milan Percic, 119 Inf
John Perez, 120 Inf
Pedro C Perez, 117 Inf
Eugene Perini, 117 Inf
Theodore T Perkes, 120 Inf
Donald G Perkins 120 Inf
Lincoln Perkins, 117 Inf
Merle L Perkins, 117 Inf
Roy O Perkins, 120 Inf
Anthony J Perkovitch, 119 Inf
John A Perrin, 120 Inf
Alessandro Perrucci, 120 Inf
Colon G Perry, 120 Inf
Joel B Perry, 120 Inf
Kloman Y Perry, 119 Inf
Glenn W Person, 120 Inf
Joseph A Perza, 120 Inf
George Pete, 120 Inf
Joe Pete, 120 Inf
John A Petenbrink, 117 Inf
Robert F Peterman, 120 Inf
George A Peters, 120 Inf
Arthur E Peterson, 119 Inf
Dale J Peterson, 119 Inf
George J Peterson, 120 Inf
Gufford T Peterson, 117 Inf
John W Peterson, 120 Inf
Reynold J Peterson, 117 Inf
Robert G Peterson, 119 Inf
William L Peterson, 120 Inf
Edward J Petraiea 119 Inf
Samuel G Pettigrew, 120 Inf

Charles B Pettyjohn, 117 Inf
Leslie D Petty, 119 Inf
Nathan D Petway, 117 Inf
Milton J Pfeffer, 117 Inf
Chester D Phillips, 117 Inf
Clyde M Phillips, 119 Inf
Daniel Phillips, 117 Inf
George W Phillips, 120 Inf
John W Phillips, 117 Inf
Mamerd E Phillips, 119 Inf
Thomas J Phillips, 187 FA
William T Phillips, 120 Inf
James W Phillis, 119 Inf
Karl E Phipps, 119 Inf
John Piazza, 120 Inf
Joseph A Picardi, 105 Eng
Stephen G Pickett, 117 Inf
Clarence E Picotte, 117 Inf
Harold A Pieper, 120 Inf
Hugh S Pierce, 120 Inf
Willie P Pierce, 117 Inf
Stanley J Pietruch, 119 Inf
Edward J Pietrzak, 117 Inf
Glen F Pigozzi, 117 Inf
Charles B Pike, 120 Inf
John M Pikolas, 119 Inf
Carroll E Pilert, 120 Inf
Floyd H Pilgrim, 120 Inf
Daniel D Pinheire, 120 Inf
Jack E Pinholster, 119 Inf
John H Pinkerton, 117 Inf
Robert L Pinkston, 120 Inf
Leonard Piojda, 119 Inf
Stanislaus J Piotruwicz, 117 Inf.
William E Pipes, 119 Inf
Matt Pirtz, 119 Inf
Walter L Pisch, 119 Inf
Archie J Piscitello, 120 Inf
Anthony F Pistilli, 119 Inf
Sherman F Pitcher, 117 Inf
Stanley J Pitt, 119 Inf
Kazimiesz W Placek, 119 Inf
Elmer Plank, 119 Inf
William G Platt, 117 Inf
Allen H Plauche, 119 Inf
Leo W Pheninger, 117 Inf
Alvin C Plocher, 120 Inf
Paul B Plowman, 117 Inf
Alvin J Pociusask, 120 Inf
John G Poland, 119 Inf
Robert C Polding, 120 Inf
Aldrich A Polehna, 117 Inf
Morris J Poliseno, 117 Inf
Joseph J Pollicino, 120 Inf
Durando J Pompey, 119 Inf
Arch R Ponder, 120 Inf
Estle Poole, 120 Inf
Samuel E Poore, 117 Inf
Sylvester C Poort, 117 Inf
Raymond C Pope, 119 Inf
William E Pope, 119 Inf
George W Porch Jr, 120 Inf
Solomon Posner, 117 Inf
Paul J Post, 117 Inf
Nick A Postupack, 117 Inf
William M Potts, 117 Inf
William O Potts, 120 Inf
James H Poules, 119 Inf
James A Pousont, 120 Inf
Cecil C Powell, 117 Inf
James P Powers, 120 Inf
Truman C Powers, 117 Inf
Bob J Prahovich, 119 Inf
Elroy F Prample, 120 Inf
Lawrence Pratt, 117 Inf
John R Presley, 120 Inf
Walter Prettyman, 117 Inf
Michael J Preziose 120 Inf
Fred Price, 117 Inf
Lloyd J Price, 117 Inf
Troy M Price, 117 Inf

William H Price, 120 Inf
Charles L Prizer, 119 Inf
Arthur C Probst, 120 Inf
Clyde V Proby, 120 Inf
Kermit W Proctor, 117 Inf
Erwin A Proehl, 117 Inf
Louis M Proto, 120 Inf
Harold F Provost, 120 Inf
Frank Prudente, 119 Inf
Richard T Pruitt, 120 Inf
Stevens Psilopoulos, 119 Inf
Henry A Pszenny, 120 Inf
Jim Puga, 119 Inf
Steve J Pulhalla, 119 Inf
Peter J Puleo, 120 Inf
Robert L Pullen, 120 Inf
James W Pullman, 117 Inf
Joseph G Puls, 120 Inf
Clark Purkey, 120 Inf
Angelo Puorto, 119 Inf
John J Pushinsky, 119 Inf
Johnnie M Puskar, 119 Inf
Walter F Puzio, 117 Inf
John M Puttroff, 120 Inf
Lawrence T Quarteman, 119 Inf
Sam Queen, 117 Inf
Samuel G Queen, 117 Inf
Thomas H Queen, 117 Inf
William Queen, 117 Inf
Arthur E Queeney, 119 Inf
Ralph Quiei, 120 Inf
Ernest J Quitta, 119 Inf
Darwin H Raatz, 117 Inf
Nathan Rabinowitz, 117 Inf
Michael F Raczius, 120 Inf
Stanley G Radzio, 117 Inf
Ben T Ragan, 119 Inf
Arnold A Rahe, 120 Inf
Melvin H Rahrig, 120 Inf
Martin N Rajala, 117 Inf
Chester Rakowski, 119 Inf
Basel G Raley, 119 Inf
Albert P Rameriz, 113 FA
John Ramey, 117 Inf
Atturo Ramirez, 117 Inf
Lucas N Ramirez, 120 Inf
Ralph Ramirez, 117 Inf
Robert Ramsey Jr, 120 Inf
Deblane Ramsey, 117 Inf
Robert W Ramsey, 119 Inf
Roy L Ramsey, 117 Inf
Robert Ran, 157 FA
Joseph R Rankin, 119 Inf
John Rapoza, 120 Inf
Charles Rappaport, 117 Inf
Dietrich F Rasetzki, 119 Inf
Henry Rasmussen, 120 Inf
Howard W Rasmussen, 117 Inf
Frank J Rastetter, 119 Inf
Thomas Raszewski, 117 Inf
Wiley Ratcliff, 113 FA
Fara L Raulerson, 119 Inf
Elmer R Ray, 117 Inf
John Reacigono, 120 Inf
Edward E Redden, 117 Inf
Arnold A Redinger, 117 Inf
George A Reed Jr, 105 Eng
Lester I Reed, 119 Inf
Orrin W Reed, 119 Inf
Glenn E Reeder, 119 Inf
John C Reeves, 119 Inf
Lewis A Reeves, 117 Inf
Walter Redzik, 119 Inf
Joseph F Regan, 119 Inf
Basil J Rehill, 119 Inf
Albert L Rehnert Jr, 119 Inf
Eugene G Reigel, 120 Inf
Herbert S Reines, 120 Inf
John Reitman, 117 Inf
Antonio C Remillard, 105 Eng
Henry E Renk, 119 Inf

Martin Renteria, 120 Inf
Lloyd C Renier, 105 Eng
Meyer Reuits, 119 Inf
Davis N Reyes, 117 Inf
Oscar R Reyes, 119 Inf
Alejandro Reyna, 117 Inf
Gordon V Reynolds, 120 Inf
Edmond J Rhanlt, 120 Inf
Scott A Rhind, 120 Inf
James H Rhodes, 119 Inf
Ollie N Rhodes, 119 Inf
Harry Rhyner, 117 Inf
Joseph J Ribet, 119 Inf
Pasquale L Riccillo, 117 Inf
Pasquale F Riccio, 117 Inf
Bernard S Rice, 119 Inf
Clayton D Rice, 119 Inf
Donald E Rice, 119 Inf
Francis M Rice, 119 Inf
Harold E Rich, 120 Inf
Clarence J Richards, 119 Inf
Dale Richards, 117 Inf
Earl V Richards, 120 Inf
Alfred O Richer, 119 Inf
Ralph B Richey, 105 Eng
Linzy A Richmond, 120 Inf
Royce Richter, 119 Inf
Johnnie C Ricker, 119 Inf
Giles Ridderger, 117 Inf
Coel N Riddle, 117 Inf
James J Rider, 120 Inf
Carl L Ridgeway, 120 Inf
Elroy F Reiger, 119 Inf
Melvin L Riesch, 119 Inf
Roy E Riickert, 117 Inf
Earl R Riley, 119 Inf
Francis J Riley, 120 Inf
Samuel E Riley, 117 Inf
Robert A Rill, 120 Inf
Robert J Rinehirt, 117 Inf
Ulys S Riner, 117 Inf
Raymond Rinfred, 119 Inf
Andres L Rios, 117 Inf
Richard L Ripper, 120 Inf
George E Ristav, 117 Inf
Frank Risley, 120 Inf
Morris O Ristvedt, 105 Eng.
Ernest M Ritchey, 117 Inf
James F Ritter, 120 Inf
Joseph A Riviello, 117 Inf
Santiago V Rizo, 120 Inf
Natale S Rizzotte, 105 Eng
Aaron W Robbins, 117 Inf
James W Robbins, 119 Inf
Lyle W Robbins, 119 Inf
Ad Robertson, 117 Inf
Edward J Roberson, 117 Inf
Allen E Roberts, 117 Inf
James H Roberts, 117 Inf
Guy E Robertson, 119 Inf
Melvin Robertson, 117 Inf
William A Robertson, 120 Inf
Oliver A Robey, 120 Inf
Adjuter Robikoux, 120 Inf
Byron L Robinnette, 119 Inf
Alvinza R Robinson, 119 Inf
Charles Robinson, 119 Inf
Charles J Robinson, 120 Inf
Chester T Robinson, 117 Inf
Clifford P Robinson, 117 Inf
Harry L Robinson, 119 Inf
James R Robinson, 119 Inf
John F Robinson, 120 Inf
Leonard V Robinson, 120 Inf
Manona T Robinson, 120 Inf
Ralph C Robinson, 119 Inf
Robert Robinson, 119 Inf
W A Robinson, 120 Inf
William H Robinson, 119 Inf
William T Robinson, 230 FA
Edward W Rochacewiz, 120 Inf.

Walter C Rodlyer, 117 Inf
David G Rodriguez, 117 Inf
Ebdon J Rodriguez, 120 Inf
Joseph M Rodriguez, 117 Inf
Frederick W Roese, 119 Inf
Kenneth J Roether, 117 Inf
Thomas P Rogan, 117 Inf
Harold Rogers, 120 Inf
Marion S Rogers, 119 Inf
Clarence N Rohrer, 120 Inf
Emil C Roilando, 119 Inf
Lester M Rolf, 120 Inf
George W Rolfe, 119 Inf
Vernon C Rollag, 119 Inf
William E Rolland Jr, 120 Inf
Jack W Rolph, 120 Inf
Lionel J Rondeau, 119 Inf
Bernard B Rosa, 120 Inf
Dominic N Rosa, 120 Inf
Ben Rosales, 120 Inf
Jorge A Rosario, 120 Inf
Archie F Rose, 117 Inf
Dale W Rose, 119 Inf
Robert Rose, 117 Inf
Robert L Rose, 120 Inf
Melvin C Rosenbaum, 117 Inf
Merlin Rosenberger, 120 Inf
Robert E Rosenberger, 117 Inf
Leo Rosenblatt, 117 Inf
John Rosholt, 119 Inf
Denver G Ross, 117 Inf
Jack E Ross, 120 Inf
Arthur S Roth, 119 Inf
Richard P Roth, 119 Inf
Alex Rother, 117 Inf
Raymond Rattar, 120 Inf
George Rounds, 117 Inf
Joseph J Rous, 117 Inf
Edward D Roust, 119 Inf
Chauncey S Rowell, 117 Inf
James D Rowell, 120 Inf
Harold D Rowell, 119 Inf
Sims A Rowland, 119 Inf
Earl N Roy, 119 Inf
Albert J Ruback, 120 Inf
John J Ruff, 117 Inf
Raymond T Rugenstien, 119 Inf
Charles M Ruggiero, 117 Inf
Amato J Rullo, 117 Inf
Umberto J Rullo, 120 Inf
Edwin H Ruona, 119 Inf
Russell T Rushing, 117 Inf
Tomlinson C. Russ, 118 FA
Arlo A Russell, 120 Inf
Charles E Russell, 117 Inf
Luther E Russell, 120 Inf
Leon Russomano, 120 Inf
Albert Rutman, 120 Inf
John E Ryan, 157 FA
Thomas J Ryan, 120 Inf
William W Ryan, 119 Inf
Frederick Rykala, 120 Inf
Frank Sabatini, 119 Inf
Jerome L Sacks, 117 Inf
Andrew C Saddher, 117 Inf
Francis E Sage, 117 Inf
Stanley J Sajdak, 120 Inf
Urho E Sakkinen, 120 Inf
James W Salvo, 119 Inf
Earl E Sams, 119 Inf
Edgar M Sanden, 120 Inf
Juddie C Sanders, 119 Inf
William D Sanders, 117 Inf
Sam Sandrowitz, 120 Inf
Willie M Sands, 119 Inf
Freeman H Sanquist, 119 Inf
Joseph J Santangelo, 120 Inf
Marselino P Santoye, 117 Inf
Nick G Sapharas, 117 Inf
John Sardiello, 119 Inf
James W Sargent, 120 Inf.

John Saucedo, 119 Inf
John Sauls, 120 Inf
Walter T. Savey, 117 Inf
Robert Savage, 117 Inf
Raymond E Savard, 117 Inf
Edward R Savich, 119 Inf
Clifton G Savoy, 117 Inf
Frederick G Sawyer, 120 Inf
William H Saylors, 117 Inf
Ralph Scalf, 117 Inf
Richard A Scavola, 120 Inf
Edward J Schaefer, 119 Inf
William E Scha, 120 Inf
Carl C Schaudt, 117 Inf.
Allen I Schell, 120 Inf
Walter Scherba, 119 Inf
Harold L Scherer, 120 Inf
Harvey B Schick, 113 FA
Frederick Schlemmer, 120 Inf
Jules D Schlichter, 119 Inf
Richard F Schmelzer, 119 Inf
William R Schmitz, 120 Inf
Kenneth F Schmook, 119 Inf
Milton V Schneider, 119 Inf
Richard R Schneider, 120 Inf
Leonard Schnessel, 120 Inf
John H Schnittker, 117 Inf
Lyle E Schoenwetter, 120 Inf.
Leonard C Scholl Jr, 120 Inf
Melvin J Schott, 120 Inf
James E Schramm, 117 Inf
Kenneth J Schreiber, 120 Inf
George H Schrepfer, 119 Inf
Lewis A Schuchard, 117 Inf
Walter S Schubert, 120 Inf.
Francis J Schulte, 120 Inf
Daniel G Schultz, 120 Inf
Lawrence Schultz, 117 Inf
Paul J Schultz, 119 Inf
Phillip L Schultz, 119 Inf
Vernon C Schultze, 120 Inf
Roy A Schuman, 119 Inf
Paul K. Schunk, 120 Inf
Ralph E Schutte, 119 Inf
Robert Schwartz, 117 Inf
John Schwet, 117 Inf
Leonard W Schweyer, 119 Inf
Salvatore A Scifo, 105 Eng
Joseph Scodella, 119 Inf ,
Gene B Scoggins, 120 Inf
Arthur L. Sconocchia, 119 Inf.
Beverly B Scott, 120 Inf
David D Scott, 120 Inf
Francis E Scott, 30 Rcn Tr
Robert D. Scott, 120 Inf.
Roy E Scott, 119 Inf
Lavion M Scotto, 119 Inf
Jesse W Scroggins, 120 Inf
Robert K Seal, 30 Rcn. Tr
Stephen L Sealey, 30 Rcn Tr
Richard L Seay, 119 Inf
Joseph L Sebeck, 117 Inf
Woodrow Secrist, 117 Inf
Robert Seddon, 120 Inf
Frank T Sedita, 120 Inf
Paul Sedlock, 120 Inf
Joe J Sedor, 117 Inf
Onais A Sellers, 120 Inf
Carlton L Sells, 117 Inf
Leon W Senobs, 119 Inf
William P Sepel, 117 Inf
Francisco Serna, 119 Inf
Andrew J Sessions, 120 Inf.
John S Setla, 119 Inf
Willard Settles, 119 Inf
George H Severin, 117 Inf
Harrow Sexton, 117 Inf
Morse G Seymour, 119 Inf
Henry J Shade, 105 Eng
Joseph L Shafer, 120 Inf
William W. Shailor, 119 Inf.

James L Shanahan, 117 Inf
William F Shanks, 120 Inf
Ernest G Sharp Jr, 120 Inf.
Eugene Sharp, 119 Inf
Wilbur B Shaver, 120 Inf
Carl E Shaw, 117 Inf
Raymond W Shaw, 120 Inf
Warren S Shaw, 120 Inf
Bart F Shea, 120 Inf
Mortimer G Shea, 119 Inf
Harvey Shearer, 119 Inf
Arthur B Shearin, 119 Inf
Charles D Sheldon, 120 Inf
Russell Shell, 117 Inf
Andrew J Shelley, 120 Inf
Robert D Shellito, 125 Eng
Wilber L Shemonia, 117 Inf
Eithel A Sheperd, 120 Inf
Michael Sherba, 120 Inf
Charles M Sherrill, 119 Inf
Milton A Sherwin, 120 Inf
Ralph E Sherwin, 119 Inf
Leo W Shields, 120 Inf
Lewis W Shields, 120 Inf
Edwin G Shifrin, 117 Inf
Joseph B Shimko, 120 Inf
Hardy H Shinault, 119 Inf
Robert G Shine, 120 Inf
Herbert O Shipley, 119 Inf
Alton S Shipp, 117 Inf
Robert S Shoaf, 117 Inf
Edward W Shoemaker, 117 Inf
Floyd C Shoemaker, 119 Inf.
Milton C Shope, 119 Inf
Elmer Short, 120 Inf
Morriss Showel, 117 Inf
Outra Shroader, 113 FA
John E Shrout, 120 Inf.
Wilbert L Shryock, 117 Inf
David J Shumaker, 117 Inf
Ollie L Shumaker, 119 Inf
Robert F Shurkey, 119 Inf
Paul J Sickler, 120 Inf
Desmond A Siddon, 119 Inf
Arthur L Sigler, 119 Inf
Rufus Sigmon, 119 Inf
Billy T Sillings, 119 Inf
Raymond Silverman, 119 Inf
August A Silvestro, 120 Inf
Gerald W Simerl, 117 Inf
Stewart R Simerly, 117 Inf
Edmond J Simmons, 119 Inf
John R Simmons, 120 Inf
Paul F Simonson, 117 Inf.
Anthony Simone, 120 Inf
Glynn Sims, 120 Inf
Jewell P Sinclair, 120 Inf.
John C Singer, 120 Inf
Leonard Singer, 117 Inf
Melvin Singer, 119 Inf
John Single, 119 Inf
James A Singleton, 1 FA
John P Sink, 119 Inf
James N Sinkler, 119 Inf
William T Sipola, 117 Inf
John H Sippola, 117 Inf
Marvin Sirotkin, 117 Inf
Michael G Sisak, 120 Inf
Craig Sisk, 120 Inf
Kenneth F Sivafford, 105 Med
Saul D Siwek, 120 Inf
John A Sojostrom, 119 Inf
George W Skaggs, 117 Inf
Kenneth L Skaggs, 119 Inf
Melvin O Skahal, 117 Inf
Grover C Skeen, 117 Inf
Gordon H Skinner, 119 Inf
Joseph B Skorupski, 119 Inf
Mathew J Skowronski, 119 Inf.
Oliver J Skvivanie, 117 Inf
Gilbert L Slagle, 117 Inf

Fred L Slater, 120 Inf
Harry Slater, 119 Inf
Goddis M Slaughter, 117 Inf
William B Slaughter, 119 Inf
John W Sleppy, 119 Inf
Donald H Sletten, 120 Inf
Paul P Slosar, 117 Inf
Ralph R Sluga, 120 Inf
Emil Slupik, 117 Inf
Charles B Slutz, 119 Inf
Donald J Small, 120 Inf
John G Smedbers, 30 Rcn Tr
Beauford L Smelser, 117 Inf
George Smetak, 117 Inf
Spencer J Smiley, 119 Inf
Albert Smith, 120 Inf
Albert N Smith, 120 Inf
Arthur A Smith, 119 Inf
Carl A Smith, 120 Inf
Clyde W Smith, 117 Inf
Edward Smith, 117 Inf
Edward M Smith, 113 FA
Elizha Smith, 30 Rcn Tr
Emmett Smith, 120 Inf
George L Smith, 117 Inf
Guy R Smith, 119 Inf
Harland Smith, 30 Rcn Tr
James Smith, 105 Eng
James R Smith, 119 Inf
James P Smith, 119 Inf
James W Smith, 117 Inf
James W Smith, 120 Inf
James W Smith, 120 Inf
John K Smith, 119 Inf
John M Smith, 117 Inf
Joseph G Smith, 119 Inf
Max R Smith, 119 Inf
Milton E Smith, 117 Inf
Miner R Smith, 120 Inf
Rex A Smith, 120 Inf
Sylvester T Smith, 117 Inf
Thomas R Smith, 120 Inf
Tom C Smith, 117 Inf
William F Smith, 119 Inf
John D Smithdeal, 117 Inf
Lehi L Smithson, 119 Inf
Robert H Smithson, 120 Inf
William S Snedegar, 120 Inf
David E Snipes, 117 Inf
Russell N Snoad, 120 Inf
Norman A Snoddy, 120 Inf
Archick Snow, 105 Eng
Cecil J Snow, 120 Inf
Albert E Snyder, 120 Inf
Frank E Snyder, 119 Inf
Jason Snyder, 117 Inf
John R Snyder, 120 Inf
Walter A Snyder, 120 Inf
Mathew Sobek, 120 Inf
Frank Soben, 120 Inf
Feliciano Solano, 119 Inf
Leo P Solenski, 117 Inf
Grover L Solesbee, 119 Inf
Ernest E Solis, MP Plat
Claro Solls, 120 Inf
David G Somers, 119 Inf
Henry J Sondel, 120 Inf
Mario Sorell, 120 Inf
Russell N Sorensen, 119 Inf
Reynaldo G Sotelo, 119 Inf
Floyd C Soto, 119 Inf
Edward M Soule, 119 Inf
Roy Sowers, 117 Inf
Raymond R Spahr, 119 Inf
Kenneth I Sparr, 117 Inf
John N Spatafore, 105 Eng
Warren P Spayd, 120 Inf
Jean S Spector, 119 Inf
Woodrow Speed, 120 Inf
Alton L Spencer, 119 Inf
Samuel M Spencer, 119 Inf

Harold O Speiberg, 119 Inf
Lawience H Spero, 117 Inf
Joseph J Spidaletto, 120 Inf
Lester E Spilde, 119 Inf
Jasper C Spivey, 120 Inf
Peter Spoganetz, 119 Inf
Clyde A Spradley, 119 Inf
Harley F Spradlin, 119 Inf
Sterling F Spiague, 120 Inf
Robert S Sprankle, 117 Inf
Thomas Squires, 117 Inf
Wm S Srp, 113 FA
John B Stabryla, 119 Inf
Edward B Stackhouse, 117 Inf
Robert V Stacy, 120 Inf
William S Staehling, 30 MP Plat
Earl Stafford, 120 Inf
Gene Stagner, 120 Inf
Oliver H Stanhnke, 120 Inf
Junius Stallings, 120 Inf
Clarence E Standen Jr, 117 Inf
Rocco Stanish, 119 Inf
Odis C Stantill, 117 Inf
John J Stanton, 113 FA
Thomas D Stanton, 119 Inf
Ervin C Staples, 120 Inf
Dennis C Staik, 120 Inf
Harry L Stark, 119 Inf
Herbert C Stark, 30 Rcn Tr
John A Stasek, 119 Inf
John Stecak, 119 Inf
Howard P Stedman, 105 Eng
Fred D Steelman, 119 Inf
Stanley T Steen, 120 Inf
George C Stegall, 119 Inf
Ralph L Stehly, 119 Inf
Herbert Steinbruegge Jr, 117 Inf
Lewis C Steiner, 120 Inf
George Steinman, 120 Inf
Leroy H Stellman, 120 Inf
Fred H Stenstrom, 30 Hq Co
Frank M Stepanek, 120 Inf
Carl Stepps, 119 Inf
Fred R Stern, 113 FA
Clyde F Sternberg, 120 Inf
Donald G Stevens, 120 Inf
Edwin C Stevens, 119 Inf
James W Stevens Jr, 117 Inf
Lan B Stevens, 120 Inf
Oscar M Stevens, 119 Inf
Everette W Stewart, 119 Inf
Harold C Stewart, 119 Inf
John A Stewart, 120 Inf
Thomas E Stewart, 120 Inf
Ray F Stiles 120 Inf
Roger B Stiles, 119 Inf
Aldrich L Still, 119 Inf
Edward A Stimpert, 120 Inf
James E Stirling, 120 Inf
Dale E Stockton, 30 Sig Co
Dewey Stoddard, 117 Inf
Gordon M Stoen, 120 Inf
Andrew J Stogher, 117 Inf
Adam Stoichick, 117 Inf
Granville M Stokes, 117 Inf
Harry W Stone, 105 Eng
James W Stone, 117 Inf
Richard S Stone, 119 Inf
Todd G Stone, 119 Inf
F Stoneham Jr, 117 Inf
John Stopka, 119 Inf
Stanley A Stopyra, 117 Inf
Louie C Storey, 117 Inf
Sam Stowe, 117 Inf
Nelson J St Peter, 120 Inf
Herbert Stracy, 117 Inf
Albert H Strahle, 117 Inf
Ora E Strait, 120 Inf
Howard Strange, 119 Inf
Michael P Stratigos, 119 Inf
Warren D Stratton, 117 Inf

Dominick Strazzante, 119 Inf
Milton S Strickland, 119 Inf
Willie J Strickland, 117 Inf
John E Stringer, 120 Inf
Victor E Strobel, 120 Inf
John Strobo, 120 Inf
Louie H Strohecker, 117 Inf
Adolphe P Strojny, 119 Inf
Ralph C Strom, 120 Inf
William E Stroud, 119 Inf
George E Strout, 120 Inf
Paul W Strutt, 117 Inf
Harold O Stults, 120 Inf
Warren L Stump, 120 Inf
Andrew S Suetta, 117 Inf
George S Sullivan, 120 Inf
Lawrence Sullivan, 120 Inf
Timothy D Sullivan, 119 Inf
Edard Fiehl L Summer, 117 Inf
Harry R Summers, 117 Inf
James B Summers, 119 Inf
Bennie Summey, 117 Inf
John Sunseri, 117 Inf
Wayne Suber, 117 Inf
Mathew S Surgenti, 120 Inf
John T Surniak, 117 Inf
Cecil Sutherland, 117 Inf
Robert D Sutter, 117 Inf
Charles W Sutton, 120 Inf
Thomas F Swan, 119 Inf
Ralph F Swangee, 117 Inf
J C Sanger, 113 FA
Gust W Swanson, 117 Inf
Maurice L Swanson, 119 Inf
Richard E Swanson, 117 Inf
Kenneth Swarm, 120 Inf
James F Swartz, 117 Inf
Joseph J Swartz, 119 Inf
Charles E Sweeney, 120 Inf
Albert L Sift, 119 Inf
Dempster Swift, 119 Inf
Donald B Switzer, 117 Inf
Robert Swottard, 117 Inf
Emerson S Symington, 120 Inf
Harvie R Synoground, 117 Inf
Joseph Szklanny, 119 Inf
Anthony W Szmocki, 117 Inf
Edmund I Szulezynski, 117 Inf
Edward R Szutowicz, 117 Inf
Alois E Szzepaniak, 117 Inf
John N Tagliaferro, 119 Inf
Lester E Talbot, 119 Inf
Ervin T Tallei, 117 Inf
David Tannenbaun, 117 Inf
Beryl E Tarwater, 119 Inf
Charles L Tate, 120 Inf
George W Tavenner, 117 Inf
Ciancento V Tavormina, 119 Inf
Clofus Taylor, 120 Inf
Felix M Taylor, 119 Inf
Harold L Taylor, 119 Inf
Jay C Taylor, 117 Inf
Lloyd R Taylor Jr, 117 Inf
Louis J Taylor, 120 Inf
Ralph M Taylor Jr, 117 Inf
Stewart C Tease, 119 Inf
Edward W Teets, 117 Inf
William J Teetsell, 113 FA
John J Teixeira, 117 Inf
Willie J Temples, 119 Inf
Homer E Tencate, 120 Inf
Dick J Tepaske, 105 Med
Marvin Terpstra, 117 Inf
Cletus N Terrell, 120 Inf
Walter E Terry, 120 Inf
Gustave Teskin, 119 Inf
Ralph C Testament, 119 Inf
Robert J Thagard, 120 Inf
Edward H Thalem, 105 Med
Roger C Thames, 105 Eng
Lloyd W Theiman, 120 Inf

Clarence E Thibodeare, 117 Inf
David J Thoke Jr, 117 Inf
Clarence D Thomas, 120 Inf
Francis J Thomas, 119 Inf
Harold F Thomas, 119 Inf
Herbert E Thomas, 120 Inf
John S Thomas, 120 Inf
Leland H Thomas, 117 Inf
Rooer W Thomas, 120 Inf
Roy W Thomas, 120 Inf
Sulian R Thomas, 120 Inf
William L Thomas, 119 Inf
Arnold W Thompson, 120 Inf
George O Thompson, 120 Inf
Gust A Thompson, 117 Inf
Paul M Thompson, 120 Inf
Peyton W Thompson, 120 Inf
Randall J Thompson, 117 Inf.
Ray E Thompson, 119 Inf
Richard O Thompson, 119 Inf
William Thorp, 120 Inf
Thoi J Thorsson, 120 Inf
Wallace W Thorton, 119 Inf
Harry D Thurley, 120 Inf
Clifton N Thurman, 119 Inf
William H Tidwell, 119 Inf
Roy G Tieken, 119 Inf
Lawrence Till, 119 Inf
Edison H Timmons, 117 Inf
L D Tippett, 117 Inf
John J Tincher, 120 Inf
Roy P Tindall, 120 Inf
Joseph J Tirpak, 119 Inf
Stephen A Tobias, 119 Inf
Edwin J Todd, 119 Inf
Felix, A Todesco, 120 Inf
Buford C Toler, 119 Inf
Frederick W Toll 119 Inf
Robert M Tommasco, 119 Inf
John J Tomsey, 120 Inf
John W Toney, 119 Inf
Robert G Toperzer, 120 Inf
Augustine F Toth, 119 Inf
David D Townsend, 113 FA
William J Tracey, 105 Eng
James A Tracy, 120 Inf
John D Trainor, 117 Inf
Gentry L Tramel, 117 Inf
Levi V Traversie, 119 Inf
Bernard J Treacy, 119 Inf
Michael G Trello, 119 Inf
Daniel H Tremper, 117 Inf
Dott Trentham, 120 Inf
James I Treposkoufes, 117 Inf
Robert Trevathan, 117 Inf
Claude W Triplew, 120 Inf
Frank E Trippenese, 120 Inf
Carllon W Trotter, 120 Inf
John J Trotter, 117 Inf
Willis M True, 120 Inf
Alexander Troup, 113 FA
Earl A Troup, 119 Inf
John L Trout, 117 Inf
Foster E Troy, 119 Inf
Pablo A Trujillo, 117 Inf
J P Tubbs, 117 Inf
Richard F Tucker, 120 Inf
Frank J Tules, 117 Inf
Raymond G Tuning, 117 Inf
Charles Turak, 119 Inf
William Turash, 120 Inf
Harley H Turner, 120 Inf
Luther Turner, 117 Inf
Samuel Turner Jr, 120 Inf
William C Turner, 117 Inf
Ignacy Turon, 119 Inf
Harry D Tuthill, 120 Inf
Virgil F Twedt, 119 Inf
James H Tweedy, 119 Inf
William A Twohig, 105 Eng
George H Tyner, 113 FA

John J Udovic, 113 FA
John Uhal, 117 Inf
James Uland, 119 Inf.
Robert F Umscheid, 119 Inf
Basil M Underhill, 117 Inf
Robert C Underwood, 117 Inf
Virgil L Underwood, 119 Inf
Francis E Unland, 120 Inf
Wilburn K Upchurch, 120 Inf.
Clyde R Upright, 120 Inf
Wellis R Upson, 117 Inf
George Ursin, 119 Inf
Edward Usis, 119 Inf
Steve C Uyhely, 120 Inf
Anthony B Vabolis, 120 Inf
Julius W Vajda, 119 Inf
William A Valenti, 119 Inf
Richard B Valentine, 119 Inf
Vincent E Van Alstine, 119 Inf
Arthur Van Auken, 119 Inf
Elbert J Vance, 105 Eng
John A Van De Baake, 117 Inf
Maurice Van Doorne, 117 Inf
Woodrow E Vanhoose, 119 Inf
John Van Nort, 120 Inf
Richard C Van Welty, 119 Inf
James F Vardy, 117 Inf
Antonio V Vasquez, 119 Inf
Veto S Vaticonis, 120 Inf
Robert B Vaughn, 117 Inf
Howard Vaught, 117 Inf
Robert A Vaught, 119 Inf
Theodore Vavoulis, 120 Inf
Joseph D Veilleux, 105 Eng
Fred J Veleta, 120 Inf
Theodore Veltman, 230 FA
Philip Venticinque, 119 Inf
Gregorio A Vera, 119 Inf
John P Vermillion, 117 Inf
James M Vernon, 117 Inf
Alvin A Vertin, 117 Inf
Wade J Verweire, 119 Inf
Adrian F Vetter, 119 Inf
Robert F Vezino, 119 Inf
Francis J Vidrine, 117 Inf
John M Viglante, 117 Inf
Eugene J Vigosky, 119 Inf
Carl G Vilsack Jr, 117 Inf
Bennie R Vincent, 120 Inf
James M Vincent, 120 Inf
John M Vinson, 120 Inf
Sam J Viviano, 119 Inf
Angleo M Voldo, 117 Inf
Charles J Voss, 117 Inf
Austin K Voyles, 117 Inf
Reuben Wacker, 119 Inf
Phillip J Wade, 119 Inf
Reuben B Wade, 119 Inf
Melvin F Wagener, 119 Inf
John A Waggoner, 117 Inf
Gresswell D Wagner, 117 Inf
Winston E Waite, 117 Inf
James L Walch, 117 Inf
Henry C Walden, 197 FA
William D Walden, 120 Inf
Anton M Walker, 197 FA
Earl E Walker, 120 Inf
Franklin E Walker, 120 Inf
Fred L Walker, 120 Inf
Hubert H Walker, 117 Inf
James J Walker, 117 Inf
Miles N Walker, 30 Rcn Tr
Omer W Walker, 117 Inf
Archie M Wallace, 117 Inf
Robert T Wallace, 119 Inf
Frank Wallenberg, 117 Inf
Finis E Walls, 119 Inf
Joseph F Walsh, 120 Inf
Harry G Walter, 120 Inf
Don C Walters, 120 Inf
Nelson M Walters, 119 Inf

Lawrence M Walthorn, 120 Inf
Edward E Wantuck, 119 Inf
Dale R Ward, 120 Inf
Harold M Ward, 230 FA
Maynard E Ward, 120 Inf
Reuben E Ward, 119 Inf
Robert A Ward, 119 Inf
George D Wark, 117 Inf
Clyde F Warlick, 120 Inf
George L Warman, 119 Inf
Clowes V Warnock, 120 Inf
James H Warren, 120 Inf
John A Warren, 117 Inf
Domonick J Wash, 119 Inf
Daniel J Waskevitz, 119 Inf
Hyman Wasserman, 117 Inf
Robert T Waters, 117 Inf
Joseph Watier, 117 Inf
James F Watkins, 117 Inf
Joseph Watkins, 117 Inf
William J Watkins, 117 Inf
Grover D Watson, 120 Inf
Lawrence V Watson, 119 Inf
Sidney E Watson, 117 Inf
Theodore L Watson, 117 Inf
Troy Watts, 120 Inf
Wesley J Watts, 119 Inf
William D Watts, 117 Inf
John W Waute, 120 Inf
Frank W Way, 119 Inf
Hailan W Way, 117 Inf
Frank L Wease, 119 Inf
Carlos A Weathers, 120 Inf
Clarence E Weaver, 117 Inf
Daniel E Weaver, 117 Inf
Eldridge R Weaver, 119 Inf
Grady O Weaver, 117 Inf
Ronald E Weaver, 117 Inf
William B Weaver, 117 Inf
William D Weaver, 119 Inf
Howard F Weavers, 120 Inf
Walter B Webb, 117 Inf
Horace G Webber, 117 Inf
Jerry W Webber, 117 Inf
Earnest R Weber, 120 Inf
Kenneth J Weber, 117 Inf
Arless A Webster, 119 Inf
Blaine Webster, 120 Inf
Grovel L Webster, 117 Inf
Everette A Weeks, 119 Inf
Harold D Weedon, 120 Inf
Hugh J Weeks, 117 Inf
Meridith B Weeks, 117 Inf
Woodrow Weeks, 117 Inf
Warren J Weeley, 120 Inf
Mathew Weglowski, 117 Inf
Harvey H Wehde, 119 Inf.
Melvin Weiner, 120 Inf
Edward C Weingerber, 120 Inf
Edward Weinmeister, 120 Inf
Jack Weinstein, 120 Inf
Frank P Weiss, 120 Inf
Eukle Welch, 117 Inf
Francis E Welch, 120 Inf
Hollis Welch, 119 Inf
Edward P Well, 117 Inf
Alvin J Wells, 117 Inf
Ivan R Wellington, 119 Inf
Harold Wellman, 120 Inf
Oakley O Wells, 120 Inf
Leo R Wencl, 117 Inf
Raymond W Werges, 119 Inf
Earl R Wescott, 120 Inf
Charlie A Wess, 119 Inf
Benjamin F Wesson, 119 Inf
Harold D West, 120 Inf
Harold L West, 119 Inf
Robert A Wetmore, 120 Inf
Ralph R Weyh, 120 Inf
Erwin L Weymuth, 120 Inf
Rober T Whalen, 117 Inf

Harold S Whaley, 117 Inf
Emmette A Wheeler, 119 Inf
Bert J Wheeles, 117 Inf
Douglas V Whitaker, 119 Inf
Earnest R Whitaker, 117 Inf
Daniel A Whitcher, 120 Inf
Charles W White, 117 Inf
Drew B White, 120 Inf
Gale S White, 120 Inf
James B White, 119 Inf
Michael F White, 113 Inf
Orvel C White, 117 Inf
Charles E Whitehari, 117 Inf
Virgil B Whitesell, 119 Inf
William H Whitson, 117 Inf
James E Whittaker, 119 Inf
Lusco Wickisen, 30 Rcn Tr
Charles J Wiederhold, 120 Inf
Owen D Wiedman, 119 Inf
Frank J Wieland, 117 Inf
Peter S Wielusz, 117 Inf
Robert A Wiemels, 119 Inf
Everett M Wiggen, 120 Inf
John A Wiggins, 117 Inf
Franklin J Wilbur, 117 Inf
Phillip M Wilburn 119 Inf
Ralph W Wiles, 117 Inf
Jack H Wilhite, 117 Inf
James C Wilhoit, 120 Inf
Robert D Wilkie, 120 Inf
William R Wilkens, 120 Inf
John F Wilkenson, 120 Inf
Jesse L Wilkins, 119 Inf
James B Wilkison, 120 Inf
Frank J Wilkolaski, 120 Inf
Frank D Willard, 117 Inf
Clifford A Willeat, 120 Inf
Dallas M Willet, 117 Inf
Buford O Williams, 117 Inf
Clement W Williams, 120 Inf
Donald M Williams, 120 Inf
Earl C Williams, 120 Inf
Earnest W Williams, 117 Inf
Glen E Williams, 117 Inf
Harry J Williams, 120 Inf
Houston W Williams, 120 Inf
Joe B Williams, 117 Inf
John D Williams, 117 Inf
John S Williams, 117 Inf
Lloyd G Williams, 119 Inf
Malcom A Williams, 120 Inf
Merlyn V Williams, 117 Inf
Orei Williams, 120 Inf.
Walter W Williams, 117 Inf
Wilson F Williams, 117 Inf
Stanley R Williamson, 117 Inf
Delma J Willis, 117 Inf
Gordon W Willoughby, 120 Inf
Samuel H Wilmarth, 119 Inf
Edward C Wilson, 197 FA
Edward R Wilson, 119 Inf.
Eugene Wilson, 119 Inf
Glenn M Wilson, 119 Inf
Hayden M Wilson, 120 Inf
Hugh S Wilson, 119 Inf
James H Wilson, 120 Inf
James A Wilkens, 113 FA
Leo M Willits, 117 Inf
Donald C Wilmot, 117 Inf
Donald E Wilson, 119 Inf
Eddie A Wilson, 117 Inf
Edwin W Wilson, 117 Inf
Orval D Wilson, 30 Rcn Tr
Pius W Wing, 119 Inf
Andrew J Wingate, 119 Inf
Norbert H Winiecki, 120 Inf.
John J Winifisky, 117 Inf.
William Winkle, 119 Inf
George H Winkler, 119 Inf
Carl M Winstead, 117 Inf
John Winstead Jr, 120 Inf

Luther H Winstead, 117 Inf
Ralph L Winstead, 120 Inf
George E Winter, 117 Inf
Lester J Winters, 120 Inf
Antoine E Wintier, 120 Inf
Alfred P Wise, 119 Inf
John C Wise, 120 Inf
Burdette M Wisel, 117 Inf
Robert E Wiseman, 119 Inf
Edgar D Wissen, 230 FA
Casimir Witalisz, 119 Inf
Roland G Withers, 120 Inf
George W Witherspoon, 119 Inf
J B Wittie, 119 Inf
Roy V Wittmer, 119 Inf
Michael B Witzman, 117 Inf
Maxwell J Wogoman, 117 Inf
Henry Wojciechowski, 119 Inf
John Wojdyla, 119 Inf
Robert R Wolf, 120 Inf
Edgar Wolfangel, 119 Inf
Clarence E Wolfe, 117 Inf
James Wolfe Jr, 120 Inf
William L Wolfe, 120 Inf
Howard A Wolpert, 117 Inf
John R Womack, 120 Inf
Simon W Wonderlin, 119 Inf
Ben P Wood, 120 Inf
Charles T Wood, 117 Inf
Daniel R Wood, 119 Inf
Donald J Wood, 120 Inf
Henry E Wood, 119 Inf
Lyal V Wood, 120 Inf
Rex L Wood, 119 Inf
Robert T Wood, 117 Inf
Stanley D Woodard, 119 Inf
Harrison W Woods, 119 Inf
Harp J Woody, 120 Inf
Harry Woody, 117 Inf
Horace J Woods, 120 Inf
James Woody, 117 Inf
James M Wooley, 117 Inf
George H Wooten, 119 Inf
Melvin K Wooten, 117 Inf
Grady W Workman, 117 Inf
Harold G Works, 30 Rcn Tr.
Edward J Worley, 120 Inf
Arnold Worthington, 117 Inf
Edward W Worthington, 117 Inf
Frank M Wozniak, 120 Inf
Leroy G Wright, 117 Inf
Stanley N Wright, 117 Inf
William H Wright, 117 Inf
John S Wronski, 117 Inf
Stanley J Wrzesien, 119 Inf
Veryl A Wurtz, 120 Inf
Addis R Wyatt, 117 Inf
G W Wyatt, 117 Inf
James B Wyatt, 119 Inf
Chester J Wycykal, 117 Inf
Homer D Wynn, 117 Inf
Vincent Yackamovich, 117 Inf.
Peter J Yalch, 113 FA
Arlie R Yarbrough, 120 Inf
Donald W Yarrow, 119 Inf
Charles H Yates, 119 Inf
Louie M Ybarra, 117 Inf
James C Yeargin, 119 Inf
Connie O Yeatts, 119 Inf
Robert D Yeazel, 230 FA
Alvin Yetchny, 119 Inf
Fred Yetsook, 119 Inf
Frank G Yonski, 120 Inf
William C York, 105 Eng.
Edward G York, 120 Inf.
Ernest Yost, 120 Inf
Alvin H Young, 117 Inf.
Deber A Young, 120 Inf.
Frederick A Young, 119 Inf.
Harry Young, 120 Inf
James H Young, 117 Inf.

Lloyd W Young, 120 Inf
Tom H Young, 120 Inf
Weston D Young, 117 Inf
Edward A Zaidins, 120 Inf
Steven Zarkovich, 230 FA
Clemont O Zavodny, 117 Inf
William J Zayance, 120 Inf
Sigmund W Zebroski, 117 Inf
Bernard A Zech, 120 Inf
Steve V Zelip, 117 Inf
Julio N Zepeda, 120 Inf
Ramon R Zepeda, 120 Inf
Fred W Ziegler, 119 Inf

Leo O Ziegler, 120 Inf
Frank G Zika, 119 Inf
William Zilinek, 120 Inf
Alton Zimmerman, 120 Inf
William E Zimmerman, 117 Inf
Lawrence Zinman, 119 Inf
Frederick Zitzer, 117 Inf
Ralph L Zortman, 119 Inf
Irving Zuckerman, 120 Inf
Irving H Zuckerman, 119 Inf
John A Zuidema, 120 Inf
Victor Zupo, 120 Inf
Andrew F Zutic, 120 Inf

HOW IT LOOKED

THE END OF THE BEGINNING. Above, 30th soldiers sit on their docked transport's deck in Southhampton, waiting for the convoy to move. Below, a headquarters truck starts ashore at Omaha Beach.

The Channel

NORMANDY'S HEDGEROWS stretched unendingly into the distance as the 30th went into combat near Isigny. This photo of the Division CP shows clearly the tracks made by trucks.

France

THICK AND HEAVY, the hedgerows provide protection to the defender and obstacles to the attacker.

PLANNING AN ATTACK. A staff sergeant tells his squad just how and where it will move.

ARMOR NEEDS HELP. Here doughboys set charges in a hedgerow to blast a path for tanks.

ARMOR GIVES HELP. A TD lumbers out of hiding in support of an infantry attack.

A BAZOOKAMAN draws a bead through a hedgerow's foliage.

HAIL TO THE CHIEF. General Eisenhower visits the 30th's CP near Isigny, July 7. General Hobbs stands bareheaded. With three stars on his helmet is General Omar N. Bradley of First Army, and behind General Hobbs is Major General Charles H. Corlett, XIX Corps commander.

VIRE ATTACK AREA. This air photo mosaic was distributed to the assault troops before the attack of July 7. The 30th's first assault came from the upper right corner, crossing the twisting black line of the Vire River just above St. Fromond, where the white line of the main highway from Airel crosses the river. Fields and orchards were numbered so that troop locations could be reported from the mosaic directly.

PONT DU ST. FROMOND. Above, infantrymen and a tank cross the Vire. Below, soldiers take over from enemy fire as a tankdozer moves up to the new treadway section of the bridge.

MEN AND MACHINES crowd the roads leading to the Vire. The engineers at the right carry plate like mine detectors.

TRAFFIC JAM. Tanks and jeeps crowded up on a narrow muddy road near the Vire.

COUNTERATTACK CASUALTY. This German tank was knocked out near the Vire crossing site.

JULY 25, 1944. Infantrymen and medics dig out a fellow-soldier buried by U. S. bombs, before starting the St. Lô breakthrough.

FIRST PURSUIT. Doughboys stream southward past St. Lô, July 27.

HABITAT: AFRICA, EUROPE. 88mm. guns, like this one destroyed in Normandy, were hated and feared by Allied troops.

BARRELS AND REST. Wine was plentiful but sleep was not in the fighting around Tessy-sur-Vir

HOME-MADE AMBULANCE. A jeep with racks built to carry stretchers takes a wounded man to the rear.

A GROUND MOUNT .50 set up near Mortain.

CLOSE SUPPORT is provided by a 105mm. howitzer of a cannon company.

WITH HIS GUN DUG IN, this mortarman is ready to fire against Germans near St. Barthelmy.

ORCHARDS ARE PRETTY, but risky under fire. This squad moves cautiously into one near Mortain.

MORTAIN BATTLEFIELD: a close-up view.

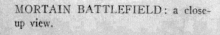

MORTAIN REVISITED, after recapture of the town. Below, troops pick their way through Dom-ont's rubble.

HOW DO YOU DO! Above, the first jeep into Evreux receives a warm welcome. Below, doughboys get individual attention.

RETREAT FROM KERKRADE. Here are some of the 30,000 civilians driven from the Dutch border town into the American lines.

THE ALBERT CANAL near Fort Eben Emael, Belgium.

OBSERVATION POSTS in water towers and atop slag piles enabled Germans to fire on anything that moved. TD fire made the holes in this Übach water tower.

GERMAN TRENCHES, GERMAN TARGETS. From positions dug by the enemy, these machine gunners fire across the open country of the Aachen plain.

The Aachen Plain

IN OFT-SHELLED ÜBACH a knocked out American TD and a battered house testify to German artillery fire.

"WOODEN" PILLBOX near tenfield, Germany. A shack camflaged the concrete structure.

HOLE IN THE WALL serves a gunner firing at Germans 300 yards away near Kohlscheid.

LITTERED STREET, FLAMING TANK provide backdrop of war as rifleman at left fires down a Würselen street.

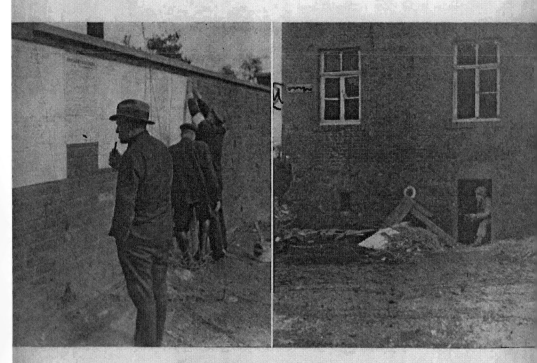

THOU SHALT NOT—"A German udies strict rules posted by AMG in Bar-nberg.

HOUSE-TO-HOUSE fighting was SOP in Würselen. A rifleman crouches before his dash to another house.

30TH ACK-ACK beside Westwall "dragon's teeth."

CHAIN OF COMMAND. Lt. Gen. William H. Simpson, center, Ninth Army commander, and Maj. Gen. Raymond S. McLain, XIX Corps commander, chat with Gen. Hobbs in Herzogenrath, before the November offensive.

GOING TO WORK. Doughboys plod dow
Alsdorf's gray streets to positions for t
November 16 attack.

EUCHEN IS NEXT. Infantrymen crou
in an orchard awaiting the attack sign
Left, mortars support the attack.

THE ATTACK BEGINS. Assault troops move out across country toward Euchen.

STREET SCENE: NOVEMBER, 1944. A column splashes through the muck and debris of Lurken, Germany.

FINAL OBJECTIVE: ALTDORF. This air photo was used by the troops which captured Altdorf at night. Note division of the town into company sectors marked A, B and C. Circles and "goose eggs" in lower part of photo denote possible enemy positions marked for artillery concentration

FIRE FOR EFFECT. A forward observer directs shells against Altdorf.

LOG BARRIERS were found in most German towns.

29

OP.
GOEBBALS ST   BROICHWEIDEN

S (CHOW)
KLOSTER ST

g Streets
ed
Possible Tank Bivouac Area
egt.

RR Station

Defended

Houses Blown fo
Fields of Fire

WURSELEN WAS FULL OF GER-MANS. This battered air photo is the one used by a regimental intelligence officer to chart German positions in the town just before the American attack of November 16. All positions shown here are German. The pie-shaped area enclosed by roads at the lower left was known as the "Bloody Triangle." Markings which show up as black were actually made with red ink. The vertical rough white line on the left side of the photo is a crease mark.

THE ARDENNES, from just south of Malmédy, Belgium.

The Ardennes

READY FOR PANZERS
is this big 90mm. AA gun.

A MACHINE GUNNER
guards against surprise.

REMAINS OF A GAS DUMP. Fuel in these cans was deliberately set afire when German tank headed up from Stavelot.

AMERICAN BOMBERS did this to Malmédy by mistake.

HOT CHOW replaced K-rations around New Year's Day as the 30th awaited orders to attack south.

STRAFING kept life from becoming monotonous.

LA GLEIZE CITY HALL, just after the battle. Note destroyed German tank in front of the building.

TWO SOLDIERS ADVANCE past a burning German tank in the La Gleize pocket.

THE BRIDGE AT STAVELOT was a key point in the 30th's battle with the 1st SS. Note the wrecked jeep on the bridge and the snow-covered German tank across the river at the left.

TANK MEN park their "frigidaires" under cover of snow-laden trees.

LIFE photograph by Florea © Time, Inc.

TRUCKS AND GUNS found snow-choked roads troublesome. This 155mm. howitzer slid into a ditc

A WINTER JEEP RIDE was an ordeal, but the little vehicles kept food and ammunition movir toward the front.

AINTED WHITE, a tankdozer leads a tank column through Malmédy, prepared to plow a
ay through the snow.

MAMMY YOKUM," a 105mm. howitzer, fires in
e Ardennes.

MINE-CLEARING ENGINEERS
probe near Recht. Knocked-out tanks in
background are German.

FOUR BLASTED AMERICAN TANKS are shown as the 30th found them near Rodt.

TROJAN HORSE, M1944. The enemy disguised this Mark VI tank as a U. S. TD. Soldiers are clearing snow from Allied white star painted on by Germans.

HERE WAS A TANK BATTLE. Note knocked-out tanks beside road and at woods' edge and tank tracks in the snow. .

PAST THE WRECKAGE OF WAR: Infantry advances between a dead German soldier and a destroyed enemy tank.

WHEN SHELL-POCKED ST. VITH fell under the 30th's gunfire, the northern part of the Bulge fight was all but over. Bombing and shelling and then capture of this road center cut off German supply lines into the Bulge.

SPRING PLOWING. Signal men plow
under telephone lines to protect them from
shellfire.

BATTLING A FLOOD, doughboys practice on the Inde River for the Roer crossing.

STRONG EMPLACE-
MENTS marked the
German Roer line. This
steel turret covered a
roomy dugout.

The Roer

ACROSS THE SOGGY LOW-
LANDS, assault troops move toward the Roer under cover of a
smoke screen.

NARROW, PRECARIOUS foot-
bridges served the assault waves.

BIG GUNS NEED BIG
BRIDGES. By H plus 24 engineers had a treadway over the river
and the 155mm. howitzers were
rolling across.

ACK-ACK crosses the swollen Roer.

TANK-RIDING INFANTRYMEN leap into position as opposition develops in the Hambach Forest.

LEAPFROG TACTICS confused the enemy. These troops are attacking Königshoven from Kirchherten, shortly after its capture by another unit. Later, still a third unit used the same street to attack Garzweiler.

FREAK. The German 360mm. self-propelled howitzer captured in the Roer drive.

ON THE MAAS RIVER the 30th practiced assault crossing before moving up to the Rhine.

ATTACK PLANS ARE STUDIED. Here Chief of Staff Stephens goes into detail with battalion commanders.

The Rhine

FERRYING TANKS came early in the Rhine assault schedule. This Sherman is squeezing into an LCM.

LONG LINES OF PRISONERS came reeling back to the Rhine.

AP photo

HORSEPLAY IN HAMELIN. German prisoners docilely follow a GI "Pied Piper" for the benefit of press photographers.

BRUNSWICK: A CONFERENCE FAILS. German General Veith, bareheaded, faces Generals Hobbs and Harrison.

12 HOURS LATER the conference room was a mess, blasted by American artillery.

APPROACHING BRUNSWICK, the infantry strings out in crooked lines, ready to deploy for the attack.

BARRICADES IN BRUNSWICK go down before blows of an engineer bulldozer.

AFTER THE BATTLE troops fall out for a short rest in Brunswick before moving on.

TRUCKING ACROSS GERMANY the 30th found many newly-released Allied soldiers.

HITTING THE DIRT to escape "burp-gun" fire these doughboys work through the maze of truck gardens on Magdeburg's outskirts.

TANK TRACKS pointing to Magdeburg on the Elbe, the 30th's final objective.

AMERICANS AND RUSSIANS meet ceremoniously in Magdeburg, in one of many gatherings before and after V-E Day.

CHURCH SERVICES are conducted in Oschersleben as the Division ends its fighting career and turns to occupation duties.

MAJOR GENERAL LELAND S. HOBBS
Commanding General, 30th Infantry Division

**BRIGADIER GENERAL
WILLIAM K. HARRISON**
Asst. Division Commander

**BRIGADIER GENERAL
RAYMOND S. McLAIN**
Div. Artillery Commander

**BRIGADIER
JAMES M**
Div. Artillery

COL. HAMMOND D. BIRKS
120th Infantry

COL. BRANNER P. PURDUE
120th Infantry

COL. EDWIN M. SUTHERLAND
119th Infantry

COL. RUSSELL A. BAKER
119th Infantry

COL. HENRY E. KELLY
117th Infantry

COL. WALTER M. JOHNSON
117th Infantry

COL. OTTO ELLIS
Executive, Division Artillery

COL. RICHARD W. STEPHENS
Chief of Staff

CPSIA information can be obtained at www.ICGtesting.com
Printed in the USA
BVOW071209050812

297111BV00004B/7/P